The
REGISTER
of the
VICTORIA
CROSS

Revised & Enlarged Edition

© This England 1988

First published in 1981. This revised and enlarged
edition published 1988 by This England Books,
Alma House, Rodney Road, Cheltenham,
Gloucestershire, GL50 1HT.

Printed in England by
The Beshara Press Ltd
Cheltenham, Gloucestershire.

ISBN 0 906324 07 6 (Hardback)

Contents

A message from the Rt. Hon. Viscount De L'Isle, V.C.

Deputy President of the Victoria Cross & George Cross Association

Queen Victoria, portrayed in 1855. The Royal Warrant instituting the award named after her was signed in January 1856, shortly after this portrait was painted.

WINDSOR, ROYAL COLLECTION

After the Centenary of the Institution of the Victoria Cross in 1956 an Association of holders of the award was formed. Five years later, holders of the George Cross were invited to join in equal partnership. In 1957 Her Majesty The Queen graciously consented to be our Patron.

Sir Winston Churchill became the first President in 1959. He was followed in office by Sir John Smyth, Founder Chairman of the Association until his death in 1983. In that year Her Majesty Queen Elizabeth The Queen Mother honoured the Association by accepting the Presidency.

Members reside in Britain, in the Commonwealth, and in other overseas countries. Reunions are held in London, usually every other year, lasting a few days and providing members with opportunities for maintaining and renewing friendships.

The first edition of the Register of the Victoria Cross was published in 1981. As Deputy President of the Association it is now my privilege to welcome this revised and enlarged edition.

Penshurst Place, Tonbridge, Kent.

Foreword

by Rear-Admiral B.C.G. PLACE, VC, CB, DSC.

Chairman of the Victoria Cross and George Cross Association

The first edition of this Register, published in 1981, coincided with the 125th anniversary of the institution of the Victoria Cross and the 124th anniversary of the first investiture of VCs in Hyde Park, London. That investiture, on 26th June, 1857, was unique, the first occasion on which officers and men were decorated by the Monarch together, and was wholly in keeping with Her Majesty's view that this decoration should be awarded regardless of rank. On that day, 62 officers and men were decorated by Queen Victoria who, mounted on a charger and leaning from her saddle, pinned the Cross on each of the soldier's and sailor's breasts. The VCs then stood opposite the Queen while the troops marched past between — the infantry twice and the cavalry and horse artillery three times.

In 1956 more than 300 VCs assembled in Hyde Park and were inspected by Her Majesty — only a handful being young enough to be still serving and in uniform. This time it was the VCs who marched past: with great pride. Out of this was born the Victoria Cross Association, very shortly after to become the Victoria Cross and George Cross Association.

The VC is essentially the most democratic of awards. Quite apart from the clause in the Warrant which decrees "that neither rank nor long service, nor wounds, nor any other circumstance or condition whatsoever, save the merit of conspicuous bravery, shall be held to establish a sufficient claim to the honour", the recommendations for the award are made by those who have seen or had direct report from those who have seen the action, and decided by the Monarch on the advice of those who have considered every report on a whole multitude of deeds. It is the decision of the holders' contemporaries and the reason behind their decisions which are often given in the *London Gazette* announcing the award . . . not infrequently in language inspired to eloquence by the deed itself.

Today, with no major war in the last 43 years, only 54 holders out of the 1350 who have received the award are still alive, but I do not think any of them would wish it to be otherwise. An essential of the award of the Victoria Cross is that it should be in the presence of an enemy, but men experienced in war are seekers of peace. Great courage has been and will continue to be shown by selfless men and women in times of adversity and disaster, with no enemy present. Another award of equal esteem is appropriate, and then there will be no more VCs . . . a progress to be highly prized.

Godfrey Place

A Short History of the Victoria Cross

The Victoria Cross was founded by Royal Warrant on January 29th, 1856, and was originally intended to be awarded solely to members of the Royal Navy and British Army who, serving in the presence of the enemy, should have performed some signal act of valour or devotion to their country.

As Queen Victoria herself pointed out, it was not an Order, such as the Garter or the Bath. It offered no knighthood or Companionage, bore no religious significance and contained no ranks within itself. It was intended solely as a decoration "to be highly prized and eagerly sought after by the officers and men of Our naval and military services".

In due course, further Royal Warrants enlarged the scope of the award to admit other categories but the over-riding requirements for winning it remained conspicuous bravery. It could not be earned in any other way, whether by influence or privilege. It was to be conferred by the Sovereign alone, upon advice, and was to be utterly beyond reproach.

An important clause laid down that "neither rank, nor long service, nor wounds, nor any other circumstance or condition whatsoever, save the merit of conspicuous bravery" should establish a sufficient claim to the honour, thereby placing "all persons on a perfectly equal footing in relation to eligibility for the decoration". The VC therefore became the most democratic honour in the annals of military and naval history. This aspect was confirmed by the elective procedure laid down in those cases where a number of "equally brave and distinguished persons" had been thought worthy of the honour. The names submitted to the Sovereign were to be chosen by their fellow men taking part in the action concerned.

Pensions were granted to all holders of the Victoria Cross below commissioned rank, and an expulsion clause allowed for a recipient's name to be erased from the official Register in certain wholly discreditable circumstances, and his pension cancelled.

Although there are eight recorded cases of forfeiture, in accordance with the terms of the original Warrant, all eight men are still included in the main total and no mention of the forfeiture is made except as a note at the bottom of the War Office List, which covers the period 1856 to August 1914.

King George V felt very strongly that the decoration should never be forfeited. In a letter written by his Private Secretary, Lord Stamfordham, on 26th July, 1920, his views are forcibly expressed: "The King feels so strongly that, no matter the crime committed by anyone on whom the VC has been conferred, the decoration should not be forfeited. Even were a VC to be sentenced to be hanged for murder, he should be allowed to wear his VC on the scaffold".

Since the original Warrant, others have been issued modifying or extending its provisions — in 1858 Queen Victoria decreed that the Cross could be won by those who "may perform acts of conspicuous courage and bravery . . . in circumstances of extreme danger, such as the occurrence of a fire on board ship, or of the foundering of a vessel at sea, or under any other circumstances in which . . . life or public property may be saved".

This Warrant was only called into use twice and then, in 1881, a new VC Warrant was signed which stated "Our Will and Pleasure is that the qualification (for the award of the Victoria Cross) shall be "conspicuous bravery or devotion to the country in the presence of the enemy". But for this stipulation there would have been no need for the institution of the George Cross.

In 1902 King Edward Vll approved the important principle of awarding it posthumously. In 1911 King George V admitted native officers and men of the Indian Army to eligibility and, in 1920, it was further extended to include the RAF, and "matrons, sisters, nurses . . . serving regularly or temporarily under the orders, direction or supervision" of the military authorities . . . emphasising, however, that the VC "shall only be awarded for most conspicuous bravery or some daring pre-eminent act of valour or self-sacrifice or extreme devotion to duty in the presence of the enemy".

Queen Victoria chose the design for the new decoration herself. It is in the form of a Maltese Cross ensigned with the Royal Crest and a scroll inscribed simply "For Valour". It is connected by a V-shaped link to a bar engraved on the face with laurel leaves, and having a space on the reverse for the recipient's name. The date of the deed for which the honour is bestowed is engraved on the back of the Cross itself. It is worn on the left breast suspended from a 1½-inch wide red ribbon . . . originally the VC ribbon was blue for the Navy, dark red for the Army, but since 1918 it has been the same crimson shade for all services.

The actual Cross itself is made of bronze and still cast from metal melted down from the cannons captured at Sevastopol in the Crimean War.

Although the Royal Warrant instituting the Victoria Cross was not issued until January 1856, the earliest deed of valour to win the award was performed 19 months earlier, on June 21st, 1854, by a 20-year-old Irishman, Charles Davis Lucas, Mate of HMS *Hecla* which was attacking the fortress of Bomarsund in the Baltic. At a range of only 500 yards a live shell with fuse still hissing landed on the deck of the *Hecla* from a Russian battery. Lucas picked it up with his bare hands and threw it overboard . . . it exploded as it entered the sea, but the ship and crew were saved from certain destruction. Lucas was promoted to Lieutenant on the spot by his commanding officer and eventually rose to the rank of Rear-Admiral.

Some 62 VCs who had been "gazetted" — i.e. their names and deeds were cited in the *London Gazette* — were present at Hyde Park, London, on the morning of June 26th, 1857, when Queen Victoria held her first Investiture ceremony for the newly-instituted decoration that bore her name. In keeping with the democratic spirit of the award all recipients stood shoulder to shoulder, regardless of rank. Since then, a total of 1,350 men or, in the case of posthumous awards, their widows or representatives, have been decorated with the VC. The last deed for which it was awarded took place on 12th June, 1982 in the Falkland Islands. The winner was Sergeant Ian McKay of the Parachute Regiment.

FREDERICK G. CARROLL
Wing Commander, RAF (Rtd.)

ACKNOWLEDGEMENTS

The publishers would like to thank the following for their valuable assistance in the preparation of this volume: The Director and Staff of the Imperial War Museum, London, for allowing facilities for extensive research, in particular the comprehensive files of Canon William Lummis, MC, and the Ranken VC Collection; Miss Rose Coombs, MBE, formerly Special Collections Officer, Imperial War Museum, for her never-failing, cheerful co-operation and invaluable advice; Wing Commander Frederick Carroll, for access to his comprehensive photographic files which form the bulk of the illustrative material contained here, and for his encyclopaedic knowledge; Mr. John Winton, for permitting access to the files of the late Mrs. Margaret Pratt, which include valuable information relating to births and deaths; The Commonwealth War Graves Commission, for their comprehensive lists relating to memorials and graves; The Victoria Cross and George Cross Association, for their encouragement and support; The Gloucestershire Regiment, for allowing us to photograph the Victoria Cross posthumously awarded to Second Lieutenant H.F. Parsons; Mr. Allan Stanistreet, Mr. Kenneth Williams, Mr. Ronald Biddle, Mr. Peter Burke, Mr. Harry Irwin, Mrs. Mary Marks and the readers of *This England* magazine — all of whom have given us much valuable information and help.

Compiled and researched for *This England* by NORA BUZZELL

AARON, Arthur Louis   **1**
A/Flight Sergeant   218 Squadron, Royal Air Force Volunteer Reserve
Other Decorations: DFM
Date of Gazette: 5 Nov. 1943
Place/Date of Birth: Leeds — 5 Mar. 1922
Place/Date of Death: Bone, N. Africa — 13 Aug. 1943
Memorials: Bone War Cemetery, Algeria; St Mary's Church Bexwell, Norfolk
Town/County Connections: Leeds, Yorkshire
Remarks: — VC in LEEDS MUSEUM
Account of Deed: On 12 Aug. 1943 during a raid on Turin, Italy, Flight Sergeant Aaron's bomber was attacked by a night fighter and was very badly damaged. The navigator was killed, other members of the crew were wounded, Flight Sergeant Aaron's jaw was broken and part of his face was torn away. He had also been hit in the lung and his right arm was useless. Despite his terrible injuries he managed to level the aircraft out at 3000ft. and then the bomb aimer took control until he rallied his failing strength enough to direct the difficult landing operation. He died nine hours after the aircraft touched down.

ABDUL HAFIZ,   **2**
Jemadar   9th Jat Infantry, Indian Army
Other Decorations: —
Date of Gazette: 27 Jul. 1944
Place/Date of Birth: Kalanaur Village, Rohtak District, Punjab — 1 Jul. 1918
Place/Date of Death: Waken Hill, near Imphal, Assam, India — 6 Apr. 1944
Memorials: Imphal Indian War Cemetery
Town/County Connections: —
Remarks: —
Account of Deed: On 6 Apr. 1944 north of Imphal, India, Jemadar Abdul Hafiz was ordered to attack with his platoon a prominent position held by the enemy, the only approach to which was across a bare slope and then up a very steep cliff. The jemadar led the assault, killing several of the enemy himself and then pressed on regardless of machine-gun fire from another feature. He received two wounds, the second of which was fatal, but he had succeeded in routing an enemy vastly superior in numbers and had captured a most important position.

ABLETT, Alfred   **3**
Private (later Sergeant)   3rd Bn., Grenadier Guards
Other Decorations: DCM
Date of Gazette: 24 Feb. 1857
Place/Date of Birth: Weybread, Suffolk — 3 Aug. 1830
Place/Date of Death: Weybread, Suffolk — 12 Mar. 1897
Memorials: Weybread Churchyard, Suffolk
Town/County Connections: Weybread, Suffolk
Remarks: Became Inspector of Police, Millwall Docks, London
Account of Deed: On 2 Sep 1855 during the siege of Sebastopol, Crimea, a burning shell fell into a trench containing two cases of ammunition. Private Ablett at once realising the danger to which all were exposed, seized the shell in his hands and threw it over the parapet, where it immediately exploded as it touched the ground, but not a man was touched.

ACKROYD, Harold   **4**
T/Captain   Royal Army Medical Corps, attd. 6th Bn., The Royal Berkshire Regt. (Princess Charlotte of Wales's)
Other Decorations: MC
Date of Gazette: 6 Sep. 1917
Place/Date of Birth: Southport, Lancashire — 18 Jul. 1877
Place/Date of Death: Glencorse Wood, Ypres — 11 Aug. 1917
Memorials: Birr Cross Roads, Belgium; War Memorial Royston Hertfordshire; Guy's Hospital; RAMC College, Millbank, London
Town/County Connections: Southport, Lancs; Royston, Herts.
Remarks: —
Account of Deed: Between 31 Jul. and 1 Aug. 1917 at Ypres, Belgium, Captain Ackroyd worked continuously, utterly regardless of danger, tending the wounded and saving the lives of officers and men in the front line. In so doing he had to move across the open under heavy machine-gun, rifle and shell fire. On one occasion he carried a wounded officer to a place of safety under heavy fire, and on another went some way in front of the advanced line and brought in a wounded man under continuous sniping. He was killed in action ten days later.

ACTON, Abraham   **5**
Private   2nd Bn., The Border Regiment
Other Decorations: —
Date of Gazette: 18 Feb. 1915
Place/Date of Birth: Whitehaven, Cumberland — 17 Dec. 1892
Place/Date of Death: Festubert, France — 16 May 1915
Memorials: Le Touret Memorial, France
Town/County Connections: Whitehaven, Cumberland
Remarks: —
Account of Deed: On 21 Dec. 1914 at Rouges Bancs, France, Private Acton and another private* went out from their trench and rescued a wounded man who had been lying exposed against the enemy's trenches for 75 hours. On the same day they again left their trench under heavy fire to bring in another wounded man. They were under fire for 60 minutes whilst conveying the wounded men to safety. (*See also SMITH, James — No. 1163)

ADAMS, James William   **6**
The Reverend   Bengal Ecclesiastical Department, Indian Army
Other Decorations: —
Date of Gazette: 26 Aug. 1881
Place/Date of Birth: Cork, Ireland — 24 Nov. 1839
Place/Date of Death: Ashwell, Rutland — 20 Oct. 1903 *Grave in Churchyard, Ashwell.*
Memorials: Stow Bardolph Church, Norfolk , *Postwick, Norfolk.*
Town/County Connections: Cork; Postwick and Stow Bardolph, Norfolk; Ashwell, Rutland
Remarks: Hon. Chaplain to Queen Victoria 1900; Chaplain in ordinary to King Edward VII 1901
Account of Deed: On 11 Dec. 1879 at Killa Kazi, (Afghan War), some men of the 9th Lancers had fallen, with their horses, into a wide, deep ditch and the enemy were close upon them. The Reverend J.W. Adams rushed into the water, dragged the horses off the men, upon whom they were lying, and extricated them. All this time he was under very heavy fire and up to his waist in water. Some of the enemy were within a few yards of him and, having let his own horse go in order to render more effectual assistance, Mr. Adams had to escape on foot.

ADAMS, Robert Bellew (later Sir Robert)   **7**
Bt/Lieutenant Colonel (later Major General)   Staff Corps and Corps of Guides, Indian Army
Other Decorations: KCB
Date of Gazette: 9 Nov. 1897
Place/Date of Birth: Murree, Punjab — 26 Jul. 1856
Place/Date of Death: Inverness, Scotland — 13 Feb. 1928
Memorials: (Cremated Glasgow)
Town/County Connections: Inverness, Scotland
Remarks: —
Account of Deed: On 17 Aug. 1897 at Nawa Kili, Upper Swat, India, (Tirah Campaign), Lieutenant Colonel Adams, with two other officers* and five men of the Guides, went under a heavy and close fire, to the rescue of a lieutenant of the Lancashire Fusiliers who was lying disabled by a bullet wound and surrounded by enemy swordsmen. While the wounded officer was being brought under cover he was unfortunately killed by a bullet. One of the officers of the rescue party was mortally wounded and Colonel Adams' horse and three others were shot. (*See also FINCASTLE, A.E.M. and MACLEAN, H.L.S.)

ADDISON, Henry   **8**
Private   43rd Regt. (later The Oxfordshire and Buckinghamshire Light Infantry)
Other Decorations: —
Date of Gazette: 2 Sep. 1859
Place/Date of Birth: Bardwell, Suffolk — Feb. 1821
Place/Date of Death: Bardwell, Suffolk — 18 Jun. 1887
Memorials: Bardwell Churchyard, Suffolk
Town/County Connections: Bardwell, Suffolk
Remarks: —
Account of Deed: On 2 Jan. 1859 near Kurrereah, India, Private Addison defended a lieutenant against a large force and saved his life when he had fallen on the ground wounded. The private received two dangerous wounds and lost a leg in this gallant service.

ADDISON, William Robert Fountains　　　　　　　　　　　**9**
The Reverend, T/Chaplain of the Forces, 4th Class (later 2nd Class), Army Chaplain's Dept.
Other Decorations: —
Date of Gazette: 26 Sep. 1916
Place/Date of Birth: Cranbrook, Kent — 18 Sep. 1883
Place/Date of Death: St. Leonards-on-Sea, Sussex — 7 Jan. 1962
Memorials: Brookwood Cemetery, Woking, Surrey
Town/County Connections: Goudhurst, Kent; St. Leonards-on-Sea, Sussex
Remarks: Order of St. George (Russia); Senior Chaplain to the Forces, Borden 1934-38 and 1939-42; Deputy Assistant Chaplain General 1942.
Account of Deed: On 9 Apr. 1916 at Sanna-i-Yat, Mesopotamia, The Reverend William Addison carried a wounded man to the cover of a trench and helped several others to the same cover after binding up their wounds under heavy rifle and machine-gun fire. In addition to these unaided efforts, his splendid example and utter disregard of personal danger, encouraged the stretcher-bearers to go forward under heavy fire and collect the wounded.

ADLAM, Tom Edwin　　　　　　　　　　　　　　　　　**10**
T/Second Lieutenant (later Lieutenant Colonel)　7th Bn., The Bedfordshire Regiment
Other Decorations: —
Date of Gazette: 25 Nov. 1916
Place/Date of Birth: Salisbury, Wiltshire — 21 Oct. 1893
Place/Date of Death: Hayling Island, Hampshire — 28 May 1975
Memorials: —
Town/County Connections: Salisbury, Wilts; Hayling Island, Hants.
Remarks: Italian Silver Medal for Military Valour; served in the Second World War with the Royal Engineers (Movement Control Section)
Account of Deed: On 27 Sep. 1916 at Thiepval, France, a portion of a village which had defied capture had to be taken at all costs and Second Lieutenant Adlam rushed from shell-hole to shell-hole under very heavy fire collecting men for a sudden rush. At this stage he was wounded in the leg, but in spite of his wound he led the rush, captured the position and killed the occupants. Throughout the day he continued to lead his men and on the following day, although wounded again he still led and encouraged them. His magnificent example and behaviour produced far-reaching results.

AGANSING RAI　　　　　　　　　　　　　　　　　**11**
Naik (later Havildar)　2nd Bn., 5th Royal Gurkha Rifles, Indian Army
Other Decorations: MM
Date of Gazette: 5 Oct. 1944
Place/Date of Birth: Assora Village, Okhaldunga District, Nepal — ?1920
Place/Date of Death: — *Died about 28.5.2000 Katmandu, Nepal*
Memorials: — *B.*
Town/County Connections: —
Remarks: —
Account of Deed: On 26 Jun. 1944 at Bishenpur, Burma, Naik Agansing Rai led his section in an attack on one of two posts which had been taken by the enemy and were now threatening our communications. Under withering fire the naik and his party charged a machine-gun, he himself killing three of the crew. The first position having been taken, he then led a dash on a machine-gun firing from the jungle, where he killed three of the crew, his men accounting for the rest. He subsequently tackled an isolated bunker single-handed, killing all four occupants. The enemy were now so demoralized that they fled and the second post was recaptured.

AGAR, Augustine William Shelton　　　　　　　　　　　**12**
Lieutenant (later Commodore)　Royal Navy
Other Decorations: DSO　*The Order of Orange Nassau.*
Date of Gazette: 22 Aug. 1919　*Framlingham School, Suffolk.*
Place/Date of Birth: Kandy, Ceylon — 4 Jan. 1890
Place/Date of Death: Alton, Hampshire — 30 Dec. 1968
Memorials: Alton Cemetery, Alton, Hampshire　*Grave No. R.238*
Town/County Connections: Kerry, Ireland; Alton, Hampshire
Remarks: Commodore and President of the Royal Naval College, Greenwich 1943-45; author of *Footprints in the Sea* (autobiography), *Showing the Flag, Baltic Episode*
Account of Deed: On 17 Jun. 1919 at Kronstadt, Russia, Lieutenant Agar took HM Coastal Motor Boat 4 into the bay, penetrated a destroyer screen and was closing a larger warship further inshore when CMB4, whose hull had been damaged by gunfire, broke down. She had to be taken alongside a breakwater to do repairs and for 20 minutes was in full view of the enemy. The attack was then resumed and a Russian cruiser was sunk, after which Lieutenant Agar retired to the safety of the open bay under heavy fire.

AIKMAN, Frederick Robertson   **13**
Lieutenant (later Colonel)   4th Bengal Native Infantry
Other Decorations: —
Date of Gazette: 3 Sep. 1858
Place/Date of Birth: Ross, Broomelton, Lanarkshire, Scotland — 6 Feb. 1828
Place/Date of Death: Hamilton, Lanarkshire, Scotland — 5 Oct. 1888
Memorials: Kensal Green Cemetery, London
Town/County Connections: Broomelton and Hamilton, Scotland; London
Remarks: Member of the Honourable Corps of Gentlemen-at-arms 1865-88.
Account of Deed: On 1 Mar. 1858 near Amethi, India, Lieutenant Aikman, commanding an advanced picket with 100 of his men, was informed of the proximity of a body of 500 rebel infantry and 200 horse and guns. The lieutenant attacked and utterly routed this large enemy force, cutting up more than 100 of them, capturing two guns and driving the survivors over the River Goomtee. This feat was carried out over broken ground and partly under flanking fire from an adjoining fort. Lieutenant Aikman himself received a severe sabre cut in the face.

AITKEN, Robert Hope Moncrieff   **14**
Lieutenant (later Colonel)   13th Bengal Native Infantry
Other Decorations: CB
Date of Gazette: 16 Apr. 1863
Place/Date of Birth: Cupar, Fife, Scotland — 14 Apr. 1828
Place/Date of Death: St. Andrews, Scotland — 18 Sep. 1887
Memorials: Eastern Cemetery, St. Andrews
Town/County Connections: Cupar and St. Andrews, Scotland
Remarks: —
Account of Deed: From 30 Jun. to 22 Nov. 1857 at Lucknow, India, Lieutenant Aitken performed various acts of gallantry during the defence of the Residency. On one occasion when the enemy had set fire to the Bhoosa Stock in the garden, the lieutenant, and other officers, cut down all the tents in order to stop the fire spreading to the powder magazine which was there. This was done close to the enemy's loopholes under the bright light of the flames. Other exploits included saving the Baillie Guard Gate, taking enemy guns and capturing the Fureed Buksh Palace.

ALBRECHT, Herman   **15**
Trooper   Imperial Light Horse (Natal)
Other Decorations: —
Date of Gazette: 8 Aug. 1902
Place/Date of Birth: Burghersdorp, Aliwal, North Cape Area, South Africa — ?1876
Place/Date of Death: Ladysmith, Natal — 6 Jan. 1900
Memorials: Buried at Wagon Hill, Ladysmith
Town/County Connections: —
Remarks: —
Account of Deed: On 6 Jan. 1900 during the attack on Wagon Hill (Ladysmith), South Africa, a lieutenant* of the Royal Engineers and Trooper Albrecht led the force which re-occupied the top of the hill at a critical moment, just as the three foremost attacking Boers reached it. The leader was shot by the lieutenant and the two others by Trooper Albrecht. (*See also JONES, R.J.T.D-)

ALEXANDER, Ernest Wright   **16**
Major (later Major General)   119th Bty., Royal Field Artillery
Other Decorations: CB, CMG
Date of Gazette: 18 Feb. 1915
Place/Date of Birth: Liverpool, Lancashire — 2 Oct. 1870
Place/Date of Death: Kingsbridge, Devon — 25 Aug. 1934
Memorials: (Cremated Putney Vale Cemetery, London — ashes in family grave)
Town/County Connections: Liverpool, Lancs; Kingsbridge, Devon
Remarks: Croix de Guerre (Belgium)   *Harrow School*
Account of Deed: On 24 Aug. 1914 at Elouges, Belgium, when the flank guard was attacked by a German corps, Major Alexander handled his battery against overwhelming odds with such conspicuous success that all his guns were saved notwithstanding that they had to be withdrawn by hand by himself and volunteers led by a Captain* of the 9th Lancers. This enabled the retirement of the 5th Division to be carried out without serious loss. Subsequently, Major Alexander rescued a wounded man under heavy fire. (*See also GRENFELL, F.O.)

No photograph available

ALEXANDER, John   **17**
Private   90th Regiment   (later The Cameronians — Scottish Rifles)
Other Decorations: —
Date of Gazette: 24 Feb. 1857
Place/Date of Birth: Mullingar, West Meath, Ireland—?
Place/Date of Death: Lucknow, India — 24 Sep. 1857
Memorials: —
Town/County Connections: Mullingar, West Meath
Remarks: —
Account of Deed: On 18 Jun. 1855 at Sebastopol, Crimea, after the attack on the Redan, Private
Alexander went out from the trenches under very heavy fire and brought in several wounded men.
Also, on 6 Sep. when he was with a working party in the most advanced trench he went out under heavy fire and helped to bring
in a captain who was severely wounded.

ALGIE, Wallace Lloyd   **18**
Lieutenant   20th Bn., 1st Central Ontario Regiment, C.E.F.
Other Decorations: —
Date of Gazette: 21 Jan. 1919
Place/Date of Birth: Alton, Ontario, Canada — 10 Jun. 1891
Place/Date of Death: Cambrai, France — 11 Oct. 1918
Memorials: Niagara Cemetery, Iwuy, France
Town/County Connections: —
Remarks: —
Account of Deed: On 11 Oct. 1918 north east of Cambrai, France, Lieutenant Algie was with
attacking troops which came under heavy enfilade machine-gun fire from a neighbouring village.
Rushing forward with nine volunteers he shot the crew of an enemy machine-gun and then turned the gun on the enemy,
enabling his party to reach the village. He rushed another machine-gun, killing the crew and capturing an officer and 10 men,
thereby clearing the end of the village. He then went back for reinforcements but was killed while leading them forward.

ALI HAIDAR   **19**
Sepoy (later Havildar)   13th Frontier Force Rifles, Indian Army
Other Decorations: —
Date of Gazette: 3 Jul. 1945
Place/Date of Birth: Shahu Village, Kohat, N.W. Frontier, India — 21 Aug. 1913
Place/Date of Death: — *Died about* 20.7.1999
Memorials: —
Town/County Connections: —
Remarks: —
Account of Deed: On 9 Apr. 1945 near Fusignano, Italy, during the crossing of the Senio River,
only Sepoy Ali Haidar and the two other men of his section managed to get across under heavy
machine-gun fire. Then, while the other two covered him, the sepoy attacked the nearest strong point and, in spite of being
wounded, put it out of action. In attacking a second strong-point he was again severely wounded but managed to crawl closer,
throw a grenade and charge the post; two of the enemy were wounded, the remaining two surrendered. The rest of the
company were then able to cross the river and establish a bridgehead.

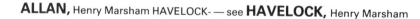

ALLAN, Henry Marsham HAVELOCK- — see **HAVELOCK,** Henry Marsham

ALLAN, William Wilson   **20**
Corporal (later Sergeant Instructor of Musketry)   2nd Bn., 24th Regt. (later The South Wales
Borderers)
Other Decorations: —
Date of Gazette: 2 May 1879
Place/Date of Birth: Newcastle upon Tyne — c.1844
Place/Date of Death: Monmouth — 12 Mar. 1890
Memorials: Monmouth Cemetery
Town/County Connections: Newcastle upon Tyne; Monmouth
Remarks: — *VC in S.W.B. Museum, Brecon*
Account of Deed: On 22 and 23 Jan. 1879 at Rorke's Drift, Natal, South Africa, Corporal Allan and
another man* kept communication with the hospital open, despite being severely wounded. Their determined conduct enabled
the patients to be withdrawn from the hospital, and when incapacitated by their wounds from fighting, they continued, as soon
as their wounds were dressed, to serve out ammunition to their comrades during the night. (*See also HITCH, F.)

ALLEN, William Barnsley 21
Captain (later Major)   Royal Army Medical Corps, attd. 246th (W. Riding) Bde., Royal Field Artillery
Other Decorations: DSO, MC & Bar
Date of Gazette: 26 Oct. 1916
Place/Date of Birth: Sheffield, Yorkshire — 8 Jun. 1892
Place/Date of Death: Bracklesham, Nr. Chichester, Sussex — 27 Oct. 1933
Memorials: Earnley Cemetery, Bracklesham Bay, Sussex
Town/County Connections: Sheffield, Yorks; Hounslow, Middlesex
Remarks: —
Account of Deed: On 3 Sep. 1916, near Mesnil, France, when gun detachments were unloading high explosive ammunition, the enemy suddenly began to shell the battery position. The first shell fell on one of the limbers, exploded the ammunition and caused several casualties. Captain Allen at once ran across under heavy shell fire and started attending to the wounded. He himself was hit four times by pieces of shell, but he went coolly on with his work until the last man had been attended to and removed. He then went to tend a wounded officer and only then reported his own injuries.

ALLMAND, Michael 22
A/Captain   Indian Armoured Corps, attd. 6th Gurkha Rifles, Indian Army
Other Decorations: —
Date of Gazette: 26 Oct. 1944
Place/Date of Birth: London — 22 Aug. 1923
Place/Date of Death: Pin Hmi, Burma — 24 Jun. 1944
Memorials: Taukkyan War Cemetery, Burma
Town/County Connections: Golders Green, London
Remarks: —
Account of Deed: On 11 Jun. 1944 in Burma, Captain Allmand's platoon came under heavy fire when attacking the Pin Hmi Road Bridge, and on being halted by casualties, he charged on alone, killing three of the enemy. Inspired by his example his surviving men followed him and captured the postion. Two days later, owing to heavy casualties among the officers, Captain Allmand took command of the company and successfully led his men to seize a ridge of high ground. Again, on 23 Jun. in the final assault on the railway bridge at Mogaung, he went forward alone, but in charging an enemy machine-gun nest, was mortally wounded.

AMEY, William 23
Lance-Corporal (later Corporal)   1/8th Bn., The Royal Warwickshire Regiment
Other Decorations: MM
Date of Gazette: 31 Jan. 1919
Place/Date of Birth: Duddeston, Birmingham — 5 Mar. 1881
Place/Date of Death: Leamington Spa, Warwickshire — 28 May 1940
Memorials: — *Buried All Saints Church, Leamington Spa.*
Town/County Connections: Birmingham; Leamington Spa
Remarks: —
Account of Deed: On 4 Nov. 1918 at Landrecies, France, when many hostile machine-gun nests were missed by the leading troops owing to fog, Lance-Corporal Amey led his section against a machine-gun nest under heavy fire and drove the garrison into a neighbouring farm, finally capturing 50 prisoners and several machine-guns. Later, single-handed and under heavy fire he attacked a machine-gun post in a farmhouse, killed two of the garrison and drove the remainder into a cellar until assistance arrived. Subsequently he rushed a strongly-held post, capturing 20 more prisoners.

ANDERSON, Charles 24
Private (later Corporal)   2nd Dragoon Guards (Queen's Bays)
Other Decorations: —
Date of Gazette: 11 Nov. 1862
Place/Date of Birth: Liverpool — 1826
Place/Date of Death: Seaham Harbour, Sunderland — 19 Apr. 1899
Memorials: —
Town/County Connections: Liverpool; Dublin
Remarks: — *VC in Queens Dragoon Guards Museum, Shrewsbury.*
Account of Deed: On 8 Oct. 1858 near Sundeela Oudh, India, a group of mutineers (30 to 40 in number) suddenly opened fire on the officer commanding the regiment and his party, and then rushed upon them with drawn swords. In the fighting which ensued the colonel was cut down, and Private Anderson and a trumpeter* immediately came to his rescue, shooting one of the assailants and driving at others with their swords, thus enabling the colonel to rise and defend himself again, until the enemy were despatched. (*See also MONAGHAN, T.)

ANDERSON, Charles Groves Wright

25

Lieutenant Colonel   Comd. 2/19th Bn., (N.S.W.), Australian Military Forces
Other Decorations: MC
Date of Gazette: 13 Feb. 1942
Place/Date of Birth: Capetown, South Africa — 12 Feb. 1897
Place/Date of Death: — *Canberra 11.11.1988.*
Memorials: Australian War Memorial, Canberra
Town/County Connections: —
Remarks: Served in First World War, with the King's African Rifles; Member of House of Representatives for Hume, New South Wales, 1949-51 and 1955-61
Account of Deed: During the period 18/22 Jan. 1942, near the Muar River, Malaya, Lieutenant Colonel Anderson was in command of a small force which destroyed 10 enemy tanks and, when later they were cut off, he led his force through enemy lines to a depth of 15 miles, being attacked by air and ground forces all the way. He was again surrounded and suffered heavy casualties, and although he attempted to fight his way back through eight miles of enemy-occupied territory, this proved impossible, and he had to destroy his equipment and work his way around the enemy. Throughout the fighting he protected his wounded and refused to leave them.

ANDERSON, Eric

26

Private   5th Bn., The East Yorkshire Regiment
Other Decorations: —
Date of Gazette: 29 Jul. 1943
Place/Date of Birth: Fagley, Eccleshill, Bradford, Yorkshire — 15 Sep. 1915
Place/Date of Death: Akarit, Tunisia — 6 Apr. 1943
Memorials: Sfax War Cemetery, Tunisia; Beverley Minster and St. John's United Reformed Church, Bradford
Town/County Connections: Bradford, Yorks.
Remarks: —
Account of Deed: On 6 Apr. 1943 on the Wadi Akarit, Tunisia, when a company of The East Yorkshire Regiment had to withdraw temporarily behind the crest of a hill, Private Anderson, a stretcher-bearer, went forward alone through heavy fire to rescue the wounded. Three times he brought in wounded comrades, and was rendering first aid to a fourth when he was mortally wounded.

ANDERSON, John Thompson McKellar

27

A/Major   8th Bn., The Argyll and Sutherland Highlanders (Princess Louise's)
Other Decorations: DSO
Date of Gazette: 29 Jun. 1943
Place/Date of Birth: Hampstead, London — 12 Jan. 1918
Place/Date of Death: Termoli, Italy — 5 Oct. 1943
Memorials: Sangro River War Cemetery, Italy
Town/County Connections: Hampstead, London; Bagshot, Surrey
Remarks: — *Name on Bagshot W.M. & in Church.*
Account of Deed: On 23 Apr. 1943 at Longstop Hill, Tunisia, Major Anderson assumed command of the battalion when his commanding officer was killed and although he himself was wounded in the leg he went on and eventually occupied the objective. His force was reduced to about 44 officers and men, but 200 prisoners were taken and he had personally led successful attacks on several machine-gun posts and mortars.

ANDERSON, William

28

Corporal   2nd Bn., The Yorkshire Regt. (Alexandra, Princess of Wales's Own)
Other Decorations: —
Date of Gazette: 22 May 1915
Place/Date of Birth: Dallas, Elgin, Morayshire, Scotland — Nov. 1885
Place/Date of Death: Neuve Chapelle, France — 13 Mar. 1915
Memorials: Le Touret Memorial, France
Town/County Connections: Dallas, Elgin, Morayshire
Remarks: —
Account of Deed: On 12 Mar. 1915 at Neuve Chapelle, France, Corporal Anderson led three men with bombs against a large party of the enemy who had entered our trenches, and by his prompt and determined action saved what might have otherwise become a serious situation. Corporal Anderson first threw his own bombs, then those in the possession of the other men (all of whom had been wounded) amongst the Germans, after which he opened rapid fire upon them with great effect, notwithstanding that he was at the time quite alone.

ANDERSON, William Herbert   **29**
A/Lieutenant Colonel   Comd. 12th (S) Bn., The Highland Light Infantry
Other Decorations: —
Date of Gazette: 3 May 1918
Place/Date of Birth: Glasgow — 29 Dec. 1881
Place/Date of Death: Nr. Maricourt, France — 25 Mar. 1918
Memorials: Peronne Road Cemetery, France
Town/County Connections: Glasgow
Remarks: —
Account of Deed: On 25 Mar. 1918 at Bois Favieres, near Maricourt, France, when the enemy attack had penetrated a wood on the right of his line and there was grave danger that the flank of the whole position would be turned, Lieutenant Colonel Anderson gathered together the remainder of his two companies, counter-attacked and drove the Germans from the wood, capturing 12 machine-guns and 70 prisoners. Later the same day, Colonel Anderson led another counter-attack which resulted in the enemy being driven from his position, but the colonel died fighting within the enemy's lines.

ANDREW, Leslie Wilton   **30**
Corporal (later Brigadier)   2nd Bn., Wellington Infantry Regiment, N.Z.E.F.
Other Decorations: DSO
Date of Gazette: 6 Sep. 1917
Place/Date of Birth: Ashurst, New Zealand — 23 Mar. 1897
Place/Date of Death: Palmerston North, New Zealand — 9 Jan. 1969
Memorials: HQ, Dunedin RSA, New Zealand
Town/County Connections: —
Remarks: NZSC (New Zealand); commanded a N.Z. Brigade in Crete in the Second World War.
Account of Deed: On 31 Jul. 1917 at La Bassee Ville, France, Corporal Andrew was in charge of a small party in an attack on the enemy's position. His objective was a machine-gun post which had been located in an isolated building, but on leading his men forward he encountered another machine-gun post which was holding up the advance of another company. He immediately attacked it, capturing the gun and killing several of the crew. He then continued with his attack on the original objective and finally captured the post, killing a number of the enemy and putting the remainder to flight.

ANDREWS, Harold Marcus ERVINE-   **31**
Captain (later Lieutenant-Colonel)   The East Lancashire Regiment
Other Decorations: —
Date of Gazette: 30 Jul. 1940
Place/Date of Birth: Keadue, Cavan, Ireland — 29 Jul. 1911
Place/Date of Death: —
Memorials: —
Town/County Connections: Keadue, Cavan; Bodmin and Gorran, Cornwall
Remarks: Attd. to RAF in U.K., 1940; on loan to Australian Military Forces 1941-3; Commanding No.61 Carrier-Borne Army Liaison Section, 1944; SALO in 21st Aircraft Carrier Squadron, 1945; Assistant Director of Public Relations to B.A.O.R., 1951
Account of Deed: During the night of 31 May/1 Jun. 1940 near Dunkirk, France, the company commanded by Captain Ervine-Andrews was heavily outnumbered and under intense German fire. When the enemy attacked at dawn and crossed the Canal de Bergues, Captain Ervine-Andrews, with volunteers from his company, rushed to a barn and from the roof shot 17 of the enemy with a rifle and many more with a Bren gun. When the barn was shattered and alight, he sent the wounded to the rear and led the remaining eight men back, wading for over a mile in water up to their chins.

ANDREWS, Henry John   **32**
T/Captain   Indian Medical Service
Other Decorations: MBE
Date of Gazette: 9 Sep. 1920
Place/Date of Birth: London — 1871
Place/Date of Death: Kajuri Post, Waziristan — 22 Oct. 1919
Memorials: Delhi Memorial, India
Town/County Connections: London
Remarks: Served with the Salvation Army for 30 years in India
Account of Deed: On 22 Oct. 1919 at Waziristan, North-west India, Captain Andrews, the senior medical officer in charge of the Khajeri Post, heard that a convoy had been attacked in the vicinity and that men had been wounded. He at once went out under heavy fire and established an Aid Post under conditions which afforded some protection to the wounded, but none to himself. He was subsequently compelled to move the Aid Post, but continued to attend the wounded. Finally when a van was available, he collected the wounded, under fire, and put them into it. He was killed whilst stepping into the van on the completion of his task.

ANGUS, William
33

Lance-Corporal   8th Bn., The Highland Light Infantry
Other Decorations: —
Date of Gazette: 29 Jun. 1915
Place/Date of Birth: Armadale, Linlithgow, West Lothian, Scotland — 28 Feb. 1888
Place/Date of Death: Carluke, Lanarkshire, Scotland — 14 Jun. 1959
Memorials: Wilton Cemetery, Carluke
Town/County Connections: Armadale, West Lothian; Carluke, Lanarkshire
Remarks: —
Account of Deed: On 12 Jun. 1915 at Givenchy, France, Lance-Corporal Angus voluntarily left his trench under very heavy bomb and rifle fire and rescued a wounded officer who was lying within a few yards of the enemy's position. The lance-corporal had no chance of escaping the enemy's fire when undertaking this gallant deed, and in effecting the rescue he received about 40 wounds, some of them being very serious.

ANNAND, Richard Wallace
34

Second Lieutenant (later Captain)   2nd Bn., The Durham Light Infantry
Other Decorations: —
Date of Gazette: 23 Aug. 1940
Place/Date of Birth: South Shields, Co. Durham — 5 Nov. 1914
Place/Date of Death: — *Christmas Eve 2004. South Shields County Durham*
Memorials: —
Town/County Connections: South Shields, Co. Durham
Remarks: Personnel Officer at Finchale Abbey Training Centre for the Disabled, near Durham, 1948; DL County of Durham, 1956
Account of Deed: On 15 May 1940, near the River Dyle, Belgium, Second Lieutenant Annand inflicted heavy casualties on the enemy with hand grenades. He was wounded, but after having his wound dressed, he made another attack on the enemy the same evening. Later, when the position became hopeless and the platoon was ordered to withdraw, Lieutenant Annand discovered that his batman was wounded and missing. He returned at once to the former position and brought him back in a wheelbarrow before fainting from loss of blood.

ANSON, The Hon. Augustus Henry Archibald
35

Captain (later Lieutenant Colonel)   84th Regt. (later The York and Lancaster Regt.)
Other Decorations: —
Date of Gazette: 24 Dec. 1858
Place/Date of Birth: Pembroke, Wales — 5 Mar. 1835
Place/Date of Death: Cannes, France — 17 Dec. 1877
Memorials: Cimitière Protestant du Grand Jas, Cannes, France; Lichfield Cathedral
Town/County Connections: Pembroke; Shugborough and Lichfield, Staffs.
Remarks: *VC with the National Trust.*
Account of Deed: On 28 Sep. 1857 at Bolandshahr, India, the 9th Light Dragoons had charged through the town and were reforming on the Serai, when the enemy tried to close the entrance by drawing their carts across it. Captain Anson, taking a lance, dashed out of the gateway and knocked the drivers off their carts. Owing to a wound in his left hand, he could not stop his horse and rode into the middle of the enemy who fired on him. At Lucknow, on 16 Nov. 1857 he again showed great gallantry when he entered with a storming party on the gates being burst open; his horse was killed and he was slightly wounded.

ARCHIBALD, Adam
36

Sapper   218th Field Coy., Corps of Royal Engineers
Other Decorations: —
Date of Gazette: 6 Jan. 1919
Place/Date of Birth: Leith, Midlothian, Scotland — 14 Jan. 1879
Place/Date of Death: Leith, Midlothian — 10 Mar. 1957
Memorials: —
Town/County Connections: Leith, Midlothian
Remarks: —
Account of Deed: On 4 Nov. 1918 near Ors, France, Sapper Archibald was with a party building a floating bridge across the canal. He was foremost in the work under a very heavy artillery barrage and machine-gun fire. The latter was directed at him from a few yards distance while he was working on the cork floats. Nevertheless he persevered in his task and his example and efforts were such that the bridge which was essential to the success of the operations was very quickly completed. Immediately afterwards Sapper Archibald collapsed from gas poisoning.

ARTHUR, (real name McARTHUR) Thomas   **37**
Gunner and Driver   Royal Regiment of Artillery
Other Decorations: —
Date of Gazette: 24 Feb. 1857
Place/Date of Birth: Abbotsham, Bideford, Devon — 1835
Place/Date of Death: Savernake, Wiltshire — 2 Mar. 1902
Memorials: Cadley Churchyard, Wiltshire
Town/County Connections: Bideford, Devon; Savernake, Wiltshire
Remarks: Médaille Militaire (France); fought in the China War, 1860
Account of Deed: On 7 Jun. 1855 in the Crimea, Gunner Arthur was in charge of the magazine in one of the left advanced batteries of the right attack, when the Quarries were taken. On his own initiative he carried barrels of infantry ammunition for the 7th Fusiliers several times during the evening, across the open. He volunteered for and formed one of the spiking party of artillery at the assault on the Redan on 18 Jun. 1855 and on numerous occasions left the trenches to bring in wounded officers and men.

ASHFORD, Thomas Elsdon   **38**
Private   The Royal Fusiliers
Other Decorations: —
Date of Gazette: 7 Oct. 1881
Place/Date of Birth: Newmarket, Suffolk — 1859
Place/Date of Death: Whitwick, Leicestershire — 21 Feb. 1913
Memorials: Whitwick Cemetery
Town/County Connections: Newmarket, Suffolk; Whitwick, Leicestershire
Remarks: —
Account of Deed: On 16 Aug. 1880 at Deh Khoja, near Kandahar, (Afghan War) Private Ashford assisted a lieutenant* in rescuing and carrying for a distance of over 200 yards under the fire of the enemy, a wounded soldier who had taken shelter in a block house. Several times they were compelled to rest, but they persevered and finally brought the wounded man to a place of safety. (*See also CHASE, W.St.L.)

ATKINSON, Alfred   **39**
Sergeant   1st Bn., The Yorkshire Regt. (Alexandra, Princess of Wales's Own)
Other Decorations: —
Date of Gazette: 8 Aug. 1902
Place/Date of Birth: Leeds, Yorkshire — 6 Feb. 1874
Place/Date of Death: Nr. Paardeberg, South Africa — 21 Feb. 1900
Memorials: —
Town/County Connections: Leeds, Yorkshire.
Remarks: —
Account of Deed: On 18 Feb. 1900 during the Battle of Paardeberg, South Africa, Sergeant Atkinson went out seven times under heavy and close fire to obtain water for the wounded. At the seventh attempt he was wounded in the head and died a few days afterwards.

AUTEN, Harold   **40**
Lieutenant (later Commander)   Royal Naval Reserve
Other Decorations: DSC
Date of Gazette: 14 Sep. 1918
Place/Date of Birth: Leatherhead, Surrey — 22 Aug. 1891
Place/Date of Death: Bushkill, Pennsylvania, USA — 3 Oct. 1964
Memorials: —
Town/County Connections: Leatherhead, Surrey; Lewisham, London
Remarks: Order of Orange Nassau (Netherlands); Legion of Merit (USA); served with the RNR again during the Second World War, routeing convoy shipping leaving New York for Europe. Author of *Q Boat Adventures*
Account of Deed: On 30 Jul. 1918 in the English Channel, Lieutenant Auten was in command of HMS *Stock Force* (one of the 'Q' or 'mystery' ships) when she was torpedoed by a U-boat and very badly damaged. The 'Panic party' took to the boats and the U-boat surfaced half a mile away, but after 15 minutes the 'Panic party' began to row back, followed by the U-boat. When it lay about 300 yards from *Stock Force* the guns opened fire, doing tremendous damage to the submarine which sank in a very short time. *Stock Force* finally sank about four hours later, Lieutenant Auten and her crew being taken off by a torpedo boat.

AXFORD, Thomas Leslie   **41**
Lance-Corporal (later Corporal)   16th Bn. (S.A. and W.A.) Australian Imperial Force
Other Decorations: MM
Date of Gazette: 17 Aug. 1918
Place/Date of Birth: Carleton, Carriston, South Australia — 18 Jun. 1894
Place/Date of Death: In the air between Dubai and Hongkong — 11 Oct. 1983 *After*
Memorials: Australian War Memorial, Canberra. *attending VC/GC Reunion*
Town/County Connections: —
Remarks: —
Account of Deed: On 4 Jul. 1918 during the attack at Vaire and Hamel Woods, France, when the advance of the adjoining platoon was being delayed in uncut wire and machine-gun fire, and his company commander had become a casualty, Lance-Corporal Axford charged and threw bombs amongst the enemy gun crews. He then jumped into the trench, and charging with his bayonet, killed 10 of the enemy and took six prisoners. He threw the machine-guns over the parapet and the delayed platoon was able to advance. He then rejoined his own platoon and fought with it during the remainder of the operations.

AYLMER Fenton John (later Sir Fenton)   **42**
Captain (later Lieutenant General)   Corps of Royal Engineers
Other Decorations: KCB
Date of Gazette: 12 Jul. 1892
Place/Date of Birth: Hastings, Sussex — 5 Apr. 1862
Place/Date of Death: Wimbledon, Surrey — 3 Sep. 1935
Memorials: (Cremated, Golders Green, London); Kilcock Church, Co. Kildare, Ireland
Town/County Connections: Hastings, Sussex; Donadea, Co. Kildare; Wimbledon, Surrey
Remarks: Served in the First World War, 1914-18; Colonel-Commandant, Corps of Royal Engineers, 1922-35
Account of Deed: On 2 Dec. 1891 during the assault on Nilt fort, India (Hunza Campaign), Captain Aylmer, with the storming party, forced open the inner gate with gun-cotton which he had placed and ignited, and although severely wounded, fired 19 shots with his revolver, killing several of the enemy, and remained fighting until, fainting from loss of blood, he was carried out of action.

BABTIE, William (later Sir William)   **43**
Major (later Lieutenant General)   Royal Army Medical Corps
Other Decorations: KCB, KCMG
Date of Gazette: 20 Apr. 1900
Place/Date of Birth: Dumbarton, Scotland — 7 May 1859
Place/Date of Death: Knocke, Belgium — 11 Sep. 1920
Memorials: —
Town/County Connections: Dumbarton, Scotland
Remarks: Knight of the Order of St. John; Deputy Director General, Army Medical Services, 1910-1914; Director, Medical Services in India, 1914-15; Director, and later Inspector, Medical Services, War Office, 1916-19
Account of Deed: On 15 Dec. 1899 at the Battle of Colenso, South Africa, Major Babtie rode up under heavy rifle fire to attend to the wounded who were lying in an advanced donga close to the rear of the guns. When he arrived at the donga, he attended to them all, going from place to place, exposed to the heavy rifle fire which greeted anyone who showed himself. Later in the day Major Babtie went out with another officer* to bring in a Lieutenant* who was lying wounded on the veldt — this also under very heavy fire. (*See also CONGREVE, W.N. and ROBERTS, F.H.S.)

BADCOE, Peter John   **44**
Major   Australian Army Training Team, Vietnam
Other Decorations: —
Date of Gazette: 13 Oct. 1967
Place/Date of Birth: Adelaide, South Australia — 11 Jan. 1934
Place/Date of Death: Huong Tra, Vietnam — 7 April 1967
Memorials: Terendak Cemetery, Malaysia; Australian War Memorial, Canberra
Town/County Connections: —
Remarks: —
Account of Deed: On 23 Feb. 1967 in Vietnam, Major Badcoe rescued, under heavy fire, a United States Medical Adviser. On 7 Mar. he led his company in an attack and turned what seemed to be certain defeat into a victory. Again, on 7 Apr. he attempted to lead his company against more powerful opposition. This final act of bravery resulted in his death.

BADLU SINGH 45
Ressaidar   14th Lancers, (The Scinde Horse) Indian Army, attd. 29th Lancers (Deccan Horse)
Other Decorations: —
Date of Gazette: 27 Nov. 1918
Place/Date of Birth: Dhakla Village, Rohtak District, Punjab, India —
Place/Date of Death: River Jordan, Palestine — 23 Sep. 1918
Memorials: The Heliopolis (Port Tewfik) Memorial, Heliopolis War Cemetery, Cairo, Egypt
Town/County Connections: —
Remarks: —
Account of Deed: On 23 Sep. 1918 on the west bank of the River Jordan, Palestine, when his squadron was charging a strong enemy position, Ressaidar Badlu Singh realised that heavy casualties were being inflicted from a small hill occupied by machine-guns and 200 infantry. Without any hesitation he collected six other ranks and with entire disregard of danger he charged and captured the position. He was mortally wounded on the very top of the hill when capturing one of the machine-guns single handed, but all the guns and infantry had surrendered to him before he died.

BAKER Charles George 46
Lieutenant   Bengal Police Battalion
Other Decorations: —
Date of Gazette: 25 Feb. 1862
Place/Date of Birth: Neocolly, Bengal — 8 Dec. 1830
Place/Date of Death: Southbourne, Hampshire — 19 Feb. 1906
Memorials: —
Town/County Connections: Southbourne, Hampshire
Remarks: Officiating Deputy Inspector General of Police, Dacca Circle of Bengal 1863; Inspector of Brigade, Imperial Ottoman Gendarmerie 1877; transferred to the Egyptian Gendarmerie in 1882, rising to the rank of Major General, Pasha.
Account of Deed: On 27 Sep. 1858 at Suhejnee, near Peroo, Bengal, Lieutenant Baker was in command of a mixed party of cavalry and mounted police (about 120 strong) which attacked and put to flight a force of about 700 rebels. The whole operation, brilliantly conceived and most gallantly carried out, resulted in the utter defeat of the enemy. (See also CHICKEN, G.B.)

BALL, Albert 47
T/Captain   7th Bn., The Sherwood Foresters (The Nottinghamshire & Derbyshire Regt.) and Royal Flying Corps.
Other Decorations: DSO & 2 Bars, MC
Date of Gazette: 8 Jun. 1917
Place/Date of Birth: Lenton, Nottinghamshire — 14 Aug. 1896
Place/Date of Death: Annoeullin, France — 7 May 1917
Memorials: Annoeullin Communal Cemetery, German extension, France; wall-garden, Nottingham Castle; memorial on site of crash, east of cemetery
Town/County Connections: Nottingham · *Scholarship at Trent College, Nottingham*
Remarks: Légion d'Honneur (France); Order of St. George, 4th Class (Russia).
Account of Deed: From 26 Apr. to 6 May 1917 over France, Captain Ball took part in 26 combats in the course of which he destroyed 11 hostile aircraft, brought down two out of control and forced several others to land. Flying alone, on one occasion he fought six hostile machines, twice he fought five and once four. When leading two other British planes he attacked an enemy formation of eight — on each of these occasions he brought down at least one enemy plane, and several times his plane was badly damaged. On returning with a damaged plane he had always to be restrained from immediately going out in another.

No photograph available

BAMBRICK, Valentine 48
Private   1st Bn., 60th Regiment (later The King's Royal Rifle Corps)
Other Decorations: —
Date of Gazette: 24 Dec. 1858
Place/Date of Birth: Cawnpore, India — 13 Apr. 1837
Place/Date of Death: Pentonville, London — 1 Apr. 1864
Memorials: (Islington Cemetery, London — unmarked grave)
Town/County Connections: Stepney, London
Remarks: —
Account of Deed: On 6 May 1858 at Bareilly, India, Private Bambrick showed conspicuous bravery when, in a serai, he was attacked by three Ghazees, one of whom he cut down. He was wounded twice on this occasion.

BAMFORD, Edward **49**
Captain (later Major) Royal Marine Light Infantry
Other Decorations: DSO
Date of Gazette: 23 Jul. 1918
Place/Date of Birth: London — 28 May 1887
Place/Date of Death: Shanghai — 29 Sep. 1928
Memorials: Bubbling Well Road Cemetery, Shanghai; Depot Church, Deal, Kent
Town/County Connections: Highgate, London. *Sherborne School, Dorset.*
Remarks: Légion d'Honneur (France); Order of St. Anne, 3rd Class (Russia); Order of the Rising Sun, 4th Class (Japan).
Account of Deed: On 22/23 Apr. 1918 at Zeebrugge, Belgium, Captain Bamford landed on the Mole from HMS *Vindictive* with three platoons of the Royal Marines storming force in the face of great difficulties. When on the Mole and under heavy fire, he commanded his company with total disregard of personal danger and showed a magnificent example to his men. He first established a strong point on the right of the disembarkation and when satisfied that it was safe, led an assault on a battery to the left. (Award by ballot.)

BANKES, William George Hawtry **50**
Cornet   7th Hussars (The Queen's Own)
Other Decorations: —
Date of Gazette: 24 Dec. 1858
Place/Date of Birth: Kingston Lacy, Dorset — 11 Sep. 1836
Place/Date of Death: Lucknow, India — 6 Apr. 1858
Memorials: Wimborne Minster, Dorest
Town/County Connections: Kingston Lacy and Corfe Castle, Dorset
Remarks: —
Account of Deed: On 19 Mar. 1858 at Lucknow, India, Cornet Bankes led three charges against a body of fanatical rebels who had rushed the guns in the vicinity of Moosa-Bagh. In the course of these charges the young officer was almost cut to pieces. He died of his wounds 18 days later.

BARBER, Edward **51**
Private   1st Bn., Grenadier Guards
Other Decorations: —
Date of Gazette: 19 Apr. 1915
Place/Date of Birth: Tring, Hertfordshire — 10 Jun. 1893
Place/Date of Death: Neuve Chapelle, France — 12 Mar. 1915
Memorials: Le Touret Memorial, France
Town/County Connections: Tring, Hertfordshire
Remarks: —
Account of Deed: On 12 Mar. 1915 at Neuve Chapelle, France, Private Barber ran in front of the grenade company to which he belonged, and threw bombs on the enemy with such effect that a very great number of them surrendered at once. When the grenade party reached Private Barber they found him alone and unsupported, with the enemy surrendering all about him. He was killed soon afterwards.

BARKER, William George **52**
A/Major   201 Squadron, Royal Air Force
Other Decorations: DSO & Bar, MC & 2 Bars
Date of Gazette: 30 Nov. 1918
Place/Date of Birth: Dauphin, Manitoba, Canada — 3 Nov. 1894
Place/Date of Death: Nr. Ottawa, Canada — 1 Mar. 1930
Memorials: Mount Pleasant Cemetery, Toronto
Town/County Connections: —
Remarks: Croix de Guerre (France); Italian Silver Medal for Military Valour; served with the Canadian Air Force (as Wing-Commander) 1920-24
Account of Deed: On 27 Oct. 1918 over the Foret de Mormal, France, Major Barker attacked a two-seater enemy aircraft causing it to break up in the air. He was afterwards attacked by formations of Fokker fighters and was wounded in both thighs and his elbow was shattered. He lost consciousness twice but each time, on recovering, went back to the attack and sent three of his opponents down in flames. Finally he brought his crippled aircraft back to our lines where he crashed on landing.

BARRATT, Thomas   **53**
Private   7th Bn., The South Staffordshire Regiment
Other Decorations: —
Date of Gazette: 6 Sep. 1917
Place/Date of Birth: Dudley, Worcestershire — 5 May 1895
Place/Date of Death: Nr. Boesinghe, Ypres, Belgium — 27 Jul. 1917
Memorials: Essex Farm Cemetery, Boesinghe, Belgium; Coseley Parish Church; Garrison
Church, Whittington Barracks, Lichfield, Staffordshire
Town/County Connections: Bilston and Tipton, Staffs; Dudley, Worcs.
Remarks: —
Account of Deed: On 27 Jul. 1917 north of Ypres, Belgium, Private Barratt, as a scout to a patrol,
worked his way towards the enemy under continuous fire from hostile snipers, which he stalked and killed. Later his patrol was
similarly held up and again he disposed of the snipers. When a party of the enemy were endeavouring to outflank the patrol on
their withdrawal, Private Barratt volunteered to cover the withdrawal which he did, his accurate shooting causing many
casualties and preventing the enemy advance. After safely regaining our lines this gallant soldier was killed by a shell.

BARRETT, John Cridlan   **54**
Lieutenant (later Colonel)   1/5th Bn., The Leicestershire Regiment
Other Decorations: TD
Date of Gazette: 14 Dec. 1918
Place/Date of Birth: Leamington Spa, Warwickshire — 10 Aug. 1897
Place/Date of Death: Leicester — 7 Mar. 1977
Memorials: —
Town/County Connections: Leamington, Warwickshire; Paddington, London; Leicester
Remarks: — *Merchant Taylor's School, Northwood, Middx*
Account of Deed: On 24 Sep. 1918 at Pontruet, France, during an attack, owing to the darkness
and smoke barrage, Lieutenant Barrett found himself advancing towards a trench containing
numerous machine-guns. He at once collected all available men and charged the nearest group of guns and in spite of being
wounded, gained the trench, personally disposing of two machine-guns and inflicting many casualties. Notwithstanding a
second wound he then climbed out of the trench to fix his position and locate the enemy, then ordered his men to cut their way
back to the battalion, which they did. He was again wounded, very seriously.

BARRON, Colin Fraser   **55**
Corporal (later Sergeant)   3rd Bn., 1st Central Ontario Regiment (Toronto Regiment), C.E.F.
Other Decorations: —
Date of Gazette: 11 Jan. 1918
Place/Date of Birth: Baldavie, Boyndie, Banff, Canada — 20 Sep. 1893
Place/Date of Death: Toronto, Canada — 15 Aug. 1958
Memorials: Prospect Cemetery, Toronto
Town/County Connections: —
Remarks: —
Account of Deed: On 6 Nov. 1917 at Passchendaele, Belgium, when his unit was held up by three
machine-guns, Corporal Barron opened fire on them at point-blank range, rushed the guns, killed
four of the crew and captured the remainder. He then turned one of the captured guns on the retiring enemy, causing severe
casualties. This action produced far-reaching results and enabled the advance to continue.

BARRY, John   **56**
Private   1st Bn., The Royal Irish Regiment
Other Decorations: —
Date of Gazette: 8 Aug. 1902
Place/Date of Birth: Kilkenny, Ireland — 1 Feb. 1873
Place/Date of Death: Belfast, South Africa — 8 Jan. 1901
Memorials: —
Town/County Connections: Kilkenny and Ballyragget, Ireland
Remarks: —
Account of Deed: On 7/8 Jan. 1901 at Monument Hill, South Africa, during a night attack, Private
Barry, although wounded and threatened by the enemy, smashed the breach of the Maxim gun,
thus rendering it useless to its captors. It was while doing this gallant act that he met his death.

BARRY, Michael — see **MAGNER,** Michael

BARTER, Frederick   **57**
Company Sergeant-Major (later Captain)   Spec. Res., attd. 1st Bn., The Royal Welch Fusiliers
Other Decorations: MC
Date of Gazette: 29 Jun. 1915
Place/Date of Birth: Cardiff — 17 Jan. 1891
Place/Date of Death: Canford Cliffs, Bournemouth — 15 May 1952
Memorials: (Cremated Bournemouth) . *Ashes scattered.*
Town/County Connections: Cardiff . *Barter Road & Barter court. Wrexham.*
Remarks: Served with the Home Guard in Second World War
Account of Deed: On 16 May 1915 at Festubert, France, Company Sergeant-Major Barter, when in the first line of German trenches, called for volunteers to enable him to extend our line, and with the eight men who responded, he attacked the German position with bombs, capturing three German officers, 102 men and 500 yards of their trenches. He subsequently found and cut 11 of the enemy's mine leads situated about 20 yards apart.

BARTON, Cyril Joe   **58**
Pilot Officer   578 Squadron, Royal Air Force Volunteer Reserve
Other Decorations: —
Date of Gazette: 27 Jun. 1944
Place/Date of Birth: Elveden, Suffolk — 5 Jun. 1921
Place/Date of Death: Ryhope, Co. Durham — 31 Mar. 1944
Memorials: Kingston-upon-Thames Cemetery, Surrey; village war memorial at Ryhope . *Durham*
Town/County Connections: Elveden, Suffolk; New Malden, Surrey
Remarks: —
Account of Deed: On 30 Mar. 1944 in an attack on Nuremburg, Germany and while 70 miles from the target, Pilot Officer Barton's Halifax bomber was badly damaged by enemy aircraft. A misinterpreted signal resulted in three of the crew baling out and Pilot Officer Barton was left with no navigator, air bomber or wireless operator. He pressed on with the attack, however, releasing the bombs himself. On the return journey, as he crossed the English coast, the fuel ran short and with only one engine working he crashed trying to avoid the houses of a village, and was killed.

BASKEYFIELD, John Daniel   **59**
Lance-Sergeant   The South Staffordshire Regiment, 1st Airborne Division
Other Decorations: —
Date of Gazette: 23 Nov. 1944
Place/Date of Birth: Burslem, Staffordshire — 18 Nov. 1922
Place/Date of Death: Arnhem, Holland — 20 Sep. 1944
Memorials: The Groesbeek Memorial, Holland; Garrison Church, Whittington Barracks, Lichfield, Staffs.
Town/County Connections: Burslem, Staffs.
Remarks: —
Account of Deed: On 20 Sep. 1944 at Arnhem, Holland, Lance-Sergeant Baskeyfield was in charge of a 6-pounder anti-tank gun and in the course of the engagement when two Tiger tanks and at least one self-propelling gun were destroyed, the lance-sergeant was wounded and all his crew became casualties. Nevertheless he continued to man his gun quite alone, keeping the enemy at bay, until it was put out of action, when he crawled to another 6-pounder and proceeded to man that single-handed. He fired two shots at a self-propelling gun, one of which was a direct hit, and was preparing to fire a third when he was killed.

BASSETT, Cyril Royston Guyton   **60**
Corporal (later Colonel)   New Zealand Divisional Signal Company, N.Z.E.F
Other Decorations: —
Date of Gazette: 15 Oct. 1915
Place/Date of Birth: Mount Eden, Auckland, New Zealand — 3 Jan. 1892
Place/Date of Death: Devonport, Auckland, New Zealand — 2 Jan. 1983
Memorials: Dunedin RSA, New Zealand
Town/County Connections: —
Remarks: —
Account of Deed: On 7 Aug. 1915 at Chunuk Bair Ridge, Gallipoli, after the New Zealand Brigade had attacked and established itself on the ridge, Corporal Bassett, in full daylight and under continuous fire, succeeded in laying a telephone line from the old position to the new one on Chunuk Bair. He also did further gallant work in connection with the repair of telephone lines by day and night under heavy fire.

BATES, Sidney   61

Corporal   The Royal Norfolk Regiment
Other Decorations: —
Date of Gazette: 2 Nov. 1944
Place/Date of Birth: Camberwell, London — 14 Jun. 1921
Place/Date of Death: Sourdeval, Normandy — 8 Aug. 1944
Memorials: Bayeux War Cemetery, France
Town/County Connections: Camberwell, London
Remarks: —
Account of Deed: On 6 Aug. 1944 near Sourdeval, north-west Europe, when the enemy had penetrated deeply in the area occupied by his section, Corporal Bates seized a light machine-gun and charged, moving foward through a hail of bullets. Although wounded twice he was undaunted and continued firing until the enemy started to withdraw before him. At this moment he was wounded for a third time mortally. He still went on firing, however, until his strength failed him, but by this time the enemy had withdrawn and the situation had been restored. He died two days later.

BATTEN-POOLL, Arthur Hugh Henry — see **POOLL,** Arthur Hugh Henry BATTEN-

BAXTER, Edward Felix   62

Second Lieutenant   1/8th Bn., The King's (Liverpool) Regiment
Other Decorations: —
Date of Gazette: 26 Sep. 1916
Place/Date of Birth: Old Swinford, Stourbridge, Worcestershire — 18 Sep. 1885
Place/Date of Death: Nr. Blairville, France — 18 Apr. 1916
Memorials: Fillievres British Cemetery, France
Town/County Connections: Kidderminster, Worcs.; Everton, Liverpool
Remarks: — *Christ's Hospital, Horsham. Sussex.*
Account of Deed: On 17/18 Apr. 1916 near Blairville, France, prior to a raid, Second Lieutenant Baxter was engaged on cutting wire close to the enemy's trenches. While doing this, he held a bomb with the pin withdrawn and once the bomb slipped and fell. He picked it up, unscrewed the base plug and dug out the detonator which he smothered in the ground, preventing the alarm being given and saving many casualties. Later, leading a storming party, he was first into the trench. After assisting in bombing dugouts, he finally climbed out, helping the last man over the parapet. He was not seen again.

BAXTER, Frank William   63

Trooper   Bulawayo Field Force
Other Decorations: —
Date of Gazette: 7 May 1897 & 15 Jan. 1907
Place/Date of Birth: Woolwich, London — 29 Dec. 1869
Place/Date of Death: Matabeleland — 22 Apr. 1896
Memorials: Buried at Bulawayo, Rhodesia; Matabeleland Rebellion Memorial, Bulawayo
Town/County Connections: Thornon Heath, Surrey
Remarks: —
Account of Deed: On 22 Apr. 1896 near Bulawayo, South Africa (Matabeleland Rebellion), Trooper Baxter gave up his horse to a wounded comrade who was being hotly pursued by an overwhelming force of the enemy. The trooper then tried to escape on foot, hanging on to the stirrup leather of another scout of the Bulawayo Field Force, until he was hit in the side, whereupon he had to let go of the stirrup and was killed a few moments later.

BAZALGETTE, Ian Willoughby   64

A/Squadron Leader   635 Squadron, Royal Air Force Volunteer Reserve
Other Decorations: DFC
Date of Gazette: 17 Aug. 1945
Place/Date of Birth: Calgary, Alberta, Canada — 19 Oct. 1918
Place/Date of Death: Senantes, France — 4 Aug. 1944
Memorials: Senantes Churchyard, France; St. Mary's church, Bexwell, Norfolk
Town/County Connections: — *New Malden, Surrey;*
Remarks: — *Plaque in Warrior Chapel, St. Mary's Church. Wimbledon*
Account of Deed: On 4 Aug. 1944 at Trossy St. Maximin, north-west Europe, Squadron Leader Bazalgette was one of the marking formation spearhead on a daylight raid. When near his target his Lancaster came under heavy anti-aircraft fire, both starboard engines were put out of action and serious fires broke out. In spite of this the squadron leader pressed on to the target, marking and bombing it accurately. He then attempted to bring the burning aircraft to safety, having ordered those of the crew who were able to do so to bale out. He managed to land the Lancaster, but it immediately exploded, killing him and his two wounded crew members.

BEACH, Thomas   **65**
Private   55th Regiment (later The Border Regiment)
Other Decorations: —
Date of Gazette: 24 Feb. 1857
Place/Date of Birth: Dundee, Scotland — Jan. 1824
Place/Date of Death: Dundee, Scotland — 24 Aug. 1864
Memorials: Eastern Necropolis, Dundee
Town/County Connections: Dundee, Fife, Scotland
Remarks: —
Account of Deed: On 5 Nov. 1854 at the Battle of Inkerman, Crimea, when on picquet duty, Private Beach attacked several Russians who were robbing a colonel who was lying wounded. He killed two of the Russians and protected the colonel until help arrived.

BEAK, Daniel Marcus William   **66**
T/Commander (later Major General)   Royal Naval Volunteer Reserve (Drake Bn., Royal Naval Division)
Other Decorations: DSO, MC & Bar
Date of Gazette: 15 Nov. 1918
Place/Date of Birth: Southampton, Hampshire — 27 Jul. 1891
Place/Date of Death: Swindon, Wiltshire — 3 May 1967
Memorials: —
Town/County Connections: Southampton, Hants; Swindon, Wilts.
Remarks: Joined the Army after the First World War (1920); commanded 1st Bn., The South Lancashire Regiment, 1938; served in France 1940; GOC Troops, Malta, 1942
Account of Deed: During the period 21/25 Aug. and on 4 Sep. 1918 at Logeast Wood, France, Commander Beak led his men and captured four enemy positions under heavy fire. Four days later, although dazed by a shell fragment, in the absence of the brigade commander, he reorganised the whole brigade under extremely heavy gun fire and led his men to their objective. When an attack was held up, accompanied by only one runner he succeeded in breaking up a nest of machine-guns, personally bringing in nine or ten prisoners. His initiative and the confidence with which he inspired all ranks, contributed very materially to the success of these operations.

BEAL, Ernest Frederick   **67**
T/Second Lieutenant   13th(S) Bn., The Yorkshire Regt. (Alexandra, Princess of Wales's Own)
Other Decorations: —
Date of Gazette: 4 Jun. 1918
Place/Date of Birth: Brighton, Sussex — 27 Jan. 1885
Place/Date of Death: St. Leger, France — 22 Mar. 1918
Memorials: Arras Memorial, France
Town/County Connections: Brighton, Sussex
Remarks: —
Account of Deed: On 21/22 Mar. 1918 at St. Leger, France, Second Lieutenant Beal was in command of a company detailed to occupy a certain section of trench. When the company was established it was found necessary to clear a gap of about 400 yards held by the enemy between the left flank of the company and the neighbouring unit. Second Lieutenant Beal therefore organised a small party and led them along the trench, capturing four machine-guns and inflicting heavy casualties. Later in the evening he brought in on his back a wounded man who was lying close to an enemy machine-gun.

BEATHAM, Robert Matthew   **68**
Private   8th Bn. (Victoria), Australian Imperial Force
Other Decorations: —
Date of Gazette: 14 Dec. 1918
Place/Date of Birth: Glassonby, Penrith, Cumberland — 16 Jun. 1894
Place/Date of Death: Rosiere, France — 11 Aug. 1918
Memorials: Heath Cemetery, Harbonnieres, France; War Memorial, Glassonby; Addingham (Addingham-with-Gamblesby) Church; Australian War Memorial, Canberra
Town/County Connections: Glassonby, Cumberland
Remarks: —
Account of Deed: On 9 Aug. 1918 at Rosiere, east of Amiens, France, when the advance was held up by heavy machine-gun fire, Private Beatham and one other man bombed and fought the crews of four enemy machine-guns, killing 10 and capturing 10. This helped the advance to go ahead, and when the final objective was reached, although wounded, he again dashed forward and bombed a machine-gun, but he was killed while doing so.

BEATTIE, Stephen Halden

69

Lieutenant-Commander (later Captain) Royal Navy
Other Decorations: —
Date of Gazette: 21 May 1942
Place/Date of Birth: Leighton, Montgomery, Wales — 29 Mar. 1908
Place/Date of Death: Mullion, Cornwall — 24 April 1975
Memorials: Ruan Minor Churchyard, Helston, Cornwall
Town/County Connections: Leighton, Montgomery; Mullion, Cornwall , *Rugby School*
Remarks: Croix de Guerre avec Palmes and Légion d'Honneur (France); Senior Naval Officer Persian Gulf, 1956-58; Naval Adviser to Ethiopian Government, 1965-69
Account of Deed: On 27 Mar. 1942, in the attack on St. Nazaire, France, Lieutenant-Commander Beattie was in command of HMS *Campbeltown*. Under intense fire directed on the bridge from a range of about 100 yards, and in the full blinding glare of many searchlights, the lieutenant-commander steamed *Campbeltown* into the lock gates, as instructed, and beached and scuttled her in the correct position. The Victoria Cross was awarded not only in recognition of Lieutenant-Commander Beattie's own valour, but also of the un-named officers and men of the ship's company, many of whom did not survive.

BEAUCHAMP-PROCTOR, Andrew Frederick Weatherby — see **PROCTOR,** Andrew Frederick Weatherby BEAUCHAMP-

BEELEY, John

70

Rifleman   The King's Royal Rifle Corps
Other Decorations: —
Date of Gazette: 21 Apr. 1942
Place/Date of Birth: Manchester, Lancashire — 8 Feb. 1918
Place/Date of Death: Sidi Rezegh, Western Desert — 21 Nov. 1941
Memorials: Knightsbridge War Cemetery, Acroma, North Africa
Town/County Connections: Manchester, Lancs.
Remarks: —
Account of Deed: On 21 Nov. 1941 at Sidi, Rezegh, Libya, at an airfield being attacked by Rifleman Beeley's company, progress was held up by short range fire. All the officers of the company were wounded so, on his own initiative the rifleman ran forward over open ground, firing his Bren gun and at 20 yards range put an anti-tank gun and two machine-guns out of action. He was killed but his bravery inspired his comrades to further efforts to reach their objective, which was eventually captured, together with 700 prisoners.

BEES, William

71

Private (later Corporal)   1st Bn., The Derbyshire Regt. (later The Sherwood Foresters — The Nottinghamshire and Derbyshire Regt.)
Other Decorations: —
Date of Gazette: 17 Dec. 1901
Place/Date of Birth: Loughborough, Leicestershire — 12 Sep. 1872
Place/Date of Death: Coalville, Leicestershire — 20 Jun. 1938
Memorials: —
Town/County Connections: Loughborough and Coalville, Leicestershire
Remarks: —
Account of Deed: On 30 Sep. 1901 at Moedwil, South Africa, Private Bees was one of a Maxim-gun detachment which suffered heavy casualties, six out of nine men being hit. Hearing his wounded comrades asking for water, Private Bees went forward under heavy fire to a spruit held by the Boers about 500 yards ahead of the men, and brought back a kettle filled with water. In doing this he had to pass within 100 yards of some rocks also held by the enemy and the kettle he was carrying was hit by several bullets.

BEESLEY, William

72

Private (later Sergeant)   13th Bn., The Rifle Brigade (Prince Consort's Own)
Other Decorations: —
Date of Gazette: 28 Jun. 1918
Place/Date of Birth: Gresley, Staffordshire — 5 Oct. 1895
Place/Date of Death: Abergavenny, Monmouthshire — 23 Sep. 1966
Memorials: (Buried at Coventry, Warwickshire); The Rifle Brigade Memorial, Winchester Cathedral. *Coventry Cemetery*
Town/County Connections: Gresley, Staffs; Nuneaton, Warwickshire.
Remarks: —
Account of Deed: On 8 May 1918 at Bucquoy, France, when Private Beesley's platoon sergeant and all the section commanders were killed he took command. Single-handed he rushed a post, shot four of the enemy, took six prisoners and sent them back to our lines. He and a comrade then brought his Lewis gun into action, inflicting many casualties and holding their position for four hours until the second private was wounded. Private Beesley, by himself, maintained his position until nightfall, when he returned to the original line with the wounded man and the Lewis gun which he kept in action until things had quietened down.

BEET, Harry Churchill   **73**
Corporal (later Captain)   1st Bn., The Derbyshire Regt. (later The Sherwood Foresters — The Nottinghamshire and Derbyshire Regt.)
Other Decorations: —
Date of Gazette: 12 Feb. 1901
Place/Date of Birth: Bingham, Nottinghamshire — 1 Apr. 1873
Place/Date of Death: Rupert, Vancouver, British Columbia, Canada — 10 Jan. 1946
Memorials: Vancouver Veterans' Cemetery
Town/County Connections: Bingham, Nottinghamshire
Remarks: —
Account of Deed: On 22 Apr. 1900 at Wakkerstroom, South Africa, an infantry company and two squadrons of the Imperial Yeomanry had to retire from near a farm under a ridge held by the Boers. A corporal was lying on the ground wounded and Corporal Beet, seeing him, remained behind and put him under cover, bound up his wounds and, by firing, prevented the enemy from coming down to the farm until dark when a medical officer came to the wounded man's assistance. Corporal Beet was exposed to very heavy fire during the whole afternoon.

BELCHER, Douglas Walter   **74**
Lance-Sergeant (later Captain)   1/5th (City of London) Bn., The London Regt. (The London Rifle Brigade)
Other Decorations: —
Date of Gazette: 23 Jun. 1915
Place/Date of Birth: Surbiton, Surrey — 15 Jul. 1889
Place/Date of Death: Claygate, Surrey — 3 Jun. 1953
Memorials: Holy Trinity Churchyard, Claygate, Surrey
Town/County Connections: Surbiton and Claygate, Surrey
Remarks: —
Account of Deed: On 13 May 1915, south of the Wieltje-St. Julien Road, Belgium, Lance-Sergeant Belcher was in charge of a portion of an advanced breastwork during continuous bombardment by the enemy. The lance-sergeant, with very few men, elected to remain and try to hold his position after the troops near him had been withdrawn, and with great skill he succeeded in his objective, opening rapid fire on the enemy, who were only 150-200 yards away, whenever he saw them collecting for an attack. This bold action prevented the enemy breaking through and averted an attack on the flank of one of our divisions.

BELL, David   **75**
Private (later Sergeant)   2nd Bn., 24th Regiment (later The South Wales Borderers)
Other Decorations: —
Date of Gazette: 17 Dec. 1867
Place/Date of Birth: Co. Down, Ireland — 1845
Place/Date of Death: Gillingham, Kent — 7 Mar. 1920   *Grave in Woodlands Cemetery*
Memorials: Woodlands Cemetery, Gillingham, Kent .   *CH 782*
Town/County Connections: Co. Down, Ireland; Gillingham, Kent
Remarks: VC not awarded for bravery in action against the enemy, but for bravery at sea in saving life in storm off Andaman Islands *VC in S.W.B Museum. Brecon*
Account of Deed: On 7 May 1867 at the island of Little Andaman, Bay of Bengal, Private Bell was one of a party of five* of the 2/24th Regiment, who risked their lives in manning a boat and proceeding through dangerous surf to rescue some of their comrades who had been sent to the island to find out the fate of the commander and seven of the crew, who had landed from the ship *Assam Valley* and were feared murdered by the cannibalistic islanders. (*See also COOPER, J., DOUGLAS, C.M., GRIFFITHS, W. and MURPHY, T.)

BELL, Donald Simpson   **76**
T/Second Lieutenant   9th Bn., The Yorkshire Regt. (Alexandra, Princess of Wales's Own)
Other Decorations: —
Date of Gazette: 9 Sep. 1917
Place/Date of Birth: Harrogate, Yorkshire — 3 Dec. 1890
Place/Date of Death: Somme, France — 10 Jul. 1916
Memorials: Gordon Dump Cemetery, France; St. Paul's Parish Church, Harrogate; Scarbeck War Memorial
Town/County Connections: Harrogate, Yorkshire
Remarks: —
Account of Deed: On 5 Jul. 1916 at Horseshoe Trench, Somme, France, a very heavy enfilade fire was opened on the attacking company by an enemy gun. Second Lieutenant Bell immediately, on his own initiative, crept up a communication trench, and then, followed by a corporal and a private, rushed across the open under very heavy fire and attacked the machine gun, shooting the firer and destroying the gun and the personnel with bombs. This officer lost his life five days later performing a very similar act of bravery.

BELL, Edward William Derrington **77**
Captain (later Major General) 23rd Regiment (later The Royal Welch Fusiliers)
Other Decorations: —
Date of Gazette: 24 Feb. 1857
Place/Date of Birth: Kempsey, Worcestershire — 18 May 1824
Place/Date of Death: Belfast, Ireland — 10 Nov. 1879
Memorials: Kempsey Churchyard, Worcs. *Grave.*
Town/County Connections: Kempsey, Worcs; Belfast
Remarks: Légion d'Honneur (France)
Account of Deed: On 20 Sep. 1854 in the Crimea, at the Battle of the Alma, Captain Bell was the first to seize upon and capture one of the enemy's guns which was limbered up and being carried off. He moreover took over the command of his regiment, which he brought out of action, all his senior officers having been killed or wounded.

BELL, Eric Norman Frankland **78**
T/Captain 9th Bn., The Royal Inniskilling Fusiliers, attd. Light Trench Mortar Bty.
Other Decorations: —
Date of Gazette: 26 Sep. 1916
Place/Date of Birth: Enniskillen, Ireland — 28 Aug. 1895
Place/Date of Death: Thiepval, France — 1 Jul. 1916
Memorials: Thiepval Memorial, France
Town/County Connections: Bootle, Lancashire; Enniskillen, Ireland
Remarks: —
Account of Deed: On 1 Jul. 1916, at Thiepval, France, when our front line was checked by enfilading machine-gun fire, Captain Bell crept forward and shot the machine-gunner. Later, on no less than three occasions, when our bombing parties were unable to advance, he went forward alone and threw trench mortar bombs among the enemy. When he had no more bombs available, he stood on the parapet, under intense fire, and used a rifle with great coolness and effect on the enemy advancing to counter-attack. Finally, he was killed rallying and reorganizing infantry parties which had lost their officers.

BELL, Frederick William **79**
Lieutenant (later Lieutenant Colonel) West Australian Mounted Infantry
Other Decorations: —
Date of Gazette: 4 Oct. 1901
Place/Date of Birth: Perth, Western Australia — 3 Apr. 1875
Place/Date of Death: Bristol — 28 Apr. 1954
Memorials: Canford Cemetery, Bristol; Australian War Memorial, Canberra
Town/County Connections: Bristol
Remarks: Served in the First World War — Commandant, Embarkation Camps, Plymouth; After the war was Political Officer, British Somaliland, then Administrative Officer, Northern Nigeria and Kenya Colony.
Account of Deed: On 16 May 1901 at Brakpan, Transvaal, South Africa, when retiring under heavy fire, Lieutenant Bell noticed a man dismounted. He returned and took him up behind him, but the horse not being equal to the weight, fell with them. The lieutenant then remained behind, covering the man's retirement until he was out of danger.

BELL, Mark Sever **80**
Lieutenant (later Colonel) Corps of Royal Engineers
Other Decorations: CB
Date of Gazette: 20 Nov. 1874
Place/Date of Birth: Sydney, New South Wales, Australia — 15 May 1843
Place/Date of Death: Windlesham, Surrey — 26 Jun. 1906
Memorials: —
Town/County Connections: Leconfield, Yorks; Windlesham, Surrey
Remarks: —
Account of Deed: On 4 Feb. 1874 at the Battle of Ordashu, Ashanti, West Africa, Lieutenant Bell was always in front, urging and exhorting an unarmed working party of Fantee labourers who were exposed not only to the fire of the enemy, but to the wild and irregular fire of the native troops to the rear. He encouraged these men to work under fire without a covering party, and this contributed very materially to the success of the day.

BELLEW, Edward Donald   **81**
Lieutenant (later Captain) 7th Bn., British Columbia Regiment, C.E.F.
Other Decorations: —
Date of Gazette: 15 May 1919
Place/Date of Birth: Bombay, India — 28 Oct. 1882
Place/Date of Death: Kamloops, British Columbia, Canada — 1 Feb. 1961
Memorials: Hillside Cemetery, Kamloops, B.C.
Town/County Connections: —
Remarks: —
Account of Deed: On 24 Apr. 1915 near Kerselaere, Belgium, the advance of the enemy was temporarily stayed by Lieutenant Bellew, the battalion machine-gun officer, who had two guns in action on high ground when the enemy's attack broke in full force. Reinforcements which were sent forward having been destroyed, and with the enemy less than 100 yards away and no further assistance in sight, Lieutenant Bellew and a sergeant decided to fight it out. The sergeant was killed and Lieutenant Bellew wounded, nevertheless, he maintained his fire until his ammunition failed, when he seized a rifle, smashed his machine-gun and, fighting to the last, was taken prisoner.

BENNETT, Eugene Paul   **82**
T/Lieutenant (later Captain) 2nd Bn., The Worcestershire Regiment
Other Decorations: MC
Date of Gazette: 30 Dec. 1916
Place/Date of Birth: Stroud, Gloucestershire — 4 Jun. 1892
Place/Date of Death: Italy — 6 Apr. 1970
Memorials: —
Town/County Connections: Stroud, Glos.
Remarks: Prosecuting Counsel on S.E. Circuit 1931-35; Metropolitan Magistrate 1935-61.
Account of Deed: On 5 Nov. 1916 near Le Transloy, France, Lieutenant Bennett was in command of the second wave of the attack, and finding that the first wave had suffered heavy casualties, its commander killed and the line wavering, he advanced at the head of the second wave and reached his objective with only 60 men. Isolated with his small party he took steps to consolidate his position under heavy rifle and machine-gun fire from both flanks, and although wounded he remained in command. But for his example of courage the attack would have been checked at the outset.

BENT, Philip Eric   **83**
T/Lieutenant Colonel Comd. 9th Bn., The Leicestershire Regiment
Other Decorations: DSO
Date of Gazette: 11 Jan. 1918
Place/Date of Birth: Halifax, Nova Scotia, Canada — 3 Jan. 1891
Place/Date of Death: Polygon Wood, Belgium — 1 Oct. 1917
Memorials: Tyne Cot Memorial, Belgium; St. Alban's Church, Hindhead, Surrey
Town/County Connections: —
Remarks: —
Account of Deed: On 1 Oct. 1917 east of Polygon Wood, Zonnebeke, Belgium, when the situation was critical owing to the confusion caused by a heavy enemy attack and the intense artillery fire, Lieutenant Colonel Bent collected a platoon that was in reserve and together with men from other companies and various regimental details, he organised and led them forward to the counter-attack, which was successful and the enemy were checked. The coolness and magnificent example of the colonel resulted in the securing of a portion of the line essential to subsequent operation, but he was killed whilst leading a charge.

BENT, Spencer John   **84**
Drummer (later Regimental Sergeant-Major) 1st Bn., The East Lancashire Regiment
Other Decorations: MM
Date of Gazette: 9 Dec. 1914
Place/Date of Birth: Stowmarket, Suffolk — 18 Mar. 1891
Place/Date of Death: London — 3 May 1977 *Cremated at West Norwood Crematorium*
Memorials: —
Town/County Connections: Stowmarket, Suffolk; Hackney, London
Remarks: — *Name on RM of Honour, Witnesham church, Suffolk.*
Account of Deed: On the night of 1/2 Nov. 1914 near Le Gheer, Belgium, when his officer, the platoon sergeant and a number of men had been struck down, Drummer Bent took command of the platoon and with great presence of mind and coolness succeeded in holding the position. He had previously distinguished himself on two occasions, on 22 and 24 Oct. by bringing up ammunition under heavy shell and rifle fire. Again, on 3 Nov. he brought into cover some wounded men who were lying, exposed to enemy fire, in the open.

BERESFORD, Lord William Leslie de la Poer   **85**
Captain (later Lieutenant Colonel)   9th Lancers (The Queen's Royal)
Other Decorations: KCIE
Date of Gazette: 23 Aug. 1879
Place/Date of Birth: Mullaghbrack, Markethill, Co. Armagh, Ireland — 20 Jul. 1847
Place/Date of Death: Dorking, Surrey — 28 Dec. 1900
Memorials: Clonagem Churchyard, Curraghmore, Ireland; Mullaghbrack Church, Co. Armagh
Town/County Connections: Mullaghbrack, Co. Armagh, Ireland; Dorking, Surrey
Remarks: —
Account of Deed: On 3 Jul. 1879 at Ulundi, Zululand, during the retirement of a reconnoitring party, Captain Lord William Beresford went to the assistance of an NCO of the 24th Regiment, whose horse had fallen and rolled on him. The Zulus were coming in great numbers, but Lord William, with help from a sergeant* of the Frontier Light Horse, managed to mount the injured man behind him. He was, however, so dizzy that the sergeant, who had been keeping back the advancing Zulus, gave up his carbine and, riding alongside, helped to hold him on. They all finally reached safety. (*See also O'TOOLE, E.).

BERGIN, James   **86**
Private   33rd Regt. (later The Duke of Wellington's (West Riding) Regt.)
Other Decorations: —
Date of Gazette: 28 Jul. 1868
Place/Date of Birth: Killbricken, Queen's Co (later Leix), Ireland — 29 Jun. 1845
Place/Date of Death: Poona, India — 1 Dec. 1880
Memorials: —
Town/County Connections: Killbricken, Leix, Ireland
Remarks: —
Account of Deed: On 13 Apr. 1868 in Abyssinia, during the assault on Magdala, when the head of the column of attack was checked by the obstacles at the gate, a small stream of officers and men of the 33rd Regiment and an officer of the Royal Engineers broke away from the main approach to Magdala, and, reaching the defences, climbed a cliff, forced their way over a wall and through a strong and thorny fence, thus turning the defenders of the gateway. The first two men to enter Magdala were Private Bergin and a Drummer*. (*See also MAGNER, M.)

BERRYMAN, John   **87**
Troop Sergeant-Major (later Major)   17th Lancers (The Duke of Cambridge's Own)
Other Decorations: —
Date of Gazette: 24 Feb. 1857
Place/Date of Birth: Dudley, Worcestershire — 18 Jul. 1825
Place/Date of Death: Woldingham, Surrey — 27 Jun. 1896
Memorials: St. Agatha's Churchyard, Woldingham
Town/County Connections: Dudley, Worcs.; Woldingham, Surrey
Remarks: Served in the Indian Mutiny and the Zulu War.
Account of Deed: On 25 Oct. 1854 at Balaclava, Crimea, (Charge of the Light Brigade) Troop Sergeant-Major Berryman, whose horse had been shot under him, stopped on the field with a wounded officer amidst a storm of shot and shell. Two sergeants* came to his assistance and between them they carried the wounded officer out of range of the guns. (*See also FARRELL, J. and MALONE, J.)

BEST-DUNKLEY, Bertram — see **DUNKLEY** Bertram BEST-

BHANBHAGTA GURUNG   **88**
Rifleman (later Lance-Naik)   3rd Bn., 2nd Gurkha Rifles, Indian Army
Other Decorations: —
Date of Gazette: 5 Jun. 1945
Place/Date of Birth: Phalbu Village, Gorkha District, Nepal — 1921
Place/Date of Death: —
Memorials: —
Town/County Connections: —
Remarks: —
Account of Deed: On 5 Mar. 1945 at Snowdon East, near Tamandu, Burma, a section was pinned down by heavy enemy fire and was also being subjected to sniping from a tree. Rifleman Bhanbhagta Gurung killed the sniper and later when the section was again attacked, he dashed forward under continuous fire personally clearing four enemy foxholes and he also silenced a light machine-gun. With the help of a Bren gunner and two riflemen he then repelled an enemy counter-attack on the captured bunker with heavy losses. His action in clearing these positions was decisive in capturing the objective.

BHANDARI RAM 89
Sepoy (later Subadar)   10th Baluch Regiment, Indian Army
Other Decorations: —
Date of Gazette: 8 Feb. 1945
Place/Date of Birth: Serunia Village, Bilaspur State, Simla Hills, India — 24 Jul. 1919
Place/Date of Death: — *About 21.5.2002*
Memorials: —
Town/County Connections: —
Remarks: PVSM (India).
Account of Deed: On 22 Nov. 1944 at East Mayu, Arakan, Burma, Sepoy Bhandari Ram's platoon was pinned down by machine-gun fire. Although wounded he crawled up to a Japanese light machine-gun in full view of the enemy and was wounded again, but continued crawling to within 5 yards of his objective. He then threw a grenade into the position, killing the gunner and two others. This action inspired his platoon to rush and capture the enemy position. Only then did he allow his wounds to be dressed.

BINGHAM, The Hon. Edward Barry Stewart 90
Commander (later Rear-Admiral)   Royal Navy
Other Decorations: OBE
Date of Gazette: 15 Sep. 1916
Place/Date of Birth: Bangor, Co. Down, Ireland — 26 Jul. 1881
Place/Date of Death: London — 24 Sep. 1939
Memorials: —
Town/County Connections: Bangor, Co. Down
Remarks: Order of St. Stanislaus (Russia); commanded the Nore Destroyer Flotilla 1925-29.
Account of Deed: On 31 May 1916, at the Battle of Jutland, Commander Bingham, of HMS *Nestor*, led his division in their attack, first on enemy destroyers and then on their battle cruisers. He finally sighted the enemy battle fleet and followed by the one remaining destroyer of his division (HMS *Nicator*), he closed to within 3,000 yards of the enemy, in order to attain a favourable position for firing the torpedoes. While making this attack *Nestor* and *Nicator* were under concentrated fire of the secondary batteries of the High Seas Fleet. *Nestor* was subsequently sunk.

BIRKS, Frederick 91
Second Lieutenant   6th Bn. (Victoria), Australian Imperial Force
Other Decorations: MM
Date of Gazette: 8 Nov. 1917
Place/Date of Birth: Buckley, Flintshire, Wales — 31 Aug. 1894
Place/Date of Death: Glencorse Wood, Ypres — 21 Sep. 1917
Memorials: Perth Cemetery (China Wall) Belgium; obelisk in Buckley, Flintshire; Australian War Memorial, Canberra *Zillebeke*
Town/County Connections: Buckley, Flintshire
Remarks: — *VC with Australian W.M. Canberra.*
Account of Deed: On 20 Sep. 1917 at Glencorse Wood, East of Ypres, Belgium, Second Lieutenant Birks, accompanied by a corporal, rushed a strong point which was holding up the advance. The corporal was wounded, but Second Lieutenant Birks went on alone, killed the remainder of the enemy and captured the machine-gun. Shortly afterwards he took a small party and attacked another strong point occupied by about 25 of the enemy, killing some and capturing an officer and 15 men. His coolness and bravery inspired his men throughout these operations. He was fatally wounded whilst trying to rescue some of his men who had been buried by a shell.

BISDEE, John Hutton 92
Trooper (later Lieutenant Colonel)   Tasmanian Imperial Bushmen
Other Decorations: OBE
Date of Gazette: 13 Nov. 1900
Place/Date of Birth: Hutton Park, Tasmania — 28 Sep. 1869
Place/Date of Death: Melton Mowbray, Tasmania — 14 Jan. 1930
Memorials: Australian War Memorial, Canberra
Town/County Connections: —
Remarks: He and Lieutenant G.G.E. Wylly were the first Australian-born men to win the VC while serving with an Australian Unit under British Command; served in the First World War with the 12th Australian Light Horse
Account of Deed: On 1 Sep. 1900 near Warm Baths, Transvaal, South Africa, Trooper Bisdee was one of an advance scouting party passing through a narrow gorge, when the enemy suddenly opened fire at close range and six out of the party of eight were wounded, including two officers. The horse of one of the wounded officers bolted and Trooper Bisdee dismounted, put him on his own horse and took him out of range of the very heavy fire.

BISHOP, William Avery **93**
Captain (later Air Marshal)   Canadian Cavalry and 60 Squadron, Royal Flying Corps
Other Decorations: CB, DSO & Bar, MC, DFC
Date of Gazette: 11 Aug. 1917
Place/Date of Birth: Owen Sound, Ontario, Canada — 8 Feb. 1894
Place/Date of Death: Palm Beach, Florida, U.S.A. — 11 Sep. 1956
Memorials: Plaque in Queen's Park, First Avenue, West Owen Sound, Ontario
Town/County Connections: —
Remarks: Criox de Guerre avec Palmes and Légion d'Honneur (France); Director of Recruiting, RCAF, 1940-44; author of *Winged Warfare*.
Account of Deed: On 2 Jun. 1917 near Cambrai, France, Captain Bishop, patrolling independently, flew to an enemy aerodrome where several machines were standing with their engines running. One of the machines took off, but Captain Bishop fired at very close range and it crashed. He fired at and missed, the second, but his fire made the pilot swerve and hit a tree. Two more aircraft then took off — he emptied his Lewis gun into the forward fuselage of the first and it crashed. He then emptied a whole drum into the fourth machine which had come up behind him and it dived away. Captain Bishop then flew back to his station.

BISSETT, William Davidson **94**
Lieutenant (later Major)   1/6th Bn., The Argyll and Sutherland Highlanders (Princess Louise's)
Other Decorations: —
Date of Gazette: 6 Jan. 1919
Place/Date of Birth: St. Martin's, Perthshire, Scotland — 7 Aug. 1893
Place/Date of Death: Wrexham, Denbighshire, Wales — 12 May 1971. *Cremated Wrexham*
Memorials: Aldershot Military Cemetery, Hampshire *Ashes in Aldershot M.C.*
Town/County Connections: Crieff, Perthshire; Overton-on-Dee, Flintshire
Remarks: Croix de Guerre avec Palme (France); served with Royal Army Ordnance Corps and Royal Pioneer Corps in Second World War. *VC in A.& S. Highlanders Museum, Stirling*
Account of Deed: On 25 Oct. 1918 East of Maing, France, Lieutenant Bissett was commanding a platoon, but owing to casualties took command of the company and handled it with great skill when an enemy counter-attack turned his left flank. Realizing the danger he withdrew to the railway, but the enemy continued to advance and when the ammunition was exhausted Lieutenant Bissett mounted the railway embankment under heavy fire and, calling for a bayonet charge, drove back the enemy with heavy loss and again charged forward, establishing the line and saving a critical situation.

BISSETT SMITH, Archibald — see **SMITH,** Archibald Bissett

BLACKBURN, Arthur Seaforth **95**
Second Lieutenant (later Brigadier)   10th Bn. (S.A.) Australian Imperial Force
Other Decorations: CMG, CBE, MC
Date of Gazette: 9 Sep. 1916
Place/Date of Birth: Adelaide, South Australia — 25 Nov. 1892
Place/Date of Death: Adelaide, South Australia — 24 Nov. 1960
Memorials: AIF Cemetery, Adelaide; Australian War Memorial, Canberra
Town/County Connections: —
Remarks: Served in the Second World War, 1939-45 — commanded 2/2 Machine Gun Bn., 2nd A.M.F., 1940; GOC A.M.F. in Java, 1941-42
Account of Deed: On 23 Jul. 1916, at Pozieres, France, Second Lieutenant Blackburn was directed with 50 men to drive the enemy from a strong point. By great determination he eventually captured 250 yards of trench, after personally leading four separate parties of bombers against it, many of whom became casualties. Then after crawling forward with a sergeant to reconnoitre, he returned, attacked and seized another 120 yards of trench, establishing communication with the battalion on his left.

BLAIR, James **96**
Captain (later General)   2nd Bombay Light Cavalry
Other Decorations: CB
Date of Gazette: 25 Feb. 1862
Place/Date of Birth: Nimach, Gwalior State, India — 27 Jan. 1828
Place/Date of Death: Melrose, Scotland — 18 Jan. 1905
Memorials: —
Town/County Connections: Melrose, Scotland
Remarks: Cousin of Lieutenant R. Blair, VC
Account of Deed: On 12 Aug. 1857 at Neemuch, India, Captain Blair volunteered to apprehend seven or eight armed mutineers who had shut themselves up in a house. He burst open the door and after a fierce encounter during which he was severely wounded, the rebels escaped through the roof. In spite of his wounds he pursued, but was unable to catch them. On 23 Oct. at Jeerum, the captain fought his way through a body of rebels who had surrounded him. In the action he broke his sword and was wounded, but nevertheless he led his men in a charge on the rebels and dispersed them.

No photograph available

BLAIR, Robert **97**

Lieutenant (later Captain)   2nd Dragoon Guards (Queen's Bays), attd. 9th Lancers (The Queen's Royal)
Other Decorations: —
Date of Gazette: 18 Jun. 1858
Place/Date of Birth: Linlithgow, West Lothian, Scotland — 13 Mar. 1834
Place/Date of Death: Cawnpore, India — 28 Mar. 1859
Memorials:
Town/County Connections: Linlithgow, W. Lothian
Remarks: Cousin of Captain J. Blair, VC   *VC in Queens Dragoon Guards H. Shrewsbury*
Account of Deed: On 28 Sep. 1857 at Bolandshahr, India, Lieutenant Blair was ordered to take a party of one sergeant and 12 men and bring in a deserted ammunition wagon. As they approached, 50 or 60 of the enemy on horseback attacked them, but without hesitation Lieutenant Blair formed up his men and gallantly led them through the rebels. He made good his retreat without losing a man, but leaving nine of the enemy dead on the field. He himself was severely wounded in this action.

BLAKER, Frank Gerald **98**

T/Major   The Highland Light Infantry, attd. 3rd. Bn., 9th Gurkha Rifles, Indian Army
Other Decorations: MC
Date of Gazette: 26 Sep. 1944
Place/Date of Birth: Meiktila, Upper Burma — 8 May 1920
Place/Date of Death: Near Taunghi, Burma — 9 Jul. 1944
Memorials: Taukkyan War Cemetery, Burma
Town/County Connections: —
Remarks: —
Account of Deed: On 9 Jul. 1944 near Taunghi, Burma, Major Blaker was commanding a company which was held up during an important advance by close-range firing from medium and light machine-guns. The major went ahead of his men through very heavy fire and in spite of being severely wounded in the arm, located the machine-guns and single-handed charged the position. Even when mortally wounded he continued to cheer on his men whilst lying on the ground. His fearless leadership inspired his men to storm and capture the objective.

BLOOMFIELD, William Anderson **99**

Captain (later Major)   Scout Corps, 2nd South African Mounted Brigade
Other Decorations: —
Date of Gazette: 30 Dec. 1916
Place/Date of Birth: Edinburgh — 30 Jan. 1873
Place/Date of Death: Ermelo, Transvaal, South Africa — 12 May 1954
Memorials: —
Town/County Connections: Edinburgh
Remarks: —
Account of Deed: On 24 Aug. 1916 at Mlali, East Africa, when consolidating his new position after being heavily attacked and being forced to retire, Captain Bloomfield found that one of the wounded — a corporal — had not been evacuated with the rest. At considerable personal risk the captain went back over 400 yards of ground swept by machine-gun and rifle fire and managed to reach the wounded man and bring him back to safety.

BOGLE, Andrew Cathcart **100**

Lieutenant (later Major)   78th Regt. (later The Seaforth Highlanders — Ross-shire Buffs, Duke of Albany's)
Other Decorations: —
Date of Gazette: 2 Sep. 1859
Place/Date of Birth: Glasgow — 20 Jan. 1829
Place/Date of Death: Sherborne, Dorset — 11 Dec. 1890
Memorials: —
Town/County Connections: Glasgow; Sherborne, Dorset
Remarks: —
Account of Deed: On 29 Jul. 1857 in the attack on Oonao, India, Lieutenant Bogle led the way into a loopholed house which was occupied by the enemy and from which a heavy fire harassed the advance of his regiment. The lieutenant was severely wounded in this action.

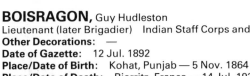

BOISRAGON, Guy Hudleston   **101**
Lieutenant (later Brigadier)   Indian Staff Corps and 5th Gurkha Rifles, Indian Army
Other Decorations: —
Date of Gazette: 12 Jul. 1892
Place/Date of Birth: Kohat, Punjab — 5 Nov. 1864
Place/Date of Death: Biarritz, France — 14 Jul. 1931
Memorials: Kensal Green Cemetery, London; Sanctum Crypt, St. Luke's Church, Chelsea,
London
Town/County Connections: —
Remarks: Served in First World War, 1914-16; Order of the Nile, 4th Class (Egypt).
Account of Deed: On 2 Dec. 1891 during the attack on Nilt Fort, India (Hunza Campaign),
Lieutenant Boisragon led the assault, forcing his way through difficult obstacles to the inner gate, when he returned for
reinforcements, moving fearlessly to and fro under heavy cross-fire until he had collected sufficient men to drive the enemy
from the fort.

BONNER, Charles George   **102**
Lieutenant (later Captain)   Royal Naval Reserve
Other Decorations: DSC
Date of Gazette: 2 Nov. 1917
Place/Date of Birth: Shuttington, Warwickshire — 29 Dec. 1884
Place/Date of Death: Edinburgh — 7 Feb. 1951
Memorials: —
Town/County Connections: Walsall, Staffs.; Edinburgh
Remarks: Became an expert in ship salvage after the war
Account of Deed: On 8 Aug. 1917 in the Bay of Biscay, Lieutenant Bonner was with HMS
Dunraven (one of the 'Q' or 'mystery' ships playing the part of an unobservant merchantman)
when she was shelled by an enemy submarine. The lieutenant was in the thick of the fighting and throughout the whole of the
action his pluck and determination had a considerable influence on the crew. (See also PITCHER, E.H.)

BOOTH, Anthony Clarke   **103**
Colour Sergeant   80th Regiment (later The South Staffordshire Regiment)
Other Decorations: —
Date of Gazette: 23 Feb. 1880
Place/Date of Birth: Carrington, Nottingham — 21 Apr. 1846
Place/Date of Death: Brierley Hill, Staffordshire — 8 Dec. 1899
Memorials: Garrison Church, Whittington Barracks, Lichfield, Staffs. *Buried Brierley Hill Churchyard.*
Town/County Connections: Carrington, Notts.; Brierley Hill, Staffs.
Remarks: —
Account of Deed: On 12 Mar. 1879 on the Intombi River, South Africa (Zulu War), during an
attack by very large numbers of the enemy, Colour-Sergeant Booth rallied a few men on the south
bank of the river and covered the retreat of 50 soldiers and others for a distance of three miles. Had it not been for the coolness
displayed by this NCO not one man would have escaped.

BOOTH, Frederick Charles   **104**
Sergeant (later Captain)   British South African Police, attd. Rhodesia Native Infantry
Other Decorations: DCM
Date of Gazette: 8 Jun. 1917
Place/Date of Birth: Upper Holloway, London — 6 Mar. 1890
Place/Date of Death: Brighton, Sussex — 14 Sep. 1960
Memorials: Bear Road Cemetery, Brighton , *Buried in Red Cross Plot.*
Town/County Connections: Bowes Park, London; Brighton, Sussex
Remarks: —
Account of Deed: On 12 Feb. 1917 at Johannesbruck, near Songea, East Africa, during an attack
in thick bush on the enemy position and under very heavy rifle fire, Sergeant Booth went forward
alone and brought in a man who was dangerously wounded. Later he rallied native troops who were badly disorganised and
brought them to the firing line. On many previous occasions this NCO had set a splendid example of pluck, and endurance.

BORELLA, Albert Chalmers   **105**
Lieutenant (later Captain)   26th Bn. (Q. and T.), Australian Imperial Force
Other Decorations: MM
Date of Gazette: 16 Sep. 1918
Place/Date of Birth: Borung, Victoria, Australia — 7 Aug. 1881
Place/Date of Death: Albury, Victoria, Australia — 7 Feb. 1968
Memorials: Australian War Memorial, Canberra
Town/County Connections: —
Remarks: —
Account of Deed: During the period 17/18 Jul. 1918 at Villers-Bretonneux, France, Lieutenant Borella, whilst leading his platoon, charged and captured an enemy machine-gun, shooting two gunners. He then led his party, by now reduced to 10 men and two Lewis guns, against a very strongly held trench, using his revolver and later a rifle with great effect and causing many casualties. Two large dug-outs were also bombed and 30 prisoners taken. On another occasion, although outnumbered ten to one, he and his men repulsed the enemy, causing heavy losses.

BORTON, Arthur Drummond   **106**
Lieutenant Colonel   Comd. 2/22nd (County of London) Bn., The London Regiment (The Queen's)
Other Decorations: CMG, DSO
Date of Gazette: 18 Dec. 1917
Place/Date of Birth: Chevening, Kent — 1 Jul. 1883
Place/Date of Death: Hunton, Kent — 5 Jan. 1933
Memorials: KRRC memorial, Winchester Cathedral
Town/County Connections: Chevening and Hunton, Kent
Remarks: — *Eton College*
Account of Deed: On 7 Nov. 1917 at Sheria, Palestine, under most difficult conditions, in darkness and in an unknown country, Lieutenant Colonel Borton deployed his battalion for attack and at dawn led his attacking companies against a strongly held position. When the leading waves were checked by withering fire, he moved freely up and down the line under heavy fire and then led his men forward, capturing the position. At a later stage he led a party of volunteers against a battery of field-guns in action at point-blank range, capturing the guns and the detachments. His fearless leadership was an example to the whole brigade.

BOUGHEY, Stanley Henry Parry   **107**
Second Lieutenant   1/4th Bn., The Royal Scots Fusiliers
Other Decorations: —
Date of Gazette: 13 Feb. 1918
Place/Date of Birth: Ayrshire, Scotland — 9 Apr. 1896
Place/Date of Death: Near Ramleh, Palestine — 4 Dec. 1917
Memorials: Gaza War Cemetery, Palestine
Town/County Connections: Ayrshire
Remarks: —
Account of Deed: On 1 Dec. 1917 at El Burf, Palestine, when the enemy in large numbers had managed to crawl up to within 30 yards of our firing line and with bombs and automatic rifles were keeping down the fire of our machine-guns, Second Lieutenant Boughey rushed forward alone with bombs right up to the enemy, killing many and causing the surrender of a party of 30. As he turned to go back for more bombs he was mortally wounded at the moment when the enemy were surrendering.

BOULGER, Abraham   **108**
Lance-Corporal (later Lieutenant Colonel)   84th Regiment (later The York and Lancaster Regt.)
Other Decorations: —
Date of Gazette: 18 Jun. 1858
Place/Date of Birth: Kilcullen, Co. Kildare, Ireland — 4 Sep. 1835
Place/Date of Death: Ireland — 23 Jan. 1900
Memorials: —
Town/County Connections: Kilcullen, Co. Kildare
Remarks: —
Account of Deed: During the period 12 Jul. to 25 Sep. 1857 in India, Lance-Corporal Boulger distinguished himself in all 12 actions fought by his regiment. He was one of the party which stormed the bridge over the canal on the relief of the Residency and shot a gunner who was in the act of firing a 68-pounder in the face of the British troops. He was also the first man to enter a masked battery. In the subsequent defence of the Residency he was severely wounded.

BOULTER, William Ewart   **109**
Sergeant (later Lieutenant) 6th Bn., The Northamptonshire Regiment
Other Decorations: —
Date of Gazette: 26 Oct. 1916
Place/Date of Birth: Wigston, Leicestershire — 14 Oct. 1892
Place/Date of Death: Wimbledon, Surrey — 1 Jun. 1955
Memorials: (Cremated Putney Vale Crematorium) *Plaque in Chapel*
Town/County Connections: Wigston, Leics.; Wimbledon, Surrey
Remarks: — *VC in Northamptonshire Regt. Museum*
Account of Deed: On 14 Jul. 1916 at Trones Wood, France, when one company and part of another was held up in the attack on a wood by a hostile machine-gun which was causing heavy casualties, Sergeant Boulter, with utter contempt of danger, and in spite of being wounded in the shoulder, advanced alone over open ground under heavy fire, in front of the gun and bombed the gun team from their position. This act not only saved many casualties, but materially helped the operation of clearing the enemy out of the wood.

BOURCHIER, Claude Thomas   **110**
Lieutenant (later Colonel) 1st Bn., The Rifle Brigade (Prince Consort's Own)
Other Decorations: —
Date of Gazette: 24 Feb. 1857
Place/Date of Birth: Brayford, Devon — 22 Apr. 1831
Place/Date of Death: Brighton, Sussex — 19 Nov. 1877
Memorials: The Rifle Brigade Memorial, Winchester Cathedral.
Town/County Connections: Brighton, Sussex
Remarks: Légion d'Honneur (France); Served in the Indian Mutiny; ADC to the Queen 1869.
Account of Deed: On 20 Nov, 1854 in the Crimea, Lieutenant Bourchier, with another lieutenant* was with a party detailed to drive the Russians from some rifle pits. Advancing on the pits after dark they launched a surprise attack and drove the Russian riflemen from their cover, but in the fierce fighting which ensued the officer in command of the party was killed. The two lieutenants, however, maintained their advantage, withstood all attacks from the enemy during the night and held the position until relieved next day. (*See also CUNINGHAME, W.J.M.)

BOURKE, Roland Richard Louis   **111**
Lieutenant (later Lieutenant-Commander) Royal Naval Volunteer Reserve
Other Decorations: DSO
Date of Gazette: 28 Aug. 1918
Place/Date of Birth: London — 28 Nov. 1885
Place/Date of Death: Esquimalt, British Columbia, Canada — 29 Aug. 1958
Memorials: Royal Oak Burial Park, Victoria, B.C.
Town/County Connections: Kensington, London
Remarks: Served with the RCNVR during the Second World War
Account of Deed: On 9 and 10 May 1918 at Ostend, Belgium, after *Vindictive's* crew had been taken off, Lieutenant Bourke, commanding Motor Launch 276 went into the harbour to check that everybody had got away. After searching and finding no one, he withdrew, but hearing cries from the water he turned back, found an officer and two seamen clinging to an up-turned boat, and rescued them. During this time the motor launch was under very heavy fire and was hit 55 times, once by a 6-inch shell which killed two of her crew and did considerable damage. Lieutenant Bourke, however, managed to take her into the open sea, and was taken in tow.

BOYD-ROCHFORT, George Arthur — see **ROCHFORT,** George Arthur BOYD-

BOYES, Duncan Gordon   **112**
Midshipman Royal Navy
Other Decorations: —
Date of Gazette: 21 Apr. 1865
Place/Date of Birth: Cheltenham, Gloucestershire — 5 Nov. 1846
Place/Date of Death: Anderson's Bay, New Zealand — 26 Jan. 1869
Memorials: Anderson's Bay Cemetery, Servicemen's section, New Zealand
Town/County Connections: Cheltenham, Glos.
Remarks: Brother-in-law of Lieutenant T.J. Young, VC.
Account of Deed: On 6 Sep. 1864 at Shimonoseki, Japan, Midshipman Boyes of HMS *Euryalus* displayed great gallantry in the capture of the enemy's stockade. He carried the Queen's Colour into action with the leading company and kept the flag flying in spite of direct fire which killed one of his colour sergeants. Mr. Boyes and the other colour sergeant* who was badly wounded, were only prevented from going further forward by direct orders from their superior officer. (*See also PRIDE, T.)

BOYLE, Edward Courtney   **113**
Lieutenant-Commander (later Rear-Admiral)   Royal Navy
Other Decorations: —
Date of Gazette: 21 May 1915
Place/Date of Birth: Carlisle, Cumberland — 23 Mar. 1883
Place/Date of Death: Ascot, Berkshire — 16 Dec. 1967. *Cremated at Woking*
Memorials: —
Town/County Connections: Carlisle, Cumberland; Southsea, Hants; Ascot, Berks.
Remarks: Chevalier, Légion d'Honneur (France); Order of St. Maurice and St. Lazarus (Italy);
King's Harbourmaster, Devonport, 1926-28; Flag Officer in Charge, London, 1939-42
Account of Deed: On 27 Apr. 1915 in the Sea of Marmara, Dardanelles, Lieutenant-Commander
Boyle, in command of Submarine E.14, dived his vessel under the enemy mine-fields and in spite of great navigational difficulties from strong currents and the presence of hostile patrols waiting to attack, he continued, during the next two weeks, to operate in the narrow waters of the straits and succeeded in sinking two Turkish gunboats and one military transport.

BRADBURY, Edward Kinder   **114**
Captain   'L' Bty., Royal Horse Artillery
Other Decorations: —
Date of Gazette: 25 Nov. 1914
Place/Date of Birth: Altrincham, Cheshire — 16 Aug. 1881
Place/Date of Death: Nery, France — 1 Sep. 1914
Memorials: Nery Communal Cemetery, France
Town/County Connections: Altrincham, Cheshire
Remarks: — *Marlborough College.*
Account of Deed: On 1 Sep. 1914 at Nery, France, during a fierce attack by the enemy, when all
the officers of 'L' Battery were either killed or wounded, Captain Bradbury, although having had
one leg taken off by a shell, continued to direct the fire of the battery until he died. (See also DORRELL, G.T. and NELSON, D.)

BRADFORD, George Nicholson   **115**
Lieutenant-Commander   Royal Navy
Other Decorations: —
Date of Gazette: 17 Mar. 1919
Place/Date of Birth: Darlington, Co. Durham — 23 Apr. 1887
Place/Date of Death: Zeebrugge, Belgium — 23 Apr. 1918
Memorials: Blankenberge Communal Cemetery, Belgium
Town/County Connections: Darlington, Co. Durham
Remarks: Brother of Lieutenant Colonel R.B. Bradford, VC.
Account of Deed: On 22/23 Apr. 1918 at Zeebrugge, Belgium, Lieutenant-Commander Bradford
commanding the naval storming parties embarked in HMS *Iris II* found there was great difficulty
in placing the parapet anchors when the ship came alongside the Mole. Although securing the ship was not part of his duties, the lieutenant-commander climbed a derrick which was projecting out over the Mole and, under heavy fire, with the derrick crashing against the Mole because of the violent tossing of the ship, he picked his moment and jumped with the anchor. He had just placed it in position when he was killed.

BRADFORD, Roland Boys   **116**
T/Lieutenant Colonel (later Brigadier General)   Comd. 9th Bn., The Durham Light Infantry
Other Decorations: MC
Date of Gazette: 25 Nov. 1916
Place/Date of Birth: Etherley, Co. Durham — 22 Feb. 1892
Place/Date of Death: Cambrai, France — 30 Nov. 1917
Memorials: Hermies British Cemetery, France
Town/County Connections: Darlington, Co. Durham
Remarks: Brother of Lieutenant-Commander G.N. Bradford, VC.
Account of Deed: On 1 Oct. 1916 at Eaucourt L'Abbaye, France, when a leading battalion had
suffered very severe casualties and the commander was wounded, its flank was dangerously
exposed to the enemy. At the request of the wounded commander, Lieutenant Colonel Bradford took command of that battalion in addition to his own. By his fearless energy under fire of all descriptions, and skilful leadership of both battalions, he succeeded in rallying the attack and capturing and defending the objective.

BRADLEY, Frederick Henry   **117**
Driver (later Captain)   69th Bty., Royal Field Artillery
Other Decorations: —
Date of Gazette: 27 Dec. 1901
Place/Date of Birth: London — 27 Sep. 1876
Place/Date of Death: Gwelo, S. Rhodesia — 10 Mar. 1943
Memorials: —
Town/County Connections: Kingsland, London
Remarks: —
Account of Deed: On 26 Sep. 1901 at Itala, South Africa, there was a call for volunteers to carry ammunition up the hill. To do this, a space of about 150 yards swept by a heavy cross-fire, had to be crossed. A driver and a gunner came forward and started, but half way across the driver fell wounded. Driver Bradley and the gunner, without hesitation, ran out, and while the injured man was carried to cover, Driver Bradley, with another volunteer, succeeded in getting the ammunition up the hill.

BRADSHAW, Joseph   **118**
Private (later Corporal) 2nd Bn., The Rifle Brigade (Prince Consort's Own)
Other Decorations: —
Date of Gazette: 24 Feb. 1857
Place/Date of Birth: Dromkeen, Limerick, Ireland — 1835
Place/Date of Death: Woolwich, London — 21 Mar. 1875
Memorials: The Rifle Brigade memorial, Winchester Cathedral.
Town/County Connections: London
Remarks: Médaille Militaire (France)
Account of Deed: On 22 Apr. 1855 in the Crimea, Private Bradshaw and another private*, on their own, attacked and captured a Russian rifle pit situated among the rocks overhanging the Woronzoff Road. The pit was occupied every night by the Russians and its capture and subsequent destruction was of great importance. (*See also HUMPSTON, J.)

BRADSHAW, William   **119**
Assistant Surgeon   90th Regt. (later The Cameronians — Scottish Rifles)
Other Decorations: —
Date of Gazette: 18 Jun. 1858
Place/Date of Birth: Thurles, Co. Tipperary, Ireland — 12 Feb. 1830
Place/Date of Death: Thurles, Tipperary — 9 Mar. 1861
Memorials: St. Mary's Church, Thurles, Tipperary
Town/County Connections: Thurles, Tipperary
Remarks: —
Account of Deed: On 26 Sep. 1857 at Lucknow, India, Assistant Surgeon Bradshaw, with another surgeon* was ordered to remove the wounded men left behind when the troops forced their way into the Residency. The dhooly-bearers had left the dhoolies, but notwithstanding the close proximity of the sepoys, the two surgeons managed to get some of the bearers together and Assistant Surgeon Bradshaw, with about 20 dhoolies, after becoming separated from the rest of the party, succeeded in reaching the Residency in safety. (*See also HOME, A.D.)

BRENNAN, Joseph Charles   **120**
Bombardier (later Sergeant)   Royal Regiment of Artillery
Other Decorations: —
Date of Gazette: 11 Nov. 1859
Place/Date of Birth: St. Probus, Truro, Cornwall — Aug. 1818
Place/Date of Death: Elham, Folkestone, Kent — 24 Sep. 1872
Memorials: —
Town/County Connections: St. Probus, Cornwall; Folkestone, Kent
Remarks: —
Account of Deed: On 3 Apr. 1858 at Jhansi, India, during the assault on the Fort, Bombardier Brennan brought up two guns manned by natives, laying each under a very heavy fire from the walls, and directing them so accurately as to compel the enemy to abandon his battery.

BRERETON, Alexander Picton   **121**
A/Corporal (later Company Quartermaster-Sergeant)   8th Bn., Manitoba Regiment, C.E.F.
Other Decorations: —
Date of Gazette: 27 Sep. 1918
Place/Date of Birth: Oak River, Manitoba, Canada — 13 Nov. 1892
Place/Date of Death: Calgary, Alberta, Canada — 11 Jun. 1976
Memorials: —
Town/County Connections: —
Remarks: —
Account of Deed: On 9 Aug. 1918 east of Amiens, France, during an attack when a line of hostile machine-guns opened fire suddenly on his platoon which was in an exposed position with no cover, Corporal Brereton realised that unless something was done, his platoon would be annihilated. On his own initiative he at once sprang forward alone and, reaching one of the enemy machine-gun posts, shot the operator of the gun and bayoneted the next one who attempted to operate it, whereupon nine others surrendered. His action inspired the platoon to charge and capture the five remaining posts.

BRILLANT, Jean   **122**
Lieutenant   22nd Bn., Quebec Regiment (Canadien Français), C.E.F.
Other Decorations: MC
Date of Gazette: 27 Sep. 1918
Place/Date of Birth: Assametquaghan, Matapadia Co., Quebec — 15 Mar. 1890
Place/Date of Death: Near Amiens, France — 10 Aug. 1918
Memorials: Villers-Bretonneux Military Cemetery, France
Town/County Connections: —
Remarks: —
Account of Deed: On 8/9 Aug. 1918 east of Meharicourt, France, Lieutenant Brillant, while capturing a machine-gun which was holding up his company, was wounded but refused to leave his command. Later his company was again held by heavy machine-gun fire and Lieutenant Brillant, with two platoons, rushed the machine-gun post, capturing 150 prisoners and 15 guns. He was wounded a second time, had his wounds dressed immediately and again refused to leave his command. Subsequently he led a "rushing" party towards a field gun and was again seriously wounded, but continued to advance until he fell unconscious. He died the next day.

BRODIE, Walter Lorrain   **123**
Captain (later Lieutenant Colonel)   2nd Bn., The Highland Light Infantry
Other Decorations: MC
Date of Gazette: 12 Dec. 1914
Place/Date of Birth: Edinburgh — 28 Jul. 1885
Place/Date of Death: Near Moeuvres, France — 23 Aug. 1918
Memorials: Bienvillers Military Cemetery, France
Town/County Connections: Edinburgh
Remarks: —
Account of Deed: On 11 Nov. 1914 near Becelaere, Belgium, Captain Brodie led a charge to evict the enemy from a portion of our trenches which they had succeeded in occupying. He bayoneted several of the enemy himself and relieved a dangerous situation. As a result of the captain's prompt action, 80 of the enemy were killed and 51 taken prisoner.

BROMHEAD, Gonville   **124**
Lieutenant (later Lieutenant Colonel)   2nd Bn., 24th Regiment (later The South Wales Borderers)
Other Decorations: —
Date of Gazette: 2 May 1879
Place/Date of Birth: Versailles, France — 29 Aug. 1844
Place/Date of Death: Allahabad, India — 10 Feb. 1891
Memorials: Name inscribed on Colour Pole of 24th Regiment *VC in S.W.B. Museum. Brecon*
Town/County Connections: Thurlby, Lincolnshire. *Mementoes in Thurlby Church.*
Remarks: — *Portrait Uniform, Magnus Grammar School, Newark*
Account of Deed: On 22 and 23 Jan. 1879 at Rorke's Drift, Natal, South Africa, Lieutenant Bromhead shared the command of the defenders of the post with an officer of the Royal Engineers*, setting a fine example and conducting himself with great gallantry in most trying circumstances. (*See also CHARD, J.R.M.)

BROMLEY, Cuthbert   **125**
T/Major   1st Bn., The Lancashire Fusiliers
Other Decorations: —
Date of Gazette: 15 Mar.1917
Place/Date of Birth: Seaford, Sussex — 19 Sep. 1878
Place/Date of Death: At sea, Eastern Mediterranean — 13 Aug. 1915
Memorials: Helles Memorial, Gallipoli; War Memorial, Seaford, Sussex
Town/County Connections: Seaford, Sussex
Remarks: — *Name on W.M, Seaford, Sussex.*
Account of Deed: On 25 Apr. 1915 west of Cape Helles, Gallipoli, three companies and the
Headquarters of the 1st Battalion, Lancashire Fusiliers, when landing on W. Beach, were met by a
very deadly fire from hidden machine-guns which caused a large number of casualties. The survivors, however, rushed up and
cut the wire entanglements notwithstanding the terrific fire from the enemy and after overcoming supreme difficulties, the cliffs
were gained and the position maintained. (Major Bromley was one of the six members of the regiment elected for the award.
See also GRIMSHAW, J.E., KENEALLY, W., RICHARDS, A.J., STUBBS, F.E. and WILLIS, R.R.)

BROOKE, James Anson Otho   **126**
Lieutenant (promotion to Captain w.e.f. Sep. 1914 notified posthumously)   2nd Bn., The Gordon
Highlanders
Other Decorations: —
Date of Gazette: 18 Feb. 1915
Place/Date of Birth: Newhills, Aberdeen, Scotland — 3 Feb. 1884
Place/Date of Death: Near Gheluvelt, Belgium — 29 Oct. 1914
Memorials: Zantvoorde British Cemetery, Belgium
Town/County Connections:
Remarks: — *Wellington College. Berkshire*
Account of Deed: On 29 Oct. 1914 near Gheluvelt, Belgium, Lieutenant Brooke led two attacks on
the German trenches under heavy rifle and machine-gun fire, regaining a lost trench at a very critical moment. By his marked
coolness and promptitude on this occasion, Lieutenant Brooke prevented the enemy from breaking through our line at a time
when a general counter-attack could not have been organised. Having regained the lost trench, he went back to bring up
supports, and while doing so, was killed.

BROOKS, Edward   **127**
Company Sergeant-Major   2/4th Bn., The Oxfordshire and Buckinghamshire Light Infantry
Other Decorations: —
Date of Gazette: 27 Jun. 1917
Place/Date of Birth: Oakley, Buckinghamshire — 11 Apr. 1883
Place/Date of Death: Oxford — 26 Jun. 1944
Memorials: Rose Hill Cemetery, Oxford
Town/County Connections: Oxford
Remarks: —
Account of Deed: On 28 Apr. 1917 at Fayet, near St. Quentin, France, Company Sergeant-Major
Brooks, while taking part in a raid on the enemy's trenches, saw that the front wave was being
checked by an enemy machine-gun. On his own initiative he rushed forward from the second wave, killed one of the gunners
with his revolver and bayoneted another. The remainder of the gun crew then made off, leaving the gun, whereupon the
company sergeant-major turned it on the retreating enemy, after which he carried it back to Allied lines. His courageous action
undoubtedly prevented many casualties and greatly added to the success of the operation.

BROOKS, Oliver   **128**
Lance-Sergeant (later Sergeant)   3rd Bn., Coldstream Guards
Other Decorations: —
Date of Gazette: 28 Oct. 1915
Place/Date of Birth: Midsomer Norton, Somerset — 1889
Place/Date of Death: Windsor, Berkshire — 29 Oct. 1940
Memorials: Windsor Cemetery, Berkshire . *Grave*
Town/County Connections: Midsomer Norton, Som.; Windsor, Berks.
Remarks: —
Account of Deed: On 8 Oct. 1915 near Loos, France, Lance-Sergeant Brooks led a party of
bombers against the enemy who had captured 200 yards of our trenches. The regaining of this lost
ground was entirely due to the bravery and presence of mind of this NCO who accomplished his task in the midst of a hail of
bombs from the enemy.

BROWN, Donald Forrester   **129**
Sergeant   2nd Bn., Otago Infantry Regiment, N.Z.E.F.
Other Decorations: —
Date of Gazette: 14 Jun. 1917
Place/Date of Birth: Dunedin, New Zealand — 23 Feb. 1890
Place/Date of Death: Near Eaucourt, L'Abbaye, France — 1 Oct. 1916
Memorials: Warlencourt British Cemetery, France; HQ Dunedin RSA, New Zealand
Town/County Connections: —
Remarks: —
Account of Deed: On 15 Sep. 1916 south-east of High Wood, France, when his company had suffered very heavy casualties from machine-gun fire, Sergeant Brown, with another man, advanced to a point within 30 yards of an enemy gun, killing four of the crew and capturing the gun. When the advance of the company was again held up, Sergeant Brown and his comrade rushed another gun and killed the crew. On a third occasion the sergeant attacked single-handed a machine-gun, killed the crew and captured the gun. Later this gallant soldier was killed.

BROWN (later BROWNE-SINGE-HUTCHINSON) Edward Douglas   **130**
Major (later Colonel)   14th Hussars (The King's)
Other Decorations: CB
Date of Gazette: 15 Jan. 1901
Place/Date of Birth: Kassouli, Dagshai, India — 6 Mar. 1861
Place/Date of Death: London — 3 Feb. 1940
Memorials: —
Town/County Connections: London
Remarks: Knight of the Order of St. John; Freeman of the City of London 1911
Account of Deed: On 13 Oct. 1900 at Geluk, South Africa, Major Brown, seeing that the horse of one of the sergeants had been shot, helped the man up behind him and carried him for about three-quarters of a mile to a place of safety. He did this under heavy fire. Afterwards he helped a lieutenant to mount his horse which was very restive under heavy fire — the officer could not have mounted without this help. Later, Major Brown carried a wounded lance-corporal out of action to safety.

BROWN, Francis David Millest   **131**
Lieutenant (later Lieutenant Colonel)   1st European Bengal Fusiliers (later The Royal Munster Fusiliers)
Other Decorations: —
Date of Gazette: 17 Feb. 1860
Place/Date of Birth: Bhagalpur, Bengal, India — 7 Aug. 1837
Place/Date of Death: Sandown, Isle of Wight — 21 Nov. 1895
Memorials: Royal Munster Fusilier memorial, Winchester Cathedral
Town/County Connections: Sandown, Isle of Wight
Remarks: —
Account of Deed: On 16 Nov. 1857 at Narnoul, India, Lieutenant Brown, at the risk of his own life, rushed to the assistance of a wounded soldier, whom he carried off under heavy fire from the enemy, whose cavalry were within 40 or 50 yards of him at the time.

BROWN, Harry   **132**
Private   10th Bn., Quebec Regiment, C.E.F.
Other Decorations: —
Date of Gazette: 17 Oct. 1917
Place/Date of Birth: Ganonoque, Ontario, Canada — 10 May 1898
Place/Date of Death: Near Loos, France — 17 Aug. 1917
Memorials: Noeux-les-Mines Communal Cemetery, France
Town/County Connections: —
Remarks: —
Account of Deed: On 16 Aug. 1917 at Hill 70, near Loos, France after the capture of a position, the enemy massed in force and counter-attacked and the situation became critical. All signal wires were cut and Private Brown and another soldier were given an important message to be delivered at all costs. The other messenger was killed and Private Brown's arm was shattered, but he struggled through to complete his mission before collapsing. He died of his wounds.

BROWN, Peter   **133**
Trooper   Cape Mounted Riflemen, South African Forces
Other Decorations: —
Date of Gazette: 12 Apr. 1880
Place/Date of Birth: Sweden — 1837
Place/Date of Death: Cape Town, South Africa — 11 Sep. 1894
Memorials: Buried in Cape Town
Town/County Connections: —
Remarks: —
Account of Deed: On 8 Apr. 1879 during the assault on Morosi's Mountain, South Africa (Basuto War), Trooper Brown spent all day carrying water to his wounded comrades who were lying under rocks where they had taken shelter. He did this within 200 yards of the enemy who were firing from redoubts up the sides of the mountain and he was severely wounded during the day, his forearm was shattered and he was also hit in the leg. Nevertheless, he did not cease his efforts until his water bottle was shot through and became useless.

BROWN, Walter Ernest   **134**
Corporal (later Sergeant)   20th Bn. (N.S.W.), Australian Imperial Force
Other Decorations: DCM & Bar
Date of Gazette: 17 Aug. 1918
Place/Date of Birth: New Norfolk, Tasmania — 2 Jul. 1885
Place/Date of Death: Malaya — 28 Feb. 1942
Memorials: Singapore Memorial; Australian War Memorial, Canberra
Town/County Connections: —
Remarks: Served with Royal Australian Artillery in Second World War
Account of Deed: On 6 Jul. 1918 at Villers-Bretonneux, France on his own initiative, Corporal Brown rushed a machine-gun post, which had been causing great inconvenience by persistent sniping. Despite being fired on by another machine-gun, he continued to his objective and with a Mills grenade in his hand, he stood at the door of the dug-out and called on the occupants to surrender. One of the enemy rushed out and scuffled with him, but was knocked down by the corporal's fist. One officer and 11 men then surrendered and he brought them back as prisoners, again under heavy machine-gun fire.

BROWNE, Edward Stevenson   **135**
Lieutenant (later Brigadier General)   1st Bn., 24th Regiment (later The South Wales Borderers)
Other Decorations: CB
Date of Gazette: 17 Jun. 1879
Place/Date of Birth: Cambridge — 23 Dec. 1852
Place/Date of Death: Montreux, Switzerland — 16 Jul. 1907
Memorials: —
Town/County Connections: —
Remarks: — *VC in SWB Museum, Brecon*
Account of Deed: On 29 Mar. 1879 at Inhlobana, South Africa, when the Mounted Infantry were being driven in by the enemy, Lieutenant Browne twice galloped back under heavy fire and helped on to his horse one of the mounted men who would otherwise have fallen into enemy hands.

BROWNE, Henry George GORE-   **136**
Captain (later Colonel)   32nd Regiment (later The Duke of Cornwall's Light Infantry)
Other Decorations: —
Date of Gazette: 20 Jun. 1862
Place/Date of Birth: Newtown, Roscommon, Ireland — 30 Sep. 1830
Place/Date of Death: Shanklin, Isle of Wight — 15 Nov. 1912
Memorials: Buried at Brook, Isle of Wight
Town/County Connections: Newtown, Roscommon, Ireland; Shanklin, Isle of Wight
Remarks: President, Isle of Wight Agricultural Society; Deputy Governor, Isle of Wight, 1912
Account of Deed: On 21 Aug. 1857 at Lucknow, India, during the Siege of the Residency, Captain Browne led a sortie for the purpose of spiking two heavy guns which were doing considerable damage to the defences. The guns were protected by high palisades, the embrasures being closed with sliding shutters. On reaching the battery, Captain Browne removed the shutters, jumped into the battery and spiked the guns. It is supposed that about 100 of the enemy were killed in this operation.

BROWNE, Samuel James (later Sir Samuel)   **137**
Captain (later General)   46th Bengal Native Infantry
Other Decorations: GCB, KCSI
Date of Gazette: 1 Mar. 1861
Place/Date of Birth: India — 3 Oct 1824
Place/Date of Death: Ryde, Isle of Wight — 14 Mar. 1901
Memorials: Ryde Cemetery, Isle of Wight; The Crypt, St. Paul's Cathedral; Lahore Cathedral, India
Town/County Connections: Ryde, Isle of Wight
Remarks: Said to be the inventor of the 'Sam Browne' belt
Account of Deed: On 31 Aug. 1858 at Seerporah, India, in an engagement with the rebels, Captain Browne, whilst advancing upon the enemy's position, pushed on with one orderly sowar upon a 9-pounder gun and attacked the gunners, preventing them from re-loading and attacking the infantry who were advancing to the attack. In the conflict which ensued, Captain Browne received two sword cuts, one on the left knee and one which severed his left arm at the shoulder, but not before he had cut down one of his assailants. The gun was eventually captured and the gunner killed.

BROWNE-SYNGE-HUTCHINSON, Edward Douglas — see **BROWN,** Edward Douglas

BRUCE, William Arthur McCrae   **138**
Lieutenant   59th Scinde Rifles, Indian Army
Other Decorations: ––
Date of Gazette: 4 Sep. 1919
Place/Date of Birth: Edinburgh — 15 Jun. 1890
Place/Date of Death: Near Givenchy, France — 19 Dec. 1914
Memorials: Neuve Chapelle Memorial, France; St. Clement's Church, Jersey, C.I.
Town/County Connections: Edinburgh
Remarks: —
Account of Deed: On 19 Dec. 1914 near Givenchy, France, during a night attack, Lieutenant Bruce was in command of a small party which captured one of the enemy trenches. In spite of being wounded in the neck he walked up and down the trench encouraging his men to hold out against several counter-attacks until he was killed. The fire from rifles and bombs was very heavy all day and it was due to his example and encouragement that the men were able to hold out until dusk when the trench was finally captured by the enemy.

BRUNT, John Henry Cound   **139**
T/Captain   The Sherwood Foresters (The Nottinghamshire and Derbyshire Regt.), attd. 6th Bn., The Lincolnshire Regiment
Other Decorations: MC
Date of Gazette: 8 Feb. 1945
Place/Date of Birth: Priest Weston, Chirbury, Shropshire — 6 Dec. 1922
Place/Date of Death: Near Faenza, Italy — 10 Dec. 1944
Memorials: Faenza War Cemetery, Italy; The Soldiers' Chapel of St. George, Lincoln Cathedral
Town/County Connections: Chirbury, Shropshire
Remarks: —
Account of Deed: On 9 Dec. 1944 near Faenza, Italy, the house round which Captain Brunt's platoon was dug in, was destroyed by intense mortar fire. The captain, rallying his remaining men and moving to an alternative position, continued to hold the enemy although heavily outnumbered. Personally firing a Bren gun he killed about 14 and then, his ammunition exhausted, he fired a Piat and 2-in. mortar left by casualties. This aggressive defence enabled him to re-occupy his previous position and to get his wounded away. Later he showed similar aggressive and inspiring leadership which caused the final withdrawal of the enemy.

BRYAN, Thomas   **140**
Lance-Corporal   25th (S) Bn., The Northumberland Fusiliers
Other Decorations: —
Date of Gazette: 8 Jun. 1917
Place/Date of Birth: Stourbridge, Worcestershire — 21 Jan. 1882
Place/Date of Death: Doncaster, Yorkshire — 13 Oct. 1945
Memorials: Arksey Cemetery, Doncaster; Castleford Civic Centre, Yorkshire. *Buried Arksey Cem*
Town/County Connections: Stourbridge, Worcs; Doncaster and Castleford, Yorks.
Remarks: —
Account of Deed: On 9 Apr. 1917 near Arras, France, during an attack Lance-Corporal Bryan although wounded, went forward alone in order to silence a machine-gun which was inflicting much damage. He worked his way along the communication trench, approached the gun from behind, disabled it and killed two of the team. The results obtained by Lance-Corporal Bryan's action were very far-reaching.

BUCHAN, John Crawford　　　　　　　　　　　　　　**141**
Second Lieutenant　7th Bn., The Argyll & Sutherland Highlanders (Princess Louise's), attd. 8th Bn.
Other Decorations: —
Date of Gazette: 22 May 1918
Place/Date of Birth: Alloa, Clackmannan, Scotland — 10 Oct. 1892
Place/Date of Death: Near Marteville, France — 22 Mar. 1918
Memorials: Roisel Communal Cemetery Extension, France
Town/County Connections: Alloa, Clackmannan, Scotland
Remarks: —
Account of Deed: On 21 Mar. 1918 east of Marteville, France, Second Lieutenant Buchan, although wounded early in the day, insisted on remaining with his platoon which was suffering heavy casualties from most severe shell fire. He continually visited all his posts, encouraging his men in the face of the approaching enemy and heavy machine-gun fire. When called on to surrender, he fought his way back to the support line where he held out until dusk. He then withdrew as ordered, but refused to have his injuries attended to. He was eventually completely cut off and was last seen fighting valiantly against overwhelming odds.

BUCHANAN, Angus　　　　　　　　　　　　　　**142**
T/Captain　4th Bn., The South Wales Borderers
Other Decorations: MC
Date of Gazette: 26 Sep. 1916
Place/Date of Birth: Coleford, Gloucestershire — 11 Aug. 1894
Place/Date of Death: Gloucester — 1 Mar. 1944
Memorials: Coleford Church; Memorial Gardens, Coleford　*· Buried Coleford*
Town/County Connections: Coleford, Gloucestershire
Remarks: Order of St. Vladimir — 4th Class, with Swords (Russia)　*VC· in SWB Museum. Brecon*
Account of Deed: On 5 Apr. 1916 at Falauyah Lines, Mesopotamia, during an attack, an officer was lying out in the open severely wounded about 150 yards from cover. Two men went out to his assistance and one of them was hit at once. Captain Buchanan immediately went out and with the help of the other man, carried the first casualty to cover under machine-gun fire. He then returned and brought in the other wounded man, again under heavy fire.

BUCKINGHAM, William　　　　　　　　　　　　　**143**
Private　2nd Bn., The Leicestershire Regiment
Other Decorations: —
Date of Gazette: 28 Apr. 1915
Place/Date of Birth: Leicester — Feb. 1886
Place/Date of Death: Somme, France — 15 Sep. 1916
Memorials: Thiepval Memorial, France
Town/County Connections: Countesthorpe, Leicestershire
Remarks: —
Account of Deed: On 10 and 12 Mar. 1915 at Neuve Chapelle, France, Private Buckingham showed great bravery and devotion to duty in rescuing and rendering aid to the wounded, while he himself was exposed to heavy fire.

BUCKLEY, Alexander Henry　　　　　　　　　　　**144**
T/Corporal　54th Bn. (N.S.W.), Australian Imperial Force
Other Decorations: —
Date of Gazette: 14 Dec. 1918
Place/Date of Birth: Warren, New South Wales, Australia — 22 Jul. 1891
Place/Date of Death: Peronne, France — 2 Sep. 1918
Memorials: Peronne Communal Cemetery Extension, France; Australian War Memorial, Canberra
Town/County Connections: —
Remarks: —
Account of Deed: On 1 and 2 Sep. 1918 at Peronne, France, Corporal Buckley, with one other man, rushed an enemy machine-gun nest, shooting four of the enemy and capturing 22. Later, on reaching a moat, it was found that another machine-gun nest commanded the only available foot-bridge. Corporal Buckley tried to cross the bridge and rush the position, but was killed in the attempt.

BUCKLEY, Cecil William
145

Lieutenant (later Captain)   Royal Navy
Other Decorations: —
Date of Gazette: 24 Feb. 1857
Place/Date of Birth: — 7 Oct. 1830
Place/Date of Death: Funchal, Madeira — 7 Dec. 1872
Memorials: —
Town/County Connections: Calcott, Somerset
Remarks: Légion d'Honneur (France); First winner of the VC to be actually gazetted
Account of Deed: On 29 May 1855 in the Sea of Azov, Crimea, Lieutenant Buckley of HMS *Miranda*, with a lieutenant* from HMS *Swallow* and a gunner* from HMS *Ardent,* volunteered to land at a beach where the Russian army were in strength. They were out of covering gunshot range of the ships offshore and met considerable enemy opposition, but managed to set fire to corn stores and ammunition dumps and destroy enemy equipment. On 3 June Lieutenant Buckley carried out another raid with a boatswain* from *Miranda*. They landed at the town of Taganrog and were successful in destroying enemy equipment and stores, whilst being under enemy fire. (*See also BURGOYNE, H.T., ROBARTS, J. and COOPER, H.)

BUCKLEY, John
146

Deputy Assistant Commissary of Ordnance   Commissariat Department (Bengal Est.)
Other Decorations: —
Date of Gazette: 18 Jun. 1858
Place/Date of Birth: Cockerhill, Stalybridge, Cheshire — 24 May 1813
Place/Date of Death: London — 14 Jul. 1876
Memorials: (City of London and Tower Hamlets Cemetery — unmarked grave)
Town/County Connections: Stalybridge, Cheshire; London
Remarks: —
Account of Deed: On 11 May 1857 at Delhi, India, Deputy Assistant Commissary Buckley was one of nine men who defended the Magazine for more than five hours against large numbers of mutineers, until, on the wall being scaled and there being no hope of help, they fired the Magazine. Five of the gallant band died in the explosion and one shortly afterwards, but many of the enemy were killed. (See also FORREST, G, and RAYNOR, W.)

BUCKLEY, (alias SEXTON, Gerald) Maurice Vincent
147

Sergeant   13th Bn. (N.S.W.), Australian Imperial Force
Other Decorations: DCM
Date of Gazette: 14 Dec. 1918 & 8 Aug. 1919
Place/Date of Birth: Upper Hawthorn, Victoria, Australia — 13 Apr. 1891
Place/Date of Death: Melbourne, Australia — 27 Jan. 1921
Memorials: Brighton Cemetery, Melbourne; Australian War Memorial, Canberra
Town/County Connections: —
Remarks: —
Account of Deed: On 18 Sep. 1918, near Le Verguier, north-west of St. Quentin, France, Sergeant Buckley and his section rushed an enemy field gun, killing the gunners. Regardless of machine-gun fire, he then fired down some dug-outs, forcing about 30 of the enemy to surrender. When the advance was again held up by machine-gun fire, Sergeant Buckley, supported by another platoon, put the enemy guns out of action. Later, he again showed conspicuous initiative in capturing hostile posts and machine-guns.

BUGDEN, Patrick Joseph
148

Private   31st Bn. (Q. and V.), Australian Imperial Force
Other Decorations: —
Date of Gazette: 26 Nov. 1917
Place/Date of Birth: Gundurimba, New South Wales, Australia — Mar. 1897
Place/Date of Death: Polygon Wood, Zonnebeke — 28 Sep. 1917
Memorials: Hooge Crater Cemetery, Belgium; Australian War Memorial, Canberra
Town/County Connections: —
Remarks: —
Account of Deed: During the period 26/28 Sep. 1917 at Polygon Wood, Zonnebeke, Belgium, an advance was held up by strongly defended pillboxes. Private Bugden despite devastating machine-gun fire twice led small parties against these strong points and, successfully silencing the guns, captured the enemy at the point of the bayonet. On another occasion, he rescued a corporal from capture, when, single-handed he rushed up, shot one of the enemy and bayoneted the other two. On five occasions he rescued wounded men under intense shell and machine-gun fire, showing an utter contempt and disregard for danger. He was killed during one of these missions.

BULLER, Redvers Henry (later Sir Redvers)   **149**
Bt/Lieutenant Colonel (later General)   60th Rifles (later The King's Royal Rifle Corps)
Other Decorations: GCB, GCMG
Date of Gazette: 17 Jun. 1879
Place/Date of Birth: Downes, Crediton, Devon — 7 Dec. 1839
Place/Date of Death: Crediton, Devon — 2 Jun. 1908   *Buried Crediton Church*
Memorials: Winchester Cathedral; Exeter Cathedral; Crediton Church; equestrian statue, Exeter
Town/County Connections: Downes and Crediton, Devon
Remarks: Family connection with Second Lieutenant A.B. Turner, VC and Lieutenant Colonel
V.B. Turner, VC; in command Aldershot 1898-99; served in South Africa 1899-1900 as general
commanding forces and then as GOC in Natal; commanded 1st Army Corps, Aldershot 1901
Account of Deed: On 28 Mar. 1879 at Inhlobana, South Africa (Zulu War), during the retreat, Lieutenant Colonel Buller, while being hotly pursued by Zulus, rescued a captain of the Frontier Light Horse and carried him on his own horse until he overtook the rearguard. On the same day, under the same circumstances, he carried a lieutenant, whose horse had been killed under him, to a place of safety. Again, on the same day, he saved a trooper whose horse was exhausted, and who would otherwise have been killed by the Zulus who were within 80 yards of him.

BURGES, Daniel   **150**
T/Lieutenant Colonel   The Gloucestershire Regt., comd. 7th (S) Bn., The South Wales Borderers
Other Decorations: DSO
Date of Gazette: 14 Dec. 1918
Place/Date of Birth: London — 1 Jul. 1873
Place/Date of Death: Bristol — 24 Oct. 1946
Memorials: —
Town/County Connections: London; Bristol
Remarks: Croix de Guerre avec Palme (France); Greek Military Cross (2nd Class)
Account of Deed: On 18 Sep. 1918 at Jumeaux, in the Balkans, valuable reconnaissance of the enemy front line trenches enabled Lieutenant Colonel Burges to bring his battalion, without casualties, to the assembly point, but later while some distance from the objective they came under severe machine-gun fire. Although he himself was wounded the colonel continued to lead his men with skill and courage until he was hit again twice and fell unconscious. He was taken prisoner by the Bulgars, but was abandoned in a dug-out with one of his legs shattered.

BURGOYNE, Hugh Talbot   **151**
Lieutenant (later Captain)   Royal Navy
Other Decorations: —
Date of Gazette: 24 Feb. 1857
Place/Date of Birth: Dublin — 17 Jul. 1833
Place/Date of Death: At Sea, near Finisterre — 7 Sep. 1870
Memorials: Plaque in St. Paul's Cathedral; family grave, Brompton Cemetery, London
Town/County Connections: Dublin   *Parish Church, Sutton. Bedfordshire.*
Remarks: Légion d'Honneur (France)
Account of Deed: On 29 May 1855 in the Sea of Azov, Crimea, Lieutenant Burgoyne of HMS *Swallow*, with a lieutenant* from HMS *Miranda* and a gunner* from HMS *Ardent*, volunteered to land at a beach where the Russian army were in strength. They were out of covering gunshot range of the ships offshore and met considerable enemy opposition, but managed to set fire to corn stores and ammunition dumps and destroy enemy equipment before embarking again. (*See also BUCKLEY, C.W. and ROBARTS, J.)   *Flag of HMS Captain in which he was drowned in Micheldever Church. Hampshire*

BURMAN, William Francis   **152**
Sergeant   16th Bn., The Rifle Brigade (Prince Consort's Own)
Other Decorations: —
Date of Gazette: 26 Nov. 1917
Place/Date of Birth: London — 30 Aug. 1897
Place/Date of Death: Cromer, Norfolk — 23 Oct. 1974
Memorials: The Rifle Brigade memorial, Winchester Cathedral.
Town/County Connections: Stepney, London; Cromer, Norfolk
Remarks: —
Account of Deed: On 20 Sep. 1917 south-east of Ypres, Belgium, when the advance of his company was held up by a machine-gun at point-blank range, Sergeant Burman shouted to the men next to him to wait a few minutes and going forward to what seemed certain death killed the enemy gunner and carried the gun to the company's objective where he used it with great effect. Fifteen minutes later it was seen that about 40 of the enemy were enfilading the battalion on the right. Sergeant Burman and two others ran and got behind them, killing six and capturing two officers and 29 other ranks.

BURSLEM, Nathaniel   **153**
Lieutenant (later Captain)   67th Regiment (later The Hampshire Regiment)
Other Decorations: —
Date of Gazette: 13 Aug. 1861
Place/Date of Birth: Limerick, Ireland — 2 Feb. 1838
Place/Date of Death: Drowned in Thames River, New Zealand — 1865
Memorials: —
Town/County Connections: Limerick, Ireland
Remarks: —
Account of Deed: On 21 Aug. 1860 at the Taku Forts, China, Lieutenant Burslem and a private*
of his regiment displayed great gallantry in swimming the ditches of the North Taku Fort and
attempting, during the assault and before an entrance had been effected by anyone, to enlarge an opening in the wall, through
which they eventually entered. In doing so, they were both severely wounded. (*See also LANE, T.)

BURT, Alfred Alexander   **154**
Corporal (later Sergeant)   1st Bn., The Hertfordshire Regiment
Other Decorations: —
Date of Gazette: 22 Jan. 1916
Place/Date of Birth: Port Vale, Hertfordshire — 3 Mar. 1895
Place/Date of Death: Chesham, Bucks — 9 Jun. 1962
Memorials: (Garston Crematorium, West Hertfordshire)
Town/County Connections: Port Vale, Hertfordshire; Chesham, Buckinghamshire
Remarks: —
Account of Deed: On 27 Sep. 1915 at Cuinchy, France, Corporal Burt's company was ready to
attack when a large minenwerfer bomb fell into the trench. Knowing full well the destructive
powers of this bomb the corporal, who might easily have got under cover behind a traverse, went forward, put his foot on the
fuse, wrenched it out of the bomb and threw it over the parapet, and so saved the lives of many of his comrades.

BURTON, Alexander Stewart   **155**
Corporal   7th Bn. (Victoria), Australian Imperial Force
Other Decorations: —
Date of Gazette: 15 Oct. 1915
Place/Date of Birth: Kyneton, Victoria, Australia — 20 Jan. 1893
Place/Date of Death: Lone Pine, Gallipoli — 9 Aug. 1915
Memorials: Lone Pine Memorial, Gallipoli; Australian War Memorial, Canberra
Town/County Connections: —
Remarks: —
Account of Deed: On 9 Aug. 1915, at Lone Pine, Gallipoli, the enemy made a determined counter
attack on the centre of the newly captured trench held by a lieutenant*, two corporals* (one of
whom was Corporal Burton) and a few men. The enemy blew in the sand-bag barricade leaving only a foot standing, but the
lieutenant and the two corporals repulsed the enemy and rebuilt the barricade. Twice more the enemy blew in the barricade and
on each occasion they were repulsed and the barricade rebuilt, but Corporal Burton was killed while most gallantly building up
the parapet under a hail of bombs. (*See also TUBB, F.H. and DUNSTAN, W.)

BURTON, Richard Henry   **156**
Private (later Corporal)   1st Bn., The Duke of Wellington's (West Riding) Regiment
Other Decorations: —
Date of Gazette: 4 Jan. 1945
Place/Date of Birth: Melton Mowbray, Leicestershire — 29 Jan. 1923
Place/Date of Death: — *About 12.7.1993*
Memorials: — *Probably Kirriemuir, Angus*
Town/County Connections: Melton Mowbray, Leicestershire
Remarks: —
Account of Deed: On 8 Oct. 1944 at Monte Ceco, Italy, when an assault was held up, Private
Burton rushed forward from his platoon and engaged a Spandau position with his tommy gun,
killing three of the crew. Later, again showing complete disregard for his own safety he disposed of the crews of two machine-
guns and thanks to his outstanding courage the company was able to consolidate the position. Afterwards, in spite of the fact
that most of his comrades were either dead or wounded, he repelled two counter-attacks, directing such accurate fire that the
enemy retired.

BUSHELL, Christopher   **157**
T/Lieutenant Colonel   Comd. 7th (S) Bn., The Queen's Royal West Surrey Regiment (S.R.)
Other Decorations: DSO
Date of Gazette: 3 May 1918
Place/Date of Birth: Neston, Cheshire — 31 Oct. 1888
Place/Date of Death: South of Morlencourt, Somme — 8 Aug. 1918
Memorials: Querrieu British Cemetery, France
Town/County Connections: Neston, Cheshire
Remarks: —   *Rugby School.*
Account of Deed: On 23 Mar. 1918 west of St. Quentin's Canal and north of Tergnier, France,
Lieutenant Colonel Bushell personally led C Company of his battalion who were co-operating with
an Allied regiment in a counter-attack. In the course of this attack he was severely wounded in the head, but continued to carry
on, walking in front of both English and Allied troops, encouraging them and visiting every portion of the lines in the face of
terrific machine-gun and rifle fire. He refused to go to the rear until he had to be removed to the dressing station in a fainting
condition.

BUTLER, John Fitzhardinge Paul   **158**
Lieutenant (later Captain)   The King's Royal Rifle Corps, attd. Pioneer Coy., Gold Coast Regt.,
West African Field Force
Other Decorations: DSO
Date of Gazette: 23 Aug. 1915
Place/Date of Birth: Berkeley, Gloucestershire — 20 Dec. 1888
Place/Date of Death: Motomba, East Africa — 5 Sep. 1916
Memorials: Morogoro Cemetery, Tanganyika
Town/County Connections: Berkeley and Wyck Hill, Gloucestershire
Remarks: Nephew of Lord Gifford, VC.   *Wellington College, Berkshire.*
Account of Deed: On 17 Nov. 1914 in the Cameroons, West Africa, Lieutenant Butler, with a party
of 13 men went into the thick bush and attacked a force of about 100 of the enemy, including several Europeans, defeated them
and captured their machine-gun and many loads of ammunition. On 27 Dec. when on patrol duty with a few men, Lieutenant
Butler swam the Ekam River, which was held by the enemy, alone and in the face of brisk fire. He completed his reconnaissance
on the further bank and returned to safety.

BUTLER, Thomas Adair   **159**
Lieutenant (later Major)   1st Bengal European Fusiliers (later The Royal Munster Fusiliers)
Other Decorations: —
Date of Gazette: 6 May 1859
Place/Date of Birth: Soberton, Hampshire — 12 Feb. 1836
Place/Date of Death: Camberley, Surrey — 17 May 1901
Memorials: St. Michael's Churchyard, Camberley; Royal Munster Fusilisers memorial,
Winchester Cathedral
Town/County Connections: Soberton, Hampshire
Remarks: —
Account of Deed: On 9 Mar. 1858 at Lucknow, India, in order to ascertain the enemy's position
and to inform his superiors, Lieutenant Butler swam the river Goomtee, on the banks of which the city stands, mounted the
parapet of a field work and remained there for a considerable time, exposed to the enemy's fire. He stayed there until the
relieving force arrived.

BUTLER, William Boynton   **160**
Private   17th Bn., The West Yorkshire Regt. (The Prince of Wales's Own), attd. 106th T.M. Bty.
Other Decorations: —
Date of Gazette: 17 Oct. 1917
Place/Date of Birth: Leeds, Yorkshire — 20 Nov. 1894
Place/Date of Death: Leeds, Yorkshire — 25 Mar. 1972
Memorials: —
Town/County Connections: Leeds, Yorkshire
Remarks: Croix de Guerre (France)
Account of Deed: On 6 Aug. 1917 east of Lempire, France, Private Butler was in charge of a
Stokes gun in trenches which were being heavily shelled. Suddenly one of the fly-off levers of a
Stokes shell came off and fired the shell in the emplacement. Private Butler picked up the shell and shouted a warning to a party
of infantry. He then turned and put himself between the party of men and the live shell, holding it until they were out of danger,
when he threw it on to the parados and took cover. The shell exploded, damaging the trench, but only contusing Private Butler.

BYE, Robert James   **161**
Sergeant   1st Bn., Welsh Guards
Other Decorations: —
Date of Gazette: 6 Sep. 1917
Place/Date of Birth: Pontypridd, Glamorgan, Wales — 12 Dec. 1889
Place/Date of Death: Warsop, Nottinghamshire — 23 Aug. 1962 _Grave Warsop Cem._
Memorials: Warsop Cemetery; Guards Chapel, Wellington Barracks, London
Town/County Connections: Pontypridd and Penrhiwceiber, Glamorgan; Warsop, Notts.
Remarks: Served with the Sherwood Foresters during the Second World War
Account of Deed: On 31 Jul. 1917 at the Yser Canal, Belgium, during an attack, Sergeant Bye saw
that the leading waves were being troubled by two enemy block-houses. He rushed at one of them
and put the garrison out of action. He then rejoined his company and went forward to the second objective. Later he volunteered
to take charge of a party detailed to clear up a line of block-houses which had been passed. He accomplished this, taking many
prisoners, and then advanced to the third objective, again taking a number of prisoners. During the action he accounted for over
70 of the enemy. _VC in Welsh Guards Memorial in Guards Chapel Wellington Barracks_

BYRNE, James   **162**
Private (later Sergeant)   86th Regiment (later The Royal Irish Rifles)
Other Decorations: —
Date of Gazette: 11 Nov. 1859
Place/Date of Birth: Newtown, Mount Kennedy, Co. Wicklow, Ireland — 1822
Place/Date of Death: Dublin — 6 Dec. 1872
Memorials:
Town/County Connections: Newtown, Mount Kennedy, Co. Wicklow
Remarks: —
Account of Deed: On 3 Apr. 1858 at Jhansi, India, Private Byrne assisted a captain of his
regiment* in removing, under very heavy fire, a lieutenant who was severely wounded. They took
the injured man to a place of safety, in the performance of which act the private was wounded. (*See also JEROME, H.E.)

No photograph available

BYRNE, John   **163**
Private (later Corporal)   68th Regiment (later The Durham Light Infantry)
Other Decorations: —
Date of Gazette: 24 Feb. 1857
Place/Date of Birth: Castlecomer, Kilkenny, Ireland — Sep. 1832
Place/Date of Death: Caerleon, Monmouthshire — 10 Jul. 1879 _Committed suicide._
Memorials: (Buried at St. Woolo's Cemetery, Newport, Monmouthshire, unmarked grave)
Town/County Connections: Castlecomer, Kilkenny; Caerleon, Monmouthshire,
Remarks: — _Grave RC E15. Block 14. is in lawn cemetery and is unmarked._
Account of Deed: On 5 Nov. 1854 in the Crimea, at the Battle of Inkerman, when the regiment
was ordered to retire, Private Byrne went back towards the enemy, and, at the risk of his own life,
brought in a wounded soldier, under fire. On 11 May 1855 he bravely engaged in a hand-to-hand contest with one of the enemy
on the parapet of the work he was defending, prevented the entrance of the enemy, killed his antagonist, and captured his arms.

BYRNE, Thomas   **164**
Private   21st Lancers (Empress of India's)
Other Decorations: —
Date of Gazette: 15 Nov. 1898
Place/Date of Birth: St. Thomas, Dublin — Dec. 1866
Place/Date of Death: Canterbury, Kent — 14 Mar. 1944
Memorials: (Buried at Canterbury)
Town/County Connections: Dublin; Canterbury, Kent
Remarks: —
Account of Deed: On 2 Sep. 1898 at the Battle of Khartoum, Sudan, Private Byrne turned back in
the middle of the charge of the 21st Lancers and went to the assistance of a lieutenant of the Royal
Horse Guards who was wounded, dismounted, disarmed and being attacked by several Dervishes. Private Byrne already
wounded, attacked these Dervishes, received a second severe wound and by his gallant conduct enabled the officer to escape.

BYTHESEA, John
Lieutenant (later Rear-Admiral)   Royal Navy
Other Decorations: CB, CIE
Date of Gazette: 24 Feb. 1857
Place/Date of Birth: Freshford, Somerset — 15 Jun. 1827
Place/Date of Death: South Kensington, London — 18 May 1906
Memorials: Bath Abbey Cemetery; Freshford Church, Somerset
Town/County Connections: Freshford and Bath, Somerset; Kensington, London
Remarks: Consulting Naval Officer to the Indian Government, 1874-80
Account of Deed: On 9 Aug. 1854 in the Baltic, Lieutenant Bythesea of HMS *Arrogant* obtained permission to land on the island of Wardo with a stoker* from the ship, in order to intercept important despatches from the Czar which were being sent via Wardo to Bomarsund. The two men spent two nights reconnoitring the island and on 12 Aug. when the despatches arrived, they ambushed the five Russians carrying them. Two of the carriers dropped their mail bags and ran, but the other three surrendered and were taken back to *Arrogant*. In this action the officer and stoker were armed with just one pistol. (*See also JOHNSTONE, W.)

CADELL, Thomas
Lieutenant (later Colonel)   2nd Bengal European Fusiliers (later The Royal Munster Fusiliers)
Other Decorations: CB
Date of Gazette: 29 Apr. 1862
Place/Date of Birth: Cockenzie, East Lothian, Scotland — 5 Sep. 1835
Place/Date of Death: Edinburgh — 6 Apr. 1919
Memorials: —
Town/County Connections: Cockenzie, East Lothian; Edinburgh
Remarks: Cousin of Lieutenant S.H. Lawrence, VC
Account of Deed: On 12 Jun. 1857 at Delhi, India, during the siege, Lieutenant Cadell brought in a wounded bugler of his own regiment under most severe fire. Later on the same day, when the Fusiliers were retiring, this officer went back of his own accord and, accompanied by three men, brought in a severely wounded man under heavy fire from the advancing enemy.

166

CAFE, William Martin
Captain (later General)   56th Bengal Native Infantry
Other Decorations: —
Date of Gazette: 17 Feb. 1860
Place/Date of Birth: London — 23 Mar. 1826
Place/Date of Death: London — 6 Aug. 1906   *Buried Brompton Cemetery*
Memorials: Brompton Cemetery, London
Town/County Connections: London
Remarks: —
Account of Deed: On 15 Apr. 1858 during the attack on Fort Ruhya, India, Captain Cafe, with other volunteers* carried away the body of a lieutenant from the top of the glacis in a most exposed position under a very heavy fire. He then went to the rescue of one of the privates who had been severely wounded. (*See also SPENCE, E. and THOMPSON, A.)

167

CAFFREY, John
Private (later Lance-Corporal)   2nd Bn., The York and Lancaster Regiment
Other Decorations: —
Date of Gazette: 22 Jan. 1916
Place/Date of Birth: Birr, King's Co. (later Offaly), Ireland — 23 Oct. 1891
Place/Date of Death: Derby — 26 Feb. 1953
Memorials: —
Town/County Connections: Birr, Offaly, Ireland
Remarks: Cross of the Order of St. George, Fourth Class (Russian)
Account of Deed: On 16 Nov. 1915 near La Brique, France, a man was badly wounded and lying in the open unable to move, in full view of and about 350 yds from the enemy's trenches. A corporal of the RAMC and Private Caffrey at once started to rescue him, but at the first attempt were driven back by shrapnel fire. They tried again and succeeded in reaching and bandaging the wounded man, but just as they were lifting him up, the RAMC corporal was shot in the head. Private Caffrey bandaged the corporal and helped him back to safety, and then returned and brought in the other wounded man.

168

CAIN, Robert Henry   **169**
T/Major   The Royal Northumberland Fusiliers, attd. The South Staffordshire Regt. — 1st
Airborne Division
Other Decorations: —
Date of Gazette: 2 Nov. 1944
Place/Date of Birth: Shanghai, China — 2 Jan. 1909
Place/Date of Death: Crowborough, Sussex — 2 May 1974
Memorials: Garrison Church, Whittington Barracks, Lichfield, Staffordshire
Town/County Connections: Crowborough, Sussex; Castletown, Isle of Man
Remarks: Became a member of the Nigerian House of Representatives after 1951 while working
with Shell in West Africa
Account of Deed: During the period 19 to 25 Sep. 1944 at Arnhem, Holland, Major Cain's company was cut off from the
battalion and throughout the whole of this time was closely engaged with enemy tanks, self-propelled guns and infantry. The
Major was everywhere danger threatened, moving among his men and encouraging them to hold out. By his leadership he not
only stopped, but demoralized the enemy attacks and although he was suffering from a perforated ear-drum and multiple
wounds, he refused medical attention.

CAIRNS, George Albert   **170**
Lieutenant   The Somerset Light Infantry (Prince Albert's) attd. The South Staffordshire Regt.
Other Decorations: —
Date of Gazette: 20 May 1949
Place/Date of Birth: London — 12 Dec. 1913
Place/Date of Death: Henu Block, Burma — 19 Mar. 1944
Memorials: Taukkyan War Cemetery, Burma; Garrison Church, Whittington Barracks, Lichfield,
Staffs; Brighstone Churchyard, Isle of Wight
Town/County Connections: London (Tooting and Fulham)
Remarks: Last VC to be gazetted for the Second World War — the original recommendation was
with General Wingate when he was killed in an air crash and the necessary information could not
be obtained again until the war was over.
Account of Deed: On 13 Mar. 1944 at Henu Block, Burma, during an attack on a hill-top held by the Japanese, Lieutenant Cairns
was attacked by a Japanese officer who with his sword hacked off the lieutenant's left arm. The latter killed the officer, picked
up the sword and continued to lead his men, slashing left and right with the captured sword, killing and wounding several of
the enemy before he himself fell to the ground. He later died of his wounds, but his action so inspired his comrades that the
Japanese were completely routed, a very rare occurrence at that time.

CAIRNS, Hugh   **171**
Sergeant   46th South Saskatchewan Bn., Saskatchewan Regiment, C.E.F.
Other Decorations: DCM
Date of Gazette: 31 Jan. 1919
Place/Date of Birth: Ashington, Northumberland — 4 Dec. 1896
Place/Date of Death: Valenciennes, France — 2 Nov. 1918
Memorials: Auberchicourt British Cemetery, France
Town/County Connections: Ashington, Northumberland
Remarks: —
Account of Deed: On 1 Nov. 1918 at Valenciennes, France, when a machine-gun opened fire on
his platoon, Sergeant Cairns seized a Lewis gun and single-handed, in the face of direct fire,
rushed the post, killed the crew of five and captured the gun. Later, after killing 12 of the enemy and capturing 18 and two guns,
he went with a small party and, although wounded, outflanked more field and machine-guns, killing many and capturing all the
guns. After consolidation he went with a battle patrol to exploit Marly and forced 60 to surrender, but was severely wounded.
He later collapsed and died next day.

CALDWELL, Thomas   **172**
Sergeant (later Company Sergeant-Major)   12th Bn., The Royal Scots Fusiliers
Other Decorations: —
Date of Gazette: 6 Jan. 1919
Place/Date of Birth: Carluke, Lanarkshire, Scotland — 10 Feb. 1894
Place/Date of Death: Adelaide, Australia — 7 Jun. 1969
Memorials: Centennial Park Crematorium, Adelaide
Town/County Connections: Carluke, Lanarkshire
Remarks: —
Account of Deed: On 31 Oct. 1918 near Audenarde, Belgium, Sergeant Caldwell was in
command of a Lewis gun section engaged in clearing a farmhouse, and when his section came
under intense fire at close range, the sergeant rushed towards the farm, captured the enemy position single-handed and took
18 prisoners. This gallant and determined exploit removed a serious obstacle from the line of advance and led to the capture
by the section of about 70 prisoners, eight machine-guns and one trench mortar.

CALVERT, Laurence 173
Sergeant   5th Bn., The King's Own Yorkshire Light Infantry
Other Decorations: MM
Date of Gazette: 15 Nov. 1918
Place/Date of Birth: Hunslet, Leeds, Yorkshire — 16 Feb. 1892
Place/Date of Death: Dagenham, Essex — 7 Jul. 1964
Memorials: South Essex Crematorium, Upminster, Essex.
Town/County Connections: Leeds and Conisborough, Yorks; Dagenham, Essex
Remarks: Chevalier de l'Ordre de Leopold II (Belgium)
Account of Deed: On 12 Sep. 1918 at Havrincourt, France, severe enfilade machine-gun fire was creating a difficult situation and Sergeant Calvert went forward alone against a machine-gun team, bayoneting three and shooting four. His valour and determination in capturing single-handed two machine-guns and killing the crews ensured the success of the operation. His personal gallantry inspired all ranks.

CAMBRIDGE, Daniel 174
Sergeant (later Master Gunner)   Royal Regiment of Artillery
Other Decorations: —
Date of Gazette: 23 Jun. 1857
Place/Date of Birth: Carrickfergus, Co. Antrim, Ireland — 1820
Place/Date of Death: London, S.E.18 — 12 Jun. 1882
Memorials: —
Town/County Connections: Carrickfergus, Co. Antrim; London
Remarks: Became one of the Yeomen of the Guard 1871.
Account of Deed: On 8 Sep. 1855 at Sebastopol, Crimea, Sergeant Cambridge volunteered for the spiking party at the assault on the Redan and remained with the party even after being severely wounded. Later on the same day he went out under heavy fire to bring in a wounded man.

CAMERON, Aylmer Spicer 175
Lieutenant (later Colonel)   1st Bn., 72nd Regt. (later The Seaforth Highlanders — Ross-shire Buffs, Duke of Albany's)
Other Decorations: CB
Date of Gazette: 11 Nov. 1859
Place/Date of Birth: — 12 Aug. 1833
Place/Date of Death: Alverstoke, Hampshire — 13 Jun. 1909
Memorials: —
Town/County Connections: Alverstoke, Hampshire
Remarks: Commanded King's Own Borderers 1881-83; Chief of Intelligence Department 1883-86; Commandant Royal Military College Sandhurst 1886-88
Account of Deed: On 30 Mar. 1858 at Kotah, India, Lieutenant Cameron headed a small party of men and attacked a body of fanatic rebels, previously posted in a loopholed house with one narrow entrance. Lieutenant Cameron stormed the house and killed three rebels in single combat. He was severely wounded, having lost half of one hand by a stroke from a tulwar.

CAMERON, Donald 176
Lieutenant (later Commander)   Royal Naval Reserve
Other Decorations: —
Date of Gazette: 22 Feb. 1944
Place/Date of Birth: Carluke, Lanarkshire, Scotland — 18 Mar. 1916
Place/Date of Death: Haslar, Hampshire — 10 Apr. 1961
Memorials: (Buried at sea.)
Town/County Connections: Carluke, Lanarkshire; Lee-on-Solent, Hampshire
Remarks: Transferred to the Royal Navy, 1946 and served mainly with submarines for the rest of his service — Commander (Submarines) at Fort Blockhouse, 1955.
Account of Deed: On 22 Sep. 1943 at Kaafjord, North Norway, Lieutenant Cameron, commanding Midget Submarine X.6, and another lieutenant* commanding Midget Submarine X.7, carried out a most daring and successful attack on the German Battleship *Tirpitz*. The two submarines had to travel at least 1,000 miles from base, negotiate a mine field, dodge nets, gun defences and enemy listening posts. Having eluded all these hazards they finally placed the charges underneath the ship where they went off an hour later, doing so much damage that the *Tirpitz* was out of action for months. (*See also PLACE, B.C.G.)

CAMPBELL, Frederick William   **177**
Lieutenant   1st Bn., Western Ontario Regiment, C.E.F.
Other Decorations: —
Date of Gazette: 23 Aug. 1915
Place/Date of Birth: Mount Forest, Ontario, Canada — 15 Jun. 1867
Place/Date of Death: Near Givenchy, France — 19 Jun. 1915
Memorials: Boulogne Eastern Cemetery, France
Town/County Connections: —
Remarks: —
Account of Deed: On 15 Jun. 1915 at Givenchy, France, Lieutenant Campbell took two machine-gun detachments forward and in face of heavy fire reached the German front line trench with one gun which he kept in action after nearly all his detachment had been killed or wounded. When the German counter-attack came, Lieutenant Campbell advanced his gun still further and by firing about 1,000 rounds succeeded in holding the enemy back, but he was mortally wounded and died four days later.

CAMPBELL, Gordon   **178**
Commander (later Vice-Admiral)   Royal Navy
Other Decorations: DSO & 2 Bars
Date of Gazette: 21 Apr. 1917
Place/Date of Birth: Croydon, Surrey — 6 Jan. 1886
Place/Date of Death: Isleworth, London — 3 Jul. 1953
Memorials: —
Town/County Connections: Croydon and Upper Norwood, Surrey
Remarks: Croix de Guerre avec Palmes and Légion d'Honneur (France); Member of Parliament for Burnley, 1931-35. Author of *My Mystery Ships*, etc. *Dulwich College.*
Account of Deed: On 17 Feb. 1917 in the north Atlantic, Commander Campbell, commanding HMS Q.5 (one of the 'mystery' ships) sighted a torpedo track. He altered course and allowed the torpedo to hit Q.5 aft by the engine-room bulkhead. The 'Panic party' got away convincingly, followed by the U-boat. When the submarine had fully surfaced and was within 100 yards of Q.5 — badly damaged and now lying very low in the water — the commander gave the order to fire. Almost all of the 45 shells fired hit the U-boat which sank. Q.5 was taken in tow just in time and was safely beached.

CAMPBELL, John Charles   **179**
A/Brigadier (later Major General)   Royal Horse Artillery, comd. 7th Armoured Division
Other Decorations: DSO & Bar, MC
Date of Gazette: 3 Feb. 1942
Place/Date of Birth: Thurso, Caithness, Scotland — 10 Jan. 1894
Place/Date of Death: Libya — 26 Feb. 1942
Memorials: Cairo War Memorial Cemetery, Egypt; All Saints' Cathedral, Cairo
Town/County Connections: Weedon, Northamptonshire
Remarks: —
Account of Deed: On 21 Nov. 1941 at Sidi Rezegh, Libya, Brigadier Campbell's small force holding important ground was repeatedly attacked and wherever the fighting was hardest he was to be seen either on foot or in his open car. Next day, under intensified enemy attacks, he was again in the forefront, encouraging his troops and personally controlling the fire of his batteries — he twice manned a gun himself to replace casualties. During the final attack, although wounded, he refused to be evacuated. His brilliant leadership was the direct cause of the very heavy casualties inflicted on the enemy, and did much to maintain the fighting spirit of his men.

CAMPBELL, John Vaughan   **180**
T/Lieutenant Colonel (later Brigadier General)   Comd. 3rd Bn., Coldstream Guards
Other Decorations: CMG, DSO
Date of Gazette: 26 Oct. 1916
Place/Date of Birth: London — 31 Oct. 1876
Place/Date of Death: Woodchester, Gloucestershire — 21 May 1944
Memorials: (Cremated, Cheltenham, Glos.); Cawdor Parish Church, Nairn, Scotland
Town/County Connections: Cawdor, Nairn; Oswestry, Shropshire; Woodchester, Glos.
Remarks: Served in South African War 1899-1902; ADC to The King, 1919-33; Member of Hon. Corps of Gentlemen-at-Arms, 1934-44 *Eton College.*
Account of Deed: On 15 Sep. 1916 at Ginchy, France, Lieutenant Colonel Campbell took personal command of the third line when the first two waves of his battalion had been decimated by machine-gun and rifle fire. He rallied his men and led them against the enemy machine-guns, capturing the guns and killing the personnel. Later in the day he again rallied the survivors of his battalion and led them through very heavy hostile fire. His personal gallantry and initiative at a very critical moment enabled the division to press on and capture objectives of the highest tactical importance.

CAMPBELL, Kenneth **181**
Flying Officer   22 Squadron, Royal Air Force Volunteer Reserve
Other Decorations: —
Date of Gazette: 13 Mar. 1942
Place/Date of Birth: Saltcoats, Ayr, Scotland — 21 Apr. 1917
Place/Date of Death: Brest, France — 6 Apr. 1941   *Sedbergh School.*
Memorials: Brest (Kerfautras) Cemetery, Lambezellec, France
Town/County Connections: Saltcoats, Ayr
Remarks: —
Account of Deed: On 6 Apr. 1941 over Brest Harbour, Flying Officer Campbell attacked the German battle-cruiser *Gneisenau.* He ran the gauntlet of concentrated anti-aircraft fire and launched a torpedo at point-blank range. The ship was severely damaged below the waterline and was obliged to return to the dock whence she had come only the day before. Flying Officer Campbell's aircraft then met a withering wall of flak and crashed into the harbour.

CAMPBELL, Lorne MacLaine **182**
T/Lieutenant Colonel (later Brigadier)   Comd. 7th Bn., The Argyll and Sutherland Highlanders (Princess Louise's)
Other Decorations: DSO & Bar, TD
Date of Gazette: 8 Jun. 1943
Place/Date of Birth: The Airds, Argyllshire, Scotland — 22 Jul. 1902
Place/Date of Death: — *Died about 26.5.1991*
Memorials: —
Town/County Connections: London; Argyllshire
Remarks: Officer, Legion of Merit (U.S.A.); Hon. Colonel, 8th Bn., Argyll and Sutherland Highlanders, 1954-67.
Account of Deed: On 6 Apr. 1943 at Wadi Akarit, Tunisia, the battalion commanded by Lieutenant Colonel Campbell had to break through an enemy minefield and anti-tank ditch in order to form a bridgehead. The battalion formed up in darkness and then attacked at an angle. This difficult operation was successfully completed and at least 600 prisoners taken. Next day the position was subjected to heavy and continuous bombardment and although the colonel was wounded, his personality dominated the battlefield. Under his inspiring leadership the attacks were repulsed and the bridgehead held.

CARLESS, John Henry **183**
Ordinary Seaman   Royal Navy
Other Decorations: —
Date of Gazette: 17 May 1918
Place/Date of Birth: Walsall, Staffordshire — 11 Nov. 1896
Place/Date of Death: At sea, off Heligoland — 17 Nov. 1917
Memorials: Portsmouth Naval Memorial; Memorial, Lichfield Street, Walsall, Staffordshire.
Town/County Connections: Walsall, Staffs.
Remarks: —
Account of Deed: On 17 Nov. 1917 at the Battle of Heligoland, Ordinary Seaman Carless of HMS *Caledon,* although mortally wounded in the abdomen, still went on serving his gun and helping to clear away the casualites. He collapsed once, but got up again and cheered on the new gun's crew. He then fell and died. He not only set a very inspiring example, but while mortally wounded continued to do effective work against the enemy.

CARLIN, Patrick **184**
Private   1st Bn., 13th Regt. (later The Somerset Light Infantry — Prince Albert's)
Other Decorations: —
Date of Gazette: 26 Oct. 1858
Place/Date of Birth: Belfast, Ireland — 1832
Place/Date of Death: Belfast — 11 May 1895
Memorials: —
Town/County Connections: Belfast
Remarks: —
Account of Deed: On 6 Apr. 1858 at Azumgurh, India, Private Carlin rescued from the field of battle a wounded naik of the 4th Madras Rifles, after killing with the naik's sword a mutineer sepoy who fired on him while he was carrying his wounded comrade on his shoulders.

CARMICHAEL, John 185
Sergeant   9th Bn., The North Staffordshire Regiment (The Prince of Wales's)
Other Decorations: MM
Date of Gazette: 17 Oct. 1917
Place/Date of Birth: Airdrie, Lanarkshire, Scotland — 1 Apr. 1893
Place/Date of Death: New Monkland, Airdrie, Lanarkshire — 26 Dec. 1977
Memorials: New Monkland Parish Churchyard; Garrison Church, Whittington Barracks, Lichfield, Staffs.
Town/County Connections: Airdrie, Lanarkshire
Remarks: —
Account of Deed: On 8 Sep. 1917 near Hill 60, Zwarteleen, Belgium, when excavating a trench, Sergeant Carmichael saw that a grenade had been unearthed and had started to burn. He immediately rushed to the spot shouting to his men to get clear, put his steel helmet over the grenade and then stood on the helmet. The grenade exploded and blew him out of the trench. He could have thrown the bomb out of the trench but realised that by doing so he would have endangered the lives of the men working on top. He was seriously injured.

CARNE, James Power 186
Lieutenant Colonel (later Colonel)   Comd. 1st Bn., The Gloucestershire Regiment
Other Decorations: DSO
Date of Gazette: 27 Oct. 1953
Place/Date of Birth: Falmouth, Cornwall — 11 Apr. 1906
Place/Date of Death: Cheltenham — 19 Apr. 1986 · *Stonebank, Cranham. Glos.*
Memorials: —
Town/County Connections: Falmouth, Cornwall; Cranham, Gloucestershire
Remarks: DSC (U.S.A.); DL, County of Gloucester. The stone cross which he carved for use at prison camp services is now preserved in Gloucester Cathedral.
Account of Deed: On 22/23 Apr. 1951 near the Imjin River, Korea, Lieutenant Colonel Carne's battalion was heavily and incessantly engaged by vastly superior numbers of the enemy Throughout this time Colonel Carne moved among the whole battalion under very heavy mortar and machine-gun fire, inspiring the utmost confidence and the will to resist among his troops. On two separate occasions, armed with rifle and grenades, he personally led assault parties which drove back the enemy and saved important situations. His courage, coolness and leadership was felt not only in his own battalion but throughout the whole brigade.

CARPENTER, Alfred Francis Blakeney 187
Captain (later Vice-Admiral)   Royal Navy
Other Decorations: Royal Humane Society's medal for life-saving
Date of Gazette: 23 Jul. 1918
Place/Date of Birth: Barnes, Surrey — 17 Sep. 1881
Place/Date of Death: St. Briavels, Gloucestershire — 27 Dec. 1955
Memorials: — *Cremated Cheltenham*
Town/County Connections: Mortlake, Surrey; St. Briavels, Gloucestershire
Remarks: Croix de Guerre and Légion d'Honneur (France); commanded 17th Glos. (Wye Valley) Bn., Home Guard, 1940-44; Director of Shipping at the Admiralty, 1945; author of *The Blocking of Zeebrugge*.
Account of Deed: On 22/23 Apr. 1918 at Zeebrugge, Belgium, Captain Carpenter was in command of HMS *Vindictive*, navigating mined waters and bringing the ship alongside the Mole in darkness. When *Vindictive* was within a few yards of the Mole, the enemy started and maintained a heavy fire from batteries, machine-guns and rifles. Captain Carpenter supervised the landing from *Vindictive* on to the Mole, walking the decks, encouraging the men. His power of command, personal bearing and encouragement to those under him greatly contributed to the success of the operation. (Award by ballot.)

CARROLL, John 188
Private (later Lance Corporal)   33rd Bn. (N.S.W.) Australian Imperial Force
Other Decorations: —
Date of Gazette: 2 Aug. 1917
Place/Date of Birth: Brisbane, Australia — 15 Aug. 1892
Place/Date of Death: Perth, Australia — 4 Oct. 1971
Memorials: Karrakatta Cemetery, Perth; Australian War Memorial, Canberra
Town/County Connections: —
Remarks: —
Account of Deed: On 7/12 Jun. 1917 at St. Yves, France, during an attack, Private Carroll rushed the enemy's trench and bayoneted four of the occupants. He then noticed a comrade in difficulties and went to his assistance, killing another of the enemy. Next he attacked single-handed a machine-gun team, killing three of them and capturing the gun. Later two of his comrades were buried by a shell and in spite of heavy shelling and machine-gun fire, he managed to rescue them.

CARTER, Herbert Augustine   **189**
Lieutenant (later Major)   Mounted Infantry, Indian Army
Other Decorations: —
Date of Gazette: 9 Dec. 1904
Place/Date of Birth: Exeter — 26 May 1874
Place/Date of Death: Mwelo Mdogo, East Africa — 13 Jan. 1916
Memorials: St. Erth Churchyard, Cornwall; York Minster; Bodmin Parish Church. *Buried in*
Town/County Connections: Exeter, Devon; St. Erth, Cornwall   *St. Erth Churchyard.*
Remarks: Served in First World War 1914-16   *W.M. Shrine in bronze.*
Account of Deed: On 19 Dec. 1903 during a reconnaissance at Jidballi, Somaliland, when two
sections were retiring before a force of Dervishes who outnumbered them by thirty to one,
Lieutenant Carter rode back alone, a distance of 400 yards, to the assistance of a private who had lost his horse and was closely
pursued by a number of the enemy. The man was so badly wounded that it took three attempts to get him on to the horse.

CARTER, Nelson Victor   **190**
Company Sergeant-Major   12th Bn., The Royal Sussex Regiment
Other Decorations: —
Date of Gazette: 9 Sep. 1916
Place/Date of Birth: Eastbourne — 9 Apr. 1887
Place/Date of Death: Richebourg l'Avoue, France — 30 Jun. 1916
Memorials: R.I. Rifles Churchyard, Laventie, France; Regimental Memorial, Chichester
Cathedral; War Memorial, Hailsham, Sussex.
Town/County Connections: Eastbourne and Hailsham, Sussex
Remarks: —
Account of Deed: On 30 Jun. 1916 at Boar's Head, Richebourg l'Avoue, France, during an attack
Company Sergeant-Major Carter was in command of the fourth wave of the assault. Under intense shell and machine-gun fire
he penetrated, with a few men, into the enemy's second line and inflicted heavy casualties with bombs. When forced to retire
into the enemy's first line, he captured a machine-gun and shot the gunner with his revolver. Finally, after carrying several
wounded men into safety, he was himself mortally wounded and died in a few minutes.

CARTON de WIART, Adrian (later Sir Adrian)   **191**
T/Lieutenant Colonel (later Lieutenant General)   4th Dragoon Guards (Royal Irish), attd. The
Gloucestershire Regiment, comd. 8th Bn.
Other Decorations: KBE, CB, CMG, DSO
Date of Gazette: 9 Sep. 1916
Place/Date of Birth: Brussels — 5 May 1880
Place/Date of Death: Killinardrish, Co. Cork, Ireland — 5 Jun. 1963
Memorials: —
Town/County Connections: Killinardrish, Co. Cork
Remarks: Croix d'Officier de l'Ordre de la Couronne and Croix de Guerre (Belgium); Croix de
Guerre and Légion d'Honneur (France); Cross of Valour (Poland), 1920 and 1939. Commanded
British Military Mission to Poland, 1918-24; served in Second World War (British Military Mission with Polish Army, Central
Norwegian Expeditionary Force; appointed to Military Mission to Yugoslavia, taken prisoner en route 1941, released from POW
camp 1943 to negotiate Italian surrender; special military representative with General Chiang-Kai-Shek, 1943). Author of *Happy
Odyssey*.
Account of Deed: On 2/3 Jul. 1916 at La Boiselle, France, Lieutenant Colonel Carton de Wiart's dauntless courage and
inspiration averted what could have been a serious reverse. He displayed the utmost energy in forcing the attack home and after
three other battalion commanders had become casualties, he controlled their commands and made sure that the ground was
held at all costs. In organising the positions to be held, he exposed himself fearlessly to enemy fire. He was wounded eight times
(including the loss of an eye and his left hand) during the course of the First World War.

CARTWRIGHT, George   **192**
Private (later Captain)   33rd Bn. (N.S.W.), Australian Imperial Force
Other Decorations: ED
Date of Gazette: 14 Dec. 1918
Place/Date of Birth: London — 9 Dec. 1894
Place/Date of Death: Epping, New South Wales, Australia — 2 Feb. 1978
Memorials: Australian War Memorial, Canberra
Town/County Connections: Camberwell, London
Remarks: Served with the 28th Infantry Training Bn., Reception Training Depot, Eastern
Command, Australia during the Second World War
Account of Deed: On 31 Aug. 1918 at Road Wood, south-west of Bouchavesnes, near Peronne,
France, when two companies were held up by machine-gun fire, Private Cartwright attacked the gun alone under intense fire.
He shot three of the crew, and, having bombed the post, captured the gun and nine of the enemy.

CASSIDY, Bernard Matthew   **193**
Second Lieutenant   2nd Bn., The Lancashire Fusiliers
Other Decorations: —
Date of Gazette: 3 May 1918
Place/Date of Birth: Manchester — 17 Aug. 1892
Place/Date of Death: Arras, France — 28 Mar. 1918
Memorials: Arras Memorial, France
Town/County Connections: Manchester
Remarks: —
Account of Deed: On 28 Mar. 1918 at Arras, France, at a time when the flank of the division was in danger, Second Lieutenant Cassidy was in command of the left company of his battalion. He had been given orders to hold on to the position at all costs and he carried out this instruction to the letter. Although the enemy came in overwhelming numbers he continued to rally and encourage his men, under terrific bombardment until the company was eventually surrounded and he was killed.

CASTLETON, Claude Charles   **194**
Sergeant   5th Machine Gun Corps, Australian Imperial Force
Other Decorations: —
Date of Gazette: 26 Sep. 1916
Place/Date of Birth: Kirkley, Lowestoft, Suffolk — 12 Apr. 1893
Place/Date of Death: Near Pozieres, France — 28 Jul. 1916
Memorials: Pozieres British Cemetery, France
Town/County Connections: Lowestoft, Suffolk
Remarks: —
Account of Deed: On 28 Jul. 1916 near Pozieres, France, during an attack the infantry was temporarily driven back by the intense machine-gun fire from the enemy trenches. Many wounded were left in "No Man's Land" lying in shell holes. Sergeant Castleton went out twice in the face of this intense fire, and each time brought in a wounded man on his back. He went out a third time and was bringing in another wounded man when he was himself hit in the back and killed instantly.

CATES, George Edward   **195**
Second Lieutenant   2nd Bn., The Rifle Brigade (Prince Consort's Own)
Other Decorations: —
Date of Gazette: 11 May 1917
Place/Date of Birth: Wimbledon, Surrey — 8 May 1892
Place/Date of Death: Bouchavesnes, France — 9 Mar. 1917
Memorials: Hem Military Cemetery, France; Wimbledon Church; The Rifle Brigade Memorial, Winchester Cathedral · *Warrior Chapel. St. Mary's Church. Wimbledon*
Town/County Connections: Wimbledon, Surrey *Name on Peace Memorial, Putney Vale*
Remarks: —
Account of Deed: On 8 Mar. 1917 east of Bouchavesnes, France, Second Lieutenant Cates was engaged with some other men in deepening a captured trench when his spade struck a buried bomb which immediately started to burn. Without hesitation he put his foot on it and it immediately exploded. This act cost him his life, but saved the lives of others with him.

CATHER, Geoffrey St. George Shillington   **196**
T/Lieutenant   9th Bn., The Royal Irish Fusiliers
Other Decorations: —
Date of Gazette: 9 Sep. 1916
Place/Date of Birth: London — 11 Oct. 1890
Place/Date of Death: Hamel, France — 2 Jul. 1916
Memorials: Thiepval Memorial, France
Town/County Connections: Streatham, London; Limpsfield, Surrey
Remarks: — *Rugby School.*
Account of Deed: On 1 Jul. 1916 near Hamel, France, from 7pm till midnight, Lieutenant Cather searched "No Man's Land" and brought in three wounded men. Next morning, at 8am, he continued his search, brought in another wounded man and gave water to others, arranging for their rescue later. Finally, at 10.30am, he took out water to another man and was proceeding further on when he was himself killed. All this was carried out in full view of the enemy and under direct machine-gun fire and intermittent artillery fire.

CATOR, Harry **197**
Sergeant (later Captain)   7th Bn., The East Surrey Regiment
Other Decorations: MM
Date of Gazette: 8 Jun. 1917
Place/Date of Birth: Drayton, Norwich — 24 Jan. 1894
Place/Date of Death: Sproston, Norwich — 7 Apr. 1966
Memorials: —
Town/County Connections: Drayton, Norwich
Remarks: Croix de Guerre (France)
Account of Deed: On 9 Apr. 1917 near Arras, France, Sergeant Cator's platoon had suffered heavy casualties from a hostile machine-gun. Under heavy fire the sergeant, with one man, advanced across the open to attack the gun and when his companion was killed, he went on alone. Picking up a Lewis gun and some drums on his way, he succeeded in reaching the enemy trench and sighting another hostile machine-gun, he killed the entire team and the officer. He held the end of the trench with such effect that the bombing squad were able to capture 100 prisoners and five machine-guns.

CHAFER, George William **198**
Private   1st Bn., The East Yorkshire Regiment
Other Decorations: —
Date of Gazette: 5 Aug. 1916
Place/Date of Birth: Bradford, Yorkshire — 16 Apr. 1894
Place/Date of Death: Rotherham, Yorkshire — 2 Mar. 1966
Memorials: —
Town/County Connections: Epworth, Lincs.; Bradford and Rotherham, Yorkshire
Remarks: —
Account of Deed: On 3/4 Jun. 1916 east of Meaulte, France, during a very heavy bombardment and attack on our trenches, a man carrying an important written message to his commanding officer was half buried and rendered unconscious by a shell. Private Chafer, at once grasping the situation, on his own initiative, took the message from the man's pocket and, although severely wounded, choking and blinded by gas, ran along the ruined parapet under heavy shell and machine-gun fire. He just succeeded in delivering the message before he collapsed from the effects of his wounds.

CHAMPION, James **199**
Troop Sergeant-Major   8th Hussars (The King's Royal Irish)
Other Decorations: MSM
Date of Gazette: 20 Jan. 1860
Place/Date of Birth: Hammersmith, London — 1834
Place/Date of Death: London — 4 May 1904
Memorials: Hammersmith Cemetery, London ｜ *Grave.*
Town/County Connections: Hammersmith, London
Remarks: Rode in the Light Brigade charge at Balaclava
Account of Deed: On 8 Sep. 1858 at Beejapore, India, when both the officers attached to the troop were disabled, Troop Sergeant-Major Champion, although severely wounded himself at the start of the action, nevertheless continued to do his duty and wounded several of the enemy. He was also commended for his distinguished conduct at Gwalior.

CHANNER, George Nicolas **200**
Captain (later General)   Bengal Staff Corps and 1st Gurkha rifles, Indian Army
Other Decorations: CB
Date of Gazette: 12 Apr. 1876
Place/Date of Birth: Allahabad, India — 7 Jan. 1843
Place/Date of Death: Westward Ho! Devon — 13 Dec. 1905
Memorials: —
Town/County Connections: Lanlivery, Cornwall; Westward Ho! Devon
Remarks: —
Account of Deed: On 20 Dec. 1875 in Perak, Malaya, Captain Channer was the first to jump into the enemy's stockade to which he had been despatched with a small party to obtain intelligence of its strength and position. The stockade was formidable and it would have been impossible to bring guns to bear on it because of the steepness of the hill and the density of the jungle. If Captain Channer and his party had not been able to take the stockade in this manner it would have been necessary to resort to the bayonet, with consequent great loss of life.

CHAPLIN, John Worthy 201

Ensign (later Colonel) 67th Regiment (later The Hampshire Regiment)
Other Decorations: —
Date of Gazette: 13 Aug. 1861
Place/Date of Birth: Ewhurst Park, Hampshire — 23 Jul. 1840
Place/Date of Death: Market Harborough, Leicestershire — 19 Aug. 1920
Memorials: —
Town/County Connections: Market Harborough, Leicestershire
Remarks: — *Harrow School.*
Account of Deed: On 21 Aug. 1860 at the Taku Forts, China, Ensign Chaplin was carrying the Queen's Colours of the Regiment and first planted the Colours on the breach made by the storming party, assisted by a private. He then planted the Colours on the bastion of the fort which he was the first to mount, but in doing so he was severely wounded.

CHAPMAN, Edward Thomas 202

Corporal (later Sergeant) 3rd Bn., The Monmouthshire Regiment
Other Decorations: BEM
Date of Gazette: 13 Jul. 1945
Place/Date of Birth: Pontlottyn, Glamorgan, Wales — 13 Jan. 1920
Place/Date of Death: — *About 4.2.2002 Probably in Wales*
Memorials: —
Town/County Connections: Pontlottyn, Glamorgan; Pontypool, Monmouthshire
Remarks: —
Account of Deed: On 2 Apr. 1945, near the Dortmund-Ems canal, Germany, Corporal Chapman's section came under heavy machine-gun fire, causing many casualties. He ordered his men to take cover and went forward alone with a Bren gun, mowing down the enemy at point-blank range, forcing them to retire. His section isolated, Corporal Chapman again halted the enemy advances with his Bren gun, at one time firing it over his shoulder, to cover those bringing him ammunition. He then carried in his company commander who was lying wounded, but on the way back the officer was killed and Corporal Chapman wounded.

CHARD, John Rouse Merriott 203

Lieutenant (later Colonel) Corps of Royal Engineers
Other Decorations: —
Date of Gazette: 2 May 1879
Place/Date of Birth: Pathe, Bridgwater, Somerset — 21 Dec. 1847
Place/Date of Death: Hatch Beauchamp, Somerset — 1 Nov. 1897. *Buried St. John's Churchyard*
Memorials: Name inscribed on Colour Pole of 24th Regiment; Jesus Chapel, Rochester Cathedral
Town/County Connections: Pathe and Hatch Beauchamp, Somerset
Remarks: —
Account of Deed: On 22 and 23 Jan. 1879 at Rorke's Drift, Natal, South Africa, Lieutenant Chard shared the command of the defenders of the post with an officer of the 2nd/24th Regiment of Foot*, setting a fine example and conducting himself with great gallantry in most trying circumstances. (*See also BROMHEAD, G.)

CHARLTON, Edward Colquhoun 204

Guardsman 2nd Bn., Irish Guards
Other Decorations: —
Date of Gazette: 2 May 1945
Place/Date of Birth: Rowlands Gill, Co. Durham — 15 Jun. 1920
Place/Date of Death: Elsdorf, Germany — 21 Apr. 1945
Memorials: Becklingen War Cemetery, Soltau, Germany; St. John's Church, Old Trafford, Manchester
Town/County Connections: Rowlands Gill, Co. Durham; Manchester
Remarks: —
Account of Deed: On 21 Apr. 1945 at Wistedt, Germany, Guardsman Charlton was a co-driver of one tank of a troop which, with a platoon of infantry, captured the village. When shortly afterwards, all the tanks were hit in a fierce enemy attack, and the infantry were in danger of being over-run, Guardsman Charlton, on his own initiative, seized a Browning and advanced firing from the hip, inflicting such heavy casualties that the enemy were halted. Although wounded in the left arm the guardsman mounted his gun on a fence and continued firing even when wounded again. He died later, but his gallantry had saved a desperate situation.

CHASE, William St. Lucien   205

Lieutenant (later Colonel)   28th Native Infantry, Indian Army
Other Decorations: CB
Date of Gazette: 7 Oct. 1881
Place/Date of Birth: St. Lucia, West Indies — 2nd Jul. 1856
Place/Date of Death: Quetta, Baluchistan — 24 Jun. 1908
Memorials: —
Town/County Connections: —
Remarks: —
Account of Deed: On 16 Aug. 1880 at Deh Khoja, near Kandahar, (Afghan War), Lieutenant Chase with the help of a private* rescued and carried for a distance of over 200 yards under the fire of the enemy, a wounded soldier who had taken shelter in a block house. Several times they were compelled to rest, but they persevered and finally brought the wounded man to a place of safety. (*See also ASHFORD, T.)

CHATTA SINGH,   206

Sepoy (later Havildar)   9th Bhopal Infantry, Indian Army
Other Decorations: —
Date of Gazette: 21 Jun. 1916
Place/Date of Birth: Talsanda District, Cawnpore, India — 1887
Place/Date of Death: India — Mar. 1961
Memorials: —
Town/County Connections: —
Remarks: PVSM (India)
Account of Deed: On 13 Jan. 1916 during the Battle of the Wadi, Mesopotamia, Sepoy Chatta Singh left cover to assist his commanding officer, who was lying wounded and helpless in the open. The sepoy bound up the officer's wounds and then dug cover for him with his entrenching tool, being exposed all the time to very heavy rifle fire. For five hours until nightfall he stayed with the wounded officer, shielding him with his body on the exposed side. He then, under cover of darkness, went back for assistance and brought the officer to safety.

CHAVASSE, Noel Godfrey   207

Captain   Royal Army Medical Corps, attd. 1/10th Bn., The King's (Liverpool) Regiment
Other Decorations: MC
Date of Gazette: 26 Oct. 1916 and BAR 14 Sep. 1917
Place/Date of Birth: Oxford — 9 Nov. 1884
Place/Date of Death: Near Ypres, Belgium — 4 Aug. 1917
Memorials: Brandhoek New Military Cemetery, Belgium; HQ, Liverpool Scottish Regiment; Liverpool Cathedral
Town/County Connections: Oxford . *Name on W.M. Bromsgrove, Worcs.*
Remarks: Family connection with Captain C.H. Upham, VC & Bar
Account of Deed: On 9 Aug. 1916, at Guillemont, France, during an attack, Captain Chavasse attended to the wounded all day under heavy fire, frequently in view of the enemy, and during the night he searched for wounded in front of the enemy's lines. Next day he took a stretcher-bearer and under heavy shell fire carried an urgent case 500 yards into safety, being wounded himself on the return journey. The same night, with 20 volunteers, he rescued three wounded men from a shell-hole 36 yards from the enemy's trenches, buried the bodies of two officers and collected many identity discs. Altogether he saved the lives of some 20 wounded men, besides the ordinary cases which passed through his hands.
BAR: During the period 31 Jul. to 2 Aug. 1917, at Wieltje, Belgium, Captain Chavasse, although severely wounded early in the action while carrying a wounded officer to the dressing station, refused to leave his post and not only continued to perform his duties, but in addition went out repeatedly under heavy fire and searched for and attended the wounded. During these searches, although practically without food, worn with fatigue and faint from his wound, he helped to carry in badly wounded men. He was instrumental in saving many wounded who would have undoubtedly died under the bad weather conditions. Captain Chavasse subsequently died of his wounds.

CHERRY, Percy Herbert   208

Captain   26th Bn. (Q. and T.), Australian Imperial Force
Other Decorations: MC
Date of Gazette: 11 May 1917
Place/Date of Birth: Murradoc, Drysdale, Victoria, Australia — 4 Jun. 1895
Place/Date of Death: Lagnicourt, France — 27 Mar. 1917
Memorials: Queant Road Cemetery, France; Australian War Memorial, Canberra
Town/County Connections: —
Remarks: —
Account of Deed: On 26 Mar. 1917 at Lagnicourt, France, Captain Cherry was commanding a company detailed to storm and clear a village. After all the other officers of the company had become casualties, he carried on in the face of fierce opposition and cleared the village of the enemy. Having done this, he beat off most resolute and heavy counter-attacks. He was wounded early next morning, but refused to leave his post and remained, encouraging his men to hold out at all costs, until in the afternoon he was killed by an enemy shell.

CHESHIRE, Geoffrey Leonard 209

Wing Commander (later Group Captain)   Royal Air Force Volunteer Reserve
Other Decorations: OM, DSO and 2 Bars, DFC
Date of Gazette: 8 Sep. 1944
Place/Date of Birth: Chester — 7 Sep. 1917
Place/Date of Death: —
Memorials: —
Town/County Connections: Chester; Abingdon, Berkshire; Cavendish, Suffolk
Remarks: Pioneered the first Cheshire Foundation Home for the incurably sick, 1948. Author of *Bomber Pilot, Pilgrimage to the Shroud, The Face of Victory.*
Account of Deed: From Jun. 1940 when his operational career began, until the end of his fourth tour in Jul. 1944, when he had completed a total of 100 missions Wing Commander Cheshire displayed the courage and determination of an exceptional leader. During his fourth tour he pioneered a new method of marking enemy targets, flying in at a very low level in the face of strong defences. In four years of fighting against the bitterest opposition he maintained a standard of outstanding personal achievement, his successful operations being the result of careful planning, brilliant execution and supreme contempt for danger.

CHHELU RAM 210

Company Havildar-Major   6th Rajputana Rifles, Indian Army
Other Decorations: —
Date of Gazette: 27 Jul. 1943
Place/Date of Birth: Dhenod Village, Hissar District, Bhiwani, Punjab — 4 May 1905
Place/Date of Death: Near Enfidaville, Tunisia — 20 Apr. 1943
Memorials: Sfax War Cemetery, Tunisia
Town/County Connections: —
Remarks: —
Account of Deed: On the night of 19/20 Apr. 1943 at Djebel Garli, Tunisia, the advance of a battalion of the 5th Indian Infantry Brigade was held up by machine-gun and mortar fire. Company Havildar-Major Chhelu Ram dashed forward with a tommy-gun and killed the occupants of a post and then went to the aid of his company commander who had become a casualty. While doing so he was himself wounded, but taking command of the company, he led them in hand-to-hand fighting. He was again wounded, but continued rallying his men until he died.

No photograph available

CHICKEN, George Bell 211

Mr.   a volunteer with the Indian Naval Brigade
Other Decorations: —
Date of Gazette: 27 Apr. 1860
Place/Date of Birth: Bishopswearmouth, Co. Durham — 6 Mar. 1838
Place/Date of Death: At sea, Bay of Bengal — May 1860
Memorials: —
Town/County Connections: —
Remarks: —
Account of Deed: On 27 Sep. 1858 at Suhednee, near Peroo, Bengal, Mr. Chicken attached himself to a mixed party of troopers of mounted police and cavalry. They routed a force of about 700 mutineers and in the pursuit which followed Mr. Chicken forged ahead and charged into the middle of about 20 of the enemy, killing five before he was knocked off his horse and badly wounded. He would have been cut to pieces if four of the troopers had not galloped up and rescued him. (See also BAKER, C.G.)

CHOWNE, Albert 212

Lieutenant   2/2nd Bn. (N.S.W.), Australian Military Forces
Other Decorations: MM
Date of Gazette: 6 Sep. 1945
Place/Date of Birth: Sydney, Australia — 19 Jul. 1920
Place/Date of Death: Wewak, New Guinea — 25 Mar. 1945
Memorials: Lae War Cemetery, New Guinea; Australian War Memorial, Canberra
Town/County Connections: —
Remarks: —
Account of Deed: On 25 Mar. 1945 near Dagua, New Guinea, Lieutenant Chowne attacked an enemy position which was holding up further movement towards Wewak. Seeing that the leading platoon was suffering heavy casualties, Lieutenant Chowne rushed forward and knocked out two light machine-guns with grenades and then, calling on his men to follow him and firing his sub-machine-gun from the hip, he charged the position. Although he was twice wounded in the chest, the impetus of his charge carried him forward 50 yards under intense machine-gun and rifle fire and he accounted for two more of the enemy before he was killed.

CHRISTIAN, Harry   **213**
Private   2nd Bn., The King's Own (Royal Lancaster) Regiment
Other Decorations: —
Date of Gazette: 3 Mar. 1916
Place/Date of Birth: Pennington, Lancashire — 17 Jan. 1892
Place/Date of Death: Lancashire — 5 Sep. 1974
Memorials: —
Town/County Connections: Pennington, Lancashire
Remarks: —
Account of Deed: On 18 Oct. 1915 at Cuinchy, France, Private Christian was holding a crater with five or six men in front of the Allied lines. The enemy started a fierce bombardment of the position, forcing a temporary withdrawal. When he found that three men were missing, Private Christian at once returned alone to the crater and although bombs were continually bursting actually on the edge of the crater, he found, dug out and carried one by one into safety, all the three men. Later he placed himself where he could see the bombs coming and directed his comrades when and where to seek cover.

CHRISTIE, John Alexander   **214**
Lance-Corporal   1/11th (County of London) Bn., The London Regt. (Finsbury Rifles)
Other Decorations: —
Date of Gazette: 27 Feb. 1918
Place/Date of Birth: Edmonton, London — 14 May 1895
Place/Date of Death: Bramhall, Cheshire — 10 Sep. 1967
Memorials: —
Town/County Connections: Bramhall, Cheshire; Edmonton, London
Remarks: —
Account of Deed: On 21/22 Dec. 1917, at Fejja, Palestine, after a position had been captured, the enemy immediately made counter-attacks up the communication trenches. Lance-Corporal Christie, seeing what was happening, took a supply of bombs and went alone about 50 yards in the open along the communication trench and bombed the enemy. He continued to do this in spite of heavy opposition until a block had been established. On his way back he bombed more of the enemy who were moving up the trench. His prompt action cleared a difficult position at a most difficult time and saved many lives.

CLAMP, William   **215**
Corporal   6th Bn., The Yorkshire Regiment (Alexandra, Princess of Wales's Own)
Other Decorations: —
Date of Gazette: 18 Dec. 1917
Place/Date of Birth: Motherwell, Lanarkshire, Scotland — 28 Oct. 1891
Place/Date of Death: Poelcapelle, Belgium — 9 Oct. 1917
Memorials: Tyne Cot Memorial, Belgium
Town/County Connections: Motherwell, Lanarkshire
Remarks: —
Account of Deed: On 9 Oct. 1917 at Poelcapelle, Belgium, when the advance was checked by intense machine-gun fire from concrete blockhouses and by snipers, Corporal Clamp attempted to rush the largest blockhouse. His first attempt failed and the two men with him became casualties, but he collected some bombs and two more men and dashing forward was the first to reach the blockhouse where he hurled his bombs, killing many of the occupants. He then entered, capturing a machine-gun and about 20 prisoners whom he brought back under heavy fire. He went forward again encouraging his men and displaying the greatest heroism until killed by a sniper.

CLARE, George William Burdett   **216**
Private   5th Lancers (Royal Irish)
Other Decorations: —
Date of Gazette: 11 Jan. 1918
Place/Date of Birth: St. Ives, Huntingdonshire — 18 May 1889
Place/Date of Death: Bourlon Wood, France — 29 Nov. 1917
Memorials: Cambrai Memorial, France; St. Peter's and St. Paul's Church, Chatteris, Cambridgeshire, War Memorial, Chatteris.
Town/County Connections: St. Ives, Huntingdonshire; Chatteris, Cambridgeshire
Remarks: —
Account of Deed: On 28/29 Nov. 1917 at Bourlon Wood, France, Private Clare, a stretcher-bearer, dressed wounds and conducted the wounded to the dressing station under most intense fire. At one period, when all the garrison of a detached post had become casualties, he crossed to them through very heavy fire and having dressed all the cases, manned the post single-handed until a relief could be sent. Then, after carrying a seriously wounded man through intense fire to the dressing station, he went, still under heavy fire, to every company post warning them that the enemy were using gas shells. This gallant soldier was subsequently killed.

CLARK-KENNEDY, William Hew — see **KENNEDY,** William Hew CLARK-

CLARKE, James

217

Sergeant   15th Bn., The Lancashire Fusiliers
Other Decorations: —
Date of Gazette: 6 Jan. 1919
Place/Date of Birth: Winsford, Cheshire — 6 Apr. 1894
Place/Date of Death: Rochdale, Lancashire — 16 Jun. 1947
Memorials: —
Town/County Connections: Winsford, Cheshire
Remarks: —
Account of Deed: On 2 Nov. 1918 at Happegarbes, France, when Sergeant Clarke's platoon was held up by heavy machine-gun fire, he rushed forward through a strongly-held ridge, capturing in succession four machine-guns and killing the crews. Later, with the remnants of his platoon he captured three more machine-guns and many prisoners and when his platoon was again held up he successfully led a tank against the enemy guns. Throughout the whole of these operations Sergeant Clarke acted with great bravery and total disregard of personal safety.

CLARKE, Leo

218

A/Corporal   2nd Bn., Eastern Ontario Regiment, C.E.F.
Other Decorations: —
Date of Gazette: 26 Oct. 1916
Place/Date of Birth: Hamilton, Ontario, Canada — 1 Dec. 1892
Place/Date of Death: Etretat France — 19 Oct. 1916
Memorials: Etretat Churchyard, France; lamp post in Valour Road, Winnipeg.
Town/County Connections: —
Remarks: —
Account of Deed: On 9 Sep. 1916 near Pozieres, France, Corporal Clarke was detailed with his section of bombers, to cover the construction of a "block" in a newly-captured trench. Most of his party had become casualties when about 20 of the enemy, with two officers, counter-attacked. The corporal advanced, emptying his revolver into them; then he picked up two enemy rifles and fired those too. One of the officers attacked with a bayonet, wounding Corporal Clarke in the leg, but he shot him dead, and pursued the rest of the Germans, shooting four more and capturing a fifth.

CLARKE, Wilwood Alexander Sandys

219

Lieutenant   The Loyal North Lancashire Regiment
Other Decorations: —
Date of Gazette: 29 Jun. 1943
Place/Date of Birth: Southport, Lancashire — 8 Jun. 1919
Place/Date of Death: Guiriat El Atach, Tunisia — 23 Apr. 1943
Memorials: Massicault War Cemetery, Tunisia
Town/County Connections: Egerton, Lancashire
Remarks: —
Account of Deed: On 23 Apr. 1943 at Guiriat El Atach, Tunisia, Lieutenant Clarke's company were counter-attacked and almost wiped out, he being the sole remaining officer. Although wounded in the head he gathered a composite platoon together and advancing to attack the position again met heavy fire from a machine-gun post. He manoeuvred his men to give covering fire and then tackled the post single-handed, killing or capturing the crew and knocking out the gun. He dealt similarly with two other posts and then led his platoon to the objective, but was killed when he later went forward to tackle two sniper posts single-handed.

CLEMENTS, John James

220

Corporal (later Sergeant)   Rimington's Guides, South African Forces
Other Decorations: —
Date of Gazette: 4 Jun. 1901
Place/Date of Birth: Middelburg, Cape Colony, South Africa — 19 Jun. 1872
Place/Date of Death: Newcastle, Natal, South Africa — 18 Jun. 1937
Memorials: —
Town/County Connections: —
Remarks: —
Account of Deed: On 24 Feb. 1901 near Strijdenburg, South Africa, Corporal Clements was dangerously wounded in the lungs and called upon to surrender, but instead he threw himself into the midst of a party of Boers, shooting three of them with his revolver, and thereby causing the whole party to surrender.

CLIFFORD, The Hon. Henry Hugh (later Sir Henry)   **221**
Lieutenant (later Major General)   1st Bn., The Rifle Brigade (Prince Consort's Own)
Other Decorations: CB, KCMG
Date of Gazette: 24 Feb. 1857
Place/Date of Birth: Irnham, Lincolnshire — 12 Sep. 1826
Place/Date of Death: Chudleigh, Devon — 12 Apr. 1883
Memorials: Buckfastleigh Abbey and family chapel, Ugbrooke, Chudleigh, Devon; The Rifle
Brigade Memorial, Winchester Cathedral.   *Buried Buckfast Abbey*
Town/County Connections: Irnham, Lincs.; Chudleigh, Devon
Remarks: Légion d'Honneur (France)
Account of Deed: On 5 Nov. 1854 at the Battle of Inkerman, Crimea, Lieutenant Clifford led one
of the charges, killing one of the enemy with his sword, disabling another and saving the life of a soldier.

CLOGSTOUN, Herbert Mackworth   **222**
Captain (later Major)   19th Madras Native Infantry
Other Decorations: —
Date of Gazette: 21 Oct. 1859
Place/Date of Birth: Port of Spain, Trinidad — 13 Jun. 1820
Place/Date of Death: Hingoli, India — 6 May 1862
Memorials: —
Town/County Connections: —
Remarks: —
Account of Deed: On 15 Jan. 1859 at Chichumbah, India, Captain Clogstoun charged the rebels
into the town with only eight men of his regiment, compelling them to re-enter and finally to
abandon their plunder. He was severely wounded himself and lost seven out of the eight men who accompanied him.

CLOUTMAN, Brett Mackay (later Sir Brett)   **223**
A/Major (later Lieutenant Colonel)   59th Field Company, Corps of Royal Engineers
Other Decorations: MC
Date of Gazette: 31 Jan. 1919
Place/Date of Birth: London — 7 Nov. 1891
Place/Date of Death: Highgate, London — 15 Aug. 1971
Memorials: —
Town/County Connections: Muswell Hill, Middlesex; Highgate, London
Remarks: The last act to win a VC in the First World War. Served in Second World War, 1939-45;
Senior Chairman, War Pensions (Special Review) Tribunals 1947; Senior Official Referee of
Supreme Court of Judicature, 1954-63   *London University*
Account of Deed: On 6 Nov. 1918 at Pont-sur-Sambre, France, Major Cloutman, after reconnoitring the river crossings, found
the Quartes Bridge almost intact but prepared for demolition. Leaving his party under cover he went forward alone, swam
across the river and having cut the 'leads' from the charges returned the same way, despite the fact that the bridge and all the
approaches were swept by enemy shells and machine-gun fire. Although the bridge was blown up later in the day by other
means, the abutments remained intact.

COBBE, Alexander Stanhope (later Sir Alexander)   **224**
Captain (local Lieutenant Colonel — later Lieutenant General)   Indian Army and King's African
Rifles
Other Decorations: GCB, KCSI, DSO
Date of Gazette: 20 Jan. 1903
Place/Date of Birth: Naini Tal, India — 5 Jun. 1870
Place/Date of Death: Sharnbrook, Bedford — 27 Jun. 1931   *Grave, Chiswick.*
Memorials: — *Name on family grave in Old Burial Ground, Chiswick* *Wellington College, Berkshire*
Town/County Connections: Sharnbrook, Bedford
Remarks: Served with distinction in First World War, particularly in Mesopotamia
Account of Deed: On 6 Oct. 1902 at Erego, Somaliland, when some of the companies had retired,
Lieutenant Colonel Cobbe was left by himself with a Maxim gun. Without assistance he brought in the Maxim and used it most
effectively at a critical time in the engagement. He then went out under very hot fire from the enemy and succeeded in bringing
in a wounded orderly.

COCHRANE, Hugh Stewart   **225**
Lieutenant and Adjutant (later Colonel)   86th Regiment (later The Royal Irish Rifles)
Other Decorations: —
Date of Gazette: 24 Dec. 1858
Place/Date of Birth: Fort William, Inverness — 4 Aug. 1829
Place/Date of Death: Southsea, Hampshire — 18 Apr. 1884
Memorials: — *Buried Highland Road Cemetery, Portsmouth*
Town/County Connections: Fort William, Inverness; Southsea, Hants.
Remarks: —
Account of Deed: On 1 Apr. 1858 near Jhansi, India, when No.1 company of the regiment was ordered to take a gun, Lieutenant Cochrane dashed forward at a gallop under heavy musketry and artillery fire, drove the enemy from the gun and kept possession of it until the company came up. He also showed conspicuous gallantry in attacking the rear guard of the enemy when he had three horses in succession shot under him.

COCKBURN, Hampden Zane Churchill   **226**
Lieutenant (later Major)   Royal Canadian Dragoons
Other Decorations: —
Date of Gazette: 23 Apr. 1901
Place/Date of Birth: Toronto, Canada — 19 Nov. 1867
Place/Date of Death: Maple Creek, Saskatchewan, Canada — 13 Jul. 1913
Memorials: St. James's Cemetery, Toronto
Town/County Connections: —
Remarks: —
Account of Deed: On 7 Nov. 1900 during the action at Komati River, South Africa, Lieutenant Cockburn with a handful of men, at a most critical moment, held off the enemy to enable the guns to get away. To do so he had to sacrifice himself and his party, all of whom were killed, wounded, or taken prisoner. He himself was slightly wounded.

No photograph available

COFFEY, William   **227**
Private (later Sergeant)   34th Regiment (later The Border Regiment)
Other Decorations: DCM
Date of Gazette: 24 Feb. 1857
Place/Date of Birth: Knocklong, Co. Limerick, Ireland — 5 Aug. 1829
Place/Date of Death: Chesterfield, Derbyshire — 13 Jul. 1875
Memorials: —
Town/County Connections: Limerick, Ireland; Chesterfield, Derbyshire
Remarks: Médaille Militaire (France)
Account of Deed: On 29 Mar. 1855 in the Crimea, Private Coffey threw a live shell, which had fallen into a trench, over the parapet and thus saved many lives.

COFFIN, Clifford   **228**
T/Brigadier General (later Major General)   Corps of Royal Engineers, comd. 25th Infantry Bde.
Other Decorations: CB, DSO and Bar
Date of Gazette: 14 Sep. 1917
Place/Date of Birth: Blackheath, London — 10 Feb. 1870
Place/Date of Death: Torquay, Devon — 4 Feb. 1959
Memorials: —
Town/County Connections: Blackheath, London; Torquay, Devon   *Haileybury School*
Remarks: ADC to The King, 1920-24; Colonel-Commandant, Corps of Royal Engineers, 1936-40; Chairman, Executive Council of the British Empire Service League during Second World War
Account of Deed: On 31 Jul. 1917 at Westhoek, Belgium, when his command was held up in attack owing to heavy machine-gun and rifle fire, Brigadier-General Coffin went forward and made an inspection of his front posts. Although under the heaviest fire from both machine-guns and rifles and in full view of the enemy, he showed an utter disregard of personal danger, walking quietly from shell-hole to shell-hole, giving advice and cheering his men by his presence. His gallant conduct had the greatest effect on all ranks and it was largely owing to his personal courage and example that the shell-hole line was held.

COGHILL, Nevill Josiah Aylmer   229
Lieutenant   1st Bn., 24th Regiment (later The South Wales Borderers)
Other Decorations: —
Date of Gazette: 2 May 1879 & 15 Jan. 1907
Place/Date of Birth: Drumcondra, Co. Dublin — 25 Jan. 1852
Place/Date of Death: Buffalo River, Zululand — 22 Jan. 1879
Memorials: Name inscribed on Colour Pole of 24th Regiment *Haileybury School.*
Town/County Connections: Drumcondra, Dublin
Remarks: *—21 Bolton Studios, Redcliffe Road London SW10. Chelsea.*
Account of Deed: On 22 Jan. 1879 after the disaster of the Battle of Isandhlwana, South Africa, Lieutenant Coghill joined another officer* who was trying to save the Queen's Colour of the Regiment. They were pursued by Zulu warriors and while crossing the swollen river Buffalo, Lieutenant Coghill went to the rescue of his brother officer, who had lost his horse and was in great danger. The two men were eventually overtaken by the enemy and following a short but gallant struggle, both were killed. (*See also MELVILL, T.) *VC in SWB Museum, Brecon. Painting in Haileybury School.*

COGHLAN, Cornelius — see COUGHLAN, Cornelius

COLEMAN, John   230
Sergeant   97th Regiment (later The Queen's Own Royal West Kent Regiment)
Other Decorations: —
Date of Gazette: 24 Feb. 1857
Place/Date of Birth: St. Mary-in-the-Marsh, Romney Marsh, Kent — 12 Jul. 1798
Place/Date of Death: Lucknow, India — 21 May 1858
Memorials: —
Town/County Connections: *— West Raynham, Norfolk (or South Raynham)*
Remarks: —
Account of Deed: On 30 Aug. 1855 in the Crimea, when the enemy attacked "New Sap" and drove the working party in, Sergeant Coleman remained in the open, exposed to the enemy's rifle pits, until all round him had been killed or wounded. He finally carried one of his officers who was mortally wounded, to the rear.

COLLEY, Harold John   231
A/Sergeant   10th Bn., The Lancashire Fusiliers
Other Decorations: MM
Date of Gazette: 22 Oct. 1918
Place/Date of Birth: Smethwick, Staffordshire — 26 May 1894
Place/Date of Death: Martinpuich, France — 25 Aug. 1918
Memorials: Mailly Wood Cemetery, France; War Memorial, Smethwick, Staffs.
Town/County Connections: Smethwick, Staffs.
Remarks: —
Account of Deed: On 25 Aug. 1918 at Martinpuich, France, during a strong counter-attack Sergeant Colley's company was holding an advanced position with two platoons in advance and two in support. The forward platoons were ordered to hold on at all costs and Sergeant Colley went, without orders, to help these two platoons. He rallied the men, then formed a defensive flank and held it, although out of the two platoons only three men remained unwounded and the sergeant himself was dangerously wounded and died the same day. It was entirely due to his action that the enemy was prevented from breaking through.

COLLIN, Joseph Henry   232
Second Lieutenant   1/4th Bn., The King's Own (Royal Lancaster) Regiment
Other Decorations: —
Date of Gazette: 28 Jun. 1918
Place/Date of Birth: Jarrow, Co. Durham — 11 Apr. 1893
Place/Date of Death: Givenchy, France — 9 Apr. 1918
Memorials: Vielle-Chapelle New Military Cemetery, France; The Priory, Lancaster
Town/County Connections: Carlisle, Cumberland
Remarks: —
Account of Deed: On 9 Apr. 1918 at Givenchy, France, after offering a gallant resistance against heavy odds in the Keep held by his platoon, Second Lieutenant Collin, with only five of his men remaining, slowly withdrew, contesting every inch of ground. Single-handed, he then attacked a machine-gun — after firing his revolver into the enemy, he seized a Mills grenade and threw it into the hostile gun team, putting the gun out of action, killing four of the team and wounding two others. He then took a Lewis gun and engaged a second hostile machine-gun, keeping the enemy at bay until he was mortally wounded.

COLLINGS-WELLS, John Stanhope — see WELLS, John Stanhope COLLINGS-

COLLINS, John   **233**
A/Corporal (later Sergeant)   25th Bn., The Royal Welch Fusiliers
Other Decorations: DCM, MM
Date of Gazette: 18 Dec. 1917
Place/Date of Birth: West Hatch, Somerset — 10 Sep. 1877
Place/Date of Death: Merthyr Tydfil, South Wales — 8 Sep. 1951
Memorials: Pant Cemetery, Merthyr Tydfil *, Grave*
Town/County Connections: West Hatch, Somerset; Merthyr Tydfil, S. Wales
Remarks: Served as Sergeant-Major in the Home Guard in Second World War
Account of Deed: On 31 Oct. 1917 at Wadi Saba, Beersheba, Palestine, Corporal Collins repeatedly went out when his battalion was forced to lie out in the open under heavy shell and machine-gun fire, and brought back many wounded. In subsequent operations he rallied his men and led the final assault with great skill in spite of heavy fire at close range and uncut wire. He killed 15 of the enemy and with a Lewis gun section covered the reorganization and consolidation most effectively, although isolated and under fire from snipers and guns.
VC in RWF Museum, Caernarvon Castle.

COLLIS, James   **234**
Gunner   Royal Horse Artillery
Other Decorations: —
Date of Gazette: 16 May 1881
Place/Date of Birth: Cambridge — 19 Apr. 1856
Place/Date of Death: Battersea, London — 28 Jun. 1918
Memorials: Wandsworth Cemetery, London (unmarked grave)
Town/County Connections: Cambridge; Battersea, London
Remarks: —
Account of Deed: On 28 Jul. 1880 during the retreat from Maiwand to Kandahar (Afghan War), when the officer commanding the battery was trying to bring in a limber with wounded men under cross-fire, Gunner Collis ran forward and drew the enemy's fire on himself, thus taking their attention from the limber.

COLTMAN, William Harold   **235**
Lance-Corporal   1/6th Bn., The North Staffordshire Regiment (The Prince of Wales's)
Other Decorations: DCM and Bar, MM and Bar
Date of Gazette: 6 Jan. 1919
Place/Date of Birth: Rangemore, Staffordshire — 17 Nov. 1891
Place/Date of Death: Burton-on-Trent, Staffordshire — 29 Jun. 1974
Memorials: Garrison Church, Whittington Barracks, Lichfield, Staffs; town park,
Burton-on-Trent
Town/County Connections: Burton-on-Trent and Burslem, Staffs.
Remarks: Most decorated NCO of the First World War; commissioned in Burton Army Cadet Force 1939-45
Account of Deed: On 3/4 Oct. 1918 during the operations at Mannequin Hill, north-east of Sequehart, France, Lance-Corporal Coltman, a stretcher-bearer, hearing that wounded had been left behind during the retirement, went forward alone in the face of fierce enfilade fire, found the casualties, dressed their wounds and on three successive occasions, carried some of them on his back to safety. This very gallant NCO tended the wounded unceasingly for 48 hours.

COLUMBINE, Herbert George   **236**
Private   9th Squadron, Machine Gun Corps
Other Decorations: —
Date of Gazette: 3 May 1918
Place/Date of Birth: London — 28 Nov. 1893
Place/Date of Death: Hervilly Wood, France — 22 Mar. 1918
Memorials: Pozieres Memorial, France; pedestal on sea-front, Walton-on-the-Naze, Essex
Town/County Connections: Penge, London
Remarks: —
Account of Deed: On 22 Mar. 1918 at Hervilly Wood, France, Private Columbine took over command of a gun and kept firing it from 9 a.m. to 1 p.m. in an isolated position with no wire in front. During this time wave after wave of the enemy failed to get up to him, but at last with the help of a low-flying aircraft, the enemy managed to gain a strong foot-hold in the trench. As the position was now untenable, Private Columbine told the two remaining men to get away, and although he was being bombed on either side, he kept his gun firing, inflicting losses, until he was killed by a bomb which blew up him and his gun.

COLVIN, Hugh   **237**
Second Lieutenant (later Major)   9th Bn., The Cheshire Regiment
Other Decorations: —
Date of Gazette: 8 Nov. 1917
Place/Date of Birth: Burnley, Lancashire — 1 Feb. 1887
Place/Date of Death: Bangor, Co. Down, Ireland — 16 Sep. 1962
Memorials: Chester Cathedral
Town/County Connections: Burnley, Lancs; Hatherlow, Cheshire; Bangor, Co. Down, Ireland
Remarks: — *Buried Carnmona, Bangor.*
Account of Deed: On 20 Sep. 1917 east of Ypres, Belgium, when all the other officers of his
company and all but one in the leading company had become casualties, Second Lieutenant
Colvin took command of both companies and led them forward under heavy fire with great success. He went with only two men
to a dug-out, when he left the men on top, entered it alone and brought out 14 prisoners. He then proceeded to clear other dug-
outs, alone or with only one man, capturing machine-guns, killing some of the enemy and taking a large number of prisoners.

COLVIN, James Morris Colquhoun   **238**
Lieutenant (later Colonel)   Corps of Royal Engineers
Other Decorations: —
Date of Gazette: 20 May 1898
Place/Date of Birth: Bijnor, North-west Frontier, India — 26 Aug. 1870
Place/Date of Death: Stanway, Colchester, Essex — 7 Dec. 1945
Memorials: —
Town/County Connections: Sutton Veny, Wiltshire
Remarks: Served in South African War 1901-2
Account of Deed: On the night of 16/17 Sep. 1897, in the Mohmand Valley, N.W. India, Lieutenant
Colvin was with another lieutenant* who collected a party of volunteers and led them into the dark
and burning village of Bilot, to try to dislodge the enemy who were inflicting losses on our troops. When his brother officer had
been incapacitated by wounds, Lieutenant Colvin continued the fight and made two more attempts to clear the enemy from the
village. He was conspicuous during the whole night for his devotion to his men, in the most exposed positions and under very
heavy fire. (*See also WATSON, T.C. and SMITH, James — No. 1162)

COLYER-FERGUSSON, Thomas Riversdale — see **FERGUSSON,** Thomas
Riversdale COLYER-

COMBE, Robert Grierson   **239**
Lieutenant   27th Bn., Manitoba Regiment, C.E.F.
Other Decorations: —
Date of Gazette: 27 Jun. 1917
Place/Date of Birth: Aberdeen, Scotland — 5 Aug. 1880
Place/Date of Death: Acheville, France — 3 May 1917
Memorials: Vimy Memorial, France
Town/County Connections: Aberdeen, Scotland
Remarks: —
Account of Deed: On 3 May 1917, south of Acheville, France, Lieutenant Combe steadied his
company under intense fire and leading them through the enemy barrage reached the objective
with only five men. He proceeded to bomb the enemy, inflicting heavy casualties and then, collecting small groups of men,
succeeded in capturing the objective, together with 80 prisoners. He repeatedly charged the enemy, driving them before him,
but while personally leading his bombers he was killed by a sniper.

COMMERELL John Edmund (later Sir John)   **240**
Commander (later Admiral)   Royal Navy
Other Decorations: GCB
Date of Gazette: 24 Feb. 1857
Place/Date of Birth: London — 13 Jan. 1829
Place/Date of Death: London — 21 May 1901
Memorials: Cheriton Road Cemetery, Folkestone, Kent
Town/County Connections: Victoria, London
Remarks: C-in-C North American and West Indies Station, 1881; C-in-C Portsmouth, 1888;
Groom-in-Waiting to The Queen, 1891; Admiral of the Fleet, 1892
Account of Deed: On 11 Oct. 1855 in the Sea of Azov, Crimea, Commander Commerell of HMS
Weser, with the Quartermaster* and a seaman, went to destroy large quantities of forage on the shore of the Putrid Sea. After
a difficult and dangerous journey they reached their objective — a magazine of corn — and managed to ignite the stacks, but
the guards were alerted and immediately opened fire and gave chase. The pursuit was so hot that the men had difficulty in
escaping, but they finally reached their ship and the look-outs later reported that the fodder store had burned to the ground.
(*See also RICKARD, W.)

CONGREVE, Walter Norris (later Sir Walter)   **241**
Captain (later Lieutenant General)   The Rifle Brigade (Prince Consort's Own)
Other Decorations: KCB, MVO
Date of Gazette: 2 Feb. 1900
Place/Date of Birth: Congreve, Staffordshire — 20 Nov. 1862
Place/Date of Death: Malta — 26 Feb. 1927
Memorials: Stone pillar between the temples of Hagar Qim and Mnajdra on South coast of
Malta; Stow-by-Chartley church, Staffordshire; The Rifle Brigade Memorial, Winchester
Cathedral
Town/County Connections: Congreve, Staffordshire; Burton, Cheshire
Remarks: Father of Major W. La T. Congreve, VC; Légion d'Honneur (France); Order of St. Anne,
1st Class (Russia); Governor of Malta 1925-27   *Harrow School.*
Account of Deed: On 15 Dec. 1899 at the Battle of Colenso, South Africa, Captain Congreve with several others, tried to save
the guns of the 14th and 66th Batteries, Royal Field Artillery, when the detachments serving the guns had all become casualties
or been driven from their guns. Some of the horses and drivers were sheltering in a donga about 500 yards behind the guns
and the intervening space was swept with shell and rifle fire. Captain Congreve, with two other officers* helped to hook a team
into a limber and then to limber up a gun. Although wounded himself, seeing one of the officers fall, he went out with an RAMC
Major* and brought him in. (*See also ROBERTS, F.H.S., SCHOFIELD, H.N. and BABTIE, W.)

CONGREVE, William La Touche   **242**
Bt/Major   The Rifle Brigade (Prince Consort's Own)
Other Decorations: DSO, MC
Date of Gazette: 26 Oct. 1916
Place/Date of Birth: Burton, Cheshire — 22 Mar. 1891
Place/Date of Death: Longueval, France — 20 Jul. 1916
Memorials: Corbie Communal Cemetery Extension, France; Stow-by-Chartley church,
Staffordshire; Corbie church, France; The Rifle Brigade Memorial, Winchester Cathedral
Town/County Connections: Burton, Cheshire
Remarks: Son of Captain W.N. Congreve, VC. Légion d'Honneur (France).   *Eton College.*
Account of Deed: During the period 6/20 Jul. 1916 at Longueval, France, Major Congreve
constantly inspired those round him by numerous acts of gallantry. As Brigade Major he not only conducted battalions up to
their positions but when the Brigade headquarters was heavily shelled he went out with the medical officer to remove the
wounded to places of safety, although he himself was suffering from gas and other shell effects. He went out again on a
subsequent occasion tending the wounded under heavy shell fire. Finally, on returning to the front line to ascertain the position
after an unsuccessful attack, he was shot and died instantly.

CONKER, Frederick — see **WHIRLPOOL,** Frederick

No photograph available

CONNOLLY, William   **243**
Gunner   Bengal Horse Artillery
Other Decorations: —
Date of Gazette: 3 Sep. 1858
Place/Date of Birth: Liverpool — May 1817
Place/Date of Death: West Derby, Liverpool, Lancashire — 31 Dec. 1891
Memorials: —
Town/County Connections: Liverpool, Lancs.
Remarks: —
Account of Deed: On 7 Jul. 1857 at Jhelum, India, during an engagement with the enemy,
Gunner Connolly, acting as second sponge-man, was felled by a musket ball through his thigh and
although suffering severely from pain and loss of blood, he insisted on mounting his horse in the gun team and riding to the
next position which the guns had taken up on retirement. He was again hit by a musket ball later the same morning but
staggered to his feet and went on wielding his sponge with energy and courage, and encouraging another wounded man, until
he was wounded yet again and fell unconscious.

CONNORS, Joseph   **244**
Private (later Corporal)   3rd Regiment (later The East Kent Regiment (The Buffs))
Other Decorations: —
Date of Gazette: 24 Feb. 1857
Place/Date of Birth: Davaugh, Listowel, Co. Kerry, Ireland — Oct. 1830
Place/Date of Death: Corfu — 22 Aug. 1858
Memorials: —
Town/County Connections: —
Remarks: —
Account of Deed: On 8 Sep. 1855 at Sebastopol in the Crimea, Private Connors showed
conspicuous gallantry at the assault on the Redan in personal conflict with the enemy. He rescued
an officer of the 30th Regiment who was surrounded by Russians, by shooting one and bayoneting another.

CONOLLY, John Augustus   **245**
Lieutenant (later Lieutenant Colonel)   49th Regt. (later The Royal Berkshire Regiment — Princess
Charlotte of Wales's)
Other Decorations: —
Date of Gazette: 5 May 1857
Place/Date of Birth: Cliff, Ballyshannon, Co. Donegal, Ireland — 30 May 1829
Place/Date of Death: Curragh, Co. Kildare, Ireland — 23 Dec. 1888
Memorials: Mount Jerome Cemetery, Dublin
Town/County Connections: Castletown, Co. Donegal; Curragh, Co. Kildare
Remarks: Transferred to the Coldstream Guards soon after the action on 26 Oct. 1854. Became Sub-Commissioner, Dublin Metropolitan Police after leaving the Army and later Resident Magistrate for the Curragh of Kildare
Account of Deed: On 26 Oct. 1854 in the Crimea, an attack by the Russians was repulsed and the enemy fell back pursued by men of the 49th Regiment, led by Lieutenant Conolly, whose gallant behaviour was most conspicuous in this action. He ultimately fell, dangerously wounded, while in personal encounter with several Russians, in defence of his post.

COOK, John   **246**
Captain (later Major)   Bengal Staff Corps and 5th Gurkha Rifles, Indian Army
Other Decorations: —
Date of Gazette: 18 Mar. 1879
Place/Date of Birth: Edinburgh — 28 Aug. 1843
Place/Date of Death: Sherpur, Afghanistan — 19 Dec. 1879
Memorials: Sanctum crypt, St Luke's Church, Chelsea, London
Town/County Connections: Edinburgh
Remarks: —
Account of Deed: On 2 Dec. 1878 at the Peiwar Kotal (Afghan War), Captain Cook, through heavy fire, charged out of the entrenchments with such impetuosity that the enemy broke and fled. At the close of the mêlée, seeing that a major was in personal conflict with an Afghan soldier, Captain Cook distracted attention to himself and a hand-to-hand encounter ensued, during which both men fell to the ground. The Afghan seized the captain's arm in his teeth until the struggle was ended by the man being shot in the head.

No photograph available

COOK, Walter   **247**
Private   42nd Regiment (later The Black Watch (Royal Highlanders))
Other Decorations: —
Date of Gazette: 18 Jun. 1859
Place/Date of Birth: Cripplegate, London — 1834
Place/Date of Death: ?Drowned in River Ravi, Punjab, India — c. 1864
Memorials: —
Town/County Connections: Cripplegate, London
Remarks: —
Account of Deed: On 15 Jan. 1859 at Maylah Ghat, India, when the fighting was most severe and the few men of the 42nd Regiment were skirmishing so close to the enemy (who were in great numbers) that some of them were wounded by sword cuts, the only officer was severely wounded and the colour-sergeant was killed. Private Cook and another private* immediately went to the front and took a prominent part in directing the company and displayed a courage, coolness and discipline which was the admiration of all who witnessed it. (*See also MILLAR, D.)

COOKE, Thomas   **248**
Private   8th Bn., (Victoria), Australian Imperial Force
Other Decorations: —
Date of Gazette: 9 Sep. 1916
Place/Date of Birth: Kaikoura, Marlborough, New Zealand — 5 Jul. 1881
Place/Date of Death: Pozieres, France — 28 Jul. 1916
Memorials: Villers-Bretonneux Memorial, France; Australian War Memorial, Canberra
Town/County Connections: —
Remarks: —
Account of Deed: On 24/25 Jul. 1916 at Pozieres, France, after a Lewis gun had been disabled, Private Cooke was ordered to take his gun to a dangerous part of the line. He did fine work, but came under very heavy fire, and finally he was the only man left. He still stuck to his post and continued to fire, but when assistance finally arrived he was found dead beside his gun.

COOKSON, Edgar Christopher   **249**
Lieutenant-Commander   Royal Navy
Other Decorations: DSO
Date of Gazette: 21 Jan. 1916
Place/Date of Birth: Tranmere, Cheshire — 13 Dec. 1883
Place/Date of Death: Nr. Kut-el-Amara, Mesopotamia — 28 Sep. 1915
Memorials: Amara War Cemetery, Iraq; Chatham Naval Memorial
Town/County Connections: Tranmere, Cheshire *, Whitchurch Canonicorum, Dorset*
Remarks: —
Account of Deed: On 28 Sep. 1915 during the advance on Kut-el-Amara, Mesopotamia, HMS
Comet, commanded by Lieutenant-Commander Cookson, and other armed vessels, were
ordered, if possible, to destroy an obstruction which had been placed across the river by the Turks. When they approached, very
heavy rifle and machine-gun fire was opened on them, and an attempt to sink the centre dhow by gun fire having failed
Lieutenant-Commander Cookson ran *Comet* alongside and he himself jumped on the dhow with an axe and tried to cut the
cables connecting it with the other two craft forming the obstruction. He was shot several times and died within a few minutes.

COOPER, Edward   **250**
Sergeant (later Major)   12th Bn., The King's Royal Rifle Corps
Other Decorations: —
Date of Gazette: 14 Sep. 1917
Place/Date of Birth: Stockton-on-Tees, Co. Durham — 4 May 1896
Place/Date of Death: Stockton-on-Tees — 19 Aug. 1985
Memorials: Stockton-on-Tees Public Library
Town/County Connections: Stockton-on-Tees, Co. Durham *Plaque in Stockton Library*
Remarks: Médaille Militaire (France)
Account of Deed: On 16 Aug. 1917 at Langemarck, Belgium, enemy machine-guns from a
concrete blockhouse 250 yards away were holding up the advance of the battalion on the left and
also causing heavy casualties to Sergeant Cooper's own battalion. With four men he rushed towards the blockhouse, but
although they fired at the garrison at very close range (100 yards) the machine-guns were not silenced, so Sergeant Cooper ran
straight at them and fired his revolver into an opening in the blockhouse. The machine-guns ceased firing and the garrison
surrendered. Seven machine-guns and 45 prisoners were captured.

COOPER, Henry   **251**
Boatswain   Royal Navy
Other Decorations: —
Date of Gazette: 24 Feb. 1857
Place/Date of Birth: Devonport, Devon — 1825
Place/Date of Death: Torpoint, Cornwall — 15 Jul. 1893
Memorials: Antony Churchyard, Torpoint, Cornwall
Town/County Connections: Torpoint, Cornwall
Remarks: Légion d'Honneur (France)
Account of Deed: On 3 Jun. 1855 at Taganrog, Sea of Azov, Crimea, Boatswain Cooper of HMS
Miranda, together with a lieutenant* landed while the town was actually under bombardment by
the Allied Squadron. It was garrisoned by 3,000 Russian troops, but the two men landed at several places and set fire to
government buildings and destroyed enemy equipment and arms. They were under fire themselves for most of the time. (*See
also BUCKLEY, C.W.)

No photograph available

COOPER, James   **252**
Private   2nd Bn., 24th Regiment (later The South Wales Borderers)
Other Decorations: —
Date of Gazette: 17 Dec. 1867
Place/Date of Birth: Birmingham — 1840
Place/Date of Death: Birmingham — 9 Aug. 1889
Memorials: Warstone Lane Cemetery, Warstone, Hockley, Birmingham *Grave 1428*
Town/County Connections: Birmingham
Remarks: VC not awarded for bravery in action against the enemy, but for bravery at sea in
saving life in storm off Andaman Islands
Account of Deed: On 7 May 1867 at the island of Little Andaman, Bay of Bengal, Private Cooper
was one of a party of five* of the 2/24th Regiment, who risked their lives in manning a boat and proceeding through dangerous
surf to rescue some of their comrades who had been sent to the island to find out the fate of the commander and seven of the
crew, who had landed from the ship *Assam Valley* and were feared murdered by the cannibalistic islanders. (*See also BELL,
David, DOUGLAS, C.M., GRIFFITHS, W. and MURPHY, T.)

COOPER, Neville Bowes ELLIOTT-   **253**
T/Lieutenant Colonel   Comd. 8th Bn., The Royal Fusiliers
Other Decorations: DSO, MC
Date of Gazette: 13 Feb. 1918
Place/Date of Birth: London — 22 Jan. 1889
Place/Date of Death: Hanover, Germany — 11 Feb. 1918
Memorials: Hamburg Cemetery, Germany; Ripon Cathedral
Town/County Connections: London . *Eton College*
Remarks: — *Name on W.M. Bentworth, Near Alton. Hampshire*
Account of Deed: On 30 Nov. 1917 east of La Vacquerie, near Cambrai, France when the enemy had broken through our outpost line, Lieutenant Colonel Elliott-Cooper seeing them advancing across the open, mounted the parapet calling upon the reserve company and details from battalion headquarters to follow. Absolutely unarmed, he made straight for the advancing enemy and under his direction his men forced them back 600 yards. While still yards in front he was severely wounded and realising that his force was greatly outnumbered, he signalled to them to withdraw, knowing that he must be taken prisoner. He died of his wounds three months later in Germany.

COPPINS, Frederick George   **254**
Corporal   8th Bn., Manitoba Regiment, C.E.F.
Other Decorations: —
Date of Gazette: 27 Sep. 1918
Place/Date of Birth: London — 25 Oct. 1889
Place/Date of Death: Livermore, California, U.S.A. — 30 Mar. 1963
Memorials: Greenlawn Cemetery, Colma, near San Francisco, California, U.S.A.
Town/County Connections: London
Remarks: —
Account of Deed: On 9 Aug. 1918 at Hackett Woods, near Amiens, France, Corporal Coppins' platoon came unexpectedly under fire of numerous machine-guns. It was not possible to advance or retire and there was no cover. Corporal Coppins, calling on four men to follow him, leapt forward in the face of intense machine-gun fire and rushed straight for the guns. The four men with him were killed and he was wounded, but going on alone, he killed the operator of the first gun and three of the crew and took four prisoners. Despite his wound, he then continued with his platoon to the final objective.

CORBETT, (alias EMBLETON, David) Frederick   **255**
Private   3rd Bn., The King's Royal Rifle Corps
Other Decorations: —
Date of Gazette: 16 Feb. 1883
Place/Date of Birth: Camberwell, London — 1856
Place/Date of Death: ?London — sometime after 1904
Memorials: —
Town/County Connections: Camberwell, London
Remarks: —
Account of Deed: On 5 Aug. 1882 at Kafr Dowar, Egypt, during a reconnaissance, a lieutenant was mortally wounded — he fell in the open and there was no time to move him. Private Corbett therefore asked, and obtained permission to remain by him, and although under constant fire, he at once tried to stop the bleeding of the officer's wounds. When orders to retreat were received, Private Corbett helped to carry the officer off the field.

CORNWELL, John Travers   **256**
Boy, First Class   Royal Navy
Other Decorations: Boy Scouts' Bronze Cross
Date of Gazette: 15 Sep. 1916
Place/Date of Birth: Leyton, Essex — 8 Jan. 1900
Place/Date of Death: Grimsby, Lincolnshire — 2 Jun. 1916
Memorials: Manor Park Cemetery, Essex; Jack Cornwell Cottage Homes, Hornchurch, Essex; memorial to HMS *Chester*, Chester Cathedral *Take Main Gate in Sebert Road,*
Town/County Connections: Leyton, Essex *Grave is on corner of first right hand turn*
Remarks: — *Jack Cornwell Ward in Star & Garter Home. Richmond*
Account of Deed: On 31 May 1916, at the Battle of Jutland, Boy First Class Cornwell, of HMS *Chester*, was mortally wounded early in the battle, but remained standing alone at a most exposed post, quietly awaiting orders, until the end of the action, with the gun's crew dead and wounded around him.

COSENS, Aubrey

257

Sergeant   The Queen's Own Rifles of Canada, Canadian Infantry Corps
Other Decorations: —
Date of Gazette: 22 May 1945
Place/Date of Birth: Latchford, Ontario, Canada — 21 May 1921
Place/Date of Death: Mooshof, Holland — 26 Feb. 1945
Memorials: Groesbeek Canadian War Cemetery, Nijmegen, Holland
Town/County Connections: —
Remarks: —
Account of Deed: On the night of 25/26 Feb. 1945 at Mooshof, Holland, Sergeant Cosens assumed command of the four survivors of his platoon whom he placed in position to give him covering fire and then, running forward alone to a tank, took up an exposed position in front of the turret and directed its fire. When a further counter-attack had been repulsed and, on his orders, the tank had rammed some farm buildings, he went in alone, killing several of the defenders and taking the rest prisoners. He then dealt similarly with the occupants of two more buildings, but soon afterwards was killed by a sniper.

COSGROVE, William

258

Corporal (later Staff-Sergeant)   1st Bn., The Royal Munster Fusiliers
Other Decorations: MSM
Date of Gazette: 23 Aug. 1915
Place/Date of Birth: Aghada, Co. Cork, Ireland — 1 Oct. 1888
Place/Date of Death: Millbank, London — 14 Jul. 1936
Memorials: —
Town/County Connections: Upper Aghada, Cork, Ireland; Millbank, London
Remarks: —
Account of Deed: On 26 Apr. 1915, east of Cape Helles, Gallipoli, Corporal Cosgrove led his section during the attack on the Turkish position. The corporal pulled down the posts of the enemy's high wire entanglements single-handed, notwithstanding the terrific fire from both front and flanks. This action greatly assisted in the successful clearing of the heights.

COSTELLO, Edmond William

259

Lieutenant (later Brigadier General)   22nd Punjab Infantry, Indian Army
Other Decorations: CMG, CVO, DSO
Date of Gazette: 9 Nov. 1897
Place/Date of Birth: Sheikhbudia, North-west Frontier, India — 7 Aug. 1873
Place/Date of Death: Eastbourne, Sussex — 7 Jun. 1949
Memorials: St. Mark's Church, Hadlow Down, Sussex   *Stonyhurst College. Lancs.*
Town/County Connections: Eastbourne, Sussex
Remarks: Served in First World War; Croix de Guerre (France). DL, Cambridgeshire; Commanded Home Guard, Eastbourne in Second World War
Account of Deed: On 26 Jul. 1897 at Malakand on the Indian Frontier, Lieutenant Costello went out from the hospital enclosure and with the assistance of two sepoys, brought in a wounded lance-havildar who was lying 60 yards away, in the open, on the football ground. This ground was at the time over-run with swordsmen and swept by a heavy fire from both the enemy and our own men who were holding the sapper lines.

COTTER, William Reginald

260

A/Corporal   6th Bn., The East Kent Regiment (The Buffs)
Other Decorations: —
Date of Gazette: 30 Mar. 1916
Place/Date of Birth: Folkestone, Kent — Mar. 1883
Place/Date of Death: Lillers, France — 14 Mar. 1916
Memorials: Lillers Communal Cemetery, France; War Memorial, Sandgate, Kent
Town/County Connections: Folkestone and Sandgate, Kent
Remarks: —
Account of Deed: On 6 Mar. 1916 near Hohenzollern Redoubt, France, Corporal Cotter's leg was blown off at the knee and he was also wounded in both arms. He nevertheless made his way unaided for 50 yards to a crater, steadied the men who were holding it, controlled their fire, issued orders and altered their dispositions to meet a fresh counter-attack. For two hours he held his position and only allowed his wounds to be roughly dressed when the attack had quietened down. He could not be moved back for 14 hours and during all this time he had a cheery word for everyone.

COUGHLAN (or COGHLAN), Cornelius   **261**
Colour-Sergeant (later Sergeant-Major)   75th Regiment (later The Gordon Highlanders)
Other Decorations: —
Date of Gazette: 11 Nov. 1862
Place/Date of Birth: Eyrecourt, Co. Galway, Ireland — 27 Jun. 1828
Place/Date of Death: Westport, Co. Mayo, Ireland — 14 Feb. 1915
Memorials: —   *HEADSTONE ON GRAVE INSTALLED   8.8.2004*
Town/County Connections: Eyrecourt, Co. Galway; Westport, Co. Mayo   *WESTPORT, MAYO*
Remarks: —
Account of Deed: On 8 Jun. 1857 at Delhi, India, Colour-Sergeant Coughlan gallantly ventured under heavy fire, with three others, into a serai occupied by the enemy in great numbers and rescued a private of their regiment who was severely wounded. On 18 Jul. he encouraged a party to charge down a lane lined on each side with huts and raked by cross-fire. He went with the party into an enclosure filled with the enemy and accounted for all of them. He then returned under cross-fire to collect dhoolies and carry off the wounded.

COULSON, Gustavus Hamilton Blenkinsopp   **262**
Lieutenant   1st Bn., The King's Own Scottish Borderers
Other Decorations: DSO
Date of Gazette: 8 Aug. 1902
Place/Date of Birth: Wimbledon, Surrey — 1 Apr. 1879
Place/Date of Death: Lambrechtfontein, South Africa — 18 May 1901
Memorials: —
Town/County Connections: Wimbledon, Surrey
Remarks: —
Account of Deed: On 18 May 1901 at Lambrechtfontein, South Africa, during a rearguard action in which Lieutenant Coulson rallied his men and saved the guns, a corporal who was the lieutenant's servant, had his horse shot. Lieutenant Coulson, seeing this, dismounted and took the man up on his own horse, but after a short distance the horse was wounded and both riders were brought to the ground. Lieutenant Coulson then told the corporal to get along with the wounded horse as best he could, while he, the lieutenant, would look after himself. He was, however, mortally wounded almost at once.

COUNTER, Jack Thomas   **263**
Private   1st Bn., The King's (Liverpool) Regiment
Other Decorations: —
Date of Gazette: 22 May 1918
Place/Date of Birth: Blandford Forum, Dorset — 3 Nov. 1898
Place/Date of Death: Blandford Forum, Dorset — 16 Sep. 1970
Memorials: Ashes interred in Jersey; Jack Counter Close, St. Helier, Jersey
Town/County Connections: Blandford, Dorset
Remarks: —
Account of Deed: On 16 Apr. 1918 near Boisieux St. Marc, France, it was necessary for information to be obtained from the front line and the only way to get it was over ground with no cover and in full view of the enemy. A small party tried without success, followed by six men, singly, each one being killed in the attempt. Private Counter then volunteered and, going out under terrific fire, got through and returned with vital information which enabled his commanding officer to organise and launch the final successful counter-attack. Subsequently he also carried five messages across the open under heavy artillery barrage to company headquarters.

COURY, Gabriel George   **264**
Second Lieutenant (later Captain)   3rd Bn., The South Lancashire Regiment (The Prince of Wales's Volunteers) attd. 1/4th Bn.
Other Decorations: —
Date of Gazette: 26 Oct. 1916
Place/Date of Birth: Liverpool, Lancashire — 13 Jun. 1896
Place/Date of Death: Liverpool, Lancashire — 23 Feb. 1956
Memorials: Cemetery of church of St. Peter and St. Paul, Crosby, Liverpool
Town/County Connections: Liverpool, Lancs.   *Stonyhurst College, Lancs*
Remarks: Served with RASC in Second World War
Account of Deed: On 8 Aug. 1916 near Arrow Head Copse, France, Second Lieutenant Coury was in command of two platoons ordered to dig a communication trench. By his fine example and utter contempt of danger he kept up the spirits of his men and completed his task under intense fire. Later when his battalion had suffered severe casualties and the Commanding Officer had been wounded he went out in broad daylight in full view of the enemy, found his Commanding Officer and brought him back to the new advanced trench over ground swept by machine-gun fire.

COVERDALE, Charles Harry   **265**
Sergeant (later Second Lieutenant)   11th Bn., The Manchester Regiment
Other Decorations: MM
Date of Gazette: 18 Dec. 1917
Place/Date of Birth: Manchester, Lancashire — 21 Apr. 1888
Place/Date of Death: Huddersfield, Yorkshire — 20 Nov. 1955
Memorials: —
Town/County Connections: Manchester, Lancs; Huddersfield, Yorks.
Remarks: —
Account of Deed: On 4 Oct. 1917 south-west of Poelcapelle, Belgium, when close to the objective, Sergeant Coverdale disposed of three snipers. He then rushed two machine-guns, killing or wounding the teams. He subsequently reorganised his platoon in order to capture another position, but after getting within 100 yards of it was held up by our own barrage and had to return. Later he went out again with five men to capture the position, but when he saw a considerable number of the enemy advancing, withdrew his detachment man by man, he himself being the last to retire.

COWLEY, Charles Henry   **266**
Lieutenant-Commander   Royal Naval Volunteer Reserve
Other Decorations: —
Date of Gazette: 2 Feb. 1917
Place/Date of Birth: Baghdad — 21 Feb. 1872
Place/Date of Death: Near Kut-el-Amara, Mesopotamia — 25 Apr. 1916
Memorials: Basra Memorial, Iraq
Town/County Connections: —
Remarks: —
Account of Deed: On the night of 24/25 Apr. 1916 in Mesopotamia, an attempt was made to reprovision the force besieged at Kut-el-Amara. Lieutenant-Commander Cowley, with a lieutenant* (commanding *SS Julnar*), a sub-lieutenant and 12 ratings, started off with 270 tons of stores up the River Tigris. Unfortunately *Julnar* was attacked almost at once by Turkish machine-guns and artillery. At Magasis, steel hawsers stretched across the river halted the expedition, the enemy opened fire at point-blank range and *Julnar's* bridge was smashed. *Julnar's* commander was killed, also several of his crew; Lieutenant-Commander Cowley was taken prisoner with the other survivors and almost certainly executed by the Turks. (*See also FIRMAN, H.O.P.)

COX, Christopher Angustus   **267**
Private   7th Bn., The Bedfordshire Regiment
Other Decorations: —
Date of Gazette: 11 May 1917
Place/Date of Birth: King's Langley, Hertfordshire — 25 Dec. 1889
Place/Date of Death: King's Langley, Hertfordshire — 24 Aug. 1959
Memorials: King's Langley cemetery
Town/County Connections: King's Langley, Hertfordshire
Remarks: —
Account of Deed: On 13 Mar. 1917 at Achiet-le-Grand, France during an attack by the battalion, the front wave was checked by very heavy artillery and machine-gun fire and the whole line had to take shelter in shell holes to avoid annihilation. Private Cox, a stretcher-bearer, went out over fire-swept ground and, single-handed, rescued four men. Having collected the wounded of his own battalion he then helped to bring in the wounded of the adjoining battalion. On two subsequent days he carried out similar work with complete disregard of his own safety.

No photograph available

CRAIG, James   **268**
Colour-Sergeant (later Lieutenant)   Scots (Fusilier) Guards
Other Decorations: —
Date of Gazette: 20 Nov. 1857
Place/Date of Birth: Perth, Scotland — 10 Sep. 1824
Place/Date of Death: Port Elizabeth, South Africa — 18 Mar. 1861
Memorials: St. Mary's Cemetery, South End, Port Elizabeth
Town/County Connections: Perth, Scotland
Remarks: —
Account of Deed: On 6 Sep. 1855 at Sebastopol, Crimea, Colour-Sergeant Craig volunteered and personally collected other volunteers, to go out under heavy fire to look for a captain of his regiment who was supposed to be wounded. Sergeant Craig brought in the body of that officer whom he found dead, and while doing so was himself wounded.

CRAIG, John Manson   **269**
Second Lieutenant   1/4th Bn., The Royal Scots Fusiliers, attd. 1/5th Bn.
Other Decorations: —
Date of Gazette: 2 Aug. 1917
Place/Date of Birth: Comrie, Perthshire, Scotland — 5 Mar. 1896
Place/Date of Death: Crieff, Perthshire, Scotland — 19 Feb. 1970
Memorials: —
Town/County Connections: Comrie, Perthshire
Remarks: Served in Royal Air Force during Second World War
Account of Deed: On 5 Jun. 1917 in Egypt, an advanced post having been rushed by the enemy, Second Lieutenant Craig immediately organised a rescue party and after tracking the enemy back to his trenches, set his party to work removing the dead and wounded under heavy rifle and machine-gun fire. An NCO was wounded and a medical officer who went to his aid was also wounded. Second Lieutenant Craig went out at once and got the NCO under cover, but while taking the medical officer to shelter was himself wounded. Nevertheless the rescue was effected, and he then scooped cover for the wounded, thus saving their lives.

CRANDON, Harry George   **270**
Private (later Corporal)   18th Hussars (Queen Mary's Own)
Other Decorations: —
Date of Gazette: 18 Oct. 1901
Place/Date of Birth: Wells, Somerset — 12 Feb. 1874
Place/Date of Death: Manchester, Lancashire — 2 Jan. 1953
Memorials: — *Buried Swinton Cemetery. Manchester.*
Town/County Connections: Wells, Somerset
Remarks: Re-enlisted in 1914 and served with 18th Hussars throughout the First World War
Account of Deed: On 4 Jul. 1901 at Springbok Laagte, South Africa, Private Crandon rode back to help another private who was wounded and whose horse became disabled. Private Crandon gave up his horse to the wounded man so that he could reach shelter, and followed on foot, having to run 1,100 yards, all the time under fire.

CREAGH, O'Moore (later Sir O'Moore)   **271**
Captain (later General)   Bombay Staff Corps, Indian Army
Other Decorations: GCB, GCSI
Date of Gazette: 17 Nov. 1879
Place/Date of Birth: Cahirbane, Co. Clare, Ireland — 2 April 1848
Place/Date of Death: South Kensington, London — 9 Aug. 1923
Memorials: East Sheen Cemetery, Surrey
Town/County Connections: Cahirebane, Co. Clare; London
Remarks: Order of the Rising Sun (Japan); Secretary, Military Department, India Office, 1907-9; C-in-C India, 1909-14. Knight of Grace of St. John of Jerusalem; Compiler and editor (with E.M. Humphris) of *The V.C. and D.S.O.*
Account of Deed: On 12/22 Apr. 1879 at Kam Dakka, on the Kabul River, (Afghan War), Captain Creagh, who had been ordered to take a detachment of 150 men to protect the village against a threatened incursion of the Mohmands, had to repel an attack by about 1,500 of the enemy. The inhabitants of Kam Dakka joined with the Mohmands and Captain Creagh's force was compelled to retire, so he took up a position in a cemetery and held it, repulsing repeated attacks with the bayonet until a relief force arrived, when the enemy was finally routed and many of them were driven into the river.

CREAN, Thomas Joseph   **272**
Surgeon Captain (later Major)   1st Imperial Light Horse (Natal)
Other Decorations: DSO
Date of Gazette: 11 Feb. 1902
Place/Date of Birth: Dublin — 19 Apr. 1873
Place/Date of Death: London — 25 Mar. 1923
Memorials: St. Mary's RC Cemetery, Kensal Green, London
Town/County Connections: Dublin; London
Remarks: —
Account of Deed: On 18 Dec. 1901, during the action at Tygerkloof Spruit, South Africa, Surgeon Captain Crean, although wounded himself, continued to attend to the wounded in the firing line, under a very heavy fire at only 150 yards range. He did not stop until hit a second time, and, as it was first thought, mortally wounded.

CRICHTON, James

273

Private (later Sergeant) 2nd Bn., Auckland Infantry Regiment, N.Z.E.F.
Other Decorations: —
Date of Gazette: 15 Nov. 1918
Place/Date of Birth: Carrickfergus, Co. Antrim, Ireland — 15 Jul. 1879
Place/Date of Death: Auckland, New Zealand — 22 Sep. 1961
Memorials: Soldiers' Cemetery, Waikumete, Auckland; HQ Dunedin RSA, New Zealand
Town/County Connections: Carrickfergus, Co. Antrim
Remarks: —
Account of Deed: On 30 Sep. 1918 at Crevecoeur, France, Private Crichton, although wounded in the foot, stayed with the advancing troops despite difficult canal and river obstacles. When his platoon was forced back by a counter-attack he succeeded in carrying a message which involved swimming a river and crossing an area swept by machine-gun fire. Subsequently he rejoined his platoon and later undertook on his own initiative to save a bridge which had been mined. Under close fire he managed to remove the charges, returning with the fuses and detonators.

CRIMMIN, John

274

Surgeon (later Colonel) Bombay Medical Service, Indian Army
Other Decorations: CB, CIE, VD
Date of Gazette: 17 Sep. 1889
Place/Date of Birth: Dublin — 19 Mar. 1859
Place/Date of Death: Wells, Somerset — 20 Feb. 1945
Memorials: —
Town/County Connections: Dublin; Wells, Somerset
Remarks: —
Account of Deed: On 1 Jan. 1889, in the action near Lwekaw, Eastern Karenni, Burma, a lieutenant and four men charged into a large body of the enemy and two men were wounded. Surgeon Crimmin attended one of them under enemy fire and he then joined the firing line and helped in driving the enemy from small clumps of trees where they had taken shelter. Later while Surgeon Crimmin was attending a wounded man several of the enemy rushed out at him. He thrust his sword through one of them, attacked a second and a third dropped from the fire of a sepoy. The remainder fled.

CRISP, Thomas

275

Skipper Royal Naval Reserve
Other Decorations: DSC
Date of Gazette: 2 Nov. 1917
Place/Date of Birth: Lowestoft, Suffolk — 28 Apr. 1876
Place/Date of Death: North Sea — 15 Aug. 1917
Memorials: Chatham Memorial; tenor bell at St. Margaret's Church, Lowestoft
Town/County Connections: Lowestoft, Suffolk
Remarks: —
Account of Deed: On 15 Aug. 1917 in the North Sea, Skipper Crisp of HM Armed Smack *Nelson* was below packing fish when a German submarine opened fire. The skipper cleared *Nelson* for action just as a shell hit her below the water-line and another shell passed through the ship, mortally wounding the skipper, who, however, went on directing operations. He gave the order to abandon ship but he himself was too badly injured to be moved and went down with *Nelson*.

CROAK, John Bernard

276

Private 13th Bn., Quebec Regt. (Royal Highlanders of Canada), C.E.F.
Other Decorations: —
Date of Gazette: 27 Sep. 1918
Place/Date of Birth: Little Bay, Newfoundland — 18 May 1892
Place/Date of Death: Near Amiens, France — 8 Aug. 1918
Memorials: Hangard Wood British Cemetery, France
Town/County Connections: —
Remarks: —
Account of Deed: On 8 Aug. 1918 at Amiens, France, Private Croak, having become separated from his section, encountered a machine-gun which he bombed and silenced, taking the gun and crew prisoners. Shortly afterwards he was severely wounded but refusing to give in, rejoined his platoon. When several more machine-guns at a strong point were encountered, the private, seeing an opportunity, dashed forward, followed almost immediately by the rest of the platoon in a brilliant charge. He was the first to arrive at the trench line into which he led his men, bayoneting or capturing the entire garrison. He was again wounded and died almost at once.

CROSS, Arthur Henry   **277**
A/Lance-Corporal   40th Bn., Machine Gun Corps
Other Decorations: MM
Date of Gazette: 4 Jun. 1918
Place/Date of Birth: Shipdham, Thetford, Norfolk — 13 Dec. 1884
Place/Date of Death: Lambeth, London — 23 Nov. 1965
Memorials:
Town/County Connections: Shipdham, Norfolk; Lambeth, London
Remarks: —
Account of Deed: On 25 Mar. 1918 at Ervillers, France, Lance-Corporal Cross volunteered to make a reconnaissance of the position of two machine-guns which had been captured by the enemy. He went alone to the enemy trench and with his revolver forced seven of the enemy to surrender and to carry their guns with the tripods and ammunition to our lines. He then handed over the prisoners and collected teams for his guns which he brought into action immediately, annihilating a very heavy attack by the enemy.

CROWE, John James   **278**
Second Lieutenant (later Captain)   2nd Bn., The Worcestershire Regiment
Other Decorations: —
Date of Gazette: 28 Jun. 1918
Place/Date of Birth: Devonport, Devon — 28 Dec. 1876
Place/Date of Death: Brighton, Sussex — 2 Mar. 1965
Memorials: (Cremated, Down's Crematorium, Bear Road, Brighton)
Town/County Connections: Brighton, Sussex
Remarks: —
Account of Deed: On 14 Apr. 1918 at Neuve Eglise, Belgium, when the enemy, having attacked a post in a village, broke past on the high ground and established a machine-gun and snipers, Second Lieutenant Crowe, with two NCOs and seven men twice engaged the enemy who on each occasion withdrew into the village, followed by the lieutenant firing on them. On the second occasion, taking only two men, he attacked two enemy machine-guns killing both gunners and several more of the enemy. The remainder withdrew and he captured the two guns.

CROWE, Joseph Petrus Hendrick   **279**
Lieutenant (later Lieutenant Colonel)   78th Regt. (later The Seaforth Highlanders — Ross-shire Buffs, Duke of Albany's)
Other Decorations: —
Date of Gazette: 15 Jan. 1858
Place/Date of Birth: Uitenhage, Cape, South Africa — 12 Jan. 1826
Place/Date of Death: Penge, London — 12 Apr. 1876
Memorials: West Norwood Cemetery, London; Re-interred at Uitenhage, 5 Feb. 1977
Town/County Connections: —
Remarks: — *Once buried at W.N.C. Grave 15950*
Account of Deed: On 12 Aug. 1857 at Boursekee Chowkee, the entrenched village in front of Busherutgunge, India, the redoubt was occupied by the enemy who were causing heavy casualties among the 78th Regiment. It was decided to take the place by storm, and the Highlanders dashed forward, Lieutenant Crowe being the first in, followed by his men. In less than a minute the redoubt was captured.

CRUICKSHANK, John Alexander   **280**
Flying Officer (later Flight Lieutenant)   210 Squadron, Royal Air Force Volunteer Reserve
Other Decorations: —
Date of Gazette: 1 Sep. 1944
Place/Date of Birth: Aberdeen, Scotland — 20 May 1920
Place/Date of Death: —
Memorials: —
Town/County Connections: Aberdeen, Scotland
Remarks: ADC to the Lord High Commissioner to the General Assembly of the Church of Scotland, 1946-48
Account of Deed: On 17/18 Jul. 1944 Flying Officer Cruickshank, on anti-submarine patrol in Northern waters, was attacking a U-boat in a hail of flak shells when one burst inside the aircraft, causing a great deal of damage. One member of the crew was killed and two wounded, and although he too had been hit — it was later found that he had 72 wounds — Flying Officer Cruickshank went in again, releasing his depth charges, which straddled the U-boat perfectly, and it sank. On the hazardous 5½-hour return journey the flying officer several times lost consciousness, but insisted on helping to land the Catalina.

CRUICKSHANK, Robert Edward   **281**
Private (later Major)   2/14th (County of London) Bn., The London Regt. (London Scottish)
Other Decorations: —
Date of Gazette: 21 Jun. 1918
Place/Date of Birth: Winnipeg, Canada — 17 Jun. 1888
Place/Date of Death: Blaby, Leicestershire — 1 Sep. 1961
Memorials:
Town/County Connections: Harringay, London; Blaby, Leics.
Remarks: —
Account of Deed: On 1 May 1918 east of Jordan, Palestine, Private Cruickshank volunteered to take a message to company headquarters from his platoon which was in the bottom of a wadi, with its officer and most of the men casualties. He rushed up the slopes but was hit, tried again and was again wounded. After his wounds had been dresed, he tried yet again, but was so badly wounded that he could make no further attempt. He lay all day in a dangerous position, being sniped at and wounded where he lay, but displayed great endurance and was cheerful and uncomplaining throughout.

CRUTCHLEY, Victor Alexander Charles (later Sir Victor)   **282**
Lieutenant (later Admiral)   Royal Navy
Other Decorations: KCB, DSC
Date of Gazette: 28 Aug. 1918
Place/Date of Birth: London — 2 Nov. 1893
Place/Date of Death: Mappercombe, Nettleton, Bridport, Dorset — 24 Jan. 1986, *Powerstock*
Memorials: — *Died near Bridport 24-1-1986 - Funeral at St. Marys, Powerstock*
Town/County Connections: London; Nettlecombe, Bridport, Dorset
Remarks: Croix de Guerre (France); Polonia Restituta (Poland); Commander, Legion of Merit (USA). Commanded Australian Naval Squadron, 1942-44; Flag Officer, Gibraltar 1945-47; DL and High Sheriff of Dorset, 1957.
Account of Deed: On 9/10 May 1918 at Ostend, Belgium, Lieutenant Crutchley took command of HMS *Vindictive* when the commanding officer had been killed and the second in command seriously wounded. He displayed great gallantry and seamanship both in *Vindictive* and M.L. 254 which rescued the crew after the former vessel had been sunk between the piers of Ostend harbour. He also took command of M.L. 254 when the commanding officer of that vessel had collapsed from his wounds*. M.L. 254 was full of wounded and in a sinking condition, but Lieutenant Crutchley kept her afloat until HMS *Warwick* came to the rescue. (*See also BOURKE, R.R.L. and DRUMMOND, G.H.)

CUBITT, William George   **283**
Lieutenant (later Colonel)   13th Bengal Native Infantry
Other Decorations: DSO
Date of Gazette: 18 Jun. 1859
Place/Date of Birth: Calcutta, India — 19 Oct. 1835
Place/Date of Death: Camberley, Surrey — 23 Jan. 1903
Memorials: St. Peter's Churchyard, Frimley, Surrey
Town/County Connections: Camberley, Surrey
Remarks: Brother-in-law of Second Lieutenant J. Hills, VC; uncle of Lieutenant Colonel L.P. Evans, VC.
Account of Deed: On 30 Jun. 1857 during the retreat from Chinhut, India, Lieutenant Cubitt saved the lives of three men of the 32nd Regiment at the risk of his own.

CUMMING, Arthur Edward   **284**
Lieutenant Colonel (later Brigadier)   Comd. 2/12th Frontier Force Regiment, Indian Army
Other Decorations: OBE, MC
Date of Gazette: 20 Feb. 1942
Place/Date of Birth: Karachi, India — 18 Jun. 1896
Place/Date of Death: Edinburgh — 10 Apr. 1971
Memorials: Sanctum crypt, St. Luke's Church, Chelsea, London.
Town/County Connections: Highbury, London; Edinburgh
Remarks: Commander, Dehra Dun Sub-Area 1944-47; Superintendent of Police, Kyrenia, Cyprus 1956-59.
Account of Deed: On 3 Jan. 1942 near Kuantan, Malaya, the Japanese made a furious attack on the battalion and a strong enemy force penetrated the position. Lieutenant Colonel Cumming, with a small party of men immediately led a counter-attack and although all his men became casualties and he himself had two bayonet wounds in the stomach he managed to restore the situation sufficiently for the major portion of the battalion and its vehicles to be withdrawn. Later he drove in a carrier under very heavy fire, collecting isolated detachments of his men and was again wounded. His gallant actions helped the brigade to withdraw safely.

CUNINGHAME, William James Montgomery (later Sir William)   **285**
Lieutenant (later Colonel)   1st Bn., The Rifle Brigade (Prince Consort's Own)
Other Decorations: —
Date of Gazette: 24 Feb. 1857
Place/Date of Birth: Ayr, Scotland — 20 May 1834
Place/Date of Death: Gunton, Suffolk — 11 Nov. 1897
Memorials: Kirkmichael Churchyard, Ayr; The Rifle Brigade Memorial, Winchester Cathedral
Town/County Connections: Corse Hill, Ayrshire, Scotland
Remarks: Member of Parliament for Ayr 1874-80   *Harrow School.*
Account of Deed: On 20 Nov. 1854 in the Crimea, Lieutenant Cuninghame, with another
lieutenant* was with a party detailed to drive the Russians from some rifle pits. Advancing on the
pits after dark they launched a surprise attack and drove the Russian riflemen from their cover, but in the fierce fighting which
ensued the officer in command of the party was killed. The two lieutenants, however, maintained their advantage, withstood
all attacks from the enemy during the night and held the position until relieved next day. (*See also BOURCHIER, C.T.)

CUNNINGHAM, John   **286**
Private   12th (S) Bn., The East Yorkshire Regiment
Other Decorations: —
Date of Gazette: 13 Jan. 1917
Place/Date of Birth: Scunthorpe, Lincolnshire — 28 Jun. 1897
Place/Date of Death: Hull, Yorkshire — 21 Feb. 1941
Memorials: — *Buried Western Cemetery. Hull.*
Town/County Connections: Scunthorpe, Lincs.; Hull, Yorks.
Remarks: —
Account of Deed: On 13 Nov. 1916 opposite Hebuterne Sector, France, after the enemy's front
line had been captured, Private Cunningham went with a bombing section up a communication
trench where much opposition was met and all the rest of the section were either killed or wounded. Collecting all the bombs
from the casualties Private Cunningham went on alone and when he had used up all the bombs he had he returned for a fresh
supply and again went up the communication trench where he met a party of 10 Germans. He killed all 10 and cleared the trench
up to the new line.

CUNNINGHAM, John   **287**
Corporal   2nd Bn., The Prince of Wales's Leinster Regiment
Other Decorations: —
Date of Gazette: 8 Jun. 1917
Place/Date of Birth: Thurles, Tipperary, Ireland — 22 Oct. 1890
Place/Date of Death: Near Barlin, France — 16 Apr. 1917
Memorials: Barlin Communal Cemetery, France; St. Mary's church, Thurles, Tipperary, Ireland
Town/County Connections: Thurles, Tipperary, Ireland
Remarks: —
Account of Deed: On 12 Apr. 1917 at Bois-en-Hache, near Barlin, France, Corporal Cunningham
was in command of a Lewis gun section which came under a very heavy enfilade fire. Although
wounded, he succeeded, almost alone, in reaching the objective with his gun which he got into action in spite of much
opposition. When counter-attacked by a party of 20 Germans, he exhausted his ammunition against them and then started
throwing bombs. He was wounded again and fell, but picked himself up and continued to fight single-handed with the enemy
until his bombs were finished. He later died from the effects of his wounds.

CUNYNGHAM, William Henry DICK-   **288**
Lieutenant (later Lieutenant Colonel)   The Gordon Highlanders
Other Decorations: —
Date of Gazette: 18 Oct. 1881
Place/Date of Birth: Prestonfield, Edinburgh — 16 Jun. 1851
Place/Date of Death: Ladysmith, Natal, South Africa — 6 Jan. 1900
Memorials: Old Windsor Cemetery, Berks. South African War Memorial, Cheltenham, Glos.
Town/County Connections: Edinburgh; Cheltenham, Glos
Remarks: —
Account of Deed: On 13 Dec. 1879 during the attack on the Sherpur Pass, (Afghan War) there was
a momentary wavering of the troops who had been beaten back at the top of the hill. Lieutenant
Dick-Cunyngham rushed forward and gallantly exposed himself to the full fire being poured upon this point. He rallied the men
by his example and cheering words, and calling on those near to follow him, charged into the middle of the enemy.

CURREY, William Matthew

Private   53rd Bn. (N.S.W.), Australian Imperial Force
Other Decorations: —
Date of Gazette: 14 Dec. 1918
Place/Date of Birth: Wallsend, Newcastle, New South Wales, Australia — 19 Sep. 1895
Place/Date of Death: New South Wales, Australia — 30 Apr. 1948
Memorials: Woronora Crematorium, Sydney, N.S.W.; Australian War Memorial, Canberra
Town/County Connections: —
Remarks: —
Account of Deed: On 1 Sep. 1918 in the attack on Peronne, France, Private Currey rushed forward under heavy machine-gun fire and captured single-handed a 77mm field gun which had been holding up the advance, killing all the crew. Later, when the advance was checked by an enemy strong-point he crept round the flank and engaged the post with a Lewis gun, then rushed at it, causing many casualties. Subsequently he volunteered to carry orders for withdrawal to an isolated company, doing so under heavy fire and bringing back valuable information.

289

CURRIE, David Vivian

Major (later Lieutenant Colonel)   29th Canadian Armoured Reconnaissance Regt. (The South Alberta Regt.), Canadian Armoured Corps
Other Decorations: —
Date of Gazette: 27 Nov. 1944
Place/Date of Birth: Sutherland, Saskatchewan, Canada — 8 Jul. 1912
Place/Date of Death: Ottawa — 24 Jun. 1986
Memorials: —
Town/County Connections: —
Remarks: Sergeant-at-Arms of the House of Commons in Ottawa until 1979. Vice-Chairman (Overseas) VC and GC Association. 1968-86
Account of Deed: During the period 18/20 Aug. 1944 at the Battle of Falaise, Normandy, Major Currie was in command of a small mixed force of tanks, self-propelled anti-tank guns and infantry which had been ordered to cut one of the main escape routes. Having attacked the village of St. Lambert-sur-Dives and consolidated a position halfway inside it, for 36 hours he repulsed repeated enemy attacks. Despite heavy casualties Major Currie never considered the possibility of failure and in the final assault 7 enemy tanks, 12 88mm guns and 40 vehicles were destroyed, 300 Germans were killed, 500 wounded and 1,100 captured. The remnants of two German armies were thus denied this escape route.

290

CURTIS, Albert Edward

Private (later Sergeant)   2nd Bn., The East Surrey Regiment
Other Decorations: —
Date of Gazette: 15 Jan. 1901
Place/Date of Birth: Guildford, Surrey — 6 Jan. 1866
Place/Date of Death: Barnet, Hertfordshire — 28 Mar. 1940
Memorials: —
Town/County Connections: Guildford, Surrey; Barnet, Hertfordshire
Remarks: —
Account of Deed: On 23 Feb. 1900 at Onderbank Spruit, South Africa, a colonel lay all day in an open space under close fire from the enemy who fired on any man that moved. The colonel was wounded eight or nine times. Private Curtis after several attempts, managed to reach him, bound his wounds and gave him his own flask, all under heavy fire. He then, with the assistance of another man, tried to move the wounded officer who, fearing that both men would be killed, told them to leave him. This they refused to do, and eventually managed to carry him to safety.

291

CURTIS, Henry

Boatswain's Mate   Royal Navy (Naval Brigade)
Other Decorations: —
Date of Gazette: 24 Feb. 1857
Place/Date of Birth: Romsey, Hampshire — 21 Dec. 1822
Place/Date of Death: Portsmouth, Hampshire — 23 Nov. 1896
Memorials: — *Buried Kingston Cemetery, Portsmouth.*
Town/County Connections: Romsey and Awbridge, Hampshire
Remarks: —
Account of Deed: On 18 Jun. 1855, in the Crimea, immediately after the assault on Sebastopol, a soldier of the 57th Regiment, who had been wounded in both legs, was observed sitting up and calling for help. At once the second-in-command of the scaling party, another seaman* and Boatswain's Mate Curtis left the shelter of their battery works and ran forward a distance of 70 yards, across open ground, through heavy gunfire and succeeded in carrying the wounded man to safety. (*See also RABY, H.J. and TAYLOR, J.)

292

CURTIS, Horace Augustus **293**
Sergeant   2nd Bn., The Royal Dublin Fusiliers
Other Decorations: —
Date of Gazette: 6 Jan. 1919
Place/Date of Birth: St. Anthony-in-Roseland, Cornwall — 7 Mar. 1891
Place/Date of Death: Redruth, Cornwall — 11 Jul. 1968
Memorials: —
Town/County Connections: St. Anthony-in-Roseland and Newlyn, Cornwall
Remarks: —
Account of Deed: On 18 Oct. 1918 east of Le Cateau, France, when his platoon was attacking and came unexpectedly under intense machine-gun fire, Sergeant Curtis realised that the guns must be silenced and went forward through our own barrage and the enemy fire. He killed and wounded the teams of two of the guns, whereupon the remaining four guns surrendered. He then turned his attention to a train loaded with reinforcements and succeeded in capturing 100 of the enemy before his comrades joined him.

CURTIS, Philip Kenneth Edward **294**
Lieutenant   The Duke of Cornwall's Light Infantry, attd. 1st Bn., The Gloucestershire Regt.
Other Decorations: —
Date of Gazette: 1 Dec. 1953
Place/Date of Birth: Devonport, Devon — 7 Jul. 1926
Place/Date of Death: Imjin River, Korea — 23 Apr. 1951
Memorials: United Nations Memorial Cemetery, Pusan, Korea; Memorial to The Gloucestershire Regiment, Korea.
Town/County Connections: Devonport, Devon
Remarks: —
Account of Deed: On 22/23 Apr. 1951 near the Imjin River, Korea, during a heavy enemy attack, No.1 platoon under the command of Lieutenant Curtis, was ordered to carry out a counter-attack which was initially successful, but was eventually held up by heavy fire and grenades. The lieutenant then ordered some of his men to give covering fire while he himself rushed the main position of resistance. In this charge he was severely wounded but he insisted on making a second attempt. While making another desperate charge he was killed when within a few yards of his objective.

CUTLER, Arthur Roden (later Sir Roden) **295**
Lieutenant   2/5th Field Artillery, Australian Military Forces
Other Decorations: KCMG, KCVO, CBE
Date of Gazette: 28 Nov. 1941
Place/Date of Birth: Manly, Sydney, New South Wales, Australia — 24 May 1916
Place/Date of Death: — *About 21.2.2002 probably in Australia.*
Memorials: Australian War Memorial, Canberra
Town/County Connections: —
Remarks: High Commissioner for Australia to New Zealand, 1946-52, to Ceylon, 1952-55; Australian Minister to Egypt, 1955-56; Secretary-General SEATO Conference, 1957; Chief of Protocol, Department of External Affairs, Canberra, 1957-58; State President of RSL (formerly RSSAILA (ACT)), 1958; Australian High Commissioner to Pakistan, 1959-61; Australian Representative to Independence of Somali Republic, 1960; Australian Consul-General, New York, 1961-65; Australian Ambassador to The Netherlands, 1965; Delegate to UN General Assembly and Australian Representative, Fifth Committee, 1962-3-4; Governor, New South Wales, 1966-81; Knight of the Order of St. John; Vice-Chairman (Overseas) VC and GC Association 1986
Account of Deed: During the period 19 Jun./6 Jul. 1941 in the Merdjayoun-Damour area, Syria, the exploits of Lieutenant Cutler included the repair of a telephone line under heavy fire, the repulse of enemy tanks with an anti-tank rifle, the setting up of an outpost to bring under fire a road used by enemy transport, and the demolishing, with a 25-pound field gun, of a post threatening to hold up the British advance. While laying a line to his outpost at Damour, he was seriously wounded, and by the time he was rescued 26 hours later, his leg had to be amputated.

DALTON, James Langley **296**
Acting Assistant Commissary   Commissariat and Transport Department (later Royal Army Service Corps)
Other Decorations: —
Date of Gazette: 17 Nov. 1879
Place/Date of Birth: London — Dec. 1832
Place/Date of Death: Port Elizabeth, South Africa — 8 Jan. 1887
Memorials: Russell Road Cemetery, Port Elizabeth, South Africa
Town/County Connections: London
Remarks: —
Account of Deed: On 22 Jan. 1879 at Rorke's Drift, Natal, South Africa, Acting Assistant Commissary Dalton actively superintended the work of defence and was amongst the foremost of those who received the first attack at the corner of the hospital, where the deadliness of his fire checked the mad rush of the enemy. He saved the life of a man in the Army Hospital Corps by shooting the Zulu who was attacking him. Although wounded himself this officer continued to give the same example of cool courage throughout the action.

DALZIEL, Henry   **297**
Driver (later Sergeant)   15th Bn. (Q & T) Australian Imperial Force
Other Decorations: —
Date of Gazette: 17 Aug. 1918
Place/Date of Birth: Irvinebank, North Queensland, Australia — 18 Feb. 1893
Place/Date of Death: Brisbane, Queensland — 24 Jul. 1965
Memorials: Mt. Thompson Crematorium, Brisbane; Australian War Memorial, Canberra
Town/County Connections: —
Remarks: —
Account of Deed: On 4 Jul. 1918 at Hamel Wood, France, when determined resistance was coming from an enemy strong-point which was also protected by strong wire entanglements, Private Dalziel, armed only with a revolver, attacked an enemy machine-gun. He killed or captured the entire crew and, although severely wounded in the hand, carried on until the final objective was captured. He twice went over open ground under heavy artillery and machine-gun fire to obtain ammunition and, suffering from loss of blood, continued to fill magazines and serve his gun until wounded in the head.

DANAHER, (or DANAGHER) John   **298**
Trooper (later Sergeant)   Nourse's (Transvaal) Horse, South African Forces
Other Decorations: —
Date of Gazette: 14 Mar. 1882
Place/Date of Birth: Limerick, Ireland — 25 Jun. 1860
Place/Date of Death: Ireland — 9 Jan. 1919   *Buried Milton Cemetery, Portsmouth*
Memorials: —
Town/County Connections: Limerick, Ireland
Remarks: —
Account of Deed: On 16 Jan. 1881 at Elandsfontein, near Pretoria, South Africa, Trooper Danaher, with a lance-corporal of the Connaught Rangers* advanced for 500 yards under heavy fire from a party of about 60 of the enemy, and brought out of action a private who had been severely wounded. (*See also MURRAY, James)

DANCOX, Frederick George   **299**
Private   4th Bn., The Worcestershire Regiment
Other Decorations: —
Date of Gazette: 26 Nov. 1917
Place/Date of Birth: Barbourne, Worcester — 1879
Place/Date of Death: Near Masnieres, France — 30 Nov. 1917
Memorials: Cambrai Memorial, France
Town/County Connections: Worcester
Remarks: —   *VC in Guildhall, Worcester*
Account of Deed: On 9 Oct. 1917 at Boesinghe Sector, Belgium, after the first objective had been captured, work was considerably hampered by an enemy machine-gun firing from a concrete emplacement. Private Dancox who was one of a party of 10 detailed as moppers-up, managed to work his way through the barrage and entered the 'pill box' from the rear, threatening the garrison with a Mills bomb. Shortly afterwards he reappeared with a machine-gun under his arm and about 40 of the enemy. He brought the gun back to our position and kept it in action throughout the day.

DANIEL, Edward St. John   **300**
Midshipman (later Lieutenant)   Royal Navy (Naval Brigade)
Other Decorations: —
Date of Gazette: 24 Feb. 1857
Place/Date of Birth: Clifton, Bristol — 17 Jan. 1837
Place/Date of Death: Hokitika, New Zealand — 20 May 1868
Memorials: (Hokitika Municipal Cemetery — unmarked grave)
Town/County Connections: Clifton, Bristol
Remarks: —
Account of Deed: On 18 Oct. 1854 at Sebastopol, Crimea, Midshipman Daniel was one of the volunteers from HMS *Diamond*, who, under the command of the captain* brought in powder to the battery from a waggon under very heavy fire, a shot having disabled the horses. On 5 Nov. at the Battle of Inkerman he, as ADC to the captain, remained by his side throughout a long and dangerous day. On 18 Jun. 1855 he was again with his captain in the first scaling party at the assault on the Redan, binding up his superior officer's severely wounded arm and taking him back to a place of safety. (*See also PEEL, W.)

DANIELS, Harry   301
Company Sergeant-Major (later Lieutenant Colonel)   2nd Bn., The Rifle Brigade (Prince Consort's Own)
Other Decorations: MC
Date of Gazette: 28 Apr. 1915
Place/Date of Birth: Wymondham, Norfolk — 13 Dec. 1884
Place/Date of Death: Leeds, Yorkshire — 13 Dec. 1953
Memorials: Lawnswood Cemetery, Leeds; The Rifle Brigade memorial, Winchester Cathedral
Town/County Connections: Wymondham, Norfolk; Leeds, Yorkshire
Remarks: Chief Recruiting Officer, North Western Division 1933-42
Account of Deed: On 12 Mar. 1915 at Neuve Chapelle, France, when the advance of the battalion was impeded by wire entanglements and by very severe machine-gun fire, Company Sergeant-Major Daniels and another man* voluntarily rushed in front and succeeded in cutting the wires. They were both wounded at once, and the other man later died of his wounds. (*See also NOBLE, C.R.)

D'ARCY, Henry Cecil Dudgeon   302
Captain (later Commandant)   Cape Frontier Light Horse, South African Forces
Other Decorations: —
Date of Gazette: 9 Oct. 1879
Place/Date of Birth: Wanganui, New Zealand — 11 Aug. 1850
Place/Date of Death: Amatola Forest, Cape Province, South Africa — Oct. 1881
Memorials: —
Town/County Connections: —
Remarks: —
Account of Deed: On 3 Jul. 1879 at Ulundi, South Africa (Zulu War), during a reconnaissance, Captain D'Arcy went to the rescue of a trooper of the Frontier Light Horse who had fallen from his horse as the troops were retiring. The captain waited for the man to mount behind him although the enemy were quite close, but the horse kicked them both off. Captain D'Arcy was hurt by the fall, and quite alone, but he still tried to lift the trooper, who was stunned, on to the horse, and only mounted and rode off when he was completely exhausted.

DARTNELL, Wilbur Taylor   303
T/Lieutenant   25th (S) Bn., The Royal Fusiliers
Other Decorations: —
Date of Gazette: 23 Dec. 1915
Place/Date of Birth: Fitzroy, Melbourne, Australia — 6 Apr. 1885
Place/Date of Death: Maktau, East Africa — 3 Sep. 1915
Memorials: Voi Cemetery, Kenya, Africa; Australian War Memorial, Canberra; plaque in foyer of Covent Garden Theatre, London
Town/County Connections: —
Remarks: —
Account of Deed: On 3 Sep. 1915, near Maktau, East Africa, during a mounted infantry engagement, the enemy were so close that it was impossible to get the more severely wounded away. Lieutenant Dartnell, who was himself being carried away wounded in the leg, seeing the situation, and knowing that the enemy's black troops murdered the wounded, insisted on being left behind, in the hope of being able to save the lives of other wounded men. He gave his own life in a gallant attempt to save others.

DARWAN SING NEGI,   304
Naik (later Subadar)   1st Bn., 39th Garhwal Rifles, Indian Army
Other Decorations: —
Date of Gazette: 7 Dec. 1914
Place/Date of Birth: Kafartir, Karakot, United Provinces, India — Nov. 1881
Place/Date of Death: Kafartir, Karakot — 24 Jun. 1950
Memorials: —
Town/County Connections: —
Remarks: PVSM (India)
Account of Deed: On the night on 23/24 Nov. 1914 at Festubert, France, the regiment was engaged in retaking and clearing the enemy out of our trenches. In this very dangerous operation Naik Darwan Sing Negi was the first to push round every traverse. Although he was wounded in the head and in the arm, he kept on going forward in the face of heavy fire from bombs and rifles at very close range.

DAUNT, John Charles Campbell   **305**
Lieutenant (later Colonel)   11th Bengal Native Infantry
Other Decorations: —
Date of Gazette: 25 Feb. 1862
Place/Date of Birth: Autranches, Normandy — 8 Nov. 1832
Place/Date of Death: Bristol — 15 Apr. 1886
Memorials: —
Town/County Connections: Brighton, Sussex
Remarks: —
Account of Deed: On 2 Oct. 1857 at Chota Behar, India, Lieutenant Daunt, with a sergeant* acted with conspicuous gallantry in the capture of two guns, particularly the second which they rushed and took, pistolling the gunners who were mowing down the detachment, one third of which was *hors de combat* at the time. On 2 Nov. the lieutenant chased mutineers across a plain into a richly cultivated area. He was dangerously wounded while attempting to drive out a large body of these rebels from an enclosure. (*See also DYNON, D.)

DAVEY, Philip   **306**
Corporal   10th Bn. (S.A.), Australian Imperial Force
Other Decorations: MM
Date of Gazette: 17 Aug. 1918
Place/Date of Birth: Goodwood, South Australia — 10 Oct. 1896
Place/Date of Death: Adelaide, South Australia — 21 Dec. 1953
Memorials: AIF Cemetery, Adelaide, Australian War Memorial, Canberra
Town/County Connections: —
Remarks: —
Account of Deed: On 28 Jun. 1918, at Merris, France, when an enemy machine-gun was causing heavy casualties, Corporal Davey moved forward in the face of fierce point-blank fire, and attacked the gun with hand grenades, putting half the crew out of action. Having used all available grenades, he fetched a further supply and again attacked the gun, the crew of which had meantime been reinforced. He killed all eight of the crew and captured the gun, which he then used to repel a determined counter-attack, during which he was severely wounded.

DAVIES, James Llewellyn   **307**
Corporal   13th Bn., The Royal Welch Fusiliers
Other Decorations: —
Date of Gazette: 6 Sep. 1917
Place/Date of Birth: Nantymoel, Glamorganshire, Wales — 16 Mar. 1886
Place/Date of Death: Pilkem, Belgium — 31 Jul. 1917   *Elverdinge Plot 2. Row B. G. 18*
Memorials: Canada Farm Cemetery, Belgium
Town/County Connections: Nantymoel, Glamorganshire
Remarks: — *Name on Nantymoel W.M.   VC in RWF Museum. Caernarvon*
Account of Deed: On 31 Jul. 1917 at Polygon Wood, Pilkem, Belgium, during an attack on the enemy line, Corporal Davies, single-handed, attacked a machine-gun emplacement after several men had been killed in attempting to take it. He bayoneted one of the gun crew and brought in another, together with a captured gun. Then, although wounded, he led a bombing party to the assault of a defended house and killed a sniper who was harassing his platoon. He died of his wounds the same day.

DAVIES, John Thomas   **308**
Corporal   11th (S) Bn., The South Lancashire Regt. (The Prince of Wales's Volunteers)
Other Decorations: —
Date of Gazette: 22 May 1918
Place/Date of Birth: Rockferry, Cheshire — 29 Sep. 1896
Place/Date of Death: St. Helens, Lancashire — 28 Oct. 1955
Memorials: —
Town/County Connections: Rockferry, Cheshire; St. Helens, Lancashire
Remarks: —
Account of Deed: On 24 Mar. 1918 near Eppeville, France, when his company was ordered to withdraw, Corporal Davies knew that the only line of withdrawal lay through a deep stream lined with a belt of barbed wire and that it was imperative to hold up the enemy as long as possible. He mounted the parapet in full view of the enemy in order to get a more effective field of fire and kept his Lewis gun in action to the last, causing many enemy casualties and enabling part of his company to get across the river, which they would otherwise have been unable to do.

DAVIES, Joseph John **309**
Corporal (later Staff-Sergeant)   10th Bn., The Royal Welch Fusiliers
Other Decorations: —
Date of Gazette: 26 Sep. 1916
Place/Date of Birth: Tipton, Staffordshire — 28 Apr. 1889
Place/Date of Death: Bournemouth, Hampshire — 23 Feb. 1976
Memorials: (Cremated, Bournemouth) Davies Court, Hightown, Wrexham, Wales
Town/County Connections: Tipton, Staffordshire; Parkstone, Dorset
Remarks: Order of St. George, 1st Class (Russia)   *VC in RWF Museum, Caernarvon.*
Account of Deed: On 20 Jul. 1916 at Delville Wood, France, prior to an attack on the enemy, Corporal Davies and eight men became separated from the rest of the company. When the enemy delivered their second counter-attack, the party was completely surrounded, but Corporal Davies got his men into a shell hole and by throwing bombs and opening rapid fire he succeeded in routing the attackers, and even followed and bayoneted them in their retreat.

DAVIES, Llewellyn Alberic Emilius PRICE- **310**
Lieutenant (later Major General)   The King's Royal Rifle Corps
Other Decorations: CB, CMG, DSO
Date of Gazette: 29 Nov. 1901
Place/Date of Birth: Chirbury, Shropshire — 30 Jun. 1878   *Born Marrington Hall*
Place/Date of Death: Sonning, Berkshire — 26 Dec. 1965   *at Cordon*
Memorials: St. Andrew's Church, Sonning, Berkshire; KRRC memorial, Winchester Cathedral
Town/County Connections: Chirbury, Shropshire; Sonning, Berkshire
Remarks: Served in First World War, 1914-18; President, Standing Committee of Enquiry regarding Prisoners of War, 1918-19; ADC to The King 1920-30; Assistant Adjutant-General, Aldershot Command, 1920-24; Commanded 145th Infantry Brigade, 1924-27; Assistant Adjutant and Quarter Master General, Gibraltar, 1927-30; Member of the Hon. Corps of Gentlemen-at-Arms, 1933-48; Battalion Commander, Upper Thames Patrol (Home Guard) 1940-45.   *VC in KRRC Museum. Winchester*
Account of Deed: On 17 Sep. 1901 at Blood River Poort, South Africa the Boers had overwhelmed the right of the British column and some 400 of them were galloping round the flank and rear of the guns calling on the drivers to surrender them. Lieutenant Price-Davies, hearing an order to fire on the charging Boers, at once drew his revolver and dashed upon them in a desperate attempt to rescue the guns. He was immediately shot and knocked off his horse, but was not mortally wounded although he had ridden to what seemed certain death.

DAVIES, Richard Bell **311**
Squadron Commander (later Vice-Admiral)   Royal Navy (3 Squadron, Royal Naval Air Service)
Other Decorations: CB, DSO, AFC
Date of Gazette: 1 Jan. 1916
Place/Date of Birth: Kensington, London — 19 May 1886
Place/Date of Death: Haslar, Hampshire — 26 Feb. 1966
Memorials: (Cremated Swaythling Crematorium, Hampshire)
Town/County Connections: Kensington, London; Lee-on-Solent, Hampshire
Remarks: Croix de Guerre avec Palme and Légion d'Honneur (France); Rear-Admiral, Naval Air Stations, 1937-41; author of *Sailor in the Air.*   *Bradfield, Berks*
Account of Deed: On 19 Nov. 1915 while carrying out an air attack at Ferrijik Junction, Bulgaria, one of the planes engaged in the bombing mission was brought down, the pilot making a safe landing. Seeing, however, that Bulgarian troops were approaching, he set fire to his aircraft. He then realised that Squadron Commander Davies was preparing to land to rescue him, so he detonated the last bomb on the burning aircraft, with a pistol shot, in case it should blow up as the rescue plane approached. The squadron commander landed as near as possible to the stranded pilot, picking him up just as the enemy came within rifle range.

DAVIS, Gronow **312**
Captain (later Major General)   Royal Regiment of Artillery
Other Decorations: —
Date of Gazette: 23 Jun. 1857
Place/Date of Birth: Bristol — 16 May 1828
Place/Date of Death: Clifton, Bristol — 18 Oct. 1891
Memorials: —
Town/County Connections: Clifton, Bristol
Remarks: —
Account of Deed: On 8 Sep. 1855 at Sebastopol, Crimea, Captain Davis commanded the spiking party in the attack on the Redan with great coolness and gallantry. Afterwards he saved the life of a lieutenant of the 39th Regiment by jumping over the parapet of a sap and going some distance across the open, under murderous fire, to help carry the wounded man to cover. He also carried several other wounded soldiers to safety.

DAVIS, (real name James Davis KELLY) James **313**
Private   42nd Regt. (later The Black Watch (Royal Highlanders))
Other Decorations: —
Date of Gazette: 27 May 1859
Place/Date of Birth: Edinburgh — Feb. 1835
Place/Date of Death: Edinburgh — 2 Mar. 1893
Memorials: —
Town/County Connections: Edinburgh
Remarks: —
Account of Deed: On 15 Apr. 1858 during the attack on Fort Ruhya, India, Private Davis, who was with an advanced party, offered to carry back to the regiment the body of a lieutenant who had been killed at the gate of the fort. He performed this gallant act under the very walls of the fort.

DAWSON, James Lennox **314**
Corporal (later Colonel)   187th Coy., Corps of Royal Engineers
Other Decorations: —
Date of Gazette: 7 Dec. 1915
Place/Date of Birth: Tillycoultry, Clackmannanshire, Scotland — 25 Dec. 1891
Place/Date of Death: Eastbourne, Sussex — 15 Feb. 1967
Memorials: —
Town/County Connections: Tillycoultry, Clackmannanshire; Eastbourne, Sussex
Remarks: Cousin of Corporal J.D. Pollock, VC
Account of Deed: On 13 Oct. 1915 at Hohenzollern Redoubt, France, during a gas attack, when the trenches were full of men, Corporal Dawson exposed himself fearlessly to the enemy's fire in order to give directions to his sappers and to clear the infantry out of sections of the trench which were full of gas. Finding three leaking cylinders, he rolled them well away from the trench, again under heavy fire, and then fired rifle bullets into them to let the gas escape. His gallantry undoubtedly saved many men from being gassed.

DAY, George Fiott **315**
Lieutenant (later Captain) Royal Navy
Other Decorations: CB
Date of Gazette: 24 Feb. 1857
Place/Date of Birth: Southampton, Hampshire — 20 Jun. 1819
Place/Date of Death: Weston-super-Mare, Somerset — 18 Dec. 1876
Memorials: Weston-super-Mare Cemetery
Town/County Connections: Southampton, Hants.; Weston-super Mare, Som.
Remarks: Légion d'Honneur (France); Order of Medjidie, 5th Class (Turkey)
Account of Deed: On 17 Sep. 1855 at Genitichi, Crimea, Lieutenant Day of HMS *Recruit* was put ashore from a rowing boat to reconnoitre the bridge, batteries and enemy gun boats on the Spit of Arabat. He went alone and after covering four or five miles of swampy ground, sometimes up to his thighs in water, he got to within 200 yards of the enemy position, where he found that the gun boats appeared to be under-manned and lightly defended. He returned to his ship convinced that a surprise attack was possible, but had to abandon this plan when he returned on 19 Sep. and found the enemy on the alert and the gun boats fully manned.

DAY, Sidney James **316**
Corporal   11th Bn., The Suffolk Regiment
Other Decorations: —
Date of Gazette: 17 Oct. 1917
Place/Date of Birth: Norwich — 3 Jul. 1891
Place/Date of Death: Portsmouth, Hampshire — 17 Jul. 1959 *Buried Milton Cemetery. Portsmouth*
Memorials: —
Town/County Connections: Norwich; Portsmouth, Hants.
Remarks: —
Account of Deed: On 26 Aug. 1917 east of Hargicourt, France, Corporal Day was in command of a bombing section detailed to clear a maze of trenches still held by the enemy; this he did, killing two machine gunners and taking four prisoners. Immediately after he returned to his section a stick bomb fell into a trench occupied by five men, one badly wounded. The corporal seized the bomb and threw it over the trench where it immediately exploded. He afterwards completed the clearing of the trench and established himself in an advanced position, remaining for 66 hours at his post which came under intense fire.

DAYKINS, John Brunton 317

A/Sergeant   2/4th Bn., The York and Lancaster Regiment
Other Decorations: —
Date of Gazette: 6 Jan. 1919
Place/Date of Birth: Ormiston, Roxburgh, Scotland — 26 Mar. 1883
Place/Date of Death: Jedburgh, Scotland — 24 Jan. 1933
Memorials: —
Town/County Connections: Jedburgh, Scotland
Remarks: —
Account of Deed: On 20 Oct. 1918 at Solesmes, France, Sergeant Daykins, with 12 remaining men of his platoon, rushed a machine-gun and during subsequent severe hand-to-hand fighting he himself disposed of many of the enemy and secured his objective. He then located another machine-gun which was holding up an operation of his company. Under heavy fire he worked his way alone to the post and shortly afterwards returned with 25 prisoners and an enemy machine-gun, which he mounted at his post. His magnificent fighting spirit and example inspired his men, saved many casualties and contributed largely to the success of the attack.

DEAN, Donald John 318

T/Lieutenant (later Colonel)   8th Bn., The Queen's Own Royal West Kent Regiment
Other Decorations: OBE
Date of Gazette: 14 Dec. 1918
Place/Date of Birth: London — 19 Apr. 1897
Place/Date of Death: Sittingbourne, Kent — 9 Dec. 1985
Memorials: —
Town/County Connections: Herne Hill, London; Sittingbourne, Kent
Remarks: Commander, Royal Danish Order of the Dannebrog; OC No.5 Group Auxiliary Pioneer Corps, France, 1940; DL, County of Kent
Account of Deed: During the period 24/26 Sep. 1918 north-west of Lens, France, Lieutenant Dean with his platoon held an advance post established in a newly-captured enemy trench. The post was ill-prepared for defence and the lieutenant worked unceasingly with his men consolidating the position, under very heavy fire. Five times in all the post was attacked and on each occasion the attack was repulsed. Throughout the whole of this time Lieutenant Dean inspired his command with his own contempt of danger and set the highest example of valour, leadership and devotion to duty.

DEAN, Percy Thompson 319

Lieutenant (later Lieutenant-Commander)   Royal Naval Volunteer Reserve
Other Decorations: —
Date of Gazette: 23 Jul. 1918
Place/Date of Birth: Blackburn, Lancashire — 20 Jul. 1877
Place/Date of Death: London — 20 Mar. 1939
Memorials: —
Town/County Connections: Blackburn, Lancashire; London
Remarks: Member of Parliament for Blackburn, 1918-22
Account of Deed: On 22 and 23 Apr. 1918 at Zeebrugge, Belgium, after *Intrepid* and *Iphigenia* had been scuttled, their crews were taken off by Motor Launch 282 commanded by Lieutenant Dean. He embarked more than 100 officers and men under constant and deadly fire from heavy and machine-guns at point blank range. This complete, he was about to clear the canal when the steering gear broke down, so he manoeuvred on his engines and was actually clear of the entrance to the harbour when he was told there was an officer in the water. He immediately turned back and rescued him.

DEASE, Maurice James 320

Lieutenant   4th Bn., The Royal Fusiliers
Other Decorations: —
Date of Gazette: 16 Nov. 1914
Place/Date of Birth: Coole, Co. West Meath, Ireland — 28 Sep. 1889
Place/Date of Death: Mons, Belgium — 23 Aug. 1914
Memorials: St. Symphorien Military Cemetery, Belgium; plaque on Nimy Bridge, Mons; Westminster Cathedral
Town/County Connections: Coole, Co. West Meath   *Stoneyhurst College, Lans*
Remarks: First VC of the First World War
Account of Deed: On 23 Aug. 1914 at Mons, Belgium, Nimy Bridge was being defended by a single company of Royal Fusiliers and a machine-gun section with Lieutenant Dease in command. The gun fire was intense, and the casualties very heavy, but the lieutenant went on firing in spite of his wounds, until he was hit for the fifth time and was carried away to a place of safety where he died. A private* of the same battalion who had been assisting the lieutenant while he was still able to operate the guns, took over, and alone he used the gun to such good effect that he covered the retreat of his comrades. (*See also GODLEY, S.F.)

Name on W.M. Exton Rutland. Memorial sited by village green was erected by 3rd Earl of Gainsborough in memory of his son Tom Noel and others. Friends and neighbours, Maurice Dease being one. (Dease was Lady Gainsborough's nephew)

DE L'ISLE, Viscount — see **SIDNEY,** William Philip

DE MONTMORENCY, The Hon. Raymond Harvey Lodge Joseph　　**321**
Lieutenant (later Captain)　21st Lancers, (Empress of India's)
Other Decorations: —
Date of Gazette: 15 Nov. 1898
Place/Date of Birth: Montreal, Canada — 5 Feb. 1867
Place/Date of Death: Dordrecht, Cape Colony, South Africa — 23 Feb. 1900
Memorials: —
Town/County Connections: — *Dewlish, Dorset*
Remarks: —
Account of Deed: On 2 Sep. 1898 at the Battle of Khartoum, Sudan, after the charge, Lieutenant
De Montmorency returned to help a second lieutenant who was lying surrounded by a great many
Dervishes. The lieutenant drove the Dervishes off and, finding that the officer was dead, put the body on his horse which then
broke away. Another lieutenant* and a corporal then came to his assistance and he was able to rejoin the regiment which had
begun to open fire on the enemy. (*See also KENNA, P.A.)

DEMPSEY, Denis　　**322**
Private　1st Bn., 10th Regiment (later The Lincolnshire Regiment)
Other Decorations: —
Date of Gazette: 17 Feb. 1860
Place/Date of Birth: Rathmichael, Bray, Co. Dublin — 1826
Place/Date of Death: Toronto, Canada — 10 Jan. 1896
Memorials: —
Town/County Connections: Bray, Dublin
Remarks: —
Account of Deed: On 12 Aug. 1857 at Lucknow, India, Private Dempsey carried a powder-bag
through a burning village for the purpose of mining a passage in the rear of the enemy's position.
During this time he was exposed to very heavy fire and to a still greater danger from the sparks which flew from the blazing
houses. He was the first man to enter the village of Jugdispore on that day under most galling fire. On 14 Mar. 1858 in the retreat
from Arrah, he helped to carry an ensign who was mortally wounded, for two miles.

de PASS, Frank Alexander　　**323**
Lieutenant　34th Prince Albert Victor's Own Poona Horse, Indian Army
Other Decorations: —
Date of Gazette: 18 Feb. 1915
Place/Date of Birth: London — 26 Apr. 1887
Place/Date of Death: Festubert, France — 25 Nov. 1914
Memorials: Bethune Town Cemetery, France
Town/County Connections: Kensington, London
Remarks: — *Rugby School.*
Account of Deed: On 24 Nov. 1914 near Festubert, France, Lieutenant de Pass entered a German
sap and destroyed a traverse in the face of the enemy's bombs. Subsequently he rescued, under
heavy fire, a wounded man who was lying exposed to enemy bullets in the open. Lieutenant de Pass lost his life in a second
attempt to capture the sap which had been reoccupied by the enemy.

DERRICK, Thomas Currie　　**324**
Sergeant (later Lieutenant)　2/48th Bn. (S.A.), Australian Military Forces
Other Decorations: DCM
Date of Gazette: 23 Mar. 1944
Place/Date of Birth: Berri, Murray River, South Australia — 20 Mar. 1914
Place/Date of Death: Tarakan, Borneo — 23 May 1945
Memorials: Labuan War Cemetery, North Borneo; Australian War Memorial, Canberra
Town/County Connections: —
Remarks: —
Account of Deed: On 24 Nov. 1943 in New Guinea, South-west Pacific, Sergeant Derrick's
platoon was ordered to take a slope by storm and then attack a point 150 yards from the township
of Sattelberg. After two hours of fruitless attempts under intense fire from the enemy posts, the company was ordered to retire,
but Sergeant Derrick, obtaining permission to make one last attempt, advanced alone and with grenades so demoralized the
enemy that they fled leaving all their weapons. He then went on to deal with the remaining posts in the area, and was so
successful that the battalion was able to capture Sattleberg the following day.

DEVEREUX, James — see **GORMAN,** James

DE WIND, Edmund   **325**
Second Lieutenant   15th Bn., The Royal Irish Rifles
Other Decorations: —
Date of Gazette: 15 May 1919
Place/Date of Birth: Comber, Co. Down, Ireland — 11 Dec. 1883
Place/Date of Death: Near Groagie, France — 21 Mar. 1918
Memorials: Pozieres Memorial, France; Mount De Wind, Alberta, Canada
Town/County Connections: Comber, Co. Down
Remarks: —
Account of Deed: On 21 Mar. 1918, at the Racecourse Redoubt, near Groagie, France, for seven hours Second Lieutenant De Wind held this important post and though twice wounded and practically single-handed, he maintained his position until another section could be sent to his help. On two occasions, with two NCOs only, he got out on top under heavy machine-gun and rifle fire and cleared the enemy out of the trench, killing many of them. He continued to repel attack after attack until he was mortally wounded and collapsed.

DIAMOND, Bernard   **326**
Sergeant   Bengal Horse Artillery
Other Decorations: —
Date of Gazette: 24 Apr. 1858
Place/Date of Birth: Port Glenone, Co. Antrim, Ireland — 1827
Place/Date of Death: Masterton, New Zealand — 24 Jan. 1892
Memorials: —
Town/County Connections: Port Glenone, Co. Antrim
Remarks: —
Account of Deed: On 28 Sep. 1857 at Bolandshahr, India, Sergeant Diamond and a gunner* worked their gun after every other man belonging to it had been either killed or wounded. They performed the action under very heavy fire of musketry, and thereby cleared the road of the enemy. (*See also FITZGERALD, R.)

DIARMID (formerly DREW) Allastair Malcolm Cluny McREADY-(formerly Arthur   **327**
Malcolm Cluny McREADY-)
A/Captain   17th (S) Bn., The Middlesex Regiment (Duke of Cambridge's Own)
Other Decorations: —
Date of Gazette: 15 Mar. 1918
Place/Date of Birth: Southgate, London — 21 Mar. 1888
Place/Date of Death: Moeuvres, France — 1 Dec. 1917
Memorials: Cambrai Memorial, France
Town/County Connections: Southgate and Acton, London; Dursley, Gloucestershire
Remarks: —
Account of Deed: On 30 Nov./1 Dec. 1917 at the Moeuvres Sector, France, when the enemy penetrated into our position, and the situation was extremely critical, Captain McReady-Diarmid led his company through a heavy barrage and immediately engaged the enemy and drove them back at least 300 yards, causing numerous casualties and taking 27 prisoners. The following day the enemy again attacked and drove back another company which had lost all its officers. The captain called for volunteers, and leading the attack, again drove them back. It was entirely due to his marvellous throwing of bombs that the ground was regained, but he was eventually killed by a bomb.

DICK-CUNYNGHAM, William Henry — see **CUNYNGHAM,** William Henry DICK-

DICKSON, Collingwood (later Sir Collingwood)   **328**
Lieutenant Colonel (later General)   Royal Regiment of Artillery
Other Decorations: GCB
Date of Gazette: 23 Jun. 1857
Place/Date of Birth: Valenciennes, France — 20 Nov. 1817
Place/Date of Death: London — 28 Nov. 1904
Memorials: Kensal Green Cemetery, London   *Name on Monument outside Woolwich Barracks*
Town/County Connections: London
Remarks: Inspector-General of Artillery, 1870-75; Colonel-Commandant, Royal Regiment of Artillery, 1875
Account of Deed: On 17 Oct. 1854 in the Crimea, when the batteries had run short of powder, Lieutenant Colonel Dickson displayed great coolness and contempt of danger in directing the unloading of several waggons of the field battery which were brought up to the trenches to supply the want. He personally helped to carry the powder-barrels under heavy fire from the enemy.

DIGBY-JONES, Robert James Thomas — see **JONES,** Robert James Thomas DIGBY-

DIMMER, John Henry Stephen   **329**
Lieutenant (later Lieutenant Colonel)   2nd Bn., The King's Royal Rifle Corps
Other Decorations: MC
Date of Gazette: 19 Nov. 1914
Place/Date of Birth: Wimbledon, Surrey — 9 Oct. 1883   *Trinity Road*
Place/Date of Death: Marteville, France — 21 Mar. 1918
Memorials: Vadencourt British Cemetery, France; KRRC Memorial, Winchester Cathedral
Town/County Connections: Wimbledon and Merton, Surrey
Remarks: —   *Name on Peace Memorial Putney Vale*
Account of Deed: On 12 Nov. 1914 at Klein Zillebeke, Belgium, Lieutenant Dimmer went on
serving his machine-gun during an attack, and stayed at his post until the gun was destroyed, in
spite of being shot five times.

DINESEN, Thomas   **330**
Private (later Lieutenant)   42nd Bn., Quebec Regiment (Royal Highlanders of Canada)
Other Decorations: —
Date of Gazette: 26 Oct. 1918
Place/Date of Birth: Copenhagen, Denmark — 9 Aug. 1892
Place/Date of Death: Leerbaek, Denmark — 10 Mar. 1979
Memorials: —
Town/County Connections: —   *Brother of Karen Blixen (Out of Africa)*
Remarks: Croix de Guerre (France); author of *No Man's Land* (translated from Danish into
English under the title *Merry Hell*), and *Twilight on the Betz*
Account of Deed: On 12 Aug. 1918 at Parvillers, France, Private Dinesen displayed conspicuous
bravery during 10 hours of hand-to-hand fighting which resulted in the capture of over a mile of strongly defended enemy
trenches. Five times in succession he rushed forward alone and put hostile guns out of action, accounting for 12 of the enemy
with bomb and bayonet. His sustained valour inspired his comrades at a very critical stage of the action.

DIVANE, (or DEVINE) John   **331**
Private   1st Bn., 60th Rifles (later The King's Royal Rifle Corps)
Other Decorations: —
Date of Gazette: 20 Jan. 1860
Place/Date of Birth: Canavane, Loughrea, Galway, Ireland — Nov. 1822
Place/Date of Death: Penzance, Cornwall — 1 Dec. 1888
Memorials: —
Town/County Connections: Loughrea, Galway
Remarks: —
Account of Deed: On 10 Sep. 1857 at Delhi, India, Private Divane headed a successful charge by
the Beeloochee and Sikh troops on one of the enemy's trenches. He leapt out of our trenches,
closely followed by the native troops and was shot down from the top of the enemy's breastworks. (Elected by the regiment.)

DIXON, Matthew Charles   **332**
Captain (later Major General)   Royal Regiment of Artillery
Other Decorations: CB
Date of Gazette: 24 Feb. 1857
Place/Date of Birth: Avranches, Brittany — 5 Feb. 1821
Place/Date of Death: Pembury, Kent — 7 Jan. 1905
Memorials: Kensal Green Cemetery, London
Town/County Connections: Pembury, Kent
Remarks: —
Account of Deed: On 17 Apr. 1855 in the Crimea, at about 2pm the battery commanded by
Captain Dixon was blown up by a shell from the enemy which burst in the magazine, destroying
the parapets, killing or wounding 10 men, disabling five guns and covering a sixth with earth. The captain reopened fire with
the remaining gun and continued firing it until sunset, despite the heavy concentration of fire from the enemy's batteries and
the ruined state of his own.

DOBSON, Claude Congreve
Commander (later Rear-Admiral)   Royal Navy
Other Decorations: DSO
Date of Gazette: 11 Nov. 1919
Place/Date of Birth: Barton Regis, Bristol — 1 Jan. 1885
Place/Date of Death: Chatham, Kent — 26 Jun. 1940
Memorials: Gillingham Cemetery, Kent
Town/County Connections: Barton Regis, Bristol; Walmer, Kent.
Remarks: Served with the Royal Australian Navy 1922-25.
Account of Deed: On 18 Aug. 1919 at Kronstadt, Russia, Commander Dobson was in command of the Coastal Motor Boat Flotilla which he led through the chain of forts to the entrance to the harbour. CMB.31 from which he directed the general operations then passed in under heavy machine-gun fire and torpedoed the battleship *Andrei Pervozvanni*, subsequently returning through heavy fire to the open sea. (See also STEELE, G.C.)

DOBSON, Frederick William
Private (later Lance-Corporal)   2nd Bn., Coldstream Guards
Other Decorations: —
Date of Gazette: 9 Dec. 1914
Place/Date of Birth: Nafferton, Stocksfield-on-Tyne, Northumberland — 9 Nov. 1886
Place/Date of Death: Newcastle-upon-Tyne, Northumberland — 15 Nov. 1935
Memorials: Ryton Cemetery, Co. Durham
Town/County Connections: Ovingham, Newcastle-upon-Tyne, Northumberland
Remarks: —
Account of Deed: On 28 Sep. 1914 at Chavanne, Aisne, France, Private Dobson twice volunteered to go out under heavy fire to bring in two wounded men. This undertaking involved crossing a good deal of open ground in full view of the enemy. Private Dobson, however, crawled out and found one of the men dead and the other wounded. He dressed the wounds and then crawled back, to return with a corporal and a stretcher, on to which they put the wounded man and then dragged him back to safety.

DONNINI, Dennis
Fusilier   4/5th Bn., The Royal Scots Fusiliers
Other Decorations: —
Date of Gazette: 20 Mar. 1945
Place/Date of Birth: Easington, Co. Durham — 17 Nov. 1925
Place/Date of Death: River Roer, Holland — 18 Jan. 1945
Memorials: Sittard War Cemetery, Limburg, Holland
Town/County Connections: Easington, Co. Durham
Remarks: —
Account of Deed: On 18 Jan. 1945 between the rivers Roer and Maas, Holland, Fusilier Donnini's platoon was ordered to attack a small village. On leaving their trench they immediately came under heavy fire from a house and the fusilier was hit in the head. After recovering consciouness he charged 30 yards down the open road and hurled a grenade through the nearest window, whereupon the enemy fled pursued by Fusilier Donnini and the survivors of his platoon. He was wounded a second time, but continued firing his Bren gun until he was killed. His gallantry had enabled his comrades to overcome twice their own number of the enemy.

No photograph available

DONOHOE, Patrick
Private   9th Lancers (The Queen's Royal)
Other Decorations: —
Date of Gazette: 24 Dec. 1858
Place/Date of Birth: Nenagh, Co. Tipperary, Ireland — 1820
Place/Date of Death: Ashbourne, Co. Meath, Ireland — 16 Aug. 1876
Memorials: —
Town/County Connections: Nenagh, Co. Tipperary
Remarks: —
Account of Deed: On 28 Sep. 1857 at Bolandshahr, India, Private Donohoe went to the assistance of a lieutenant who was severely wounded, and with some other men he brought that officer to safety through a large body of the enemy's cavalry.

DOOGAN, John   **337**
Private   1st Dragoon Guards (The King's)
Other Decorations: —
Date of Gazette: 14 Mar. 1882
Place/Date of Birth: Aughrim, Co. Galway, Ireland — Mar. 1853
Place/Date of Death: Folkestone, Kent — 24 Jan. 1940
Memorials: Military Cemetery, Shorncliffe, Kent
Town/County Connections: Cork, Ireland; Folkestone, Kent
Remarks: —
Account of Deed: On 28 Jan. 1881 at Laing's Nek, South Africa, during the charge of the mounted men, Private Doogan saw an officer to whom he was servant dismounted and in danger among the Boers because his horse had been shot. Private Doogan rode up, although he was himself severely wounded, dismounted and pressed the officer to take his horse, receiving another wound while doing so.

DORRELL, George Thomas   **338**
Battery Sergeant-Major (later Lieutenant Colonel)   'L' Bty., Royal Horse Artillery
Other Decorations: MBE
Date of Gazette: 16 Nov. 1914
Place/Date of Birth: Paddington, London — 7 Jul. 1880
Place/Date of Death: Cobham, Surrey — 7 Jan. 1971
Memorials: —
Town/County Connections: Paddington, London
Remarks: Served with the Home Guard 1940-45
Account of Deed: On 1 Sep. 1914 at Nery, France, during a fierce attack by the enemy, all the officers of 'L' Battery were either killed or wounded, including the officer* in command, who, although having had one leg taken off by a shell, continued to direct the firing until he died. Battery Sergeant-Major Dorrell then took over command with the support of a sergeant* and continued to fire one of the guns until all the ammunition was expended. (*See also BRADBURY, E.K. and NELSON, D.)

DOUGALL, Eric Stuart   **339**
A/Captain   Special Reserve, attd. 'A' Bty., 88th Bde., Royal Field Artillery
Other Decorations: MC
Date of Gazette: 4 Jun. 1918
Place/Date of Birth: Tunbridge Wells, Kent — 13 Apr. 1886
Place/Date of Death: Kemmel, Belgium — 14 Apr. 1918
Memorials: Westoutre British Cemetery, Belgium
Town/County Connections: Tunbridge Wells, Kent.
Remarks: — _Tonbridge School._
Account of Deed: On 10 Apr. 1918 at Messines, Belgium, Captain Dougall, on the withdrawal of our line, ran his guns to the top of the ridge to fire over open sights. By now the infantry had been pressed back in line with the guns, so Captain Dougall supplied them with Lewis guns and armed some of his gunners with rifles. He managed to maintain the line throughout the day, thereby delaying the German advance for over 12 hours, and when his battery was at last ordered to withdraw, the guns were manhandled over half a mile of shell-cratered country under intense machine-gun fire.

DOUGHTY-WYLIE, Charles Hotham Montagu — see **WYLIE,** Charles Hotham Montagu DOUGHTY-

DOUGLAS, Campbell Mellis   **340**
Assistant Surgeon (later Lieutenant Colonel)   2nd Bn., 24th Regiment (later The South Wales Borderers)
Other Decorations: Silver Medal of the Royal Humane Society
Date of Gazette: 17 Dec. 1867
Place/Date of Birth: Quebec, Canada — 5 Aug. 1840
Place/Date of Death: Horrington, near Wells, Somerset — 31 Dec. 1909
Memorials: — _Buried Wells Cemetery_  _VC at Camp Bordon Military Museum_
Town/County Connections: Dunmow, Essex
Remarks: VC not awarded for bravery in action against the enemy, but for bravery at sea in saving life in storm off Andaman Islands
Account of Deed: On 7 May 1867 at the island of Little Andaman, Bay of Bengal, Assistant Surgeon Douglas and four Privates* of the 2/24th Regiment risked their lives in manning a boat and proceeding through dangerous surf to rescue some of their comrades who had been sent to the island to find out the fate of the commander and seven of the crew, who had landed from the ship _Assam Valley_ and were feared murdered by the cannibalistic islanders. (*See also BELL, David, COOPER, J., GRIFFITHS, W. and MURPHY, T.)

DOUGLAS, Henry Edward Manning   **341**
Lieutenant (later Major General)   Royal Army Medical Corps
Other Decorations: CB, CMG, DSO
Date of Gazette: 29 Mar. 1901
Place/Date of Birth: Gillingham, Kent — 11 Jul. 1875
Place/Date of Death: Droitwich, Worcestershire — 14 Feb. 1939
Memorials: —
Town/County Connections: Droitwich, Worcestershire
Remarks: Served in the First World War; Croix de Guerre avec Palme (France); Order of Red Cross, Order of Samaritan and Order of St. Sava (Serbia); Commandant, Royal Army Medical College 1926-29; Deputy Director Medical Services, Southern Command, India 1929-33
Account of Deed: On 11 Dec. 1899, at Magersfontein, South Africa, Lieutenant Douglas went out in the open and attended to wounded officers and men under intense enemy fire. He performed many similar acts of gallantry on the same day.

DOUGLAS-HAMILTON, Angus Falconer — see **HAMILTON,** Angus Falconer DOUGLAS-

DOWELL, George Dare   **342**
Lieutenant (later Bt/Lieutenant Colonel)   Royal Marine Artillery
Other Decorations: —
Date of Gazette: 24 Feb. 1857
Place/Date of Birth: Chichester, Sussex — 15 Feb. 1831
Place/Date of Death: Remuera, Auckland, New Zealand — 3 Aug. 1910
Memorials: Purewa Cemetery, Auckland
Town/County Connections: Chichester, Sussex
Remarks: —
Account of Deed: On 13 Jul. 1855 at the Fort of Viborg in the Gulf of Finland, when an explosion occurred in one of the cutters of HMS *Arrogant*, Lieutenant Dowell, who was on board HMS *Ruby*, took three volunteers and went, under very heavy fire to the assistance of the cutter. He took up three of the crew, and having rescued the rest and also the Captain of the Mast*, he then towed the stricken boat out of enemy gun range. (*See also INGOUVILLE, G.)

No photograph available

DOWLING, William   **343**
Private   32nd Regiment (later The Duke of Cornwall's Light Infantry)
Other Decorations: —
Date of Gazette: 21 Nov. 1859
Place/Date of Birth: Thomastown, Co. Kilkenny, Ireland — 1825
Place/Date of Death: Liverpool, Lancashire — 17 Feb. 1887
Memorials: —
Town/County Connections: Thomastown, Kilkenny
Remarks: —
Account of Deed: On 4 Jul. 1857 at Lucknow, India, Private Dowling went out with two other men and spiked the enemy's guns and killed a subadar of the enemy by one of the guns. On 9 Jul. he again went out, with three men, to spike one of the enemy's guns, but had to retire as the spike was too small. He was, however, exposed to the same dangers. Also on 27 Sep. he spiked an 18-pounder gun during a sortie, under very heavy fire.

DOWN, John Thornton   **344**
Ensign   57th Regt. (later The Middlesex Regiment — Duke of Cambridge's Own)
Other Decorations: —
Date of Gazette: 22 Sep. 1864
Place/Date of Birth: Fulham, London — 2 Mar. 1842
Place/Date of Death: Otahuhu, New Zealand — 28 Apr. 1866
Memorials: 57th (West Middlesex) Regiment brass tablet, St Paul's Cathedral
Town/County Connections: Fulham, London
Remarks: —
Account of Deed: On 2 Oct. 1863 at Pontoko, New Zealand, Ensign Down and a drummer* volunteered to rescue a wounded comrade from the rebel natives. They succeeded in bringing in this wounded man who was lying about 50 yards from the bush, although the enemy kept up a very heavy fire at short range and from fallen logs close at hand. (*See also STAGPOOLE, D.)

Name on Westminster School Memorial outside Westminster Abbey

DOWNIE, Robert   **345**
Sergeant   2nd Bn., The Royal Dublin Fusiliers
Other Decorations: MM
Date of Gazette: 25 Nov. 1916
Place/Date of Birth: Glasgow — 12 Jan. 1894
Place/Date of Death: Glasgow — 18 Apr. 1968
Memorials: —
Town/County Connections: Glasgow
Remarks: —
Account of Deed: On 23 Oct. 1916 east of Lesboeufs, France, when most of the officers had become casualties, Sergeant Downie, utterly regardless of personal danger and under very heavy fire, organised the attack which had been temporarily checked. At the critical moment he rushed forward shouting "Come on the Dubs!" which had an immediate response and the line rushed forward at this call. Sergeant Downie accounted for several of the enemy and in addition captured a machine gun, killing the team. Although wounded early in the fight, he remained with his company, giving valuable assistance while the position was being consolidated.

DOXAT, Alexis Charles   **346**
Lieutenant (later Major)   3rd Bn., Imperial Yeomanry
Other Decorations: —
Date of Gazette: 15 Jan. 1901
Place/Date of Birth: Surbiton, Surrey — 9 Apr. 1867
Place/Date of Death: Cambridge — 29 Nov. 1942
Memorials: —
Town/County Connections: Surbiton, Surrey; Cambridge; Cheshunt, Herts.
Remarks: Served in the First World War 1914-18.
Account of Deed: On 20 Oct. 1900 near Zeerust, South Africa, Lieutenant Doxat, with a party of mounted infantry was reconnoitring a position held by 100 Boers on a ridge of kopjes. When the enemy opened a heavy fire on the reconnaissance party they had to retire, but Lieutenant Doxat, seeing that one of his men had lost his horse, galloped back under very heavy fire and took him on his own horse to a place of safety.

DOYLE, Martin   **347**
Company Sergeant-Major   1st Bn., The Royal Munster Fusiliers
Other Decorations: MM
Date of Gazette: 31 Jan. 1919
Place/Date of Birth: New Ross, Co. Wexford, Ireland — 25 Oct. 1891
Place/Date of Death: Dublin — 20 Nov. 1940
Memorials: —
Town/County Connections: New Ross, Co. Wexford
Remarks: —
Account of Deed: On 2 Sep. 1918 at Reincourt, France, when command of the company fell on Company Sergeant-Major Doyle, all the officers having become casualties, he extricated a party of his men who were surrounded by the enemy, and carried back, under heavy fire, a wounded officer. Later he went forward under intense fire to the assistance of a tank and when an enemy machine-gun opened fire on the tank, making it impossible to get the wounded away, he captured it single-handed and took three prisoners. Subsequently when the enemy counter-attacked, he drove them back, taking many more prisoners.

DRAIN, Job Henry Charles   **348**
Driver (later Sergeant)   37th Bty., Royal Field Artillery
Other Decorations: —
Date of Gazette: 25 Nov. 1914
Place/Date of Birth: Barking, Essex — 15 Oct. 1895
Place/Date of Death: Dagenham, Essex — 26 Jul. 1975
Memorials: —
Town/County Connections: Barking and Dagenham, Essex
Remarks: —
Account of Deed: On 26 Aug. 1914 at Le Cateau, France, when a captain* of the same battery was trying to recapture two guns, Driver Drain and another driver* volunteered to help and gave great assistance in the eventual saving of one of the guns. At the time they were under heavy artillery and infantry fire from the enemy who were only 100 yards away. (*See also REYNOLDS, D. and LUKE, F.)

DRAKE, Alfred George　　　　　　　　　　　　　　　　　**349**
Corporal　8th Bn., The Rifle Brigade (Prince Consort's Own)
Other Decorations:　—
Date of Gazette:　22 Jan. 1916
Place/Date of Birth:　Mile End, Old Town, London — 10 Dec. 1893
Place/Date of Death:　La Brique, Belgium — 23 Nov. 1915
Memorials:　La Brique Military Cemetery, Belgium; The Rifle Brigade Memorial, Winchester Cathedral
Town/County Connections:　Stepney, London
Remarks:　—
Account of Deed:　On 23 Nov. 1915, near La Brique, Belgium, Corporal Drake was one of a patrol of four which was reconnoitring towards the German lines. The patrol was discovered when close to the enemy who opened fire with rifles and machine-gun, wounding the officer and one of the men. The latter was carried back by the last remaining man and Corporal Drake stayed with his officer, bandaging his wounds regardless of the enemy's fire. Later, a rescue party found the officer, alive and bandaged, but the corporal was dead.

DRESSER, Tom　　　　　　　　　　　　　　　　　　　**350**
Private　7th Bn., The Yorkshire Regiment (Alexandra, Princess of Wales's Own)
Other Decorations:　—
Date of Gazette:　27 Jun. 1917
Place/Date of Birth:　Westgate, Pickering, Yorkshire — 21 Jul. 1892
Place/Date of Death:　Middlesbrough, Yorkshire — 9 Apr. 1982
Memorials:　Thorntree Cemetery, Middlesbrough
Town/County Connections:　Middlesbrough and Pickering, Yorkshire.
Remarks:　—
Account of Deed:　On 12 May 1917 near Roeux, France, Private Dresser, in spite of having been twice wounded on the way and suffering great pain, succeeded in conveying an important message from battalion headquarters to the front line trenches, which he eventually reached in an exhausted condition. His fearlessness and determination to deliver this message at all costs proved of the greatest value to his battalion at a crititcal period.

DREW, Arthur Malcolm Cluny McREADY- — see **DIARMID,** Allastair Malcolm Cluny McREADY-

DREWRY, George Leslie　　　　　　　　　　　　　　　**351**
Midshipman (later Lieutenant)　Royal Naval Reserve
Other Decorations:　—
Date of Gazette:　16 Aug. 1915
Place/Date of Birth:　Forest Gate, London — 3 Nov. 1894
Place/Date of Death:　Scapa Flow, Orkney Islands — 3 Aug. 1918　*Grave No 90251 square 197*
Memorials:　City of London Cemetery, Manor Park; All Saints' Church, Forest Gate
Town/County Connections:　Forest Gate, London.
Remarks:　— *Merchant Taylor's School, Northwood, Middx.*
Account of Deed:　On 25 Apr. 1915 during the landing at V Beach, Cape Helles, Gallipoli, Midshipman Drewry and three others* of HMS *River Clyde*, assisted the commander of the ship* at the work of securing the lighters under a very heavy rifle and Maxim fire. He was wounded in the head, but continued his work and twice subsequently attempted to swim from lighter to lighter with a line. (*See also UNWIN, E., MALLESON, W. St A., SAMSON, G.M. and WILLIAMS, W.C.)

DRUMMOND, Geoffrey Heneage　　　　　　　　　　　**352**
Lieutenant　Royal Naval Volunteer Reserve
Other Decorations:　—
Date of Gazette:　28 Aug. 1918
Place/Date of Birth:　St. James's Place, London — 25 Jan. 1886
Place/Date of Death:　Rotherhithe, London — 21 Apr. 1941
Memorials:　Chalfont St. Peter Cemetery, Buckinghamshire　*Name on Town W.M.*
Town/County Connections:　Chalfont St. Peter, Buckinghamshire　*Eton College*
Remarks:　Served as a Seaman in River Thames Patrol Service in Second World War.
Account of Deed:　On 9/10 May 1918 at Ostend, Belgium, Lieutenant Drummond commanding HM M.L. 254, volunteered for rescue work and was following HMS *Vindictive* to the harbour when a shell burst on board killing an officer and a deck hand and badly wounding the coxswain and Lieutenant Drummond. Notwithstanding his wounds, this officer brought M.L. 254 alongside *Vindictive* and then took off two officers and 38 men, some of whom were killed or wounded while embarking. He retained consciousness long enough to back his vessel away from the piers and towards the open sea before collapsing exhausted from his wounds. (See also BOURKE R.R.L. and CRUTCHLEY, V.A.C.)

DUFFY, James

353

Private   6th Bn., The Royal Inniskilling Fusiliers
Other Decorations: —
Date of Gazette: 28 Feb. 1918
Place/Date of Birth: Gweedore, Co. Donegal, Ireland — 17 Nov. 1889
Place/Date of Death: Letterkenny, Co. Donegal — 8 Apr. 1969
Memorials: —
Town/County Connections: Letterkenny, Co. Donegal
Remarks: —
Account of Deed: On 27 Dec. 1917 at Kereina Peak, Palestine, whilst the company was holding a very exposed position, Private Duffy, a stretcher-bearer, and another stretcher-bearer went out to bring in a seriously wounded comrade. When the other stretcher-bearer was wounded, Private Duffy returned to get another man, who was killed almost immediately. The private then went forward alone and, under very heavy fire, succeeded in getting both wounded men under cover and attended to their injuries. His gallantry undoubtedly saved both men's lives.

No photograph available

DUFFY, Thomas

354

Private   1st Madras Fusiliers (later The Royal Dublin Fusiliers)
Other Decorations: —
Date of Gazette: 18 Jun. 1858
Place/Date of Birth: Caulry, Athlone, Co. Westmeath, Ireland — 1805
Place/Date of Death: Dublin — 23 Dec. 1868
Memorials: —
Town/County Connections: Athlone, Co. Westmeath
Remarks: —
Account of Deed: On 26 Sep. 1857 at Lucknow, India, a 24-pounder gun which had been used against the enemy on the previous day was left in an exposed position and all efforts to reach it were unsuccessful, so heavy was the fire maintained on it by the mutineers. Private Duffy, however, who went out with two others, managed to fasten a rope to the gun in such a manner that it could be pulled away and was saved from falling into the hands of the enemy.

DUGDALE, Frederic Brooks

355

Lieutenant   5th Lancers (Royal Irish)
Other Decorations: —
Date of Gazette: 17 Sep. 1901
Place/Date of Birth: Burnley , Lancashire — 21 Oct. 1877
Place/Date of Death: Blakemore, Gloucestershire — 13 Nov. 1901
Memorials: Buried at Longborough, Gloucestershire
Town/County Connections: Burnley, Lancs.; Moreton-in-Marsh, Glos.
Remarks: —
Account of Deed: On 3 Mar. 1901 near Derby, South Africa, Lieutenant Dugdale was in command of a small outpost when, having been ordered to retire, his patrol came under heavy fire at a range of about 250 yards, and a sergeant, two men and a horse were hit. Lieutenant Dugdale dismounted and put one of the wounded men on his own horse. He then caught another horse, galloped up to another wounded man and took him up behind him, then brought both men safely out of action.

DUNBAR-NASMITH, Martin Eric — see NASMITH, Martin Eric DUNBAR-

DUNDAS, James

356

Lieutenant (later Captain)   Bengal Engineers, Indian Army
Other Decorations: —
Date of Gazette: 31 Dec. 1867
Place/Date of Birth: Edinburgh — 10 Sep. 1842
Place/Date of Death: Sherpur, Afghanistan — 23 Dec. 1879
Memorials: St. Mary's Cathedral, Edinburgh, Rochester Cathedral, Kent
Town/County Connections: Edinburgh
Remarks: —
Account of Deed: On 30 Apr. 1865 at Dewan-Giri, Bhootan, India, a number of the enemy, about 200 strong, had barricaded themselves in the blockhouse, which they continued to defend after the main body was in retreat. The blockhouse, which was loopholed, was the key of the enemy's position and on the orders of the general in command, Lieutenant Dundas and another officer* had to climb a 14ft. wall and then go head first through an opening only 2 feet wide. The two officers scaled the wall, followed, after they had set the example, by the Sikh soldiers, but they were both wounded. (*See also TREVOR, W.S.)

DUNKLEY, Bertram BEST-　　　　　　　　　　　　　　　　**357**
T/Lieutenant Colonel　Comd. 2/5th Bn., The Lancashire Fusiliers
Other Decorations:　—
Date of Gazette:　6 Sep. 1917
Place/Date of Birth:　York — 3 Aug. 1890
Place/Date of Death:　Near Ypres, Belgium — 5 Aug. 1917
Memorials:　Mendingham Military Cemetery, Belgium
Town/County Connections:　York
Remarks:　—
Account of Deed:　On 31 Jul. 1917 at Wieltje, Belgium, when the leading waves of the attack had become disorganised by rifle and machine-gun fire at very close range from positions which were believed to be in our hands, Lieutenant Colonel Best-Dunkley dashed forward, rallied his men and personally led them to the assault of these positions, which despite heavy losses, were carried. He continued to lead his battalion until all their objectives had been gained. Later in the day when our position was threatened he collected his battalion headquarters, led them to the attack and beat off the advancing enemy. He later died of his wounds.

No photograph available

DUNLAY, (or DUNLEY, or DUNLEA) John　　　　　　　　　**358**
Lance-Corporal　93rd Regt. (later The Argyll and Sutherland Highlanders — Princess Louise's)
Other Decorations:　—
Date of Gazette:　24 Dec. 1858
Place/Date of Birth:　Douglas, Co. Cork, Ireland — 1831
Place/Date of Death:　Cork, Ireland — 17 Oct. 1890
Memorials:　—
Town/County Connections:　Douglas, Co. Cork
Remarks:　—
Account of Deed:　On 16 Nov. 1857 at Lucknow, India, Lance-Corporal Dunlay was the first man of the Regiment to enter one of the breaches in the Secundra Bagh, with a captain whom he most gallantly supported against superior numbers. (Elected by the Regiment.)

DUNMORE, Earl of — see **FINCASTLE,** Viscount

DUNN, Alexander Roberts　　　　　　　　　　　　　　　**359**
Lieutenant (later Colonel)　11th Hussars (Prince Albert's Own)
Other Decorations:　—
Date of Gazette:　24 Feb. 1857
Place/Date of Birth:　Dunstable, York (now Toronto) Canada — 15 Sep. 1833
Place/Date of Death:　Senafe, Abyssinia — 25 Jan. 1868
Memorials:　Military Cemetery at Senafe, Abyssinia; Regimental Memorial, York Minster
Town/County Connections:　— *Harrow School*
Remarks:　First Canadian-born man to win the VC.
Account of Deed:　On 25 Oct. 1854 at Balaclava, Crimea, (Charge of the Light Brigade) Lieutenant Dunn saved the life of a sergeant of his regiment, by cutting down two or three Russian Lancers who were attacking from the rear. He later killed a Russian Hussar who was attacking a private.

DUNSIRE, Robert　　　　　　　　　　　　　　　　　　**360**
Private (later Corporal)　13th Bn., The Royal Scots (The Lothian Regiment)
Other Decorations:　—
Date of Gazette:　18 Nov. 1915
Place/Date of Birth:　Buckhaven, Fife, Scotland — 24 Nov. 1891
Place/Date of Death:　Mazingarbe, France — 30 Jan. 1916
Memorials:　Mazingarbe Communal Cemetery, France; War Memorial, Kirkcaldy, Fife
Town/County Connections:　Kirkcaldy, Fife
Remarks:　—
Account of Deed:　On 26 Sep. 1915 on Hill 70, France, Private Dunsire went out under very heavy fire and rescued a wounded man from between the firing lines. Later another man, considerably nearer the German lines, was heard shouting for help and Private Dunsire crawled out again, with complete disregard for the enemy and carried the wounded man in. Shortly afterwards the Germans attacked over this ground.

DUNSTAN, William   **361**
Corporal (later Lieutenant)   7th Bn. (Victoria) Australian Imperial Force
Other Decorations: —
Date of Gazette: 15 Oct. 1915
Place/Date of Birth: Ballarat, Victoria, Australia — 8 Mar. 1895
Place/Date of Death: Melbourne, Australia — 3 Mar. 1957
Memorials: Australian War Memorial, Canberra
Town/County Connections: —
Remarks: —
Account of Deed: On 9 Aug. 1915, at Lone Pine, Gallipoli, the enemy made a determined counter-attack on the centre of the newly captured trench held by a lieutenant*, two corporals* (one of whom was Corporal Dunstan) and a few men. The enemy blew in the sand-bag barricade, leaving only a foot standing, but the lieutenant and the two corporals repulsed the enemy and rebuilt the barricade. Twice more the enemy blew in the barricade and on each occasion they were repulsed and the barricade rebuilt. (*See also TUBB, F.H. and BURTON, A.S.)

DUNVILLE, John Spencer   **362**
Second Lieutenant   1st Royal Dragoons
Other Decorations: —
Date of Gazette: 2 Aug. 1917
Place/Date of Birth: Marylebone, London — 7 May 1896
Place/Date of Death: Near Epehy, France — 26 Jun. 1917
Memorials: Villiers-Faucon Communal Cemetery, France; War Memorial, Holywood, Co. Antrim, Ireland
Town/County Connections: Marylebone, London; Holywood, Co. Antrim
Remarks: — Eton College
Account of Deed: On 24/25 Jun. 1917 near Epehy, France, in order to ensure the absolute success of the demolition of the enemy's wire, Second Lieutenant Dunville placed himself between an NCO of the Royal Engineers and the enemy's fire and, thus protected, the NCO was enabled to complete a work of great importance. Second Lieutenant Dunville, although severely wounded, continued to direct his men in the wire cutting and general operations until the raid was successfully completed. He subsequently died of his wounds.

DURRANT, Alfred Edward   **363**
Private (later Lance-Corporal)   2nd Bn., The Rifle Brigade (Prince Consort's Own)
Other Decorations: ISM
Date of Gazette: 18 Oct. 1901
Place/Date of Birth: St. James's, Westminster, London — 4 Nov. 1864
Place/Date of Death: Tottenham, London — 29 Mar. 1933
Memorials: The Rifle Brigade memorial, Winchester Cathedral, Hants.
Town/County Connections: Westminster, London
Remarks: —
Account of Deed: On 27 Aug. 1900 at Bergendal, South Africa, a corporal having been wounded and somewhat dazed, got up from his prone position in the firing line and started to run towards the enemy. Private Durrant rose and, pulling him down, tried to keep him quiet, but finding this impossible, he took him up and carried him back for 200 yards under heavy fire to shelter. The private then returned immediately to his place in the line.

DURRANT, Thomas Frank   **364**
Sergeant   Corps of Royal Engineers, attd. No. 1 Commando
Other Decorations: —
Date of Gazette: 19 Jun. 1945
Place/Date of Birth: Green Street Green, Farnborough, Kent — 17 Oct. 1918
Place/Date of Death: St. Nazaire, France — 29 Mar. 1942
Memorials: Escoublac-la-Baule War Cemetery, France
Town/County Connections: Green Street Green, Farnborough, Kent
Remarks: —
Account of Deed: On 27 Mar. 1942 at St. Nazaire, France, Sergeant Durrant was in charge of a Lewis gun on HM Motor Launch 306 which came under heavy fire during the raid. Although he had no protection and was wounded in several places he continued firing until the launch was boarded and those who were still alive were taken prisoner. He died of his wounds the next day.

DWYER, Edward   **365**
Private (later Corporal) 1st Bn., The East Surrey Regiment
Other Decorations: —
Date of Gazette: 22 May 1915
Place/Date of Birth: Fulham, London — 25 Nov. 1895
Place/Date of Death: Guillemont, France — 3 Sep. 1916
Memorials: Flatiron Copse Cemetery, France
Town/County Connections: Fulham, London
Remarks: — *Memorial in Regimental Chapel, All Saints. Kingston*
Account of Deed: On 20 Apr. 1915 at Hill 60, Belgium, when his trench was heavily attacked by German grenade-throwers, Private Dwyer climbed on to the parapet and although subjected to a hail of bombs at close quarters, succeeded in dispersing the enemy by the effective use of hand-grenades. Earlier in the day he had left his trench under heavy shell-fire to bandage his wounded comrades.

DWYER, John James (later The Hon.)   **366**
Sergeant (later Lieutenant) 4th Coy., Machine Gun Corps, Australian Imperial Force
Other Decorations: —
Date of Gazette: 26 Nov. 1917
Place/Date of Birth: Lovett, Port Cygnet, Tasmania — 9 Mar. 1890
Place/Date of Death: Bruny Island, Tasmania — 17 Jan. 1962
Memorials: Hobart Cemetery, Tasmania; Australian War Memorial, Canberra
Town/County Connections: —
Remarks: Speaker of Tasmanian House of Assembly 1941-48; Minister of Agriculture and Fisheries 1948-61; Deputy Premier 1958-61
Account of Deed: On 26 Sep. 1917, at Zonnebeke, Belgium, Sergeant Dwyer, in charge of a Vickers machine-gun, during an advance, rushed his gun forward to within 30 yards of an enemy machine-gun, fired point blank at it and killed the crew. He then seized the gun and carried it back across shell-swept ground to our front line. On the following day, when the position was being heavily shelled, and his Vickers gun was blown up, he took his team through the enemy barrage and fetched a reserve gun which he put into use in the shortest possible time.

No photograph available

DYNON, Denis   **367**
Sergeant 53rd Regiment (later The King's Shropshire Light Infantry)
Other Decorations: —
Date of Gazette: 25 Feb. 1862
Place/Date of Birth: Kilmannon, Queen's Co. (later Leix), Ireland — Sep. 1822
Place/Date of Death: Dublin — 16 Feb. 1863
Memorials: —
Town/County Connections: Fullamore, Dublin
Remarks: —
Account of Deed: On 2 Oct. 1857 at Chota Behar, India, Sergeant Dynon, with a lieutenant*, acted with conspicuous gallantry in the capture of two guns, particularly the second which they rushed and took, pistolling the gunners who were mowing down the detachment, one third of which was *hors de combat* at the time. (*See also DAUNT, J.C.C.)

EARDLEY, George Harold   **368**
A/Sergeant (later Company Sergeant-Major) 4th Bn., The King's Shropshire Light Infantry
Other Decorations: MM
Date of Gazette: 2 Jan. 1945
Place/Date of Birth: Congleton, Cheshire — 6 May 1912
Place/Date of Death: — *About 12.9.1991*
Memorials: —
Town/County Connections: Congleton, Cheshire
Remarks: —
Account of Deed: On 16 Oct. 1944 east of Overloon, Holland, Sergeant Eardley's platoon was ordered to clear some orchards where a strong opposition was holding up the advance, but 80 yards away from the objective the platoon was halted by automatic fire from machine-gun posts. Sergeant Eardley spotted one of these posts and moving forward under heavy fire killed the officer at the post with a grenade. He went on to destroy two more posts single-handed, under fire so intense that it daunted those who were with him, but his action enabled the platoon to achieve its objective and thus ensured the success of the whole attack.

EDMONDSON, John Hurst 369

Corporal   2/17th Bn., Australian Military Forces
Other Decorations: —
Date of Gazette: 4 Jul. 1941
Place/Date of Birth: Wagga Wagga, New South Wales, Australia — 8 Oct. 1914
Place/Date of Death: Tobruk, North Africa — 14 Apr. 1941
Memorials: Tobruk War Cemetery, Libya; Australian War Memorial, Canberra
Town/County Connections: —
Remarks: —
Account of Deed: During the night of 13/14 Apr. 1941 at Tobruk, Libya, Corporal Edmondson was severely wounded while serving with a party which was counter-attacking the enemy who had broken through the barbed wire defences. He continued to advance, however, under heavy fire and went to the assistance of his officer who was in difficulties — he had his bayonet through one of the enemy, who in turn was clasping the officer round his legs, and another of the enemy was attacking from behind. Corporal Edmondson, in spite of his wounds, immediately came to the rescue and killed both of the enemy. He died shortly afterwards.

EDWARDS, Alexander 370

Sergeant   1/6th Bn., The Seaforth Highlanders (Ross-shire Buffs, Duke of Albany's)
Other Decorations: —
Date of Gazette: 14 Sep. 1917
Place/Date of Birth: Lossiemouth, Morayshire, Scotland — 4 Nov. 1885
Place/Date of Death: East of Arras, France — 24 Mar. 1918
Memorials: Arras Memorial
Town/County Connections: Lossiemouth, Morayshire
Remarks: —
Account of Deed: On 31 Jul. 1917 north of Ypres, Belgium, Sergeant Edwards located a machine-gun in a wood, led some men against it, captured the gun and killed all the team. Later, when a sniper was causing casualties, he stalked him and although badly wounded in the arm, went on and killed him. There being only one officer now left with the company, Sergeant Edwards, regardless of his wound, led his men on until the objective was captured. He continued to show great daring, particularly in personal reconnaissance and although again wounded twice the next day he still maintained a complete disregard for personal safety.

EDWARDS, Frederick Jeremiah 371

Private (later Corporal)   12th Bn., The Middlesex Regiment (Duke of Cambridge's Own)
Other Decorations: —
Date of Gazette: 25 Nov. 1916
Place/Date of Birth: Queenstown, Co. Cork, Ireland — 3 Oct. 1894
Place/Date of Death: Richmond, Surrey — 9 Mar. 1964
Memorials: Richmond Cemetery
Town/County Connections: Queenstown, Co. Cork; Richmond, Surrey
Remarks: —
Account of Deed: On 26 Sep. 1916 at Thiepval, France, part of the line was held up by machine-gun fire and all the officers had become casualties. There was confusion and indication of retirement. Private Edwards, grasping the situation and on his own initiative, dashed out towards the gun, which he knocked out with his bombs. This very gallant act, coupled with great presence of mind and disregard of personal danger, made further advance possible and cleared up a dangerous situation.

EDWARDS, Hughie Idwal (later Sir Hughie) 372

Wing Commander (later Air Commodore)   105 Squadron, Royal Air Force
Other Decorations: KCMG, CB, DSO, OBE, DFC
Date of Gazette: 22 Jul. 1941
Place/Date of Birth: Fremantle, Western Australia — 1 Aug. 1914
Place/Date of Death: Sydney, New South Wales — 5 Aug. 1982 , *Cremated.*
Memorials: Australian War Memorial, Canberra
Town/County Connections: — *VC in Australian W.M. Canberra.*
Remarks: Commandant, Central Fighter Establishment 1958-60; ADC to The Queen 1960-63; Director of Establishments Air Ministry 1962-63; Australian Representative, Selection Trust 1964-74; Governor, Western Australia 1974-75; Knight of the Order of St. John
Account of Deed: On 4 Jul. 1941 over Bremen, Germany, Wing Commander Edwards led a force of bombers, in daylight, at a height of about 50 feet through telephone wires and high tension cables, to attack the heavily defended port. The bombers successfully penetrated fierce A.A. fire and a dense balloon barrage, but further fire over the port itself resulted in the loss of four of the attacking force. His task completed, Wing Commander Edwards brought his remaining aircraft safely back, although all had been hit.

EDWARDS, Thomas   **373**
Private   1st Bn., The Royal Highlanders (The Black Watch)
Other Decorations: —
Date of Gazette: 21 May 1884
Place/Date of Birth: Brill, Aylesbury, Buckinghamshire — 19 Apr. 1863
Place/Date of Death: Woodford, Essex — 27 Mar. 1953
Memorials: —
Town/County Connections: Brill, Aylesbury, Bucks.
Remarks: —
Account of Deed: On 13 Mar. 1884 at the Battle of Tamai, Sudan, when both members of the crew of one of the guns had been killed, Private Edwards, after bayoneting two Arabs and himself receiving a wound from a spear, remained with the gun, defending it throughout the action.

EDWARDS, Wilfred   **374**
Private (later Captain)   7th Bn., The King's Own Yorkshire Light Infantry
Other Decorations: —
Date of Gazette: 14 Sep. 1917
Place/Date of Birth: Norwich — 16 Feb. 1893
Place/Date of Death: Leeds, Yorkshire — 4 Jan. 1972
Memorials: —
Town/County Connections: Leeds, Yorkshire
Remarks: —
Account of Deed: On 16 Aug. 1917 at Langemarck, Belgium, when all the company officers were lost, Private Edwards, without hesitation and under heavy machine-gun and rifle fire from a strong concrete fort, dashed forward at great personal risk, bombed through the loopholes, surmounted the fort and waved to his company to advance. Three officers and 30 other ranks were taken prisoner by him in the fort. Later he did most valuable work as a runner and eventually guided most of the battalion out through very difficult ground. Throughout he set a splendid example and was utterly regardless of danger.

EDWARDS, William Mordaunt Marsh   **375**
Lieutenant (later Major)   2nd Bn., The Highland Light Infantry
Other Decorations: —
Date of Gazette: 13 Feb. 1883
Place/Date of Birth: Hardingham, Norfolk — 7 May 1855
Place/Date of Death: Hardingham, Norfolk — 17 Sep. 1912
Memorials: St. George's Church, Hardingham
Town/County Connections: Hardingham, Norfolk
Remarks: Officer of the Hon. Corps of Gentlemen-at-Arms; DL County of Norfolk
Account of Deed: On 13 Sep. 1882 at Tel-el-Kebir, Egypt, Lieutenant Edwards led a party of the Highland Light Infantry to storm a redoubt. The lieutenant who was in advance of his party, rushed alone into the battery, killed the artillery officer in charge and was himself knocked down by a gunner with a rammer and was only rescued by the timely arrival of three men of his regiment.

EGERTON, Ernest Albert   **376**
Corporal (later Sergeant)   16th Bn., The Sherwood Foresters (The Nottinghamshire and Derbyshire Regiment)
Other Decorations: —
Date of Gazette: 26 Nov. 1917
Place/Date of Birth: Longton, Staffordshire — 10 Nov. 1897
Place/Date of Death: Stoke-on-Trent, Staffordshire — 14 Feb. 1966
Memorials: Buried at Forsbrook, Stoke-on-Trent
Town/County Connections: Longton, Staffordshire
Remarks: —
Account of Deed: On 20 Sep. 1917 south-east of Ypres, Belgium, during an attack, visibility was bad owing to fog and smoke. As a result the two leading waves of the attack passed over certain hostile dug-outs without clearing them and enemy rifles and machine-guns from these dug-outs were inflicting severe casualties. Corporal Egerton at once responded to a call for volunteers to help in clearing up the situation and he dashed for the dug-outs under heavy fire at short range. He shot a rifleman, a bomber and a gunner, by which time support had arrived and 29 of the enemy surrendered.

ELCOCK, Roland Edward   **377**
A/Corporal (later Major)   11th Bn., The Royal Scots (The Lothian Regiment)
Other Decorations: MM
Date of Gazette: 26 Dec. 1918
Place/Date of Birth: Wolverhampton, Staffordshire — 5 Jun. 1899
Place/Date of Death: Dehra Dun, India — 6 Oct. 1944
Memorials: —
Town/County Connections: Wolverhampton, Staffordshire
Remarks: —
Account of Deed: On 15 Oct. 1918 south-east of Capelle St. Catherine, France, Corporal Elcock was in charge of a Lewis gun team, and entirely on his own initiative he rushed his gun up to within 10 yards of enemy guns which were causing heavy casualties and holding up the advance. He put both guns out of action, capturing five prisoners and undoubtedly saved the whole attack from being held up. Later, near the River Lys, this NCO again attacked an enemy machine-gun and captured the crew.

ELLIOTT, Keith   **378**
Sergeant   22nd Bn., 2nd N.Z.E.F.
Other Decorations: —
Date of Gazette: 24 Sep. 1942
Place/Date of Birth: Apiti, New Zealand — 25 Apr. 1916
Place/Date of Death: _Died at Lower Hutt about 9.10.1989_
Memorials: HQ, Dunedin RSA, New Zealand
Town/County Connections: —
Remarks: —
Account of Deed: On 15 Jul. 1942 at Ruweisat, Western Desert, Sergeant Elliott, while leading his platoon in an attack under heavy machine-gun and mortar fire, was wounded in the chest. Nevertheless, he carried on and led his men in a bayonet charge which resulted in the capture of four enemy machine-gun posts and an anti-tank gun. Seven of the enemy were killed and 50 taken prisoner. In spite of his wounds Sergeant Elliott refused to leave his platoon until he had reformed them and handed over the prisoners, the number of which had by then increased to 130.

ELLIOTT-COOPER, Neville Bowes — see **COOPER,** Neville Bowes ELLIOTT-

ELPHINSTONE, Howard Craufurd (later Sir Howard)   **379**
Lieutenant (later Major General)   Corps of Royal Engineers
Other Decorations: KCB (Civ.), CMG, CB (Mil.)
Date of Gazette: 2 Jun. 1858
Place/Date of Birth: Sunzel, near Riga, North Russia — 12 Dec. 1829
Place/Date of Death: At sea, near Ushant — 8 Mar. 1890
Memorials: Devonport Chapel, Devon; Bagshot Parish Church, Surrey; Exeter Cathedral; St. George's Garrison Church, Aldershot
Town/County Connections: Bagshot, Surrey; Windsor, Berks. _West Woodhay, Berks_
Remarks: Governor, Comptroller and Treasurer to HRH Prince Arthur, Duke of Connaught, 1859-90
Account of Deed: On 18 Jun. 1855 at Sebastopol, Crimea, on the night following the unsuccessful attack on the Redan, Lieutenant Elphinstone commanded a party of volunteers who searched for the scaling ladders left behind after the repulse. While performing this task he also conducted a search close to the enemy for wounded men, 20 of whom he rescued and took back to the trenches.

ELSTOB, Wilfrith   **380**
T/Lieutenant Colonel   Comd. 16th Bn., The Manchester Regiment
Other Decorations: DSO, MC
Date of Gazette: 9 Jun. 1919
Place/Date of Birth: Chichester, Sussex — 8 Sep. 1888
Place/Date of Death: Near St. Quentin, France — 21 Mar. 1918
Memorials: Pozieres Memorial, France; All Saints' Church, Siddington, Cheshire
Town/County Connections: Chelford, Cheshire _Christ's Hospital, Horsham._ ↑ _Father was vicar for 38 years_
Remarks: —
Account of Deed: On 21 Mar. 1918 at the Manchester Redoubt, near St. Quentin, France, Lieutenant Colonel Elstob encouraged his men during the preliminary bombardment, giving personal support with revolver, rifle and bombs. Single-handed, he repulsed one bombing assault and later when ammunition was required, made several journeys under heavy fire to replenish the supply. By means of a buried cable he sent a message to his brigade commander that the Manchesters would hold the position to the last, and although he was wounded twice he inspired his men to do this until he was killed, in the final assault.

ELTON, Frederick Cockayne · **381**
Bt/Major (later Lieutenant Colonel)   55th Regiment (later The Border Regiment)
Other Decorations: —
Date of Gazette: 24 Feb. 1857
Place/Date of Birth: Whitestaunton, Chard, Somerset — 23 Apr. 1832
Place/Date of Death: London — 24 Mar. 1888
Memorials: Parish Church, Whitestaunton, Somerset
Town/County Connections: Whitestaunton, Chard, Somerset
Remarks: —
Account of Deed: On 29 Mar. 1855 in the Crimea, Major Elton, with a small number of men, drove off a party of Russians who were destroying one of the new detached works, taking one prisoner himself. On 7 Jun. he was the first to lead his men from the trenches. On 4 Aug. he was in command of a working party in the advanced trenches in front of the Quarries, encouraging his men to work under very heavy fire and even used a pick and shovel himself to set an example.

EMBLETON, David — see **CORBETT,** Frederick

EMERSON, James Samuel · **382**
T/Second Lieutenant   9th Bn., The Royal Iniskilling Fusiliers
Other Decorations: —
Date of Gazette: 13 Feb. 1918
Place/Date of Birth: Collon, Drogheda, Co. Louth, Ireland — 3 Aug. 1895
Place/Date of Death: La Vacquerie, France — 6 Dec. 1917
Memorials: Cambrai Memorial, France
Town/County Connections: Collon, Drogheda, Co. Louth, Ireland
Remarks: —
Account of Deed: On 6 Dec. 1917, on the Hindenberg Line north of La Vacquerie, France, Second Lieutenant Emerson led his company in an attack and cleared 400 yards of trench. Though wounded, when the enemy attacked in superior numbers he met their attack with eight men, killing many and taking six prisoners. For three hours afterwards, all other officers having become casualties, he remained with his company, refusing to go to the dressing station, and repeatedly repelling bombing attacks. Later, leading his men to repel another attack, he was mortally wounded. His heroism inspired his men to hold out until reinforcements arrived.

ENGLEHEART, Henry William · **383**
Sergeant (later Quarter Master-Sergeant)   10th Hussars (Prince of Wales's Own Royal)
Other Decorations: —
Date of Gazette: 5 Oct. 1900
Place/Date of Birth: Blackheath, London — 14 Nov. 1863
Place/Date of Death: Datchet, Berkshire — 9 Aug. 1939
Memorials: (Cremated Woking, Surrey)
Town/County Connections: Blackheath, London; Datchet, Berkshire
Remarks: —
Account of Deed: On 13 Mar. 1900 north of Bloemfontein, South Africa, the party which had destroyed the railway had to get over four deep spruits in order to make their way back through enemy lines. At the fourth spruit the horse of one of the sappers failed to get up the bank and he was left in a very dangerous position. In the face of very heavy fire Sergeant Engleheart went to the rescue of the sapper and his horse. Shortly before this he had shown great gallantry in dashing into the first spruit and dealing with the Boers there, before they had time to rally.

ENGLISH, William John · **384**
Lieutenant (later Lieutenant Colonel)   2nd Scottish Horse
Other Decorations: —
Date of Gazette: 4 Oct. 1901
Place/Date of Birth: Cork, Ireland — 6 Oct. 1882
Place/Date of Death: At sea, near Egypt — 4 Jul. 1941
Memorials: Maala Military Cemetery, Aden
Town/County Connections: Upper Norwood, Surrey
Remarks: Served with the Royal Army Service Corps in the First World War and The Royal Ulster Rifles in the Second
Account of Deed: On 3 Jul. 1901 at Vlakfontein, South Africa, Lieutenant English was holding a position under attack by the enemy. Two of his men were killed and two wounded, but the position was still held, largely owing to the lieutenant's personal pluck. When the ammunition ran short, he went over to the next party to get more, over 15 yards of open ground, under very heavy fire at a range of 20 to 30 yards.

ERSKINE, John   **385**
Sergeant   5th Bn., The Cameronians (Scottish Rifles)
Other Decorations: —
Date of Gazette: 5 Aug. 1916
Place/Date of Birth: Dunfermline, Scotland — 13 Jan. 1894
Place/Date of Death: Arras, France — 14 Apr. 1917
Memorials: Arras Memorial, France
Town/County Connections: Dunfermline, Scotland
Remarks: —
Account of Deed: On 22 Jun. 1916 at Givenchy, France, whilst the near lip of a crater caused by the explosion of a large mine was being consolidated, Sergeant Erskine rushed out under continuous fire and rescued a wounded sergeant and a private. Later, seeing his officer, who was believed to be dead, showing signs of movement, he ran to him, bandaged his head and remained with him for fully an hour, being repeatedly fired on. When assistance arrived, he helped to bring in the officer, shielding him with his own body to lessen the chance of his being hit again.

ERVINE-ANDREWS, Harold Marcus — see **ANDREWS,** Harold Marcus ERVINE-

ESMONDE, Eugene Kingsmill   **386**
Lieutenant-Commander   Royal Navy (825 Squadron, Fleet Air Arm)
Other Decorations: DSO
Date of Gazette: 3 Mar. 1942
Place/Date of Birth: Thurgoland, Wortley, Yorkshire — 1 Mar. 1909
Place/Date of Death: Straits of Dover — 12 Feb. 1942
Memorials: Woodlands Cemetery, Gillingham, Kent
Town/County Connections: Borrisokane, Co. Tipperary, Ireland
Remarks: Great-nephew of Lieutenant Colonel T. Esmonde, VC.
Account of Deed: On 12 Feb. 1942 in the Straits of Dover, Lieutenant Commander Esmonde led his squadron of six Swordfish to the attack of two German battle cruisers and the cruiser *Prinz Eugen*, which were entering the Straits strongly escorted by surface craft. Detached from their escorting fighters (just 10 in number) by enemy fighters, all the aircraft of the squadron were damaged, but even after Lieutenant-Commander Esmonde's plane sustained a direct hit he still continued the run-in towards his target until it burst into flames and crashed into the sea. The squadron went on to launch a gallant attack, but none of the six aircraft returned.

ESMONDE, Thomas   **387**
Captain (later Lieutenant Colonel)   18th Regiment (later The Royal Irish Regiment)
Other Decorations: —
Date of Gazette: 25 Sep. 1857
Place/Date of Birth: Pembrokestown, Co. Waterford, Ireland — 25 May 1829
Place/Date of Death: Bruges, Belgium — 14 Jan. 1873
Memorials: —
Town/County Connections: Pembrokestown, Co. Waterford and Borrisokane, Co. Tipperary
Remarks: Great-uncle of Lieutenant-Commander E.K. Esmonde, VC
Account of Deed: On 18 Jun. 1855 at Sebastopol, Crimea, after being engaged in the attack on the Redan, Captain Esmonde repeatedly assisted, at great personal risk, in rescuing wounded men from exposed situations. Also, on 20 Jun. while in command of a covering party he rushed to a spot where a fireball from the enemy had just lodged, and extinguished it before it could betray the position of his men, thus saving the party from a murderous fire of shell and grape which was immediately opened where the fireball had fallen.

EVANS, Arthur (alias SIMPSON, Walter)   **388**
Lance-Sergeant   6th Bn., The Lincolnshire Regiment
Other Decorations: DCM
Date of Gazette: 30 Oct. 1918 & 31 Mar. 1919
Place/Date of Birth: Everton, Liverpool, Lancashire — 8 Apr. 1891
Place/Date of Death: Sydney, Australia — 31 Oct. 1936
Memorials: Buried Sydney, New South Wales, Australia, re-interred Park Cemetery, Lytham-St.-Annes, Lancashire
Town/County Connections: Liverpool and Bolton, Lancashire
Remarks: —
Account of Deed: On 2 Sep. 1918 south west of Etaing, France, a patrol reconnoitring on the west bank of a river sighted an enemy machine-gun on the east bank. The river being very deep at that point, Lance-Sergeant Evans volunteered to swim across and having done so crawled up behind the machine-gun post, where he shot the sentry and another man and made four more surrender. After a crossing had been found and one officer and one man joined him, machine-gun and rifle fire was opened on them. The officer was wounded and Sergeant Evans covered his withdrawal under very heavy fire.

EVANS, George   **389**
Company Sergeant-Major   18th Bn., The Manchester Regiment
Other Decorations: —
Date of Gazette: 30 Jan. 1920
Place/Date of Birth: Kensington, London — 16 Feb. 1876
Place/Date of Death: Sydenham, Kent — 28 Sep. 1937
Memorials: Elmers End Cemetery, Beckenham, Kent
Town/County Connections: Kensington, London; Sydenham, Kent
Remarks: Last VC to be gazetted for the First World War.
Account of Deed: On 30 Jul. 1916 at Guillemont, France, Company Sergeant-Major Evans volunteered to take back an important message after five runners had been killed in attempting to do so. He had to cover about 700 yards, the whole of which was under observation from the enemy. He succeeded in delivering the message in spite of being wounded and rejoined his company although advised to go to the dressing station. The return journey had again meant facing 700 yards of severe rifle and machine-gun fire, but by dodging from shell-hole to shell-hole he managed it.

EVANS, Lewis Pugh   **390**
A/Lieutenant Colonel (later Brigadier General)   The Black Watch (Royal Highlanders), comd. 1st Bn., The Lincolnshire Regiment
Other Decorations: CB, CMG, DSO & Bar
Date of Gazette: 26 Nov. 1917
Place/Date of Birth: Aberystwyth, Cardiganshire, Wales — 3 Jan. 1881
Place/Date of Death: Paddington, London — 30 Nov. 1962   *Paddington Station*
Memorials: Llanbadarn Churchyard, Cardiganshire
Town/County Connections: Aberystwyth, Cardiganshire
Remarks: Nephew of Lieutenant W.G. Cubitt, VC; Order of Leopold (Belgium); Croix de Guerre (France); commanded 159th Welsh Infantry Brigade 1933-37; Military Liaison Officer, Wales Region Headquarters 1939-41; DL Cardiganshire 1937-62   *Eton College*
Account of Deed: On 4 Oct. 1917 near Zonnebeke, Belgium, Lieutenant Colonel Evans took his battalion through a terrific enemy barrage, and while his troops were working round the flank of a machine-gun emplacement, rushed at it himself, firing his revolver through the loophole, and forcing the garrison to capitulate. Although severely wounded in the shoulder he refused to be bandaged and again led his battalion forward and was again wounded. Nevertheless he carried on until the next objective was achieved, and then collapsed. As there were numerous casualties he again refused assistance and managed unaided to reach the dressing station.

EVANS, Samuel   **391**
Private   19th Regt. (later The Yorkshire regiment — Alexandra, Princess of Wales's Own)
Other Decorations: —
Date of Gazette: 23 Jun. 1857
Place/Date of Birth: Paisley, Renfrewshire, Scotland — 1821
Place/Date of Death: Edinburgh — Oct. 1901
Memorials: —
Town/County Connections: Paisley, Renfewshire; Edinburgh
Remarks: —
Account of Deed: On 13 Apr. 1855 at Sebastopol, Crimea, Private Evans volunteered to go into an embrasure to repair a breach. He and another private went into the battery and leapt into the embrasure, where they carried out the necessary repairs under very heavy fire.

FARMER, Donald Dickson   **392**
Sergeant (later Lieutenant Colonel)   1st Bn., The Queen's Own Cameron Highlanders
Other Decorations: MSM
Date of Gazette: 12 Apr. 1901
Place/Date of Birth: Kelso, Roxburghshire, Scotland — 28 May 1877
Place/Date of Death: Liverpool, Lancashire — 23 Dec. 1956
Memorials: —
Town/County Connections: Edinburgh; Liverpool, Lancashire
Remarks: —
Account of Deed: On 13 Dec. 1900 during an attack at Nooitgedacht, South Africa, a lieutenant with 15 men went to the assistance of a picquet which was heavily engaged, most of the men having been killed or wounded. The enemy immediately opened fire on the relief party, killing two and wounding five, including the lieutenant. Sergeant Farmer at once went to the officer who was quite helpless, and carried him away under heavy fire to a place of comparative safety, after which he returned to the firing line and was eventually taken prisoner.

FARMER, Joseph John   **393**
Provisional Lance-Corporal (later Corporal)   Army Hospital Corps (later Royal Army Medical Corps)
Other Decorations: —
Date of Gazette: 16 May 1881
Place/Date of Birth: King's Cross, London — 5 May 1854
Place/Date of Death: Northwood, Middlesex — 30 Jun. 1930
Memorials: Brompton Cemetery, London
Town/County Connections: London
Remarks: —
Account of Deed: On 27 Feb. 1881, at the Majuba Mountain in South Africa, when the Boers closed with the British troops near the Wells, Corporal Farmer held a white flag over the wounded and when the arm holding the flag was shot through, he then raised the flag with the other arm and continued to do so until that one also was shot through.

FARQUHARSON, Francis Edward Henry   **394**
Lieutenant (later Major)   42nd Regiment (later The Black Watch (Royal Highlanders))
Other Decorations: —
Date of Gazette: 16 Jun. 1859
Place/Date of Birth: Glasgow — 25 Mar. 1837
Place/Date of Death: Harberton, Devon — 12 Sep. 1875
Memorials: Buried Harberton Churchyard
Town/County Connections: Harberton, Devon
Remarks: —
Account of Deed: On 9 Mar. 1858 at Lucknow, India, Lieutenant Farquharson led a portion of his company and stormed a bastion mounting two guns and then spiked them. This meant that the advanced positions held during the night were rendered secure from artillery fire. Lieutenant Farquharson was severely wounded while holding an advanced position the following morning.

No photograph available

FARRELL, John   **395**
Sergeant (later Quartermaster-Sergeant)   17th Lancers (Duke of Cambridge's Own)
Other Decorations: —
Date of Gazette: 20 Nov. 1857
Place/Date of Birth: Dublin — Mar. 1826
Place/Date of Death: Secunderabad, India — 31 Aug. 1865
Memorials: —
Town/County Connections: Dublin
Remarks: —
Account of Deed: On 25 Oct. 1854 at Balaclava, Crimea (Charge of the Light Brigade), Sergeant Farrell, whose horse had been killed under him, stopped on the field and amidst a storm of shot and shell helped a troop sergeant-major* and another sergeant* to move a severely wounded officer (who subsequently died) out of range of the guns. (*See also BERRYMAN, J. and MALONE, J.)

FAULDS, William Frederick   **396**
Private (later Captain)   1st Bn., South African Infantry
Other Decorations: MC
Date of Gazette: 9 Sep. 1916
Place/Date of Birth: Cradock, Cape Province, South Africa — 19 Feb. 1895
Place/Date of Death: Salisbury, Rhodesia — 16 Aug. 1950
Memorials: —
Town/County Connections: —
Remarks: First South African-born man serving with South African Forces to win the VC. Served in Second World War in East Africa.
Account of Deed: On 18 Jul. 1916 at Delville Wood, France, a bombing party came under very heavy rifle and machine-gun fire and the majority were killed or wounded, including the lieutenant in charge, who lay unable to move midway between the two lines of trench. In full daylight Private Faulds, accompanied by two other men, climbed over the parapet, ran out, picked up the officer and carried him back. Two days later Private Faulds went out alone, under intense artillery fire, and brought in a wounded man and then rejoined his platoon.

No photograph available

FAZAL DIN   397

A/Naik   10th Baluch Regiment, Indian Army
Other Decorations: —
Date of Gazette: 24 May 1945
Place/Date of Birth: Hussianpur Village, Hoshiapur District, Punjab — 1 Jul. 1921
Place/Date of Death: Near Meiktila, Burma — 2 Mar. 1945
Memorials: The Rangoon Memorial, Burma
Town/County Connections: —
Remarks: —
Account of Deed: On 2 Mar. 1945 near Meiktila, Burma, during an attack, Naik Fazal Din's section was held up by fire from the enemy bunkers, whereupon he personally attacked the nearest bunker and silenced it, then led his men against the other. Suddenly six Japanese, led by two officers wielding swords rushed out and Naik Fazal Din was run through the chest by one of them. As the sword was withdrawn, the naik wrested it from the hands of its owner and killed him with it. Having killed another Japanese with the sword he waved it aloft, continuing to encourage his men before staggering back to make his report and collapsing.

FEGEN, Edward Stephen Fogarty   398

A/Captain   Royal Navy
Other Decorations: SGM (in silver); Lloyd's Medal for life-saving
Date of Gazette: 22 Nov. 1940
Place/Date of Birth: Southsea, Hampshire — 8 Oct. 1891
Place/Date of Death: Atlantic Ocean — 5 Nov. 1940
Memorials: Chatham Naval Memorial; sundial, Hamilton, Bermuda; column in grounds of hospital, St. John, New Brunswick, Canada; Seamen's Institute, Wellington, New Zealand
Town/County Connections: —
Remarks: Dutch life-saving medal
Account of Deed: On 5 Nov. 1940 in the Atlantic, Captain Fegen, commanding HMS *Jervis Bay*, was escorting 37 merchantmen, when they were attacked by the German pocket battleship *Admiral Scheer*. Captain Fegen immediately engaged the enemy head-on, thus giving the ships of the convoy time to scatter. Out-gunned and on fire *Jervis Bay* maintained the unequal fight for three hours, although the captain's right arm was shattered and his bridge was shot from under him. He went down with his ship but it was due to him that 31 ships of the convoy escaped.

FERGUSSON, Thomas Riversdale COLYER-   399

A/Captain   2nd Bn., The Northamptonshire Regiment
Other Decorations: —
Date of Gazette: 6 Sep. 1917
Place/Date of Birth: Ightham, Kent — 18 Feb. 1896
Place/Date of Death: Bellewaarde, Belgium — 31 Jul. 1917
Memorials: Menin Road South Military Cemetery, Belgium; Ightham Parish Church; Ightham War memorial
Town/County Connections: Ightham, Kent
Remarks: — Harrow School
Account of Deed: On 31 Jul. 1917 at Bellewaarde, Belgium, Captain Colyer-Fergusson unexpectedly found himself with a sergeant and five men only. He carried out the planned attack nevertheless and succeeded in capturing the enemy trench. During an enemy counter-attack, assisted only by his orderly, he attacked and captured an enemy machine-gun, turning it on the assailants. Later, assisted only by his sergeant, he again attacked and captured a second enemy machine-gun, but shortly afterwards he was killed by a sniper.

FFRENCH, Alfred Kirke   400

Lieutenant (later Captain)   53rd Regiment (later The King's Shropshire Light Infantry)
Other Decorations: —
Date of Gazette: 24 Dec. 1858
Place/Date of Birth: Meerut, India — 25 Feb. 1835
Place/Date of Death: Chiswick, London — 28 Dec. 1872
Memorials: —
Town/County Connections: Chiswick, London
Remarks: —
Account of Deed: On 16 Nov. 1857 at Lucknow, India, Lieutenant Ffrench was in command of the Grenadier Company and behaved with conspicuous bravery at the taking of the Secundra Bagh. He was one of the first to enter the building. (Elected by the regiment.)

FIELDING, John — see **WILLIAMS,** John

FINCASTLE, Viscount, (later The Earl of DUNMORE) Alexander Edward Murray   **401**
Lieutenant (later Major)   16th Lancers (The Queen's)
Other Decorations: DSO, MVO
Date of Gazette: 9 Nov. 1897
Place/Date of Birth: Portland Place, London — 22 Apr. 1871
Place/Date of Death: London — 29 Jan. 1962
Memorials: —
Town/County Connections: London
Remarks: Served in South African War 1899-1900; served in First World War 1914-16; Captain of the Hon. Corps of Gentlemen-at-Arms 1924
Account of Deed: On 17 Aug. 1897 at Nawa Kili, Upper Swat, India (Tirah Campaign), Lieutenant Fincastle with two other officers* and five men of the Guides, went under a heavy and close fire, to the rescue of a lieutenant of the Lancashire Fusiliers who was lying disabled by a bullet wound and surrounded by enemy swordsmen. While the wounded officer was being brought under cover he was unfortunately killed by a bullet. One of the officers of the rescue party was mortally wounded and four horses were shot. (*See also ADAMS, R.B. and MACLEAN, H.L.S.)

FINCH, Norman Augustus   **402**
Sergeant (later Lieutenant and Quartermaster)   Royal Marine Artillery
Other Decorations: MSM
Date of Gazette: 23 Jul. 1918
Place/Date of Birth: Handsworth, Birmingham — 26 Dec. 1890
Place/Date of Death: Portsmouth, Hampshire — 15 Mar. 1966   *Cremated Porchester.*
Memorials: St. Andrew's Church, Eastney Barracks (RM), Southsea, Hampshire
Town/County Connections: Birmingham; Southsea, Hampshire
Remarks: Sergeant-Major in the Queen's Bodyguard of Yeoman of the Guard 1961
Account of Deed: On 22/23 Apr. 1918 at Zeebrugge, Belgium, Sergeant Finch was second in command of the pom-poms and Lewis gun in the foretop of HMS *Vindictive*. At one period *Vindictive* was being hit every few seconds, but Sergeant Finch and the officer in command kept up a continuous fire, until two heavy shells made direct hits on the foretop killing or disabling everyone except Sergeant Finch who was, however, severely wounded. Nevertheless he remained in his battered and exposed position, harassing the enemy on the Mole until the foretop received another direct hit, putting the remainder of the armament completely out of order. (Award by ballot.)

FINDLATER, George   **403**
Piper (later Pipe-Major)   1st Bn., The Gordon Highlanders
Other Decorations: —
Date of Gazette: 20 May 1898
Place/Date of Birth: Forgue, Huntly, Aberdeenshire, Scotland — 15 Feb. 1872
Place/Date of Death: Turriff, Aberdeenshire — 11 Mar. 1942
Memorials: —
Town/County Connections: Forgue, Huntly, Aberdeenshire
Remarks: —
Account of Deed: On 20 Oct. 1897 during the attack on the Dargai Heights, Indian Frontier (Tirah Campaign), Piper Findlater, after being shot through both feet and unable to stand, propped himself against a boulder and went on playing the regimental march under heavy fire, to encourage the advance.

FINDLAY, George de Cardonnel Elmsall   **404**
A/Major (later Colonel)   409 (Low) Field Coy., Corps of Royal Engineers
Other Decorations: MC & Bar
Date of Gazette: 15 May 1919
Place/Date of Birth: Boturich, Balloch, Dunbartonshire, Scotland — 20 Aug. 1889
Place/Date of Death: Helensburgh, Renfrewshire, Scotland — 26 Jun. 1967
Memorials: —
Town/County Connections: Balloch, Dunbartonshire
Remarks: Served in Second World War; DL, County of Dunbarton.   *Harrow School.*
Account of Deed: On 4 Nov. 1918 during the forcing of the Sambre-Oise Canal at the lock south of Catillon, France, Major Findlay was with the leading bridging and assaulting parties which came under heavy fire and the advance was stopped. Nevertheless he collected what men he could and repaired the bridges, under incessant fire. Although wounded he continued with his task and after two unsuccessful efforts managed to place the bridge in position across the lock and was the first man across, remaining at this dangerous post until further work was completed.

FINLAY, David **405**
Lance-Corporal (later Sergeant)   2nd Bn., The Black Watch (Royal Highlanders)
Other Decorations: —
Date of Gazette: 29 Jun. 1915
Place/Date of Birth: Guardbridge, Fife, Scotland — 25 Jan. 1893
Place/Date of Death: Persian Gulf — 21 Jan. 1916
Memorials: Basra Memorial, Iraq
Town/County Connections: Guardbridge, Fife
Remarks: —
Account of Deed: On 9 May 1915 near Rue du Bois, France, Lance-Corporal Finlay led a bombing party of 12 men in the attack until 10 of them had fallen. He then ordered the two survivors to crawl back and he himself went to the assistance of a wounded man and carried him over a distance of 10 yards of fire-swept ground into cover, quite regardless of his own safety.

FIRMAN, Humphrey Osbaldston Brooke **406**
Lieutenant   Royal Navy
Other Decorations: —
Date of Gazette: 2 Feb. 1917
Place/Date of Birth: Kensington, London — 24 Nov. 1886
Place/Date of Death: Near Kut-el-Amara, Mesopotamia — 25 Apr. 1916
Memorials: Basra Memorial, Iraq
Town/County Connections: Kensington, London
Remarks: —
Account of Deed: On the night of 24/25 Apr. 1916 in Mesopotamia, an attempt was made to reprovision the force besieged at Kut-el-Amara. Lieutenant Firman, commanding SS *Julnar*, with a lieutenant-commander*, a sub-lieutenant and 12 ratings, started off with 270 tons of stores up the River Tigris. Unfortunately *Julnar* was attacked almost at once by Turkish machine-guns and heavy artillery. At Magasis, steel hawsers stretched across the river halted the expedition, the enemy opened fire at point-blank range and *Julnar's* bridge was smashed. Lieutenant Firman and several of his crew were killed, the survivors and supplies being captured. (*See also COWLEY, C.H.)

FIRTH, James **407**
Sergeant   1st Bn., The Duke of Wellington's (West Riding) Regiment
Other Decorations: —
Date of Gazette: 11 Jun. 1901
Place/Date of Birth: Jarrow, Co. Durham — 15 Jan. 1874
Place/Date of Death: Sheffield, Yorkshire — 29 May 1921
Memorials: Burngreave Cemetery, Sheffield
Town/County Connections: Sheffield, Yorkshire
Remarks: —
Account of Deed: On 24 Feb. 1900 at Plewman's Farm, near Arundel, Cape Colony, South Africa, Sergeant Firth picked up and carried to cover a lance-corporal who was lying wounded and exposed to heavy fire. Later in the day, when the enemy had advanced to within a short distance of the firing line, Sergeant Firth rescued a second lieutenant who was dangerously wounded, and carried him over the crest of a ridge to safety. He himself was shot through the nose and eye while doing so.

FISHER, Frederick **408**
Lance-Corporal   13th Bn., Quebec Regiment (Royal Highlanders of Canada), C.E.F.
Other Decorations: —
Date of Gazette: 23 Jun. 1915
Place/Date of Birth: St. Catherine's Ontario, Canada — 3 Aug. 1894
Place/Date of Death: St. Julien, Ypres — 24 Apr. 1915
Memorials: Menin Gate Memorial, Belgium
Town/County Connections:
Remarks: First Canadian-born man to win VC while serving in the Canadian Army
Account of Deed: On 23 Apr. 1915 in the neighbourhood of St. Julien, Belgium, Lance-Corporal Fisher went forward with the machine-gun of which he was in charge, under heavy fire, and covered the retreat of a battery, losing four of his gun team. Later, when he had obtained four more men, he went forward again to the firing line and was killed while bringing his machine gun into action under very heavy fire.

FitzCLARENCE, Charles

409

Captain (later Brigadier General) The Royal Fusiliers
Other Decorations: —
Date of Gazette: 6 Jul. 1900
Place/Date of Birth: Bishopscourt, Co. Kildare, Ireland — 8 May 1865
Place/Date of Death: Polygon Wood, Zonnebeke, Belgium — 12 Nov. 1914
Memorials: Menin Gate Memorial, Belgium; St. George's Memorial Church, Ypres
Town/County Connections: Bishopscourt, Co. Kildare
Remarks: Commanded 1st Guards Brigade 1914 *Wellington College, Berks*
Account of Deed: On 14 Oct. 1899 near Mafeking, South Africa, Captain FitzClarence went with a partially-trained squadron to the assistance of an armoured train. The enemy was in greatly superior numbers and the squadron was, for a time, surrounded and in great danger. The captain, however, so inspired his men that not only was the train relieved, but a heavy defeat was inflicted on the Boers. On 27 Oct. he led his squadron in a successful night attack and on 26 Dec. he again distinguished himself, and was severely wounded.

No photograph available

FitzGERALD, Richard

410

Gunner Bengal Horse Artillery
Other Decorations: —
Date of Gazette: 24 Apr. 1858
Place/Date of Birth: St. Finbars, Cork, Ireland — Dec. 1831
Place/Date of Death: India — 1884
Memorials: —
Town/County Connections: St. Finbars, Cork, Ireland
Remarks: —
Account of Deed: On 28 Sep. 1857 at Bolandshahr, India, Gunner Fitzgerald and a sergeant* worked their gun after every other man belonging to it had been either killed or wounded. They were under very heavy fire, but cleared the road of the enemy. (See also DIAMOND, B.)

FITZGIBBON, Andrew

411

Hospital Apprentice (later Apothecary) Indian Medical Establishment, attd. 67th Regt. (later The Hampshire Regiment)
Other Decorations: —
Date of Gazette: 13 Aug. 1861
Place/Date of Birth: Gogerat, India — 13 May 1845
Place/Date of Death: Delhi, India — 7 Mar. 1883
Memorials: —
Town/County Connections: Tipperary, Ireland
Remarks: Acknowledged to be one of the two youngest winners of the VC (aged 15 years, 3 months), the other being Drummer T. Flinn, VC, also aged 15 years, 3 months.
Account of Deed: On 21 Aug. 1860 at the capture of the North Taku Fort, India, Hospital Apprentice Fitzgibbon accompanied a wing of the 67th Regiment when it took up a position within 500 yards of the fort. He then proceeded, under heavy fire, to attend a dhoolie-bearer, whose wound he had been directed to bind up, and while the regiment was advancing under the enemy's fire, he ran across the open ground to attend to another wounded man. In doing so he was himself severely wounded.

FITZPATRICK, Francis

412

Private 94th Regiment (later The Connaught Rangers)
Other Decorations: —
Date of Gazette: 23 Feb. 1880
Place/Date of Birth: Tullycorbet, Co. Monaghan, Ireland — 1859
Place/Date of Death: Ireland — 10 Jul. 1933
Memorials: —
Town/County Connections: Tullycorbet, Co. Monaghan
Remarks: —
Account of Deed: On 28 Nov. 1879 during an attack on Sekukuni's Town, South Africa (Basuto War), Private Fitzpatrick and another private* with six men of the Native Contingent, were with a lieutenant of the 1st Dragoon Guards when he was badly wounded. The natives carried the wounded officer at first, but when the party was pursued by about 30 of the enemy they deserted and the lieutenant would have been killed but for the gallantry of the two privates — one carrying him and the other covering the retreat and firing on the enemy. (*See also FLAWN, T.)

FLAWN, Thomas 413

Private   94th Regiment (later The Connaught Rangers)
Other Decorations: —
Date of Gazette: 23 Feb. 1880
Place/Date of Birth: Finedon, Irthlingborough, Northamptonshire — 22 Dec. 1857
Place/Date of Death: Plumstead, Kent — 19 Jan. 1925
Memorials: Plumstead Cemetery, Kent
Town/County Connections: Irthlingborough, Northants; Plumstead, Kent
Remarks: —
Account of Deed: On 28 Nov. 1879 during an attack on Sekukuni's Town, South Africa (Basuto War), Private Flawn and another private* with six men of the Native Contingent, were with a lieutenant of the 1st Dragoon Guards when he was badly wounded. The natives carried the wounded officer at first, but when the party was pursued by about 30 of the enemy they deserted and the lieutenant would have been killed but for the gallantry of the two privates — one carrying him and the other covering the retreat and firing on the enemy. (*See also FITZPATRICK, F.)

FLEMING-SANDES, Arthur James Terence
— see **SANDES, Arthur James Terence FLEMING-**

FLINN, Thomas 414

Drummer   64th Regt. (later The North Staffordshire Regiment — The Prince of Wales's)
Other Decorations: —
Date of Gazette: 12 Apr. 1859
Place/Date of Birth: Athlone, Ireland — Aug. 1842
Place/Date of Death: Athlone, Ireland — 10 Aug. 1892
Memorials: Garrison Church, Whittington Barracks, Lichfield
Town/County Connections: Athlone, Ireland
Remarks: Acknowledged to be one of the two youngest winners of the VC (aged 15 years, 3 months), the other being Hospital Apprentice A. Fitzgibbon, VC, also aged 15 years, 3 months
Account of Deed: On 28 Nov. 1851 at Cawnpore, India, during a charge on the enemy's guns, Drummer Flinn, although wounded himself, engaged in a hand-to-hand encounter with two of the rebel artillerymen.

FLOWERDEW, Gordon Muriel 415

Lieutenant   Lord Strathcona's Horse, C.E.F.
Other Decorations: —
Date of Gazette: 24 Apr. 1918
Place/Date of Birth: Billingford, Norfolk — 2 Jan. 1885
Place/Date of Death: Bois de Moreuil, France — 31 Mar. 1918
Memorials: Namps-au-Val British Cemetery, France; Billingford Church, Norfolk
Town/County Connections: Billingford, Norfolk
Remarks: —
Account of Deed: On 30 Mar. 1918 north east of Bois de Moreuil, France, Lieutenant Flowerdew, commanding a squadron detailed for special service, reached the first objective and saw two lines of the enemy, each about 60 strong, armed with machine-guns. He ordered one troop to dismount and engage the enemy while he led the remaining three troops to the charge, passing over the lines, killing many of the enemy then wheeling about and galloping at them again. Although the squadron had about 70 per cent casualties, including Lieutenant Flowerdew who was dangerously wounded, the enemy broke and fled, and the position was captured.

FOOTE, Henry Robert Bowreman 416

T/Lieutenant Colonel (later Major General)   Comd. 7th Royal Tank Regiment
Other Decorations: CB, DSO
Date of Gazette: 18 May 1944
Place/Date of Birth: Ishapur, Bengal, India — 5 Dec. 1904
Place/Date of Death: — *Died about 23.11.1993*
Memorials: — *lived in Sussex*
Town/County Connections: Birmingham; West Chiltington, Pulborough, Sussex
Remarks: OC 2nd Royal Tank Regt. 1947-48; OC Automotive Wing Fighting Vehicles Proving Establishment, Min. of Supply 1948-49; Comd. 7th Armoured Bde. 1949-50; Comd. 11th Armoured Div. 1950-53; Director-General of Fighting Vehicles, Min. of Supply 1953-55; Dir. Royal Armoured Corps at the War Office 1955-58; Vice-Chairman (UK), VC and GC Association 1968
Account of Deed: During the period 27 May/15 Jun. 1942 in Libya, Lieutenant Colonel Foote commanded his battalion with outstanding courage and leadership, always being at the crucial point at the right time. On 6 Jun., although wounded, he continued to lead his battalion from an exposed position on the outside of a tank, and succeeded in defeating the enemy's attempt to encircle two of our divisions. On 13 Jun. when a number of our tanks had been destroyed, he went on foot, from one tank to another, encouraging the crews under intense artillery and anti-tank fire. By his magnificent example the corridor was kept open for the brigade to march through.

FOOTE, John Weir

417

Hon. Captain (later Major)   Canadian Chaplains' Service, attd. The Royal Hamilton Light Infantry, Canadian Army
Other Decorations: —
Date of Gazette: 14 Feb. 1946
Place/Date of Birth: Madoc, Ontario, Canada — 5 May 1904
Place/Date of Death: — *Died in Canada about 4.5.1988*
Memorials: —
Town/County Connections: —
Remarks: Minister of Reform Institutions, Ontario 1950-57
Account of Deed: On 19 Aug. 1942 at Dieppe, France, Captain Foote coolly and calmly during the eight hours of the battle walked about collecting the wounded, saving many lives by his gallant efforts and inspiring those around him by his example. At the end of this gruelling time he climbed from the landing craft that was to have taken him to safety and deliberately walked into the German position in order to be taken prisoner so that he could be a help to those men who would be in captivity until the end of the war.

FORBES-ROBERTSON, James — see ROBERTSON, James FORBES-

No photograph available

FORREST, George

418

Lieutenant (later Captain)   Bengal Veteran Establishment
Other Decorations: —
Date of Gazette: 18 Jun. 1858
Place/Date of Birth: St. Michael's, Dublin — 1800
Place/Date of Death: Dehra Dun, India — 3 Nov. 1859
Memorials: Tablet over gateway, Delhi Magazine
Town/County Connections: Dublin
Remarks: —
Account of Deed: On 11 May 1857 at Delhi, India, Lieutenant Forrest was one of nine men who defended the Magazine for more than five hours against large numbers of rebels and mutineers, until, on the wall being scaled and there being no hope of help, they fired the Magazine. Five of the gallant band died in the explosion and one shortly afterwards, but many of the enemy were killed. (See also BUCKLEY, J. and RAYNOR, W.)

FORSHAW, William Thomas

419

Lieutenant (later Major)   1/9th Bn., The Manchester Regiment
Other Decorations: —
Date of Gazette: 9 Sep. 1915
Place/Date of Birth: Barrow-in-Furness, Lancashire — 20 Apr. 1890
Place/Date of Death: Holyport, Berkshire — 26 May 1943
Memorials: ~~Buried at Ashton-under-Lyne, Lancashire~~ Blue plaque, Ladysmith Barracks, Ashton-under-Lyne
Town/County Connections: Barrow-in-Furness, Lancs.; Ipswich, Suffolk; Holyport, Berks.
Remarks: — Buried at Touchen End, near Maidenhead. Headstone installed 1995.
Account of Deed: During the period 7/9 Aug. 1915 in Gallipoli, when holding the north-west corner of "The Vineyard" against heavy attacks by the Turks, Lieutenant Forshaw not only directed his men but personally threw bombs continuously for over 40 hours. When his detachment was relieved, he volunteered to continue directing the defence. Later, when the Turks captured a portion of the trench, he shot three of them and recaptured it. It was due to his fine example and magnificent courage that this very important position was held.

FORSYTH, Samuel

420

Sergeant   New Zealand Engineers, attd. 2nd Bn., Auckland Infantry Regiment, N.Z.E.F.
Other Decorations: —
Date of Gazette: 22 Oct. 1918
Place/Date of Birth: Wellington, New Zealand — 3 Apr. 1891
Place/Date of Death: Grevillers, France — 24 Aug. 1918
Memorials: Adanac Military Cemetery, France; HQ, Dunedin RSA, New Zealand
Town/County Connections: —
Remarks: —
Account of Deed: On 24 Aug. 1918 at Grevillers, France, when Sergeant Forsyth's company was under heavy machine-gun fire on nearing their objective, he led attacks on three machine-gun positions and took the crews prisoner before they could inflict many casualties on our troops, Subsequently, in endeavouring to gain support from a tank to deal with several machine-guns, he was wounded and the tank put out of action. He then led the tank crew and several of his own men in an attack which brought about the retirement of the enemy machine-guns and enabled the advance to continue. At this moment he was killed by a sniper.

FOSBERY, George Vincent **421**
Lieutenant (later Colonel)   4th Bengal European Regiment, Indian Army
Other Decorations: —
Date of Gazette: 7 Jul. 1865
Place/Date of Birth: Stert, Devizes, Wiltshire — 1833
Place/Date of Death: Bath, Somerset — 8 May 1907
Memorials: —
Town/County Connections: Stert, Devizes, Wiltshire; Bath, Somerset
Remarks: Invented the "Paradox Gun" and an automatic revolver
Account of Deed: On 30 Oct. 1863 during the Umbeyla Campaign, North-West India, Lieutenant Fosbery led a party of his regiment to recapture the Crag Picquet, after its garrison had been driven in by the enemy and 60 of them killed. The approach to the Crag was very narrow, but the lieutenant led his party with great coolness, and was the first man to gain the top of the Crag from his side of the attack. Subsequently, when the commanding officer was wounded, Lieutenant Fosbery assembled a party and pursued the routed enemy, inflicting on them further losses. (See also PITCHER, H.W.)

FOSS, Charles Calveley **422**
Captain (later Brigadier)   2nd Bn., The Bedfordshire Regiment
Other Decorations: DSO
Date of Gazette: 23 Aug. 1915
Place/Date of Birth: Kobe, Japan — 9 Mar. 1885
Place/Date of Death: London — 9 Apr. 1953
Memorials: —
Town/County Connections: Bedford   *Marlborough College, Wilts*
Remarks: Served in the Home Guard 1940-45; County Cadet Commandant, Bedfordshire Army Cadet Force 1942-47; DL, County of Bedford
Account of Deed: On 12 Mar. 1915 at Neuve Chapelle, France, after the enemy had captured a part of one of our trenches and a counter-attack made with one officer and 20 men had failed (all but two of the party having been killed or wounded in the attempt) Captain Foss on his own initiative dashed forward with only eight men under heavy fire and attacked the enemy with bombs and captured the position and the 52 Germans occupying it.

FOSTER, Edward **423**
Corporal   13th Bn., The East Surrey Regiment
Other Decorations: —
Date of Gazette: 27 Jun. 1917
Place/Date of Birth: Streatham, London — 4 Feb. 1886
Place/Date of Death: Wandsworth, London — 22 Jan. 1946
Memorials: —
Town/County Connections: Streatham and Wandsworth, London
Remarks: —
Account of Deed: On 24 Apr. 1917 at Villers Plouich, France, during an attack, the advance was held up in a portion of the village by two machine-guns which were entrenched and strongly covered by wire entanglements. Corporal Foster who was in charge of two Lewis guns succeeded in entering the trench and engaged the enemy guns. One of the Lewis guns was lost, but the corporal rushed forward, bombed the enemy and recovered the gun. Then, getting his two guns into action, he killed the enemy gun team and captured their guns.

FOWLER, Edmund John **424**
Private (later Colour-Sergeant)   2nd Bn., The Cameronians (Scottish Rifles)
Other Decorations: —
Date of Gazette: 5 Apr. 1882
Place/Date of Birth: Waterford, Ireland — 1861
Place/Date of Death: Colchester, Essex — 26 Mar. 1926
Memorials: —
Town/County Connections: Waterford, Ireland
Remarks: —
Account of Deed: On 28 Mar. 1879 at the Zlobane Mountain, South Africa (Zulu War), Private Fowler, with a captain and a lieutenant* dashed forward in advance of the party which had been ordered to dislodge the enemy from a commanding position in natural caves up the mountain. The path was so narrow that they had to advance in single file and the captain who arrived first at the mouth of the cave was instantly killed. The lieutenant and Private Fowler undismayed by the death of their leader, immediately sprang forward and cleared the enemy out of their stronghold. (*See also LYSONS, H.)

FRASER, Charles Craufurd (later Sir Charles)   **425**
Major (later Lieutenant General)   7th Hussars (The Queen's Own)
Other Decorations: KCB
Date of Gazette: 8 Nov. 1860
Place/Date of Birth: ? — 31 Aug. 1829
Place/Date of Death: London — 7 Jun. 1895
Memorials: Brompton Cemetery, London; All Saints' Garrison Church, Aldershot
Town/County Connections: London
Remarks: Served in the Abyssinian war; ADC to the Duke of Cambridge 1873-77; MP for North
Lambeth 1884-92
Account of Deed: On 31 Dec. 1858 at the River Raptee, India, Major Fraser volunteered, at great
personal risk and under a sharp fire of musketry, to swim to the rescue of a captain and some men who were in imminent danger
of being drowned while in pursuit of the rebels. Major Fraser succeeded in this mission, although still partially disabled from a
wound received while leading a charge against the enemy some months earlier.

FRASER, Ian Edward   **426**
Lieutenant (later Lieutenant-Commander)   Royal Naval Reserve
Other Decorations: DSC, RD & Bar
Date of Gazette: 13 Nov. 1945
Place/Date of Birth: Ealing, London — 18 Dec. 1920
Place/Date of Death: —
Memorials: —
Town/County Connections: Ealing, London; Burnham, Buckinghamshire
Remarks: Legion of Merit (USA)
Account of Deed: On 31 Jul. 1945 in the Johore Straits, Singapore, Lieutenant Fraser, in
command of HM Midget Submarine XE.3, went to attack the Japanese cruiser *Takao*, which was
located after a long and hazardous journey. Lieutenant Fraser slid the submarine under the target which lay over a depression
in the sea bed, and his diver* went out to fix the limpet mines to the bottom of the ship. The two side-charges then had to be
released, but the starboard charge stuck and the diver climbed out again and after a nerve-wracking five minutes released the
charge. XE.3 then made for home. (*See also MAGENNIS, J.J.)

No photograph available

FREEMAN, John   **427**
Private   9th Lancers (The Queen's Royal)
Other Decorations: —
Date of Gazette: 24 Dec. 1858
Place/Date of Birth: Sittingbourne, Kent — 1832
Place/Date of Death: Hackney, London — 1 Jul. 1913
Memorials: —
Town/County Connections: Sittingbourne, Kent
Remarks: —
Account of Deed: On 10 Oct. 1857 at Agra, India, Private Freeman went to the assistance of a
lieutenant who had been shot. He killed the leader of the enemy's cavalry, and defended the
lieutenant against several of the enemy.

FRENCH, John Alexander   **428**
Corporal   2/9th Bn. (Q), Australian Military Forces
Other Decorations: —
Date of Gazette: 14 Jan. 1943
Place/Date of Birth: Crow's Nest, Toowoomba, Queensland, Australia — 15 Jul. 1914
Place/Date of Death: Milne Bay, Papua, New Guinea — 4 Sep. 1942
Memorials: Port Moresby (Bomana) War Cemetery, New Guinea; Australian War Memorial,
Canberra
Town/County Connections: —
Remarks: —
Account of Deed: On 4 Sep. 1942 at Milne Bay, New Guinea, the advance of Corporal French's
section was held up by fire from three enemy machine-gun posts, whereupon he ordered the section to take cover, advanced
and silenced the first two posts with grenades. He then attacked the third post with a sub-machine-gun, and although obviously
badly wounded, continued to advance. The enemy guns ceased to fire and the section pushed on to find that all members of
their crews had been killed and that Corporal French had died in front of the third gun. His courageous action enabled the
section to complete its task.

FREYBERG, Bernard Cyril   **429**
T/Lieutenant Colonel (later Lieutenant General)   The Queen's Royal West Surrey Regt., comd.
Hood Bn., Royal Naval Division
Other Decorations: GCMG, KCB,KBE, DSO & 3 Bars
Date of Gazette: 15 Dec. 1916
Place/Date of Birth: Richmond Hill, Surrey — 21 Mar. 1889
Place/Date of Death: Windsor, Berkshire — 4 Jul. 1963
Memorials: St. Martha's churchyard, Chilworth, Surrey;Crypt, St. Paul's Cathedral; St.
George's Chapel, Windsor; bust in Guildhall, London
Town/County Connections: Chilworth, Surrey; Windsor, Berkshire
Remarks: GOC New Zealand Forces 1939-45; C-in-C Crete 1941; Governor-General, New
Zealand 1946-52; Deputy Constable and Lieutenant Governor, Windsor Castle 1953-63
Account of Deed: On 13 Nov. 1916 at Beaucourt sur Ancre, France, after carrying the initial attack through the enemy's front
system of trenches, Lieutenant Colonel Freyberg's battalion was much disorganised, but after rallying and re-forming his own
men and some others, he led them on a successful assault of the second objective, during which he was twice wounded, but
remained in command and held his ground throughout the day and the following night. When reinforced the next morning he
attacked and captured a strongly fortified village, taking 500 prisoners. He was wounded twice more, the second time severely,
but he refused to leave the line until he had issued final instructions.

FRICKLETON, Samuel   **430**
Lance-Corporal (later Captain)   3rd Bn., 3rd N.Z. (Rifle) Brigade, N.Z.E.F.
Other Decorations: —
Date of Gazette: 2 Aug. 1917
Place/Date of Birth: Slamannan, Stirlingshire, Scotland — 1 Apr. 1891
Place/Date of Death: Wellington, New Zealand — 1 Sep. 1971
Memorials: Taita Servicemen's Cemetery, Naenae, New Zealand; HQ, Dunedin RSA, New
Zealand
Town/County Connections: Slamannan, Stirlingshire
Remarks: —
Account of Deed: On 7 Jun. 1917 at Messines, Belgium, Lance-Corporal Frickleton, although
slightly wounded, dashed forward at the head of his section, pushed into our barrage and personally destroyed with bombs an
enemy machine-gun and crew which was causing heavy casualties. He then attacked a second gun killing all the crew of 12. By
the destruction of these two guns he undoubtedly saved his own and other units from very severe casualties. During the
consolidation of this position he received a second severe wound.

FRISBY, Cyril Hubert   **431**
A/Captain   1st Bn., Coldstream Guards
Other Decorations: —
Date of Gazette: 27 Nov. 1918
Place/Date of Birth: New Barnet, Hertfordshire — 17 Sep. 1885
Place/Date of Death: Guildford, Surrey — 10 Sep. 1961
Memorials: Brookwood Cemetery, Woking, Surrey   *Buried Brookwood Cemetery*
Town/County Connections: New Barnet, Hertfordshire; Guildford, Surrey
Remarks: — *Haileybury School.*
Account of Deed: On 27 Sep. 1918 at the Canal du Nord, near Graincourt, France, Captain Frisby
was in command of a company detailed to capture a canal crossing, but when the canal was
reached, the leading platoon came under annihilating fire from a strong enemy post under the bridge on the far side of the canal.
Captain Frisby with a lance-corporal* and two others, climbed down into the canal under intense fire and succeeded in
capturing the post with two machine-guns and 12 men. Then having consolidated his objective he gave timely support to a
company which had lost all its officers and sergeants, organising the defences and beating off a heavy counter-attack. (*See
also JACKSON, T.N.)

FULLER, Wilfred Dolby   **432**
Lance-Corporal (later Corporal)   1st Bn., Grenadier Guards
Other Decorations: —
Date of Gazette: 19 Apr. 1915
Place/Date of Birth: East Kirkby, Greasley, Nottinghamshire — 28 Jul. 1893
Place/Date of Death: Frome, Somerset — 22 Nov. 1947
Memorials: Buried at Frome, Somerset
Town/County Connections: East Kirkby, Greasley, Nottinghamshire; Frome, Somerset
Remarks: —
Account of Deed: On 12 Mar. 1915 at Neuve Chapelle, France, Lance-Corporal Fuller saw a party
of the enemy trying to escape along a communication trench. He ran towards them and killed the
leading man with a bomb; the remainder (nearly 50) seeing no means of evading his bombs, all surrendered to him. Lance-
Corporal Fuller was quite alone at the time.

FULLER, William Charles **433**
Lance-Corporal (later Sergeant)   2nd Bn., The Welch Regiment
Other Decorations: Royal Humane Society Medal for Life-saving
Date of Gazette: 23 Nov. 1914
Place/Date of Birth: Laugharne, Carmarthen, Wales — 24 Mar. 1884
Place/Date of Death: Swansea, Glamorganshire, Wales — 29 Dec. 1974
Memorials: Oystermouth Cemetery, Mumbles, Swansea *Grave 373, Section R.*
Town/County Connections: Laugharne, Carmarthen; Swansea, Glamorgan
Remarks: —
Account of Deed: On 14 Sep. 1914 near Chivy-sur-Aisne, France, Lance-Corporal Fuller
advanced under very heavy rifle and machine-gun fire to pick up an officer who was mortally
wounded, and carried him back to cover.

FURNESS, The Hon. Christopher **434**
Lieutenant   1st Bn., Welsh Guards
Other Decorations: —
Date of Gazette: 7 Feb. 1946
Place/Date of Birth: London — 17 May 1912
Place/Date of Death: Near Arras, France — 24 May 1940 *→ Column 34*
Memorials: The Dunkirk Memorial, France; Guards Chapel, Wellington Barracks
Town/County Connections: London
Remarks: — *Eton College   VC. with Welsh Guards*
Account of Deed: During the period 17/24 May 1940 near Arras, France, Lieutenant Furness
commanded the Carrier Platoon when his battalion formed part of the garrison of the town. On 23
May the platoon was ordered to cover the withdrawal of the transport (over 40 vehicles) to Douai. Early on 24 May the enemy
were advancing along the road where the transport columns were moving and Lieutenant Furness decided to attack. He
reached the enemy position under heavy fire and when the light tanks and all the carriers and their crews had become casualties
he engaged the enemy in hand-to-hand combat until he was killed. His fight against hopeless odds made the enemy withdraw
temporarily and enabled the vehicles to get clear.

FYNN (or FINN) James Henry **435**
Private   4th Bn., The South Wales Borderers
Other Decorations: —
Date of Gazette: 26 Sep. 1916
Place/Date of Birth: Truro, Cornwall — 24 Nov. 1893
Place/Date of Death: Mesopotamia — 30 Mar. 1917
Memorials: Basra Memorial, Iraq; The Guildhall, Bodmin, Cornwall
Town/County Connections: Bodmin, Cornwall
Remarks: — *VC in Bodmin Town Hall*
Account of Deed: On 9 Apr. 1916 at Sanna-i-Yat, Mesopotamia, Private Fynn was one of a small
party which dug in, in front of our advanced line and about 300 yards from the enemy's trenches.
He went out and bandaged a number of wounded men under heavy fire, making several journeys in order to do so. Being unable
to get a stretcher, he carried on his back a badly wounded man to safety.

GABY, Alfred Edward **436**
Lieutenant   28th Bn. (W.A.), Australian Imperial Force
Other Decorations: —
Date of Gazette: 30 Oct. 1918
Place/Date of Birth: Springfield, Tasmania — 25 Jan. 1892
Place/Date of Death: Villers-Bretonneux, France — 11 Aug. 1918
Memorials: Heath Cemetery, Harbonnieres, France; Australian War Memorial, Canberra
Town/County Connections: —
Remarks: —
Account of Deed: On 8 Aug. 1918 at Villers-Bretonneux, France, when the advance was checked
by a large force of the enemy about 40 yards beyond the wire, Lieutenant Gaby found a gap and
approached the strong point under heavy machine-gun and rifle fire. He emptied his revolver into the garrison, drove the crews
from their guns and captured 50 prisoners and four machine-guns. Three days later, while leading his men during an attack, he
was killed.

GAJE GHALE 437

Havildar (later Subadar) 2nd Bn., 5th Royal Gurkha Rifles, Indian Army
Other Decorations: —
Date of Gazette: 30 Sep. 1943
Place/Date of Birth: Borpak Village, Gorkha District, Nepal — 1 Jul. 1922
Place/Date of Death: — *About 29.3.2000*
Memorials: —
Town/County Connections: —
Remarks: —
Account of Deed: During the period 24/27 May 1943 in the Chin Hills, Burma, Havildar Gaje Ghale was in charge of a platoon of young soldiers engaged in attacking a strong Japanese position. Wounded in the arm, chest and leg he nevertheless continued to lead assault after assault, encouraging his men by shouting the Gurkha's battle-cry. Spurred on by the irresistible will of their leader, the platoon stormed and captured the position which the havildar then held and consolidated under heavy fire, refusing to go to the Regimental Aid post until ordered to do so.

GANJU LAMA 438

Rifleman (later Subadar) 1st Bn., 7th Gurkha Rifles, Indian Army
Other Decorations: MM
Date of Gazette: 7 Sep. 1944
Place/Date of Birth: Samgmo Busty, Sikkim — 7 Jul. 1922
Place/Date of Death: — *About July 1st 2000.*
Memorials: —
Town/County Connections: —
Remarks: — *He was neither a Gurkha nor a Nepalese. He was of Bhutan.*
Account of Deed: On 12 Jun. 1944 at Ninthoukhong, Burma, 'B' Company was attempting to stem the enemy's advance when it came under heavy machine-gun and tank machine-gun fire. Rifleman Ganju Lama, with complete disregard for his own safety, took his Piat gun and crawling forward succeeded in bringing the gun into action within 30 yards of the enemy tanks, knocking out two of them. Despite a broken wrist and two other serious wounds to his right and left hands he then moved forward and engaged the tank crew who were trying to escape. Not until he had accounted for all of them did he consent to have his wounds dressed.

GARDINER, George 439

Sergeant (later Colour-Sergeant) 57th Regt. (later The Middlesex Regiment — Duke of Cambridge's Own)
Other Decorations: DCM
Date of Gazette: 2 Jun. 1858
Place/Date of Birth: Gelwallen, Warrenpoint, Co. Down, Ireland — 1821
Place/Date of Death: Lifford, Co. Donegal, Ireland — 17 Nov. 1891
Memorials: Lifford Cemetery, Co. Donegal
Town/County Connections: Warrenpoint, Co. Down
Remarks: —
Account of Deed: On 22 Mar. 1855 at Sebastopol, Crimea, Sergeant Gardiner acted with great gallantry upon the occasion of a sortie by the enemy, in having rallied the covering parties which had been driven in by the Russians, thus regaining the trenches. On 18 Jun. during the attack on the Redan he himself remained and encouraged others to remain in the holes made by the explosions of the shells, and from whence they were able to keep up a continuous fire until their ammunition was exhausted, and the enemy cleared away from the parapet.

GARDNER, Philip John 440

A/Captain Royal Tank Regiment, R.A.C.
Other Decorations: MC
Date of Gazette: 10 Feb. 1942
Place/Date of Birth: Sydenham, London — 25 Dec. 1914
Place/Date of Death: — *13.2.2003*
Memorials: —
Town/County Connections: Sydenham and Dulwich, London
Remarks: —
Account of Deed: On 23 Nov. 1941 at Tobruk, Libya, Captain Gardner took two tanks to the rescue of two armoured cars of the King's Dragoon Guards, which were out of action and under heavy attack. Whilst one tank gave covering fire the captain dismounted from the other, hitched a tow rope to one of the cars, then lifted into it an officer, both of whose legs had been blown off. The tow rope broke, so Captain Gardner returned to the armoured car, but was immediately wounded in the arm and leg. Despite this he managed to transfer the wounded man to the second tank and returned to British lines through intense shell-fire.

GARDNER, William   **441**
Colour-Sergeant (later Sergeant-Major)   42nd Regiment (later The Black Watch (Royal Highlanders))
Other Decorations: MSM
Date of Gazette: 23 Aug. 1858
Place/Date of Birth: Nemphlar, Lanarkshire, Scotland — 3 Mar. 1821
Place/Date of Death: Bothwell, Lanarkshire, Scotland — 24 Oct. 1897
Memorials: Bothwell Park Cemetery, Lanarkshire
Town/County Connections: Nemphlar, Lanarkshire
Remarks: —
Account of Deed: On 5 May 1858 at Bareilly, India, Colour-Sergeant Gardner saved the life of his commanding officer who, during the action had been knocked from his horse when three fanatics rushed upon him. The colour-sergeant ran out and bayoneted two of the assailants and was in the act of attacking the third when he was killed by another soldier of the regiment.

GARFORTH, Charles Ernest   **442**
Corporal (later Sergeant)   15th Hussars (The King's)
Other Decorations: —
Date of Gazette: 16 Nov. 1914
Place/Date of Birth: Willesden Green, London — 23 Oct. 1891
Place/Date of Death: Beeston, Nottinghamshire — 1 Jul. 1973
Memorials: —
Town/County Connections: Willesden Green and Harrow, London; Beeston, Nottinghamshire
Remarks: —
Account of Deed: On 23 Aug. 1914 at Harmingnies, France, Corporal Garforth volunteered to cut wire under fire, which enabled his squadron to escape. On 2 Sep. when under constant fire, he extricated a sergeant who was lying under his dead horse, and carried him to safety. The next day, when another sergeant had lost his horse in a similar way, Corporal Garforth drew off the enemy fire and enabled the sergeant to get away.

GARLAND, Donald Edward   **443**
Flying Officer   12 Squadron, Royal Air Force
Other Decorations: —
Date of Gazette: 11 Jun. 1940
Place/Date of Birth: Ballinacor, Co. Wicklow, Ireland — 28 Jun. 1918
Place/Date of Death: Maastricht, Holland — 12 May 1940
Memorials: Heverlee War Cemetery, Louvain, Belgium
Town/County Connections: Ballinacor, Co. Wicklow
Remarks: —
Account of Deed: On 12 May 1940, over the Albert Canal, Belgium, one bridge in particular was being used by the invading army, with protection from fighter aircraft, anti-aircraft and machine-guns. The RAF was ordered to demolish this vital bridge, and five Fairey Battle bombers were despatched with Flying Officer Garland leading the attack. They met an inferno of anti-aircraft fire, but the mission was accomplished, due to the expert leadership of Flying Officer Garland and the coolness and resource of his navigator*. Only one bomber managed to get back to base, the leading aircraft and three others did not return. (*See also GRAY, T.)

GARVIN, Stephen   **444**
Colour-Sergeant   1st Bn., 60th Rifles (later The King's Royal Rifle Corps)
Other Decorations: —
Date of Gazette: 20 Jun. 1860
Place/Date of Birth: Cashel, Co. Tipperary, Ireland — 1826
Place/Date of Death: Chesterton, Oxfordshire — 23 Nov. 1874
Memorials: —
Town/County Connections: Cashel, Co. Tipperary; Chesterton, Oxfordshire
Remarks: —
Account of Deed: On 23 Jun. 1857 at Delhi, India, Colour-Sergeant Garvin volunteered to lead a small party of men under heavy fire to the 'Sammy House' in order to dislodge a number of the enemy who were keeping up a destructive fire on the advanced battery of heavy guns. This action was successful. Colour-Sergeant Garvin was also commended for gallant conduct throughout the operations before Delhi.

GEARY, Benjamin Handley   **445**
Second Lieutenant (later Major)   4th Bn., The East Surrey Regiment, attd. 1st Bn.
Other Decorations: —
Date of Gazette: 15 Oct. 1915
Place/Date of Birth: Marylebone, London — 29 Jun. 1891
Place/Date of Death: Niagara-on-the-Lake, Ontario, Canada — 26 May 1976
Memorials: —
Town/County Connections: Marylebone, London
Remarks: Chaplain to the Forces 1926; served with the Canadian Army during Second World War
Account of Deed: On 20 and 21 Apr. 1915 on Hill 60 near Ypres, Belgium, Second Lieutenant
Geary led his men across exposed open ground swept by fierce enemy fire to join survivors of the
Bedfordshire Regiment in a crater at the top of the hill, which he held against artillery and bomb attacks during the evening and
night. Each attack was repulsed mainly owing to the fine example and personal gallantry of Second Lieutenant Geary. He
deliberately exposed himself to enemy fire in order to see by the light of flares the whereabouts of the enemy. He was severely
wounded early on 21 April.

GEE, Robert   **446**
T/Captain   2nd Bn., The Royal Fusiliers
Other Decorations: MC
Date of Gazette: 11 Jan. 1918
Place/Date of Birth: Leicester — 7 May 1876
Place/Date of Death: Perth, Western Australia — 2 Aug. 1960
Memorials: Fountain at War Veterans' House, Perth, Western Australia
Town/County Connections: Countesthorpe, Leicestershire
Remarks: —
Account of Deed: On 30 Nov. 1917 at Masnieres and Les Rues Vertes, France, an attack by the
enemy captured brigade headquarters and ammunition dump. Captain Gee, finding himself a
prisoner, managed to escape and organised a party of the brigade staff with which he attacked the enemy, closely followed by
two companies of infantry. He cleared the locality and established a defensive flank, then finding an enemy machine-gun still
in action, with a revolver in each hand, he went forward and captured the gun, killing eight of the crew. He was wounded, but
would not have his wound dressed until the defence was organised.

GIAN SINGH   **447**
Naik   15th Punjab Regiment, Indian Army
Other Decorations: —
Date of Gazette: 22 May 1945
Place/Date of Birth: Shapur, Jullundur, Punjab — 5 Oct. 1920
Place/Date of Death: — Died about 14.10.1996
Memorials: —
Town/County Connections: —
Remarks: PVSM (India)
Account of Deed: On 2 Mar. 1945 on the road between Kamye and Myingyan, Burma, where the
Japanese were strongly positioned, Naik Gian Singh who was in charge of the leading section of
his platoon, went on alone firing his tommy gun, and rushed the enemy foxholes. In spite of being wounded in the arm he went
on, hurling grenades. He attacked and killed the crew of a cleverly concealed anti-tank gun, and then led his men down a lane
clearing all enemy positions. He went on leading his section until the action had been satisfactorily completed.

GIBSON, Guy Penrose   **448**
Wing Commander   617 Squadron, Royal Air Force
Other Decorations: DSO & Bar, DFC & Bar
Date of Gazette: 28 May 1943
Place/Date of Birth: Simla, India — 12 Aug. 1918
Place/Date of Death: Near Bergen-op-Zoom, Holland — 19 Sep. 1944
Memorials: Steenbergen-en-Kruisland R.C. Churchyard, Holland
Town/County Connections: Porthleven, Cornwall
Remarks: Legion of Merit (USA); author of *Enemy Coast Ahead*.
Account of Deed: On 16/17 May 1943 over Germany, Wing Commander Gibson led the raid on
the Möhne Dam, descending to within a few feet of the water and taking the full brunt of the enemy
defences. He delivered his attack with great accuracy and afterwards circled very low for 30 minutes, drawing the enemy's fire
on himself in order to leave as free a run as possible to the following aircraft. He then led the remainder of his force to the Eder
Dam where with complete disregard for his own safety he repeated his tactics and once again drew the enemy fire so that the
attack could be successfully developed.

GIFFORD Lord Edric Frederick   449
Lieutenant (later Major) 2nd Bn., 24th Regiment (later The South Wales Borderers)
Other Decorations: —
Date of Gazette: 28 Mar. 1874
Place/Date of Birth: Ropley, Hampshire — 5 Jul. 1849
Place/Date of Death: Chichester, Sussex — 5 Jun. 1911
Memorials: Bosham Church, Sussex *Buried Bosham, alternatively Ampney P Cirencester*
Town/County Connections: Ropley, Hampshire; Chichester and Bosham, Sussex
Remarks: Uncle of Captain J.F.P. Butler, VC; Colonial Secretary for Western Australia and Senior
Member Legislative Council 1880-1883; Colonial Secretary for Gibraltar 1883-88 *Harrow School.*
Account of Deed: During the 1873-74 Ashanti Campaign, Lieutenant Lord Gifford was in charge
of Scouts after the army crossed the Prah, and he daily took his life in his hands, performing his dangerous duties. He ferreted
out the enemy's intentions, discovered their positions and took numerous prisoners. His courage was particularly conspicuous
at the taking of Becquah, into which he penetrated with his scouts before the troops carried it.

GILL, Albert   450
Sergeant 1st Bn., The King's Royal Rifle Corps
Other Decorations: —
Date of Gazette: 26 Oct. 1916
Place/Date of Birth: Birmingham — 8 Sep. 1879
Place/Date of Death: Delville Wood, France — 27 Jul. 1916
Memorials: Delville Wood Cemetery, France
Town/County Connections: Birmingham
Remarks: —
Account of Deed: On 27 Jul. 1916 at Delville Wood, France, the enemy made a very strong
counter-attack on the right flank of the battalion and rushed the bombing post after killing all the
company bombers. Sergeant Gill rallied the remnants of his platoon, none of whom were skilled bombers, and reorganised his
defences. Soon afterwards the enemy nearly surrounded his men and started sniping at about 20 yards range. Although it was
almost certain death, Sergeant Gill stood boldly up in order to direct the fire of his men. He was killed almost at once, but his
gallant action held up the enemy advance.

No photograph available

GILL, Peter   451
Sergeant-Major (later Lieutenant and Barrack-Master) Loodiana Regiment
Other Decorations: —
Date of Gazette: 23 Aug. 1858
Place/Date of Birth: St. Paul's, Dublin — Sep. 1831
Place/Date of Death: Morar, Central India — 26 Jul. 1868
Memorials: —
Town/County Connections: Dublin
Remarks: —
Account of Deed: On 4 Jun. 1857 at Benares, India, Sergeant-Major Gill volunteered, with
another sergeant-major and a private* to rescue a paymaster and his family from their bungalow
and take them to the safety of the barracks. During the same evening he saved the life of a quartermaster-sergeant by cutting
off the head of the sepoy who had just bayoneted him. He is also said to have twice saved the life of a major who was being
attacked by sepoys. (*See also ROSAMUND, M. and KIRK, John).

GLASOCK, Horace Henry   452
Driver 'Q' Bty., Royal Horse Arillery
Other Decorations: —
Date of Gazette: 26 Jun. 1900
Place/Date of Birth: Islington, London — 16 Oct. 1880
Place/Date of Death: South Africa — 13 Feb. 1920
Memorials: Maitland Cemetery, Cape Town, South Africa
Town/County Connections: Islington, London
Remarks: — *Picture on staircase in Islington Town Hall*
Account of Deed: On 31 Mar. 1900 at Korn Spruit, South Africa, two batteries of the Royal Horse
Artillery were ambushed with the loss of most of the baggage column and five guns of the leading
battery. When the alarm was given, 'Q' Battery went into action 1150 yards from the spruit, until the order to retire was received,
when the major* commanding the battery ordered the guns and their limbers to be run back by hand to a safe place. This most
exhausting operation was carried out by, among others, Driver Glasock, a sergeant* and a gunner* and when at last all but one
of the guns and one limber had been moved to safety, the battery was reformed. (Awarded by ballot. *See also HORNBY, E.J.
Phipps-,PARKER, C.E.H. and LODGE, I.)

GLENN, James Alexander — see **SMITH,** James

GOAT, William
453

Lance-Corporal (later Corporal)   9th Lancers (The Queen's Royal)
Other Decorations: —
Date of Gazette: 24 Dec. 1858
Place/Date of Birth: Fritton, near Long Stratton, Norfolk — 12 Jan. 1836
Place/Date of Death: Jarrow, Co. Durham — 24 Oct. 1901
Memorials: —
Town/County Connections: Norwich; Jarrow, Co. Durham
Remarks: —
Account of Deed: On 6 Mar. 1858 at Lucknow, India, Lance-Corporal Goat dismounted in the presence of the enemy in order to take up the body of a major, which he then attempted to take off the field, but was forced to relinquish as he was surrounded by hostile cavalry. He did not, however, give up, but went a second time under heavy fire and recovered the body.

No photograph available

GOBAR SING NEGI
454

Rifleman   2/39th Garhwal Rifles, Indian Army
Other Decorations: —
Date of Gazette: 28 Apr. 1915
Place/Date of Birth: Manjaur, Takti State, Garhwal, India — 7 Oct. 1893
Place/Date of Death: Near Neuve Chapelle, France — 10 Mar. 1915
Memorials: Neuve Chapelle Memorial, France
Town/County Connections: —
Remarks: —
Account of Deed: On 10 Mar. 1915 at Neuve Chapelle, France, during an attack on the German position Rifleman Gobar Sing Negi was one of a bayonet party with bombs who entered their main trench, and was the first man to go round each traverse, driving back the enemy until they were eventually forced to surrender. He was killed during this engagement.

GOBIND SINGH
455

Lance-Dafadar (later Jemadar)   28th Light Cavalry, attd. 2nd Lancers, Indian Army
Other Decorations: —
Date of Gazette: 11 Jan. 1918
Place/Date of Birth: Damoe Village, Jodhpur, India — 7 Dec. 1887
Place/Date of Death: Nagaur, Rajputana, India — 9 Dec. 1942
Memorials: —
Town/County Connections: —
Remarks: —
Account of Deed: On 1 Dec. 1917 east of Peizieres, France, Lance-Dafadar Gobind Singh three times volunteered to carry messages between the regiment and brigade headquarters, a distance of 1½ miles over open ground which was under heavy fire from the enemy. He succeeded each time in delivering the message, although on each occasion his horse was shot and he was compelled to finish the journey on foot.

GODLEY, Sidney Frank
456

Private   4th Bn., The Royal Fusiliers
Other Decorations: —
Date of Gazette: 25 Nov. 1914
Place/Date of Birth: East Grinstead, Sussex — 14 Aug. 1889
Place/Date of Death: Epping, Essex — 29 Jun. 1957
Memorials: Manor Park Cemetery, London; plaque on Nimy Bridge, Mons.
Town/County Connections: East Grinstead, Sussex; Sidcup, Kent; Epping, Essex
Remarks: First private soldier to be awarded the VC in the First World War, and thought to be the original of Bruce Bairnsfather's character 'Old Bill'; presented in 1938 with special gold medal struck by Mons
Account of Deed: On 23 Aug. 1914 at Mons, Belgium, Private Godley took over a machine-gun on Nimy Bridge when the lieutenant* in charge of the section had been mortally wounded. Private Godley held the enemy from the bridge single-handed for two hours under very heavy fire and was wounded twice. His gallant action covered the retreat of his comrades, but he was eventually taken prisoner. His final act was to destroy the gun and throw the pieces into the canal. (*See also DEASE, M.J.)

Buried in Grave 3051, Loughton Cemetery attached to St. John's Church, Loughton Essex. Take main pathway from Main Gate, then second section on left. Grave is off the main pathway

GOOD, Herman James   **457**

Corporal   13th Bn., Quebec Regiment (Royal Highlanders of Canada)
Other Decorations: —
Date of Gazette: 27 Sep. 1918
Place/Date of Birth: South Bathurst, New Brunswick, Canada — 29 Nov. 1887
Place/Date of Death: Bathurst, New Brunswick — 18 Apr. 1969
Memorials: St. Alban's Cemetery, Bathurst, New Brunswick
Town/County Connections: —
Remarks: —
Account of Deed: On 8 Aug. 1918 at Hangard Wood, France, when his company was held up by heavy fire from three machine-guns, Corporal Good dashed forward alone, killing several of the garrison and capturing the remainder. Later on, the corporal, while alone, encountered a battery of 5.9-inch guns which were in action at the time. Collecting three men of his section he charged the battery under point-blank fire and captured the entire crews of three guns.

GOODFELLOW, Charles Augustus   **458**

Lieutenant (later Lieutenant General)   Bombay Engineers
Other Decorations: CB
Date of Gazette: 16 Apr. 1863
Place/Date of Birth: Essex — 27 Nov. 1836
Place/Date of Death: Leamington, Warwickshire — 1 Sep. 1915
Memorials: —
Town/County Connections: Leamington, Warwickshire
Remarks: —
Account of Deed: On 6 Oct. 1859 during an attack on the Fort of Beyt, India, a soldier was shot under the walls in a sharp fire of matchlock. Lieutenant Goodfellow carried away the body of the man who was then dead, but whom he had at first thought was only wounded.

GOODLAKE, Gerald Littlehales   **459**

Bt/Major (later Lieutenant General)   Coldstream Guards
Other Decorations: —
Date of Gazette: 24 Feb. 1857
Place/Date of Birth: Wadley, Berkshire — 14 May 1832
Place/Date of Death: Denham, Middlesex — 5 Apr. 1890
Memorials: Harefield Churchyard, Middlesex
Town/County Connections: Wadley, Berkshire; Denham, Middlesex
Remarks: Légion d'Honneur (France)   *Newstead Abbey. Notts*
Account of Deed: On 28 Oct. 1854 at Inkerman, Crimea, Major Goodlake was in command of a party of sharpshooters which held Windmill Ravine against a much larger force of the enemy, killing 38 (including an officer) and taking three prisoners. He also showed conspicuous gallantry on a later occasion when his sharpshooters surprised a picquet and seized the knapsacks and rifles of the enemy.

GORDON, Bernard Sidney   **460**

Lance-Corporal   41st Bn. (Queensland), Australian Imperial Force
Other Decorations: MM
Date of Gazette: 26 Dec. 1918
Place/Date of Birth: Launceston, Tasmania — 16 Aug. 1891
Place/Date of Death: Launceston, Tasmania — 19 Oct. 1963
Memorials: Australian War Memorial, Canberra
Town/County Connections: —
Remarks: —
Account of Deed: On 26/27 Aug. 1918, east of Bray, France, after leading his section through heavy shellfire, Lance-Corporal Gordon, single-handed, attacked an enemy machine-gun, killed the gunner and captured the post, which contained an officer and 10 men. He then cleared more trenches and captured a further 51 prisoners, including one officer, and six machine-guns.

GORDON, James Heather   **461**
Private (later Warrant Officer Class II)   2/31st Bn. (Q. & V.) Australian Military Forces
Other Decorations: —
Date of Gazette: 28 Oct. 1941
Place/Date of Birth: Rockingham, Western Australia — 7 Mar. 1909
Place/Date of Death: Perth, Western Australia — 24 Jul. 1986
Memorials: Australian War Memorial, Canberra
Town/County Connections: —
Remarks: —
Account of Deed: On 10 Jul. 1941 at Djezzine, Syria, Private Gordon's company was held up by intense machine-gun and grenade fire, but on his own initiative, he crept forward alone and succeeded in getting close to the machine-gun post. He then charged it and killed the four machine-gunners. His action completely demoralized the enemy in this sector and the company advanced and took the position.

GORDON, William Eagleson   **462**
Captain (later Colonel)   1st Bn., The Gordon Highlanders
Other Decorations: CBE
Date of Gazette: 28 Sep. 1900
Place/Date of Birth: Bridge of Allan, Stirlingshire, Scotland — 4 May 1866
Place/Date of Death: London — 10 Mar. 1941
Memorials: —
Town/County Connections: Bridge of Allan, Stirlingshire, Scotland
Remarks: ADC to The King 1913; served in the First World War; commanded Northern District, Scottish Command 1917-20
Account of Deed: On 11 Jul. 1900 near Krugersdorp, South Africa, a party of men had succeeded in dragging an artillery waggon under cover when its horses were unable to do so, because of heavy and accurate firing by the enemy. Captain Gordon then went out alone to the nearest gun under heavy fire and then having fastened a drag rope to the gun, he called for volunteers to come and help. While the gun was being moved, however, a captain* and three men were hit, and to save further casualties, Captain Gordon ordered the remainder of the party to take cover, and having seen the wounded safely away, he himself retired. (*See also YOUNGER, D.R.)

GORDON, William James   **463**
Lance-Corporal (later Sergeant)   West India Regiment
Other Decorations: —
Date of Gazette: 9 Dec. 1892
Place/Date of Birth: Jamaica, West Indies — 19 May 1864
Place/Date of Death: Jamaica — 15 Aug. 1922
Memorials: —
Town/County Connections: —
Remarks: —
Account of Deed: On 13 Mar. 1892 at Toniataba, West Africa, the major who was in command of the troops was superintending a party of 12 men who were trying, with a heavy beam, to break down the south gate of the town. Suddenly a number of musket-muzzles appeared through a double row of loopholes, some of them being only two or three yards from the major's back and before he realised what had happened, Lance-Corporal Gordon threw himself between the major and the muskets, pushing that officer out of the way. At the same moment the NCO was shot through the lungs.

GORE-BROWNE, Henry George — see **BROWNE,** Henry George GORE-

GORLE, Robert Vaughan   **464**
T/Lieutenant   'A' Bty., 50th Brigade, Royal Field Artillery
Other Decorations: —
Date of Gazette: 14 Dec. 1918
Place/Date of Birth: Southsea, Hampshire — 6 May 1896
Place/Date of Death: Durban, Natal, South Africa — 9 Jan. 1937
Memorials: —
Town/County Connections: Southsea, Hampshire
Remarks: —   *Rugby School.*
Account of Deed: On 1 Oct. 1918 at Ledeghem, Belgium, Lieutenant Gorle was in command of an 18-pounder gun working in close conjunction with the infantry. He brought his gun into action in the most exposed position on four separate occasions and disposed of enemy machine-guns by firing over open sights under direct fire. Later, when the infantry were driven back, he galloped his gun in front of the leading troops and twice knocked out enemy machine-guns which were causing the trouble. His disregard of personal safety was a magnificent example to the wavering line which rallied and re-took the northern end of the village.

GORMAN, (born DEVEREUX), James **465**
Seaman (later Able Seaman)   Royal Navy (Naval Brigade)
Other Decorations: —
Date of Gazette: 24 Feb. 1857
Place/Date of Birth: ?London, ?Essex — ?1832
Place/Date of Death: Southwark, London — 27 Dec. 1889
Memorials: —
Town/County Connections: Southwark, London
Remarks: —
Account of Deed: On 5 Nov. 1854 at the Battle of Inkerman, Crimea, when the Right Lancaster Battery was attacked and many of the soldiers were wounded, Seaman Gorman, with two other seamen* and two others who were killed during the action, mounted the defence work banquette and, under withering attack from the enemy, kept up a rapid, repulsing fire. Their muskets were re-loaded for them by the wounded soldiers under the parapet and eventually the enemy fell back and gave no more trouble. (*See also REEVES, T. and SCHOLEFIELD, M.)

GORT, Viscount, John Standish Surtees Prendergast Vereker **466**
A/Lieutenant Colonel (later Field Marshal)   Comd. 1st Bn., Grenadier Guards
Other Decorations: GCB,CBE,DSO & 2 Bars,MVO,MC
Date of Gazette: 27 Nov. 1918
Place/Date of Birth: Isle of Wight — 10 Jul. 1886
Place/Date of Death: London — 31 Mar. 1946
Memorials: St. John the Baptist Church, Penshurst, Kent *Buried there.*
Town/County Connections: Cowes, Isle of Wight; London *Ebchester (Hamsterley Hall) Durham*
Remarks: Father-in-law of Major W.P. Sidney (Viscount De L'Isle, VC; Chief of the Imperial General Staff 1937-39; C-in-C British Field Force 1939-40; Inspector-General to the Forces for Training and Inspector-General Home Guard 1940-41) ADC General to The King 1940-44; Governor and C-in-C Gibraltar 1941-42; Governor and C-in-C Malta 1942-44; Colonel Commandant Honourable Artillery Company 1943-46; High Commissioner and C-in-C Palestine and High Commissioner for Trans-Jordan 1944-45 *Harrow School*
Account of Deed: On 27 Sep. 1918 at the Canal du Nord, near Flesquieres, France, Lieutenant Colonel Gort led his battalion under very heavy fire and although wounded, when the battalion was held up, he went across open ground to obtain assistance from a tank and personally led it to the best advantage. He was again wounded but after lying on a stretcher for a while, insisted on getting up and directing the further attack which resulted in the capture of over 200 prisoners, two batteries of field-guns and numerous machine-guns. He refused to leave the field until the success signal had gone up on the final objective.

GOSLING, William **467**
Sergeant (later Major)   3rd Wessex Brigade, Royal Field Artillery
Other Decorations: —
Date of Gazette: 14 Jun. 1917
Place/Date of Birth: Wanborough, near Swindon, Wiltshire — 15 Aug. 1892
Place/Date of Death: Wroughton, Wiltshire — 12 Feb. 1945
Memorials: —
Town/County Connections: Wanborough and Wroughton, Wiltshire
Remarks: —
Account of Deed: On 5 Apr. 1917 near Arras, France, a bomb which had a faulty cartridge, fell 10 yards from the mortar. Sergeant Gosling sprang out, lifted the nose of the bomb which had sunk into the ground, unscrewed the fuse and threw it on the ground where it immediately exploded. This very gallant action undoubtedly saved the lives of the whole detachment.

GOUGH, Charles John Stanley (later Sir Charles) **468**
Major (later General)   5th Bengal European Cavalry
Other Decorations: GCB
Date of Gazette: 21 Oct. 1859
Place/Date of Birth: Chittagong, India — 28 Jan. 1832
Place/Date of Death: Clonmel, Tipperary, Ireland — 6 Sep. 1912
Memorials: —
Town/County Connections: Rathronan and Clonmel, Tipperary, Ireland
Remarks: Brother of Lieutenant H.H. Gough, VC; father of Bt/Major J.E. Gough, VC
Account of Deed: On 15 Aug. 1857 at Khurkowdah, India, Major Gough saved the life of his brother* who was wounded, and killed two of the enemy. On 18 Aug. he led a troop of the Guide Cavalry in a charge and cut down two of the enemy's sowars after a hand-to-hand combat with one of them. On 27 Jan. 1858, in a charge, he attacked one of the enemy's leaders and pierced him with his sword which was carried out of his hand in the mêlée. He defended himself with his revolver and shot two of the enemy. On 23 Feb. at Meangunge he went to the assistance of a major and killed his opponent. (*Lieutenant H.H. Gough, VC)

GOUGH, Hugh Henry (later Sir Hugh)   **469**
Lieutenant (later General)   1st Bengal European Light Cavalry
Other Decorations: GCB
Date of Gazette: 24 Dec. 1858
Place/Date of Birth: Calcutta, India — 14 Nov. 1833
Place/Date of Death: London — 12 May 1909
Memorials: Kensal Green Cemetery, London
Town/County Connections: Rathronan, Tipperary, Ireland; London
Remarks: Brother of Major C.J.S. Gough, VC; uncle of Bt/Major J.E. Gough, VC; Keeper of the Crown Jewels, Tower of London 1898-1909
Account of Deed: On 12 Nov. 1857 at Alumbagh, India, Lieutenant Gough charged across a swamp and captured two guns which were defended by a vastly superior body of the enemy. His horse was wounded in two places and he himself received sword cuts through his turban. On 25 Feb. 1858 at Jellalabad he set a magnificent example to his regiment when ordered to charge the enemy's guns. He engaged himself in a series of single combats until at length he was disabled by a musket ball through his leg while charging two sepoys with fixed bayonets.

GOUGH, John Edmund (later Sir John)   **470**
Bt/Major (later Brigadier General)   The Rifle Brigade (Prince Consort's Own)
Other Decorations: KCB, CMG
Date of Gazette: 15 Jan. 1904
Place/Date of Birth: Muree, India — 25 Oct. 1871
Place/Date of Death: Estaires, France — 22 Feb. 1915
Memorials: Estaires Communal Cemetery, France; Winchester Cathedral
Town/County Connections: —
Remarks: Son of Major C.J.S. Gough, VC; nephew of Lieutenant H.H. Gough, VC; Inspector-General, King's African Rifles 1907-09
Account of Deed: On 22 Apr. 1903 after the action at Daratoleh, Somaliland, Major Gough who was in charge of the column, came back to help two captains* who were with a mortally wounded officer. They managed to get him on to a camel, but he was wounded again and died immediately. (*See also WALKER, W.G. and ROLLAND, G.M.)

GOULD, Thomas William   **471**
Petty Officer   Royal Navy
Other Decorations: —
Date of Gazette: 9 Jun. 1942
Place/Date of Birth: Dover — 28 Dec. 1914
Place/Date of Death: — *About 6.12.2001*
Memorials: —
Town/County Connections: Dover and Bromley, Kent; St. Albans, Hertfordshire; London
Remarks: —
Account of Deed: On 16 Feb. 1942 north of Crete, HM Submarine *Thrasher*, after attacking and sinking a supply ship, was itself attacked, and later, after surfacing, two unexploded bombs were discovered in the gun-casing. The first lieutenant* and Petty Officer Gould removed the first one without too much difficulty, but the second was lying in a very confined space and they had to approach it lying full length. Petty Officer Gould then lay on his back with the bomb in his arms while the lieutenant dragged him along by the shoulders. It was 40 minutes before they got the bomb clear and dropped it over the side. (*See also ROBERTS, P.S.W.)

GOURLEY, Cyril Edward   **472**
Sergeant (later Captain)   'D' Bty., 276th (West Lancashire) Brigade, Royal Field Artillery
Other Decorations: MM
Date of Gazette: 13 Feb. 1918
Place/Date of Birth: Wavertree, Liverpool, Lancashire — 19 Jan. 1893
Place/Date of Death: Haslemere, Surrey — 30 Jan. 1982 *Buried in Grange Cemetery. West Kirby. L*
Memorials: Grayswood College, Chiddingfold, Surrey; Memorial College at West Kirby, Wirral
Town/County Connections: Wavertree, Liverpool; Grayswood, Surrey
Remarks: — *Scholarship named after him by Liverpool University.*
Account of Deed: On 30 Nov. 1917 at Little Priel Farm, east of Epehy, France, Sergeant Gourley was in command of a section of howitzers. During an enemy advance, when their forces were within a few hundred yards of him, both to the front and on one flank, and though plagued by snipers, Sergeant Gourley managed to keep one gun firing. At one point he pulled the gun out of the pit and engaged a machine-gun at 500 yards, knocking it out with a direct hit. All day he held the Germans in check, firing over open sights on enemy parties, thereby saving his guns, which were withdrawn at nightfall.

GOWRIE, Earl of — see **RUTHVEN,** The Hon. Alexander Gore Arkwright HORE-

GRADY, Thomas	**473**
Private (later Sergeant)   4th Regiment (later The King's Own (Royal Lancaster) Regiment)
Other Decorations: DCM
Date of Gazette: 23 Jun. 1857
Place/Date of Birth: Cheddah, Galway, Ireland — 18 Sep. 1835
Place/Date of Death: Victoria, Australia — 18 May 1891
Memorials: Melbourne General Cemetery, Melbourne, Victoria; The Priory, Lancaster
Town/County Connections: Cheddah, Galway
Remarks: —
Account of Deed: On 18 Oct. 1854 in the Crimea, Private Grady volunteered to repair the embrasures of the Sailors' Battery on the Left Attack and carried out this task under very heavy fire from a line of batteries. On 22 Nov. during the repulse of a Russian attack, although severely wounded, Private Grady refused to leave the front and his example encouraged the weak force which was engaging the enemy to maintain their position.

GRAHAM, Gerald (later Sir Gerald)	**474**
Lieutenant (later Lieutenant General)   Corps of Royal Engineers
Other Decorations: GCB, GCMG
Date of Gazette: 24 Feb. 1857
Place/Date of Birth: Acton, London — 27 Jun. 1831
Place/Date of Death: Acton, London — 17 Dec. 1899
Memorials: —   *Buried Bideford Parish Churchyard*
Town/County Connections: Acton, London
Remarks: Légion d'Honneur, France
Account of Deed: On 18 Jun. 1855 in the Crimea, Lieutenant Graham, accompanied by a sapper* showed determined gallantry at the head of a ladder party at the assault on the Redan at Sebastopol. He also went out on numerous occasions to bring in wounded officers and men. (*See also PERIE, J.)

GRAHAM, John Reginald Noble(later Sir Reginald)	**475**
Lieutenant (later Lieutenant Colonel)   9th Bn., The Argyll and Sutherland Highlanders (Princess Louise's), attd. 136th Coy., Machine Gun Corps
Other Decorations: OBE
Date of Gazette: 14 Sep. 1917
Place/Date of Birth: Calcutta, India — 17 Sep. 1892
Place/Date of Death: Edinburgh — 6 Dec. 1980
Memorials: —
Town/County Connections: Lochlomondside, Dumbarton, Scotland
Remarks: Served in the Second World War; Gentleman Usher of the Green Rod to the Most Noble Order of the Thistle 1959-79   *Eton College*
Account of Deed: On 22 Apr. 1917 at Istabulat, Mesopotamia, Lieutenant Graham was in command of a machine-gun section which came under very heavy fire. When his men became casualties he insisted on carrying the ammunition and although twice wounded, he continued in control and with one gun opened accurate fire on the enemy. This gun was put out of action and he was again wounded and forced to retire, but before doing so he disabled his gun and then brought a Lewis gun into action with excellent effect until all the ammunition was expended. He was wounded yet again and was again forced to retire.

No photograph available

GRAHAM, Patrick	**476**
Private   90th Regiment (later The Cameronians — Scottish Rifles)
Other Decorations: —
Date of Gazette: 24 Dec. 1858
Place/Date of Birth: St. Michael's, Dublin — 1837
Place/Date of Death: Dublin — 3 Jun. 1875
Memorials: —
Town/County Connections: Dublin
Remarks: —
Account of Deed: On 17 Nov. 1857 at Lucknow, India, Private Graham brought in a wounded comrade under very heavy fire. (Elected by the regiment.)

GRANT, Charles James William   **477**
Lieutenant (later Bt/Colonel)   Indian Staff Corps
Other Decorations: —
Date of Gazette: 26 May 1891
Place/Date of Birth: Bourtie, Aberdeenshire, Scotland — 14 Oct. 1861
Place/Date of Death: Sidmouth, Devon — 23 Nov. 1932
Memorials: —
Town/County Connections: Bourtie, Aberdeenshire
Remarks: Served in First World War
Account of Deed: During the period 21 Mar. to 9 Apr. 1891 after the disaster at Manipur, Burma,
Lieutenant Grant volunteered to attempt the relief of the British captives with 80 native soldiers.
Inspiring his men with his example of personal daring and resource, the lieutenant captured Thobal near Manipur, and held it
against a large force of the enemy.

GRANT, John Duncan   **478**
Lieutenant (later Colonel)   8th Gurkha Rifles, Indian Army
Other Decorations: CB, DSO
Date of Gazette: 24 Jan. 1905
Place/Date of Birth: Roorkee, United Provinces, India — 28 Dec. 1877
Place/Date of Death: Tunbridge Wells, Kent — 20 Feb. 1967
Memorials: —
Town/County Connections: Tunbridge Wells, Kent
Remarks: Served in First World War 1914-18; Asst. Adj. General, AHQ, India 1925-28; Dep.
Director, Auxiliary and Territorial Forces in India 1928-29; Colonel, 10th Gurkha Rifles 1934-47
Account of Deed: On 6 Jul. 1904 at the storming of the Gyantse Jong, Tibet, the storming
company, led by Lieutenant Grant, had to advance up a bare, almost precipitous rock-face with little cover and under heavy fire.
Showers of rock and stones were being hurled down the hillside by the enemy and only one man could go up at a time, crawling
on hands and knees. Lieutenant Grant and a havildar attempted to scale the final defensive curtain, but on reaching the top they
were both wounded and hurled back. Regardless of their injuries, they made another attempt and, covered by the fire of men
below, were at last successful.

GRANT, John Gilroy   **479**
Sergeant (later Lieutenant)   1st Bn., Wellington Infantry Regiment, N.Z.E.F.
Other Decorations: —
Date of Gazette: 27 Nov. 1918
Place/Date of Birth: Hawera, New Zealand — 26 Aug. 1889
Place/Date of Death: Auckland, New Zealand — 25 Nov. 1970
Memorials: HQ, Dunedin RSA, New Zealand
Town/County Connections: —
Remarks: —
Account of Deed: On 1 Sep. 1918 near Bancourt, France, the leading waves of the battalion on
reaching a crest of high ground, found that a line of enemy machine-gun posts offered a serious
obstacle to further advance. The company, however, advanced against these posts under point-blank fire, and when about 20
yards away Sergeant Grant, closely followed by a comrade, rushed ahead of his platoon, entering the centre post and
demoralising the garrison so that the platoon were able to mop up the position. In the same manner he rushed the post on the
left and the remaining posts were quickly occupied and cleared by his company.

GRANT, Peter   **480**
Private   93rd Regt. (later The Argyll and Sutherland Highlanders — Princess Louise's)
Other Decorations: —
Date of Gazette: 24 Dec. 1858
Place/Date of Birth: Ireland — ?1824
Place/Date of Death: Dundee, Scotland — 10 Jan. 1868
Memorials: —
Town/County Connections: —
Remarks: —
Account of Deed: On 16 Nov. 1857 at Lucknow, India, Private Grant showed great personal
gallantry at the Secundra Bagh in killing five of the enemy with one of their own swords when they
were attempting to follow the colonel as that officer was carrying a Colour which he had captured. (Elected by the regiment.)

GRANT, Robert   **481**
Sergeant   1st Bn., 5th Regiment (later The Northumberland Fusiliers)
Other Decorations: —
Date of Gazette: 19 Jun. 1860
Place/Date of Birth: Harrogate, Yorkshire — 1837
Place/Date of Death: London — 23 Nov. 1874
Memorials: Regimental Museum of The Royal Northumberland Fusiliers, Alnwick Castle, Northumberland
Town/County Connections: Harrogate, Yorkshire; London
Remarks: —
Account of Deed: On 24 Sep. 1857 at Alumbagh, India, Sergeant Grant went, under very heavy fire, to save the life of a private whose leg had been shot away. With the help of a lieutenant, Sergeant Grant carried the wounded man to the safety of the camp.

GRATWICK, Percival Eric   **482**
Private   2/48th Bn. (S.A.), Australian Military Forces
Other Decorations: —
Date of Gazette: 28 Jan. 1943
Place/Date of Birth: Katanning, Western Australia — 19 Oct 1902
Place/Date of Death: Miteiriya Ridge, Libya — 25/26 Oct. 1942
Memorials: El Alamein War Cemetery, Egypt; Australian War Memorial, Canberra
Town/County Connections: —
Remarks: —
Account of Deed: On 25/26 Oct. 1942 during the attack at Miteiriya Ridge, Western Desert, the platoon to which Private Gratwick belonged suffered a considerable number of casualties, including the platoon commander and sergeant. Private Gratwick, realizing the seriousness of the situation, charged on alone and with hand grenades, killed the crew of an enemy machine-gun and an entire mortar crew. Under heavy machine-gun fire he then charged the second post with rifle and bayonet. In inflicting further casualties he was killed by machine-gun fire, but his brave and determined action enabled his company to capture the final objective.

GRAY, Robert Hampton   **483**
T/Lieutenant   Royal Canadian Naval Volunteer Reserve (1841 Squadron, Fleet Air Arm)
Other Decorations: DSC
Date of Gazette: 13 Nov. 1945
Place/Date of Birth: Trail, British Columbia, Canada — 2 Nov. 1917
Place/Date of Death: Honshu, Japan — 9 Aug. 1945
Memorials: Halifax Memorial, Nova Scotia, Canada
Town/County Connections: —
Remarks: —
Account of Deed: On 9 Aug. 1945 at Onagawa Wan, Honshu, Japan, Lieutenant Gray led an attack on a Japanese destroyer. In the face of fire from shore batteries and heavy concentration of fire from some five warships, he pressed home his attack, flying very low in order to ensure success. Although he was wounded and his aircraft in flames he obtained at least one direct hit, sinking the destroyer. His aircraft crashed into the bay.

GRAY, Thomas   **484**
Sergeant   12 Squadron, Royal Air Force
Other Decorations: —
Date of Gazette: 11 Jun. 1940
Place/Date of Birth: Urchfont, Devizes, Wiltshire — 17 May 1914
Place/Date of Death: Maastrichht, Holland — 12 May 1940
Memorials: Heverlee War Cemetery, Louvain, Belgium
Town/County Connections: Urchfont, Devizes, Wiltshire . *Bath*
Remarks: —
Account of Deed: On 12 May 1940, over the Albert Canal, Belgium, one bridge in particular was being used by the invading army, with protection from fighter aircraft, anti-aircraft and machine-guns. The RAF was ordered to demolish this vital bridge, and five Fairey Battle bombers were despatched with Sergeant Gray as the navigator in the plane leading the bombing attack. They met an inferno of anti-aircraft fire, but the mission was accomplished, much of the success being due to the coolness and resource of the pilot* of the leading aircraft and the navigation of Sergeant Gray. Unfortunately the leading aircraft and three others did not return. (*See also GARLAND, D.E.)

GRAYBURN, John Hollington 485
Lieutenant   The Parachute Regiment (Army Air Corps)
Other Decorations: —
Date of Gazette: 25 Jan. 1945
Place/Date of Birth: Manora (island off Karachi Harbour), India — 30 Jan. 1918
Place/Date of Death: Arnhem — 20 Sep. 1944
Memorials: Arnhem Oosterbeek War Cemetery Holland; Hong Kong & Shanghai Bank,
Gracechurch Street, London E.C.
Town/County Connections: Chalfont St. Giles, Buckinghamshire
Remarks: —
Account of Deed: During the period 17/20 Sep. 1944 at Arnhem, Holland, at the assault on the
bridge over the Rhine, Lieutenant Grayburn led his men with supreme gallantry and determination. Although wounded
early in the action, in pain, short of food and without sleep, his courage never flagged. He constantly exposed himself to the enemy's
fire, moving among his men encouraging them, and seemed oblivious to danger. If it had not been for his inspiring leadership
and personal bravery, the Arnhem bridge could never have been held for this time.

GREAVES, Fred 486
A/Corporal (later Sergeant)   9th Bn., The Sherwood Foresters (The Nottinghamshire and
Derbyshire Regiment)
Other Decorations: —
Date of Gazette: 26 Nov. 1917
Place/Date of Birth: Killamarsh, Derbyshire — 16 May 1890
Place/Date of Death: Chesterfield, Derbyshire — 11 Jun. 1973
Memorials: Buried at Brimington, Derbyshire
Town/County Connections: Killamarsh and Chesterfield, Derbyshire
Remarks: —
Account of Deed: On 4 Oct. 1917 at Poelcapelle, east of Ypres, Belgium, when the platoon was
held up by machine-gun fire from a concrete stronghold and the platoon commander and sergeant were casualties, Corporal
Greaves, followed by another NCO, rushed forward, reached the rear of the building and bombed the occupants, killing or
capturing the garrison and the machine-gun. Later, at a most critical period of the battle, during a heavy counter-attack, all the
officers of the company became casualties and Corporal Greaves collected his men, threw out extra posts on the threatened
flank and opened up rifle and machine-gun fire to enfilade the advance.

GREEN, John Leslie 487
Captain   Royal Army Medical Corps, attd. 1/5th Bn., The Sherwood Foresters (The
Nottinghamshire and Derbyshire Regiment)
Other Decorations: —
Date of Gazette: 5 Aug 1916
Place/Date of Birth: St. Neots, Huntingdonshire — 4 Dec 1888
Place/Date of Death: Foncquevillers, France — 1 Jul. 1916
Memorials: Foncquevillers Military Cemetery, France
Town/County Connections: St. Neots and Houghton, Huntingdonshire
Remarks: Name on W.H Buckden, Hunts' Felsted School, Essex
Account of Deed: On 1 Jul. 1916 at Foncquevillers, France, Captain Green, although wounded
himself, rescued an officer who had been wounded and was caught up in the enemy's wire entanglements. He dragged him to
a shell hole where he dressed his wounds, notwithstanding the bombs and grenades being thrown at him the whole time.
Captain Green then tried to bring the wounded officer to safety and had nearly succeeded when he was himself killed.

GREEN, Patrick 488
Private (later Colour-Sergeant)   75th Regiment (later The Gordon Highlanders)
Other Decorations: —
Date of Gazette: 26 Oct. 1858
Place/Date of Birth: Ballinasloe, Co. Galway, Ireland — 1824
Place/Date of Death: Cork, Ireland — 19 Jul. 1889
Memorials: —
Town/County Connections: The Curragh, Co. Kildare and Cork, Ireland
Remarks: —
Account of Deed: On 11 Sep. 1857 at Delhi, India, when a picket at Koodsia Bagh, Private Green
although surrounded by many of the enemy, successfully rescued a comrade who had fallen,
wounded, as a skirmisher.

GREENWOOD, Harry   **489**
A/Lieutenant Colonel   Comd. 9th Bn., The King's Own Yorkshire Light Infantry
Other Decorations: OBE, DSO & Bar, MC
Date of Gazette: 26 Dec. 1918
Place/Date of Birth: Windsor, Berkshire — 25 Nov. 1881
Place/Date of Death: Wimbledon, Surrey — 6 May 1948
Memorials: Putney Vale Cemetery
Town/County Connections: Windsor, Berkshire; Wimbledon, Surrey
Remarks: —
Account of Deed: On 23 Oct. 1918 at Ovillers, France, when the advance of the battalion was
checked by enemy machine-gun fire, Lieutenant Colonel Greenwood single-handed rushed the
position and killed the crew. Subsequently, accompanied by two runners he took another machine-gun post, but then found
that his command was almost surrounded by the enemy who started to attack. Repulsing this attack, the colonel led his troops
forward, capturing the last objective with 150 prisoners, eight machine-guns and one field gun. On 24 Oct. he again inspired his
men to such a degree that the last objective was captured and the line held in spite of heavy casualties.

GREGG, Milton Fowler (later The Hon. Milton)   **490**
Lieutenant (later Brigadier)   Royal Canadian Regiment, C.E.F.
Other Decorations: CBE, MC & Bar
Date of Gazette: 6 Jan. 1919
Place/Date of Birth: Mountain Dale, New Brunswick, Canada — 10 Apr. 1892
Place/Date of Death: New Brunswick, Canada — 13 Mar. 1978
Memorials: —
Town/County Connections: —
Remarks: SM (Canada); served in Second World War 1939-45 — Commandant, Canadian OCTU,
England 1941; Colonel-Commandant Officers' Training Centre, Canada 1942; Brigadier-
Commandant Canadian School of Infantry 1943; Minister of Fisheries, Canada 1947-48; Minister
of Veterans' Affairs 1948-50; Minister of Labour 1950-57; UN Technical Assistance in Iraq 1958-59; UN Children's Fund in
Indonesia 1960-63; Canadian Commissioner to Guyana 1964-67
Account of Deed: During the period 27 Sep. to 1 Oct. 1918 near Cambrai, France, Lieutenant Gregg showed most conspicuous
bravery and initiative. Although wounded twice, he led his men against enemy trenches in which he personally killed or
wounded 11 Germans, took 25 prisoners and captured 12 machine-guns. In spite of his wounds he stayed with his company and
a few days later again led his men in attack until severely wounded for the third time.

GREGG, William   **491**
Sergeant (later Company Sergeant-Major)   13th Bn., The Rifle Brigade (Prince Consort's Own)
Other Decorations: DCM, MM
Date of Gazette: 28 Jun. 1918
Place/Date of Birth: Heanor, Derbyshire — 27 Jan. 1890
Place/Date of Death: Heanor, Derbyshire — 10 Aug. 1969
Memorials: The Rifle Brigade memorial, Winchester Cathedral
Town/County Connections: Heanor, Derbyshire
Remarks: —
Account of Deed: On 6 May 1918 at Bucquoy, France, when all the officers of Sergeant Gregg's
company had been hit during an attack on an enemy outpost, he took command, rushing two
enemy posts, killing some of the gun teams, taking prisoners and capturing a machine-gun. He then started to consolidate his
position until driven back by a counter-attack, but as reinforcements had by now come up, he led a charge, personally bombed
a hostile machine-gun, killed the crew and captured the gun. When driven back again, he led another successful attack and held
on to his position until ordered to withdraw.

GRENFELL, Francis Octavus   **492**
Captain   9th Lancers (The Queen's Royal)
Other Decorations: —
Date of Gazette: 16 Nov. 1914
Place/Date of Birth: Hatchlands, Guildford, Surrey — 4 Sep. 1880
Place/Date of Death: Hooge, Belgium — 24 May 1915
Memorials: Vlamertinghe Military Cemetery, Belgium; St. George's Memorial Church, Ypres;
9th Lancers Memorial, Canterbury Cathedral; Beaconsfield Parish Church, Bucks.
Town/County Connections: Clandon, Surrey; Beaconsfield, Buckinghamshire
Remarks: — Eton College. Name on Beaconsfield W.M. Memorial window in Chu
Account of Deed: On 24 Aug. 1914 at Audregnies, Belgium, Captain Grenfell rode with the Chu
regiment in a charge against a large body of unbroken German infantry. The casualties were very heavy and the captain was
left as the senior officer. He was rallying part of the regiment behind a railway embankment when he was twice hit and severely
wounded. In spite of his injuries, however, when asked for help in saving the guns, by the commander* of the 119th Battery,
Royal Field Artillery, he and some volunteers, under a hail of bullets, helped to manhandle and push the guns out of range of
enemy fire. (*See also ALEXANDER, E.W.)

GRIBBLE, Julian Royds

493

T/Captain   10th (S) Bn., The Royal Warwickshire Regiment
Other Decorations: —
Date of Gazette: 28 Jun. 1918
Place/Date of Birth: London — 5 Jan. 1897
Place/Date of Death: Germany — 25 Nov. 1918
Memorials: Niederzwehren Cemetery, Germany
Town/County Connections: London   *Long Bredy, Dorset*
Remarks: — *Eton College*
Account of Deed: On 23 Mar. 1918 at Beaumetz, Hermies Ridge, France, Captain Gribble was in command of a company which was ordered to hold on at all costs. They were eventually entirely isolated and he could easily have withdrawn when the battalion on his left was driven back, but he obeyed his orders to the letter and when his company was finally surrounded by the enemy he was seen fighting to the last. He was taken prisoner and died in Germany of his wounds.

GRIEVE, John

494

Sergeant-Major (later Lieutenant and Adjutant)   2nd Dragoons (Royal Scots Greys)
Other Decorations: —
Date of Gazette: 24 Feb. 1857
Place/Date of Birth: Musselburgh, Midlothian, Scotland — 3 May 1822
Place/Date of Death: Inveresk, Midlothian, Scotland — 1 Dec. 1863
Memorials: —
Town/County Connections: Musselburgh, Scotland
Remarks: Uncle of Captain R.C. Grieve, VC
Account of Deed: On 25 Oct. 1854 at Balaclava, Crimea, an officer in the Heavy Cavalry charge was surrounded by Russian cavalry and in great danger. Sergeant-Major Grieve rode up to his rescue, cutting off the head of one Russian and dispersing the others.

GRIEVE, Robert Cuthbert

495

Captain   37th Bn. (Victoria), Australian Imperial Force
Other Decorations: —
Date of Gazette: 2 Aug. 1917
Place/Date of Birth: Brighton, Melbourne, Victoria, Australia — 19 Jun. 1889
Place/Date of Death: Melbourne, Australia — 4 Oct. 1957
Memorials: Springvale Cemetery, Melbourne; Australian War Memorial, Canberra
Town/County Connections: —
Remarks: Nephew of Sergeant-Major J. Grieve, VC
Account of Deed: On 7 Jun. 1917 at Messines, Belgium, during an attack on the enemy's position, and after his own company had suffered very heavy casualties, Captain Grieve located two hostile machine-guns which were holding up his advance. Under continuous heavy fire from the two guns, he succeeded in bombing and killing the two gun crews, then reorganized the remnants of his own company and gained his original objective. Captain Grieve set a splendid example and when he finally fell, wounded, the position had been secured.

No photograph available

GRIFFITHS, William

496

Private   2nd Bn., 24th Regiment (later The South Wales Borderers)
Other Decorations: —
Date of Gazette: 17 Dec. 1867
Place/Date of Birth: Co. Roscommon, Ireland — 1841
Place/Date of Death: Isandhlwana, Zululand — 22 Jan. 1879
Memorials: Regimental Memorial, Isandhlwana, Zululand   *Buried in mass grave on the Battlefield*
Town/County Connections: —
Remarks: VC not awarded for bravery in action against the enemy, but for bravery at sea in saving life in storm off Andaman Islands
Account of Deed: On 7 May 1867 at the island of Little Andaman, Bay of Bengal, Private Griffiths was one of a party of five* of the 2/24th Regiment, who risked their lives in manning a boat and proceeding through dangerous surf to rescue some of their comrades who had been sent to the island to find out the fate of the commander and seven of the crew, who had landed from the ship *Assam Valley* and were feared murdered by the cannibalistic islanders. (*See also BELL, David, COOPER, J., DOUGLAS, C.M. and MURPHY, T)

VC in S.W.B. Museum, Brecon

GRIMBALDESTON, William Henry 497

A/Company Quartermaster-Sergeant   1st Bn., The King's Own Scottish Borderers
Other Decorations: —
Date of Gazette: 14 Sep. 1917
Place/Date of Birth: Blackburn, Lancashire — 19 Sep. 1889
Place/Date of Death: Blackburn, Lancashire — 13 Aug. 1959
Memorials: —
Town/County Connections: Blackburn, Lancashire
Remarks: Croix de Guerre (France)
Account of Deed: On 16 Aug. 1917 at Wijdendrift, Belgium, Company Quartermaster-Sergeant Grimbaldeston noticed that the unit on his left was held up by enemy machine-gun fire from a blockhouse. Arming himself with a rifle and hand grenade he started to crawl towards his objective, and when he had advanced about 100 yards another soldier came forward to give covering support. Although wounded, he pushed on to the blockhouse, threatened the machine-gun teams inside with a hand grenade and forced them to surrender. This action resulted in the capture of 36 prisoners, six machine-guns and one trench mortar.

GRIMSHAW, John Elisha 498

Corporal (later Sergeant)   1st Bn., The Lancashire Fusiliers
Other Decorations: —
Date of Gazette: 15 Mar. 1917
Place/Date of Birth: Abram, Wigan, Lancashire — 20 Jan. 1893
Place/Date of Death: Isleworth, London — 20 Jul. 1980
Memorials: (Cremated S.W. London Crematorium, Hanwell, Middlesex) · *No memorial*
Town/County Connections: Abram, Wigan, Lancashire; Isleworth, London
Remarks: —
Account of Deed: On 25 Apr. 1915 west of Cape Helles, Gallipoli, three companies and the Headquarters of the 1st Battalion, Lancashire Fusiliers, when landing on W Beach, were met by a very deadly fire from hidden machine guns which caused a large number of casualties. The survivors, however, rushed up and cut the wire entanglements notwithstanding the terrific fire from the enemy and after overcoming supreme difficulties, the cliffs were gained and the position maintained. (Corporal Grimshaw was one of the six members of the regiment elected for the award. See also BROMLEY, C., KENEALLY, W., RICHARDS, A.J., STUBBS, F.E. and WILLIS, R.R.)

GRISTOCK, George 499

Company Sergeant-Major   The Royal Norfolk Regiment
Other Decorations: —
Date of Gazette: 23 Aug. 1940
Place/Date of Birth: Pretoria, Transvaal, South Africa — 14 Jan. 1905
Place/Date of Death: Brighton, Sussex — 16 Jun. 1940
Memorials: Bear Road Cemetery, Brighton
Town/County Connections: Sandhurst, Surrey
Remarks: —
Account of Deed: On 21 May 1940 near the River Escaut, Belgium, Company Sergeant-Major Gristock organised a party of eight riflemen and went forward to cover the company's right flank, where the enemy had broken through. He then went on with one man under heavy fire and was severely wounded in both legs, but having gained his fire position undetected, he managed to put out of action a machine-gun which was inflicting heavy casualties and kill the crew of four. He then dragged himself back to the right flank position but refused to be evacuated until contact with the battalion had been established. He later died of his wounds.

GROGAN, George William St. George 500

T/Brigadier General   The Worcestershire Regiment, comd. 23rd Infantry Brigade
Other Decorations: CB,CMG,DSO & Bar
Date of Gazette: 25 Jul. 1918
Place/Date of Birth: Plymouth, — 1 Sep. 1875
Place/Date of Death: Sunningdale, Berkshire — 3 Jan. 1962
Memorials: —
Town/County Connections: St. Andrews, Fife, Scotland; Sunningdale, Berkshire
Remarks: Colonel, The Worcestershire Regiment 1938-45; Member of the Hon. Corps of Gentlemen-at-Arms, HM Body Guard 1933-45
Account of Deed: On 27 May 1918 at the River Aisne, France, Brigadier General Grogan was in command of the remnants of the infantry of a division and attached troops. His utter disregard for personal safety combined with sound practical ability helped to stay the onward thrust of the enemy. He rode up and down the front line encouraging his troops under artillery, trench mortar, rifle and machine-gun fire and when one horse was shot under him, he continued encouraging his men on foot until another horse was brought. As a result of his actions the line held.

GUISE, John Christopher (later Sir John)   **501**
Major (later Lieutenant General)   90th Regiment (later The Cameronians — Scottish Rifles)
Other Decorations: CB
Date of Gazette: 24 Dec. 1858
Place/Date of Birth: Highnam, Gloucestershire — 27 Jul. 1826
Place/Date of Death: Gorey, Co. Wexford, Ireland — 5 Feb. 1895
Memorials: Elmore Church, Gloucestershire
Town/County Connections: Highnam and Elmore, Gloucestershire
Remarks: Colonel, The Leicestershire Regiment 1890
Account of Deed: On 16 and 17 Nov. 1857 at Lucknow, India, Major Guise, together with a sergeant*, saved the life of a captain at the storming of the Secundra Bagh and also went in under heavy fire to help two wounded men. In fact he acted with gallantry throughout the operations for the Relief of the Lucknow garrison. (Elected by the regiment. *See also HILL,S.)

GUNN, George Ward   **502**
Second Lieutenant   3rd Regiment, Royal Horse Artillery
Other Decorations: MC
Date of Gazette: 21 Apr. 1942
Place/Date of Birth: Muggleswick, Co. Durham — 26 Jul. 1912
Place/Date of Death: Sidi Rezegh, Western Desert — 21 Nov. 1941
Memorials: Knightsbridge War Cemetery, Acroma, Libya
Town/County Connections: Neston, Wirral, Cheshire
Remarks: —
Account of Deed: On 21 Nov. 1941 at Sidi Rezegh, Libya, an attack by 60 German tanks was countered by four anti-tank guns under the command of Second Lieutenant Gunn. During the engagement this officer drove from gun to gun in an unarmoured vehicle, encouraging his men, and when three of his guns were destroyed and the crew of the fourth, except the sergeant, were all dead or disabled, he took charge of this remaining weapon the portee of which was alight. There was danger of the flames exploding the ammunition with which the portee was loaded, but he managed to fire 50 rounds and set two enemy tanks on fire before he himself was killed.

GURNEY, Arthur Stanley   **503**
Private   2/48th Bn. (S.A.) Australian Military Forces
Other Decorations: —
Date of Gazette: 14 Sep. 1942
Place/Date of Birth: Day Dawn, Murchison Goldfields, Western Australia — 15 Dec. 1908
Place/Date of Death: Tel-el-Eisa, Egypt — 22 Jul. 1942
Memorials: El Alamein War Cemetery, Egypt; Australian War Memorial, Canberra
Town/County Connections: —
Remarks: —
Account of Deed: On 22 Jul. 1942 at Tel-el-Eisa, Egypt, the company to which Private Gurney belonged was held up by intense machine-gun fire, heavy casualties being suffered, including all the officers. Private Gurney, realizing the seriousness of the situation, charged the nearest machine-gun post, silencing the guns and bayoneting three of the crew. He bayoneted two more at a second post, and was then knocked down by a grenade, but picked himself up and charged a third post. Nothing more was seen of him until later, when his body was found by his comrades, whose advance he had made possible.

GUY, Basil John Douglas   **504**
Midshipman (later Commander)   Royal Navy
Other Decorations: DSO
Date of Gazette: 1 Jan. 1901
Place/Date of Birth: Bishop Auckland, Co. Durham — 9 May 1882
Place/Date of Death: London — 29 Dec. 1956
Memorials: Buried Pirbright, Surrey; Family memorial Christ Church, Harrogate
Town/County Connections: Bishop Auckland, Co. Durham; Pirbright, Surrey; Harrogate, Yorkshire
Remarks: Served in the First and Second World Wars
Account of Deed: On 13 Jul. 1900 during the attack on Tientsin, China, a very heavy crossfire was brought to bear on the Naval Brigade and there were several casualties. Among those who fell was an able seaman, shot about 50 yards short of cover. Midshipman Guy stopped with him and tried, unsuccessfully, to lift him up, so after bandaging his wound he ran to get help — during this time the enemy were concentrating their fire on the two men. Shortly after Mr. Guy got under cover the stretchers arrived, and he again ran out and helped to bring in the wounded man, who was unfortunately shot again and died before he could be got to safety.

HACKETT, Thomas Bernard   **505**
Lieutenant (later Lieutenant Colonel)   23rd Regiment (later The Royal Welch Fusiliers)
Other Decorations: —
Date of Gazette: 12 Apr. 1859
Place/Date of Birth: ?Riverstown, Co. Tipperary, Ireland — 15 Jun. 1836
Place/Date of Death: Arrabeg, King's Co. (later Offaly), Ireland — 5 Oct. 1880
Memorials: Marshall family vault, Lockeen Churchyard, Borrisokane, Co. Tipperary
Town/County Connections: Riverstown, Co. Tipperary; Arrabeg, King's Co. (Offaly)
Remarks: —
Account of Deed: On 18th Nov. 1857 at Secundra Bagh, Lucknow, India, Lieutenant Hackett, with others*, rescued a corporal of the 23rd Regiment, who was lying wounded and exposed to very heavy fire. He also showed conspicuous bravery when, under heavy fire, he ascended the roof and cut the thatch of a bungalow, to prevent its being set on fire. (*See also MONGER, G.)

HACKETT, William   **506**
Sapper   254th Tunnelling Coy., Corps of Royal Engineers
Other Decorations: —
Date of Gazette: 5 Aug. 1916
Place/Date of Birth: Nottingham — 11 Jun. 1873
Place/Date of Death: Givenchy, France — 27 Jun. 1916
Memorials: Ploegsteert Memorial, Belgium; Market Hall, Mexborough, Yorkshire.
Town/County Connections: Nottingham; Mexborough, Yorkshire.
Remarks: —
Account of Deed: On 22/23 Jun. 1916 at Shaftesbury Avenue Mine, near Givenchy, France, Sapper Hackett was entombed with four others in a gallery, owing to the explosion of an enemy mine. After working for 24 hours a hole was made and the rescue party outside contacted. Sapper Hackett helped three of the men through the hole and could easily have followed, but refused to leave the fourth man who had been seriously injured. The hole gradually got smaller, but he still refused to leave his injured comrade. Finally the gallery collapsed and although the rescue party worked desperately for four days, they were unable to reach the two men.

HAINE, Reginald Leonard   **507**
Second Lieutenant (later Lieutenant Colonel)   1st Bn., Honourable Artillery Company
Other Decorations: MC & Bar
Date of Gazette: 8 Jun. 1917
Place/Date of Birth: Wandsworth, London — 10 Jul. 1896
Place/Date of Death: London — 12 Jun. 1982
Memorials: —
Town/County Connections: East Horsley and Richmond, Surrey
Remarks: Served with the Home Guard in Second World War.
Account of Deed: On 28/29 Apr. 1917 near Gavrelle, France, when our troops were holding a salient which was being repeatedly counter-attacked by the enemy Second Lieutenant Haine organised and led six bombing attacks against a German strong point and captured the position, together with 50 prisoners and two machine-guns. The enemy at once counter-attacked and regained the lost ground, but Second Lieutenant Haine formed a "block" in his trench and for the whole of the following night maintained his position. Next morning he again attacked and recaptured the position. His splendid example inspired his men during more than 30 hours of continuous fighting.

HALE, Thomas Egerton   **508**
Assistant Surgeon (later Lieutenant Colonel)   1st Bn., 7th Regiment (later The Royal Fusiliers)
Other Decorations: CB
Date of Gazette: 5 May 1857
Place/Date of Birth: Faddiley, Nantwich, Cheshire — 24 Sep. 1832
Place/Date of Death: Faddiley, Nantwich, Cheshire — 25 Dec. 1909
Memorials: Acton Church, Cheshire
Town/County Connections: Faddiley, Nantwich, Cheshire
Remarks: Served in the Indian Mutiny; medical officer in charge at Cherat in 1860; medical charge of 2nd Punjab Infantry and European detachments on Punjab frontier 1864-66
Account of Deed: On 8 Sep. 1855, in the Crimea, at Sebastopol, during the attack on the Redan, Assistant Surgeon Hale remained with an officer who was dangerously wounded, when everyone except one other officer had retreated. Again, on the same day, after the regiment had retired to the trenches, Assistant Surgeon Hale cleared the most advanced sap of the wounded and then carried into the sap, under heavy fire, several wounded men from the open ground.

HALL, Arthur Charles   **509**
Corporal   54th Bn. (N.S.W.), Australian Imperial Force
Other Decorations: —
Date of Gazette: 14 Dec. 1918
Place/Date of Birth: Granville, New South Wales, Australia — 11 Aug. 1896
Place/Date of Death: New South Wales, Australia — 25 Feb. 1978
Memorials: West Bogan Cemetery Coolabah, New South Wales; Australian War Memorial, Canberra
Town/County Connections: —
Remarks: —
Account of Deed: On 1 Sep. 1918 at Peronne, France, Corporal Hall rushed a machine-gun post, shooting four of the enemy and capturing nine, with two guns. Continuously in advance of the main party, he personally led assault parties, capturing many small parties of the enemy and machine-guns. On the morning of 2 Sep. during a heavy barrage, he carried to safety a comrade who had been dangerously wounded and was in urgent need of medical attention.

HALL, Frederick William   **510**
Company Sergeant-Major   8th Manitoba Regiment, C.E.F.
Other Decorations: —
Date of Gazette: 23 Jun. 1915
Place/Date of Birth: Kilkenny, Ireland — 8 Feb. 1885
Place/Date of Death: Gravenstafel, Ypres — 25 Apr. 1915
Memorials: Menin Gate Memorial, Belgium; lamp post in Valour Road, Winnipeg
Town/County Connections: —
Remarks: —
Account of Deed: On 24 Apr. 1915, near Ypres, Belgium when a wounded man, who was lying some 15 yards from the trench, called for help, Company Sergeant-Major Hall endeavoured to reach him in the face of a very heavy enfilade fire by the enemy. He then made a second most gallant attempt, and was in the act of lifting up the wounded man to bring him in when he fell mortally wounded in the head.

HALL, William   **511**
Able Seaman (later Quartermaster and Petty Officer)   Royal Navy (Naval Brigade)
Other Decorations: —
Date of Gazette: 1 Feb. 1859
Place/Date of Birth: Horton's Bluff, Nova Scotia, Canada — 28 Apr. 1827
Place/Date of Death: Hantsport, Nova Scotia — 25 Aug. 1904
Memorials: Cairn monument at Hantsport, Nova Scotia
Town/County Connections: —
Remarks: First coloured man to win the VC
Account of Deed: On 16 Nov. 1857 at Lucknow, India, naval guns were brought up close to the Shah Nujeff mosque, and the gun crews kept up a steady fire in an attempt to breach the walls, while a hail of musket balls and grenades from the mutineers inside the mosque caused heavy casualties. Able Seaman Hall and the lieutenant* in command of the gun crews were, after a time, the only survivors, all the rest having been killed or wounded, and between them they loaded and served the last gun. (*See also YOUNG, T.J.)

HALLIDAY, Lewis Stratford Tollemache (later Sir Lewis)   **512**
Captain (later Lieutenant General)   Royal Marine Light Infantry
Other Decorations: KCB
Date of Gazette: 1 Jan. 1901
Place/Date of Birth: Medstead, Hampshire — 14 May 1870
Place/Date of Death: Dorking, Surrey — 9 Mar. 1966
Memorials: Eastney Barracks (RM), Southsea, Hampshire
Town/County Connections: Medstead, Hampshire; Dorking, Surrey; Kingsbridge, Devon
Remarks: Served in the First World War; member of the British Delegation to the Peace Conference; Adjutant General, Royal Marines 1927-30; Honorary Colonel Commandant Royal Marines 1930-40
Account of Deed: On 24 Jun. 1900 at Peking, China, an attack was made on the British Legation by the Boxers who set fire to the stables and occupied some of the other buildings. It being imperative to drive the enemy out, a hole was knocked in the Legation wall and 20 men of the RMLI went in. Captain Halliday, leading a party of six men, was involved in desperate fighting and was severely wounded, but despite his injuries, he killed four of the enemy. Finally, unable to carry on any further, he ordered his men to go on without him, after which he was taken to hospital.

HALLIWELL, Joel   **513**
Lance-Corporal   11th Bn., The Lancashire Fusiliers
Other Decorations: —
Date of Gazette: 25 Jul. 1918
Place/Date of Birth: Chadderton, Oldham, Lancashire — 29 Dec. 1873
Place/Date of Death: Manchester, Lancashire — 14 Jun. 1956
Buried Middleton Cemetery, Manchester
Memorials: —
Town/County Connections: Middleton, Lancashire
Remarks: —
Account of Deed: On 27 May 1918 at Muscourt, France, when the remnants of the battalion were withdrawing and being closely engaged by the enemy, Lance-Corporal Halliwell, having captured a stray horse, rode out under heavy rifle and machine-gun fire and rescued a man from No Man's Land. He repeated this performance several times and succeeded in rescuing an officer and nine other ranks. He made a last effort to reach a wounded man but was driven back by the very close advance of the enemy.

HALLOWES, Rupert Price   **514**
T/Second Lieutenant   4th Bn., The Middlesex Regiment (Duke of Cambridge's Own)
Other Decorations: MC
Date of Gazette: 18 Nov. 1915
Place/Date of Birth: Redhill, Surrey, 5 May 1881
Place/Date of Death: Hooge, Belgium — 30 Sep. 1915
Memorials: Bedford House Cemetery, Belgium; gateway to Port Talbot Public Park, Glamorgan
Town/County Connections: Redhill, Surrey; Port Talbot, Glamorgan   *Haileybury School*
Remarks: — *Enclosure 4. Plot 16 Row B. Grave 36*
Account of Deed: Between 25 and 30 Sept. 1915 at Hooge, Belgium, Second Lieutenant Hallowes set a magnificent example to his men during four heavy and prolonged bombardments. More than once he climbed upon the parapet, utterly regardless of danger in order to put fresh heart into his men. He made daring reconnaissances of the German positions in our lines and when the supply of bombs was running short he went back under very heavy fire and brought up a fresh supply. Even when mortally wounded, he continued to cheer those round him and to inspire them with fresh courage. *VC with Middlesex Regt. He worked in Aberavon & worked in Port Talbot*

HALTON, Albert   **515**
Private   1st Bn., The King's Own (Royal Lancaster) Regiment
Other Decorations: —
Date of Gazette: 26 Nov. 1917
Place/Date of Birth: Warton, Carnforth, Lancashire — 1 May 1893
Place/Date of Death: Lancaster — 24 Jul. 1971
Memorials: —
Town/County Connections: Warton, Lancashire
Remarks: —
Account of Deed: On 12 Oct. 1917 near Poelcapelle, Belgium, after the objective had been reached, Private Halton rushed forward about 300 yards under very heavy fire and captured a machine-gun and its crew which was causing heavy losses to our men. He then went out again and brought in 12 prisoners, showing the greatest disregard for his own safety and setting a fine example to those round him.

HAMILTON, Angus Falconer DOUGLAS-   **516**
T/Lieutenant Colonel   Reserve of Officers, comd. 6th Bn., The Queen's Own Cameron Highlanders
Other Decorations: —
Date of Gazette: 18 Nov. 1915
Place/Date of Birth: Brighton, Sussex — 20 Aug. 1863
Place/Date of Death: Hill 70, France — 26 Sep. 1915
Memorials: Loos Memorial, France
Town/County Connections: Brighton, Sussex
Remarks: —
Account of Deed: On 25/26 Sep. 1915 during operations on Hill 70, France, Lieutenant Colonel Douglas-Hamilton, when the battalions on his right and left had retired, rallied his own battalion again and again and led his men forward four times. The last time he led all that remained, about 50 men, in a most gallant manner, and was killed at their head. It was due to his bravery, and splendid leadership that the line at this point was able to check the enemy's advance.

HAMILTON, John Brown   **517**
A/Lance-Corporal (later Sergeant)   1/9th Bn., The Highland Light Infantry
Other Decorations: —
Date of Gazette: 26 Nov. 1917
Place/Date of Birth: Dumbarton, Scotland — 26 Aug. 1896
Place/Date of Death: East Kilbride, Scotland — 23 Jul. 1973
Memorials: —
Town/County Connections: East Kilbride, Scotland
Remarks: —
Account of Deed: On 25/26 Sep. 1917 north of the Ypres-Menin Road, Belgium, great difficulty was experienced in keeping the front and support line supplied with small arm ammunition, owing to the intense artillery fire. At a time when this supply had reached a seriously low level, Lance-Corporal Hamilton on several occasions, on his own initiative, carried bondoliers of ammunition through the enemy's belts of fire and then, in full view of their snipers and machine-guns which were lying out in the front of our line at close range, he distributed the ammunition.

HAMILTON, John   **518**
Private   3rd Bn., (N.S.W.) Australian Imperial Force
Other Decorations: —
Date of Gazette: 15 Oct. 1915
Place/Date of Birth: Orange, Penshurst, New South Wales, Australia — 29 Jan. 1896
Place/Date of Death: Sydney, Australia 27 Feb. 1961
Memorials: Woronora Cemetery, Sydney; Australian War Memorial, Canberra
Town/County Connections: —
Remarks: —
Account of Deed: On 9 Aug. 1915, at Lone Pine, Gallipoli, during a heavy bomb attack by the enemy on the newly captured position, Private Hamilton, with utter disregard for personal safety, exposed himself to heavy enemy fire on the parados, in order to secure a better fire position against the enemy's bomb throwers. His daring example had an immediate effect. The defence was encouraged and the enemy driven off with heavy loss.

HAMILTON, Thomas de Courcy   **519**
Captain (later Major General)   68th Regt. (later The Durham Light Infantry)
Other Decorations: —
Date of Gazette: 24 Feb. 1857
Place/Date of Birth: Stranraer, Wigtownshire, Scotland — 20 Jul. 1825
Place/Date of Death: Cheltenham, Gloucestershire — 3 Mar. 1908
Memorials: Cheltenham Cemetery; Garrison Church, Whittington Barracks, Lichfield, Staffordshire
Town/County Connections: Stranraer, Wigtownshire; Cheltenham, Gloucestershire
Remarks: Légion d'Honneur (France); comd. 64th (later The North Staffordshire) Regt. 1862
Account of Deed: On 11 May 1855 in the Crimea, in a most determined sortie, Captain Hamilton boldly charged great numbers of the enemy with a small force, driving them from a battery of which they had taken possession. He was conspicuous for his gallantry on this occasion and his action saved the works from falling into enemy hands.

HAMILTON, Walter Richard Pollock   **520**
Lieutenant   Bengal Staff Corps/Corps of Guides, Indian Army
Other Decorations: —
Date of Gazette: 1 Sep. 1879
Place/Date of Birth: Inistioge, Kilkenny, Ireland — 18 Aug. 1856
Place/Date of Death: Kabul, Afghanistan — 3 Sep. 1879
Memorials: Horse Show Hall at Ballsbridge, Dublin; sanctum crypt, St. Luke's Church, Chelsea, London   *Plaque from Punjab Frontier Force chapel in Pakistan now housed*
Town/County Connections: Inistioge, Kilkenny   *in above crypt, Chelsea*
Remarks: —
Account of Deed: On 2 Apr. 1879 at Futtehabad, (Afghan War), Lieutenant Hamilton led a charge of the Guide Cavalry against very superior numbers of the enemy. When his commanding officer fell, the lieutenant, the only officer left with the regiment, assumed command and cheered his men on to avenge the death of the commanding officer. In this charge, seeing that a sowar was down, entangled with his dead horse and being attacked by three of the enemy, Lieutenant Hamilton rushed to the rescue, cutting down all three and saving the life of the sowar.

HAMMOND, Arthur George (later Sir Arthur)   **521**
Captain (later Brigadier General)   Bengal Staff Corps/Corps of Guides, Indian Army
Other Decorations: KCB, DSO
Date of Gazette: 18 Oct. 1881
Place/Date of Birth: Dawlish, Devon — 28 Sep. 1843
Place/Date of Death: Camberley, Surrey — 20 Apr. 1919
Memorials: St. Michael's Churchyard, Camberley, Surrey. *Buried there.*
Town/County Connections: Camberley, Surrey
Remarks: Commanded a Brigade during the Tirah Campaign 1897-98.
Account of Deed: On 14 Dec. 1879 at the action on the Asmai Heights, near Kabul, (Afghan War), Captain Hammond defended the top of the hill with a rifle and fixed bayonet against large numbers of the enemy, while the 72nd Highlanders and Guides were retiring. Again, on the retreat down the hill he stopped and helped to carry a wounded sepoy, the enemy being only 60 yards off and firing heavily all the time.

HAMPTON, Harry   **522**
Sergeant (later Colour-Sergeant)   2nd Bn., The King's (Liverpool) Regiment
Other Decorations: —
Date of Gazette: 18 Oct. 1901
Place/Date of Birth: Richmond, Surrey — 14 Dec. 1870
Place/Date of Death: Richmond, Surrey — 4 Feb. 1920
Memorials: Richmond Cemetery   *Buried there. VC Headstone dedicated by the Regt 17.3.1986*
Town/County Connections: Richmond, Surrey
Remarks: —
Account of Deed: On 21 Aug. 1900 at Van Wyk's Vlei, South Africa, Sergeant Hampton, who was in command of a small party of mounted infantry, held an important position for some time against heavy odds, and when compelled to retire saw all his men into safety and then, although he himself had been wounded in the head, supported a lance-corporal who was unable to walk until the latter was hit again and apparently killed. Sergeant Hampton received another wound some time later.

HANCOCK, Thomas   **523**
Private (later Corporal)   9th Lancers (The Queen's Royal)
Other Decorations: —
Date of Gazette: 15 Jan. 1858
Place/Date of Birth: Kensington, London — Jul. 1823
Place/Date of Death: London — 12 Mar. 1871
Memorials: Buried Brompton Cemetery, London (unmarked grave)
Town/County Connections: Kensington, London
Remarks: —
Account of Deed: On 19 Jun. 1857 at Delhi, India during the Mutiny, when a waggon of one of the batteries was blown up and the horse of a brigadier was shot, Private Hancock with another private* and a sowar of the 4th Irregular Cavalry stayed with the officer until he could be dragged to safety by the sowar's horse. Private Hancock was severely wounded and the other private's horse was killed under him. (*See also PURCELL, J.)

HANNA, Robert Hill   **524**
Company Sergeant-Major (later Lieutenant)   29th Bn., British Columbia Regiment, C.E.F.
Other Decorations: —
Date of Gazette: 8 Nov. 1917
Place/Date of Birth: Kilkeel, Co. Down, Ireland — 6 Aug. 1887
Place/Date of Death: Mount Lehman, British Columbia, Canada — 15 Jun. 1967
Memorials: Masonic Cemetery, Burnaby, British Columbia
Town/County Connections: Kilkeel, Co. Down
Remarks: —
Account of Deed: On 21 Sep. 1917, at Lens, France, Company Sergeant-Major Hanna's company met with most severe enemy resistance at a heavily protected strong point, which had beaten off three assaults and all the officers of the company had become casualties. This warrant officer, under heavy machine-gun and rifle fire, coolly collected and led a party against the strong point, rushed through the wire and personally killed four of the enemy, capturing the position and silencing the machine-gun. This courageous action was responsible for the capture of a most important tactical point.

HANNAH, John   **525**
Sergeant   83 Squadron, Royal Air Force
Other Decorations: —
Date of Gazette: 1 Oct. 1940
Place/Date of Birth: Paisley, Renfrewshire, Scotland — 27 Nov. 1921 . *lived in Glasgow pre-war*
Place/Date of Death: Birstall, Leicestershire — 7 Jun. 1947
Memorials: St. James's Churchyard, Birstall
Town/County Connections: Birstall, Leicestershire
Remarks: Youngest recipient of the VC for aerial operations
Account of Deed: On 15 Sep. 1940 over Antwerp, Belgium, after a successful attack on German barges, the bomber in which Sergeant Hannah was wireless operator/air gunner, was subjected to intense anti-aircraft fire, starting a fire which spread quickly. The rear-gunner and navigator had to bale out and Sergeant Hannah could have acted likewise, but instead he remained to fight the fire, first with two extinguishers and then with his bare hands. He sustained terrible injuries, but succeeded in putting out the fire and the pilot was able to bring the almost wrecked aircraft back safely.

HANSEN, Percy Howard   **526**
Captain (later Brigadier)   6th Bn., The Lincolnshire Regiment
Other Decorations: DSO, MC
Date of Gazette: 1 Oct. 1915
Place/Date of Birth: Dresden, Germany — 26 Oct. 1890
Place/Date of Death: London — 12 Feb. 1951
Memorials: — *Eton College*
Town/County Connections: Kensington, London
Remarks: Croix de Guerre (France); Deputy Assistant Adjutant General, Western Command 1934-35; served in Second World War 1939-45; SHAEF Mission to Norway 1943-45; Commander, Royal Order of St. Olaf (Norway); Officer, Legion of Merit (USA)
Account of Deed: On 9 Aug. 1915 at Yilghin Burnu, Gallipoli, Captain Hansen's battalion was forced to retire leaving some wounded behind, owing to the intense heat from the scrub which had been set on fire. After the retirement Captain Hansen, with three or four volunteers dashed forward several times over 300-400 yards of open scrub, under a terrific fire and succeeded in rescuing six wounded men from inevitable death by burning.

HARDEN, Henry Eric   **527**
Lance-Corporal   Royal Army Medical Corps, attd. 45 Royal Marine Commando
Other Decorations: —
Date of Gazette: 8 Mar. 1945
Place/Date of Birth: Northfleet, Kent — 23 Feb. 1912
Place/Date of Death: Brachterbeek, Holland — 23 Jan. 1945
Memorials: Nederweert War Cemetery, Holland; plaque on bridge over Montforterbeek at Brachterbeek, Holland
Town/County Connections: —
Remarks: —
Account of Deed: On 23 Jan. 1945, at Brachterbeek, Holland, three marines of the leading section of the Royal Marine Commando Troop to which Lance-Corporal Harden was attached fell, wounded. He at once ran across the 100 yards of open ground, gave first aid and, carrying one marine on his back, brought him to safety. Although slightly wounded, this NCO insisted on going out again with two stretcher-bearers to rescue the others. On the next journey the second wounded marine was hit again and killed, but the rescue party returned to collect the third man, and in so doing Lance-Corporal Harden was killed.

HARDHAM, William James   **528**
Farrier-Major (later Captain)   4th New Zealand Contingent
Other Decorations: —
Date of Gazette: 4 Oct. 1901
Place/Date of Birth: Wellington, New Zealand — 31 Jul. 1876
Place/Date of Death: Wellington, New Zealand — 13 Apr. 1928
Memorials: HQ, Dunedin RSA, New Zealand
Town/County Connections: —
Remarks: First New Zealand-born man to win the VC. Served in First World War in Gallipoli
Account of Deed: On 28 Jan. 1901 near Naauwpoort, South Africa, Farrier-Major Hardham was with a section which was hotly engaged with a party of about 20 Boers. Just before the force started to retire, a trooper was wounded and his horse killed. The Farrier-Major at once went, under heavy fire, to his assistance, dismounted and put him on his own horse, and then ran alongside until he had guided the wounded man to a place of safety.

HARDING, Israel 529
Gunner (later Chief Gunner) Royal Navy
Other Decorations: —
Date of Gazette: 15 Sep. 1882
Place/Date of Birth: Portsmouth, Hampshire — 21 Oct. 1833
Place/Date of Death: Billingshurst, Sussex — 22 May 1917
Memorials: Highland Road Cemetery, Portsmouth
Town/County Connections: Portsmouth, Hampshire
Remarks: Served in minesweepers in the First World War
Account of Deed: On 11 Jul. 1882 at Alexandria, Egypt, HMS *Alexandra*, with other ships, was bombarding the forts of the city and suffering damage and casualties from the enemy's guns. During the engagement a 10-inch shell passed through the ship's side and lodged on the main deck. Gunner Harding, hearing a shout that there was a live shell just above the hatchway (which led to the magazine) rushed up from below, picked it up and flung it into a tub of water. Had the shell burst it would probably have caused many deaths.

HARDY, Theodore Bailey 530
The Reverend T/Chaplain to the Forces, 4th Class Army Chaplains' Department, attd. 8th Bn., The Lincolnshire Regiment
Other Decorations: DSO, MC
Date of Gazette: 11 Jul. 1918
Place/Date of Birth: Southernhay, Exeter — 20 Oct. 1863
Place/Date of Death: Rouen, France — 18 Oct. 1918
Memorials: St. Sever Cemetery Extension, France; Carlisle Cathedral; Hutton Roof Church (Near Kirkby Lonsdale) *Name in WM in Church*
Town/County Connections: Nottingham; Bentham, Yorkshire; Hutton Roof
Remarks: —
Account of Deed: On 5, 25 and 27 Apr. 1918 near Bucquoy and east of Gommecourt, France, The Reverend Theodore Hardy showed most conspicious bravery, tending the wounded under very heavy fire, absolutely regardless of his personal safety. Once he helped to bring in a wounded officer from 400 yards beyond the front line. Then, when an enemy shell exploded in one of our posts and several men were buried, he immediately went, under heavy fire, and managed to dig two of them out. On a third occasion he went out with a sergeant and brought in a wounded man who was lying within 10 yards of a German pill-box.

HARINGTON, Hastings Edward 531
Lieutenant (later Captain) Bengal Artillery
Other Decorations: —
Date of Gazette: 24 Dec. 1858
Place/Date of Birth: Hinton Parva, Wiltshire — 9 Nov. 1832
Place/Date of Death: Agra, India — 20 Jul. 1861
Memorials: Monument over his grave in Agra
Town/County Connections: Hinton Parva, Wiltshire
Remarks: — *Road named after him in Formby, Lancashire*
Account of Deed: During the whole of the period 14 to 22 Nov. 1857, at the Relief of Lucknow, India, Lieutenant Harington acted with conspicuous gallantry. (Elected by the regiment.)

HARLOCK, Ernest George — see **HORLOCK,** Ernest George

HARMAN, John Pennington 532
Lance-Corporal 4th Bn., The Queen's Own Royal West Kent Regiment
Other Decorations: —
Date of Gazette: 22 Jun. 1944
Place/Date of Birth: Beckenham, Kent — 20 Jul. 1914
Place/Date of Death: Kohima, Assam, India — 9 Apr. 1944
Memorials: Kohima War Cemetery, India; Lundy Island, Bristol Channel.
Town/County Connections: Beckenham, Kent; Lundy Island, Devon
Remarks: —
Account of Deed: On 8/9 Apr. 1944 at Kohima, India, Lance-Corporal Harman was commanding a section of a forward platoon where the enemy had established a machine-gun post within 50 yards of his company and were becoming a menace. As it was not possible to bring fire on to the enemy post the lance-corporal went forward by himself and threw a grenade into the position, annihilating it. Early next morning, having ordered covering fire from his Bren gun he went alone, with fixed bayonet and charged a party of Japanese who were digging in, shooting four and bayoneting one. On returning to his position he was fatally wounded.

HARPER, John William **533**
Corporal   4th Bn., The York and Lancaster Regiment
Other Decorations: —
Date of Gazette: 2 Jan. 1945
Place/Date of Birth: Doncaster, Yorkshire — 6 Aug. 1915
Place/Date of Death: Near Antwerp, Belgium — 29 Sep. 1944
Memorials: Leopoldsburg War Cemetery, Belgium
Town/County Connections: Doncaster, Yorkshire
Remarks: —
Account of Deed: On 29 Sep. 1944 during an assault on the Depot de Mendicite, Antwerp, Corporal Harper led his section across 300 yards of completely exposed ground, with utter disregard for the hail of mortar bombs and small arms fire from the enemy. He was killed in the action, but the subsequent capture of the position was largely due to his self-sacrifice.

HARRIS, Thomas James **534**
Sergeant   6th Bn., The Queen's Own Royal West Kent Regiment
Other Decorations: MM
Date of Gazette: 22 Oct. 1918
Place/Date of Birth: Halling, Kent — 30 Jan. 1892
Place/Date of Death: Morlancourt, France — 9 Aug. 1918
Memorials: Dernancourt Communal Cemetery Extension, France
Town/County Connections: Halling, Kent
Remarks: —
Account of Deed: On 9 Aug. 1918 at Morlancourt, France, when the advance was much impeded by hostile machine-guns concealed in crops and shell-holes, Sergeant Harris led his section against one of these, capturing it and killing seven of the enemy. Later, on two successive occasions he attacked two enemy machine-guns which were causing heavy casualties. He captured the first gun and killed the crew, but was himself killed when attacking the second. It was largely due to the great courage and initiative of this NCO that the advance of the battalion continued without delay and undue casualties.

HARRISON, Arthur Leyland **535**
Lieutenant-Commander   Royal Navy
Other Decorations: —
Date of Gazette: 17 Mar. 1919
Place/Date of Birth: Torquay, Devon — 3 Feb. 1886
Place/Date of Death: Zeebrugge, Belgium — 23 Apr. 1918
Memorials: Zeebrugge Memorial, Belgium
Town/County Connections: Torquay, Devon; Wimbledon, Surrey
Remarks: —Name on Peace Memorial + Putney Vale. Name on W.H. Ealing
Account of Deed: On 22/23 Apr. 1918 at Zeebrugge, Belgium, Lieutenant-Commander Harrison was in command of the naval storming parties, but immediately before coming alongside the Mole he was struck on the head by a fragment of shell which broke his jaw and knocked him senseless. Regaining consciousness, he resumed command, leading his men in the attack on the seaward batteries, but was killed almost at once. Although in great pain he had continued to press his attack, knowing that any delay in silencing the enemy guns might jeopardise the main object of the expedition. (See also McKENZIE, A.E.) *Plaque in St. Marys Church, Wimbledon.*

HARRISON, John **536**
T/Second Lieutenant   11th (S) Bn., The East Yorkshire Regiment
Other Decorations: MC
Date of Gazette: 14 Jun. 1917
Place/Date of Birth: Drypool, Sculcoates, Kingston-upon-Hull, Yorkshire — 2 Nov. 1890
Place/Date of Death: Oppy, France — 3 May 1917
Memorials: Arras Memorial, France
Town/County Connections: Sculcoates, Kingston-upon-Hull
Remarks: —
Account of Deed: On 3 May 1917 at Oppy, France, owing to darkness, to smoke from the enemy barrage and our own, and to the fact that the objective was in a dark wood, it was impossible to see when our barrage had lifted off the enemy front line. Nevertheless, Second Lieutenant Harrison twice led his company against the enemy trench under terrific rifle and machine-gun fire, but was repulsed. Then finally he made a dash at the machine-gun, hoping to knock it out of action and so save the lives of many of his company. (He was later reported missing, believed killed.)

HARRISON, John   **537**
Leading Seaman (later Boatswain's Mate and Petty Officer)   Royal Navy (Naval Brigade)
Other Decorations: —
Date of Gazette: 24 Dec. 1858
Place/Date of Birth: Castleborough, Co. Wexford, Ireland — 24 Jan. 1832
Place/Date of Death: London — 27 Dec. 1865
Memorials: (Brompton Cemetery, London, unmarked grave)
Town/County Connections: Castleborough, Co. Wexford; Westminster, London
Remarks: —
Account of Deed: On 16 Nov. 1857 at Lucknow, India, volunteers were called for to climb a tree near the wall of the Shah Nujeff mosque in order to spot the enemy's position and then to dislodge the mutineers who were throwing grenades and firing on the gun crews below. Leading Seaman Harrison, together with a lieutenant* and an able seaman responded to the call and succeeded in performing this dangerous service, but the lieutenant was wounded in the thigh and the able seaman was killed. (*See also SALMON, N.)

HART, Reginald Clare (later Sir Reginald)   **538**
Lieutenant (later General)   Corps of Royal Engineers
Other Decorations: GCB, KCVO, Royal Humane Society's Silver Medal
Date of Gazette: 10 Jun. 1879
Place/Date of Birth: Scarriff, Co. Clare, Ireland — 11 Jun. 1848
Place/Date of Death: Bournemouth, Hampshire — 10 Oct. 1931
Memorials: Buried at Netherbury, Dorset
Town/County Connections: Scarriff, Co. Clare; Guernsey; Netherbury, Dorset
Remarks: GOC Thames District 1902-6; Commandant, School of Military Engineers 1902-06; C-in-C South Africa 1912-14; Lieutenant Governor, Guernsey 1914-18
Account of Deed: On 31 Jan. 1879 in the Bazar Valley, (Afghan War), Lieutenant Hart, while on convoy duty, ran some 1,200 yards to the rescue of a wounded sowar of the 13th Bengal Lancers, lying in a river bed exposed to the fire of the enemy on all sides. He reached the wounded man, drove off the enemy and with the help of some soldiers who had accompanied him, carried the casualty to safety.

No photograph available

HARTIGAN, Henry   **539**
Pensioned Sergeant (later Lieutenant)   9th Lancers (The Queen's Royal)
Other Decorations: —
Date of Gazette: 19 Jun. 1860
Place/Date of Birth: Drumlea, Enniskillen, Co. Fermanagh, Ireland — Mar. 1826
Place/Date of Death: Calcutta, India — 29 Oct. 1886
Memorials: —
Town/County Connections: Enniskillen, Co. Fermanagh
Remarks: —
Account of Deed: On 8 Jun. 1857 at the Battle of Badle-ke-Serai, near Delhi, India, Pensioned Sergeant Hartigan went to the assistance of another sergeant who was wounded, dismounted and surrounded by the enemy, and at the risk of his own life, carried the casualty to safety. On 10 Oct at Agra, Sergeant Hartigan went to the assistance of another sergeant who was being attacked by four rebels. He seized a tulwar from one of them, hitting him in the mouth, then, defending himself from the other three, killed one and wounded two. He was himself dangerously wounded during this action.

HARTLEY, Edmund Barron   **540**
Surgeon Major (later Colonel)   Cape Mounted Riflemen, South African Forces
Other Decorations: CMG
Date of Gazette: 7 Oct. 1881
Place/Date of Birth: Ivybridge, Devon — 6 May 1847
Place/Date of Death: Ash, Hampshire — 20 Mar. 1919
Memorials: Brookwood Cemetery, Woking, Surrey
Town/County Connections: Seaton, Devon; Ash, Hampshire
Remarks: —
Account of Deed: On 5 Jun. 1879 during the Basuto War in South Africa, Surgeon Major Hartley attended the wounded under fire at the unsuccessful attack at Morosi's Mountain. From an exposed position, on open ground, he carried in his arms a wounded corporal of the Cape Mounted Riflemen. The surgeon major then returned under severe enemy fire in order to dress the wounds of the other men of the storming party.

HARVEY, Francis John William **541**
Major   Royal Marine Light Infantry
Other Decorations: —
Date of Gazette: 15 Sep. 1916
Place/Date of Birth: Sydenham, Surrey — 29 Apr. 1873
Place/Date of Death: North Sea, near Jutland — 31 May 1916
Memorials: Chatham Naval Memorial
Town/County Connections: Sydenham, Surrey
Remarks: —
Account of Deed: On 31 May 1916, at the Battle of Jutland, Major Harvey of HMS *Lion*, although mortally wounded and almost the only survivor after the explosion of an enemy shell in a gunhouse, ordered the magazine to be flooded. His presence of mind saved the ship, but he died shortly afterwards.

HARVEY, Frederick Maurice Watson **542**
Lieutenant (later Brigadier)   Lord Strathcona's Horse, C.E.F.
Other Decorations: MC
Date of Gazette: 8 Jun. 1917
Place/Date of Birth: Athboy, Co. Meath. Meath, Ireland — 1 Sep. 1888
Place/Date of Death: Calgary, Alberta, Canada — 24 Aug. 1980
Memorials: —
Town/County Connections: Athboy, Co. Meath; Enniskillen, Co. Fermanagh, Ireland
Remarks: —
Account of Deed: On 27 Mar. 1917 at Guyencourt, France, during an attack by the regiment, the leading troop, commanded by Lieutenant Harvey, had suffered heavy casualties from rapid fire at close range. He was riding in front of his men when he came upon a wired trench containing a machine-gun and a strong garrison. He at once swung from his saddle and ran straight for the trench, jumped the wire, shot the gunner and captured the gun.

HARVEY, Jack **543**
Private (later Corporal)   1/22nd (County of London) Bn., The London Regt. (The Queen's)
Other Decorations: —
Date of Gazette: 15 Nov. 1918
Place/Date of Birth: Peckham, London — 24 Aug. 1891
Place/Date of Death: Redhill, Surrey — 15 Aug. 1940
Memorials: Redhill Cemetery, Surrery; Stone memorial outside Redhill Town Hall
Town/County Connections: Peckham, London; Redhill, Surrey
Remarks: — *Buried in Redstone Cemetery, Redhill*
Account of Deed: On 2 Sep. 1918 north of Peronne, France, when the advance of his company was held up by machine-gun fire, Private Harvey dashed forward a distance of 50 yards alone, through our barrage and in the face of heavy enemy fire and rushed a machine-gun post, shooting two of the team and bayoneting another. He then destroyed the gun and continued his way along the enemy trench. Single-handed he rushed an enemy dug-out which contained 37 Germans and compelled them to surrender. The two acts of gallantry saved the company heavy casualties and materially assisted in the success of the operation.

HARVEY, Norman **544**
Private (later Company Quartermaster-Sergeant)   1st Bn., The Royal Inniskilling Fusiliers
Other Decorations: —
Date of Gazette: 6 Jan. 1919
Place/Date of Birth: Newton-le-Willows, Lancashire — 6 Apr. 1899
Place/Date of Death: Near Haifa, Palestine — 16 Feb. 1942
Memorials: Khayat Beach War Cemetery, Haifa
Town/County Connections: Newton-le-Willows, Lancashire
Remarks: Served with Corps of Royal Engineers in Second World War.
Account of Deed: On 25 Oct. 1918 at Ingoyghem, Belgium, when the battalion was held up and suffering heavy casualties from enemy machine-guns, Private Harvey on his own initiative rushed forward and engaged the enemy single-handed, disposing of 20 of them and capturing the guns. Later when his company was checked by another enemy strong point he again rushed forward and put the enemy to flight. Subsequently, after dark he voluntarily carried out a single-handed and important reconnaissance and gained valuable information.

HARVEY, Samuel **545**
Private   1st Bn., The York and Lancaster Regiment
Other Decorations: —
Date of Gazette: 18 Nov. 1915
Place/Date of Birth: Basford, Bulwell, Nottinghamshire — 17 Sep. 1881
Place/Date of Death: Onehouse, Stowmarket, Suffolk — 24 Sep. 1960
Memorials: Old Cemetery, Ipswich, Suffolk
Town/County Connections: Stowmarket, Suffolk
Remarks: —
Account of Deed: On 29 Sep. 1915 in the "Big Willie" Trench near the Hohenzollern Redoubt, France, during a heavy bombing attack, more bombs were urgently required and Private Harvey volunteered to fetch them. The communication trench was blocked with wounded and reinforcements and he went backwards and forwards across open ground under intense fire and succeeded in bringing up 30 boxes before he was wounded in the head. It was largely owing to his cool bravery in supplying the bombs that the enemy was eventually driven back.

HAVELOCK, (later HAVELOCK-ALLAN) Henry Marsham (later Sir Henry) **546**
Lieutenant (later Lieutenant General)   10th Regiment (later The Lincolnshire Regiment)
Other Decorations: GCB
Date of Gazette: 15 Jan. 1858
Place/Date of Birth: Chinsurah, Bengal, India — 6 Aug. 1830
Place/Date of Death: Rawalpindi, India — 30 Dec. 1897
Memorials: —
Town/County Connections: Durham
Remarks: Served in New Zealand 1863-66; DL County of Durham
Account of Deed: On 16 Jul. 1857 at Cawnpore, India, the 64th Regiment had suffered badly under artillery fire. When the enemy was seen rallying their last 24-pounder, the order was given to advance, and Lieutenant Havelock immediately placed himself, on his horse, in front of the centre of the 64th, opposite the muzzle of the gun and moved on at a foot pace, in the face of shot and grape fired by the enemy. The advance went steadily on, led by the lieutenant and finally the gun was rushed and taken by the 64th.

HAWKER, Lanoe George **547**
Captain (later Major)   Corps of Royal Engineers and 6 Squadron, Royal Flying Corps
Other Decorations: DSO
Date of Gazette: 24 Aug. 1915
Place/Date of Birth: Longparish, Hampshire — 30 Dec. 1890
Place/Date of Death: Near Bapaume, France — 23 Nov. 1916
Memorials: Arras Memorial, France; Longparish church, Hampshire
Town/County Connections: Longparish, Hampshire
Remarks: —
Account of Deed: On 25 Jul. 1915 when on patrol over France, Captain Hawker attacked three German aircraft in succession. The first, after he had emptied a complete drum of bullets into it, went spinning down, the second was driven to the ground damaged, and the third which he attacked at a height of about 10,000 feet burst into flames and crashed. This particular sortie was just one of the many courageous exploits which Captain Hawker had undertaken during almost a year of constant operational flying and fighting.

No photograph available

HAWKES, David **548**
Private   2nd Bn., The Rifle Brigade (Prince Consort's Own)
Other Decorations: —
Date of Gazette: 24 Dec. 1858
Place/Date of Birth: Witham, Essex — 1822
Place/Date of Death: Fyzabad, India — 14 Aug. 1858
Memorials: Rifle Brigade memorial, Winchester Cathedral, Hampshire
Town/County Connections: Witham, Essex
Remarks: —
Account of Deed: On 11 Mar. 1858 at Lucknow, India, Private Hawkes' company was engaged with a large number of the enemy near the Iron Bridge. At one stage a captain* found himself at the end of a street with only four of his men, opposed to a considerable body of the enemy. One of the men was shot through both legs and Private Hawkes, although severely wounded, lifted him up with the help of a corporal* and they then carried their comrade for a considerable distance, the captain firing with the men's rifles and covering the retreat of the party. (*See also WILMOT, H. and NASH W.)

HAWTHORNE, Robert   **549**
Bugler   52nd Regt. (later The Oxfordshire and Buckinghamshire Light Infantry)
Other Decorations: —
Date of Gazette: 27 Apr. 1858
Place/Date of Birth: Maghera, near Londonderry, Ireland — 1822
Place/Date of Death: Manchester, Lancashire — 2 Feb. 1879
Memorials: Ardwick Cemetery, Manchester
Town/County Connections: Maghera, Londonderry; Manchester, Lancs.
Remarks: —
Account of Deed: On 14 Sep. 1857 at Delhi, India, Bugler Hawthorne accompanied the explosion
party* in the desperate task of blowing in the Kashmir Gate. He not only performed the dangerous
duty on which he was employed, but, under heavy musketry fire, bound up the wounds of one of the officers of the party, who
had been badly hurt. (*See also HOME, D.C., SALKFELD, P. and SMITH, John — No. 1164).

HAYWARD, Reginald Frederick Johnson   **550**
A/Captain (later Lieutenant Colonel)   1st Bn., The Wiltshire Regiment
Other Decorations: MC & Bar, ED
Date of Gazette: 24 Apr. 1918
Place/Date of Birth: Beersheba, East Griqualand, South Africa — 17 Jun. 1891
Place/Date of Death: London — 17 Jan. 1970
Memorials: — *Cremated at Putney Vale Cemetery. No memorial.*
Town/County Connections: Limpley Stoke, Wiltshire
Remarks: Served in Second World War, CRASC (AA Command); Commandant, Prisoner of War
Camps 1945-47
Account of Deed: On 21/22 Mar. 1918 near Fremicourt, France, while commanding a company,
Captain Hayward displayed almost superhuman powers of endurance. In spite of the fact that he was buried, wounded in the
head and rendered deaf on the first day of operations and had his arm shattered two days later, he refused to leave his men
(even though he received a third serious injury to his head) until he collapsed from sheer exhaustion. Throughout this period
the enemy were attacking the company's front without cessation, but Captain Hayward continued to move across the open
from one trench to another with absolute disregard for his own safety.

HEAPHY, Charles   **551**
Major   Auckland Militia, New Zealand Military Forces
Other Decorations: —
Date of Gazette: 8 Feb. 1867
Place/Date of Birth: St John's Wood, London — 1822
Place/Date of Death: Toowong, Queensland, Australia — 3 Aug. 1881
Memorials: Toowong Cemetery, Brisbane, Queensland; HQ, Dunedin RSA, New Zealand
Town/County Connections: St. John's Wood, London
Remarks: First Man serving with New Zealand Forces to win the VC
Account of Deed: On 11 Feb. 1864 on the banks of the Mangapiko River, New Zealand, Major
Heaphy went to the assistance of a soldier who had fallen into a hollow where there were a great
many Maoris concealed. While doing this, the major became a target for a volley from only a few feet away. Five musket balls
pierced his clothes and cap and he was hit in three places, but in spite of this he stayed with the wounded man all day.

HEATHCOTE, Alfred Spencer   **552**
Lieutenant (later Captain)   60th Rifles (later The King's Royal Rifle Corps)
Other Decorations: —
Date of Gazette: 20 Jan. 1860
Place/Date of Birth: London — 29 Mar. 1832
Place/Date of Death: Bowral, New South Wales, Australia — 21 Feb. 1912
Memorials: St. James' Anglican Church, Sydney, New South Wales
Town/County Connections: London; Winchester, Hampshire
Remarks: —
Account of Deed: From Jun. to Sep. 1857, throughout the Siege of Delhi, India, during which he
was wounded, Lieutenant Heathcote's conduct was most gallant. He volunteered for services of
extreme danger, especially during the six days of severe fighting in the streets after the assault. (Elected by the regiment)

HEATON, William Edward
553

Private (later Sergeant)   1st Bn., The King's (Liverpool) Regiment
Other Decorations: —
Date of Gazette: 18 Jan. 1901
Place/Date of Birth: Ormskirk, Lancashire — 1875
Place/Date of Death: Southport, Lancashire — 5 Jun. 1941
Memorials: —
Town/County Connections: Ormskirk and Southport, Lancashire
Remarks: —
Account of Deed: On 23 Aug. 1900 at Geluk, South Africa, a company of the 1st Bn. The King's (Liverpool) Regiment became surrounded by the enemy and was suffering severely. Private Heaton volunteered to take a message back to explain the position of the company and he carried out this mission successfully at imminent risk to his own life. Had it not been for his courage, the remainder of his company would almost certainly have had to surrender.

HEAVISIDE, Michael
554

Private   15th Bn., The Durham Light Infantry
Other Decorations: —
Date of Gazette: 8 Jun. 1917
Place/Date of Birth: Durham — 20 Oct. 1880
Place/Date of Death: Durham — 26 Apr. 1939
Memorials: —
Town/County Connections: Durham
Remarks: —
Account of Deed: On 6 May 1917 near Fontaine-les-Croiselles, France, a wounded man was seen, at about 2pm, in a shell hole some 40 yards from the enemy line. It was impossible to rescue him during daylight, but Private Heaviside volunteered to take water and food to him. This he succeeded in doing, in spite of heavy gun fire, and found that the man was nearly demented with thirst and had been lying in the shell hole for four days and three nights. The arrival of the water undoubtedly saved his life. Private Heaviside succeeded the same evening, with the help of two comrades, in rescuing the man.

HEDGES, Frederick William
555

T/Lieutenant   The Bedfordshire Regiment, attd. 6th Bn., The Northamptonshire Regiment
Other Decorations: —
Date of Gazette: 31 Jan. 1919
Place/Date of Birth: Umballa, India — 6 Jun. 1896
Place/Date of Death: Harrogate, Yorkshire — 29 May 1954 *Buried Stonefall Cemetery,*
Memorials: — *Name on Roll of Honour, Stewart County school. Harrogate*
Town/County Connections: Hounslow, Middlesex; Harrogate, Yorkshire
Remarks: Served with the Civil Defence in the Second World War
Account of Deed: On 24 Oct. 1918 north-east of Bousies, France, Lieutenant Hedges led his company with great skill towards the final objective, maintaining direction under the most difficult conditions. When the advance was held up by enemy machine-gun posts the lieutenant, accompanied by one sergeant and followed at some considerable distance by a Lewis gun section, again advanced, capturing six machine-guns and 14 prisoners. His gallantry and initiative enabled the whole line to advance and contributed largely to the success of subsequent operations.

HENDERSON, Arthur
556

A/Captain   4th Bn., The Argyll and Sutherland Highlanders (Princess Louise's) attd. 2nd Bn.
Other Decorations: MC
Date of Gazette: 5 Jul. 1917
Place/Date of Birth: Paisley, Scotland — 6 May 1893
Place/Date of Death: Fontaine-les-Croiselles, France — 24 Apr. 1917
Memorials: Cojeul British Cemetery, France
Town/County Connections: Paisley, Scotland
Remarks: —
Account of Deed: On 23 Apr. 1917 near Fontaine-les-Croiselles, France, during an attack on enemy trenches, Captain Henderson, although almost immediately wounded in the left arm, led his company through the front enemy line until he gained his final objective. He then proceeded to consolidate his position, which owing to heavy gun and machine-gun fire and bombing attacks was in danger of becoming isolated. By his cheerful courage and coolness he was able to maintain the spirit of his men under most trying circumstances. Captain Henderson was killed after he had successfully accomplished his task.

HENDERSON, Edward Elers Delaval
T/Lieutenant Colonel   The North Staffordshire Regt. (The Prince of Wales's), attd. The Royal Warwickshire Regiment, comd. 9th Bn.
Other Decorations: —
Date of Gazette: 8 Jun. 1917
Place/Date of Birth: Simla, India — 2 Oct. 1878
Place/Date of Death: River Hai, Mesopotamia — 25 Jan. 1917
Memorials: Amara War Cemetery, Iraq; Garrison Church, Whittington Barracks, Lichfield, Staffordshire.
Town/County Connections: —
Remarks: —
Account of Deed: On 25 Jan. 1917 on the west bank of the River Hai, near Kut, Mesopotamia, Lieutenant Colonel Henderson brought his battalion up to the two first line trenches and they suffered heavy casualties when the enemy made a strong counter-attack, penetrating the line in several places. The situation was critical and Colonel Henderson, although wounded, jumped on to the parapet and then advanced alone in front of his battalion, cheering them on under most intense fire over 500 yards of open ground. Again wounded, he nevertheless captured the position by a bayonet charge, but he was twice more wounded and died later the same day. (See also PHILLIPS, R.E.)

HENDERSON, George Stuart   **558**
Captain   2nd Bn., The Manchester Regiment
Other Decorations: DSO & Bar, MC
Date of Gazette: 29 Oct. 1920
Place/Date of Birth: East Gordon, Berwickshire — 5 Dec. 1893
Place/Date of Death: Near Hillah, Mesopotamia — 24 Jul. 1920
Memorials: Basra Memorial, Iraq; Jedburgh Memorial; Regimental Memorial, Sandhurst
Town/County Connections: Jedburgh, Scotland
Remarks: — *Rossall School, Fleetwood, Lancs*
Account of Deed: On 24 Jul. 1920 near Hillah, Mesopotamia, Captain Henderson led his company in three charges against the enemy who had opened fire from the flank. At one time when the situation was extremely critical, the captain, by sheer pluck and coolness, steadied his command and prevented his company from being cut up. During the second charge he fell wounded but refused to leave his command and just as the company reached the trench, he was again wounded, this time mortally.

HENDERSON, Herbert Stephen   **559**
Trooper   Bulawayo Field Force, South African Forces
Other Decorations: —
Date of Gazette: 7 May 1897
Place/Date of Birth: Hillhead, Glasgow — 30 Mar. 1870
Place/Date of Death: Bulawayo, Rhodesia — 10 Aug. 1942
Memorials: —
Town/County Connections: Glasgow
Remarks: —
Account of Deed: On 30 Mar. 1896 at Campbell's Store, near Bulawayo, Rhodesia, a patrol which had been sent to the rescue of another beleagured patrol, was surprised by rebels and Trooper Henderson and another trooper were cut off from the main party. The second trooper was shot through the knee and his horse killed, so Trooper Henderson put the wounded man on his own horse, and, walking beside it, made his way to Bulawayo, 35 miles away. They had to move principally by night, as the country was full of marauding rebels and they had no food for two days and one night.

HENEAGE, Clement Walker   **560**
Captain   8th Hussars (King's Royal Irish)
Other Decorations: —
Date of Gazette: 26 Jan. 1859
Place/Date of Birth: Compton Bassett, Wiltshire — 6 Mar. 1831
Place/Date of Death: Compton Bassett, Wiltshire — 9 Dec. 1901
Memorials: — *Buried in vault in Compton Bassett Church.*
Town/County Connections: Compton Bassett, Wiltshire
Remarks: Rode in the Light Brigade charge at Balaclava
Account of Deed: On 17 Jun. 1858 at Gwalior, India, Captain Heneage (together with a sergeant, a farrier and a private)* was in a gallant charge made by a squadron of the 8th Hussars when, supported by a division of the Bombay Horse Artillery and the 95th Regiment, they routed the enemy. Charging through a rebel camp into two batteries, they captured and brought into their own camp two of the enemy's guns, under a heavy and converging fire from the fort and town. (*See also WARD, Joseph, HOLLIS, G. and PEARSON, John).

Rode in the Charge of the Light Brigade, Balaclava.

HENRY, Andrew   **561**
Sergeant-Major (later Captain)   Royal Regiment of Artillery
Other Decorations: —
Date of Gazette: 24 Feb. 1857
Place/Date of Birth: Woolwich, London — 1 Nov. 1823
Place/Date of Death: Plymouth, Devon — 14 Oct. 1870
Memorials: Ford Park Cemetery, Plymouth
Town/County Connections: Woolwich, London; Plymouth, Devon
Remarks: —
Account of Deed: On 5 Nov. 1854 at the Battle of Inkerman, Crimea, Sergeant-Major Henry defended the guns of his battery against overwhelming numbers of the enemy, and continued to do so until he had received 12 bayonet wounds and became unconscious.

HERRING, Alfred Cecil   **562**
T/Second Lieutenant (later Major)   Royal Army Service Corps, attd. 6th (S) Bn., The Northamptonshire Regiment
Other Decorations: —
Date of Gazette: 7 Jun. 1918
Place/Date of Birth: Tottenham, Middlesex — 26 Oct. 1888
Place/Date of Death: Weybridge, Surrey — 10 Aug. 1966
Memorials: —
Town/County Connections: Tottenham, Middlesex; Weybridge, Surrey
Remarks: —
Account of Deed: On 23/24 Mar. 1918 at Montagne Bridge, France, the enemy had gained a position on the south bank of the canal and Second Lieutenant Herring's post was surrounded, but he immediately counter-attacked and recaptured the position, together with 20 prisoners and six machine-guns. During the night the post was continually attacked, but all attacks were beaten off, largely due to the fact that Lieutenant Herring was frequently visiting his men and cheering them up. It was owing to his bravery and magnificent handling of his troops that the enemy advance was held up for 11 hours at a very critical period.

HEWETT William Nathan Wrighte (later Sir William)   **563**
Lieutenant (later Vice-Admiral)   Royal Navy (Naval Brigade)
Other Decorations: KCB
Date of Gazette: 24 Feb. 1857
Place/Date of Birth: Brighton, Sussex — 2 Aug. 1834
Place/Date of Death: Portsmouth, Hampshire — 13 May 1888   *Buried at Highland Road Cemetery Portsmouth*
Memorials: Highland Road Cemetery, Portsmouth
Town/County Connections: Brighton, Sussex
Remarks: —
Account of Deed: On 26 Oct. 1854 at Sebastopol, Crimea, Lieutenant Hewett, commander of HMS *Beagle*, was in charge of the Right Lancaster Battery which was being threatened by the enemy, when through a misunderstanding he was ordered to spike his gun and retreat. The lieutenant, however, took on himself the responsibility of disregarding the order. He then pulled down the parapet of the battery and with the assistance of some soldiers slewed his gun round and poured on the advancing enemy a most destructive and effectual fire. On 5 Nov. at the Battle of Inkerman he again acted with great bravery.

HEWITSON, James   **564**
Lance-Corporal (later Corporal)   1/4th Bn., The King's Own (Royal Lancaster) Regiment
Other Decorations: —
Date of Gazette: 28 Jun. 1918
Place/Date of Birth: Coniston, Lancashire — 15 Oct. 1892
Place/Date of Death: Ulverston, Lancashire — 2 Mar. 1963
Memorials: Coniston Churchyard, Lancashire
Town/County Connections: Coniston and Ulverston, Lancashire
Remarks: —
Account of Deed: On 26 Apr. 1918 at Givenchy, France, in a daylight attack on a series of crater posts, Lance-Corporal Hewitson led his party to their objective, clearing the enemy from both trench and dug-outs, killing six who would not surrender. After capturing the final objective he saw a hostile machine-gun team coming into action against his men and working his way round the edge of the crater he attacked the team, killing four and capturing one. Shortly afterwards he routed a bombing party which was attacking a Lewis gun, killing six of them.

HEWITT, Dennis George Wyldbore **565**
Second Lieutenant   14th Bn., The Hampshire Regiment
Other Decorations: —
Date of Gazette: 14 Sep. 1917
Place/Date of Birth: Mayfair, London — 18 Dec. 1897
Place/Date of Death: Near Ypres, Belgium — 31 Jul. 1917
Memorials: Menin Gate Memorial, Belgium
Town/County Connections: London; Hursley, Hampshire
Remarks: —
Account of Deed: On 31 Jul. 1917 north-east of Ypres, Belgium, when his first objective had been captured, Second Lieutenant Hewitt reorganised his company and moved forward. Whilst waiting for the barrage to lift, he was hit by a piece of shell which exploded the signal lights in his haversack and set fire to his equipment and clothes. He extinguished the flames and then, in spite of his wound and severe pain, he led forward the remnants of the company under a very heavy machine-gun fire and captured and consolidated his objective. He was subsequently killed by a sniper while inspecting the consolidation and encouraging his men.

HEWITT, William Henry **566**
Lance-Corporal (later Major)   2nd South African Light Infantry
Other Decorations: —
Date of Gazette: 26 Nov. 1917
Place/Date of Birth: Copdock, Suffolk — 19 Jun. 1884
Place/Date of Death: Cheltenham, Gloucestershire — 7 Dec. 1966
Memorials: — *Cremated Cheltenham.*
Town/County Connections: Copdock, Ipswich, Suffolk; Southsea, Hants., Cheltenham, Glos.
Remarks: Served in East Africa in Second World War
Account of Deed: On 20 Sep. 1917 east of Ypres, Lance-Corporal Hewitt attacked a pill box with his section and tried to rush the doorway. The garrison, however, proved very stubborn and in the attempt the lance-corporal received a severe wound. Nevertheless he proceeded to the loophole of the pill box where, in his attempts to put a bomb in it, he was again wounded in the arm. Undeterred, he finally managed to get the bomb inside where it dislodged the occupants and they were successfully dealt with by the rest of the section.

HILL (later HILL-WALKER) Alan Richard **567**
Lieutenant (later Major)   2nd Bn. The Northamptonshire Regiment
Other Decorations: —
Date of Gazette: 14 Mar. 1882
Place/Date of Birth: Northallerton, Yorkshire — 12 Jul. 1859
Place/Date of Death: Thirsk, Yorkshire — 21 Apr. 1944
Memorials: —
Town/County Connections: Richmond and Thirsk, Yorkshire
Remarks: —
Account of Deed: On 28 Jan. 1881 at Laing's Nek, South Africa, when the retreat was ordered, Lieutenant Hill remained behind and tried to carry out of action another lieutenant who was lying on the ground severely wounded. He was unable to lift the man into the saddle and carried him in his arms until he was shot dead. Lieutenant Hill then brought another wounded man out of action on his horse and afterwards returned and rescued another. All this was done under very heavy fire.

HILL, Albert **568**
Private   10th Bn., The Royal Welch Fusiliers
Other Decorations: —
Date of Gazette: 26 Sep. 1916
Place/Date of Birth: Manchester, Lancashire — 24 May 1895
Place/Date of Death: Pawtucket, Rhode Island, U.S.A. — 30 Mar. 1971 *Buried there*
Memorials: Highland Memorial Park, Johnston, Rhode Island, U.S.A.
Town/County Connections: Manchester
Remarks: — *VC with RWF Museum Caernarvon Castle*
Account of Deed: On 20 Jul. 1916 at Delville Wood, France when his battalion was under very heavy fire, Private Hill dashed forward when the order to charge was given and bayoneted two of the enemy. Later, finding himself cut off and almost surrounded by some 20 of the enemy, he attacked them with bombs, killing and wounding many and scattering the rest. He then joined a sergeant of his company and helped him to find the way back to the lines, where he heard that his company commander and a scout were wounded. He helped to bring in the wounded officer, and finally captured and brought in two prisoners.

No photograph available

HILL, Samuel   **569**
Sergeant   90th Regiment (later The Cameronians — Scottish Rifles)
Other Decorations: —
Date of Gazette: 24 Dec. 1858
Place/Date of Birth: Glenavy, Co. Antrim, Ireland — 1826
Place/Date of Death: Meerut, India — 21 Feb. 1863
Memorials: —
Town/County Connections: Glenavy, Co. Antrim
Remarks: —
Account of Deed: On 16 and 17 Nov. 1857 at Lucknow, India, Sergeant Hill went with a major*
to save the life of a captain at the storming of the Secundra Bagh and also went in under heavy fire
to help two wounded men. In fact he acted with gallantry throughout the operations for the relief of the Lucknow garrison.
(Elected by the Regiment. *See also GUISE, J.C.)

HILLS, (later HILLS-JOHNES) James (later Sir James)   **570**
Second Lieutenant (later Lieutenant General)   Bengal Horse Artillery
Other Decorations: GCB
Date of Gazette: 24 Apr. 1858
Place/Date of Birth: Neechindipur, Bengal, India — 20 Aug. 1833
Place/Date of Death: Dolaucothy, Carmarthenshire, Wales — 3 Jan. 1919
Memorials: Caio Churchyard, Carmarthenshire; St. George's Royal Garrison Church, Woolwich
Town/County Connections: Dolaucothy, Carmarthenshire
Remarks: Brother-in-law of Lieutenant W.G. Cubitt, VC; Hon. Colonel, 4th Bn., The Welch
Regiment; Chairman, Carmarthen County Association Territorial Forces, and of Joint Counties
Association; DL, County of Carmarthen *Portrait in Edinburgh Academy*
Account of Deed: On 9 Jul. 1857, at the siege of Delhi, India, Second Lieutenant Hills most gallantly defended the position
assigned to him when attacked by enemy cavalry. Single-handed he charged the head of the enemy's column and fought
fiercely — on foot after he and his horse had been ridden down. He was about to be killed with his own sword which one of the
enemy had wrested from him, when his senior officer* saw what was happening and twice in a short space of time came to the
rescue of his subaltern. (*See also TOMBS, H.) *VC with Royal Artillery Association*

HINCKLEY, George   **571**
Able Seaman (later Quartermaster)   Royal Navy (Naval Brigade)
Other Decorations: —
Date of Gazette: 6 Feb. 1863
Place/Date of Birth: Liverpool, Lancashire — 22 Jun. 1819
Place/Date of Death: Plymouth, Devon — 31 Dec. 1904
Memorials: Ford Park Cemetery, Plymouth
Town/County Connections: Liverpool, Lancs.; Devonport, Devon
Remarks: —
Account of Deed: On 9 Oct. 1862 at Fung Wha, China, Able Seaman Hinckley of HMS *Sphinx*
volunteered to go to the rescue of the assistant master of *Sphinx,* who was lying in the open
severely wounded. The able seaman went out under heavy and continuous fire and carried the assistant master to the shelter
of a joss-house 150 yards away. He then returned and carried a wounded army captain to safety.

HINTON, John Daniel   **572**
Sergeant   20th Bn., 2nd N.Z.E.F. (The Canterbury Regiment)
Other Decorations: —
Date of Gazette: 17 Oct. 1941
Place/Date of Birth: Colac Bay, Near Riverton, Southland, New Zealand — 17 Sep. 1908
Place/Date of Death: — *Christchurch, NZ. about 2.7.1997*
Memorials: HQ, Dunedin RSA, New Zealand
Town/County Connections:
Remarks: —
Account of Deed: On 28/29 Apr. 1941 at Kalamai, Greece, New Zealand troops heading for the
port to await evacuation were attacked by enemy machine-gun fire and self-propelled 6-inch guns.
Although the order to retire had been given, Sergeant Hinton rushed forward to the nearest gun and, hurling two grenades,
killed the crew. He continued towards the quay, clearing out two light machine-guns and a mortar with grenades, then dealt
with the garrison of a house where some of the enemy were sheltering. Later, when they were attacked by the main enemy
force, Sergeant Hinton, was only subdued and captured after being severely wounded.

HIRSCH, David Philip

573

A/Captain 4th Bn., The Yorkshire Regiment (Alexandra, Princess of Wales's Own)
Other Decorations: —
Date of Gazette: 14 Jun. 1917
Place/Date of Birth: Leeds, Yorkshire — 28 Dec. 1896
Place/Date of Death: Wancourt, France — 23 Apr. 1917
Memorials: Arras Memorial, France
Town/County Connections: Leeds, Yorkshire
Remarks: —
Account of Deed: On 23 Apr. 1917 near Wancourt, France, during an attack, Captain Hirsch having arrived at the first objective, although wounded, returned over fire-swept slopes to satisfy himself that the defensive flank was being established. Machine-gun fire was so intense that it was necessary for him to be continuously up and down the line encouraging and steadying his men. He stood on the parapet, in the face of machine-gun fire and counter-attack, until he was killed.

HITCH, Frederick

574

Private 2nd Bn., 24th Regiment (later The South Wales Borderers)
Other Decorations: —
Date of Gazette: 2 May 1879
Place/Date of Birth: Edmonton, London — 28 Nov. 1856
Place/Date of Death: Ealing, London — 7 Jan. 1913
Memorials: St. Nicholas' Churchyard, Old Chiswick, London *No.17. Block P. Chiswick old Burial ground*
Town/County Connections: Ealing and Chiswick, London
Remarks: —
Account of Deed: On 22 and 23 Jan. 1879 at Rorke's Drift, Natal, South Africa, Private Hitch and another man* kept communication with the hospital open, despite being severely wounded. Their determined conduct enabled the patients to be withdrawn from the hospital, and when incapacitated by their wounds from fighting, they continued, as soon as their wounds were dressed, to serve out ammunition to their comrades during the night. (*See also ALLAN, W.W.) *VC with SWB Museum, Brecon*

HOBSON, Frederick

575

Sergeant 20th Bn., 1st Central Ontario Regiment, C.E.F.
Other Decorations: —
Date of Gazette: 17 Oct. 1917
Place/Date of Birth: Brigg, Lincolnshire — 23 Nov. 1875
Place/Date of Death: Near Lens, France — 18 Aug. 1917
Memorials: Vimy Memorial, France
Town/County Connections: Norwood, Surrey; Brigg, Lincs.
Remarks: —
Account of Deed: On 18 Aug. 1917 north-west of Lens, France, during a strong enemy counter-attack the Lewis gun in a forward position was buried by a shell and the crew, with the exception of one man killed. Sergeant Hobson, although not a gunner, grasping the great importance of the post, rushed from his trench, dug out the gun and got it into action. The gun then jammed and so Sergeant Hobson rushed forward at the advancing enemy with bayonet and clubbed rifle, holding them back until he himself was killed by a rifle shot.

No photograph available

HODGE, Samuel

576

Private (later Lance-Corporal) 4th West India Regiment
Other Decorations: —
Date of Gazette: 4 Jan. 1867
Place/Date of Birth: Tortola, Virgin Islands, West Indies — ?1840
Place/Date of Death: Belize, Honduras — 14 Jan. 1868
Memorials: —
Town/County Connections: —
Remarks: —
Account of Deed: On 30 Jun. 1866 at Tubabecelong, near the River Gambia, West Africa, at the storming and capture of the stockaded town, Private Hodge and another man, who was afterwards killed, volunteered to hew down the stockade. After the colonel had effected an entrance Private Hodge followed him through the town, opening with his axe two barricaded gates and so allowing the support troops to enter. On reaching the other side of the town Private Hodge was acclaimed as the bravest man in the regiment, but he was very severely wounded.

HOEY, Charles Ferguson   **577**
T/Major   1st Bn., The Lincolnshire Regiment
Other Decorations: MC
Date of Gazette: 18 May 1944
Place/Date of Birth: Duncan, Vancouver Island, British Columbia, Canada — 29 Mar. 1914
Place/Date of Death: Ngakyedauk, Arakan, Burma — 17 Feb. 1944
Memorials: Taukkyan War Cemetery; War Memorial, Cowichigan, Vancouver; The Soldiers'
Chapel of St. George, Lincoln Cathedral
Town/County Connections: —
Remarks: —
Account of Deed: On 16 Feb. 1944 near the Ngakyedauk Pass, Arakan, Burma, Major Hoey's
company came under devastating machine-gun fire, but Major Hoey did not waver in his advance on the objective. Although wounded in the head and leg he went forward alone and tackled a troublesome enemy strong point, destroying it and killing all the occupants, but he was mortally wounded.

HOGAN, John   **578**
Sergeant   The 2nd Bn., The Manchester Regiment
Other Decorations: —
Date of Gazette: 22 Dec. 1914
Place/Date of Birth: Oldham, Lancashire — 8 Apr. 1884
Place/Date of Death: Oldham, Lancashire — 6 Oct. 1943
Memorials: Chadderton Cemetery, Oldham, Lancs.
Town/County Connections: Oldham, Lancashire
Remarks: —
Account of Deed: On 29 Oct. 1914 near Festubert, France, after their trench had been taken by the
enemy and two attempts to recapture it had failed, Sergeant Hogan went with a second lieutenant* and a party of 10 volunteers to recover it themselves. They took the Germans by surprise with a sudden bayonet attack and then, working from traverse to traverse, they gradually succeeded in regaining possession, killing eight of the enemy, wounding two and taking 16 prisoners. (*See also LEACH, J.)

HOLBROOK, Norman Douglas   **579**
Lieutenant (later Commander)   Royal Navy
Other Decorations: —
Date of Gazette: 22 Dec. 1914
Place/Date of Birth: Southsea, Hampshire — 9 Jul. 1888
Place/Date of Death: Midhurst, Sussex — 3 Jul. 1976
Memorials: —
Town/County Connections: Southsea, Hampshire; Midhurst, Sussex
Remarks: Served in the Second World War at the Admiralty.
Account of Deed: On 13 Dec. 1914 in the Dardanelles, Lieutenant Holbrook was in command of
the submarine B.11, an old and obsolete craft built in 1905. Notwithstanding the difficulties of a treacherous current in the Straits, he dived under five rows of mines and torpedoed and sank the Turkish battleship *Messudiyeh*, which was guarding the mine-field. He then succeeded in bringing the B.11 back to the Mediterranean, in spite of being attacked by gun fire and torpedo boats. When they got back to safety the B.11 had been submerged for 9 hours.

HOLLAND, Edward James Gibson   **580**
Sergeant (later Lieutenant Colonel)   Royal Canadian Dragoons
Other Decorations: —
Date of Gazette: 23 Apr. 1901
Place/Date of Birth: Ottawa, Canada — 2 Feb. 1878
Place/Date of Death: Cobalt, Ontario, Canada — 18 Jun. 1948
Memorials: (Cremated, ashes scattered on Island 17, Lake Temagami, Ontario)
Town/County Connections: Athy, Co. Kildare, Ireland
Remarks: —
Account of Deed: On 7 Nov. 1900 in South Africa, Sergeant Holland kept the Boers away from
two 12-pounder guns with his Colt gun. When he saw that the enemy were too near for him to escape with the carriage, as the horse was blown, he calmly lifted the gun off and galloped away with it under his arm.

HOLLAND, John Vincent   **581**
Lieutenant   3rd Bn., The Prince of Wales's Leinster Regiment, attd. 7th Bn.
Other Decorations: —
Date of Gazette: 26 Oct. 1916
Place/Date of Birth: Athy, Co. Kildare, Ireland — 19 Jul. 1889
Place/Date of Death: Hobart, Tasmania — 27 Feb. 1975
Memorials: Cornelian Bay Cemetery, Hobart
Town/County Connections: Athy, Co. Kildare
Remarks: —
Account of Deed: On 3 Sep. 1916 at Guillemont, France, during a heavy engagement, Lieutenant Holland, not content with bombing hostile dug-outs within the objective, fearlessly led his bombers through our own artillery barrage and cleared a great part of the village in front. He started out with 26 bombers and finished with only five after capturing some 50 prisoners. By this gallant action he undoubtedly broke the spirit of the enemy and saved many casualties. He was far from well at the time and later had to go to hospital.

No photograph available

HOLLIS, George   **582**
Farrier   8th Hussars (King's Royal Irish)
Other Decorations: —
Date of Gazette: 26 Jan. 1869
Place/Date of Birth: Chipping Sodbury, Gloucestershire — Oct. 1833
Place/Date of Death: St. Thomas, Devon — 16 May 1879
Memorials: —
Town/County Connections: Chipping Sodbury, Glos.; St. Thomas, Devon
Remarks: —
Account of Deed: On 17 Jun. 1858 at Gawlior, India, Farrier Hollis (together with a captain, a sergeant and a private)* was in a gallant charge made by a squadron of the 8th Hussars when, supported by a division of the Bombay Horse Artillery and the 95th Regiment, they routed the enemy. Charging through a rebel camp into two batteries, they captured and brought into their own camp two of the enemy's guns, under a heavy and converging fire from the fort and town. (*See also HENEAGE, C.W., WARD, Joseph and PEARSON, John)

HOLLIS, Stanley Elton   **583**
Company Sergeant-Major   6th Bn., The Green Howards (Alexandra Princess of Wales's Own Yorkshire Regiment)
Other Decorations: —
Date of Gazette: 17 Aug. 1944
Place/Date of Birth: Middlesbrough, Yorkshire — 21 Sep. 1912
Place/Date of Death: Middlesbrough, Yorkshire — 8 Feb. 1972
Memorials: — *The Only D-DAY VC*
Town/County Connections: Middlesbrough, Yorkshire
Remarks: The only VC awarded at the D-Day landings
Account of Deed: On 6 Jun. 1944 in Normandy, France, Company Sergeant-Major Hollis went with his company commander to investigate two German pill-boxes which had been by-passed as the company moved inland from the beaches. He rushed forward to the first pill-box, taking all but five of the occupants prisoner and then dealt with the second, taking 26 prisoners. Throughout the day, wherever the fighting was heaviest he appeared, displaying the utmost gallantry. It was through his heroism and resource that the company's objectives were gained and casualties were not heavier. He saved the lives of many of his men.

HOLLOWELL, (or HOLLIWELL), James   **584**
Private (later Lance-Corporal)   78th Regt. (later The Seaforth Highlanders — Ross-shire Buffs, Duke of Albany's)
Other Decorations: —
Date of Gazette: 18 Jun. 1858
Place/Date of Birth: Lambeth, London — 1823
Place/Date of Death: London (Holborn District) — 4 Apr. 1876
Memorials: —
Town/County Connections: Lambeth, London
Remarks: —
Account of Deed: On 26. Sep. 1857 at Lucknow, India, Private Hollowell was one of a party which was shut up and besieged in one of the houses. He behaved throughout the day in a most admirable manner, encouraging the other nine men, who were in low spirits, to keep going. His cheerful persuasion prevailed and they made a successful defence in a burning house with the enemy firing through four windows.

HOLMES, Frederick William   **585**
Lance-Corporal (later Captain)   2nd Bn., The King's Own Yorkshire Light Infantry
Other Decorations: —
Date of Gazette: 25 Nov. 1914
Place/Date of Birth: Tottenham, Middlesex — 13 Sep. 1889
Place/Date of Death: Port Augusta, South Australia — 22 Oct. 1969
Memorials: (Cremated Stirling North Garden Cemetery, Port Augusta, South Australia)
Town/County Connections: Bermondsey, London; Tottenham, Middlesex
Remarks: Médaille Militaire (France)
Account of Deed: On 26 Aug. 1914 at Le Cateau, France, Lance-Corporal Holmes carried a
wounded man out of the trenches under heavy fire and later helped to drive a gun out of action by
taking the place of a driver who was wounded. *Town Hall, Spa Road, Bermondsey, London has two drawings of him in the Council Chamber*

No photograph available

HOLMES, Joel   **586**
Private   84th Regiment (later The York and Lancaster Regiment)
Other Decorations: —
Date of Gazette: 18 Jun. 1858
Place/Date of Birth: Great Comershall, Halifax, Yorkshire — 1821
Place/Date of Death: Halifax, Yorkshire — 27 Jul. 1872
Memorials: All Souls' Cemetery, Halifax
Town/County Connections: Halifax, Yorkshire
Remarks: —
Account of Deed: On 25 Sep. 1857 at Lucknow, India, Private Holmes was the first man to
respond to a call for volunteers to assist in working under very heavy enemy fire one of the guns
from which all the artillerymen had become casualties.

HOLMES, Thomas William   **587**
Private   4th Canadian Mounted Rifles, 2nd Central Ontario Regiment, C.E.F.
Other Decorations: —
Date of Gazette: 11 Jan. 1918
Place/Date of Birth: Montreal, Canada — 14 Oct. 1898
Place/Date of Death: Toronto, Canada — 4 Jan. 1950
Memorials: Buried at Owen Sound, Canada; Queen's Park, West Owen Sound, Ontario
Town/County Connections: —
Remarks: —
Account of Deed: On 26 Oct. 1917 near Passchendaele, Belgium, when the right flank of our
attack was held up by heavy machine-gun fire from a pill box strong point and heavy casualties
were producing a critical situation, Private Holmes, on his own initiative and single-handed, ran forward and threw two bombs,
killing and wounding the crews of two machine-guns. He then fetched another bomb and threw this into the entrance of the pill
box, causing the 19 occupants to surrender.

HOLMES, William Edgar   **588**
Private   2nd Bn., Grenadier Guards
Other Decorations: —
Date of Gazette: 26 Dec. 1918
Place/Date of Birth: Wood Stanway, Gloucestershire — 26 Jun. 1895
Place/Date of Death: Cattenieres, France — 9 Oct. 1918
Memorials: Carnieres Communal Cemetery Extension, France: Didbrook Church, Glos.
Town/County Connections: Wood Stanway, Gloucestershire
Remarks: —
Account of Deed: On 9 Oct. 1918 at Cattenieres, France, Private Holmes carried in two men under
the most intense fire and while he was attending to a third case he was severely wounded. In spite
of this he continued to carry in the casualties, and was shortly afterwards mortally wounded. By his self-sacrifice this man was
the means of saving the lives of several of his comrades.

HOME, Anthony Dickson (later Sir Anthony)   **589**
Surgeon (later Surgeon General)   90th Regiment (later The Cameronians — Scottish Rifles)
Other Decorations: KCB
Date of Gazette: 18 Jun. 1858
Place/Date of Birth: Dunbar, Scotland — 30 Nov. 1826
Place/Date of Death: London — 10 Aug. 1914
Memorials: Brompton Cemetery, London   *grave*
Town/County Connections: Dunbar, Scotland; London
Remarks: Principal Medical Officer, Ashanti 1873, Cyprus 1878-79, to forces in India 1881-85
Account of Deed: On 26 Sep. 1857 at Lucknow, India, Surgeon Home was in charge of the wounded men left behind when the troops forced their way into the Residency. The escort left with the wounded had been reduced, by casualties, to a small party, who with the wounded, were forced into a house which they defended until it was set on fire. They then retreated to a shed nearby and defended this for more than 22 hours until relieved. At last only six men with Surgeon Home in charge, remained to fire, and the fact that the wounded were safe and the defence was successful was mainly attributable to his brave conduct throughout. (See also BRADSHAW, W.)

HOME, Duncan Charles   **590**
Lieutenant   Bengal Engineers
Other Decorations: —
Date of Gazette: 18 Jun. 1858
Place/Date of Birth: Jubbulpore, Central Provinces, India — 10 Jun. 1828
Place/Date of Death: Malagarh, India — 1 Oct. 1857
Memorials: Tomb at Bolandsharh; Kashmir Gate, Delhi; St. Paul's Cathedral, Calcutta
Town/County Connections: —
Remarks: —
Account of Deed: On 14 Sep. 1857 at Delhi, India, Lieutenant Home, with another lieutenant, a sergeant and a bugler* showed conspicuous gallantry in the desperate task of blowing in the Kashmir Gate in broad daylight under heavy and destructive musket fire, preparatory to the assault. (*See also SALKELD, P., SMITH, John (No. 1164) and HAWTHORNE, R.)

HONEY, Samuel Lewis   **591**
Lieutenant   78th Bn., Manitoba Regiment (Winnipeg Grenadiers), C.E.F.
Other Decorations: DCM, MM
Date of Gazette: 6 Jan. 1919
Place/Date of Birth: Conn, Wellington Co., Ontario, Canada — 9 Feb. 1894
Place/Date of Death: Bourlon Wood, France — 30 Sep. 1918
Memorials: Queant Communal Cemetery, British Extension, France
Town/County Connections: —
Remarks: —
Account of Deed: On 27 Sep. 1918 at Bourlon Wood, France, when his company commander and all the other officers of his company became casualties, Lieutenant Honey took command, continuing the advance and gaining the objective. Then, finding his company suffering casualties from enfilade machine-gun fire he made a personal reconnaissance and locating the machine-gun nest, rushed it single-handed, capturing the guns and 10 prisoners. Later, after repelling four enemy counter-attacks, he captured another machine-gun post. He continued to lead his company with great initiative and daring, but died of his wounds on the last day of the attack by his battalion.

HOOK, Alfred Henry   **592**
Private (later Sergeant)   2nd Bn., 24th Regiment (later The South Wales Borderers)
Other Decorations: —
Date of Gazette: 2 May 1879
Place/Date of Birth: Churcham, Gloucestershire — 6 Aug. 1850
Place/Date of Death: Churcham, Gloucestershire — 12 Mar. 1905
Memorials: Churcham, Glos; Brecon Cathedral
Town/County Connections: Churcham, Gloucestershire; Monmouth   *Buried Churcham*
Remarks: Later served with the 1st Volunteer Bn., The Royal Fusiliers
Account of Deed: On 22/23 Jan. 1879 at Rorke's Drift, Natal, South Africa, a distant room of the hospital had been held for more than an hour by three privates, and when finally they had no ammunition left the Zulus burst in, and killed one of the men and two patients. One of the privates* however, succeeded in knocking a hole in the partition and taking the last two patients through into the next ward, where he found Private Hook. These two men then worked together — one holding the enemy at bayonet point while the other broke through three more partitions — and they were then able to bring eight patients into the inner line of defence. (*See also WILLIAMS, John).

VC with SWB Museum, Brecon

HOPE, William   **593**
Lieutenant (later Colonel)   7th Regiment (later The Royal Fusiliers)
Other Decorations: —
Date of Gazette: 5 May 1857
Place/Date of Birth: Edinburgh — 12 Apr. 1834
Place/Date of Death: Chelsea, London — 17 Dec. 1909
Memorials: Brompton Cemetery, London (family plot)
Town/County Connections: Edinburgh; London; Dagenham, Essex
Remarks: —
Account of Deed: On 18 Jun. 1855 at Sebastopol, Crimea, Lieutenant Hope went to the assistance of the adjutant, who was lying outside the trenches badly wounded. Having found that it was impossible to move him, even with the help of four men, he ran back across the open ground under very heavy fire from the enemy batteries, and procured a stretcher to bring the wounded officer in.

HORE-RUTHVEN, The Hon. Alexander Gore Arkwright —
see **RUTHVEN,** The Hon. Alexander Gore Arkwright HORE-

HORLOCK, (or HARLOCK) Ernest George   **594**
Bombardier (later Battery Sergeant-Major)   113th Bty., Royal Field Artillery
Other Decorations: —
Date of Gazette: 25 Nov. 1914
Place/Date of Birth: Alton, Hampshire — 24 Oct. 1885
Place/Date of Death: At sea, near Egypt — 30 Dec. 1917
Memorials: Alexandria (Hadra) War Memorial Cemetery; Langrish Church, Hants.
Town/County Connections: Alton and Langrish, Hampshire
Remarks: —   *Name on Roll of Honour, Langrish Church.*
Account of Deed: On 15 Sep. 1914 at Vendresse, France, when the 113th Battery, Royal Field Artillery was in action under heavy shell fire, Bombardier Horlock, although twice wounded, returned to lay his gun on each occasion after his wound had been dressed, in spite of the fact that the medical officer twice ordered him to go to hospital.

HORNBY, Edmund John PHIPPS-   **595**
Major (later Brigadier General)   'Q' Battery, Royal Horse Artillery
Other Decorations: CB, CMG
Date of Gazette: 26 Jun. 1900
Place/Date of Birth: Lordington, Emsworth, Hampshire — 31 Dec. 1857
Place/Date of Death: Sonning, Berkshire — 13 Dec. 1947
Memorials: —
Town/County Connections: Emsworth, Hampshire
Remarks: Served in First World War, 1914-15; DL County of Berkshire
Account of Deed: On 31 Mar. 1900 at Korn Spruit, South Africa, two batteries of the Royal Horse Artillery were ambushed with the loss of most of the baggage column and five guns of the leading battery. When the alarm was given 'Q' Battery, commanded by Major Phipps-Hornby, went into action 1150 yards from the spruit, until the order to retire was received, when the major commanded that the guns and their limbers be run back by hand to a safe place — a most exhausting operation over a considerable distance, but at last all but one of the guns and one limber had been moved to safety and the battery reformed. (See also PARKER, C.E.H., LODGE, I. and GLASOCK,.H.H.)

HORNELL, David Ernest   **596**
Flight Lieutenant   162 Squadron, Royal Canadian Air Force
Other Decorations: —
Date of Gazette: 28 Jul. 1944
Place/Date of Birth: Mimico, Ontario, Canada — 26 Jan. 1910
Place/Date of Death: Near Faroes, North Atlantic — 25 Jun. 1944
Memorials: Lerwick New Cemetery, Shetland Islands
Town/County Connections: —
Remarks: —
Account of Deed: On 24 Jun. 1944 on sea patrol in the North Atlantic, Flight Lieutenant Hornell's twin-engined amphibian aircraft was attacked and badly damaged by an enemy submarine; nevertheless he succeeded in sinking it and then with superhuman effort managed to bring his aircraft down on the heavy swell, blazing furiously. There was only one serviceable dinghy which could not hold all the crew so they took it in turns in the water. By the time the survivors were rescued after 21 hours, Flight Lieutenant Hornell was blinded and weak from exposure and cold. He died shortly after being picked up.

HORSFALL, Basil Arthur **597**
Second Lieutenant   3rd Bn., The East Lancashire Regiment, attd. 11th Bn.
Other Decorations: —
Date of Gazette: 22 May 1918
Place/Date of Birth: Colombo, Ceylon — 4 Oct. 1887
Place/Date of Death: Near Ablainzeville, France — 27 Mar. 1918
Memorials: Arras Memorial, France
Town/County Connections: Hedingham, Essex
Remarks: —
Account of Deed: On 27 Mar. 1918 between Moyenville and Ablainzeville, France, when the enemy first attacked Second Lieutenant Horsfall's centre platoon, his three forward sections were driven back and he was wounded in the head. Nevertheless he immediately reorganised the remainder of his men and made a counter-attack which recovered his original position. Despite the severity of his wound, he refused to go to the dressing station, as the three remaining officers in his company were casualties. Later, he made a second successful counter-attack but when finally ordered to withdraw, he was the last to leave the position. He was killed almost immediately afterwards.

HORWOOD, Alec George **598**
Lieutenant   1/6th Bn., The Queen's Royal Regt. (West Surrey), attd. 1st Bn., The Northamptonshire Regiment
Other Decorations: DCM
Date of Gazette: 30 Mar. 1944
Place/Date of Birth: Deptford, London — 6 Jan. 1914
Place/Date of Death: Kyauchaw, Burma — 20 Jan. 1944
Memorials: Rangoon Memorial
Town/County Connections: —
Remarks: —
Account of Deed: On 18 Jan. 1944 at Kyauchaw, Burma, Lieutenant Horwood accompanied a company into action with his forward mortar observation post. Throughout the day he was in an exposed position and under intense fire, but he came back at night with most valuable information about the enemy. On 19 Jan. he moved forward and established another observation post, directing accurate mortar fire in support of two attacks, and also carrying out personal reconnaissance, deliberately drawing the enemy fire so that their position could be definitely located. On 20 Jan. he volunteered to lead the attack and while doing so was mortally wounded.

HOUSE, William **599**
Private (later Lance-Corporal)   2nd Bn., The Royal Berkshire Regiment (Princess Charlotte of Wales's)
Other Decorations: —
Date of Gazette: 7 Oct. 1902
Place/Date of Birth: Thatcham, near Newbury, Berkshire — 7 Oct. 1879
Place/Date of Death: Dover, Kent — 28 Feb. 1912
Memorials: St. James's Cemetery, Dover
Town/County Connections: Thatcham, Newbury, Berkshire; Dover, Kent
Remarks: —
Account of Deed: On 2 Aug. 1900 at Mosilikatse Nek, South Africa, when a sergeant who had gone forward to reconnoitre was wounded, Private House rushed out from cover (although cautioned not to do so as the fire from the enemy was very hot) picked up the wounded sergeant and tried to bring him into shelter. In doing this he was severely wounded, but he warned his comrades not to come to his assistance as the fire was so heavy.

HOWELL, George Julian **600**
Corporal (later Staff-Sergeant)   1st Bn. (N.S.W.), Australian Imperial Force
Other Decorations: MM
Date of Gazette: 27 Jun. 1917
Place/Date of Birth: Enfield, Sydney, New South Wales, Australia — 23 Nov. 1893
Place/Date of Death: Perth, Western Australia — 23 Dec. 1964
Memorials: Karrakatta Cemetery, Hollywood, Perth, Western Australia; Australian War Memorial, Canberra
Town/County Connections: —
Remarks: —
Account of Deed: On 6 May 1917, near Bullecourt, France, seeing that a party of the enemy were likely to outflank his battalion, Corporal Howell, on his own initiative and exposed to heavy bomb and rifle fire, climbed to the top of the parapet and bombed the enemy, pressing them back along the trench. When his stock of bombs was exhausted, he continued the attack with his bayonet, but was then severely wounded. This prompt and gallant action was seen by the whole battalion and inspired them in the subsequent successful counter-attack.

HOWSE, Neville Reginald (later Sir Neville)   **601**
Captain   New South Wales Medical Staff Corps, Australian Forces
Other Decorations: KCB, KCMG
Date of Gazette: 4 Jun. 1901
Place/Date of Birth: Stogursey, Somerset — 26 Oct. 1863
Place/Date of Death: London — 19 Sep. 1930
Memorials: Kensal Green Cemetery, London; Australian War Memorial, Canberra
Town/County Connections: —
Remarks: First man to win a VC while serving with an Australian unit. Served in the First World War; DMS Australian Imperial Force; DGMS Australian Military Forces; Minister for Defence and Health, Australian Government 1927-28; Minister for Health and Repatriation, Australian Commonwealth 1925-29; Minister for Home and Territories 1928; Knight of the Order of St. John
Account of Deed: On 24 Jul. 1900 during the action at Vredefort, South Africa, Captain Howse saw a trumpeter fall and went through very heavy cross-fire to rescue the man. His horse was soon shot from under him and the captain continued on foot, reached the casualty and dressed his wound. He then carried him to safety.

HUDSON, Charles Edward   **602**
T/Lieutenant Colonel (later Major General)   Comd. 11th Bn., The Sherwood Foresters (The Nottinghamshire and Derbyshire Regiment)
Other Decorations: CB, DSO & Bar, MC
Date of Gazette: 11 Jul. 1918
Place/Date of Birth: Derby, — 29 May 1892
Place/Date of Death: Scilly Isles — 4 Apr. 1959
Memorials: —
Town/County Connections: Derby; Scilly Isles   *Sherborne School. Dorset*
Remarks: Croix de Guerre (France); Italian Silver Medal for Valour; Chief Instructor, Royal Military College 1933-37; Commanded 2nd Infantry Brigade 1938; County Commissioner, St. John Ambulance Association 1949-54; Knight of the Order of St. John; DL, County of Devon
Account of Deed: On 15 Jun. 1918 near Asiago, Italy, during an attack when the enemy had penetrated our front line, Lieutenant Colonel Hudson collected and personally led various headquarter details such as orderlies, servants, runners, etc. to deal with the situation. He rushed a position with only two men, shouting to the enemy to surrender, some of whom did. He was severely wounded by a bomb which exploded on his foot and although in great pain gave directions for the counter-attack which was successful, about 100 prisoners and six machine-guns being taken.

HUFFAM, James Palmer   **603**
Second Lieutenant (later Major)   5th Bn., The Duke of Wellington's (West Riding) Regiment, attd. 2nd Bn.
Other Decorations: —
Date of Gazette: 26 Dec. 1918
Place/Date of Birth: Dunblane, Perthshire, Scotland — 31 Mar. 1897
Place/Date of Death: Stanmore, Middlesex — 16 Feb. 1968
Memorials: —
Town/County Connections: Dunblane, Perthshire; Stanmore, Middlesex
Remarks: Served in the Second World War — Assistant Provost Marshal, France 1940
Account of Deed: On 31 Aug. 1918 at St. Servin's Farm, France, Second Lieutenant Huffam with three men rushed an enemy machine-gun post and put it out of action. His position was then heavily attacked and he withdrew, carrying back a wounded comrade. Again in the night, accompanied by two men only he rushed an enemy machine-gun, capturing eight prisoners and enabling the advance to continue.

HUGHES, Matthew   **604**
Private (later Corporal)   7th Regiment (later The Royal Fusiliers)
Other Decorations: —
Date of Gazette: 24 Feb. 1857
Place/Date of Birth: Bradford, Yorkshire — 1822
Place/Date of Death: Bradford, Yorkshire — 9 Jan. 1882
Memorials: —
Town/County Connections: Bradford, Yorkshire
Remarks: —
Account of Deed: On 7 Jun. 1855 in the Crimea, at the storming of the Quarries, Private Hughes went twice for ammunition across open ground, under heavy fire. He also went to the front and brought in a soldier who was severely wounded. On 18 Jun. he volunteered to bring in a badly wounded lieutenant, and in so doing was severely wounded himself.

HUGHES, Thomas   **605**
Private (later Corporal)   6th Bn., The Connaught Rangers
Other Decorations: —
Date of Gazette: 26 Oct. 1916
Place/Date of Birth: Coravoo, Near Castleblaney, Co. Monaghan, Ireland — 30 May 1885
Place/Date of Death: Near Carrickmacross, Ireland — 8 Jan. 1942
Memorials: —
Town/County Connections: Castleblaney, Co Monoghan
Remarks: —
Account of Deed: On 3 Sep. 1916 at Guillemont, France, Private Hughes was wounded in an attack but returned at once to the firing line after having his wounds dressed. Later, seeing a hostile machine-gun, he dashed out in front of his company, shot the gunner and, single-handed, captured the gun. Though again wounded, he brought back three or four prisoners.

HULL, Charles   **606**
Private — Shoeing Smith (later Corporal)   21st Lancers, (Empress of India's)
Other Decorations: —
Date of Gazette: 3 Mar. 1916
Place/Date of Birth: Harrogate, Yorkshire — 24 Jul. 1890
Place/Date of Death: Leeds, Yorkshire — 13 Feb. 1953
Memorials: —
Town/County Connections: Harrogate and Leeds, Yorkshire
Remarks: —
Account of Deed: On 5 Sep. 1915 at Hafiz Kor, N.W. Frontier, India, Private Hull rescued an officer from certain death at the hands of the tribesmen. The latter's horse had been shot and Private Hull took the officer up behind on his own horse, under heavy fire at close range, and galloped away to safety.

HULME, Alfred Clive   **607**
Sergeant   23rd Bn., 2nd N.Z.E.F. (The Canterbury Regiment)
Other Decorations: —
Date of Gazette: 14 Oct. 1941
Place/Date of Birth: Dunedin, New Zealand — 24 Jan. 1911
Place/Date of Death: Tauranga, New Zealand — 3 Sep. 1982
Memorials: Dunedin RSA, New Zealand
Town/County Connections: —
Remarks: —
Account of Deed: During the period 20/28 May 1941 in Crete, Sergeant Hulme displayed outstanding leadership and courage. At Maleme he led a party against the enemy who were attacking with rifles, machine-guns and mortars. At Galatos he drove the enemy away from a school building with hand grenades. At Suda Bay he killed five snipers and at Stylos he wiped out a mortar crew and accounted for three more snipers.

HUMPSTON, Robert   **608**
Private   2nd Bn., The Rifle Brigade (Prince Consort's Own)
Other Decorations: —
Date of Gazette: 24 Feb. 1857
Place/Date of Birth: Derby — 1832
Place/Date of Death: Derby — 22 Dec. 1884
Memorials: The Rifle Brigade memorial, Winchester Cathedral
Town/County Connections: Derby
Remarks: —
Account of Deed: On 22 Apr. 1855 in the Crimea Private Humpston and another private*, on their own, attacked and captured a Russian rifle pit situated among the rocks overhanging the Woronzoff Road. The pit was occupied every night by the Russians and its capture and subsequent destruction was of great importance. (*See also BRADSHAW, J.)

HUNTER, David Ferguson   **609**
Corporal (later Sergeant)   1/5th Bn., The Highland Light Infantry
Other Decorations: —
Date of Gazette: 23 Oct. 1918
Place/Date of Birth: Kingseat, Dunfermline, Scotland — 28 Nov. 1891
Place/Date of Death: Dunfermline, Scotland — 14 Feb. 1965
Memorials: —
Town/County Connections: Dunfermline, Scotland
Remarks: —
Account of Deed: On 16/17 Sep. 1918 at Moeuvres, France, Corporal Hunter was detailed to take on an advanced post which was established in shell holes close to the enemy. There was no opportunity for reconnoitring the adjacent ground, and the following afternoon Corporal Hunter found that the enemy had established posts all round him, isolating his command. He determined to hold out and despite being exceedingly short of food and water this NCO managed to maintain his position for over 48 hours until a counter-attack relieved him. He repelled frequent enemy attacks and also barrage from our own attacks, which came right across his post.

HUNTER, Thomas Peck   **610**
T/Corporal   43rd Royal Marine Commando
Other Decorations: —
Date of Gazette: 12 Jun. 1945
Place/Date of Birth: Aldershot, Hampshire — 6 Oct. 1923
Place/Date of Death: Lake Comacchio, Italy — 2 Apr. 1945
Memorials: Argenta Gap War Cemetery, Italy
Town/County Connections: —
Remarks: —
Account of Deed: On 2 Apr. 1945 at Lake Comacchio, Italy, Corporal Hunter, who was in charge of a Bren gun section, offered himself as a target to save his troop. Seizing the Bren gun he charged alone across 200 yards of open ground under most intense fire towards a group of houses where three Spandau machine-guns were lodged. So determined was his charge that the enemy were demoralized and six of the gunners surrendered, the remainder fled. He cleared the house, changing magazines as he ran and continued to draw the enemy fire until most of the troop had reached cover and he was killed, firing accurately to the last.

HUTCHESON, Bellenden Seymour   **611**
Captain   Canadian Army Medical Corps, attd. 75th Bn., 1st Central Ontario Regiment, C.E.F.
Other Decorations: MC
Date of Gazette: 14 Dec. 1918
Place/Date of Birth: Mount Carmel, Illinois, U.S.A. — 16 Dec. 1883
Place/Date of Death: Cairo, Illinois, U.S.A. — 9 Aril 1954
Memorials: Mount Carmel Cemetery, Mount Carmel, Illinois, U.S.A.
Town/County Connections: —
Remarks: —
Account of Deed: On 2 Sep. 1918 in France, Captain Hutcheson went through the Queant-Drocourt Support Line with his battalion, remaining on the field until every wounded man had been attended to. He dressed the wounds of a seriously hurt officer under terrific machine-gun and shell fire, and with the help of prisoners and his own men succeeded in evacuating the officer to safety. Immediately afterwards he rushed forward in full view of the enemy to attend a wounded sergeant and having placed him in a shell-hole, dressed his wounds.

HUTCHINSON, James   **612**
Private (later Corporal)   2/5th Bn., The Lancashire Fusiliers
Other Decorations: —
Date of Gazette: 9 Sep. 1916
Place/Date of Birth: Bank Top, Radcliffe, Lancashire — 9 Jul. 1895
Place/Date of Death: Torquay, Devon — 22 Jan. 1972
Memorials: —
Town/County Connections: Radcliffe, Lancashire; Torquay, Devon
Remarks: —
Account of Deed: On 28 Jun. 1916 opposite Ficheux, France, during an attack on the enemy's position, Private Hutchinson was the leading man, and entering their trench, shot two sentries and cleared two of the traverses. Afterwards, when the objective had been gained and the retirement ordered, Private Hutchinson, on his own initiative, undertook the dangerous task of covering the retirement thus ensuring that the wounded could be removed to safety. All the time he was exposed to fierce fire from machine-guns and rifles at close quarters.

HUTT, Arthur   **613**
Private (later Corporal)   1/7th Bn., The Royal Warwickshire Regiment
Other Decorations: —
Date of Gazette: 26 Nov. 1917
Place/Date of Birth: Earlsden, Coventry, Warwickshire — 12 Feb. 1889
Place/Date of Death: Coventry — 14 Apr. 1954
Memorials: War Memorial Park, Coventry   *Grave*
Town/County Connections: Earlsden, Coventry, Warwickshire
Remarks: —
Account of Deed: On 4 Oct. 1917 at Terrier Farm, south-east of Poelcapelle, Belgium, when all
the officers and NCOs of No. 2 Platoon had become casualties, Private Hutt took command of and
led the platoon. He was held up by a strong post but immediately ran forward alone and shot the officer and three men in the
post; between 40 and 50 others surrendered. Later, having pushed too far, he withdrew his party, covering them by sniping the
enemy, and then carried back a wounded man to shelter. After he had consolidated his position, he then went out and carried
in four more wounded under heavy fire.

IND, Alfred Ernest   **614**
Shoeing Smith (later Farrier-Sergeant)   Royal Horse Artillery
Other Decorations: —
Date of Gazette: 15 Aug. 1902
Place/Date of Birth: Tetbury, Gloucestershire — 16 Sep. 1872
Place/Date of Death: Eccleston, Cheshire — 29 Nov. 1916
Memorials: —
Town/County Connections: Tetbury, Gloucestershire; Eccleston, Cheshire
Remarks: —
Account of Deed: On 20 Dec. 1901 near Tafelkop, Orange River Colony, South Africa, Shoeing
Smith Ind stuck to his pompom gun under very heavy fire when the whole of the remainder of the
team had been shot down, and continued to fire into the advancing enemy until the last possible moment. A captain who was
mortally wounded on this occasion, requested that Shoeing Smith Ind's gallant conduct on this and in every other action since
he joined the pompom service be brought to notice.

INGHAM, Samuel — see **MEEKOSHA,** Samuel

INGOUVILLE George   **615**
Captain of the Mast   Royal Navy
Other Decorations: —
Date of Gazette: 24 Feb. 1857
Place/Date of Birth: St. Saviour, Jersey, Channel Islands — 7 Oct. 1826
Place/Date of Death: ? — 13 Jan. 1869
Memorials: —
Town/County Connections: St. Saviour, Jersey
Remarks: —
Account of Deed: On 13 Jul. 1855 at the Fort of Viborg in the Gulf of Finland, while the boats of
HMS *Arrogant* were engaged with the enemy, her second cutter was swamped by the blowing up
of her magazine and drifted inshore under enemy guns. Captain of the Mast Ingouville, although wounded, jumped overboard,
swam round to the boat's bows, took hold of the painter and tried to turn the cutter out to sea. A lieutenant of the Royal Marine
Artillery* came to his assistance, when with three volunteers, he took off the crew from the cutter, rescued Mr. Ingouville from
the water and then towed the stricken boat out of gun range. (*See also DOWELL, G.D.)

INGRAM, George Morby   **616**
Lieutenant   24th Bn. (Victoria), Australian Imperial Force
Other Decorations: MM
Date of Gazette: 6 Jan. 1919
Place/Date of Birth: Bendigo, Victoria, Australia — 18 Mar. 1889
Place/Date of Death: Hastings, Victoria, Australia — 1 Jul. 1961
Memorials: Frankston Cemetery, Victoria; Australian War Memorial, Canberra
Town/County Connections: —
Remarks: Served in Royal Australian Engineers in Second World War
Account of Deed: On 5 Oct. 1918, at Montbrehain, east of Peronne, France, Lieutenant Ingram,
at the head of his men, rushed and captured nine enemy machine-guns, and killed 42 of the enemy
after stubborn resistance. Later, when his company had suffered severe casualties, including many of the leaders, he again
rushed a machine-gun post, shot six of the enemy and captured the gun. On two subsequent occasions he attacked enemy
posts, inflicting many casualties and taking 62 prisoners.

INKSON, Edgar Thomas **617**
Lieutenant (later Colonel)   Royal Army Medical Corps, attd. The Royal Inniskilling Fusiliers
Other Decorations: DSO
Date of Gazette: 15 Jan. 1901
Place/Date of Birth: Naini Tal, India — 5 Apr. 1872
Place/Date of Death: Chichester, Sussex — 19 Feb. 1947
Memorials: —
Town/County Connections: Chichester, Sussex
Remarks: Served in the First World War 1914-18
Account of Deed: On 24 Feb. 1900, at Hart's Hill, Colenso, South Africa, Lieutenant Inkson carried a young officer, who was severely wounded and unable to walk, for three or four hundred yards, under very heavy fire, to a place of safety.

INNES, James John McLeod **618**
Lieutenant (later Lieutenant General)   Bengal Engineers
Other Decorations: CB
Date of Gazette: 24 Dec. 1858
Place/Date of Birth: Baghalpur, Bengal, India — 5 Feb. 1830
Place/Date of Death: Cambridge — 13 Dec. 1907
Memorials: —
Town/County Connections: Cambridge
Remarks: Became Inspector-General of Military Works, India, and served on the India Defence Committee Enquiry
Account of Deed: On 23 Feb. 1858 at Sultanpore, India, Lieutenant Innes, far in advance of the leading skirmishers, was the first to secure a gun which the enemy were abandoning. They then rallied round another gun from which the shot would have ploughed through our advancing columns. Lieutenant Innes rode up, unsupported, shot the gunner and remained at his post keeping the enemy at bay until assistance reached him.

INSALL, Gilbert Stuart Martin **619**
Second Lieutenant (later Group Captain)   11 Squadron, Royal Flying Corps (later Royal Air Force)
Other Decorations: MC
Date of Gazette: 23 Dec. 1915
Place/Date of Birth: Paris — 14 May 1894
Place/Date of Death: Scrooby, Bawtry, Yorkshire — 17 Feb. 1972
Memorials: —
Town/County Connections: Scrooby, Bawtry, Yorkshire
Remarks: Served in the Second World War; commanded RAF Uxbridge 1940
Account of Deed: On 7 Nov. 1915 near Achiet, France, Second Lieutenant Insall, on patrol in a Vickers fighter, engaged an enemy machine, the pilot of which was eventually forced to make a rough landing in a ploughed field. Seeing the Germans scramble out preparing to fire, the lieutenant dived to 500ft and his gunner opened fire, whereupon they fled. After dropping an incendiary bomb on the German aircraft he flew through heavy fire, at 2000ft over enemy trenches. The Vickers' petrol tank was hit, but the lieutenant managed to land near a wood 500ft inside Allied lines and he and his gunner, after repairing the machine during the night, flew back to base at dawn.

INWOOD, Reginald Roy **620**
Private (later Sergeant)   10th Bn. (S.A.), Australian Imperial Force
Other Decorations: —
Date of Gazette: 26 Nov. 1917
Place/Date of Birth: Renmark, North Adelaide, South Australia — 14 Jul. 1890
Place/Date of Death: Adelaide, Australia — 23 Oct. 1971
Memorials: AIF Cemetery, Adelaide; Australian War Memorial, Canberra
Town/County Connections: —
Remarks: —
Account of Deed: During the period 19/22 Sep. 1917 in an attack at Polygon Wood, near Ypres, Belgium, Private Inwood moved forward alone through the allied barrage, capturing an enemy strong-point, killing several and taking nine prisoners. During the evening, he volunteered for a special all-night patrol which went out 600 yards in front of the allied line, and succeeded in bringing back valuable information. In the early morning of 21 Sep. he again went out in company with another man and they located a machine-gun which was causing much trouble. They bombed it so effectively that only one gunner survived and he was brought in as a prisoner, with the gun.

IRWIN, Charles   **621**
Private   53rd Regiment (later The King's Shropshire Light Infantry)
Other Decorations: —
Date of Gazette: 24 Dec. 1858
Place/Date of Birth: Manorhamilton, Co. Leitrim, Ireland — 1824
Place/Date of Death: Newton Butler, Co. Fermanagh, Ireland — 8 Apr. 1873
Memorials: —
Town/County Connections: Manorhamilton, Co. Leitrim; Newton Butler, Co. Fermanagh
Remarks: —
Account of Deed: On 16 Nov. 1857 at Lucknow, India, Private Irwin showed conspicuous bravery at the assault on the Secundra Bagh when, although severely wounded through the right shoulder, he was one of the first to enter the building under heavy fire. (Elected by the regiment.)

ISHAR SINGH,   **622**
Sepoy (later Captain)   28th Punjab Regiment, Indian Army
Other Decorations: —
Date of Gazette: 25 Nov. 1921
Place/Date of Birth: Nenwan, Hoshiarpur District, Punjab, India — 30 Dec. 1895
Place/Date of Death: Nenwan, Punjab, India — 2 Dec. 1963
Memorials: —
Town/County Connections: —
Remarks: PVSM (India)
Account of Deed: On 10 Apr. 1921 near Haidari Kach, North West Frontier, India, Sepoy Ishar Singh was No. 1 of a Lewis gun section. Early in the fighting he was severely wounded, all the officers and havildars of his company became casualties and his Lewis gun was seized. He recovered the gun and went into action again although his wound was bleeding profusely, but when ordered to have it dressed, he went instead to help the medical officer, carrying water to the wounded, taking a rifle and helping to keep down enemy fire and acting as a shield while the medical officer was dressing a wound. It was nearly three hours before he submitted to being evacuated.

JACKA, Albert   **623**
Lance-Corporal (later Captain)   14th Bn. (Victoria), Australian Imperial Force
Other Decorations: MC & Bar
Date of Gazette: 24 Jul. 1915
Place/Date of Birth: Winchelsea District, Geelong, Victoria, Australia — 10 Jan. 1893
Place/Date of Death: Melbourne, Australia — 17 Jan. 1932
Memorials: St. Kilda Cemetery, Melbourne; Australian War Memorial, Canberra
Town/County Connections: —
Remarks: First Australian-born man to win VC while serving with Australian Army
Account of Deed: On 19/20 May 1915, at "Courtney's Post," Gallipoli, Lance-Corporal Jacka, while holding a portion of our trench with four other men, was heavily attacked. When all except himself were killed or wounded, and the trench was rushed and occupied by seven Turks, Lance-Corporal Jacka most gallantly attacked them single handed, killing the whole party, five by rifle and two with the bayonet.

JACKMAN, James Joseph Bernard   **624**
T/Captain   The Royal Northumberland Fusiliers
Other Decorations: —
Date of Gazette: 31 Mar. 1942
Place/Date of Birth: Dublin — 19 Mar. 1916
Place/Date of Death: El Duda, Tobruk, North Africa — 26 Nov. 1941
Memorials: Tobruk War Cemetery
Town/County Connections: Dunloaghaire, Dublin
Remarks: —
Account of Deed: On 25 Nov. 1941 at Tobruk, Libya, the assault on El Duda ridge was being slowed down by fierce enemy fire from anti-tank guns and Captain Jackman as calmly as though on manoeuvres, led his machine-gun company to ease the situation on the right flank of our tanks. Then, standing up in his vehicle, he led the trucks across the front between the tanks and the guns and got them into action on the left flank. His coolness and complete disregard of danger not only inspired his own men but also the tank crews. He was killed next day.

JACKSON, Harold

625

Sergeant   7th (S) Bn., The East Yorkshire Regiment
Other Decorations: —
Date of Gazette: 8 May 1918
Place/Date of Birth: Kirton, Boston, Lincolnshire — 2 Jun. 1892
Place/Date of Death: Flers, France — 24 Aug. 1918
Memorials: A.I.F. Burial Ground, Glas Lane, Flers, France;War Memorials at Kirton, Boston, Lincolnshire and Wood Green, London
Town/County Connections: Kirton, Boston, Lincolnshire; Wood Green, London
Remarks: —
Account of Deed: On 22 Mar. 1918 at Hermies, France, Sergeant Jackson volunteered and went through the hostile barrage and brought back valuable information regarding the enemy's movements. Later when the enemy had established themselves in our line, the sergeant single-handed bombed them out into the open. Again single-handed he stalked an enemy machine-gun, threw Mills bombs at the detachments and put the gun out of action. On a subsequent occasion when all his officers had become casualties he led his company to the attack, withdrawing them successfully when ordered to do so. He repeatedly went out under fire and carried in wounded.

JACKSON, Norman Cyril

626

Sergeant (later Warrant Officer)   106 Squadron, Royal Air Force Volunteer Reserve
Other Decorations: —
Date of Gazette: 26 Oct. 1945
Place/Date of Birth: Ealing, London — 8 Apr. 1919
Place/Date of Death: — *Died? 1994?*
Memorials: —
Town/County Connections: Ealing, London; Twickenham, Middlesex
Remarks: —
Account of Deed: On 26 Apr. 1944 after bombing Schweinfurt, Germany, the Lancaster in which Sergeant Jackson was flight engineer, was hit by an enemy fighter and fire broke out. Having asked permission to try to deal with it, Sergeant Jackson clipped on his parachute and, with a fire extinguisher, climbed on to the fuselage of the aircraft which was travelling at 200mph at 20,000ft. He tried to put out the fire, but his parachute partly opened and he slipped on to the wing. The fire spread and he was badly burned, then he was swept from the wing with his partly-inflated, burning parachute trailing behind him. He landed heavily, breaking an ankle, and was taken prisoner.

JACKSON, Thomas Norman

627

Lance-Corporal   1st Bn., Coldstream Guards
Other Decorations: —
Date of Gazette: 27 Nov. 1918
Place/Date of Birth: Swinton, Yorkshire — 11 Feb. 1897
Place/Date of Death: Graincourt, France — 27 Sep. 1918
Memorials: Sanders Keep Military Cemetery, France
Town/County Connections: Swinton, Lancashire; Swinton, Yorkshire
Remarks: —
Account of Deed: On 27 Sep. 1918 at the Canal du Nord, near Graincourt, France, Lance-Corporal Jackson was the first to volunteer to follow his company commander* across the canal in his rush against an enemy machine-gun post. With two comrades he followed his officer, rushed the post and captured two machine-guns. Later in the morning Corporal Jackson was the first to jump into a German trench which his platoon had to clear, but almost immediately he was killed. Throughout the day this NCO showed the greatest valour. (*See also FRISBY, C.H.)

JACKSON, William

628

Private   17th Bn., (N.S.W.), Australian Imperial Force
Other Decorations: —
Date of Gazette: 9 Sep. 1916
Place/Date of Birth: Gimbar, Near Hay, New South Wales, Australia — 13 Sep. 1897
Place/Date of Death: Melbourne, Australia — 4 Aug. 1959
Memorials: Spring Vale Crematorium, Melbourne; Australian War Memorial, Canberra
Town/County Connections: —
Remarks: —
Account of Deed: On 25/26 Jun. 1916 near Armentieres, France, returning from a successful raid, several members of the raiding party were seriously wounded. Private Jackson got back safely and after handing over a prisoner he had brought in, immediately went out again under very heavy fire and helped to bring in a wounded man. He then went out again with a sergeant, to bring in another wounded man when his arm was blown off by a shell and the sergeant rendered unconscious. Private Jackson then returned for assistance and went out again to look for his wounded comrades.

JAMES, Frederick Humphrey — see **WHIRLPOOL,** Frederick

JAMES, Herbert   **629**
Second Lieutenant (later Major)   4th Bn., The Worcestershire Regiment
Other Decorations: —
Date of Gazette: 1 Sep. 1915
Place/Date of Birth: Edgbaston, Birmingham — 13 Nov. 1888
Place/Date of Death: Kensington, London — 15 Aug. 1958
Memorials: —
Town/County Connections: Edgbaston, Birmingham; Kensington, London
Remarks: —
Account of Deed: On 28 Jun. 1915 in the southern zone of Gallipoli, when the advance of part of the regiment had been checked, Second-Lieutenant James, from a neighbouring unit, gathered together a body of men and led them forward under heavy fire. He then returned, organised a second party and again advanced, putting fresh life into the attack. On 3 Jul. he headed a party of bomb throwers up a Turkish communication trench and when all his party had been killed or wounded, he remained alone, under murderous fire and kept back the enemy until a barrier had been built behind him and the trench secured.

JAMES, Manley Angell   **630**
T/Captain (later Brigadier)   8th (S) Bn., The Gloucestershire Regiment
Other Decorations: DSO, MC, MBE
Date of Gazette: 28 Jun. 1918
Place/Date of Birth: Odiham, Hampshire — 12 Jul. 1896
Place/Date of Death: Bristol — 23 Sep. 1975
Memorials: —
Town/County Connections: Odiham, Hampshire; Westbury-on-Trym, Bristol
Remarks: GSO 1, 45 Division 1940; Commanded 128 Infantry Brigade 1940-43; BGS (Trg.) Home Forces 1944-45; Commanded 140 Infantry Brigade 1945; CRO, Air HQ, BAFO (Germany) 1945-48; Director of Ground Defence, Air Ministry 1948-51; DL, County of Gloucester
Account of Deed: On 21 Mar. 1918 near Velu Wood, France, Captain James led his company forward, capturing 27 prisoners and two machine-guns. Although wounded, he refused to leave his company and repulsed three enemy assaults next day. Two days later the enemy having broken through, he made a determined stand, inflicting heavy losses and gaining valuable time for the withdrawal of the guns. After holding out to the last to enable the brigade to be extricated, he led his company forward in a local counter-attack, being again wounded. He was last seen working a machine-gun single-handed, was wounded a third time and eventually taken prisoner.

JAMIESON, David Auldgo   **631**
Captain (later Major)   The Royal Norfolk Regiment
Other Decorations: —
Date of Gazette: 26 Oct. 1944
Place/Date of Birth: Thornham, near King's Lynn, Norfolk — 1 Oct. 1920
Place/Date of Death: — About 6.5.2001.
Memorials: —
Town/County Connections: Thornham, King's Lynn, Norfolk
Remarks: One of HM Body Guard, Hon. Corps of Gentleman-at-Arms 1968-. High Sheriff of Norfolk 1980.
Account of Deed: On 7/8 Aug. 1944 south of Grimbosq, Normandy, Captain Jamieson was in command of a company which established a bridgehead over the River Orne. The enemy made seven counter-attacks on the company's position, but throughout 36 hours of bitter and close fighting Captain Jamieson showed superb qualities of leadership and great personal bravery. There were times when the situation appeared hopeless but on each occasion it was restored by his coolness and determination. He personally was largely responsible for holding the bridgehead over the river and although wounded twice he refused to be evacuated.

JARRATT, George   **632**
Corporal   8th Bn., The Royal Fusiliers
Other Decorations: —
Date of Gazette: 8 Jun. 1917
Place/Date of Birth: Kennington, Surrey — 22 Jul. 1891
Place/Date of Death: Near Pelves, France — 3 May 1917
Memorials: Arras Memorial, France
Town/County Connections: Kennington, Surrey
Remarks: —
Account of Deed: On 3 May 1917 near Pelves, France, Corporal Jarratt had, together with some wounded men, been taken prisoner and placed under guard in a dug-out. The same evening the enemy were driven back by our troops and the leading infantry started to bomb the dug-outs. A grenade fell in the dug-out and without hesitation Corporal Jarratt put both feet on it and the subsequent explosion blew off both his legs. The wounded were later safely removed to Allied lines, but Corporal Jarratt died before he could be removed.

JARRETT, Hanson Chambers Taylor   **633**
Lieutenant (later Colonel)   26th Bengal Native Infantry
Other Decorations: —
Date of Gazette: 18 Jun. 1859
Place/Date of Birth: Madras, India — 2 Mar. 1837
Place/Date of Death: India — 11 Apr. 1890
Memorials: —
Town/County Connections: —
Remarks: —
Account of Deed: On 14 Oct. 1858 at the village of Baroun, India, when about 70 sepoys were defending themselves in a brick building, the only approach to which was up a very narrow street, Lieutenant Jarrett called on the men of his regiment to follow him, and backed up by four men, he made a dash at the narrow entrance. He was met by a very heavy fire, but pushed his way up to the wall of the house and, beating up the bayonets of the rebels with his sword, forced his way in.

JARVIS, Charles Alfred   **634**
Lance-Corporal   57th Field Coy., Corps of Royal Engineers
Other Decorations: —
Date of Gazette: 16 Nov. 1914
Place/Date of Birth: Fraserburgh, Scotland — 29 Mar. 1881
Place/Date of Death: Dundee, Scotland — 19 Nov. 1948
Memorials: Cupar Cemetery, Fife
Town/County Connections: Carnoustie, Scotland; Chelmsford, Essex
Remarks: —
Account of Deed: On 23 Aug. 1914 at Jemappes, Belgium, Lance-Corporal Jarvis worked for 1½ hours under heavy fire, in full view of the enemy and finally succeeded in firing charges for the demolition of a bridge.

JEE, Joseph   **635**
Surgeon (later Deputy Surgeon General)   78th Regt. (later The Seaforth Highlanders — Ross-shire Buffs, Duke of Albany's)
Other Decorations: CB
Date of Gazette: 8 Nov. 1860
Place/Date of Birth: Hartshill, Atherstone, Warwickshire — 9 Feb. 1819
Place/Date of Death: Queniborough, Leicestershire — 17 Mar. 1899
Memorials: —
Town/County Connections: Atherstone, Warwickshire; Queniborough, Leicestershire
Remarks: Deputy Inspector General of Hospitals 1868; Hon. Surgeon to Queen Victoria 1899
Account of Deed: On 25 Sep. 1857, at the relief of Lucknow, India, Surgeon Jee attended to a large number of men wounded in the charge, getting them removed on cots and on the backs of their comrades, until he had found the dhooli-bearers, who had fled. Later, when trying to reach the Residency with the casualties, he was besieged and forced to remain in the Mote Mehal all night. Next day, under heavy fire, he continued to attend the wounded and eventually succeeded in taking many of them through heavy cross-fire safely into the Residency, although repeatedly warned not to make the attempt.

JEFFERSON, Francis Arthur   **636**
Fusilier (later Lance-Corporal)   2nd Bn., The Lancashire Fusiliers
Other Decorations: —
Date of Gazette: 13 Jul. 1944
Place/Date of Birth: Ulverston, Lancashire — 18 Aug. 1921
Place/Date of Death: Bolton, Lancashire — 4 Sep. 1982
Memorials: —
Town/County Connections: Ulverston, Lancashire
Remarks: —
Account of Deed: On 16 May 1944 during an attack on the Gustav Line, Monte Casino, Italy, the leading company of Fusilier Jefferson's battalion had to dig in without protection. The enemy counter-attacked opening fire at short range, and Fusilier Jefferson, on his own initiative, seized a P.I.A.T. gun and, running forward under a hail of bullets, fired on the leading tank. It burst into flames and all the crew were killed. The fusilier then reloaded and went towards the second tank which withdrew before he could get within range. By this time our own tanks had arrived and the enemy counter-attack was smashed.

JEFFRIES, Clarence Smith **637**
Captain   34th Bn. (N.S.W.), Australian Imperial Force
Other Decorations: —
Date of Gazette: 18 Dec. 1917
Place/Date of Birth: Wallsend, Newcastle, New South Wales, Australia — 26 Oct. 1894
Place/Date of Death: Passchendaele, Belgium — 12 Oct. 1917
Memorials: Tyne Cot Cemetery, Passchendaele, Belgium; Australian War Memorial, Canberra
Town/County Connections: —
Remarks: —
Account of Deed: On 12 Oct. 1917 at Passchendaele, Belgium, with a party of men he had organized, Captain Jeffries rushed a machine-gun emplacement, capturing four machine-guns and 35 prisoners. He then led his company forward under extremely heavy artillery barrage and enfilading machine-gun fire to the objective. Later, he again organized a successful attack on a machine-gun position, capturing two machine-guns and 30 more prisoners. He was killed during this second attack.

JENNINGS, Edward **638**
Rough-Rider   Bengal Artillery
Other Decorations: —
Date of Gazette: 24 Dec. 1858
Place/Date of Birth: Ballinrobe, Co. Mayo, Ireland — 1815
Place/Date of Death: North Shields, Northumberland — 10 May 1889
Memorials: Preston Cemetery, North Shields
Town/County Connections: Ballinrobe, Co. Mayo
Remarks: —
Account of Deed: During the whole of the period 14 to 22. Nov. 1857, at the Relief of Lucknow, India, Rough-Rider Jennings acted with conspicuous gallantry. (Elected by the regiment.)

JENSEN, Jorgan Christian **639**
Private   50th Bn., (S.A.) Australian Imperial Force
Other Decorations: —
Date of Gazette: 8 Jun. 1917
Place/Date of Birth: Logstor, Aalborg, Denmark — 15 Jan. 1891
Place/Date of Death: Adelaide, Australia — 31 May 1922
Memorials: AIF Cemetery, Adelaide; Australian War Memorial, Canberra
Town/County Connections: —
Remarks: —
Account of Deed: On 2 Apr. 1917 at Noreuil, France, Private Jensen, with five comrades, attacked a barricade behind which were about 45 of the enemy and a machine-gun. One of the party shot the gunner and Private Jensen rushed the post and threw in a bomb. Then, with a bomb in each hand, he threatened the rest and made them surrender. He sent one of his prisoners to another group of the enemy, ordering them to surrender, which they did, but our troops began firing on them, whereupon Private Jensen, regardless of danger, stood on the barricade waving his helmet, and the firing stopped. He then sent his prisoners back to our lines.

JEROME, Henry Edward **640**
Captain (later Major General)   86th Regiment (later The Royal Irish Rifles)
Other Decorations: —
Date of Gazette: 11 Nov. 1859
Place/Date of Birth: Antigua, West Indies — 2 Feb. 1830
Place/Date of Death: Bath, Somerset — 25 Feb. 1901
Memorials: Lansdown Cemetery, Bath
Town/County Connections: Bath, Somerset
Remarks: —
Account of Deed: On 3 Apr. 1858 at Jhansi, India, Captain Jerome, with the assistance of a private* removed under very heavy fire a lieutenant of the regiment who was severely wounded, at a very exposed point of the attack upon the Fort. He also displayed great gallantry at the capture of the Fort of Chandairee, the storming of Jhansi and in action with a superior rebel force at Jumna on 28 May, when he was severely wounded. (*See also BYRNE, James).

JERRARD, Alan — 641
Lieutenant (later Flight Lieutenant)   66 Squadron, Royal Flying Corps (later Royal Air Force)
Other Decorations: —
Date of Gazette: 1 May 1918
Place/Date of Birth: Lewisham, London — 3 Dec. 1897
Place/Date of Death: Lyme Regis, Dorset — 14 May 1968
Memorials: Ashes interred at Hillingdon, Uxbridge
Town/County Connections: Lewisham and Uxbridge, London; Lyme Regis, Dorset
Remarks: — *According to Chaz Bowyer he was buried at Lyme Regis*
Account of Deed: On 30 Mar. 1918 near Mansue, Italy, Lieutenant Jerrard, with two other officers on offensive patrol, shot down one of five enemy aircraft. Then flying at 50 ft. he attacked an aerodrome with some 19 machines either landing or attempting to take off. After destroying one of these he was attacked by more enemy aircraft but, seeing a brother-officer in difficulties, went to assist him, destroying a third enemy machine, then continued his attacks, only retreating, with five machines in pursuit, on the orders of the patrol leader. Even then he repeatedly turned to beat off the enemy until finally forced down.

JOHNSON, Dudley Graham — 642
A/Lieutenant Colonel (later Major General)   The South Wales Borderers, attd. 2nd Bn., The Royal Sussex Regiment
Other Decorations: CB, DSO & Bar, MC
Date of Gazette: 6 Jan. 1919
Place/Date of Birth: Bourton-on-the-Water, Gloucestershire — 13 Feb. 1884
Place/Date of Death: Church Crookham, Hampshire — 21 Dec. 1975
Memorials: Church Crookham church and churchyard, Hampshire; Brecon Cathedral; General Johnson Homes (Royal British Legion) near Guildford, Surrey *Bradfield Berkshire*
Town/County Connections: Bourton-on-the-Water, Glos; Church Crookham, Hants.
Remarks: Comd. 2nd Bn. The North Staffs. Regt. 1928-32; comd. 12th (Secunderabad) Infantry Bde. 1933-36; comd. 4th Div. 1938-40; GOC Aldershot Command 1940; Hon. Colonel The South Wales Borderers 1944-49.
Account of Deed: On 4 Nov. 1918 at Sambre Canal, France, the 2nd Infantry Brigade, of which the 2nd Bn. The Royal Sussex Regiment formed part, was ordered to cross by the lock south of Catillon. The position was strong and the assaulting and bridging parties were halted on arrival at the waterway 100 yards from the canal by a heavy barrage. At this point Lieutenant Colonel Johnson arrived and personally led an assault but heavy fire again broke up the attack. He reorganized the assaulting and bridging parties and this time effected a crossing but the success of this dangerous operation was entirely due to his splendid leadership. *VC in SWB Museum, Brecon*

JOHNSON, Frederick Henry — 643
T/Second Lieutenant (later Major)   73rd Field Coy., Corps of Royal Engineers
Other Decorations: —
Date of Gazette: 18 Nov. 1915
Place/Date of Birth: Streatham, London — 15 Aug. 1890
Place/Date of Death: France — 26 Nov. 1917
Memorials: Cambrai Memorial, France
Town/County Connections: Streatham, London
Remarks: —
Account of Deed: On 25 Sep. 1915 during the attack on Hill 70, France, Second Lieutenant Johnson was with a section of his company, and although wounded in the leg, he stuck to his duty throughout the attack, led several charges on the German redoubt, and at a very critical time, under heavy fire, repeatedly rallied the men who were near to him. By his splendid example and cool courage he was mainly instrumental in saving the situation and in establishing firmly his part of the position which had been taken. He remained at his post until relieved.

JOHNSON, James — 644
Second Lieutenant   2nd Bn., The Northumberland Fusiliers, attd. 36th Bn.
Other Decorations: —
Date of Gazette: 26 Dec. 1918
Place/Date of Birth: Widdrington, Northumberland — 31 Dec. 1889
Place/Date of Death: Plymouth, Devon — 23 Mar. 1943
Memorials: —
Town/County Connections: Bedlington, Northumberland; Plymouth, Devon
Remarks: —
Account of Deed: On 14 Oct. 1918 south west of Wez Macquart, France, during operations by strong patrols, Second Lieutenant Johnson repelled frequent counter-attacks and for six hours, under heavy fire, he held back the enemy. When at length he was ordered to retire he was the last to leave the advanced position carrying a wounded man. Three times subsequently this officer returned and brought in badly wounded men under intense enemy machine-gun fire.

JOHNSON, William Henry

645

Sergeant   1/5th Bn., The Sherwood Foresters (The Nottinghamshire and Derbyshire Regt.)
Other Decorations: —
Date of Gazette: 14 Dec. 1918
Place/Date of Birth: Worksop, Nottinghamshire — 15 Oct. 1890
Place/Date of Death: Arnold, Nottingham — 25 Apr. 1945
Memorials: —
Town/County Connections: Worksop and Nottingham
Remarks: —
Account of Deed: On 3 Oct. 1918 at Ramicourt, France, when the platoon was held up by a nest of machine-guns at very close range, Sergeant Johnson worked his way forward under heavy fire and single-handed charged the post, bayoneting several gunners and capturing two machine-guns. During the attack he was severely wounded by a bomb, but continued to lead his men forward. Shortly afterwards the line was again held up by machine-guns and again single-handed the sergeant attacked the post, bombing the garrison, putting the guns out of action and capturing the teams.

JOHNSTON, Robert

646

Captain (later Major)   Imperial Light Horse (Natal)
Other Decorations: —
Date of Gazette: 12 Feb. 1901
Place/Date of Birth: Laputa, Co Donegal, Ireland — 13 Aug. 1872
Place/Date of Death: Kilkenny, Ireland — 25 Mar. 1950
Memorials:
Town/County Connections: Laputa, Co. Donegal; Kilkenny, Ireland
Remarks: Commandant, Prisoners-of-War, Oldcastle, Co. Meath, Ireland 1914-15
Account of Deed: On 21 Oct. 1899 at Elandslaagte, South Africa, at a most critical moment, when the advance was momentarily checked by very severe fire at point-blank range, Captain Johnston and another officer* gallantly rushed forward under very heavy fire and rallied the men, thus enabling the decisive flanking movement to be carried out. (*See also MULLINS, C.H.)

JOHNSTON, William Henry

647

Captain (later Major)   59th Field Coy., Corps of Royal Engineers
Other Decorations: —
Date of Gazette: 25 Nov. 1914
Place/Date of Birth: Leith, Scotland — 21 Dec. 1879
Place/Date of Death: Ypres, Belgium — 8 Jun. 1915
Memorials: Perth Cemetery (China Wall), Zillebeke, Belgium
Town/County Connections: Leith, Scotland
Remarks: *Name on Richmond-upon-Thames W.M.*
Account of Deed: On 14 Sep. 1914 at Missy, France, Captain Johnston worked with his own hands two rafts on the River Aisne. He returned with wounded from one side and took back ammunition. He continued to do this under heavy fire all day, thus enabling an advanced brigade to maintain its position across the river.

No photograph available

JOHNSTONE, William

648

Stoker   Royal Navy
Other Decorations: —
Date of Gazette: 24 Feb. 1857
Place/Date of Birth: Hanover, Germany — 1821
Place/Date of Death: Not known
Memorials: —
Town/County Connections: —
Remarks: —
Account of Deed: On 9 Aug. 1854 in the Baltic, Stoker Johnstone and a lieutenant* from HMS *Arrogant*, landed on the island of Wardo in order to intercept important despatches from the Czar which were being sent via Wardo to Bomarsund. The two men spent two nights reconnoitring the island and on 12 Aug. when the despatches arrived, they ambushed the five Russians carrying them. Two of the carriers dropped their mail bags and ran, but the other three surrendered and were taken to *Arrogant*. In this action the officer and stoker were armed with just one pistol. (*See also BYTHESEA, J.)

JONES, Alfred Stowell   **649**
Lieutenant (later Lieutenant Colonel)   9th Lancers (The Queen's Royal)
Other Decorations: —
Date of Gazette: 18 Jun. 1858
Place/Date of Birth: Liverpool, Lancashire — 24 Jan. 1832
Place/Date of Death: Finchampstead, Berkshire — 29 May 1920
Memorials: —
Town/County Connections: Liverpool, Lancs; Finchampstead, Berks.
Remarks: M. Inst. CE; Manager of all sewage works of 1st Army Corps, Aldershot 1895-1912
Account of Deed: On 8 Jun. 1857 at Delhi, India, Lieutenant Jones, with his squadron, captured one of the enemy's guns, killing the drivers, and then, with help from a lieutenant colonel, turned it upon a village occupied by the rebels, and dislodged them.

JONES, Conwyn MANSEL-   **650**
Captain   The West Yorkshire Regiment (Prince of Wales's Own)
Other Decorations: CMG, DSO
Date of Gazette: 27 Jul. 1900
Place/Date of Birth: Beddington, Surrey — 14 Jun. 1871
Place/Date of Death: Brockenhurst, Hampshire — 29 May 1942
Memorials: —   *Buried St. Nicholas Church, Brockenhurst*
Town/County Connections: Beddington, Surrey; Brockenhurst, Hampshire
Remarks: Served in the First World War; Officier de Légion d'Honneur (France); Member of the Hon. Corps of the Gentlemen-at-Arms 1920-42
Account of Deed: On 27 Feb. 1900 north of Tugela, Natal, South Africa, the companies of The West Yorkshire Regiment met with severe shell and rifle fire on the northern slope of Terrace Hill and their advance was temporarily checked. Captain Mansel-Jones, however, by his strong initiative and example restored confidence and in spite of his falling very seriously wounded, the men took the whole ridge without further check.

JONES, David   **651**
Sergeant   12th Bn., The King's (Liverpool) Regiment
Other Decorations: —
Date of Gazette: 26 Oct. 1916
Place/Date of Birth: Liverpool, Lancashire — 10 Jan. 1891
Place/Date of Death: Bancourt, Somme, France — 7 Oct. 1916
Memorials: Bancourt British Cemetery, France
Town/County Connections: Everton, Liverpool
Remarks: —
Account of Deed: On 3 Sep. 1916 at Guillemont, France, the platoon to which Sergeant Jones belonged was ordered to a forward position and during the advance came under heavy machine-gun fire, the officer being killed and the platoon suffering a great many casualties. The sergeant led forward the survivors, occupied the position and held it for two days and two nights, without food or water, until relieved. On the second day he drove back three counter-attacks, inflicting heavy losses.

JONES, Henry Mitchell   **652**
Captain   7th Regiment (later The Royal Fusiliers)
Other Decorations: —
Date of Gazette: 25 Sep. 1857
Place/Date of Birth: Dublin — 11 Feb. 1831
Place/Date of Death: Eastbourne, Sussex — 18 Dec. 1916
Memorials: —
Town/County Connections: Eastbourne, Sussex
Remarks: Légion d'Honneur (France); Entered Diplomatic Service 1858
Account of Deed: On 7 Jun. 1855 at Sebastopol, Crimea, Captain Jones distinguished himself while serving with the party which stormed and took the Quarries. He repeatedly led his men to repel the continual assaults of the enemy during the night and although wounded early in the evening, he remained at his post until after daylight the following morning.

JONES, Herbert (known only as 'H') *Code Name: SUNRAY* **653**
Lieutenant Colonel   Comd. 2nd Bn., The Parachute Regiment
Other Decorations: OBE
Date of Gazette: 11 Oct. 1982
Place/Date of Birth: London — 14 May 1940 · *81. Whitehall court, SW1.*
Place/Date of Death: Darwin, East Falkland — 28 May 1982
Memorials: San Carlos Cemetery, East Falkland · *Eton College, Eton College chapel*
Town/County Connections: Church Crookham, Hampshire; Kingswear, Devon ·
Remarks: -- *Memorial at M.O.T.H.S Sheffield*
Account of Deed: On 28 May 1982 at Darwin, East Falkland, the battalion commanded by Lieutenant Colonel Jones, was held up in its attack by very well prepared enemy positions. Colonel Jones and his reconnaissance party managed to gain the top of a recently secured re-entrant, but the enemy continued to pour fire on the battalion advance which was in danger of faltering. Colonel Jones, now at the very front of his men, charged the nearest enemy position. He fell, picked himself up and charged again, but was hit and fell dying only a few feet from the enemy. A company of the battalion then attacked and the enemy quickly surrendered — devastated by Colonel Jones' courage.

Before marriage, lived at The Grange, Kingswear. VC in National Army Museum

JONES, Loftus William **654**
Commander   Royal Navy
Other Decorations: —
Date of Gazette: 6 Mar. 1917
Place/Date of Birth: Petersfield, Hampshire — 13 Nov. 1879
Place/Date of Death: At sea, near Jutland — 31 May 1916
Memorials: Kviberg Cemetery, Sweden
Town/County Connections: Petersfield, Hampshire
Remarks: —
Account of Deed: On 31 May 1916, at the Battle of Jutland, Commander Jones of HMS *Shark*, led a division of destroyers to attack the enemy Battle Cruiser Squadron. In the course of this attack *Shark* became disabled by shell-fire and was lying helpless between two enemy fleets. Commander Jones was badly wounded in the leg, but with the help of three surviving seamen he kept the midships gun in action until he was hit by a shell which took off his leg. He continued, however, to give orders to his gun's crew, until *Shark* was hit by a torpedo and sank. Commander Jones was not among the survivors.

JONES, Richard Basil Brandram **655**
T/Lieutenant   8th Bn., The Loyal North Lancashire Regiment
Other Decorations: —
Date of Gazette: 5 Aug. 1916
Place/Date of Birth: Honor Oak Rise, London — 30 Apr. 1897
Place/Date of Death: Vimy, France — 21 May 1916
Memorials: Arras Memorial, France
Town/County Connections: Anerley, Bromley, Kent
Remarks: —
Account of Deed: On 21 May 1916 at Broadmarsh Crater, Vimy, France, Lieutenant Jones was in charge of a platoon holding the position recently captured from the enemy. Forty yards away the enemy exploded a mine and isolated the platoon by a heavy barrage of fire. Being attacked by overwhelming numbers, the platoon was in great danger, but Lieutenant Jones organised his men and set a fine example by shooting 15 of the enemy as they advanced. When all his ammunition had been used, he was about to throw a bomb when he was shot through the head.

JONES, Robert **656**
Private   2nd Bn., 24th Regiment (later The South Wales Borderers)
Other Decorations: —
Date of Gazette: 2 May 1879
Place/Date of Birth: Raglan, Monmouthshire — 19 Aug. 1857
Place/Date of Death: Madley, Herefordshire — 6 Sep. 1898 *Buried Peterchurch, Committed suicide*
Memorials: Peterchurch, Herefordshire
Town/County Connections: Raglan, Monmouthshire; Madley, Herefordshire
Remarks: — *May be buried in Kingstone?*
Account of Deed: On 22/23 Jan. 1879 at Rorke's Drift, Natal, South Africa, Private Robert Jones and another man* defended one of the wards in the hospital to the last, until six out of the seven patients had been removed. The seventh was delirious and although they managed to dress him, they could not induce him to move and when they returned to carry him away he was being stabbed to death in his bed. (*See also JONES, William)

VC Sold at auction 11.6.1996 raised £88,000. Private buyer.

JONES, Robert James Thomas DIGBY-   **657**
Lieutenant   Corps of Royal Engineers
Other Decorations: —
Date of Gazette: 8 Aug. 1902
Place/Date of Birth: Edinburgh — 27 Sep. 1876
Place/Date of Death: Ladysmith, Natal, South Africa — 6 Jan. 1900
Memorials: —
Town/County Connections: Edinburgh
Remarks: —
Account of Deed: On 6 Jan. 1900 during the attack on Wagon Hill (Ladysmith), South Africa, Lieutenant Digby-Jones and a trooper of the Imperial Light Horse* led the force which re-occupied the top of the hill at a critical moment, just as the three foremost attacking Boers reached it. The leader was shot by Lieutenant Digby-Jones and the two others by the trooper. (*See also ALBRECHT, H.)

JONES, Thomas Alfred   **658**
Private   1st Bn., The Cheshire Regiment
Other Decorations: DCM
Date of Gazette: 26 Oct. 1916
Place/Date of Birth: Runcorn, Cheshire — 25 Dec. 1880
Place/Date of Death: Runcorn, Cheshire — 30 Jan 1956
Memorials: Runcorn Cemetery; Chester Cathedral
Town/County Connections: Runcorn, Cheshire
Remarks: —
Account of Deed: On 25 Sep. 1916 at Morval, France, Private Jones was with his company covering the advance in front of a village, when he noticed an enemy sniper 200 yards away. He went out and, although one bullet went through his helmet and another through his coat, he returned the sniper's fire and killed him. He then saw two more Germans firing on him although they were displaying a white flag. Both these he shot. On reaching the enemy trench he found several occupied dug-outs and single-handed disarmed 102 of the enemy, including three or four officers, and took them prisoner.

JONES, William   **659**
Private   2nd Bn., 24th Regiment (later The South Wales Borderers)
Other Decorations: —
Date of Gazette: 2 May 1879
Place/Date of Birth: Evesham, Worcestershire — 1840
Place/Date of Death: Ardwick, Lancashire — 15 Apr. 1913
Memorials: Philips Park Cemetery, Manchester *Bradford Ward. Grave D887*
Town/County Connections: Evesham, Worcestershire; Ardwick, Lancashire
Remarks: —
Account of Deed: On 22/23 Jan. 1879 at Rorke's Drift, Natal, South Africa, Private William Jones and another man* defended one of the wards in the hospital to the last, until six out of the seven patients had been removed. The seventh was delirious and although they managed to dress him, they could not induce him to move and when they returned to carry him away he was being stabbed to death in his bed. (*See also JONES, Robert).
VC in SWB Museum. Brecon.

JOTHAM, Eustace   **660**
Captain   51st Sikhs (F.F.), Indian Army
Other Decorations: —
Date of Gazette: 24 Jul. 1915
Place/Date of Birth: Kidderminster, Worcestershire — 28 Nov. 1883
Place/Date of Death: Spina Khaisora, India — 7 Jan. 1915
Memorials: Delhi Memorial, India; Garrison Church, Whittington Barracks, Lichfield, Staffordshire; St. Luke's Church, Chelsea, London
Town/County Connections: Kidderminster, Worcestershire
Remarks: —
Account of Deed: On 7 Jan. 1915 at Spina Khaisora (Tochi Valley), India during operations against the Khostwal tribesmen, Captain Jotham, who was commanding a party of about a dozen of the North Waziristan Militia, was attacked in a nullah and almost surrounded by an overwhelming force of some 1,500 tribesmen. He gave the order to retire and could have escaped himself, but sacrificed his life in trying to rescue one of his own men who had lost a horse.

JOYNT, William Donovan   **661**
Lieutenant (later Lieutenant Colonel)   8th Bn. (Victoria), Australian Imperial Force
Other Decorations: —
Date of Gazette: 27 Nov. 1918
Place/Date of Birth: Elsternwick, Melbourne, Victoria, Australia — 19 Mar. 1889
Place/Date of Death: Melbourne, Victoria, Australia — 5 May 1986
Memorials: Australian War Memorial, Canberra
Town/County Connections: —
Remarks: —
Account of Deed: On 23 Aug. 1918 at Herleville Wood, near Chuignes, Peronne, France, Lieutenant Joynt took charge when his company commander had been killed. When the leading battalion had been demoralized by heavy casualties, he rushed forward and reorganized the remnants of the battalion. Having discoverd that heavy fire on the flanks was causing delay and casualties, he led a frontal bayonet attack on the wood, thus saving a critical situation. Later, at Plateau Wood, after severe hand-to-hand fighting, he turned a stubborn defence into an abject surrender. He was subsequently badly wounded by a shell.

JUDSON, Reginald Stanley   **662**
Sergeant (later Major)   1st Bn., Auckland Infantry Regiment, N.Z.E.F.
Other Decorations: DCM, MM
Date of Gazette: 30 Oct. 1918
Place/Date of Birth: Wharehine, New Zealand — 29 Sep. 1881
Place/Date of Death: Auckland, New Zealand — 26 Aug. 1972
Memorials: HQ, Dunedin RSA, New Zealand
Town/County Connections: —
Remarks: —
Account of Deed: On 26 Aug. 1918 south of Bapaume, France, during an attack, Sergeant Judson led a small bombing party under heavy fire and captured an enemy machine-gun. He then proceeded up the sap alone, bombing three machine-gun crews. Jumping out of the trench he then ran ahead of the enemy and, standing on a parapet, ordered a group of two officers and 10 men to surrender. They immediately opened fire and he threw a bomb and jumped amongst them, killing two and putting the rest to flight, and so captured two machine-guns.

KAEBLE, Joseph   **663**
Corporal   22nd Bn., Quebec Regiment (Canadien Français) C.E.F.
Other Decorations: MM
Date of Gazette: 16 Sep. 1918
Place/Date of Birth: St. Moise, Quebec, Canada — 5 May 1893
Place/Date of Death: Neuville-Vitasse, France — 9 Jun. 1918
Memorials: Wanquetin Communal Cemetery Extension, France
Town/County Connections: —
Remarks: —
Account of Deed: On 8/9 Jun. 1918 at Neuville-Vitasse, France, Corporal Kaeble was in charge of a Lewis gun section during a strong enemy attack, when all but one of his section became casualties. As soon as the barrage lifted and about 50 of the enemy advanced, Corporal Kaeble jumped over the parapet with his Lewis gun, emptying one magazine after another into the advancing enemy. Although hit several times, he continued to fire and blocked the enemy advance, until he fell mortally wounded. Even while lying on his back in the trench, he fired his last cartridges over the parapet at the retreating enemy.

KAMAL RAM   **664**
Sepoy (later Subadar)   8th Punjab Regiment, Indian Army
Other Decorations: —
Date of Gazette: 27 Jul. 1944
Place/Date of Birth: Bholunpura Village, Karauli State, India — 18 Dec. 1924
Place/Date of Death: —
Memorials: —
Town/County Connections: —
Remarks: PVSM (India)
Account of Deed: On 12 May 1944 at the River Gari, Italy, the company advance was held up by heavy machine-gun fire from four posts on the front and flanks. The capture of the position was essential and Sepoy Kamal Ram volunteered to get round the rear of the right post and silence it. He attacked the first two posts single-handed, killing or taking prisoner the occupants and together with a havildar he then went on and completed the destruction of a third. His outstanding bravery unquestionably saved a difficult situation at a critical period of the battle.

KARAMJEET SINGH JUDGE 665

Lieutenant   4th Bn., 15th Punjab Regiment, Indian Army
Other Decorations: —
Date of Gazette: 3 Jul. 1945
Place/Date of Birth: Kapurthala, Kapurthala State, India — 25 May 1923
Place/Date of Death: Near Meiktila, Burma — 18 Mar. 1945
Memorials: The Taukkyan Cremation Memorial, Burma
Town/County Connections: —
Remarks: —
Account of Deed: On 18 Mar. 1945 near Meiktila, Burma, Lieutenant Karamjeet Singh Judge, a platoon commander of a company ordered to capture a cotton mill, dominated the battlefield by his numerous acts of gallantry. After eliminating ten enemy bunkers he directed one tank to within 20 yards of another and asked the tank commander to cease fire while he went in to mop up. While doing so he was mortally wounded.

KARANBAHADUR RANA 666

Rifleman   2nd Bn., 3rd Q.A.O. Gurkha Rifles, Indian Army
Other Decorations: —
Date of Gazette: 21 Jun. 1918
Place/Date of Birth: Mangalthan, Gulmi, Litung, Baghlung District, Nepal — 20 Dec. 1898
Place/Date of Death: Litung, Baghlung District, Nepal — 6 Aug. 1973
Memorials: —
Town/County Connections: —
Remarks: —
Account of Deed: On 10 Apr. 1918 at El Kefr, Egypt, during an attack, Rifleman Karanbahadur Rana and a few other men crept forward with a Lewis gun under intense fire to engage an enemy machine-gun. No. 1 of the Lewis gun team opened fire but was shot almost immediately, whereupon the rifleman pushed the dead man off the gun, opened fire, knocked out the enemy gun crew and then silenced the fire of the enemy bombers and riflemen in front of him. During the remainder of the day he did magnificent work and finally assisted with covering fire in the withdrawal, until the enemy were close on him.

KAVANAGH, Thomas Henry 667

Mr.   Bengal Civil Service
Other Decorations: —
Date of Gazette: 6 Jul. 1859
Place/Date of Birth: Mullingar, Co. West Meath, Ireland — 15 Jul. 1821
Place/Date of Death: Gibraltar — 11 Nov. 1882
Memorials: North Front Cemetery, Gibraltar
Town/County Connections: Mullingar, Co. West Meath
Remarks: —
Account of Deed: On 9 Nov. 1857 at Lucknow, India, Mr. Kavanagh volunteered to go through the city (in disguise) to the camp of the relieving force outside, so that he could guide them to the beleaguered garrison in the Residency. This mission, performed against overwhelming odds, was successful and the garrison was relieved.

KEATINGE, Richard Harte 668

Major (later Lieutenant General)   Bombay Artillery, Indian Army
Other Decorations: CSI
Date of Gazette: 25 Feb. 1862
Place/Date of Birth: Dublin — 17 Jun. 1825
Place/Date of Death: Horsham, Sussex — 25 May 1904
Memorials: —
Town/County Connections: Horsham, Sussex
Remarks: —
Account of Deed: On 17 Mar. 1858 at the assault of Chundairee, India, Major Keatinge voluntarily led the column through the breach which was protected by heavy cross-fire. He was one of the first to enter and was severely wounded, but the column was saved from serious loss which would probably have resulted but for the major's knowledge of the area. Having cleared the breach, he led the column into the fort where he was again wounded.

KELLAWAY, Joseph **669**
Boatswain Third Class (later Chief Boatswain)   Royal Navy
Other Decorations: —
Date of Gazette: 24 Feb. 1857
Place/Date of Birth: Kingston, Dorset — 1 Sep. 1824
Place/Date of Death: Chatham, Kent — 2 Oct. 1880
Memorials: — *Buried Maidstone Road Cemetery, Chatham.*
Town/County Connections: Kingston, Dorset; Chatham, Kent
Remarks: Légion d'Honneur (France)
Account of Deed: On 31 Aug. 1855 in the Sea of Azov, Crimea, Boatswain Kellaway of HMS *Wrangler*, with the mate and three seamen, was put ashore to burn some boats, fishing stations and haystacks on the opposite side of a small lake. They had nearly reached the spot when they were ambushed by 50 Russians. One man fell into their hands, but Mr. Kellaway and the two other seamen had escaped when the mate accidentally fell. Mr. Kellaway immediately returned to help him, but they were surrounded by the enemy and notwithstanding a gallant resistance by Mr. Kellaway they were taken prisoner.

KELLIHER, Richard **670**
Private   2/25th Bn. (Queensland), Australian Military Forces
Other Decorations: —
Date of Gazette: 30 Dec. 1943
Place/Date of Birth: Ballybeggan, Tralee, Co. Kerry, Ireland — 1 Sep. 1910
Place/Date of Death: Melbourne, Australia — 28 Jan. 1963
Memorials: Springvale Lawn Cemetery, Melbourne; Australian War Memorial, Canberra
Town/County Connections: Ballybeggan, Tralee, Co. Kerry
Remarks: —
Account of Deed: On 13 Sep. 1943 in New Guinea, south-west Pacific, the platoon to which Private Kelliher was attached came under very heavy fire from a concealed machine-gun which inflicted severe casualties and prevented the platoon's advance. Private Kelliher suddenly, on his own initiative, dashed towards the post and hurled two grenades at it, which killed some of the enemy but not all. He returned to his section, seized a Bren gun, dashed back to the enemy post and silenced it. He then asked permission to go out again to rescue his wounded section leader, which he accomplished successfully under heavy fire from another enemy position.

KELLS, Robert **671**
Lance-Corporal (later Sergeant)   9th Lancers (The Queen's Royal)
Other Decorations: RVM
Date of Gazette: 24 Dec. 1858
Place/Date of Birth: Meerut, India — 7 Apr. 1832
Place/Date of Death: London SE11 — 14 Apr. 1905
Memorials: —
Town/County Connections: London
Remarks: Trumpet-Major and Sergeant Yeoman of the Guard after he left the 9th Lancers
Account of Deed: On 28 Sep. 1857 at Bolandshahr, India, when his commanding officer was lying in a street with his collar bone broken and his horse disabled, Lance-Corporal Kells defended him against a number of the enemy and stayed with him until the danger was over.

KELLY, Henry **672**
T/Second Lieutenant (later Major)   10th Bn., The Duke of Wellington's (West Riding) Regiment
Other Decorations: MC & Bar
Date of Gazette: 25 Oct. 1916
Place/Date of Birth: Moston, Manchester, Lancashire — 10 Jul. 1887
Place/Date of Death: Prestwich, Lancashire — 18 Jan. 1960
Memorials: —
Town/County Connections: Moston, Manchester; Prestwich, Lancashire
Remarks: Grand laurelled Cross of San Fernando (Spain — Civil War)
Account of Deed: On 4th Oct. 1916 at Le Sars, France, Second Lieutenant Kelly twice rallied his company under the heaviest fire and eventually led the only three available men of his company into the enemy's trench, remaining there bombing, until two of his men became casualties and enemy reinforcements arrived from the rear. He then carried his wounded company sergeant-major back to our trenches, a distance of 70 yards, and subsequently brought in more wounded.

KELLY, James Davis — see **DAVIS,** James

KELLY, John SHERWOOD-   **673**
A/Lieutenant Colonel   The Norfolk Regiment, comd. 1st Bn., The Royal Inniskilling Fusiliers
Other Decorations: CMG, DSO
Date of Gazette: 11 Jan. 1918
Place/Date of Birth: Queenstown, Cape Province, South Africa — 13 Jan. 1880
Place/Date of Death: Kensington, London — 18 Aug. 1931
Memorials: Brookwood Cemetery, Woking, Surrey
Town/County Connections: Kensington, London
Remarks: Served in South African war, 1899-1902; with expeditionary force to Russia, 1919
Account of Deed: On 20 Nov. 1917 at Marcoing, France, when a party of men were held up on the near side of a canal by heavy rifle fire, Lieutenant Colonel Sherwood-Kelly at once ordered covering fire, personally led his leading company across the canal and then reconnoitred, under heavy fire, the high ground held by the enemy. He took a Lewis gun team, forced his way through obstacles and covered the advance of his battalion, enabling them to capture the position. Later he led a charge against some pits from which heavy fire was coming, capturing five machine-guns and 46 prisoners.

KENEALLY, William   **674**
Private (later Sergeant)   1st Bn., The Lancashire Fusiliers
Other Decorations: —
Date of Gazette: 24 Aug. 1915
Place/Date of Birth: Wexford, Ireland — 26 Dec. 1886
Place/Date of Death: Gallipoli — 29 Jun. 1915
Memorials: Lancashire Landing Cemetery, Gallipoli
Town/County Connections: Wexford, Ireland; Wigan, Lancashire
Remarks: —
Account of Deed: On 25 Apr. 1915 west of Cape Helles, Gallipoli, three companies and the Headquarters of the 1st Battalion, Lancashire Fusiliers, when landing on W Beach, were met by a very deadly fire from hidden machine-guns which caused a large number of casualties. The survivors, however, rushed up and cut the wire entanglements notwithstanding the terrific fire from the enemy and after overcoming supreme difficulties, the cliffs were gained and the position maintained. (Private Keneally was one of the six members of the regiment elected for the award. See also BROMLEY, C., GRIMSHAW, J.E., RICHARDS, A.J., STUBBS, F.E. and WILLIS, R.R.)

KENNA, Edward   **675**
Private   2/4th Bn. (N.S.W), Australian Military Forces
Other Decorations: —
Date of Gazette: 6 Sep. 1945
Place/Date of Birth: Hamilton, Victoria, Australia — 6 Jul. 1919
Place/Date of Death: —
Memorials: Australian War Memorial, Canberra
Town/County Connections: —
Remarks: —
Account of Deed: On 15 May 1945 near Wewak, New Guinea, when fire from a Japanese bunker was holding up the company's advance, Private Kenna stood up in full view of the enemy less than 50 yards away and engaged the bunker, firing his Bren gun from the hip. The enemy returned the fire and bullets actually passed between Private Kenna's arms and body. Undeterred, he remained completely exposed and went on firing until his magazine was exahusted, when he continued with a rifle. As a result of his gallantry the bunker was taken without further loss.

KENNA, Paul Aloysius   **676**
Captain (later Brigadier General)   21st Lancers (Empress of India's)
Other Decorations: DSO
Date of Gazette: 15 Nov. 1898
Place/Date of Birth: Everton, Liverpool — 2 Feb. 1862
Place/Date of Death: Suvla, Gallipoli — 30 Aug. 1915   *North Kilworth, Leics. Name on WM*
Memorials: Lala Baba Cemetery, Gallipoli   *Stonyhurst College, Lancs*
Town/County Connections: Liverpool
Remarks: Commanded the Nottinghamshire and Derbyshire Division in the First World War
Account of Deed: On 2 Sep. 1898 at the Battle of Khartoum, Sudan, when a major of the 21st Lancers was in danger, as his horse had been shot in the charge, Captain Kenna took the major up on his own horse, to a place of safety. After the charge Captain Kenna returned to help a lieutenant* who was trying to recover the body of an officer who had been killed. (*See also DE MONTMORENCY, R.H.L.J.)

KENNEALLY, John Patrick   **677**
Lance-Corporal (later Company Quartermaster-Sergeant)   Irish Guards
Other Decorations: —
Date of Gazette: 17 Aug. 1943
Place/Date of Birth: Birmingham — 15 Mar. 1921
Place/Date of Death: — About 29.9.2000
Memorials: —
Town/County Connections: Birmingham
Remarks: —
Account of Deed: On 28 Apr. 1943 at Dj. Arada, Tunisia, Lance-Corporal Kenneally charged alone down the bare forward slope straight into the main body of the enemy about to make an attack, firing his Bren gun from the hip; the enemy were so surprised that they broke up in disorder. The lance-corporal repeated his exploit on 30 Apr. when, accompanied by a sergeant, he charged the enemy forming up for assault, inflicting many casualties. Even when wounded he refused to give up, but hopped from one fire position to another, carrying his gun in one hand and supporting himself on a comrade with the other.

KENNEDY, Charles Thomas   **678**
Private   2nd Bn., The Highland Light Infantry
Other Decorations: —
Date of Gazette: 18 Oct. 1901
Place/Date of Birth: Westport, Edinburgh — 6 Jan. 1876
Place/Date of Death: Edinburgh — 24 Apr. 1907
Memorials: Merchiston Cemetery, Edinburgh
Town/County Connections: Edinburgh
Remarks: —
Account of Deed: On 22 Nov. 1900 at Dewetsdorp, South Africa, Private Kennedy carried a wounded comrade who was bleeding to death, from Gibraltar Hill to the hospital, a distance of three-quarters of a mile, under very heavy fire. On the following day, he volunteered to carry a message to the commandant across a space over which it was almost certain death to venture. He did not, however, succeed in delivering the message, as he was severely wounded before he had gone 20 yards.

KENNEDY, William Hew CLARK-   **679**
Lieutenant-Colonel   Comd. 24th Bn., Quebec Regiment (Victoria Rifles), C.E.F.
Other Decorations: CMG, DSO & Bar, ED
Date of Gazette: 14 Dec. 1918
Place/Date of Birth: Dunskey, Wigtownshire, Scotland — 3 Mar. 1879
Place/Date of Death: Montreal, Canada — 25 Oct. 1961
Memorials: Mount Royal Cemetery, Montreal
Town/County Connections: Croix de Guerre (France)
Remarks: —
Account of Deed: On 27/28 Aug. 1918 on the Fresnes-Rouvroy line, France, the brigade of which Lieutenant Colonel Clark-Kennedy's battalion was a central unit suffered heavy casualties. At this juncture the colonel encouraged his men and led them forward, then by controlling the direction of neighbouring units and collecting stragglers he enabled the whole brigade front to advance. Next day he was severely wounded, but despite intense pain and loss of blood, he refused to be evacuated until he had gained a position from which the advance could be resumed.

KENNY, Henry Edward   **680**
Private (later Sergeant)   1st Bn., The Loyal North Lancashire Regiment
Other Decorations: —
Date of Gazette: 30 Mar. 1916
Place/Date of Birth: Hackney, London — 27 Jul. 1888
Place/Date of Death: Chertsey, Surrey — 6 May 1979
Memorials: St. John's Cemetery, Woking, Surrey
Town/County Connections: Woolwich, London; Chertsey, Surrey
Remarks: — Whitley Village, Near Woking   Name on board in Hackney Town Hall
Account of Deed: On 25 Sep. 1915 near Loos, France, Private Kenny went out on six different occasions under very heavy shell, rifle and machine-gun fire. Each time he carried in to a place of safety a wounded man who had been lying in the open. He was himself wounded as he handed the last wounded soldier over the parapet.

No photograph available

KENNY, James　　　　　　　　　　　　　　　　　　　　　　　**681**
Private　53rd Regiment (later The King's Shropshire Light Infantry)
Other Decorations: —
Date of Gazette: 24 Dec. 1858
Place/Date of Birth: ? — c.1826
Place/Date of Death: Mooltan, India — 3 Oct. 1862
Memorials: —
Town/County Connections: —
Remarks: —
Account of Deed: On 16 Nov. 1857 at Lucknow, India, Private Kenny showed conspicuous bravery at the assault on the Secundra Bagh, when, in spite of most heavy cross-fire he volunteered to bring up fresh ammunition to his company. (Elected by the regiment).

KENNY, Thomas　　　　　　　　　　　　　　　　　　　　　　**682**
Private (later Lance-Sergeant)　13th Bn., The Durham Light Infantry
Other Decorations: —
Date of Gazette: 7 Dec. 1915
Place/Date of Birth: South Wingate, Co. Durham — 4 Apr. 1882
Place/Date of Death: Durham — 29 Nov. 1958
Memorials: —
Town/County Connections: South Wingate, Co. Durham
Remarks: —
Account of Deed: On 4 Nov. 1915 near La Houssoie, France, in thick mist, an officer in charge of a patrol was shot through both thighs. Private Kenny, although repeatedly fired on by the enemy, crawled about for more than an hour with his wounded officer on his back, trying to find his way through the fog to our trenches. He refused to leave the officer, although told several times to do so, and at last, utterly exhausted, left him in a comparatively safe ditch and went for help. He found a rescue party and guided them to the wounded officer who was then brought to safety.

KENNY, Thomas James Bede　　　　　　　　　　　　　　　**683**
Private (later Corporal)　2nd Bn. (N.S.W.) Australian Imperial Force
Other Decorations: —
Date of Gazette: 8 Jun. 1917
Place/Date of Birth: Paddington, Sydney, New South Wales, Australia — 29 Sep. 1896
Place/Date of Death: Sydney, Australia — 15 Apr. 1953
Memorials: Eastern Suburbs Cemetery, Sydney; Australian War Memorial, Canberra
Town/County Connections:
Remarks: —*Bede Kenny Memorial Ward at Wentworth Hospital. Randwick Sydney*
Account of Deed: On 9 Apr. 1917, at Hermies, France, when the platoon was held up by an enemy strong point, and severe casualties prevented progress, Private Kenny, under very heavy fire and at close range, dashed alone towards the enemy's position, and killed one man who tried to bar his way. He then bombed the position, captured the gun crew, all of whom he had wounded, killed an officer and seized the gun.

KENNY, William　　　　　　　　　　　　　　　　　　　　　　**684**
Drummer (later Drum-Major)　2nd Bn., The Gordon Highlanders
Other Decorations: —
Date of Gazette: 18 Feb. 1915
Place/Date of Birth: Malta — 24 Aug. 1880
Place/Date of Death: London — 10 Jan. 1936
Memorials: — *Buried Brookwood Cemetery, Surrey*
Town/County Connections: Drogheda, Co. Louth, Ireland
Remarks: —
Account of Deed: On 23 Oct. 1914 near Ypres, Belgium, Drummer Kenny rescued wounded men on five occasions under very heavy fire. Twice previously he had saved machine-guns by carrying them out of action, and on numerous occasions he conveyed urgent messages under very dangerous circumstances over fire-swept ground.

KENNY, William David   **685**
Lieutenant   4/39th Garhwal Rifles, Indian Army
Other Decorations: —
Date of Gazette: 9 Sep. 1920
Place/Date of Birth: Saintfield, Co. Down, Ireland — 1 Feb. 1899
Place/Date of Death: Kot Kai, North West Frontier, India — 2 Jan. 1920
Memorials: Delhi Memorial, India
Town/County Connections: Donaghadee, Co. Down, Ireland
Remarks: —
Account of Deed: On 2 Jan. 1920 near Kot Kai, North West Frontier, India, Lieutenant Kenny was in command of a company holding an advanced covering position which was repeatedly attacked by the Mahsuds in greatly superior numbers. For over four hours this officer maintained his position repulsing three determined attacks, being foremost in the hand-to-hand fighting which took place. In the subsequent withdrawal, recognising that a diversion was necessary in order that some of the wounded could be got away, he turned back with a handful of men and counter-attacked the pursuing enemy and with the rest of his men was killed fighting to the last.

KER, Allan Ebenezer   **686**
Lieutenant (later Major)   3rd Bn., The Gordon Highlanders, attd. 61st Bn., Machine Gun Corps
Other Decorations: —
Date of Gazette: 4 Sep. 1919
Place/Date of Birth: Edinburgh — 5 Mar. 1883
Place/Date of Death: London — 12 Sep. 1958
Memorials: —
Town/County Connections: Edinburgh; London
Remarks: —
Account of Deed: On 21 Mar. 1918 near St. Quentin, France, when the enemy had penetrated our line, Lieutenant Ker, with one Vickers gun, succeeded in holding up the attack, inflicting many casualties. He then stayed at his post with a sergeant and several men who had been badly wounded, beating off bayonet attacks with revolvers, the Vickers gun having been destroyed. Although exhausted from want of food and gas poisoning, as well as from fighting and attending to the wounded, Lieutenant Ker only surrendered when all his ammunition was spent and the position over-run — he had managed to hold 500 of the enemy off for three hours.

KERR, George Fraser   **687**
Lieutenant (later Captain)   3rd Bn., 1st Central Ontario Regiment (Toronto Regiment), C.E.F.
Other Decorations: MC & Bar, MM
Date of Gazette: 6 Jan. 1919
Place/Date of Birth: Deseronto, Ontario, Canada — 8 Jun. 1894
Place/Date of Death: Toronto, Canada — 8 Dec. 1929
Memorials: Mount Pleasant Cemetery, Toronto
Town/County Connections: —
Remarks: —
Account of Deed: On 27 Sep. 1918 at Bourlon Wood, France, Lieutenant Kerr acted with conspicuous bravery and leadership during operations, giving timely support by outflanking a machine-gun which was impeding the advance. Later, when the advance was again held up by a strong point, and being far in advance of his company, he rushed the strong point single-handed, capturing four machine-guns and 31 prisoners.

KERR, John Chipman   **688**
Private   49th Bn., Alberta Regiment, C.E.F.
Other Decorations: —
Date of Gazette: 26 Oct. 1916
Place/Date of Birth: Fox River, Cumberland Co., Nova Scotia, Canada — 11 Jan. 1887
Place/Date of Death: Port Moody, British Columbia, Canada — 19 Feb. 1963
Memorials: —
Town/County Connections: —
Remarks: —
Account of Deed: On 16 Sep. 1916 at Courcelette, France, during a bombing attack, Private Kerr was acting as bayonet man and noting that bombs were running short, he ran along the parados under heavy fire until he was in close contact with the enemy when he opened fire at point-blank range, inflicting heavy losses. The enemy, thinking that they were surrounded, surrendered — 62 prisoners were taken and 250 yards of enemy trench captured. Earlier, Private Kerr's fingers had been blown off, but he did not have his wound dressed until he and two other men had escorted the prisoners back under fire and reported for duty.

KERR, William Alexander **689**
Lieutenant (later Captain)   24th Bombay Native Infantry
Other Decorations: —
Date of Gazette: 24 Apr. 1858
Place/Date of Birth: Melrose, Roxburghshire, Scotland — 18 Jul. 1831
Place/Date of Death: Folkestone, Kent — 19 May 1919
Memorials: Cheriton Road Cemetery, Folkestone, Kent   *Grave*
Town/County Connections: Melrose, Roxburghshire; Folkestone, Kent
Remarks: —
Account of Deed: On 10 Jul. 1857 at Kolapore, India, Lieutenant Kerr, with a small party went to attack the position taken up by mutineers in the stronghold near the town. The attacking party had no guns and the enemy kept up a ceaseless fire, but Lieutenant Kerr made a dash at one of the gateways with some dismounted horsemen and forced an entrance. The attack was successful and the defenders were all either killed, wounded or captured.

KEYES, Geoffrey Charles Tasker **690**
T/Lieutenant Colonel   Royal Scots Greys, Royal Armoured Corps (11th Scottish Commando)
Other Decorations: MC
Date of Gazette: 19 Jun. 1942
Place/Date of Birth: Aberdour, Fifeshire, Scotland — 18 May 1917
Place/Date of Death: Beda Littoria, Libya — 18 Nov. 1941
Memorials: Benghazi War Cemetery, Libya; St. James's Cemetery, Dover, Kent
Town/County Connections: Aberdour, Fifeshire
Remarks: Croix de Guerre (France)
Account of Deed: On 17/18 Nov. 1941 at Beda Littoria, Libya, Lieutenant Colonel Keyes, commanding a detachment of a force which had landed 250 miles behind enemy lines, led his men, without guides, in dangerous and precipitous country to attack the house which was believed to be General Rommel's headquarters. When they reached their objective, Colonel Keyes took only one officer and one NCO with him and having evaded the guards and dealt with the sentry, he dashed into the first room he encountered and shot the occupants. He then rushed into the second room where the occupants were the first to fire and Colonel Keyes was mortally wounded. *Roger Keyes' Son*

KEYSOR (or KEYZOR), Leonard **691**
Private (later Lieutenant)   1st Bn. (N.S.W.), Australian Imperial Force
Other Decorations: —
Date of Gazette: 15 Oct. 1915
Place/Date of Birth: Maida Vale, London — 3 Nov. 1885
Place/Date of Death: London — 12 Oct. 1951
Memorials: (Cremated, St. John's Wood Crematorium, London); Australian War Memorial, Canberra
Town/County Connections: Paddington, London
Remarks: —
Account of Deed: On 7 Aug. 1915 at Lone Pine, Gallipoli, Private Keysor was in a trench which was being heavily bombed by the enemy. He picked up two live bombs and threw them back at the enemy at great risk to himself, and continued throwing bombs until wounded. On 8 Aug. at the same place, he successfully bombed the enemy out of a position where they had gained temporary mastery over his own trench, again being wounded. He refused to go to hospital and, volunteering to throw bombs for another company which had lost its bomb throwers, continued bombing until the situation was relieved.

KEYWORTH, Leonard James **692**
Lance-Corporal (later Corporal)   24th (County of London) Bn., The London Regt. (The Queen's)
Other Decorations: —
Date of Gazette: 3 Jul. 1915
Place/Date of Birth: Lincoln — 12 Aug. 1893
Place/Date of Death: Abbeville, France — 19 Oct. 1915
Memorials: Abbeville Communal Cemetery, France
Town/County Connections: Lincoln
Remarks: —
Account of Deed: On 25/26 May 1915 at Givenchy, France, after a successful assault on the German position by the battalion a bombing attack was launched in the course of which 58 men out of 75 became casualties. During this very fierce encounter Lance-Corporal Keyworth stood fully exposed to the enemy for two hours on the top of their parapet and threw about 150 bombs amongst the Germans who were only a few yards away.

KHUDADAD KHAN **693**

Sepoy (later Subadar)   129th Duke of Connaught's Own Baluchis, Indian Army
Other Decorations: —
Date of Gazette: 7 Dec. 1914
Place/Date of Birth: Dabb Village, Chakwal, Jhelum District, Punjab — 26 Oct. 1888
Place/Date of Death: Pakistan — 8 Mar. 1971
Memorials: —
Town/County Connections: —
Remarks: The first native-born Indian to win the VC
Account of Deed: On 31 Oct. 1914 at Hollebeke, Belgium, Sepoy Khudadad Khan was in the machine-gun section of his battalion and was working one of the two guns. The British officer in charge of the detachment was wounded and the other gun was put out of action by a shell. Sepoy Khudadad Khan, although himself wounded, continued working his gun after all the other five men of the detachment had been killed. He was left by the enemy for dead, but later managed to crawl away and rejoin his unit.

KIBBY, William Henry **694**

Sergeant   2/48th Bn. (S.A.), Australian Military Forces
Other Decorations: —
Date of Gazette: 28 Jan. 1943
Place/Date of Birth: Winlaton, Co. Durham — 15 Apr. 1903
Place/Date of Death: Miteiriya Ridge, Libya — 31 Oct. 1942
Memorials: El Alamein War Cemetery, Egypt; Australian War Memorial, Canberra
Town/County Connections: —
Remarks: —
Account of Deed: During the period 23/31 Oct. 1942 with the initial attack at Miteiriya Ridge, Western Desert, Sergeant Kibby brilliantly distinguished himself leading the platoon when his commander had been killed. On 23 Oct. he silenced an enemy machine-gun, killing three of the enemy and capturing 12 others. During the following days he moved among his men directing fire and cheering them on. Several times under intense fire he went and mended the platoon line communications. On 30/31 Oct. in order to achieve his company's objective he went forward alone, throwing grenades to destroy the enemy only a few yards away. Just as success appeared certain, he was killed.

KILBY, Arthur Forbes Gordon **695**

Captain   2nd Bn., The South Staffordshire Regiment
Other Decorations: MC
Date of Gazette: 30 Mar. 1916
Place/Date of Birth: Cheltenham, Gloucestershire — 3 Feb. 1885
Place/Date of Death: Near Cuinchy, France — 25 Sep. 1915
Memorials: Arras Road Cemetery, France; York Minster; Garrison Church, Whittington Barracks, Lichfield, Staffordshire
Town/County Connections: Cheltenham, Gloucestershire; Leamington, Warwickshire
Remarks: —
Account of Deed: On 25 Sep. 1915 near Cuinchy France, Captain Kilby was selected, at his own request, to attack with his company a strong enemy redoubt. The company charged along the narrow tow-path, headed by the captain, who, although wounded at the outset, continued to lead his men right up to the enemy wire under a devastating machine-gun fire and a shower of bombs. Here he was shot down, but although his foot had been blown off, he continued to cheer his men on and to use his rifle. He was missing after this action and was later presumed killed.

KINGSBURY, Bruce Steel **696**

Private   2/14th Bn. (Victoria), Australian Military Forces
Other Decorations: —
Date of Gazette: 9 Feb. 1943
Place/Date of Birth: Armadale, Melbourne, Victoria, Australia — 8 Jan. 1918
Place/Date of Death: New Guinea, South-West Pacific — 29 Aug. 1942
Memorials: Port Moresby (Bomana) War Cemetery, New Guinea; Australian War Memorial, Canberra
Town/County Connections: —
Remarks: —
Account of Deed: On 29 Aug. 1942 in Isurava, Papua, New Guinea, when the enemy had broken through the battalion's right flank, creating serious threats to the rest of the battalion and to its headquarters, Private Kingsbury volunteered to join a platoon which had been ordered to counter-attack. He rushed forward, firing the Bren gun from his hip and succeeded in clearing a path through the enemy and inflicting an extremely large number of casualties. He was then seen to fall, shot dead by a sniper's bullet. His superb courage made possible the recapture of a position which saved Battalion Headquarters.

KINROSS, Cecil John   **697**
Private   49th Bn., Alberta Regiment, C.E.F.
Other Decorations: —
Date of Gazette: 11 Jan. 1918
Place/Date of Birth: Hillhead, Clackmannan, Scotland — 13 Jul. 1897
Place/Date of Death: Loughead, Alberta, Canada — 21 Jun. 1957
Memorials: —
Town/County Connections: Hillhead, Clackmannan, Scotland
Remarks: —
Account of Deed: On 30 Oct. 1917 at Passchendaele, Belgium, shortly after the attack was launched, the company to which Private Kinross belonged came under heavy fire and further advance was held up by very severe fire from an enemy machine-gun. Private Kinross, after making a careful survey of the situation, deliberately divested himself of all his equipment except his rifle and bandolier and then advanced alone over open ground in broad daylight. He charged the enemy machine-gun, killing the crew of six and seized and destroyed the gun. His superb example and courage enabled a highly important position to be established.

KIRBY, Frank Howard   **698**
Corporal (later Lieutenant Colonel)   Corps of Royal Engineers
Other Decorations: CBE, DCM
Date of Gazette: 5 Oct. 1900
Place/Date of Birth: Thame, Oxfordshire — 12 Nov. 1871
Place/Date of Death: Sidcup, Kent — 8 Jul. 1956
Memorials: Chatham Garrison Church, Kent
Town/County Connections: Thame, Oxfordshire; Sidcup, Kent
Remarks: Served with the Royal Flying Corps 1914-18; Group Captain, R.A.F. 1918-26
Account of Deed: On 2 Jun. 1900 near Delagoa Bay Railway, South Africa, during the retirement of a small party being hotly pressed by superior numbers of the enemy, Corporal Kirby turned and rode back to help a man whose horse had been shot. Although by the time he reached the man they were under heavy fire at close range, Corporal Kirby managed to get the man up behind him and took him clear of the firing. This was the third occasion on which Corporal Kirby had shown gallantry in the face of the enemy.

KIRK, James   **699**
Second Lieutenant   10th Bn., The Manchester Regiment, attd. 2nd Bn.
Other Decorations: —
Date of Gazette: 6 Jan. 1919
Place/Date of Birth: Adswood, Cheadle Hulme, Cheshire — 27 Jan. 1897
Place/Date of Death: Ors, France — 4 Nov. 1918
Memorials: Ors Communal Cemetery, France
Town/County Connections: Cheadle Hulme, Cheshire
Remarks: —
Account of Deed: On 4 Nov. 1918 north of Ors, France, the battalion was attempting to bridge the Oise Canal. In order to cover this difficult operation, Second Lieutenant Kirk took a Lewis gun and under intense machine-gun fire paddled across the canal and opened fire. Further ammunition was paddled across to him and he continued to provide cover for the bridging party until he was killed. His courage and self-sacrifice enabled two platoons to cross the bridge and prevented many casualties.

KIRK, John   **700**
Private   10th Regiment (later The Lincolnshire Regiment)
Other Decorations: —
Date of Gazette: 20 Jan. 1860
Place/Date of Birth: Liverpool, Lancashire — Jul. 1827
Place/Date of Death: Liverpool — 30 Aug. 1865
Memorials: —
Town/County Connections: Liverpool
Remarks: —
Account of Deed: On 4 Jun. 1857 at Benares, India, Private Kirk volunteered, with two sergeant-majors* to go to the rescue of a paymaster and his family who were surrounded by rebels in the compound of their house. At the risk of his own life, the rescue was successfully accomplished. (*See also GILL, P. and ROSAMUND, M.)

KNIGHT, Alfred Joseph   **701**
Sergeant (later Second Lieutenant)   2/8th (City of London) Bn., The London Regt. (Post Office Rifles)
Other Decorations: MBE
Date of Gazette: 8 Nov. 1917
Place/Date of Birth: Ladywood, Birmingham — 24 Aug. 1888
Place/Date of Death: Birmingham — 4 Dec. 1960
Memorials: —
Town/County Connections: Ladywood, Birmingham
Remarks: —
Account of Deed: On 20 Sep. 1917 at Alberta Section, Ypres, Belgium, when his platoon came under very heavy fire from an enemy machine-gun, Sergeant Knight rushed through our own barrage and captured it single-handed. He performed several other acts of conspicuous bravery single-handed, all under heavy machine-gun and rifle fire and without regard to personal safety. All the platoon officers of the company had become casualties before the first objective was reached, and this NCO took command not only of all the men of his own platoon but of the platoons without officers and his energy in consolidating and reorganising was untiring.

KNIGHT, Arthur George   **702**
A/Sergeant   10th Bn., Alberta Regiment, C.E.F.
Other Decorations: —
Date of Gazette: 15 Nov. 1918
Place/Date of Birth: Haywards Heath, Sussex — 26 Jun. 1886
Place/Date of Death: Villers-les-Cagnicourt, France — 3 Sep. 1918
Memorials: Dominion Cemetery, France
Town/County Connections: —
Remarks: Croix de Guerre (France)
Account of Deed: On 2 Sep. 1918 at Villers-les-Cagnicourt, France, when a bombing section which he was leading was held up, Sergeant Knight went forward alone, bayoneting several machine-gunners and trench mortar crews, and forcing the rest to retire. Then bringing forward a Lewis gun he directed his fire on the retreating enemy; his platoon went in pursuit and the sergeant, seeing about 30 of the enemy going into a tunnel leading off the trench, again went forward alone, killing an officer and two NCOs and taking 20 prisoners. After this, again single-handed, he routed another hostile party. Later he was fatally wounded.

KNIGHT, Henry James   **703**
Corporal (later Captain)   1st Bn., The King's (Liverpool) Regiment
Other Decorations: —
Date of Gazette: 4 Jan. 1901
Place/Date of Birth: Yeovil, Somerset — 5 Nov. 1878
Place/Date of Death: Anderson, near Blandford, Dorset — 24 Nov. 1955
Memorials: —
Town/County Connections: Yeovil, Somerset; Anderson, Blandford, Dorset
Remarks: —
Account of Deed: On 21 Aug. 1900 during the operations near Van Wyk's Vlei, South Africa, Corporal Knight and four men were covering the right rear of a detachment of their company when they were attacked by the enemy. The corporal held his ground, directing his men to retire one by one to better cover, where he maintained his position for nearly an hour, covering the withdrawal of part of their company, and losing two of his four men. He then retired, taking with him two wounded men, one of whom he left in a place of safety and the other he carried himself for nearly two miles.

KNOWLAND, George Arthur   **704**
Lieutenant   The Royal Norfolk Regiment, attd. No. 1 Commando
Other Decorations: —
Date of Gazette: 12 Apr. 1945
Place/Date of Birth: Catford, Kent — 16 Aug. 1922
Place/Date of Death: Kangaw, Burma — 31 Jan. 1945
Memorials: Taukkyan War Cemetery, Burma
Town/County Connections: Catford, Kent; Croydon, Surrey
Remarks: —
Account of Deed: On 31 Jan. 1945 near Kangaw, Burma, Lieutenant Knowland was in command of a forward platoon of a troop which was being heavily attacked — some 300 of the enemy concentrating on his 24 men. When all the crew of one of his forward Bren guns had been wounded, the lieutenant manned it himself, standing up to fire at 10 yards range, until the casualties had been evacuated. For 12 hours he held his ground, until he was eventually mortally wounded.

KNOX, Cecil Leonard　　　　　　　　　　　　　　　　　　　　**705**
T/Second Lieutenant (later Major)　150th Field Coy., Corps of Royal Engineers
Other Decorations:　—
Date of Gazette:　4 Jun. 1918
Place/Date of Birth:　Nuneaton, Warwickshire — 9 May 1888
Place/Date of Death:　Nuneaton, Warwickshire — 4 Feb. 1943
Memorials:　—
Town/County Connections:　Nuneaton, Warwickshire
Remarks:　Served with 605 Squadron, Royal Auxiliary Air Force (Flight Lieutenant) 1926-32
Account of Deed:　On 22 Mar. 1918 at Tugny, France, Second Lieutenant Knox was entrusted with the demolition of 12 bridges. He successfully carried out this task, but in the case of one steel girder bridge the time fuse failed to act, and without hesitation he ran to the bridge under heavy fire, and when the enemy were actually on it, he tore away the time fuse and lit the instantaneous fuse, to do which he had to get under the bridge. As a practical civil engineer, Second Lieutenant Knox undoubtedly realised the grave risk he took in doing this.

KNOX, John Simpson　　　　　　　　　　　　　　　　　　　　**706**
Sergeant (later Bt/Major)　Scots (Fusilier) Guards and The Rifle Brigade
Other Decorations:　—
Date of Gazette:　24 Feb. 1857
Place/Date of Birth:　Calton, Glasgow — 30 Sep. 1828
Place/Date of Death:　Cheltenham, Gloucestershire — 8 Jan. 1897
Memorials:　Cheltenham Cemetery; Rifle Brigade Memorial, Winchester Cathedral
Town/County Connections:　Glasgow, Scotland; Cardiff, Wales; Cheltenham, Gloucestershire
Remarks:　Légion d'Honneur (France)
Account of Deed:　On 20 Sep. 1854 at the Battle of the Alma, Crimea, Sergeant Knox, while serving with the Scots (Fusilier) Guards, behaved with conspicuous courage in re-forming the ranks of the Guards at a decisive moment of the action. Subsequently, when he was a lieutenant in the Rifle Brigade, on 18 Jun. 1855, he volunteered for the ladder party in the attack on the Redan, acting with great gallantry and remaining on the field until twice wounded.

KONOWAL, Filip　　　　　　　　　　　　　　　　　　　　　**707**
A/Corporal　47th Bn., British Columbia Regiment, C.E.F.
Other Decorations:　—
Date of Gazette:　26 Nov. 1917
Place/Date of Birth:　Podolsky, Ukraine, Russia — 15 Sep. 1888
Place/Date of Death:　Ottawa, Canada — 3 Jun. 1959
Memorials:　Notre Dame Cemetery, Ottawa
Town/County Connections:　—
Remarks:　—
Account of Deed:　During the period 22/24 Aug. 1917 at Lens, France, Corporal Konowal was in charge of a section which had the difficult task of mopping up cellars, craters and machine-gun emplacements. Under his able direction all resistance was overcome successfully and heavy casualties inflicted on the enemy. He attacked several of the enemy single-handed and on one occasion entered a gun emplacement, killed the crew and brought back the machine-gun to our lines. The next day he killed the crew of another machine-gun and then destroyed the gun and emplacement with explosives. He carried on in this manner until he was severely wounded.

KULBIR THAPA,　　　　　　　　　　　　　　　　　　　　**708**
Rifleman (later Havildar)　2nd Bn., 3rd Gurkha Rifles, Indian Army
Other Decorations:　—
Date of Gazette:　18 Nov. 1915
Place/Date of Birth:　Nigalpani, Palba, Nepal — 15 Dec. 1888
Place/Date of Death:　Nepal — 3 Oct. 1956
Memorials:　—
Town/County Connections:　—
Remarks:　—
Account of Deed:　On 25 Sep. 1915 south of Fauquissart, France, Rifleman Kulbir Thapa, having been wounded himself, found a wounded soldier of The Leicestershire Regiment behind the first-line German trench. Although urged to save himself, the Gurkha stayed with the wounded man all day and night. Early next day, in misty weather, he took him through the German wire and, leaving him in a place of comparative safety, returned and brought in two wounded Gurkhas, one after the other. He then went back and, in broad daylight, fetched the British soldier, carrying him most of the way under enemy fire.

LACHHIMAN GURUNG, 709

Rifleman   8th Gurkha Rifles, Indian Army
Other Decorations: —
Date of Gazette: 27 Jul. 1945
Place/Date of Birth: Dakhani Village, Tanhu, Nepal — 30 Dec. 1917
Place/Date of Death: —
Memorials: —
Town/County Connections: —
Remarks: —
Account of Deed: On 12/13 May 1945 at Taungdaw, Burma, Rifleman Lachhiman Gurung was manning the most forward post of his platoon which bore the brunt of an attack by at least 200 of the enemy. Twice he hurled back grenades which had fallen on his trench, but the third exploded in his right hand, blowing off his fingers, shattering his arm and severely wounding him in the face, body and right leg. His two comrades were also badly wounded, but the rifleman, now alone and disregarding his wounds, loaded and fired his rifle with his left hand for four hours, calmly waiting for each attack which he met with fire at point blank range.

LAFONE, Alexander Malins 710

Major   1/1st County of London Yeomanry
Other Decorations: —
Date of Gazette: 18 Dec. 1917
Place/Date of Birth: Cressfield, Waterloo, Liverpool, Lancashire — 19 Aug. 1870
Place/Date of Death: Near Beersheba, Palestine — 27 Oct. 1917
Memorials: Beersheba War Cemetery, Palestine
Town/County Connections: Liverpool; Knockholt, Kent; Southwark, London
Remarks: —   *Dulwich College*
Account of Deed: On 27 Oct. 1917 at Beersheba, Palestine, Major Lafone held a position for over seven hours against vastly superior forces. All the time the enemy were shelling the position, making it difficult to see, but their cavalry charges were beaten off with heavy losses. When all his men, with the exception of three had been hit, Major Lafone ordered those who could walk to move to a trench slightly in the rear and from his own position maintained a most heroic resistance. When finally surrounded and charged by the enemy he stepped into the open and continued to fight until he was mortally wounded and fell unconscious.

LAIDLAW, Daniel 711

Piper (later Sergeant-Piper)   7th Bn., The King's Own Scottish Borderers
Other Decorations: —
Date of Gazette: 18 Nov. 1915
Place/Date of Birth: Little Swinton, near Berwick-upon-Tweed, Northumberland — 26 Jul. 1875
Place/Date of Death: Shoresdean, near Berwick-upon-Tweed — 2 Jun. 1950
Memorials: Norham Church, Northumberland
Town/County Connections: Little Swinton and Shoresdean, near Berwick-upon-Tweed
Remarks: —
Account of Deed: On 25 Sep. 1915 near Loos and Hill 70, France, prior to an assault on enemy trenches and during the worst of the bombardment, Piper Laidlaw, seeing that his company was shaken with the effects of gas, with complete disregard for danger, mounted the parapet and, marching up and down, played his company out of the trench. The effect of his splendid example was immediate and the company dashed to the assault. Piper Laidlaw continued playing his pipes even after he was wounded and until the position was won.

LALA, 712

Lance-Naik (later Jemadar)   41st Dogras, Indian Army
Other Decorations: —
Date of Gazette: 13 May 1916
Place/Date of Birth: Parol, Hamipur District, Kangra, Punjab, India — 20 Feb. 1882
Place/Date of Death: Not known
Memorials: —
Town/County Connections: —
Remarks: —
Account of Deed: On 21 Jan. 1916 at El Orah, Mesopotamia, finding a British officer lying close to the enemy, Lance-Naik Lala dragged him into a temporary shelter. After bandaging his wounds, the lance-naik heard calls from his own adjutant who was lying wounded in the open. The enemy was only 100 yards away, nevertheless Lance-Naik Lala insisted on going to help. He stripped off his own clothing to keep the wounded officer warm and stayed with him until just before dark when he returned to the shelter. After dark he carried the first wounded officer to safety and then, returning with a stretcher, carried back his adjutant.

LALBAHADUR THAPA

713

Subadar (later Subadar-Major)　1st Bn, 2nd Gurkha Rifles, Indian Army
Other Decorations: —
Date of Gazette:　15 Jun. 1943
Place/Date of Birth:　Thant Hup Village, Baghlung, Parbat District, Nepal — Feb. 1906
Place/Date of Death:　Paklehawa, Nepal — 19 Oct. 1968
Memorials: —
Town/County Connections: —
Remarks: —
Account of Deed:　On 5/6 Apr. 1943 during the silent attack on Rass-es-Zouai, Tunisia, Subadar Lalbahadur Thapa, taking command of two sections, made his first contact with the enemy at the foot of a pathway winding up a narrow cleft which was thickly studded with enemy posts. The garrison of the out-posts were all killed by the subadar and his men, by kukri or bayonet and the next machine-gun posts were dealt with similarly. This officer then continued to fight his way up the bullet-swept approaches to the crest where he and the riflemen with him killed four — the rest fled. Thus secured, advance by the whole division was made possible.

No photograph available

LAMBERT, George

714

Sergeant-Major (later Lieutenant and Adjutant)　84th Regiment (later The York and Lancaster Regiment
Other Decorations: —
Date of Gazette:　18 Jun. 1858
Place/Date of Birth:　Markethill, Co. Armagh, Ireland — Dec. 1819
Place/Date of Death:　Sheffield — 10 Feb. 1860　*Buried St. Phillips' Burial Ground Sheffield*
Memorials:　Mullaghbrack Church, Co. Armagh
Town/County Connections:　Mullaghbrack, Co. Armagh; Sheffield, Yorkshire
Remarks: —
Account of Deed:　On 29 Jul. 1857 at Oonao, India, Sergeant-Major Lambert acted with distinguished bravery. Also on 16 Aug. at Bithoor when the rebels were driven at the point of the bayonet out of a strong position, and on 25 Sep. at the passage through Lucknow to the Residency.

LANE, Thomas

715

Private　67th Regiment (later The Hampshire Regiment)
Other Decorations: —
Date of Gazette:　13 Aug. 1861
Place/Date of Birth:　Cork, Ireland — May 1836
Place/Date of Death:　Kimberley, South Africa — 13 Apr. 1889
Memorials: —
Town/County Connections: —
Remarks:　Became a member of the Kimberley Police Force after leaving the Army
Account of Deed:　On 21 Aug. 1860 at the Taku Forts, China, Private Lane and a lieutenant* of his regiment displayed great gallantry in swimming the ditches of the North Taku Fort and attempting, during the assault and before an entrance had been effected by anyone, to enlarge an opening in the wall, through which they eventually entered. In doing so, they were both severely wounded. (*See also BURSLEM, N.)

LASCELLES, Arthur Moore

716

A/Captain　3rd Bn., The Durham Light Infantry, attd. 14th Bn.
Other Decorations:　MC
Date of Gazette:　11 Jan. 1918
Place/Date of Birth:　London — 12 Oct. 1880　*Wilby Lodge, Nightingale Lane, Streatha...*
Place/Date of Death:　Fontaine, France — 7 Nov. 1918
Memorials:　Dourlers Communal Cemetery Extension, France; Pennal Parish Church and War Memorial, Merionethshire; University College of N. Wales and Edinburgh University War Memorials　*Pennal Parish Church. Pennal Co. M.*
Town/County Connections:　Pennal, Merionethshire, Wales
Remarks: — *Malvern School. Uppingham School. UC of North Wales. Edinbur... Co. M.*
Account of Deed:　On 3 Dec. 1917 at Masnieres, France, during a very heavy bombardment Captain Lascelles, although wounded, continued to encourage his men and organize the defence until the attack ws driven off. Shortly afterwards the enemy attacked again and captured the trench, taking several prisoners. Captain Lascelles at once jumped on to the parapet and followed by his 12 remaining men rushed across under very heavy machine-gun fire and drove over 60 of the enemy back. Later the enemy attacked again and captured the trench and Captain Lascelles, who later managed to escape in spite of having received two further wounds. *VC with DLI Museum*

LASSEN, Anders Frederik Emil Victor Schau   717

T/Major   General List, attd. Special Boat Service, No.1 S.A.S. Regiment
Other Decorations: MC & 2 Bars
Date of Gazette: 7 Sep. 1945
Place/Date of Birth: Baekkeskov, South Zealand, Denmark — 22 Sep. 1920
Place/Date of Death: Near Lake Comacchio, Italy — 9 Apr. 1945
Memorials: Argenta Gap War Cemetery, Italy; stone memorial outside St. Peter's Chapel, Praesto Fjord, Norway; forest named after him in Israel
Town/County Connections: —
Remarks: —
Account of Deed: On 8 Apr. 1945 at Lake Comacchio, Italy, Major Lassen was ordered to take a patrol and raid the north shore of the lake, causing as many casualties and as much confusion as possible to give the impression of a major landing. In the face of overwhelming enemy numbers he fulfilled his mission, three positions being wiped out, and when he was mortally wounded he refused to be evacuated so that the withdrawal should not be impeded and his men's lives endangered.

LAUDER, David Ross   718

Private   1/4th Bn., The Royal Scots Fusiliers
Other Decorations: —
Date of Gazette: 13 Jan. 1917
Place/Date of Birth: East Glentire, Airdrie, Scotland — 21 Jan. 1894
Place/Date of Death: Glasgow — 4 Jun. 1972
Memorials: —
Town/County Connections: Dalry, Ayr, Scotland
Remarks: Serbian Medal for Bravery
Account of Deed: On 13 Aug. 1915 at Cape Helles, Gallipoli, Private Lauder was with a bombing party retaking a sap when he threw a bomb which failed to clear the parapet and fell amongst the bombing party. There was no time to smother the bomb and Private Lauder at once put his foot on it, thereby localising the explosion. His foot was blown off, but the remainder of the party escaped unhurt.

No photograph available

LAUGHNAN, Thomas   719

Gunner   Bengal Artillery, Indian Army
Other Decorations: —
Date of Gazette: 24 Feb. 1858
Place/Date of Birth: Kilmadaugh, Gort, Co. Galway, Ireland — Aug. 1824
Place/Date of Death: Co. Galway — 23 Jul. 1864
Memorials: —
Town/County Connections: Gort, Co. Galway, Ireland
Remarks: —
Account of Deed: During the whole of the period 14 to 22 Nov. 1857 at the Relief of Lucknow, India, Gunner Laughnan acted with conspicuous gallantry. (Elected by the regiment.)

LAURENT, Harry John   720

Sergeant   2nd Bn., N.Z. (Rifle) Brigade, NZ.E.F.
Other Decorations: —
Date of Gazette: 15 Nov. 1918
Place/Date of Birth: Tarata, Taranaki, New Zealand — 15 Apr. 1895
Place/Date of Death: Hastings, New Zealand — 9 Dec. 1987
Memorials: Ashes interred in Memorial Wall named in his honour in the Servicemen's Cemetery, Hawera, Taraniki; HQ Dunedin RSA, New Zealand
Town/County Connections: —
Remarks: Served in the Second World War — Area commander, Home Guard 1940-42; commanded No. 47 Air Training Corps 1943-45
Account of Deed: On 12 Sep. 1918 east of Gouzeaucourt Wood, France, during an attack, Sergeant Laurent was detailed to exploit an initial success and keep in touch with the enemy. With a party of 12 he located the very strong enemy support line and at once charged the position followed by his men completely disorganising the enemy by the suddenness of his attack. In the hand-to-hand fighting which ensued, 30 of the enemy were killed and the remainder, totalling one officer and 111 other ranks, surrendered. His party suffered four casualties.

LAWRENCE, Brian Turner Tom   **721**
Sergeant (later Lieutenant Colonel)   17th Lancers (Duke of Cambridge's Own)
Other Decorations: —
Date of Gazette: 15 Jan. 1901
Place/Date of Birth: Bewdley, Worcestershire — 9 Nov. 1873
Place/Date of Death: Nakuru, Kenya — 7 Jun. 1949
Memorials: —
Town/County Connections: Bewdley, Worcestershire
Remarks: Served in the First World War 1914-18; served in the Second World War 1939-42;
Military Knight of Windsor 1934-38; member of the English Riding Team at the Olympic Games,
Stockholm 1912
Account of Deed: On 7 Aug. 1900 near Essenbosch Farm, South Africa, Sergeant Lawrence and a private were attacked by a
group of Boers. The private's horse was shot and the man thrown, dislocating his shoulder. Sergeant Lawrence at once went
to his assistance, put him on his own horse and sent him on to the picket. He then took the soldier's carbine, and with his own
as well, kept the enemy off until the wounded man was safely out of range. The sergeant then retired for some two miles on
foot, followed by the Boers, keeping them off until help arrived.

LAWRENCE, Samuel Hill   **722**
Lieutenant (later Major)   32nd Regiment (later The Duke of Cornwall's Light Infantry)
Other Decorations: —
Date of Gazette: 21 Nov. 1859
Place/Date of Birth: Cork, Ireland — 22 Jan. 1831
Place/Date of Death: Montevideo, Uruguay — 17 Jun. 1868
Memorials: —
Town/County Connections: Cork, Ireland
Remarks: Cousin of Lieutenant T. Cadell, VC
Account of Deed: On 7 Jul. 1857 at Lucknow, India, Lieutenant Lawrence was the first person to
mount a ladder to examine a house held by the enemy, in order to discover whether or not a mine
was being driven from it. His pistol was knocked from his hand by one of the enemy while he was accomplishing this task. Also,
on 26 Sep. the Lieutenant charged, with two of his men, in advance of his company, and captured a 9-pounder gun.

LAWSON, Edward   **723**
Private   1st Bn., The Gordon Highlanders
Other Decorations: —
Date of Gazette: 20 May 1898
Place/Date of Birth: Newcastle upon Tyne, Northumberland — 11 Apr. 1873
Place/Date of Death: Walker, Northumberland — 2 Jul. 1955
Memorials: —
Town/County Connections: Newcastle upon Tyne and Walker, Northumberland
Remarks: —
Account of Deed: On 20 Oct. 1897, during the attack on the Dargai Heights, Indian Frontier (Tirah
Campaign), Private Lawson carried a lieutenant of The Gordon Highlanders, who was severely
wounded, out of a heavy fire. Subsequently, although wounded himself, he returned and brought in another casualty.

LEACH, Edward Pemberton (later Sir Edward)   **724**
Captain (later General)   Corps of Royal Engineers
Other Decorations: KCB, KCVO
Date of Gazette: 6 Dec. 1879
Place/Date of Birth: Londonderry, Ireland — 2 Apr. 1847
Place/Date of Death: Caddenabbia, Italy — 27 Apr. 1913
Memorials: —
Town/County Connections: Londonderry, Ireland
Remarks: Commanded 9th Div. 3rd Army Corps, Belfast 1900-5; GOC-in-C, Scotland 1905-9
Account of Deed: On 17 Mar. 1879 near Maidanah, (Afghan War), Captain Leach, with some men
of the 45th Sikhs, was covering the retirement of the Survey Escort who were carrying a mortally
wounded lieutenant. The captain charged with his small band a very large number of the enemy and in the encounter he killed
two or three himself while receiving a severe wound in his left arm. His action saved the whole party from annihilation.

LEACH, James

725

Second Lieutenant (later Captain)   2nd Bn., The Manchester Regiment
Other Decorations: —
Date of Gazette: 22 Dec. 1914
Place/Date of Birth: North Shields, Northumberland — 27 Jul. 1892
Place/Date of Death: Shepherd's Bush, London — 15 Aug. 1958
Memorials: — *Cremated at Mortlake Crematorium, London*
Town/County Connections: Manchester; London
Remarks: —
Account of Deed: On 29 Oct. 1914 near Festubert, France, after their trench had been taken by the enemy and two attempts to recapture it had failed, Second Lieutenant Leach and a sergeant* with a party of 10 volunteers went to recover it themselves. They took the Germans by surprise with a sudden bayonet attack and then working from traverse to traverse they gradually succeeded in regaining possession, killing eight of the enemy, wounding two and taking 16 prisoners. (*See also HOGAN, J.)

LEAK, John

726

Private   9th Bn. (Queensland), Australian Imperial Force
Other Decorations: —
Date of Gazette: 9 Sep. 1916
Place/Date of Birth: ?Portsmouth, Hampshire — 1892
Place/Date of Death: Adelaide, Australia — 20 Oct. 1972
Memorials: Stirling Cemetery, Adelaide; Australian War Memorial, Canberra
Town/County Connections: Portsmouth, Hampshire
Remarks: —
Account of Deed: On 23 Jul. 1916 at Pozieres, France, Private Leak was one of a party which finally captured an enemy strong point. At one assault, when the enemy's bombs were outranging ours, Private Leak ran forward under heavy fire, threw bombs into the enemy's bombing post, then jumped into the post and killed three of the bombers. Later, when the enemy in overwhelming numbers was driving his party back, Private Leak was always the last to withdraw at each stage and kept on throwing bombs. His actions had such an effect that when reinforcements arrived, the whole trench was recaptured.

LEAKE, Arthur MARTIN-

727

Surgeon Captain (later Lieutenant Colonel)   South African Constabulary then Royal Army Medical Corps, attd. 5th Field Ambulance
Other Decorations: —
Date of Gazette: 13 May 1902 and BAR 18 Feb. 1915
Place/Date of Birth: Standen, near Ware, Hertfordshire — 4 Apr. 1874
Place/Date of Death: Ware, Hertfordshire — 22 Jun. 1953
Memorials: High Cross Churchyard, near Ware, Hertfordshire *Grave.*
Town/County Connections: Ware, Hertfordshire
Remarks: Awarded British Medical Association's Gold Medal; commanded a mobile ARP unit in the Second World War.
Account of Deed: On 8 Feb. 1902, at Vlakfontein, South Africa, Surgeon Captain Martin-Leake went out into the firing line to dress a wounded man under very heavy enemy fire only 100 yards off. He then attended a badly wounded officer and while doing so was shot himself. He only gave up when thoroughly exhausted and then refused water until other wounded men had been served.
BAR: During the period 29 Oct. to 8 Nov. 1914 near Zonnebeke, Belgium, Lieutenant Martin-Leake showed most conspicuous bravery and devotion to duty in rescuing, whilst exposed to constant fire, a large number of the wounded who were lying close to the enemy's trenches.

LEAKEY, Nigel Gray

728

Sergeant   1/6th Bn., King's African Rifles
Other Decorations: —
Date of Gazette: 15 Nov. 1945
Place/Date of Birth: Kenya — 1 Jan. 1913
Place/Date of Death: Near Colito, Abyssinia — 19 May 1941
Memorials: The East Africa Memorial, Nairobi, Kenya
Town/County Connections: — *Bromsgrove School, Worcester*
Remarks: —
Account of Deed: On 19 May 1941 near Colito, Abyssinia, when two allied companies had established a bridgehead against strong opposition, the enemy made a sudden counter-attack with light and medium tanks. In the face of withering fire, Sergeant Leakey leaped on top of one of the tanks, wrenched open the turret and shot all the crew except the driver, whom he forced to drive to cover. He then, with three other men, stalked the rest of the tanks, jumping on one of them and killing a member of its crew before he himself was killed. His superb courage was responsible for the enemy's defeat in this action.

LEARMONTH, Okill Massey   **729**
A/Major   2nd Bn., Eastern Ontario Regiment, C.E.F.
Other Decorations: MC
Date of Gazette: 8 Nov. 1917
Place/Date of Birth: Quebec City, Canada — 22 Feb. 1894
Place/Date of Death: Near Loos, France — 19 Aug. 1917
Memorials: Noeux-les Mines Communal Cemetery, France
Town/County Connections: —
Remarks: —
Account of Deed: On 18 Aug. 1917 east of Loos, France, during a determined counter-attack on our new positions, Major Learmouth, when his company was momentarily surprised, instantly charged and personally disposed of the attackers. Later, although under intense barrage fire and mortally wounded, he stood on the parapet of the trench, bombing the enemy and on several occasions he actually caught bombs thrown at him and threw them back. When unable to carry on the fight, he still refused to be evacuated and continued giving instructions and invaluable advice, finally handing over all his duties before he was moved to hospital where he died.

LEAROYD, Roderick Alastair Brook   **730**
Flight Lieutenant (later Wing Commander) 49 Squadron, Royal Air Force
Other Decorations: —
Date of Gazette: 20 Aug. 1940
Place/Date of Birth: Folkestone, Kent — 5 Feb. 1913
Place/Date of Death: — *Died about 27.1.1996*
Memorials: —
Town/County Connections: Folkestone and Littlestone-on-Sea, Kent
Remarks: —
Account of Deed: On 12 Aug. 1940 Flight Lieutenant Learoyd was one of the pilots briefed to bomb the Dortmund-Ems Canal in Germany. Of the four other aircraft which had already made the attack on that night, two were destroyed and two were badly hit. Flight Lieutenant Learoyd took his plane into the target at only 150 feet, in the full glare of the searchlights and flak barrage all round him. The aircraft was very badly damaged but the bombs were duly dropped and he managed to get his crippled plane back to England where he flew round until first light, finally landing without causing injury to his crew or further damage to his aircraft.

LEE, Bernard Armitage Warburton WARBURTON-   **731**
Captain Royal Navy
Other Decorations: —
Date of Gazette: 7 Jun. 1940
Place/Date of Birth: Redbrook, Maelor, Flintshire, Wales — 13 Sep. 1895
Place/Date of Death: Norway — 10 Apr. 1940
Memorials: Ballangen New Cemetery, Norway; Iscoed War Memorial, Flintshire; Whitewell Church, Maelor   *Narvik. British Plot 5. Row B. Grave 9*
Town/County Connections: Iscoed, Flintshire, Wales
Remarks: First VC to be gazetted in the Second World War; Norwegian War Cross
Account of Deed: On 10 Apr. 1940 in Ofot Fjord, Narvik, Norway, Captain Warburton-Lee of HMS *Hardy* led a flotilla of five destroyers in a surprise attack on German destroyers and merchant ships in a blinding snowstorm. This was successful, and was almost immediately followed by an engagement with five more German destroyers, during which Captain Warburton-Lee was mortally wounded by a shell which hit *Hardy's* bridge.

LEET, William Knox   **732**
Major (later Major General) 1st Bn., 13th Regiment (later The Somerset Light Infantry — Prince Albert's)
Other Decorations: CB
Date of Gazette: 17 Jun. 1879
Place/Date of Birth: Dalkey, Co. Dublin, Ireland — 3 Nov. 1833
Place/Date of Death: Great Chart, Kent — 27 Jun. 1898
Memorials: Great Chart churchyard, Kent
Town/County Connections: Dalkey, Co. Dublin; Great Chart, Kent
Remarks: —
Account of Deed: On 28 Mar. 1879 at Inhlobana, Zululand, during the retreat, a lieutenant of the Frontier Light Horse whose horse had been shot under him, was on foot and being closely pursued by the Zulus. He would have been killed had not Major Leet taken him upon his horse and rode with him under fire of the enemy to a place of safety.

LEITCH, Peter   **733**
Colour-Sergeant   Corps of Royal Engineers
Other Decorations: —
Date of Gazette: 2 Jun. 1858
Place/Date of Birth: Orwell, Kinross, Scotland — 1820
Place/Date of Death: Fulham, London — 6 Dec. 1892
Memorials: —
Town/County Connections: Orwell, Kinross, Scotland
Remarks: Légion d'Honneur (France)
Account of Deed: On 18 Jun. 1855 at Sebastopol, Crimea, Colour-Sergeant Leitch, after approaching the Redan with the leading ladders, formed a caponnière across the ditch as well as a ramp by fearlessly tearing down gabions from the parapet and placing and filling them until he was disabled from wounds.

LEITH, James   **734**
Lieutenant (later Major)   14th Light Dragoons (later 14th Hussars — The King's)
Other Decorations: —
Date of Gazette: 24 Dec. 1858
Place/Date of Birth: Glenkindie, Aberdeenshire, Scotland — 26 May 1826
Place/Date of Death: London — 13 May 1869
Memorials: —
Town/County Connections: Glenkindie, Aberdeenshire
Remarks: —
Account of Deed: On 1 Apr. 1858 at Betwa, India, when a captain of his regiment was surrounded by a large number of rebel infantry, Lieutenant Leith charged alone and rescued him.

LENDRIM (or LENDRUM), William James   **735**
Corporal (later Sergeant-Major)   Corps of Royal Engineers
Other Decorations: —
Date of Gazette: 24 Feb. 1857
Place/Date of Birth: Ireland — 1 Jan. 1830
Place/Date of Death: Camberley, Surrey — 28 Nov. 1891
Memorials: Camberley, Surrey   *Buried R.M.A. Sandhurst.*
Town/County Connections: —
Remarks: Légion d'Honneur and Médaille Militaire (France).
Account of Deed: On 14 Feb. 1855 in the Crimea, Corporal Lendrim superintended 150 French Chasseurs in building No.9 Battery left attack and replacing the whole of the capsized gabions under a heavy fire. On 11 Apr. he got on top of a magazine under fire, and extinguished burning sandbags, making good the breach. On 20 Apr. he was one of four volunteers who destroyed the screen which the Russians had erected to conceal their advance rifle-pits.

LENNOX, Wilbraham Oates (later Sir Wilbraham)   **736**
Lieutenant (later Lieutenant General)   Corps of Royal Engineers
Other Decorations: KCB
Date of Gazette: 24 Feb. 1857
Place/Date of Birth: Goodwood, Sussex — 4 Aug. 1830
Place/Date of Death: London — 7 Feb. 1897
Memorials: —
Town/County Connections: Chichester, Sussex
Remarks: —
Account of Deed: On 20 Nov. 1854 in the Crimea, Lieutenant Lennox, with a working party of 100 men entrenched themselves in rifle pits which had just been captured from the enemy. Despite extreme exposure to attack, they successfully repulsed all attempts to dislodge them during the night.

LENON, Edmund Henry **737**
Lieutenant (later Lieutenant Colonel)   67th Regiment (later The Hampshire Regiment)
Other Decorations: —
Date of Gazette: 13 Aug. 1861
Place/Date of Birth: Mortlake, Surrey — 26 Aug. 1830
Place/Date of Death: Lambeth, London — 15 Apr. 1893
Memorials: —
Town/County Connections: Mortlake, Surrey
Remarks: —
Account of Deed: On 21 Aug. 1860 at the Taku Forts, China, Lieutenant Lenon, with a lieutenant and a private of the 44th Regiment*, displayed great gallantry in the ditches and entering the North Taku Fort by an embrasure during the assault. They were the first of the English troops established on the walls of the Fort. (*See also ROGERS, R.M. and McDOUGALL, John)

LE PATOUREL, Herbert Wallace **738**
T/Major (later Brigadier)   2nd Bn. The Hampshire Regiment (later The Royal Hampshire Regt.)
Other Decorations: —
Date of Gazette: 9 Mar. 1943
Place/Date of Birth: Guernsey, Channel Islands — 20 Jun. 1916
Place/Date of Death: Chewton Mendip, Somerset — 4 Sep. 1979
Memorials: — *South Bristol Crematorium*
Town/County Connections: Chewton Mendip, Somerset; Guernsey; Bristol .
Remarks: GSO 1 British Joint Services Mission to Washington D.C. 1958-60; Deputy Commander Ghana Army 1960-61; Deputy Commander 43 Div./Dis. 1961-62; DL, Avon
Account of Deed: On 3 Dec. 1942 at Tebourba, Tunisia, enemy forces were holding high ground and resisting all efforts to dislodge them. Major Le Patourel called for four volunteers to go with him and they attacked and silenced several of the machine-gun posts. When all his men became casualties, he went on alone to engage the enemy, using his pistol and hurling hand grenades. He was eventually wounded and taken prisoner.

LE QUESNE, Ferdinand Simeon **739**
Surgeon (later Lieutenant Colonel)   Medical Staff (later Royal Army Medical Corps)
Other Decorations: —
Date of Gazette: 29 Oct. 1889
Place/Date of Birth: Jersey, Channel Islands — 25 Dec. 1863
Place/Date of Death: Bristol — 14 Apr. 1950
Memorials: Canford Cemetery, Westbury-on-Trym, Bristol
Town/County Connections: Jersey; Bristol
Remarks: Served in the South African War 1899-1902
Account of Deed: On 4 May 1889 in the Burma Expedition, during the attack on the village of Tartan by a column of the Chin Field Force, Surgeon Le Quesne remained for the space of about ten minutes within five yards of the loopholed stockade, from which the enemy was firing, dressing with perfect coolness and self-possession, the wounds of an officer who shortly afterwards died. Surgeon Le Quesne was himself severely wounded later while attending to the wounds of another officer.

LESTER, Frank **740**
Private   10th Bn., The Lancashire Fusiliers
Other Decorations: —
Date of Gazette: 14 Dec. 1918
Place/Date of Birth: Huyton, Liverpool, Lancashire — 18 Feb. 1896
Place/Date of Death: Neuvilly, France — 12 Oct. 1918
Memorials: Neuvilly Communal Cemetery Extension, France; plaque in Public Library, Irby
Town/County Connections: Huyton, Liverpool; Irby, Cheshire
Remarks: —
Account of Deed: On 12 Oct. 1918 at Neuvilly, France, during the clearing of the village, Private Lester, with a party of seven men and an officer, was the first to enter a house from the back door and shot two Germans who were inside. As the party started to leave the house they found the street was swept by fire and an enemy sniper was covering the exit. Private Lester volunteered to tackle the sniper, which he did, but in killing him was himself mortally wounded.

LEWIS, Allan Leonard   **741**
Lance-Corporal   6th Bn., The Northamptonshire Regiment
Other Decorations: —
Date of Gazette: 31 Jan. 1919
Place/Date of Birth: Brilley, Near Whitney-on-Wye, Herefordshire — 28 Feb. 1895
Place/Date of Death: Near Lempire, France — 21 Sep. 1918   *Whitney church and Brilley*
Memorials: Vis-en-Artois Memorial, France   *W.M.*
Town/County Connections: Whitney-on-Wye, Herefordshire
Remarks: — *Convalescence at Longleat House, early 1917*
Account of Deed: On 18 Sep. 1918 at Rossnoy, near Lempire, France, Lance-Corporal Lewis was
in command of a section on the right of the attacking line, held up by intense machine-gun fire. He
saw that two guns were enfilading the line and crawled forward alone, successfully bombed the guns and by rifle fire made the
whole team surrender. On 21 Sep. he rushed his company through the enemy barrage, but was killed while getting his men
under cover from heavy machine-gun fire.

LEWIS, Hubert William   **742**
Private   11th Bn., The Welch Regiment
Other Decorations: —
Date of Gazette: 15 Dec. 1916
Place/Date of Birth: Milford Haven, Pembrokeshire, Wales — 1 May 1896
Place/Date of Death: Milford Haven, Pembrokeshire — 22 Feb. 1977
Memorials: Milford Cemetery, Milford Haven; War Memorial, Haverfordwest; Milford Haven
Museum *Grave.*
Town/County Connections: Milford Haven, Pembrokeshire
Remarks: Médaille Militaire (France); served in the Milford Haven Home Guard during Second
World War *Memorial: Haverfordwest W.M.*
Account of Deed: On 22/23 Oct. 1916 at Macukovo, near Seres, Salonika, when on duty during a raid, Private Lewis was twice
wounded on reaching the enemy trenches, but refused to be attended to. He was wounded again while searching enemy dug-
outs and again refused assistance. At this point three of the enemy approached and Private Lewis immediately attacked them
single-handed, capturing all three. Later, during the retirement he went to the assistance of a wounded man and, under heavy
shell and rifle fire, brought him back safely, after which he collapsed.

LIDDELL, Ian Oswald   **743**
T/Captain   5th Bn., Coldstream Guards
Other Decorations: —
Date of Gazette: 7 Jun. 1945
Place/Date of Birth: Shanghai, China — 19 Oct. 1919
Place/Date of Death: Near Rothenburg, Germany — 21 Apr. 1945
Memorials: Becklingen War Cemetery, Soltau, Germany; Mounton Church, Chepstow and St.
Thomas's Church, Shirenewton, Monmouthshire; Guards Chapel, Wellington Barracks
Town/County Connections: Chepstow, Monmouthshire *Harrow School*
Remarks: — *Name on W.M. Shirenewton, Mons. Guards Chapel.*
Account of Deed: On 3 Apr. 1945 near Lingen, Germany, a bridge over the River Ems was
covered by an enemy strong point and prepared for demolition with 500lb. bombs. Captain Liddell, in command of a company
which had been ordered to capture the bridge intact, ran forward alone and, scaling a 10ft. high road block, crossed the bridge
under intense fire. In full view of the enemy he disconnected the wires at both ends and also the charges under the bridge. His
task completed, he climbed on the road block and signalled to the leading platoon that the way was clear for the advance across
the river.

LIDDELL, John Aiden   **744**
Captain   3rd Bn., The Argyll and Sutherland Highlanders (Princess Louise's) and Royal Flying
Corps
Other Decorations: MC
Date of Gazette: 23 Aug. 1915
Place/Date of Birth: Newcastle upon Tyne, Northumberland — 3 Aug. 1888
Place/Date of Death: La Panne, Flanders — 31 Aug. 1915
Memorials: Basingstoke Old Cemetery, Hampshire; Sherfield-on-Lodden church, Hants.
Town/County Connections: Newcastle upon Tyne; Sherfield-on-Lodden, Hants.
Remarks: — *Name on W.M. Sherfield-on-Lodden. Stonyhurst College, Hants*
Account of Deed: On 31 Jul. 1915 while on flying reconnaissance over Ostend-Bruges-Ghent,
Captain Liddell was severely wounded in his right thigh. This caused momentary unconsciousness, but by great effort he
recovered partial control of his machine when it had dropped nearly 3,000ft. and succeeded, although fired on, in completing
the course and brought the plane back into the Allied lines. The control wheel and throttle control were smashed and also part
of the undercarriage and cockpit, but the machine and life of the observer were saved. Captain Liddell died a month later.

LINDSAY (later Lord WANTAGE), Robert James (LOYD- added later)   **745**
Captain (later Brigadier General)   Scots (Fusilier) Guards
Other Decorations: KCB
Date of Gazette: 24 Feb. 1857
Place/Date of Birth: Balcarres, Fife, Scotland — 17 Apr. 1832
Place/Date of Death: Lockinge, Berkshire — 10 Jun. 1901
Memorials: — Ardington, Berkshire.
Town/County Connections: Balcarres, Fife; Lockinge, Berkshire
Remarks: Légion d'Honneur (France); one of the founders of the British Red Cross Society;
Lieutenant-Colonel Commandant, Honourable Artillery Company 1866-81; Lord Lieutenant of
Berkshire, 1886
Account of Deed: On 20 Sep. 1854 at the Battle of the Alma, Crimea, Captain Lindsay, with a group of other officers, rallied a
party of NCOs and men round the Colours and they held their ground against an overwhelming force. On 5 Nov. at Inkerman,
Captain Lindsay, with a few men, charged a large party of Russians, driving them back and killing one of them himself.

LINTON, John Wallace   **746**
Commander   Royal Navy
Other Decorations: DSO, DSC
Date of Gazette: 25 May 1943
Place/Date of Birth: Malpas, Near Newport, Monmouthshire — 15 Oct. 1905
Place/Date of Death: Maddelina Harbour, Italy — 23 Mar. 1943
Memorials: Portsmouth Naval Memorial, Hampshire; Newport, Monmouthshire
Town/County Connections: Malpas, Newport, Monmouthshire
Remarks: — Panel 42 Column 3
Account of Deed: From the outbreak of the war in 1939 to May 1943 which was the month of
HMS *Turbulent's* last patrol in the Mediterranean, Commander Linton was responsible for sinking
approximately 100,000 tons of enemy shipping, including a cruiser, a destroyer, a U-boat and 28 other ships. In addition
Turbulent destroyed three trains by gun fire. In his last year Commander Linton spent 254 days at sea, submerged for nearly
half the time, his ship was hunted 13 times and had 250 depth charges aimed at her.

LISLE PHILLIPPS, Everard Aloysius — see **PHILLIPPS,** Everard Aloysius Lisle

LISTER, Joseph   **747**
Sergeant   1st Bn., The Lancashire Fusiliers
Other Decorations: —
Date of Gazette: 26 Nov. 1917
Place/Date of Birth: Higher Broughton, Salford, Lancashire — 19 Oct. 1886
Place/Date of Death: Reddish, Stockport, Cheshire — 19 Jan. 1963
Memorials: Willow Grove Cemetery, Reddish, Stockport   Grave.
Town/County Connections: Salford, Lancashire; Stockport, Cheshire
Remarks: —
Account of Deed: On 9 Oct. 1917 east of Ypres, Belgium, seeing that the advance of his company
was held up by machine-gun fire from the direction of a pill box, Sergeant Lister dashed ahead of
his men and found the gun — he shot two of the gunners and the remainder surrendered. He then went to the pill box and
shouted to the occupants to surrender. They did so with the exception of one man whom the sergeant shot, whereupon about
100 of the enemy emerged from the shell-holes further to the rear and surrendered.

LLOYD, Owen Edward Pennefather (later Sir Owen)   **748**
Surgeon Major (later Major General)   Army Medical Service (later Royal Army Medical Corps)
Other Decorations: KCB
Date of Gazette: 2 Jan. 1894
Place/Date of Birth: Co. Roscommon, Ireland — 1 Jan. 1854
Place/Date of Death: St. Leonards-on-Sea, Sussex — 5 Jul. 1941
Memorials: Kensal Green Cemetery, London
Town/County Connections: St. Leonards-on-Sea, Sussex
Remarks: —
Account of Deed: On 6 Jan. 1893, during the Kachin Expedition, Burma, while an attack was in
progress on Fort Sima, Surgeon Major Lloyd went, with an Indian NCO to the assistance of the
commanding officer who was wounded. Surgeon Major Lloyd then stayed with the officer while the NCO went back to fetch
further help in carrying the wounded man back to the fort, where he died a few minutes later. The enemy were within 10 to 15
paces during this time, keeping up a heavy fire, and Surgeon Major Lloyd was wounded while returning to the fort.

LODGE, Isaac   **749**
Gunner (later Bombardier)   'Q' Bty., Royal Horse Artillery
Other Decorations: —
Date of Gazette: 26 Jun. 1900
Place/Date of Birth: Great Canfield, near Dunmow, Essex — 6 May 1866
Place/Date of Death: Hyde Park, London — 13 Jun. 1923
Memorials: — Hendon Cemetery. Headstone erected by Artillery on 31·3·1995
Town/County Connections: Great Canfield, Dunmow, Essex
Remarks: —
Account of Deed: On 31 Mar. 1900 at Korn Spruit, South Africa, two batteries of the Royal Horse Artillery were ambushed with the loss of most of the baggage column and five guns of the leading battery. When the alarm was given, 'Q' Battery went into action 1150 yards from the spruit, until the order to retire was received, when the major* commanding the battery ordered the guns and their limbers to be run back by hand to a safe place. This most exhausting operation was carried out by, among others, Gunner Lodge, a sergeant and a driver* and when at last all but one of the guns and one limber had been moved to safety, the battery was reformed. (Award by ballot. *See also HORNBY, E.J.P-., PARKER, C.E.H. and GLASOCK, H.H.)

LOOSEMORE, Arnold   **750**
Private (later Sergeant)   8th Bn., The Duke of Wellington's (West Riding) Regiment
Other Decorations: DCM
Date of Gazette: 14 Sep. 1917
Place/Date of Birth: Sheffield, Yorkshire — 7 Jun. 1896
Place/Date of Death: Sheffield, Yorkshire — 11 Apr. 1924
Memorials: Cross in churchyard at Ecclesall, Sheffield
Town/County Connections: Sheffield, Yorkshire
Remarks: —
Account of Deed: On 11 Aug. 1917 south of Langemarck, Belgium, during the attack on a strongly-held enemy position and his platoon having been held up by heavy machine-gun fire, Private Loosemore crawled through partially-cut wire, dragging his Lewis gun with him and single-handed dealt with a strong party of the enemy, killing about 20 of them. Immediately afterwards his Lewis gun was destroyed and three of the enemy rushed at him, but he shot them with his revolver. Later he shot several enemy snipers, and on returning to the original post he brought back a wounded comrade under heavy fire.

LORD, David Samuel Anthony   **751**
Flight Lieutenant   271 Squadron, Royal Air Force
Other Decorations: DFC
Date of Gazette: 13 Nov. 1945
Place/Date of Birth: Cork, Ireland — 18 Oct. 1913
Place/Date of Death: Arnhem — 19 Sep. 1944 → Plot 4. Row B. Grave 5
Memorials: Arnhem (Oosterbeek) War Cemetery, Holland; St. Mary's R.C. Pro-Cathedral, Wrexham; Down Ampney Church, Gloucestershire
Town/County Connections: Wrexham, Denbighshire, Wales; Cork Ireland
Remarks: Memorial Down Ampney Church Glos.
Account of Deed: On 19 Sep. 1944 at Arnhem, Holland, the British 1st Airborne Division were in desperate need of supplies. Flight Lieutenant Lord, flying a Dakota through intense enemy A.A. fire was twice hit, and had one engine burning. He managed to drop his supplies, but at the end of the run found that there were two containers remaining. Although he knew that one of his wings might collapse at any moment he nevertheless made a second run to drop the last supplies, then ordered his crew to bale out. A few seconds later the Dakota crashed in flames with its pilot.

LOUDOUN-SHAND, Stewart Walter — see **SHAND,** stewart Walter LOUDOUN-

LOWERSON, Albert David   **752**
Sergeant   21st Bn. (Victoria), Australian Imperial Force
Other Decorations: —
Date of Gazette: 14 Dec. 1918
Place/Date of Birth: Myrtleford, Bogong, Victoria, Australia — 2 Aug. 1896
Place/Date of Death: Myrtleford, Victoria — 15 Dec. 1945
Memorials: Myrtleford Cemetery, Victoria, Australia; Australian War Memorial, Canberra
Town/County Connections: —
Remarks: —
Account of Deed: On 1 Sep. 1918 at Mont St. Quentin, France, an attacking party was held up by a strong-point manned by 12 machine-guns. Sergeant Lowerson took seven men and, attacking the flanks of the post, rushed the strong-point and captured it, together with the 12 guns and 50 prisoners. He was severely wounded in the right thigh, but refused to leave the front line until the position had been consolidated.

LOYD-LINDSAY, Robert James — see **LINDSAY,** Robert James (LOYD-)

LUCAS, Charles Davis   **753**
Mate (later Rear-Admiral)   Royal Navy
Other Decorations: —
Date of Gazette: 24 Feb. 1857
Place/Date of Birth: Drumargole, Armagh, Ireland — 19 Feb. 1834
Place/Date of Death: Great Culverden, Kent — 7 Aug. 1914
Memorials: St. Lawrence's Church, Mereworth, near Maidstone, Kent
Town/County Connections: Drumargole, Armagh; Great Culverden, near Tunbridge Wells,
Kent; Kensington, London; Argyllshire, Scotland
Remarks: The first act of bravery to be rewarded with the VC. Commanded the Ballachulish
Corps in Scotland 1873-83 (with the rank of Brigadier General)
Account of Deed: On 21 Jun. 1854 in the Baltic, HMS *Hecla*, with two other ships, was bombarding Bomarsund, a fort in the
Aland Islands. The fire was returned from the shore, and at the height of the action a live shell landed on *Hecla's* upper deck,
with its fuse still hissing. All hands were ordered to fling themselves flat on the deck, but Mr. Lucas with great presence of mind
ran forward and hurled the shell into the sea, where it exploded with a tremendous roar before it hit the water. Thanks to Mr.
Lucas's action no one was killed or seriously wounded.

LUCAS, John   **754**
Colour-Sergeant (later Sergeant-Major)   40th Regiment (later The South Lancashire Regiment —
The Prince of Wales's Volunteers)
Other Decorations: —
Date of Gazette: 17 Jul. 1861
Place/Date of Birth: Clashgonny, Bagnalstown, Carlow, Ireland — 1827
Place/Date of Death: Dublin — 29 Feb. 1892
Memorials: —
Town/County Connections: Bagnalstown, Carlow; Dublin
Remarks: —
Account of Deed: On 18 Mar. 1861 in New Zealand, Colour-Sergeant Lucas was with a party
employed as skirmishers, when they were suddenly ambushed. Three men were wounded, two of them mortally and help was
called for, but when a relief party arrived one of them fell and a lieutenant was also wounded. Sergeant Lucas, under heavy fire
from the rebels, who were not more than 30 yards away, immediately ran to the assistance of the officer and sent a man with
him to the rear. He then took charge of the arms belonging to the killed and wounded until the arrival of support troops.

LUKE, Frederick   **755**
Driver (later Sergeant)   37th Bty., Royal Field Artillery
Other Decorations: —
Date of Gazette: 25 Nov. 1914
Place/Date of Birth: West Tytherley, near Romsey, Hampshire — 29 Sep. 1895
Place/Date of Death: Glasgow — 11 Mar. 1983
Memorials: —
Town/County Connections: West Tytherley and Lockerley, Hampshire; Glasgow
Remarks: Served with the R.A.F. Regiment in Second World War
Account of Deed: On 26 Aug. 1914 at Le Cateau, France, when a captain* of the same battery was
trying to save two guns which had been recaptured, Driver Luke and another driver* volunteered
to help and gave great assistance in the eventual saving of one of the guns. At the time they were under heavy fire from the
enemy who were only 100 yards away. (*See also REYNOLDS, D. and DRAIN, J.H.C.)

LUMLEY, Charles   **756**
Captain (later Major)   97th Regiment (later The Queen's Own Royal West Kent Regiment)
Other Decorations: —
Date of Gazette: 24 Feb. 1857
Place/Date of Birth: Forres, Morayshire — 1824
Place/Date of Death: Brecon, Wales — 17 Oct. 1858   *Committed Suicide. Buried Brecon*
Memorials: Brecon Cathedral Churchyard   *Cathedral Churchyard*
Town/County Connections: Forres, Morayshire; Brecon, Wales   *(NE Corner)*
Remarks: Légion d'Honneur (France)
Account of Deed: On 8 Sep. 1855 in the Crimea at the assault on the Redan, Captain Lumley was
among the first inside the work, where he was immediately attacked by three Russian gunners
who were reloading a field piece. He shot two of them with his revolver when he was knocked down by a stone which stunned
him for a moment, but on recovery, he drew his sword and was in the act of cheering his men on, when he was severely
wounded in the mouth.

LUMSDEN, Frederick William   **757**
Major (later Brigadier General)   Royal Marine Artillery
Other Decorations: CB, DSO & 3 Bars
Date of Gazette: 8 Jun. 1917
Place/Date of Birth: Fyzabad, India — 14 Dec. 1872
Place/Date of Death: Blairvill, near Arras, France — 4 Jun. 1918
Memorials: Berles New Military Cemetery, France
Town/County Connections: —
Remarks: Croix de Guerre (France)
Account of Deed: On 3/4 Apr. 1917 at Francilly, France, Major Lumsden undertook to bring in six captured enemy field-guns which had been left in dug-in positions 300 yards in front of our own troops, and the enemy were keeping these guns under very heavy fire. Major Lumsden led four artillery teams and a party of infantry through the hostile barrage, and despite casualties they eventually got all the guns away. The major himself made three journeys to the guns and then stayed there directing operations until the last gun had been taken back.

LYALL, Graham Thomson   **758**
Lieutenant (later Colonel)   102nd Bn., 2nd Central Ontario Regiment, C.E.F.
Other Decorations: —
Date of Gazette: 14 Dec. 1918
Place/Date of Birth: Manchester, Lancashire — 8 Mar. 1892
Place/Date of Death: Mersa Matruh, Egypt — 28 Nov. 1941
Memorials: Halfaya Sollum War Cemetery, Egypt
Town/County Connections: Nelson, Lancashire
Remarks: Served with Royal Army Ordnance Corps in the Second World War
Account of Deed: On 27 Sep. 1918 north of Cambrai, France, Lieutenant Lyall led his platoon in the capture of a strong point, together with 13 prisoners, one field gun and four machine-guns. Later, leading his men against another strong point he rushed forward alone and captured the position single-handed, taking 45 prisoners and five machine-guns. The completion of his final objective resulted in the capture of 47 prisoners. On 1 Oct. in the neighbourhood of Blecourt, he captured a strongly defended position which yielded 60 prisoners and 17 machine-guns. During both these operations, on attaining his objectives, Lieutenant Lyall tended the wounded under fire.

LYELL, The Lord, Charles Anthony   **759**
T/Captain   1st Bn., Scots Guards
Other Decorations: —
Date of Gazette: 12 Aug. 1943
Place/Date of Birth: Cadogan Gardens, London — 14 Jun. 1913
Place/Date of Death: Bou Arada, Tunisia — 27 Apr. 1943
Memorials: Massicault War Cemetery, Tunisia
Town/County Connections: London; Kirriemuir, Angus, Scotland
Remarks: —
Account of Deed: During the period 22/27 Apr. 1943 near Dj Bou Arada, Tunisia, Captain Lord Lyell's outstanding leadership and gallantry enabled his company to take its objective. On 27 Apr. accompanied by a sergeant, a lance-corporal and two guardsmen, he led an attack on an enemy post consisting of an 88mm. gun and a heavy machine-gun in two separate pits. He destroyed the crew of the machine-gun with a hand grenade and then, three of the party having become casualties, and with the lance-corporal to give covering fire he leapt into the second pit, killing several of the crew before being overwhelmed and killed. Both the guns had been silenced.

LYNN, John   **760**
Private   2nd Bn., The Lancashire Fusiliers
Other Decorations: DCM
Date of Gazette: 29 Jun. 1915
Place/Date of Birth: Forest Hill, London — 1887
Place/Date of Death: St. Julien, Ypres — 2 May 1915
Memorials: Grootebeek British Cemetery, Belgium
Town/County Connections: Forest Hill, London
Remarks: Cross of the Order of St. George, 4th Class (Russia)
Account of Deed: On 2 May 1915 near Ypres, Belgium, when the Germans were advancing behind their wave of asphyxiating gas, Private Lynn, although almost overcome by the deadly fumes, handled his machine-gun with great effect against the enemy, and when he could not see them, he moved his gun higher up the parapet so that he could fire more effectively. This eventually checked any further advance and the outstanding courage displayed by this soldier had a great effect upon his comrades in the very trying circumstances. Private Lynn died later from the effects of gas poisoning. *Flanders X in Church, Bury, Lancs*

LYONS, John
Private (later Corporal)   19th Regiment (later The Yorkshire Regiment — Alexandra, Princess of Wales's Own)
Other Decorations: —
Date of Gazette: 24 Feb. 1857
Place/Date of Birth: Carlow, Ireland — 1823
Place/Date of Death: Naas, Co. Kildare, Ireland — 20 Apr. 1867
Memorials: —
Town/County Connections: Carlow and Naas, Ireland
Remarks: Légion d'Honneur (France)
Account of Deed: On 10 Jun. 1855 in the Crimea, Private Lyons picked up a live shell which had fallen among the guard of the trenches, and threw it over the parapet, thus saving many lives.

761

LYSONS, Henry
Lieutenant (later Colonel)   2nd Bn., The Cameronians (Scottish Rifles)
Other Decorations: CB
Date of Gazette: 5 Apr. 1882
Place/Date of Birth: Morden, Surrey — 30 Jul. 1858
Place/Date of Death: London — 24 Jul. 1907
Memorials: St. Peter's Churchyard, Rodmarton, Cirencester, Glos. *Grave*
Town/County Connections: Morden, Surrey; Rodmarton, Cirencester, Glos.
Remarks: — *Wellington College, Berks*
Account of Deed: On 28 Mar. 1879 at the Zlobane Mountain, South Africa (Zulu War), Lieutenant Lysons, with a captain and a private* dashed forward in advance of the party which had been ordered to dislodge the enemy from a commanding position in natural caves up the mountain. The path was so narrow that they had to advance in single file and the captain who arrived first at the mouth of the cave was instantly killed. Lieutenant Lysons and the private, undeterred by the death of their leader, immediately sprang forward and cleared the enemy out of their stronghold. (*See also FOWLER, E.J.)

762

LYSTER, Harry Hammon
Lieutenant (later Lieutenant General)   72nd Bengal Native Infantry
Other Decorations: CB
Date of Gazette: 21 Oct. 1859
Place/Date of Birth: Black Rock, Co. Dublin — 24 Dec. 1830
Place/Date of Death: London — 1 Feb. 1922
Memorials: —
Town/County Connections: Black Rock, Dublin; London
Remarks: Uncle of Captain H.L. Reed, VC.
Account of Deed: On 23 May 1858 at Calpee, India, Lieutenant Lyster charged alone and broke the skirmishing square of the retreating rebel army and killed two or three sepoys in the conflict.

763

McARTHUR, Thomas — see **ARTHUR,** Thomas

McAULAY, John
Sergeant   1st Bn., Scots Guards
Other Decorations: DCM
Date of Gazette: 11 Jan. 1918
Place/Date of Birth: Kinghorn, Fife, Scotland — 27 Dec. 1888
Place/Date of Death: Glasgow — 14 Jan. 1956
Memorials: —
Town/County Connections: Kinghorn, Fife; Plean, Stirling, Scotland
Remarks: —
Account of Deed: On 27 Nov. 1917 at Fontaine Notre Dame, France, when all his officers had become casualties, Sergeant McAulay assumed command of the company and under shell and machine-gun fire successfully held and consolidated the objectives gained. He reorganised the company and noticing a counter-attack developing, repulsed it by the skilful and bold use of machine-guns, causing heavy enemy casualties. The sergeant also carried his company commander, who was mortally wounded, to a place of safety.

764

McBEAN, William   765
Lieutenant and Adjutant (later Major General)   93rd Regiment (later The Argyll and Sutherland Highlanders — Princess Louise's)
Other Decorations: —
Date of Gazette: 24 Dec. 1858
Place/Date of Birth: Inverness, Scotland — 1 Jan. 1818
Place/Date of Death: Shooter's Hill, London — 23 Jun. 1878
Memorials: (Buried in Edinburgh)
Town/County Connections: Inverness; London
Remarks: He held every rank from Private to Major General
Account of Deed: On 11 Mar. 1858 at Lucknow, India, Lieutenant McBean killed 11 of the enemy with his own hand in the main breach of the Begum Bagh.

McBEATH, Robert   766
Lance-Corporal   1/5th Bn., The Seaforth Highlanders (Ross-shire Buffs, Duke of Albany's)
Other Decorations: —
Date of Gazette: 11 Jan. 1918
Place/Date of Birth: Kinlochbervie, Lairg, Sutherland, Scotland — 22 Dec. 1897
Place/Date of Death: Vancouver, Canada — 9 Oct. 1922
Memorials: —
Town/County Connections: Kinlochbervie, Lairg
Remarks: —
Account of Deed: On 20 Nov. 1917 west of Cambrai, France, when the advance was checked by a nest of machine-guns and heavy casualties resulted, Lance-Corporal McBeath volunteered to deal with these guns and moved off alone, armed with a Lewis gun and a revolver. Finding that several other machine-guns were in action, he attacked them, with the assistance of a tank, and drove the gunners to ground in a deep dug-out. The lance-corporal rushed in after them, shot the first man who opposed him then drove the remainder of the garrison out of the dug-out, capturing three officers and 30 men.

McCARTHY, Lawrence Dominic   767
Lieutenant   16th Bn. (S.A. & W.A.), Australian Imperial Force
Other Decorations: —
Date of Gazette: 14 Dec. 1918
Place/Date of Birth: York, Western Australia — 21 Jan. 1892
Place/Date of Death: Heidelberg, Victoria, Australia — 25 May 1975
Memorials: Springvale Crematorium, Melbourne; Australian War Memorial, Canberra
Town/County Connections: —
Remarks: —
Account of Deed: On 23 Aug. 1918, near Madam Wood, east of Vermandovillers, France, the battalion was heavily opposed by well-posted machine-guns. Lieutenant McCarthy, realizing the situation, dashed across the open ground with two men to the nearest post, where, having out-distanced his companions, he put the gun out of action, then continued fighting his way down the trench. Later, having been joined by one of his men, together they bombed their way along the trench until contact was established with an adjoining unit. During this action Lieutenant McCarthy had killed 22 of the enemy, taken 50 prisoners and captured 5 machine-guns.

No photograph available

McCORRIE (or McCURRY), Charles   768
Private   57th Regiment (later The Middlesex Regiment — Duke of Cambridge's Own)
Other Decorations: —
Date of Gazette: 24 Feb. 1857
Place/Date of Birth: Killeard, Co. Antrim, Ireland — 1830
Place/Date of Death: Malta — 9 Apr. 1857
Memorials: —
Town/County Connections: Killeard, Co. Antrim
Remarks: —
Account of Deed: On 23 Jun. 1855 in the Crimea Private McCorrie threw over the parapet a live shell which had been thrown from the enemy's battery.

McCREA, John Frederick   **769**
Surgeon (later Surgeon Major)   1st Cape Mounted Yeomanry, South African Forces
Other Decorations: —
Date of Gazette: 28 Jun. 1881
Place/Date of Birth: St. Peter Port, Guernsey, Channel Islands — 2 Apr. 1854
Place/Date of Death: Kokstad, East Griqualand — 16 Jul. 1894
Memorials: Kokstad Cemetery, East Griqualand
Town/County Connections: St. Peter Port, Guernsey
Remarks: —
Account of Deed: On 14 Jan. 1881, at Tweefontein, Basutoland, South Africa, the burghers had been forced to retire under a most determined enemy attack, with a loss of 16 killed and 21 wounded. Surgeon McCrea was the only doctor present and notwithstanding a serious wound on the breast bone, which he dressed himself, he most gallantly took the casualties into shelter and continued to attend to the wounded throughout the day. Had it not been for this devotion to duty on the part of Surgeon McCrea, there would undoubtedly have been much greater suffering and loss of life.

McCUDDEN, James Thomas Byrford   **770**
T/Captain (later Major)   General List and 56 Squadron, Royal Flying Corps
Other Decorations: DSO & Bar, MC & Bar, MM
Date of Gazette: 2 Apr. 1918
Place/Date of Birth: Gillingham, Kent — 28 Mar. 1895
Place/Date of Death: Marquise, France — 9 Jul. 1918
Memorials: Wavans British Cemetery, France; Sheerness Parish Church and War Memorial, Gillingham, Kent
Town/County Connections: Gillingham, Kent
Remarks: Croix de Guerre (France); Author of *Five Years in the RFC*
Account of Deed: During the period Aug. 1917 to Mar. 1918, on aerial patrols, Captain McCudden showed conspicuous bravery, exceptional perseverance and a high devotion to duty. As patrol leader he exercised the utmost skill not only in the manner in which he attacked and destroyed the enemy, but in the way in which, during aerial fights, he protected the newer members of his flight, thus keeping down the casualties to a minimum. By Mar. 1918 he had accounted for 57 enemy aircraft, some single-handed, some while leading his men. As an example of his exploits, on 16 Feb. 1918 he destroyed three two-seater aeroplanes in the morning patrol and added a fourth on his second sortie.

McDERMOND, John   **771**
Private   47th Regiment (later The Loyal North Lancashire Regiment)
Other Decorations: —
Date of Gazette: 24 Feb. 1857
Place/Date of Birth: Clackmannan, Scotland — 1832
Place/Date of Death: Glasgow — 22nd Jul. 1868
Memorials: —
Town/County Connections: Clackmannan and Glasgow
Remarks: —
Account of Deed: On 5 Nov. 1854 at the Battle of Inkerman, Crimea, Private McDermond saved the life of a colonel who was lying wounded on the ground surrounded by the enemy. Private McDermond rushed to the rescue and killed the man who had wounded the colonel.

MacDONALD, Henry   **772**
Colour-Sergeant (later Hon. Captain)   Corps of Royal Engineers
Other Decorations: —
Date of Gazette: 2 Jun. 1858
Place/Date of Birth: Inverness, Scotland — 28 May 1823
Place/Date of Death: Glasgow — 15 Feb. 1893
Memorials: Western Necropolis, Glasgow   *Grave*
Town/County Connections: Inverness and Glasgow
Remarks: —
Account of Deed: On 19 Apr. 1855 at Sebastopol, Crimea, Colour-Sergeant MacDonald acted with great gallantry when engaged in effecting a lodgement in the enemy's rifle pits in front of the left advance of the Right Attack. Subsequently when the Engineer officers were badly wounded Colour-Sergeant MacDonald took command and he determinedly persisted in carrying on the sap notwithstanding the repeated attacks of the enemy.

McDONELL, William Fraser **773**
Mr.   Bengal Civil Service
Other Decorations: —
Date of Gazette: 17 Feb. 1860
Place/Date of Birth: Cheltenham, Gloucestershire — 17 Dec. 1829
Place/Date of Death: Cheltenham, Gloucestershire — 31 Jul. 1894
Memorials: St. Peter's Churchyard, Leckhampton, Cheltenham
Town/County Connections: Cheltenham, Gloucestershire
Remarks: Judge of the High Court of Judicature, Calcutta 1874-86
Account of Deed: On 30 Jul. 1857 during the retreat from Arrah, India, Mr. McDonell and 35 soldiers were in a boat hoping to escape, but the oars had been taken away by the rebels and the rudder tied to the side of the boat. Mr. McDonell climbed out of the boat under incessant fire from the enemy and with considerable difficulty cut through the lashing which secured the rudder. He then guided the boat himself, and helped by a breeze, crossed the river to safety.

No photograph available

McDOUGALL, John **774**
Private   44th Regiment (later The Essex Regiment)
Other Decorations: —
Date of Gazette: 13 Aug. 1861
Place/Date of Birth: Old Town, Edinburgh — 1840
Place/Date of Death: Edinburgh — 10 Mar. 1869
Memorials: —
Town/County Connections: Edinburgh
Remarks: —
Account of Deed: On 21 Aug. 1860 at the Taku Forts, China, Private McDougall with an officer of his regiment* and a lieutenant of the 67th Regiment* displayed great gallantry in swimming the ditches and entering the North Taku Fort by an embrasure during the assault. They were the first of the English established on the walls of the Fort. (*See also ROGERS, R.M. and LENON, E.H.)

McDOUGALL, Stanley Robert **775**
Sergeant   47th Bn. (Queensland), Australian Imperial Force
Other Decorations: MM
Date of Gazette: 3 May 1918
Place/Date of Birth: Recherche, Tasmania — 23 July 1890
Place/Date of Death: Hobart, Tasmania — 7 Jul. 1968
Memorials: Norwood Crematorium, Mitchell, Canberra; Australian War Memorial, Canberra
Town/County Connections: —
Remarks: —
Account of Deed: On 28 Mar. 1918 at Dernancourt, France, when an enemy attack succeeded in securing a foothold in the Allied line, Sergeant McDougall charged the second wave single-handed, killing seven and capturing a machine-gun, which he turned on the attackers, routing them and causing many casualties. He continued his attack until his ammunition ran out, when he seized a bayonet and charged again, killing three men and an officer. Then, using a Lewis gun, he killed many more of the enemy and made it possible for 33 prisoners to be taken. His prompt action saved the line and halted the enemy advance.

MacDOWELL, Thain Wendell **776**
Captain (later Colonel)   38th Ottawa Bn., Eastern Ontario Regiment, C.E.F.
Other Decorations: DSO
Date of Gazette: 8 Jun. 1917
Place/Date of Birth: Lachute, Quebec, Canada — 16 Sep. 1890
Place/Date of Death: Nassau, Bahamas — 29 Mar. 1960
Memorials: Oakland Cemetery, Brockville, Ontario, Canada (Richardson Plot)
Town/County Connections: —
Remarks: —
Account of Deed: On 9 Apr. 1917 at Vimy Ridge, France, Captain MacDowell, with the assistance of two runners, was able, in the face of great difficulties, to capture two machine-guns besides two officers and 75 men. Although wounded in the hand, he continued for five days to hold the position gained, in spite of heavy shell-fire, until eventually relieved by his battalion.

McFADZEAN, William Frederick   **777**
Private   14th Bn., The Royal Irish Rifles
Other Decorations: —
Date of Gazette: 8 Jun. 1917
Place/Date of Birth: Lurgan, Co.Armagh, Ireland — 9 Oct. 1895
Place/Date of Death: Thiepval, France — 1 July 1916
Memorials: Thiepval Memorial, France; Newtonbreda Presbyterian church, Belfast
Town/County Connections: Lurgan, Co. Armagh; Cregagh, Belfast
Remarks: —
Account of Deed: On 1 Jul. 1916, near Thiepval Wood, France, in a concentration trench, a box of bombs being opened for distribution prior to an attack slipped down into the trench, which was crowded with men, and two of the safety pins fell out. Private McFadzean, instantly realizing the danger to his comrades, with heroic courage threw himself on the top of the bombs, which exploded, blowing him to pieces, but only one other man was injured. He well knew the danger, being himself a bomber, but without a moment's hesitation he gave his life for his comrades.

McGAW, Samuel   **778**
Lance-Sergeant (later Sergeant)   42nd Regiment (later The Black Watch (Royal Highlanders))
Other Decorations: —
Date of Gazette: 28 Mar. 1874
Place/Date of Birth: Kirkmichael, Ayrshire, Scotland — 1838
Place/Date of Death: Larnaca, Cyprus — 22 Jul. 1878
Memorials: English Cemetery, Kyrenia, Cyprus
Town/County Connections: Kirkmichael, Ayrshire
Remarks: —
Account of Deed: On 21 Jan. 1874 at the Battle of Amoaful, (Ashanti War), West Africa, Lance-Sergeant McGaw led his section through the bush in a most excellent manner and continued to do so throughout the day, although badly wounded early in the engagement.

McGEE, Lewis   **779**
Sergeant   40th Bn. (Tasmania), Australian Imperial Force
Other Decorations: —
Date of Gazette: 26 Nov. 1917
Place/Date of Birth: Ross, Tasmania — 13 May 1888
Place/Date of Death: Passchendaele, Ypres — 13 Oct. 1917
Memorials: Tyne Cot Cemetery, Passchendaele, Belgium; Australian War Memorial, Canberra
Town/County Connections: —
Remarks: —
Account of Deed: On 4 Oct. 1917, east of Ypres, Belgium, Sergeant McGee's platoon was suffering severely and the advance of the company was stopped by machine-gun fire from a pill box post. Sergeant McGee rushed to the post armed only with a revolver, shooting some of the crew and capturing the rest, which enabled the advance to proceed. He reorganized the remnants of his platoon and did splendid work during the consolidation of the position. His coolness and bravery contributed largely to the success of the company's operation. He was killed in action shortly afterwards.

McGOVERN, John   **780**
Private   1st Bengal Fusiliers (later The Royal Munster Fusiliers)
Other Decorations: —
Date of Gazette: 18 Jun. 1859
Place/Date of Birth: Templeport, Co. Cavan, Ireland — 16 May 1825
Place/Date of Death: Hamilton, Ontario, Canada — 22 Nov. 1888
Memorials: —
Town/County Connections: Templeport, Co. Cavan
Remarks: —
Account of Deed: On 23 Jun. 1857 at Delhi, India, Private McGovern carried into the camp a wounded comrade under heavy fire from the enemy's battery, at the risk of his own life. His gallantry was conspicuous during the whole period of these operations.

McGREGOR, David Stuart
781

Lieutenant   6th Bn., The Royal Scots (The Lothian Regiment) and 29th Bn., Machine Gun Corps
Other Decorations: —
Date of Gazette: 14 Dec. 1918
Place/Date of Birth: Edinburgh — 16 Oct. 1895
Place/Date of Death: Hoogemolen, Belgium — 22 Oct. 1918
Memorials: Staceghem Communal Cemetery, Belgium
Town/County Connections: Edinburgh
Remarks: —
Account of Deed: On 22 Oct. 1918 near Hoogemolen, Belgium, Lieutenant McGregor concealed his guns on a limber under the bank of a sunken road, but immediately the troops advanced they were subjected to such intense enfilade machine-gun fire that he realised it was impossible to get the guns carried forward without great delay. Having ordered the teams to take a safer route, he lay flat on the limber, the driver then galloped forward under the heaviest machine-gun fire to cover beyond, the guns were put into action and the advance resumed. Lieutenant McGregor continued directing the fire until he was killed.

MacGREGOR, John
782

T/Captain (later Lieutenant Colonel)   2nd Canadian Mounted Rifles, 1st Central Ontario Regiment, C.E.F.
Other Decorations: MC & Bar, DCM, ED
Date of Gazette: 6 Jan. 1919
Place/Date of Birth: Cawdor, Nairn, Scotland — 1 Feb. 1889
Place/Date of Death: Powell River, British Columbia, Canada — 9 Jun. 1952
Memorials: Cranberry Lake Cemetery, Powell River, British Columbia
Town/County Connections: Cawdor, Nairn, Scotland
Remarks: —
Account of Deed: During the period 29 Sep./3 Oct. 1918 near Cambrai, France, Captain MacGregor acted with most conspicuous bravery and leadership. He led his company under intense fire, and although wounded, located and put out of action enemy machine-guns which were checking progress, killing four and taking eight prisoners. He then reorganised his command under heavy fire and in the face of stubborn resistance continued the advance. Later, after a personal daylight reconnaissance under heavy fire, he established his company in Neuville St. Remy, thereby greatly assisting the advance into Tilloy.

No photograph available

McGREGOR, Roderick
783

Private   1st Bn., The Rifle Brigade (Prince Consort's Own)
Other Decorations: —
Date of Gazette: 24 Feb. 1857
Place/Date of Birth: Inverness, Scotland — 1824
Place/Date of Death: Buntoit, Urquhart, Inverness-shire, Scotland — 10 Aug. 1888
Memorials: The Rifle Brigade memorial, Winchester Cathedral
Town/County Connections: Inverness, Scotland
Remarks: —
Account of Deed: On 22 Apr. 1855 at the Quarries, Crimea, a bandsman going to fetch water from a well in front of the advanced trench, was killed. A number of men at once rushed out determined to drive the Russian riflemen from the pits which they occupied. Private McGregor and two others were the first to reach the Russians, whom they drove out, killing some. Later, in July, Private McGregor was employed as a sharpshooter in the advance trenches before Sebastopol. He crossed an open space under fire and, taking cover under a rock, dislodged two Russians who were occupying a rifle pit.

McGUFFIE, Louis
784

A/Sergeant   1/5th Bn., The King's Own Scottish Borderers
Other Decorations: —
Date of Gazette: 14 Dec. 1918
Place/Date of Birth: Wigtown, Scotland — 15 Mar. 1893
Place/Date of Death: Wytschaete, Belgium — 4 Oct. 1918
Memorials: Zantvoorde British Cemetery, Belgium
Town/County Connections: Wigtown, Scotland
Remarks: —
Account of Deed: On 28 Sep. 1918 near Wytschaete, Belgium, during an advance Sergeant McGuffie entered several enemy dug-outs and, single-handed, took many prisoners. During subsequent operations he dealt similarly with dug-out after dug-out, forcing one officer and 25 other ranks to surrender. During the consolidation of the first objective, he pursued and brought back several of the enemy who were slipping away and was also instrumental in rescuing some British soldiers who were being led off as prisoners. Later in the day, while commanding a platoon, he took many more prisoners, but was killed a few days later.

No photograph available

McGUIRE, James   **785**
Sergeant   1st Bengal Fusiliers (later The Royal Munster Fusiliers)
Other Decorations: —
Date of Gazette: 24 Dec. 1858
Place/Date of Birth: Enniskillen, Ireland — 1827
Place/Date of Death: Londonderry, Ireland — 22 Dec. 1862
Memorials: —
Town/County Connections: Enniskillen and Londonderry
Remarks: —
Account of Deed: On 14 Sep. 1857 at Delhi, India, when the troops were waiting at the Kabul Gate, reserve ammunition was being carried up on to the ramparts to be put into a small magazine, but before it could be safely stowed away, three boxes exploded and two were set on fire by enemy shot. Sergeant McGuire and a drummer* who were part of the ammunition guard, seeing the danger of the fire spreading, seized the two boxes which were alight and threw them over the ramparts into the canal, thus saving many lives. (*See also RYAN, M.)

McHALE, Patrick   **786**
Private   1st Bn., 5th Regiment (later The Northumberland Fusiliers)
Other Decorations: —
Date of Gazette: 19 Jun. 1860
Place/Date of Birth: Killala, Co. Mayo, Ireland — 1826
Place/Date of Death: Shorncliffe, Kent — 26 Oct. 1866
Memorials: Shorncliffe Military Cemetery, Folkestone *grave*
Town/County Connections: Killala, Co. Mayo; Shorncliffe, Kent
Remarks: —
Account of Deed: On 2 Oct. 1857 at Lucknow, India, Private McHale was the first man at the capture of one of the guns at the Cawnpore Battery. On 22 Dec. he was the first to take possession of one of the guns which had sent several rounds of grape through his company. On every occasion of attack Private McHale was the first to meet the enemy, amongst whom he caused such consternation, by the boldness of his attack that those who followed him had little to do. His daring and sustained bravery became a byword among his comrades.

No photograph available

McINNES, Hugh   **787**
Gunner   Bengal Artillery
Other Decorations: —
Date of Gazette: 24 Dec. 1858
Place/Date of Birth: Anderston, Glasgow — Oct. 1815
Place/Date of Death: Glasgow — 7 Dec. 1879
Memorials: —
Town/County Connections: Anderston, Glasgow
Remarks: —
Account of Deed: During the whole of the period 14 to 22 Nov. 1857 at the Relief of Lucknow, India, Gunner McInnes acted with conspicuous gallantry. (Elected by the Regiment.)

McINTOSH, George Imlach   **788**
Private (later Flight Sergeant)   1/6th Bn., The Gordon Highlanders
Other Decorations: —
Date of Gazette: 6 Sep. 1917
Place/Date of Birth: Buckie, Banff, Scotland — 24 Apr. 1897
Place/Date of Death: Aberdeen, Scotland — 20 Jun. 1960
Memorials: New Cemetery, Buckie, Banff
Town/County Connections: Buckie, Banff; Aberdeen
Remarks: Served in Royal Air Force during Second World War.
Account of Deed: On 31 Jul. 1917 at Ypres, Belgium, during the consolidation of a position, the company came under machine-gun fire at close range and Private McIntosh immediately rushed forward under heavy fire and reaching the emplacement, threw a Mills grenade into it, killing two of the enemy and wounding a third. Subsequently entering the dug-out he found two light machine-guns which he carried back with him. His quick grasp of the situation and the rapidity with which he acted undoubtedly saved many of his comrades and enabled the consolidation to proceed unhindered by machine-gun fire.

MacINTYRE, David Lowe   789

T/Lieutenant (later Major General)   The Argyll and Sutherland Highlanders (Princess Louise's), attd. 1/6th Bn., The Highland Light Infantry
Other Decorations: CB
Date of Gazette: 26 Oct. 1918
Place/Date of Birth: Portnahaven, Islay, Scotland — 18 Jun. 1895
Place/Date of Death: Edinburgh — 31 Jul. 1967
Memorials: —
Town/County Connections: Portnahaven, Islay; Edinburgh
Remarks: —
Account of Deed: During the period 24/27 Aug. 1918 near Henin and Fontaine, Croisilles, France, Lieutenant MacIntyre, when acting as adjutant of his battalion, was constantly in evidence in the firing line and by his coolness under most heavy shell and machine-gun fire inspired the confidence of all ranks. On one occasion when extra strong entanglements were encountered, he organised and took forward a party and under heavy fire supervised the making of gaps. Subsequently, when relieved of command of the firing line and an enemy machine-gun opened fire close to him, he rushed it single-handed, putting the team to flight, and then brought in the gun.

MACINTYRE, Donald   790

Major (later Major General)   Bengal Staff Corps and 2nd Gurkha Rifles, Indian Army
Other Decorations: —
Date of Gazette: 27 Sep. 1872
Place/Date of Birth: Kincraig, Ross & Cromarty, Scotland — 12 Sep. 1831
Place/Date of Death: Fortrose, Ross & Cromarty Scotland — 15 Apr. 1903
Memorials: —
Town/County Connections: Kincraig and Fortrose , Ross & Cromarty
Remarks: Fellow of the Royal Geographic Society
Account of Deed: On 4 Jan. 1872 during the Looshai Campaign, North-East India, Major Macintyre led the assault on the stockaded village of Lalgnoora. He was the first to reach the stockade, at that time about 9 feet high, and successfully stormed it under heavy fire from the enemy.

McIVER, Hugh   791

Private   2nd Bn., The Royal Scots (The Lothian Regiment)
Other Decorations: MM & Bar
Date of Gazette: 15 Nov. 1918
Place/Date of Birth: Linwood, Kilbarchan, Renfrewshire, Scotland — 21 Jun. 1890
Place/Date of Death: Near Courcelles, France — 2 Sep. 1918
Memorials: Vraucourt Copse Cemetery, France
Town/County Connections: Kilbarchan, Renfrewshire
Remarks: —
Account of Deed: On 23 Aug. 1918 east of Courcelle-le Compte, France, Private McIver was employed as a company-runner and under heavy artillery and machine-gun fire carried messages regardless of his own safety. Single-handed he pursued an enemy scout into a machine-gun post and having killed six of the garrison, captured 20 prisoners and two machine-guns. Later he succeeded, at great personal risk, in stopping the fire of a British tank which was directed in error against our own troops. He was killed in action 10 days later.

No photograph available

MACKAY, David   792

Private   93rd Regiment (later The Argyll and Sutherland Highlanders — Princess Louise's)
Other Decorations: —
Date of Gazette: 24 Dec. 1858
Place/Date of Birth: Thurso, Caithness, Scotland — Nov. 1830
Place/Date of Death: Lesmahagow, Lanarkshire, Scotland — 18 Nov. 1880
Memorials: Buried at Lesmahagow, Lanarkshire
Town/County Connections: Thurso, Caithness; Lesmahagow, Lanarkshire
Remarks: —
Account of Deed: On 16 Nov. 1857 at Lucknow, India, Private Mackay showed great personal gallantry in capturing an enemy's Colour after a most obstinate resistance at the Secundra Bagh. He was severely wounded afterwards at the capture of the Shah Nujjiff. (Elected by the regiment.)

McKAY, Ian John   **793**

Sergeant   3rd Bn., The Parachute Regiment
Other Decorations: —
Date of Gazette: 11 Oct. 1982
Place/Date of Birth: Wortley, near Sheffield, Yorkshire — 7 May 1953
Place/Date of Death: Mount Longdon, East Falkland — 12 Jun. 1982
Memorials: Aldershot Military Cemetery, Hampshire *Grave*
Town/County Connections: Rotherham, Yorkshire; Aldershot, Hampshire
Remarks: — *VC in Imperial War Museum, London*
Account of Deed: On 12 Jun. 1982 on Mount Longdon, East Falkland, Sergeant McKay was in command of his platoon, its commander having been wounded in the leg. They were pinned down by heavy enemy fire and several of the men had been either killed or wounded. Sergeant McKay realized that something must be done and he charged the enemy position alone. He was killed in the moment of his victory, but his action enabled his comrades to extricate themselves from a most dangerous situation.

MACKAY, John Frederick   **794**

Lance-Corporal (later Lieutenant Colonel)   1st Bn., The Gordon Highlanders
Other Decorations: —
Date of Gazette: 10 Aug. 1900
Place/Date of Birth: Edinburgh — 6 Jun. 1873
Place/Date of Death: Nice, France — 9 Jan. 1930
Memorials: —
Town/County Connections: Edinburgh
Remarks: Served in the First World War 1914-18
Account of Deed: On 20 May 1900 during the action on Crow's Nest Hill, Johannesburg, South Africa, Corporal Mackay repeatedly rushed forward under withering fire at short range to attend to wounded comrades and dress their wounds. He was himself without shelter and on one occasion he carried a wounded man from the open, under fire, to the shelter of a boulder.

McKEAN, George Burdon   **795**

Lieutenant (later Captain)   14th Bn., Quebec Regiment, C.E.F.
Other Decorations: MC, MM
Date of Gazette: 28 Jun. 1918
Place/Date of Birth: Willington, Bishop Auckland, Co. Durham — 4 Jul. 1888
Place/Date of Death: Cuffley, Hertfordshire — 28 Nov. 1926
Memorials: Brighton Extra-Mural Cemetery, Sussex; Canadian War Museum
Town/County Connections: Willington, Bishop Auckland, Co. Durham; Cuffley, Hertfordshire
Remarks: —
Account of Deed: On 27/28 Apr. 1918 at the Gavrelle Sector, France, when Lieutenant McKean's party was held up at a block in the communication trench by intense fire, he ran into the open, leaping over the block head first on top of one of the enemy. Whilst lying there, he was attacked by another with a fixed bayonet. He shot both of these men, captured the position, then sent back for more bombs, and until they arrived he engaged the enemy single-handed. He then rushed a second block, killing two of the enemy, capturing four others, and driving the remainder into a dug-out, which he tnen destroyed.

McKECHNIE, James   **796**

Sergeant   Scots (Fusilier) Guards
Other Decorations: —
Date of Gazette: 24 Feb. 1857
Place/Date of Birth: High Church, Paisley, Renfrewshire, Scotland — Jun. 1826
Place/Date of Death: Glasgow — 5 Jul. 1886
Memorials: Eastern Necropolis, Gallowgate, Glasgow *Grave*
Town/County Connections: Paisley, Renfrewshire; Glasgow
Remarks: —
Account of Deed: On 20 Sep. 1854 at the Battle of the Alma, Crimea, when the shot and fire from the batteries just in front of the battalion threw it into momentary disorder, it was forced out of its formation, becoming something of a huge triangle, with one corner pointing towards the enemy. A captain was carrying the Queen's Colour which had the pole smashed and 20 bullet holes through the silk. Sergeant McKechnie held up his revolver and dashed forward, rallying the men round the Colours. He was wounded in the action.

McKENNA, Edward   **797**
Colour-Sergeant (later Ensign)   65th Regiment (later The York and Lancaster Regiment)
Other Decorations: —
Date of Gazette: 16 Jan. 1864
Place/Date of Birth: Leeds, Yorkshire — 15 Feb. 1827
Place/Date of Death: Palmerston North, New Zealand — 8 Jun. 1908
Memorials: —
Town/County Connections: Leeds, Yorkshire
Remarks: —
Account of Deed: On 7 Sep. 1863 near Cameron Town, New Zealand, after both his officers had been shot, Colour-Sergeant McKenna, with a small force, heavily outnumbered by the enemy, charged through their position with the loss of one man killed and one missing. The colour-sergeant's coolness and intrepidity amply justified the confidence placed in him by the soldiers brought so suddenly under his command.

McKENZIE, Albert Edward   **798**
Able Seaman   Royal Navy
Other Decorations: —
Date of Gazette: 23 Jul. 1918
Place/Date of Birth: Bermondsey, London — 23 Oct. 1898
Place/Date of Death: Southwark, London — 3 Nov. 1918
Memorials: Camberwell (Forest Hill Road) Cemetery, London
Town/County Connections: Bermondsey and Southwark, London
Remarks: —
Account of Deed: On 22/23 Apr. 1918 at Zeebrugge, Belgium, Able Seaman McKenzie was a member of a storming party on the night of the operation. He landed with his machine-gun in the face of great difficulties, advancing down the Mole with his commanding officer* who with most of his party was killed. The seaman accounted for several of the enemy running for shelter to a destroyer alongside the Mole, and was severely wounded whilst working his gun in an exposed position. (Award by ballot. *See also HARRISON, A.L.)

McKENZIE, Hugh   **799**
Lieutenant   7th Coy., Canadian Machine Gun Corps, C.E.F.
Other Decorations: DCM
Date of Gazette: 13 Feb. 1918
Place/Date of Birth: Inverness, Scotland — 5 Dec. 1885
Place/Date of Death: Passchendaele, Belgium — 30 Oct. 1917
Memorials: Menin Gate Memorial, Belgium
Town/County Connections: Inverness, Scotland
Remarks: Croix de Guerre (France)
Account of Deed: On 30 Oct. 1917 at Meetscheele Spur, near Passchendaele, Belgium, Lieutenant McKenzie was in charge of a section of four machine-guns accompanying the infantry in an attack. Seeing that all the officers and most of the NCOs of an infantry company had become casualties and that the men were hesitating before a nest of enemy machine-guns, the lieutenant handed over his command to an NCO, rallied the infantry, organised an attack and captured the strong point. He then led a frontal attack on a pill box which was causing casualties. The pill box was captured but he was killed.

MACKENZIE, James   **800**
Private   2nd Bn., Scots Guards
Other Decorations: —
Date of Gazette: 18 Feb. 1915
Place/Date of Birth: West Glen, New Abbey, Kirkcudbright, Scotland — 2 Apr. 1889
Place/Date of Death: Rouges Bancs, France — 19 Dec. 1914
Memorials: Ploegsteert Memorial, Belgium; Troqueer Parish Church Maxwelltown, Dumfries
Town/County Connections: New Abbey, Kirkcudbright; Lochbushart, Ross & Cromarty; Dumfries, Scotland
Remarks: —
Account of Deed: On 19 Dec. 1914 at Rouges Bancs, France, Private Mackenzie rescued a severely wounded man from the front of the German trenches under a very heavy fire and after a stretcher party had been compelled to abandon the attempt. Private Mackenzie was killed later on that day while trying to carry out a similar act.

MACKENZIE, John **801**

Sergeant (later Major)   2nd Bn., The Seaforth Highlanders (Ross-shire Buffs, Duke of Albany's), employed West African Field Force
Other Decorations: —
Date of Gazette: 15 Jan. 1901
Place/Date of Birth: Contin, Ross-shire, Scotland — 22 Nov. 1870
Place/Date of Death: Near Cuinchy, France — 17 May 1915
Memorials: Guards Cemetery, Windy Corner, Cuichy, France
Town/County Connections: Contin, Ross-shire
Remarks: Served with The Bedfordshire Regiment in the First World War
Account of Deed: On 6 Jun. 1900 at Dompoassi (Ashanti War), Sergeant Mackenzie, after working two Maxim guns under heavy fire and being wounded while doing so, volunteered to clear the stockade of the enemy. This he did, most gallantly, leading the charge himself and driving the enemy headlong into the bush.

MACKEY, John Bernard **802**

Corporal   2/3rd Pioneer Bn., Australian Military Forces
Other Decorations: —
Date of Gazette: 8 Nov. 1945
Place/Date of Birth: Leichhardt, Sydney, New South Wales, Australia — 16 May 1922
Place/Date of Death: Tarakan, North Borneo — 12 May 1945
Memorials: Labuan War Cemetery, North Borneo; Australian War Memorial, Canberra
Town/County Connections: —
Remarks: —
Account of Deed: On 12 May 1945 at Tarakan Island, North Borneo, Corporal Mackey led his men along a very narrow spur where it was almost impossible to move to a flank. The section came under fire from three well-sited enemy positions, but Corporal Mackey went ahead, charging the first position, wrestling with and killing one of the enemy and he then rushed a heavy machine-gun post, killing the crew. He again attacked a third position further along the spur and was killed, but not before he had accounted for two more of the enemy.

MACKINTOSH, Donald **803**

Lieutenant   3rd Bn., The Seaforth Highlanders (Ross-shire Buffs, Duke of Albany's)
Other Decorations: —
Date of Gazette: 8 Jun. 1917
Place/Date of Birth: Glasgow — 7 Feb. 1896
Place/Date of Death: Fampoux, France — 11 Apr. 1917
Memorials: Brown's Copse Cemetery, France
Town/County Connections: Glasgow; Partick, Lanarkshire, Scotland
Remarks: —
Account of Deed: On 11 Apr. 1917 north of Fampoux, France, during the initial advance, Lieutenant Mackintosh was shot through the right leg, but although crippled, continued to lead his men, and captured the trench. He then collected men of another company who had lost their leader and drove back a counter-attack, when he was again wounded and although unable to stand, nevertheless continued to control the situation. With only 15 men left he ordered them to be ready to advance to the final objective and with great difficulty got out of the trench, encouraging them to advance. He was wounded yet again and fell.

MACLEAN, Hector Lachlan Stewart **804**

Lieutenant   Staff Corps and Corps of Guides, Indian Army
Other Decorations: —
Date of Gazette: 9 Nov. 1897 & 15 Jan. 1907
Place/Date of Birth: Bannu, North-west Frontier, India — 13 Sep. 1870
Place/Date of Death: Nawa Kili, Upper Swat, India — 17 Aug. 1897
Memorials: St. Alban's Church, Marden, Kent; Sanctum Crypt, St. Luke's Church, Chelsea, London
Town/County Connections: Marden, Kent
Remarks: —
Account of Deed: On 17 Aug. 1897 at Nawa Kili, Upper Swat, India (Tirah Campaign), Lieutenant Maclean, with two other officers* and five men of the Guides, went under a heavy and close fire, to the rescue of a lieutenant of the Lancashire Fusiliers who was lying disabled by a bullet wound and surrounded by enemy swordsmen. While the wounded officer was being brought under cover he was unfortunately killed by a bullet. Lieutenant Maclean was mortally wounded and four of the horses were shot. (*See also ADAMS, R.B. and FINCASTLE, A.E.M.)

McLEOD, Alan Arnett
Second Lieutenant   2 Squadron, Royal Flying Corps (later Royal Air Force)
Other Decorations: —
Date of Gazette: 1 May 1918
Place/Date of Birth: Stonewall, Winnipeg, Manitoba, Canada — 20 Apr. 1899
Place/Date of Death: Winnipeg, Canada — 6 Nov. 1918
Memorials: Kildonan Cemetery, Winnipeg, Canada
Town/County Connections: —
Remarks: —
Account of Deed: On 27 Mar. 1918 over Albert, France, Second Lieutenant McLeod, with his observer, in an FK8 destroyed an enemy triplane and was immediately attacked by eight more, two of which they brought down, but the petrol tank of the bomber was hit, the machine burst into flames and both pilot and observer were badly wounded. The lieutenant, by side slipping steeply, tried to keep the flames away from his observer, and when the machine finally crashed in No Man's Land, the young pilot, notwithstanding his own injuries, dragged his comrade from the burning wreckage and under heavy fire carried him to comparative safety, before collapsing from exhaustion.

No photograph available

806

McMANUS, Peter
Private (later Sergeant)   1st Bn., 5th Regiment (later The Northumberland Fusiliers)
Other Decorations: —
Date of Gazette: 18 Jun. 1858
Place/Date of Birth: Tynan, Co. Armagh, Ireland — Mar. 1829
Place/Date of Death: Allahabad, India — 27 Apr. 1859
Memorials: —
Town/County Connections: Tynan, Co. Armagh
Remarks: —
Account of Deed: On 26 Sep. 1857 at Lucknow, India, when a party of men was shut up and besieged in a house in the city, Private McManus stayed outside the house until he himself was wounded, and under cover of a pillar kept firing on the sepoys and prevented their rushing the house. He also, in conjuction with another private* dashed into the street and took a wounded captain out of a dhooly and carried him into the house in spite of heavy fire in which the captain was again wounded. (*See also RYAN, John (No. 1092))

807

McMASTER, Valentine Munbee
Assistant Surgeon (later Surgeon)   78th Regiment (later The Seaforth Highlanders — Ross-shire Buffs, Duke of Albany's)
Other Decorations: —
Date of Gazette: 18 Jun. 1858
Place/Date of Birth: Trichinopoly, India — 16 May 1834
Place/Date of Death: Belfast, Ireland — 22 Jan. 1872
Memorials: City Cemetery, Belfast; Londonderry Cathedral, Ireland
Town/County Connections: —
Remarks: —
Account of Deed: On 25 Sep. 1857, at the relief of Lucknow, India, Assistant Surgeon McMaster showed great bravery in exposing himself to the fire of the enemy when bringing in and attending to the wounded.

808

McNAIR, Eric Archibald
T/Lieutenant (later Captain)   9th (S) Bn., The Royal Sussex Regiment
Other Decorations: —
Date of Gazette: 30 Mar. 1916
Place/Date of Birth: Calcutta, India — 16 Jun. 1894
Place/Date of Death: Genoa, Italy — 12 Aug. 1918
Memorials: Staglieno Cemetery, Italy; Regimental Memorial, Chichester Cathedral
Town/County Connections: — *Charterhouse School.*
Remarks: —
Account of Deed: On 14 Feb. 1916 near Hooge, Belgium, when the enemy exploded a mine, Lieutenant McNair and a number of men were flung into the air and many were buried. Although much shaken, the lieutenant at once organised a party with a machine-gun to man the near edge of the crater and opened rapid fire on the enemy who were advancing. They were driven back with many dead. Lieutenant McNair then ran back for reinforcements, but the communication trench being blocked, he went across the open under heavy fire and led up the reinforcements the same way. His prompt and plucky action undoubtedly saved a critical situation.

McNALLY, William   **809**
Sergeant   8th (S) Bn., The Yorkshire Regiment (Alexandra, Princess of Wales's Own)
Other Decorations: MM
Date of Gazette: 14 Dec. 1918
Place/Date of Birth: Murton, Near Seaham, Co. Durham — 16 Dec. 1894
Place/Date of Death: Murton, Near Seaham, Co. Durham — 5 Jan. 1976
Memorials: Stone memorial in small public park at Murton.
Town/County Connections: Murton, Co. Durham
Remarks: —
Account of Deed: On 27 Oct. 1918 at Piave, Italy, when his company was most seriously hindered by machine-gun fire, Sergeant NcNally, regardless of personal safety, rushed the machine-gun post single-handed, killing the team and capturing the gun. Later, at Vazzola on 29 Oct. the sergeant crept up to the rear of an enemy post, put the garrison to flight and captured the machine-gun. On the same day, when holding a newly-captured ditch, he was strongly counter-attacked from both flanks, but coolly controlling the fire of his party, he frustrated that attack, inflicting heavy casualties on the enemy.

McNAMARA Frank Hubert   **810**
Lieutenant (later Air Vice-Marshal)   1 Squadron, Australian Flying Corps (later Royal Australian Air Force)
Other Decorations: CB, CBE
Date of Gazette: 8 Jun. 1917
Place/Date of Birth: Waranga, Rushworth, Victoria, Australia — 4 Apr. 1894
Place/Date of Death: Gerrards Cross, Buckinghamshire — 2 Nov. 1961
Memorials: The Priory, Gerrards Cross; Australian War Memorial, Canberra   *Grave*
Town/County Connections: Gerrards Cross, Buckinghamshire
Remarks: Served with the RAF during the Second World War — AOC, RAAF HQ in London 1939-42; AOC British Forces in Aden 1942-45; Director of Education, HQ British Occupation Forces Administration in Westphalia, Germany 1945-47
Account of Deed: On 20 Mar. 1917 in Egypt, during an aerial bomb attack, a pilot was forced to land behind enemy lines, with hostile cavalry approaching. Lieutenant McNamara, seeing the situation, came down through heavy fire to the rescue, despite the fact that he himself was wounded. He landed about 200 yards from the damaged plane, and the pilot climbed into his machine, but owing to his injury he could not keep it straight and it turned over. The two officers extricated themselves, set fire to the machine and made their way to the damaged one, which they succeeded in starting. Finally, Lieutenant McNamara, although weak from loss of blood, flew the machine back to the aerodrome (70 miles away).

McNAMARA, John   **811**
Corporal   9th Bn., The East Surrey Regiment
Other Decorations: —
Date of Gazette: 15 Nov. 1918
Place/Date of Birth: Walton-le-Dale, Preston, Lancashire — 28 Oct. 1887
Place/Date of Death: Near Solesmes, France — 16 Oct. 1918
Memorials: Romeries Communal Cemetery Extension, France
Town/County Connections: Walton-le-Dale, Preston, Lancashire; Kingston, Surrey
Remarks: —   *Name in Warrior chapel, All Saints Church, Kingston-on-Thame*
Account of Deed: On 3 Sep. 1918 north west of Lens, France, when operating a telephone in evacuated enemy trenches occupied by his battalion, Corporal McNamara realised that a determined enemy counter-attack was gaining ground. Rushing to the nearest post he made very good use of a revolver taken from a wounded officer and then seizing a Lewis gun he fired it until it jammed. By this time he was alone in the post and having destroyed the telephone he joined the nearest post and maintained a Lewis gun until reinforcements arrived.

McNEILL, John Carstairs (later Sir John)   **812**
Lieutenant Colonel (later Major General)   107th Regiment (Bengal Infantry — later The Royal Sussex Regiment)
Other Decorations: GCVO, KCB, KCMG
Date of Gazette: 16 Aug. 1864
Place/Date of Birth: Colonsay, Argyllshire, Scotland — 29 Mar. 1831
Place/Date of Death: London — 25 May 1904
Memorials: —
Town/County Connections: Colonsay, Argyllshire
Remarks: Knight of the Medjidie (Turkey); Bath King at Arms 1898; DL, County of Forfar, Scotland
Account of Deed: On 30 Mar. 1864 near Ohanpu, New Zealand. Lieutenant Colonel McNeill was proceeding to Te Awamutu on duty, with two privates when they saw a party of the enemy in front. The colonel sent one of the privates back to bring up the infantry, but before help could arrive the officer and private were attacked by about 50 natives. In trying to escape the private's horse fell, throwing its rider, and the colonel, seeing his plight, returned, caught the horse and helped the man to mount. Although the enemy were very close and firing sharply, by galloping hard they managed to get away.

McNESS, Frederick   **813**
Lance-Sergeant (later Sergeant)   1st Bn., Scots Guards
Other Decorations: —
Date of Gazette: 26 Oct. 1916
Place/Date of Birth: Bramley, Near Leeds — 22 Jan. 1892
Place/Date of Death: Bournemouth, Hampshire — 4 May 1956
Memorials: —
Town/County Connections: Leeds, Yorkshire; Bournemouth, Hampshire
Remarks: —
Account of Deed: On 15 Sep. 1916 near Ginchy, France, during a period of severe fighting, Lance-Sergeant McNess led his men with great dash in the face of heavy shell and machine-gun fire. When the first line of the enemy trenches was reached, it was found that the left flank was exposed and that the enemy were bombing down the trench. Sergeant McNess thereupon organised and led a counter-attack and although he was very severely wounded in the neck and jaw, did not give up. Finally he established a "block" and continued encouraging his men and throwing bombs until exhausted by loss of blood.

MACPHERSON, Herbert Taylor   **814**
Lieutenant (later Major General)   78th Regiment (later The Seaforth Highlanders — Ross-shire Buffs, Duke of Albany's)
Other Decorations: GCB, KCSI
Date of Gazette: 18 Jun. 1858
Place/Date of Birth: Ardersier, Inverness-shire, Scotland — 22 Jan. 1827
Place/Date of Death: Prome, Burma — 20 Oct. 1886
Memorials: —
Town/County Connections: Ardersier, Inverness-shire
Remarks: —
Account of Deed: On 25 Sep. 1857 at Lucknow, India, Lieutenant Macpherson set an example of heroic gallantry to the men of his regiment at the period of the action in which they captured two brass 9-pounders at the point of the bayonet.

McPHERSON, Stewart   **815**
Colour-Sergeant   78th Regiment (later The Seaforth Highlanders — Ross-shire Buffs, Duke of Albany's)
Other Decorations: —
Date of Gazette: 12 Apr. 1859
Place/Date of Birth: Culross, Dunfermline, Scotland — 1822
Place/Date of Death: Culross, Dunfermline — 7 Dec. 1892
Memorials: —
Town/County Connections: Culross, Dunfermline
Remarks: —
Account of Deed: On 26 Sep. 1857 in the Residency at Lucknow, India, Colour-Sergeant McPherson rescued, under very heavy fire and at great personal risk, a wounded private of his company, who was lying in a most exposed position. The colour-sergeant was distinguished on many occasions for his coolness and gallantry in action.

McPHIE, James   **816**
Corporal   416th (Edinburgh) Field Coy., Corps of Royal Engineers
Other Decorations: —
Date of Gazette: 31 Jan. 1919
Place/Date of Birth: Edinburgh — 18 Dec. 1894
Place/Date of Death: Aubencheul-au-Bac, France — 14 Oct. 1918
Memorials: Naves Communal Cemetery Extension, France
Town/County Connections: Edinburgh
Remarks: —
Account of Deed: On 14 Oct. 1918 at the Canal de la Sensee near Aubencheul-au-Bac, France, Corporal McPhie was with a party of sappers maintaining a cork float bridge, which when our infantry started to cross it just before dawn began to break away and sink. Corporal McPhie jumped into the water and tried to hold the cork and timbers together but this proved impossible so he swam back and collected the materials for repair. Although it was daylight and the bridge was under close fire he then led the way to the bridge, axe in hand. He was severely wounded and died almost at once.

No photograph available

McQUIRT, Bernard   **817**
Private   95th Regiment (later The Sherwood Foresters — The Nottinghamshire and Derbyshire Regiment)
Other Decorations: —
Date of Gazette: 11 Nov. 1859
Place/Date of Birth: Donacloney, Lurgan, Co. Armagh, Ireland — 1829
Place/Date of Death: Co. Down or Co. Armagh, Ireland — 5 Oct. 1888
Memorials: —
Town/County Connections: Donacloney, Lurgan, Co. Armagh
Remarks: —
Account of Deed: On 6 Jan. 1858 at the capture of the town of Rowa, India, Private McQuirt was dangerously wounded in a hand-to-hand fight with three men, of whom he killed one and wounded another. He himself was wounded by five sabre-cuts and a musket-shot.

McREADY-DIARMID, (and McREADY-DREW) Arthur Malcolm Cluny — see **DIARMID,** Allastair Malcolm Cluny

MACTIER, Robert   **818**
Private   23rd Bn. (Victoria), Australian Imperial Force
Other Decorations: —
Date of Gazette: 14 Dec. 1918
Place/Date of Birth: Tatura, Victoria, Australia — 17 May 1890
Place/Date of Death: Near Peronne, France — 1 Sep. 1918
Memorials: Hem Farm Military Cemetery, France; Australian War Memorial, Canberra
Town/County Connections: —
Remarks: —
Account of Deed: On 1 Sep. 1918 during the attack on Mont St. Quentin, near Peronne, France, the bombing patrols had failed to clear up several enemy strong-points and the battalion could not advance. Private Mactier thereupon rushed out of the trench, closed with and killed the machine-gun crew of eight men and threw the gun over the parapet. He then moved to another strong-point and captured six men. He disposed of a third machine-gun, but in tackling a fourth was killed. This action enabled the battalion to capture Mont St. Quentin a few hours later.

McWHEENEY, William   **819**
Sergeant   44th Regiment (later The Essex Regiment)
Other Decorations: —
Date of Gazette: 24 Feb. 1857
Place/Date of Birth: Bangor, Co. Down, Ireland — 1837
Place/Date of Death: Dover, Kent — 17 May 1866
Memorials: St. James's Cemetery, Dover
Town/County Connections: Bangor and Newtownards, Co. Down, Ireland; Dover, Kent
Remarks: —
Account of Deed: On 20 Oct. 1854 in the Crimea, a party of sharpshooters were being repulsed from the Quarries, and a private from the 44th Regiment was dangerously wounded. Sergeant McWheeney took the wounded man on his back and carried him to a place of safety under very heavy fire. On 5 Dec. he saved the life of a corporal, bringing him in under fire and digging a slight cover with his bayonet, where the two of them remained until dark. On 18 Jun. 1855 Sergeant McWheeney volunteered for the advanced guard in the Cemetery and was never absent from duty during the war.

No photograph available

MADDEN, Ambrose   **820**
Sergeant (later Lieutenant)   41st Regiment (later The Welch Regiment)
Other Decorations: —
Date of Gazette: 24 Feb. 1857
Place/Date of Birth: Cork, Ireland — 1820
Place/Date of Death: Jamaica — 1 Jan. 1863
Memorials: —
Town/County Connections: Cork, Ireland
Remarks: —
Account of Deed: On 26 Oct. 1854, in the Crimea, at Little Inkerman, Sergeant Madden headed a party of men of the 41st Regiment which cut off and took prisoner one Russian officer and 14 privates, three of whom were personally captured by the sergeant. *VC in Welch Regt. Museum, Cardiff Castle*

MAGENNIS, James Joseph   **821**
A/Leading Seaman   Royal Navy
Other Decorations: —
Date of Gazette: 13 Nov. 1945
Place/Date of Birth: Belfast, Ireland — 27 Oct. 1919
Place/Date of Death: Halifax, Yorkshire — 12 Feb. 1986
Memorials: —
Town/County Connections: Belfast, Ireland; Bradford, Yorkshire
Remarks: —
Account of Deed: On 31 Jul. 1945 in the Johore Straits, Leading Seaman Magennis, a diver in the midget submarine XE.3, attached limpet mines to the Japanese cruiser *Takao* under particularly difficult circumstances. He had to squeeze through a narrow space in the partly-open diving hatch, and then scrape barnacles off the bottom of the cruiser before attaching the limpets. During this time his breathing apparatus was leaking and he returned to the submarine after completion of his task very exhausted. On withdrawing, his commander* found that one of the limpet carriers which was being jettisoned, would not release itself and Magennis immediately volunteered to free it. This he did, after five minutes of nerve-racking work with a heavy spanner. (*See also FRASER, I.A.)

MAGNER, (alias BARRY) Michael   **822**
Drummer (later Corporal)   33rd Regiment (later The Duke of Wellington's (West Riding) Regt.)
Other Decorations: —
Date of Gazette: 28 Jul. 1868
Place/Date of Birth: Fermanagh, Ireland — 21 Jun. 1840
Place/Date of Death: Melbourne, Australia — 6 Feb. 1897
Memorials: Melbourne General Cemetery, Victoria, Australia
Town/County Connections: Fermanagh, Ireland
Remarks: —
Account of Deed: On 13 Apr. 1868 in Abyssinia, during the assault on Magdala, when the head of the column of attack was checked by the obstacles at the gate, a small stream of officers and men of the 33rd Regiment and an officer of the Royal Engineers broke away from the main approach to Magdala and, reaching the defences, climbed a cliff, forced their way over a wall and through a strong and thorny fence, thus turning the defenders of the gateway. The first two men to enter Magdala were Drummer Magner and a private*. (See also BERGIN, J.)

MAHONEY, John Keefer   **823**
Major   The Westminster Regiment (Motor), Canadian Infantry Corps
Other Decorations: —
Date of Gazette: 13 Jul. 1944
Place/Date of Birth: New Westminster, British Columbia, Canada — 30 Jun. 1911
Place/Date of Death: — *Died London, Ontario 18.12.1990*
Memorials: —
Town/County Connections: —
Remarks: Liaison Officer, US Department of the Army, Washington D.C. 1954; Assistant Adjutant and Quartermaster General Alberta Area 1963.
Account of Deed: On 24 May 1944 at the River Melfa, Italy, Major Mahoney and his company were ordered to establish the initial bridgehead over the river. This was accomplished and for five hours the company maintained its position in the face of enemy fire and attack until the remaining companies and supporting weapons were able to reinforce them. Early in the action Major Mahoney was wounded in the head and twice in the leg, but he refused medical aid and continued to direct the defence of the bridgehead. The enemy saw that this officer was the soul of the defence and consequently made him their particular target.

No photograph available

MAHONEY, Patrick   **824**
Sergeant   1st Madras Fusiliers (later The Royal Dublin Fusiliers)
Other Decorations: —
Date of Gazette: 18 Jun. 1858
Place/Date of Birth: Waterford, Ireland — 1827
Place/Date of Death: Lucknow, India — 30 Oct. 1857
Memorials: —
Town/County Connections: Waterford, Ireland
Remarks: —
Account of Deed: On 21 Sep. 1857 at Mungulwar, India, Sergeant Mahoney, whilst doing duty with the Volunteer Cavalry, helped in the capture of the Regimental Colour of the 1st Regiment Native Infantry.

MAILLARD, William Job   **825**
Surgeon (later Staff Surgeon)   Royal Navy
Other Decorations: —
Date of Gazette: 2 Dec. 1898
Place/Date of Birth: Banwell, Axbridge, Somerset — 10 Mar. 1863
Place/Date of Death: Bournemouth, Hampshire — 10 Sep. 1903
Memorials: Wimborne Cemetery, Dorset; Royal Naval Hospital, Haslar, Hampshire
Town/County Connections: Banwell, Axbridge, Somerset; Bournemouth, Hampshire
Remarks: First and only naval medical officer to win VC
Account of Deed: On 6 Sep. 1898 at Candia, Crete, two parties of men from HMS *Hazard* went to the assistance of the Customs House Garrison which was being besieged. Later, when medical help was called for, Surgeon Maillard, who had disembarked and reached a place of safety, went back through a deluge of bullets in an attempt to rescue one of the seamen who was wounded and had fallen back into the boat. He was, however, almost dead and it was impossible for the surgeon to lift him, as the boat was drifting. He returned to his post unhurt, but his clothes were riddled with bullets.

MALCOLM, Hugh Gordon   **826**
Wing Commander   18 Squadron, Royal Air Force
Other Decorations: —
Date of Gazette: 27 Apr. 1943
Place/Date of Birth: Broughty Ferry, Dundee, Scotland — 2 May 1917
Place/Date of Death: Chougui, Tunisia — 4 Dec. 1942
Memorials: Beja War Cemetery, Tunisia
Town/County Connections: Broughty Ferry, Dundee
Remarks: —
Account of Deed: From Nov. to Dec. 1942 in North Africa, Wing Commander Malcolm commanded a squadron of light bombers. Throughout his service in that sector his skill and daring were of the highest order. He led two attacks on Bizerta airfield, pressing his attacks to effective conclusion and on 4 Dec. he led an attack on an enemy fighter airfield near Chougui. On reaching the target, however and starting the attack, the squadron was intercepted by an overwhelming force of enemy fighters. One by one his bombers were shot down, until he himself was shot down in flames.

MALCOLMSON, John Grant   **827**
Lieutenant (later Captain)   3rd Bombay Light Cavalry
Other Decorations: MVO
Date of Gazette: 3 Aug. 1860
Place/Date of Birth: Muchrach, Inverness, Scotland — 9 Feb. 1835
Place/Date of Death: London — 14 Aug. 1902
Memorials: Kensal Green Cemetery, London
Town/County Connections: Muchrach, Inverness; London
Remarks: Became a Gentleman-at-Arms 1870
Account of Deed: On 8 Feb. 1857 at the Battle of Khoosh-ab, Persia, the adjutant of the regiment* was probably the first in the attack, but his horse, on leaping into the square, fell dead, crushing his rider and breaking his sword. The adjutant extricated himself and tried with his broken sword to force his way through the enemy, but he would almost certainly have lost his life had not Lieutenant Malcolmson seen his plight, fought his way to his dismounted comrade and, giving him his stirrup, carried him to safety. (*See also MOORE, A.T.)

MALING, George Allen   **828**
T/Lieutenant (later Captain)   Royal Army Medical Corps, attd. 12th Bn., The Rifle Brigade (Prince Consort's Own)
Other Decorations: —
Date of Gazette: 18 Nov. 1915
Place/Date of Birth: Sunderland, Co. Durham — 6 Oct. 1888
Place/Date of Death: Lee, London — 9 Jul. 1929
Memorials: — *Buried Chislehurst Cemetery.*
Town/County Connections: Sunderland, Co. Durham; London
Remarks: —
Account of Deed: On 25 Sep. 1915, near Fauquissart, France, Lieutenant Maling worked for over 24 hours with untiring energy, collecting and treating in the open, under heavy shell fire, more than 300 men. During the morning of the 25th he was temporarily stunned by the bursting of a large high explosive shell which wounded his only assistant and killed several of his patients. A second shell covered him and his instruments with débris, but he continued his gallant work single-handed.

MALLESON, Wilfred St. Aubyn
829

Midshipman (later Captain)   Royal Navy
Other Decorations: —
Date of Gazette: 16 Aug. 1915
Place/Date of Birth: Kirkee, India — 17 Sep. 1896
Place/Date of Death: St. Clements, Truro, Cornwall — 21 Jul. 1975
Memorials: —
Town/County Connections: Guildford, Surrey; Truro, Cornwall
Remarks: Served in the Second World War.
Account of Deed: On 25 Apr. 1915 during the landing at V Beach, Cape Helles, Gallipoli, Midshipman Malleson and three others* of HMS *River Clyde* assisted the commander* of the ship at the work of securing the lighters under very heavy rifle and Maxim fire. When the other midshipman with the party had failed, through sheer exhaustion to get a line from lighter to lighter, Midshipman Malleson swam with it himself and succeeded. The line subsequently broke and he afterwards made two further unsuccessful attempts at his self-imposed task. (*See also UNWIN, E., DREWRY, G.L., SAMSON, G.M. and WILLIAMS, W.C.)

MALONE, Joseph
830

Sergeant (later Captain and Riding Master)   13th Light Dragoons (later 13th Hussars)
Other Decorations: —
Date of Gazette: 25 Sep. 1857
Place/Date of Birth: Eccles, Manchester — 11 Jan. 1833
Place/Date of Death: Pinetown, Natal, South Africa — 28 Jun. 1883
Memorials: Christ Church Cemetery, Pinetown, Natal
Town/County Connections: Eccles, Manchester
Remarks: —
Account of Deed: On 25 Oct. 1854 at Balaclava, Crimea (Charge of the Light Brigade), Sergeant Malone, while returning on foot from the charge, in which his horse had been shot, stopped under very heavy fire and helped a troop sergeant-major* and another sergeant* to move a very severely wounded officer (who subsequently died) out of range of the guns. (*See also BERRYMAN, J. and FARRELL, J.)

MANGLES, Ross Lowis
831

Mr.   Bengal Civil Service
Other Decorations: —
Date of Gazette: 6 Jul. 1859
Place/Date of Birth: Calcutta, India — 14 Apr. 1833
Place/Date of Death: Pirbright, Surrey — 28 Feb. 1905
Memorials: Parish church, Pirbright, Surrey
Town/County Connections: Pirbright, Surrey
Remarks: Buried Brookwood Cemetery. This is not certain. May be Pirbright
Account of Deed: On 30 Jul. 1857 at Arrah, India, Mr. Mangles, who had volunteered to serve with the force engaged in the relief of the city, behaved with great gallantry. Notwithstanding the fact that he had himself previously been wounded, he carried a wounded soldier for several miles over swampy ground, after binding his wounds under murderous fire which killed or wounded almost the whole detachment, and got the casualty safely into a boat. VC embedded in wall of Pirbright Church.

MANLEY, William George Nicholas
832

Assistant Surgeon (later Surgeon General)   Royal Regiment of Artillery
Other Decorations: CB
Date of Gazette: 22 Sep. 1864
Place/Date of Birth: Dublin — 17 Dec. 1831
Place/Date of Death: Cheltenham, Gloucestershire — 16 Nov. 1901
Memorials: Cheltenham Cemetery
Town/County Connections: Cheltenham, Gloucestershire
Remarks: He served with the British Ambulance in the Franco-Prussion War 1870-1 and attended wounded on both sides; received Prussian Iron Cross (2nd Class), Bavarian Order of Merit and Geneva Cross; Knight of the Order of St. John
Account of Deed: On 29 Apr. 1864 near Tauranga, New Zealand, during the assault on the Rebel Pah, Assistant Surgeon Manley risked his own life in an endeavour to save that of a naval officer and others. Having volunteered to accompany the storming party into the Pah, he attended the naval officer when he was carried away mortally wounded and then volunteered to return in order to see if he could find any more wounded. He was one of the last officers to leave the Pah.

MANNERS-SMITH, John — see **SMITH,** John Manners

MANNOCK, Edward   **833**
Major   85 Squadron, Royal Air Force
Other Decorations: DSO & 2 Bars, MC & Bar
Date of Gazette: 18 Jul. 1919
Place/Date of Birth: Brighton, Sussex — 24 May 1887
Place/Date of Death: Near Lillers, France — 26 Jul. 1918
Memorials: Arras Memorial, France; Canterbury War Memorial; Canterbury Cathedral;
Mannock House, Military Road, Canterbury
Town/County Connections: Brighton, Sussex; Canterbury, Kent
Remarks: —
Account of Deed: By the end of Jul. 1918, in flying operations over France and Flanders, Major
Mannock had been officially accredited with 73 combat victories. In May 1918 he scored no less than 24 victories and on one
occasion in July whilst leading an attack on a formation of Fokker aircraft, he shot down one, sent another crashing to earth and
was the cause of another pair colliding. The whole of his career in the Royal Air Force was an outstanding example of fearless
courage, remarkable skill, devotion to duty and self-sacrifice.

MANSEL-JONES, Conwyn — see **JONES,** Conwyn MANSEL-

MANSER, Leslie Thomas   **834**
Flying Officer   50 Squadron, Royal Air Force Volunteer Reserve
Other Decorations: —
Date of Gazette: 23 Oct. 1942
Place/Date of Birth: New Delhi, India — 11 May 1922
Place/Date of Death: Belgium — 31 May 1942
Memorials: Heverlee War Cemetery, Belgium; Christ Church, Radlett, Hertfordshire
Town/County Connections: Radlett, Hertfordshire
Remarks: Brother-in-law of Captain J.N. Randle, VC.
Account of Deed: On 30 May 1942 over Germany, Flying Officer Manser was captain and first
pilot of a Manchester bomber which took part in a raid on Cologne. He bombed the target
successfully but the aircraft was hit repeatedly, the rear gunner was wounded, the front cabin filled with smoke and the port
engine was overheating. Flying Officer Manser was determined to save his aircraft and crew from falling into enemy hands and
it was not until he knew that a crash was inevitable that he gave the order to bale out. As the crew parachuted down, they saw
the bomber, still carrying their captain, crash in flames.

MANTLE, Jack Foreman   **835**
A/Leading Seaman   Royal Navy
Other Decorations: —
Date of Gazette: 3 Sep. 1940
Place/Date of Birth: Wandsworth, London — 12 Apr. 1917
Place/Date of Death: Portland, Dorset — 4 Jul. 1940
Memorials: Portland Royal Naval Cemetery, Dorset; plaque to HMS *Foylebank* in St. Paul's
Church, HMS *Osprey*, Portland
Town/County Connections: Clapham, London; Southampton, Hampshire
Remarks: —
Account of Deed: On 4 Jul. 1940 during an air raid on Portland, England, Leading Seaman
Mantle of HMS *Foylebank*, who was manning the starboard 20mm pom-pom gun, had his left leg shattered by the blast from
a bomb early in the action. Although wounded again many times, he remained at his gun, training and firing by hand when
Foylebank's electric power failed, until he collapsed and died.

MARINER, (not his original name — changed before he joined the Army)   William   **836**
Rifleman   2nd Bn., The King's Royal Rifle Corps
Other Decorations: —
Date of Gazette: 23 Jun. 1915
Place/Date of Birth: Chorley, Preston, Lancashire — 29 May 1882
Place/Date of Death: France — 1 Jul. 1916
Memorials: Thiepval Memorial, France
Town/County Connections: Chorley, Preston, Lancashire
Remarks: —
Account of Deed: On 22nd May 1915 near Cambrin, France, during a violent thunder storm,
Private Mariner left his trench and crept out through German wire entanglements until he reached
the emplacement of an enemy gun which had been hindering progress. He climbed on top of a German parapet and threw a
bomb under the roof of the emplacement and after 15 minutes he threw another bomb. He then waited while the guns opened
fire on the wire entanglements behind him and eventually he was able to return to his own trench. He had been out alone for
one and a half hours.

MARLING, Percival Scrope (later Sir Percival)   **837**
Lieutenant (later Colonel)   3rd Bn., The King's Royal Rifle Corps, attd. Mounted Infantry
Other Decorations: CB
Date of Gazette: 21 May 1884
Place/Date of Birth: King's Stanley, Stroud, Gloucestershire — 6 Mar. 1861
Place/Date of Death: Stanley Park, Stroud, Gloucestershire — 29 May 1936
Memorials: Buried at Stanley Park; Great Rissington Church, Glos.; KRRC Memorial in
Winchester Cathedral   *Harrow School*
Town/County Connections: King's Stanley and Great Rissington, Glos.
Remarks: Served in South African War 1899-1902 (18th Hussars); served with HQ Staff, Indian
Army Corps in France 1914-15; High Sheriff of County of Gloucester 1928
Account of Deed: On 13 Mar. 1884 in the Sudan, Lieutenant Marling risked his life to save that of a private of The Royal Sussex
Regiment who had been shot. The private fell off the lieutenant's horse as soon as he was put up in front, so, although the
enemy were pressing closely, Lieutenant Marling carried the wounded man to a place of comparative safety.

MARSHALL, John Neville   **838**
A/Lieutenant Colonel   Irish Guards (S.R.) attd. The Lancashire Fusiliers, comd. 16th Bn.
Other Decorations: MC & Bar
Date of Gazette: 13 Feb. 1919
Place/Date of Birth: Acocks Green, Birmingham — 12 Jun. 1887
Place/Date of Death: Catillon, France — 4 Nov. 1918
Memorials: Ors Communal Cemetery, France; War Memorial, Old Harlow, Essex
Town/County Connections: Harlow, Essex
Remarks: Crois de Guerre (Belgium); Chevalier of the Order of Leopold (Belgium)
Account of Deed: On 4 Nov. 1918 at the Sambre-Oise Canal, near Catillon, France, when a partly
constructed bridge was badly damaged before the advanced troops of his battalion could cross,
Lieutenant Colonel Marshall organised repair parties. The first party were soon killed or wounded, but the colonel's personal
example was such that more volunteers were instantly forthcoming. Under intense fire and with complete disregard of his own
safety he stood on the bank encouraging his men and helping in the work. When the bridge was repaired he attempted to lead
his men across, but was killed while so doing.

MARSHALL, William Thomas   **839**
Quartermaster-Sergeant (later Lieutenant Colonel and Quartermaster), 19th Hussars (Princess of
Wales's Own)
Other Decorations: —
Date of Gazette: 21 May 1884
Place/Date of Birth: Newark, Nottinghamshire — 5 Dec. 1854
Place/Date of Death: Kirkcaldy, Fife, Scotland — 11 Sep. 1920
Memorials: Kirkcaldy Cemetery, Fife
Town/County Connections: Newark, Nottinghamshire; Kirkcaldy, Fife
Remarks: Served in South African War 1899-1900
Account of Deed: On 29 Feb. 1884 at El Teb, Sudan, the Commanding Officer of the 18th Hussars
was severely wounded, his horse was killed and he was on the ground surrounded by the enemy. Quartermaster-Sergeant
Marshall, who stayed behind with him, seized his hand and dragged him through the enemy back to the regiment, saving him
from certain death.

MARTIN, Cyril Gordon   **840**
Lieutenant (later Brigadier)   56th Field Coy., Corps of Royal Engineers
Other Decorations: CBE, DSO
Date of Gazette: 19 Apr. 1915
Place/Date of Birth: Foochow, China — 19 Dec. 1891
Place/Date of Death: Woolwich, London — 14 Aug. 1980
Memorials: —
Town/County Connections: —
Remarks: Deputy Chief Engineer, Northern Command, India 1939; Chief Engineer, British
Troops in Iraq 1941; Chief Engineer, N.W. Army India 1945-47; ADC to The King 1945-47
Account of Deed: On 12 Mar. 1915 at Spanbroek Molen, Belgium, Lieutenant Martin volunteered
to lead a small bombing party against a section of the enemy trenches which was holding up the advance. Before he started he
was wounded, but, taking no notice, he carried on with the attack which was completely successful. He and his small party held
the trench against all counter-attacks for two and a half hours until a general withdrawal was ordered.

MARTINEAU, Horace Robert   **841**
Sergeant (later Lieutenant)   Protectorate Regiment (N.W. Cape Colony), South African Forces
Other Decorations: —
Date of Gazette: 6 Jul. 1900
Place/Date of Birth: Bayswater, London — 31 Oct. 1874
Place/Date of Death: Dunedin, New Zealand — 8 Apr. 1916
Memorials: —
Town/County Connections: Bayswater, London
Remarks: Served in Transport Service with the Anzacs at Suez and Gallipoli in First World War
Account of Deed: On 26 Dec. 1899 near Mafeking, South Africa, during the action at Game Tree, when the order to retire had been given, Sergeant Martineau rescued a corporal who had been struck down near the Boer trenches. The sergeant managed to half-drag, half-carry the wounded man to a bush where he attended to his wounds. He was shot in the side himself, but took no notice and carried on helping the corporal until he was wounded a second time and was forced to give up.

MARTIN-LEAKE, Arthur — see **LEAKE,** Arthur MARTIN-

MASTERS, Richard George   **842**
Private   Royal Army Service Corps, attd. 141st Field Ambulance
Other Decorations: —
Date of Gazette: 8 May 1918
Place/Date of Birth: Southport, Lancashire — 30 Mar. 1877
Place/Date of Death: Southport, Lancashire — 4 Apr. 1963
Memorials: —
Town/County Connections: Southport and Formby, Lancashire
Remarks: —
Account of Deed: On 9 Apr. 1918 near Bethune, France, owing to an enemy attack, communications were cut off and the wounded could not be evacuated. The road was reported impassable but Private Masters volunteered to try to get through and after great difficulty succeeded, although he had to clear the road of all sorts of debris. He made journey after journey throughout the afternoon over a road consistently shelled and swept by machine-gun fire and once he was bombed by an aeroplane. The greater number of wounded were evacuated by him as his was the only car which got through.

MASTERSON, James Edward Ignatius   **843**
Lieutenant (later Major)   1st Bn., The Devonshire Regiment
Other Decorations: —
Date of Gazette: 4 Jun. 1901
Place/Date of Birth: ? — 20 Jun. 1862
Place/Date of Death: Waterlooville, Hampshire — 24 Dec. 1935
Memorials: Tablet in Exeter Cathedral
Town/County Connections: Waterlooville, Hampshire
Remarks: Served in First World War 1914-15
Account of Deed: On 6 Jan. 1900 at Wagon Hill, Ladysmith, South Africa, Lieutenant Masterson was commanding one of the three companies of his regiment which captured a position held by the enemy. The companies were then exposed to very heavy fire from the right and left front, so the lieutenant undertook to get a message to the Imperial Light Horse, to fire to the left front in order to check the enemy's fire. To do this he had to cross an open space of 100 yards swept by heavy cross-fire, but although wounded in both thighs, he managed to deliver his message before falling, exhausted.

MAUDE, Francis Cornwallis   **844**
Captain (later Colonel)   Royal Regiment of Artillery
Other Decorations: CB
Date of Gazette: 18 Jun. 1858
Place/Date of Birth: London — 28 Oct. 1828
Place/Date of Death: Windsor, Berkshire — 19 Oct. 1900   *Windsor Cemetery, St. Leonard Road, Windsor*
Memorials: St. George's Chapel, Windsor · *Plaque.*
Town/County Connections: London; Windsor, Berkshire
Remarks: Cousin of Bt/Lieutenant Colonel F.F. Maude, VC; Military Knight of Windsor 1895
Account of Deed: On 25 Sep. 1857 at Lucknow, India, Captain Maude steadily and cheerfully pushed on with his men and bore down the desperate opposition of the enemy, though with the loss of one third of his artillerymen. He fully appreciated the dangers of the task he had undertaken, and but for his nerve and coolness, the Army could not have advanced.

MAUDE, Frederick Francis (later Sir Frederick)　　　　　　　　**845**
Bt/Lieutenant Colonel (later General)　3rd Regiment (later East Kent Regiment — The Buffs)
Other Decorations:　GCB
Date of Gazette:　24 Feb. 1857
Place/Date of Birth:　Lisnadill, Co. Armagh, Ireland — 20 Dec. 1821
Place/Date of Death:　Torquay, Devon — 20 Jun. 1897
Memorials:　Brompton Cemetery, London
Town/County Connections:　Lisnadill, Co. Armagh; Torquay, Devon
Remarks:　Cousin of Captain F.C. Maude, VC; Adjutant General, Gibraltar 1861-66; Inspector General of Militia in Ireland 1867-73; Légion d'Honneur (France).
Account of Deed:　On 5 Sep. 1855 at Sebastopol, Crimea, Lieutenant Colonel Maude was in charge of the covering and ladder party of the 2nd Division in the assault on the Redan. He held a position with only nine or ten men and did not retire until all hope of support was at an end and he himself was dangerously wounded.

MAUFE, Thomas Harold Broadbent　　　　　　　　**846**
Second Lieutenant (later Captain)　124th Siege Bty., Royal Garrison Artillery
Other Decorations:　—
Date of Gazette:　2 Aug. 1917
Place/Date of Birth:　Ilkley, Yorkshire — 6 May 1898
Place/Date of Death:　Ilkley, Yorkshire — 28 Mar. 1942
Memorials:　Ilkley Cemetery, Yorkshire
Town/County Connections:　Ilkley, Yorkshire
Remarks:　Served in the Home Guard in the Second World War.
Account of Deed:　On 4 Jun. 1917 at Feuchy, France, Second Lieutenant Maufe, on his own initiative and under intense artillery fire repaired, unaided, the telephone wire between the forward and rear positions, thereby enabling his battery to open fire on the enemy. He also saved what could have been a disastrous occurrence by extinguishing a fire in an advanced ammunition dump caused by a heavy explosion, regardless of the risk he ran from the effects of gas shells in the dump.

MAXWELL, Francis Aylmer　　　　　　　　**847**
Lieutenant (later Brigadier General)　Indian Staff Corps, attd. Roberts's Light Horse
Other Decorations:　CSI, DSO & Bar
Date of Gazette:　8 Mar. 1901
Place/Date of Birth:　Guildford, Surrey — 7 Sep. 1871
Place/Date of Death:　Ypres, Belgium — 21 Sep. 1917
Memorials:　Ypres Reservoir Cemetery, Belgium; St. Giles' Cathedral, Edinburgh
Town/County Connections:　Guildford, Surrey
Remarks:　Military Secretary to Lord Hardinge, 1911; served with the 12th Bn., The Middlesex Regiment during the First World War 1916-17
Account of Deed:　On 31 Mar. 1900 at Korn Spruit, South Africa, Lieutenant Maxwell carried out the self-imposed duty of saving the guns. He went out on five different occasions and helped to bring in two guns and three limbers, one of which he, another officer and some gunners dragged in by hand. He also went out with two other officers and tried to get the last gun in and remained there until the attempt had to be abandoned. During a previous campaign, (the Chitral Expedition, 1895) he had removed the body of a lieutenant colonel of the Corps of Guides, under fire.

MAXWELL, Joseph　　　　　　　　**848**
Lieutenant　18th Bn. (N.S.W.) Australian Imperial Force
Other Decorations:　MC & Bar, DCM
Date of Gazette:　6 Jan. 1919
Place/Date of Birth:　Forest Lodge, Sydney, New South Wales, Australia — 10 Feb. 1896
Place/Date of Death:　Sydney, Australia — 6 Jul. 1967
Memorials:　Eastern Suburbs Crematorium, Sydney; Australian War Memorial, Canberra
Town/County Connections:　—
Remarks:　—
Account of Deed:　On 3 Oct. 1918 on the Beaurevoir-Fonsomme line near Estrees, north of St. Quentin, France, Lieutenant Maxwell's company commander was severely wounded early in the advance and he at once took charge. On two occasions he advanced alone, through heavy wire entanglements, killing and taking prisoner a number of the enemy and capturing a machine-gun. Later he skilfully extricated his men from an encounter with a strong party of the enemy. Throughout the day, he set a high example of personal bravery.

MAY, Henry   **849**
Private (later Lieutenant)　1st Bn., The Cameronians (Scottish Rifles)
Other Decorations: —
Date of Gazette: 19 Apr. 1915
Place/Date of Birth: Glasgow — 2 Sep. 1885
Place/Date of Death: Niddrie, Scotland — 26 Jul. 1941
Memorials: —
Town/County Connections: Glasgow and Niddrie
Remarks: —
Account of Deed: On 22 Oct. 1914 near La Boutillerie, France, Private May tried to rescue, under very heavy fire, a wounded man who was killed before he could save him. Later, on the same day, he carried a wounded officer 300 yards into safety while exposed to very severe fire.

MAYGAR, Leslie Cecil   **850**
Lieutenant (later Lieutenant Colonel)　5th Victorian Mounted Rifles, Australian Forces
Other Decorations: DSO, VD
Date of Gazette: 11 Feb. 1902
Place/Date of Birth: Dean Station, Milmore, Victoria, Australia — 26 May 1872
Place/Date of Death: Karm, Palestine — 17 Nov. 1917
Memorials: Beersheba War Cemetery, Palestine; Australian War Memorial, Canberra
Town/County Connections: —
Remarks: Served with 8th Australian Light Horse in the First World War
Account of Deed: On 23 Nov. 1901 at Geelhoutboom, Natal, South Africa, Lieutenant Maygar galloped out and ordered men of a detached post, which was being outflanked, to retire. The horse of one of the men was shot under him when the enemy were within 200 yards and Lieutenant Maygar dismounted and lifted the man on to his own horse which bolted into boggy ground, making them both dismount. As the horse could not carry two, the lieutenant again put the man on its back and told him to gallop for cover at once, while he himself went on foot. All this took place under very heavy fire. *Memorial tree in Avenue of Honour at Eurora, Victoria. Nearby hill now after him*

MAYO, Arthur   **851**
Midshipman　Indian Navy (Naval Brigade)
Other Decorations: —
Date of Gazette: 25 Feb. 1862
Place/Date of Birth: Oxford — 18 May 1840
Place/Date of Death: Boscombe, Hampshire — 18 May 1920
Memorials: Boscombe Cemetery, Hampshire
Town/County Connections: Oxford; Torquay, Devon; Boscombe, Hampshire
Remarks: —
Account of Deed: On 22 Nov. 1857 at Dacca, India, Midshipman Mayo headed the charge when the Indian Naval Brigade was ordered to charge two 6-pounder guns manned by the mutineers which were keeping up a heavy fire. Mr. Mayo was nearly 20 yards in front of everyone else during the advance.

MAYSON, Tom Fletcher   **852**
Lance-Sergeant　1/4th Bn., The King's Own (Royal Lancaster) Regiment
Other Decorations: —
Date of Gazette: 14 Sep. 1917
Place/Date of Birth: Silecroft, Cumberland — 3 Nov. 1893
Place/Date of Death: Barrow-in-Furness, Lancashire — 21 Feb. 1958
Memorials: St. Mary's Churchyard, Whicham, near Silecroft; The Priory, Lancaster; St. Mary's Church, Whicham.
Town/County Connections: Silecroft, Cumberland; Barrow-in-Furness, Lancashire
Remarks: —
Account of Deed: On 31 Jul. 1917 at Wieltje, Belgium, when his platoon was held up by machine-gun fire, Lance-Sergeant Mayson, without waiting for orders, at once made for the gun which he put out of action with bombs, wounding four of the team; the remaining three of the team fled, pursued by Lance-Sergeant Mayson to a dug-out where he killed them. Later, when clearing up a strong point, this NCO again tackled a machine-gun single-handed, killing six of the team. Finally during an enemy counter-attack he took charge of an isolated post and successfully held it until ordered to withdraw and his ammunition was exhausted.

MEEKOSHA, (later changed name to INGHAM) Samuel   **853**
Corporal (later Captain)   1/6th Bn., The West Yorkshire Regiment (The Prince of Wales's Own)
Other Decorations: —
Date of Gazette: 22 Jan. 1916
Place/Date of Birth: Leeds, Yorkshire — 16 Sep. 1893
Place/Date of Death: Blackwood, Monmouthshire — 8 Dec. 1950
Memorials: — *Cremated at Pontypridd, Glamorganshire*
Town/County Connections: Leeds and Bradford, Yorkshire; Penarth, Glamorgan; Oakdale, Monmouthshire
Remarks: —
Account of Deed: On 19 Nov. 1915 near the Yser, France, Corporal Meekosha was with a platoon of about 20 NCOs and men holding an isolated trench. During a very heavy bombardment six of the platoon were killed and seven wounded, while the rest were more or less buried. When there were no senior NCOs left in action Corporal Meekosha took command, sent for help and in spite of more big shells falling within 20 yards of him, continued to dig out the wounded and buried men in full view of and at close range from the enemy. His courage saved at least four lives.

MEIKLE, John   **854**
Sergeant   4th Bn., The Seaforth Highlanders (Ross-shire Buffs, Duke of Albany's)
Other Decorations: MM
Date of Gazette: 16 Sep. 1918
Place/Date of Birth: Kirkintilloch, Dunbartonshire, Scotland — 11 Sep. 1898
Place/Date of Death: Marfaux, France — 20 Jul. 1918
Memorials: Marfaux British Cemetery, France; Station Square, Dingwall, Ross and Cromarty, Scotland
Town/County Connections: Nitshill, Lanarkshire, Scotland
Remarks: —
Account of Deed: On 20 Jul. 1918 near Marfaux, France, Sergeant Meikle, single-handed and armed only with a revolver and a stick, rushed and put out of action a machine-gun which was delaying his company's advance. Shortly afterwards, seizing a rifle and bayonet from a fallen comrade, he charged another machine-gun post, but was killed almost on the gun position. His bravery enabled two other men who followed him to put this gun out of action.

MEIKLEJOHN, Matthew Fontaine Maury   **855**
Captain (later Major)   2nd Bn., The Gordon Highlanders
Other Decorations: —
Date of Gazette: 20 Jul. 1900
Place/Date of Birth: Clapham, London — 27 Nov. 1870
Place/Date of Death: London — 4 Jul. 1913
Memorials: Brookwood Cemetery, Woking, Surrey *Grave*
Town/County Connections: St. Andrews, Fife, Scotland; Richmond, Surrey
Remarks: —
Account of Deed: On 21 Oct. 1899 at the Battle of Elandslaagte, South Africa, after the main Boer position had been captured, some men of the Gordon Highlanders who were about to assault a kopje were exposed to heavy cross-fire, and having lost their leaders started to waver. Seeing this, Captain Meiklejohn rushed to the front and called on the Gordons to follow him. By his conspicuous bravery and example he rallied the men and led them against the enemy's position, where he fell, desperately wounded in four places.

MELLISH, Edward Noel   **856**
Captain The Reverend, T/Chaplain   Army Chaplains' Department
Other Decorations: MC
Date of Gazette: 20 Apr. 1916
Place/Date of Birth: Barnet, Hertfordshire — 24 Dec. 1880
Place/Date of Death: South Petherton, Somerset — 8 Jul. 1962
Memorials: —
Town/County Connections: Barnet, Hertfordshire; South Petherton, Somerset; Lewisham, London; Dunmow, Essex. *One time Vicar of Great Dunmow, Essex.*
Remarks: Served in South African War (as a trooper in Baden Powell's Police) 1900-02; served as an Air Raid Warden during the Second World War. *Lewisham, London.*
Account of Deed: During the period 27/29 Mar. 1916 at St. Eloi, Belgium, Captain The Reverend Noel Mellish went backwards and forwards under continuous and very heavy shell and machine-gun fire between our original trenches and those captured from the enemy, in order to tend and rescue wounded men. He brought in 10 badly wounded men on the first day from ground swept by machine-gun fire. He went back on the second day and brought in 12 more and on the night of the third day he took charge of a party of volunteers and once more returned to the trenches to rescue the remaining wounded.

He was curate at St Pauls Church Deptford. Look for tablet or window.
He was married here after the Armistice.

MELLISS, Charles John (later Sir Charles)   **857**
Captain (later Major General)   Indian Staff Corps, attd. West African Force
Other Decorations: KCB, KCMG
Date of Gazette: 15 Jan. 1901
Place/Date of Birth: Mhow, India — 12 Sep. 1862
Place/Date of Death: Camberley, Surrey — 6 Jun. 1936
Memorials: St. Peter's Churchyard, Frimley, Surrey; Sanctum Crypt, St. Luke's Church, Chelsea,
London
Town/County Connections: Camberley, Surrey
Remarks: Served in the First World War 1914-16   *Wellington College, Berks*
Account of Deed: On 30 Sep. 1900 at Obassa (Ashanti War), Captain Melliss gathered together
a party of men and charged into the bush at the head of them, into the thick of the enemy. Although wounded in a hand-to-hand
encounter, his bold rush caused panic among the enemy who were at the same time charged by the Sikhs.

MELVILL, Teignmouth   **858**
Lieutenant   1st Bn., 24th Regiment (later The South Wales Borderers)
Other Decorations: —
Date of Gazette: 2 May 1878 and 15 Jan. 1907
Place/Date of Birth: London — 8 Sep. 1842
Place/Date of Death: Buffalo River, Zululand — 22 Jan. 1879
Memorials: Name inscribed on Colour pole of the 24th Regiment; St Winnow's Church,
Cornwall   *Window/plaque in St. Winnows Church, Near Lostwithiel.*
Town/County Connections: London; Cornwall   *Harrow School.*
Remarks: —   *VC in SWB Museum, Brecon.*
Account of Deed: On 22 Jan. 1879 after the disaster of the Battle of Isandhlwana, South Africa,
Lieutenant Melvill made gallant efforts to save the Queen's Colour of his Regiment. He and another officer* were pursued by
Zulu warriors and after experiencing great difficulty in crossing the swollen River Buffalo (during which time the Colour was
unfortunately carried downstream) the two men were overtaken by the enemy and following a short but gallant struggle both
were killed. (*See also COGHILL, N.) Note: The Colour was retrieved from the river 10 days later.

MELVIN, Charles   **859**
Private   2nd Bn., The Black Watch (Royal Highlanders)
Other Decorations: —
Date of Gazette: 26 Nov. 1917
Place/Date of Birth: Boddin Craig, Montrose, Angus, Scotland — 2 May 1885
Place/Date of Death: Kirriemuir, Scotland — 17 Jul. 1941
Memorials: —
Town/County Connections: Kirriemuir, Scotland
Remarks: —
Account of Deed: On 21 Apr. 1917 at Istabulat, Mesopotamia, Private Melvin's company were
waiting for reinforcements before attacking a front-line trench, but he rushed on by himself over
ground swept by rifle and machine-gun fire. On reaching the trench and having killed one or two of the enemy, he jumped into
it and attacked the rest with his bayonet. Most of the enemy then fled but not before Private Melvin had killed two more and
disarmed eight unwounded and one wounded. He bound up the wounded man and took him and his other prisoners back to
an officer before reporting back to his platoon sergeant.

MERRIFIELD, William   **860**
Sergeant   4th Bn., 1st Central Ontario Regiment, C.E.F.
Other Decorations: MM
Date of Gazette: 6 Jan. 1919
Place/Date of Birth: Brentwood, Essex — 9 Oct. 1890
Place/Date of Death: Toronto, Canada — 8 Aug. 1943
Memorials: West Korah Cemetery, Sault Ste. Marie, Ontario, Canada
Town/County Connections: Brentwood, Essex
Remarks: —
Account of Deed: On 1 Oct. 1918 at Abancourt, France, Sergeant Merrifield attacked two
machine-gun emplacements single-handed, when they were holding up the advance of his
platoon. Dashing from shell-hole to shell-hole he killed the occupants of the first post and, although wounded, continued to
attack the second post and with a bomb killed the occupants. He refused to be evacuated and led his platoon until he was again
severely wounded.

MERRITT, Charles Cecil Ingersoll **861**
Lieutenant Colonel   Comd. The South Saskatchewan Regiment, Canadian Infantry Corps
Other Decorations: —
Date of Gazette: 2 Oct. 1942
Place/Date of Birth: Vancouver, Canada — 10 Nov. 1908
Place/Date of Death: — *About 16.7.2000*
Memorials: —
Town/County Connections: —
Remarks: —
Account of Deed: On 19 Aug. 1942 at Dieppe, France, Lieutenant Colonel Merritt's unit had to advance across a bridge swept by very heavy machine-gun, mortar and artillery fire. The first parties had mostly been destroyed but the colonel rushed forward and personally led the survivors of at least four parties, in turn, across the bridge, and then led them in successful attacks on German pill-boxes. Although twice wounded he continued to direct the unit's operations and having collected Bren and tommy guns, prepared a defensive position to cover the withdrawal from the beach.

METCALF, William Henry **862**
Lance-Corporal   16th Bn., Manitoba Regiment (Canadian Scottish), C.E.F.
Other Decorations: MM
Date of Gazette: 15 Nov. 1918
Place/Date of Birth: Waite Township, Walsh Co., Maine, U.S.A. — 29 Jan. 1885
Place/Date of Death: Lewiston, Maine, U.S.A. — 8 Aug. 1968
Memorials: Bayside Cemetery, Eastport, Maine, U.S.A.
Town/County Connections: —
Remarks: —
Account of Deed: On 2 Sep. 1918 at Arras, France, when the right flank of the battalion was held up, Lance-Corporal Metcalf rushed forward under intense machine-gun fire to a passing tank and with his signal flag walked in front of the tank directing it along the trench in a perfect hail of bullets and bombs. The machine-gun strong-point was overcome, very heavy casualties were inflicted and a critical situation was relieved. Later, although wounded, Corporal Metcalf continued to advance until ordered to get into a shell-hole and have his wounds dressed.

MEYNELL, Godfrey **863**
Captain   Corps of Guides, 12 Frontier Force Regiment, Indian Army
Other Decorations: MC
Date of Gazette: 24 Dec. 1935
Place/Date of Birth: Meynell Langley, Derbyshire — 20 May 1904
Place/Date of Death: Mohmand, North West Frontier, India — 29 Sep. 1935
Memorials: Guides' Cemetery, Mardan, India; Kirk Langley Church, Derbyshire; Sanctum crypt, St. Luke's church, Chelsea, London
Town/County Connections: Meynell Langley, Derbyshire
Remarks: The VC was given to Captain Meynell's widow by King Edward VIII — the only one of his reign.
Account of Deed: On 29 Sep. 1935 on the North West Frontier, India, in the final phase of an attack, Captain Meynell, seeking information on the most forward troops, found them involved in a struggle against an enemy vastly superior in numbers. He at once took command and with two Lewis guns and about 30 men maintained a heavy and accurate fire on the advancing enemy, but their overwhelming numbers nevertheless succeeded in reaching the position and putting the Lewis gun out of action. In the hand-to-hand struggle which ensued, Captain Meynell was mortally wounded, but the heavy casualties inflicted on the enemy prevented them from exploiting their success.

MIDDLETON, Rawdon Hume **864**
Flight Sergeant (promotion to Pilot Officer w.e.f. 14 Nov. 1942 notified posthumously)   Royal Australian Air Force, serving with 149 Squadron, Royal Air Force
Other Decorations: —
Date of Gazette: 15 Jan. 1943
Place/Date of Birth: Waverley, New South Wales, Australia — 22 Jul. 1916
Place/Date of Death: At sea, near Dymchurch, Kent — 29 Nov. 1942
Memorials: St. John's Churchyard, Mildenhall, Suffolk; Australian War Memorial, Canberra
Town/County Connections: —
Remarks: —
Account of Deed: On 28/29 Nov. 1942 during a raid on Turin, Italy, Flight Sergeant Middleton was captain of a Stirling bomber which was damaged by A.A. fire over the target. One shell burst in the cockpit, destroying the captain's right eye and also wounding the second pilot and the wireless operator. Although there was heavy flak and the aircraft was hit many times, the bombs were released and then the aircraft, badly damaged and with insufficient fuel, made its difficult return journey over the Alps. Near the English coast Flight Sergeant Middleton ordered his crew to bale out, then turned and crashed into the sea to avoid causing civilian casualties.

MIERS, Anthony Cecil Capel (later Sir Anthony)   **865**
Commander (later Rear-Admiral)   Royal Navy
Other Decorations: KBE, CB, DSO & Bar
Date of Gazette: 7 Jul. 1942
Place/Date of Birth: Birchwood, Inverness, Scotland — 11 Nov. 1906
Place/Date of Death: Inverness, Scotland — 30 Jun. 1985
Memorials: — *Buried Tamnahurich Cemetery, Glenurquhart Road, Inverness*
Town/County Connections: Inverness, Scotland.
Remarks: Officer of the U.S. Legion of Merit; Flag Officer, Middle East 1956-59; National President, Submarine Old Comrades' Association.
Account of Deed: On 4 Mar. 1942 in Corfu Harbour, Commander Miers, commanding HM Submarine *Torbay*, having followed an enemy convoy into the harbour the previous day, fired torpedoes at a destroyer and two 5000-ton transports, scoring hits on the two supply ships, which almost certainly sank. *Torbay* then had a very hazardous withdrawal to the open sea, enduring 40 depth-charges. The submarine had been in closely patrolled enemy waters for 17 hours.

MILBANKE, Sir John Peniston   **866**
Lieutenant (later Lieutenant Colonel)   10th Hussars (Prince of Wales's Own Royal)
Other Decorations:
Date of Gazette: 6 Jul. 1900
Place/Date of Birth: London — 9 Oct. 1872
Place/Date of Death: Suvla, Gallipoli — 21 Aug. 1915
Memorials: Helles Memorial, Gallipoli
Town/County Connections: — *Harrow School. Eartham, Sussex. (see in church*
Remarks: Served with The Nottinghamshire Yeomanry in the First World War
Account of Deed: On 5 Jan. 1900 near Colesberg, South Africa, during a reconnaissance, Lieutenant Milbanke, when retiring under fire, with a small patrol, rode back to help one of his men whose horse was exhausted. Notwithstanding the fact that he was severely wounded in the thigh, the lieutenant took the man up on his own horse under very heavy fire and got him safely back to camp.

MILES, Francis George   **867**
Private   1/5th Bn., The Gloucestershire Regiment
Other Decorations: —
Date of Gazette: 6 Jan. 1919
Place/Date of Birth: Clearwell, near Coleford, Gloucestershire — 9 Jul. 1896
Place/Date of Death: Clearwell, near Coleford, Gloucestershire — 8 Nov. 1961
Memorials: —
Town/County Connections: Clearwell, near Coleford, Gloucestershire
Remarks: —
Account of Deed: On 23 Oct. 1918 at Bois de l'Eveque, Landrecies, France, when his company was held up by a line of enemy machine-guns in a sunken road, Private Miles, alone and on his own initiative went forward under exceptionally heavy fire, located a machine-gun, shot the gunner and put the gun out of action. Then seeing another gun near by, he again went forward alone, shot the gunner and captured the team of eight. Finally he stood up and beckoned to his company who, acting on his signals, were able to capture 16 machine-guns, one officer and 50 other ranks.

MILLAR, (or MILLER) Duncan   **868**
Private   42nd Regiment (later The Black Watch (Royal Highlanders))
Other Decorations: —
Date of Gazette: 18 Jun. 1859
Place/Date of Birth: Kilmarnock, Ayrshire, Scotland — 19 Jun. 1824
Place/Date of Death: Glasgow — 15 Jul. 1881
Memorials: —
Town/County Connections: Kilmarnock, Ayrshire; Glasgow
Remarks: —
Account of Deed: On 15 Jan. 1859 at Maylah Ghat, India, when the fighting was most severe and the few men of the 42nd Regiment were skirmishing so close to the enemy (who were in great numbers) that some of them were wounded by sword cuts, the only officer was severely wounded and the colour-sergeant was killed. Private Millar and another private* immediately went to the front and took a prominent part in directing the company and displayed a courage, coolness and discipline which was the admiration of all who witnessed it. (*See also COOK, W.)

No photograph available

MILLER, Frederick   **869**

Lieutenant (later Lieutenant Colonel)   Royal Regiment of Artillery
Other Decorations: —
Date of Gazette: 6 May 1859
Place/Date of Birth: Radway-under-Edge Hill, Warwickshire — 10 Nov. 1831
Place/Date of Death: Cape Town, South Africa — 17 Feb. 1874
Memorials: Obelisk in graveyard of Radway Parish Church, Warwickshire
Town/County Connections: Radway, Warwickshire
Remarks: Légion d'Honneur (France)
Account of Deed: On 5 Nov. 1854 at the Battle of Inkerman, Crimea, Lieutenant Miller personally attacked three Russians and with the gunners of his division of the battery prevented the enemy from doing mischief to the guns which they had surrounded. Part of a regiment of English infantry had previously retired through the battery in front of this body of Russians.

MILLER, James   **870**

Conductor (later Hon. Lieutenant)   Bengal Ordnance Depot
Other Decorations: —
Date of Gazette: 25 Feb. 1862
Place/Date of Birth: Glasgow — 1820
Place/Date of Death: Simla, India — 12 Jun. 1892
Memorials: —
Town/County Connections: Glasgow
Remarks: —
Account of Deed: On 28 Oct. 1857 at Futtehpore, Sikra, near Agra, India, Conductor Miller at great personal risk, went to the assistance of a wounded officer and carried him out of action. He himself was subsequently wounded.

MILLER, James   **871**

Private   7th Bn., The King's Own (Royal Lancaster) Regiment
Other Decorations: —
Date of Gazette: 9 Sep. 1916
Place/Date of Birth: Withnell, near Chorley, Lancashire — 4 May 1890
Place/Date of Death: Bazentin-le-Petit, France — 31 Jul. 1916
Memorials: Dartmoor Cemetery, France; The Priory, Lancaster.
Town/County Connections: Hoghton and Chorley, Lancashire
Remarks: —
Account of Deed: On 30/31 Jul. 1916 at Bazentin-le-Petit, France, the battalion was consolidating its position and Private Miller was ordered to take an important message under heavy shell and rifle fire and to bring back a reply at all costs. He was compelled to cross the open and on leaving the trench was almost immediately mortally wounded. In spite of this he managed to deliver the message and to stagger back with the answer, falling dead at the feet of the officer to whom he delivered it.

MILLS, Walter   **872**

Private   1/10th Bn., The Manchester Regiment
Other Decorations: —
Date of Gazette: 13 Feb. 1918
Place/Date of Birth: Oldham, Lancashire — 20 Jun. 1894
Place/Date of Death: Givenchy, France — 11 Dec. 1917
Memorials: Gorre British Cemetery, France
Town/County Connections: Oldham, Lancashire
Remarks: — *Name on W.M. inside and outside St. Mary's Church, Oldham*
Account of Deed: On 10/11 Dec. 1917 at Givenchy, France, after an intense gas attack a strong enemy patrol tried to rush our posts, the garrisons of which had been overcome. Private Mills, although badly gassed himself, met the attack single-handed and continued to throw bombs until the arrival of reinforcements and remained at his post until the enemy had been finally driven off. While being carried away he died of gas poisoning but it was entirely due to him that the enemy was defeated and the line retained intact.

MILNE, William Johnstone   **873**
Private   16th Bn., Manitoba Regiment (Canadian Scottish), C.E.F.
Other Decorations: —
Date of Gazette: 8 Jun. 1917
Place/Date of Birth: Wishaw, Lanarkshire, Scotland — 21 Dec. 1892
Place/Date of Death: Vimy, France — 9 Apr. 1917
Memorials: Vimy Memorial, France
Town/County Connections: Cambusnethan, Lanarkshire, Scotland
Remarks: —
Account of Deed: On 9 Apr. 1917 near Thelus, France, on approaching the first objective, Private Milne noticed an enemy machine-gun firing on our advancing troops. Crawling on hands and knees he managed to reach the gun which he captured, killing the crew. Later, he again located a machine-gun in the support line, but stalking this gun, as he had the first, he put the crew out of action and captured it. He was killed shortly afterwards.

MINER, Harry Garnet Bedford   **874**
Corporal   58th Bn., 2nd Central Ontario Regiment, C.E.F.
Other Decorations: —
Date of Gazette: 26 Oct. 1918
Place/Date of Birth: Cedar Springs, Ontario, Canada — 24 Jun. 1891
Place/Date of Death: Demuin, France — 8 Aug. 1918
Memorials: Grouy British Cemetery, France
Town/County Connections: —
Remarks: Croix de Guerre (France)
Account of Deed: On 8 Aug. 1918 at Demuin, France, Corporal Miner rushed an enemy machine-gun post single-handed, killed the entire crew and turned the gun on the enemy. Later, with two others, he attacked another machine-gun post and put it out of action. Then again, this NCO rushed an enemy bombing post alone, bayoneting two of the garrison and putting the remainder to flight. He was mortally wounded during this action but refused to withdraw. He died later that day.

MIR DAST,   **875**
Jemadar   55 Coke's Rifles (F.F.), attd. 57th Wilde's Rifles (F.F.) Indian Army
Other Decorations: IOM
Date of Gazette: 29 Jun. 1915
Place/Date of Birth: Landai, Tirah, India — 3 Dec. 1874
Place/Date of Death: Pakistan — 24 Jun. 1950
Memorials: —
Town/County Connections: —
Remarks: —
Account of Deed: On 26 Apr. 1915 at Wieltje, Belgium, Jemadar Mir Dast led his platoon with great bravery during the attack, and afterwards collected various parties of the regiment (when no British officers were !eft) and kept them under his command until the retirement was ordered. He also displayed great courage that day when he helped to carry eight British and Indian officers to safety while exposed to heavy fire.

MITCHELL, Coulson Norman   **876**
Captain (later Lieutenant Colonel)   1st Tunnelling Coy., 4th Canadian Engineers, C.E.F.
Other Decorations: MC
Date of Gazette: 31 Jan. 1919
Place/Date of Birth: Winnipeg, Canada — 11 Dec. 1889
Place/Date of Death: Mount Royal, Quebec, Canada — 17 Nov. 1978
Memorials: —
Town/County Connections: —
Remarks: —
Account of Deed: On 8/9 Oct. 1918 at the Canal de l'Escaut, north-east of Cambrai, France, Captain Mitchell led a small party to examine the bridges and if possible prevent their demolition. He managed to cut a number of 'lead' wires on one bridge, then in total darkness he dashed across the main bridge which was heavily charged. While he and his NCO were cutting the wires the enemy attacked, whereupon the captain at once went to the assistance of his sentry who had been wounded, killing three of the enemy and capturing 12. Under heavy fire he then continued to cut the wires and remove charges.

MITCHELL, George Allan   **877**
Private   The London Scottish (Gordon Highlanders)
Other Decorations: —
Date of Gazette: 10 Aug. 1944
Place/Date of Birth: Highgate, London — 30 Aug. 1911
Place/Date of Death: Damiano, Italy — 24 Jan. 1944
Memorials: Minturno War Cemetery, Italy; George Mitchell School, Walthamstow, London.
Town/County Connections: Highgate and Walthamstow, London
Remarks: —
Account of Deed: On 23/24 Jan. 1944 at Damiano Ridge, Italy, when an advance was held up by enemy machine-guns firing at point-blank range, Private Mitchell charged alone up the hill through intense Spandau fire, jumped into the weapon pit and killed the crew. The advance then continued, but shortly afterwards was again held up and this time Private Mitchell's assault on the position resulted in six of the enemy killed and 12 taken prisoner. He led two more successful attacks before falling dead, shot by one of the enemy who had surrendered.

MITCHELL, Samuel   **878**
Captain of the Foretop   Royal Navy
Other Decorations: —
Date of Gazette: 23 Jul. 1864
Place/Date of Birth: Apsley Guise, Woburn, Bedfordshire — 8 Sep. 1841
Place/Date of Death: Mikonui River, near Hokitika, New Zealand — 16 Mar. 1894
Memorials: Grave on hillside, near Ross, New Zealand
Town/County Connections: Woburn, Bedfordshire
Remarks: —
Account of Deed: On 29 Apr. 1864 near Te Papa, Tauranga, New Zealand, a storming party of 150 sailors and marines from HMS *Harrier*, together with the same number of soldiers of the 43rd Light Infantry, succeeded in establishing themselves inside a fortified position known as the Gate Pah. The enemy's fire, however, was heavy and accurate and all the officers were either killed or wounded. Captain of the Foretop Mitchell went into the pah with the commander of *Harrier*, and when that officer was mortally wounded Mitchell insisted on bringing him out to safety although ordered to go and save himself.

MOFFATT, Martin   **879**
Private   2nd Bn., The Prince of Wales's Leinster Regiment
Other Decorations: —
Date of Gazette: 26 Dec. 1918
Place/Date of Birth: Sligo, Ireland — 15 Apr. 1884
Place/Date of Death: Sligo, Ireland — 5 Jan. 1946
Memorials: —
Town/County Connections: Sligo, Ireland
Remarks: —
Account of Deed: On 14 Oct. 1918 near Ledeghem, Belgium, Private Moffat was advancing with five others across the open when they suddenly came under heavy rifle fire at close range from a strongly held house. Rushing towards the house through a hail of bullets, Private Moffat threw bombs and then, working to the back of the house, rushed the door, killing two and capturing 30 of the enemy.

MOLYNEUX, John   **880**
Sergeant   2nd Bn., The Royal Fusiliers
Other Decorations: —
Date of Gazette: 26 Nov. 1917
Place/Date of Birth: Peasley Cross, St. Helens, Lancashire — 22 Nov. 1890
Place/Date of Death: St. Helens, Lancashire — 25 Mar. 1972
Memorials: —
Town/County Connections: St. Helens, Lancashire
Remarks: Croix de Guerre (Belgium)
Account of Deed: On 9 Oct. 1917 east of Langemarck, Belgium, during an attack which was held up by machine-gun fire and causing many casualties, Sergeant Molyneux organised a bombing party to clear the trench in front of a house. Many of the enemy were killed and a machine-gun captured. The sergeant then called for someone to follow him and rushed for the house. By the time the extra men arrived he was in the thick of a hand-to-hand fight which only lasted a short time and the enemy surrendered. In addition to the dead and wounded between 20 and 30 prisoners were taken.

MONAGHAN, Thomas   881

Trumpeter (later Sergeant-Trumpeter)   2nd Bn., Dragoon Guards (Queen's Bays)
Other Decorations: —
Date of Gazette: 11 Nov. 1862
Place/Date of Birth: Abergavenny, Monmouthshire — 18 Oct. 1833
Place/Date of Death: Woolwich, London — 10 Nov. 1895
Memorials: Woolwich Cemetery, London   *R C Section 33 . Plot 826*
Town/County Connections: Abergavenny, Monmouthshire; Woolwich, London
Remarks: — *VC with Queens Dragoon Guards, Shrewsbury*
Account of Deed: On 8 Oct. 1858 at Jamo, near Sundeela, Oudh, India, a group of mutineers (30 to 40 in number) suddenly opened fire on the officer commanding the regiment and his party, and then rushed upon them with drawn swords. In the fighting which ensued the colonel was cut down by two sword cuts, and Trumpeter Monaghan and a dragoon* immediately came to his rescue, shooting one of the assailants and driving at others with swords, enabling the colonel to rise and defend himself, until the enemy were despatched. (*See also ANDERSON, C.)

MONGER, George   882

Private   23rd Regiment (later The Royal Welch Fusiliers)
Other Decorations: —
Date of Gazette: 12 Apr. 1859
Place/Date of Birth: Woodmancott, Hampshire — 3 Mar. 1840
Place/Date of Death: St. Leonards-on-Sea, Sussex — 9 Aug. 1887
Memorials: Hastings Borough Cemetery; Woodmancott Church, Hampshire   *Plaque in church*
Town/County Connections: Woodmancott, Hampshire; Hastings, Sussex
Remarks: — *Grave Space E. Section H. No. E18. Hastings Borough Cemetery*
Account of Deed: On 18 Nov. 1857 at Secundra Bagh, Lucknow, India, Private Monger volunteered to accompany an officer* whom he assisted in rescuing a corporal of the 23rd Regiment, who was lying wounded and exposed to very heavy fire. (*See also HACKETT, T.B.)
VC in RWF Museum. Caernarvon Castle

MOON, Rupert Vance   883

Lieutenant (later Captain)   58th Bn. (Victoria) Australian Imperial Force
Other Decorations: —
Date of Gazette: 14 Jun. 1917
Place/Date of Birth: Bacchus Marsh, Victoria, Australia — 14 Aug. 1892
Place/Date of Death: Melbourne, Victoria, Australia — 28 Feb. 1986   *Died Barwonhead Victoria*
Memorials: Australian War Memorial, Canberra
Town/County Connections: —
Remarks: —
Account of Deed: On 12 May 1917 near Bullecourt, France, Lieutenant Moon's immediate objective was a position in advance of a hostile trench, and then against the trench itself, after the capture of which it was intended that his men should co-operate in a further assault. Although wounded in the initial advance, he reached the first objective, but was again wounded in the assault on the trench. He nevertheless continued to inspire and encourage his men and captured the trench, but was again wounded when consolidating the position. It was not until he was severely wounded for a fourth time that he agreed to retire from the fight.

MOOR, George Raymond Dallas   884

Second Lieutenant (later Lieutenant)   2nd Bn. The Hampshire Regiment
Other Decorations: MC & Bar
Date of Gazette: 24 Jul. 1915
Place/Date of Birth: Melbourne, Victoria, Australia — 22 Oct. 1896
Place/Date of Death: Mouveaux, France — 3 Nov. 1918
Memorials: Y Farm Military Cemetery, France;
Town/County Connections: Bournemouth, Hampshire
Remarks: —
Account of Deed: On 5 Jun. 1915 south of Krithia, Gallipoli, when a detachment of the battalion which had lost all its officers was rapidly retiring before a heavy Turkish attack, Second Lieutenant Moor, realising the danger to the rest of the line, dashed back some 200 yards, stemmed the retirement, led back the men and recaptured the lost trench. This brave act saved a dangerous situation.

MOORE, Arthur Thomas   **885**
Lieutenant (later Major General)   3rd Bombay Light Cavalry
Other Decorations: CB
Date of Gazette: 3 Aug. 1860
Place/Date of Birth: Carlingford, Louth, Ireland — 20 Sep. 1830
Place/Date of Death: Dublin — 25 Apr. 1913
Memorials: —
Town/County Connections: Carlingford, Louth; Dublin
Remarks: —
Account of Deed: On 8 Feb. 1857 at the Battle of Khoosh-ab, Persia, Lieutenant Moore who was
Adjutant of the Regiment, was probably the first in the attack, but his horse, on leaping into the
square, fell dead, crushing his rider and breaking his sword. Lieutenant Moore extricated himself, but he would almost certainly
have lost his life had not another lieutenant* fought his way to his dismounted comrade and carried him to safety. In this battle
Lieutenant Moore also charged an infantry square of 500 Persians at the head of his regiment and jumped his horse over the
enemy's bayonets. (*See also MALCOMSON, J.G.)

MOORE, Hans Garrett   **886**
Major (later Colonel)   88th Regiment (later The Connaught Rangers)
Other Decorations: CB
Date of Gazette: 27 Jun. 1879
Place/Date of Birth: Richmond Barracks, Dublin — 31 Mar. 1834
Place/Date of Death: Lough Derg, Tipperary, Ireland — 6 Oct. 1889
Memorials: —
Town/County Connections: Dublin; Cloghan, King's Co. (later Offaly)
Remarks: —
Account of Deed: On 29 Dec. 1877 near Komgha, South Africa, during an action with the Gaikas,
Major Moore saw that a private of the Frontier Mounted Police was unable to mount his horse and
was left at the mercy of the Kaffirs. Realising the danger, Major Moore rode back alone in the midst of the enemy, and continued
in his efforts to save the man's life until the latter was killed. The major shot two Kaffirs and received an assegai in the arm during
this gallant attempt.

MOORE, Montague Shadworth Seymour   **887**
Second Lieutenant (later Major)   15th Bn., The Hampshire Regiment
Other Decorations: —
Date of Gazette: 8 Nov. 1917
Place/Date of Birth: Bournemouth, Hampshire — 9 Oct. 1896
Place/Date of Death: Kugenzo, Kenya — 12 Sep. 1966
Memorials: (Ashes scattered in game park.)
Town/County Connections: Bournemouth, Hampshire *Bedford School.*
Remarks: Game Ranger, 1926-44; Game Warden, Tanganyika 1944-51.
Account of Deed: On 20 Aug. 1917 near Tower Hamlets, east of Ypres, Belgium, Second
Lieutenant Moore volunteered to make a fresh attack on a final objective and went forward with
some 70 men, but they met such heavy opposition that when he arrived at his objective he had only one sergeant and four men.
Nothing daunted he at once bombed a large dug-out, taking 28 prisoners, two machine-guns and a light field-gun. Gradually
more officers and men arrived, numbering about 60 and he held the post for 36 hours beating off counter-attacks, until his force
was reduced to 10 men. He eventually got away his wounded and withdrew under cover of thick mist.

MOORHOUSE, William Bernard RHODES-   **888**
Second Lieutenant (promotion to Lieutenant w.e.f 24 Apr. 1915 notified posthumously)
2 Squadron, Royal Flying Corps
Other Decorations: —
Date of Gazette: 22 May 1915
Place/Date of Birth: London — 26 Sep. 1887
Place/Date of Death: Merville, France — 27 Apr. 1915
Memorials: Buried at his family home, Parnham House, Dorset
Town/County Connections: London; Beaminster, Dorset *Harrow School*
Remarks: The first airman to perform an action subsequently rewarded with the VC; the ashes
of his son (Flying-Officer W. Rhodes-Moorhouse), killed in action during the Battle of Britain, are
interred by the side of his father at Parnham.
Account of Deed: On 26 Apr. 1915 at Courtrai, Belgium, Second Lieutenant Rhodes-Moorhouse swept low over the rail
junction which he had been ordered to attack. He released his 100lb. bomb, but was immediately plunged into a heavy barrage
of small arms fire from rifles and a machine-gun in the belfry of Courtrai Church; he was severely wounded by a bullet in his
thigh and his plane was also badly hit. Returning to the Allied lines, he again ran into heavy fire from the ground and was
wounded twice more. He managed to get his aircraft back, and insisted on making his report before being taken to the Casualty
Clearing Station where he died the next day.

MORLEY, Samuel   **889**
Private   2nd Bn., Military Train (later Royal Army Service Corps)
Other Decorations: —
Date of Gazette: 7 Aug. 1860
Place/Date of Birth: East Retford, Nottinghamshire — Dec. 1839
Place/Date of Death: Nottingham — 16 Jun. 1888
Memorials: —
Town/County Connections: Radcliffe, Nottinghamshire
Remarks: —
Account of Deed: On 15 Apr. 1858 at Azimgurh, India, when Koer Singh's army was being
pursued, an adjutant of the Sikh Cavalry was dismounted and wounded by the enemy. Private
Morley, whose own horse had been shot under him, nevertheless immediately went to his aid, together with a farrier* and cut
down one of the sepoys. The two men shielded the adjutant's body, staying close to him until further assistance arrived, thereby
saving him from being killed on the spot. (*See also MURPHY, M.)

MORRELL, Thomas — see **YOUNG,** Thomas

MORROW, Robert   **890**
Private   1st Bn., The Royal Irish Fusiliers
Other Decorations: —
Date of Gazette: 22 May 1915
Place/Date of Birth: Coalisland, near Dungannon, Co Tyrone, Ireland — 7 Sep. 1891
Place/Date of Death: St. Jan, Ypres Salient, Belgium — 26 Apr. 1915
Memorials: White House Cemetery, Belgium
Town/County Connections: New Mills, near Dungannon, Co. Tyrone
Remarks: —
Account of Deed: On 12 Apr. 1915 near Messines, Belgium, Private Morrow rescued and carried
to places of comparative safety several men who had been buried in the débris of trenches
wrecked by shell fire. He carried out this work on his own initiative and under heavy fire from the enemy.

MOTT, Edward John   **891**
Sergeant   1st Bn., The Border Regiment
Other Decorations: DCM
Date of Gazette: 10 Mar. 1917
Place/Date of Birth: Drayton, near Abingdon, Berkshire — 4 Jul. 1893
Place/Date of Death: Withay, Oxfordshire — 20 Oct. 1967
Memorials: —
Town/County Connections: Drayton, Abingdon, Berkshire; Withay, Oxfordshire
Remarks: —
Account of Deed: On 27 Jan. 1917 south of Le Transloy, France, an attack by Sergeant Mott's
company was held up at a strong point by machine-gun fire. Although severely wounded in the
eye, Sergeant Mott made a rush for the gun and after a fierce struggle seized the gunner and took him prisoner, capturing the
gun. It was due to the dash and initiative of this NCO that the left flank attack succeeded.

MOTTERSHEAD, Thomas   **892**
Sergeant   20 Squadron, Royal Flying Corps
Other Decorations: DCM
Date of Gazette: 12 Feb. 1917
Place/Date of Birth: Widnes, Lancashire — 17 Jan. 1892
Place/Date of Death: Bailleul, France — 12 Jan. 1917
Memorials: Bailleul Communal Cemetery Extension, France; obelisk in Victoria Park, Widnes.
Town/County Connections: Widnes, Lancashire
Remarks: —
Account of Deed: On 7 Jan. 1917 near Ploegsteert Wood, Belgium, Sergeant Mottershead was
on flying patrol when he was attacked at an altitude of 9,000ft, the petrol tank pierced and the
machine set on fire. Enveloped in flames which his observer was unable to subdue, the sergeant nevertheless managed to take
his aircraft back to the Allied lines and made a successful landing. The undercarriage collapsed on touching the ground
however, throwing the observer clear but pinning the pilot in his cockpit. He was subsequently rescued but died four days later.

MOUAT, James (later Sir James)   **893**
Surgeon (later Surgeon General)   6th Dragoons (Inniskilling)
Other Decorations: KCB
Date of Gazette: 2 Jun. 1858
Place/Date of Birth: Chatham, Kent — 14 Apr. 1815
Place/Date of Death: Kensington, London — 4 Jan. 1899
Memorials: Kensal Green Cemetery, London   · *Grave*
Town/County Connections: Chatham, Kent; Kensington, London
Remarks: Légion d'Honneur (France)
Account of Deed: On 26 Oct. 1854 in the Crimea, at Balaclava, Surgeon Mouat went with a corporal* to the assistance of an officer who was lying seriously wounded in an exposed position, after the retreat of the Light Cavalry. He dressed the officer's wounds under heavy fire from the enemy, and by stopping a severe haemorrhage, helped to save his life. (*See also WOODEN, C)

MOUNTAIN, Albert   **894**
Sergeant   15/17th Bn., The West Yorkshire Regiment (The Prince of Wales's Own)
Other Decorations: —
Date of Gazette: 7 Jun. 1918
Place/Date of Birth: Leeds, Yorkshire — 19 Apr. 1895
Place/Date of Death: Leeds, Yorkshire — 7 Jan. 1967
Memorials: —
Town/County Connections: Leeds, Yorkshire
Remarks: Croix de Guerre and Médaille Militaire (France).
Account of Deed: On 26 Mar. 1918 at Hamelincourt, France, when the situation was critical, Sergeant Mountain with a party of 10 men attacked an advance enemy patrol of about 200 strong with a Lewis gun, killing half of them. The sergeant then rallied his men in the face of overwhelming numbers of the main body of the enemy, to cover the retirement of the rest of the company — this party of one NCO and four men held at bay 600 of the enemy for half an hour. Sergeant Mountain later took command of the flank post of the battalion, holding on for 27 hours until finally surrounded.

MOYNEY, John   **895**
Lance-Sergeant (later Sergeant)   2nd Bn., Irish Guards
Other Decorations: —
Date of Gazette: 17 Oct. 1917
Place/Date of Birth: Rathdowney, Queen's Co. (later Leix), Ireland — 8 Jan. 1885
Place/Date of Death: Roscrea, Tipperary, Ireland — 10 Nov. 1980
Memorials: —
Town/County Connections: Rathdowney, Queen's Co. (Leix)
Remarks: —
Account of Deed: On 12/13 Sep. 1917 north of Broembeek, Belgium, Lance-Sergeant Moyney was in command of 15 men forming two advanced posts. Surrounded by the enemy he held his post for 96 hours, having no water and very little food. On the fifth day, on the enemy advancing to dislodge him, he attacked them with bombs, while also using his Lewis gun with great effect. Finding himself surrounded, he led his men in a charge through the enemy and reached a stream, where he and a private* covered his party while they crossed unscathed, before crossing themselves under a shower of bullets. (*See also WOODCOCK, T.)

MOYNIHAN, Andrew   **896**
Sergeant (later Captain)   90th Regiment (later The Cameronians — Scottish Rifles)
Other Decorations: —
Date of Gazette: 24 Feb. 1857
Place/Date of Birth: Wakefield, Yorkshire — 8 Sep. 1831
Place/Date of Death: Malta — 19 May 1867
Memorials: —
Town/County Connections: Wakefield, Yorkshire
Remarks: —
Account of Deed: On 8 Sep. 1855 in the Crimea, Sergeant Moynihan, who was with the storming party at the assault on the Redan, personally encountered and killed five Russians. He also rescued from near the Redan a wounded officer under very heavy fire.

MUGFORD, Harold Sandford **897**
Lance-Corporal 8th Sqdn., Machine Gun Corps
Other Decorations: —
Date of Gazette: 26 Nov. 1917
Place/Date of Birth: St. James' London — 31 Aug. 1894
Place/Date of Death: Chelmsford, Essex — 16 Jun. 1958
Memorials: —
Town/County Connections: St. James' and East Ham, London; Chelmsford, Essex
Remarks: —
Account of Deed: On 11 Apr. 1917 at Monchy-le-Preux, France, under intense fire, Lance-Corporal Mugford got his machine-gun into a forward, very exposed position from which he dealt very effectively with the enemy. Almost immediately his No. 2 was killed and he was severely wounded. He was ordered to go to a new position and then have his wounds dressed but this he refused to do, staying to inflict severe damage on the enemy with his gun. Soon afterwards a shell broke both his legs, but he still remained with his gun and when he was at last removed to the dressing station he was again wounded.

MUIR, Kenneth **898**
Major 1st Bn., The Argyll and Sutherland Highlanders (Princess Louise's)
Other Decorations: —
Date of Gazette: 5 Jan. 1951
Place/Date of Birth: Chester — 6 Mar. 1912
Place/Date of Death: Near Songju, Korea — 23 Sep. 1950
Memorials: United Nations Memorial Cemetery, Pusan, Korea; St. Peter's Churchyard, Frimley, Surrey
Town/County Connections: Chester; Camberley, Surrey
Remarks: United Nations Silver Star
Account of Deed: On 23 Sep. 1950 near Songju, Korea, there was difficulty in evacuating the wounded after a position had been captured, until Major Muir arrived with a stretcher party. When the enemy started to launch a series of attacks on the positions, the major took over command and after a direct hit from a fire bomb, causing further casualties, he led a counter-attack and the crest of the position was regained. He was determined to hold it until all the wounded had been evacuated and moved about his small force shouting encouragement and firing a 2-in. mortar himself until he was mortally wounded.

MULLANE, Patrick **899**
Sergeant (later Regimental Sergeant-Major) Royal Horse Artillery
Other Decorations: —
Date of Gazette: 16 May 1881
Place/Date of Birth: Ahmednuggar, Deccan, India — Oct. 1858
Place/Date of Death: Plaistow, Sussex — 20 Nov. 1919
Memorials: —
Town/County Connections: —
Remarks: —
Account of Deed: On 27 Jul. 1880 during the action at Maiwand, (Afghan War), Sergeant Mullane's battery was on the point of retiring and the enemy was within 10 or 15 yards when the sergeant ran back and picked up a wounded driver and placed him on the limber, where unfortunately he died almost immediately. Again, during the retreat, Sergeant Mullane volunteered to procure water for the wounded and succeeded in doing so by going into one of the villages in which so many men lost their lives.

MULLIN, George Harry **900**
Sergeant (later Major) Princess Patricia's Canadian Light Infantry, Eastern Ontario Regiment, C.E.F.
Other Decorations: MM
Date of Gazette: 11 Jan. 1918
Place/Date of Birth: Portland, Oregon, U.S.A. — 15 Aug. 1892
Place/Date of Death: Regina, Saskatchewan, Canada — 5 Apr. 1963
Memorials: South Cemetery Legion Plot, Moosomin, Saskatchewan
Town/County Connections: —
Remarks: —
Account of Deed: On 30 Oct. 1917 at Passchendaele, Belgium, Sergeant Mullin single-handed captured a pill box which had withstood heavy bombardment and was causing heavy casualties and holding up the attack. He rushed the snipers' post in front, destroyed the garrison with bombs, shot two gunners and then compelled the remaining 10 men to surrender. All the time rapid fire was directed on him and his clothes were riddled with bullets, but he never faltered in his purpose and he not only helped to save the situation, but indirectly saved many lives.

MULLINS, Charles Herbert   **901**
Captain (later Major)   Imperial Light Horse (Natal), South African Forces
Other Decorations: CMG
Date of Gazette: 12 Feb. 1901
Place/Date of Birth: Grahamstown, Cape Colony, South Africa — 28 Jun. 1869
Place/Date of Death: Johannesburg, South Africa — 24 May 1916
Memorials: Grahamstown War Monument; St. Andrew's Chapel, Grahamstown
Town/County Connections: —
Remarks: —
Account of Deed: On 21 Oct. 1899 at Elandslaagte, South Africa, at a most critical moment, when the advance was momentarily checked by very severe fire at point-blank range, Captain Mullins and another officer* gallantly rushed forward under very heavy fire and rallied the men, thus enabling the decisive flanking movement to be carried out. Captain Mullins was wounded during the action. (*See also JOHNSTON, R.)

MUNRO, James   **902**
Colour-Sergeant   93rd Regiment (later The Argyll and Sutherland Highlanders — Princess Louise's)
Other Decorations: —
Date of Gazette: 8 Nov. 1860
Place/Date of Birth: Nigg, Cromarty, Ross, Scotland — 1827
Place/Date of Death: Inverness, Scotland — 15 Feb. 1871
Memorials: —
Town/County Connections: Nigg, Cromarty, Ross
Remarks: —
Account of Deed: On 16 Nov. 1857 at Lucknow, India, Colour-Sergeant Munro rushed to the rescue of a captain of his regiment who was severely wounded at the Secundra Bagh. The colour-sergeant carried the wounded officer to a place of safety — the same place to which the sergeant himself was carried shortly afterwards, badly wounded.

MURPHY, Michael   **903**
Farrier (later Farrier Major)   2nd Bn., Military Train (later Royal Army Service Corps)
Other Decorations: —
Date of Gazette: 27 May 1859
Place/Date of Birth: Cahir, Tipperary, Ireland — 1831
Place/Date of Death: Darlington, Co. Durham — 4 Apr. 1893
Memorials: Darlington North Municipal Cemetery
Town/County Connections: Cahir, Tipperary; Darlington, Co. Durham
Remarks: —
Account of Deed: On 15 Apr. 1858 near Azimgurh, India when Koer Singh's army was being pursued, the adjutant of the 3rd Sikh Cavalry was wounded, dismounted and surrounded by the enemy. Farrier Murphy, together with a private*, immediately went to his aid. The farrier cut down several of the enemy and although he himself was severely wounded, the two men never left the wounded officer, until further assistance arrived, thereby saving him from being killed on the spot. (*See also MORLEY, S.)

MURPHY, Thomas   **904**
Private   2nd Bn., 24th Regiment (later The South Wales Borderers)
Other Decorations: —
Date of Gazette: 17 Dec. 1867
Place/Date of Birth: Dublin — 1839
Place/Date of Death: Philadelphia, U.S.A. — 22 Mar. 1900
Memorials: —
Town/County Connections: Dublin
Remarks: VC not awarded for bravery in action against the enemy, but for bravery at sea in saving life in storm off Andaman Islands
Account of Deed: On 7 May 1867 at the island of Little Andaman, Bay of Bengal, Private Murphy was one of a party of five* of the 2/24th Regiment, who risked their lives in manning a boat and proceeding through dangerous surf to rescue some of their comrades who had been sent to the island to find out the fate of the commander and seven of the crew, who had landed from the ship *Assam Valley* and were feared murdered by the cannibalistic islanders. (*See also BELL, David, COOPER, J., DOUGLAS, C.M. and GRIFFITHS, W.)

MURRAY, The Rt. Hon. Alexander Edward — see **FINCASTLE,** Viscount

MURRAY, Henry William   **905**
Captain (later Lieutenant Colonel)   13th Bn. (N.S.W.), Australian Imperial Force
Other Decorations: CMG, DSO & Bar, DCM
Date of Gazette: 10 Mar. 1917
Place/Date of Birth: Launceston, Tasmania — 30 Dec. 1884
Place/Date of Death: Brisbane, Queensland, Australia — 7 Jan. 1966
Memorials: Mt. Thompson Crematorium, Brisbane; Australian War Memorial, Canberra
Town/County Connections: —
Remarks: Croix de Guerre (France); Organized defence force of Queensland bushmen during
Second World War
Account of Deed: On 4/5 Feb. 1917, at Stormy Trench, north-east of Gueudecourt, France,
Captain Murray led his company to the assault and quickly captured an enemy position. Very heavy fighting followed, and three
times counter-attacks were beaten back owing to this officer's wonderful work. During the night the company suffered heavy
casualties and on one occasion gave ground, but Captain Murray saved the situation, encouraging his men, leading bayonet
charges and carrying the wounded to places of safety.

MURRAY, James   **906**
Lance-Corporal   2nd Bn., The Connaught Rangers
Other Decorations: —
Date of Gazette: 14 Mar. 1882
Place/Date of Birth: St. Michael's, Cork City, Ireland — Feb. 1859
Place/Date of Death: Dublin — 19 Jul. 1942
Memorials: —
Town/County Connections: Cork; Dublin
Remarks: —
Account of Deed: On 16 Jan. 1881 at Elandsfontein, near Pretoria, South Africa, Lance-Corporal
Murray, with a trooper of Nourse's Horse* advanced for 500 yards under heavy fire from a party
of about 60 of the enemy, and brought out of action a private who was severely wounded. (*See also DANAHER, J.)

MURRAY, John   **907**
Sergeant   68th Regiment (later The Durham Light Infantry)
Other Decorations: —
Date of Gazette: 4 Nov. 1864
Place/Date of Birth: Birr, King's Co. (later Offaly), Ireland — Feb. 1837
Place/Date of Death: Derrinlogh, King's Co. (Offaly) — 7 Nov. 1911
Memorials: —
Town/County Connections: Birr, King's Co. (Offaly)
Remarks: —
Account of Deed: On 21 Jun. 1864 at Tauranga, New Zealand, when the enemy's position was
being stormed, Sergeant Murray ran up to a rifle pit containing eight to ten of the enemy and,
without any assistance, killed or wounded all of them. He then went on up the works, fighting with his bayonet.

MYLES, Edgar Kinghorn   **908**
Second Lieutenant (later Captain)   8th Bn., The Welch Regt., attd. 9th Bn., The Worcestershire
Regt.
Other Decorations: DSO
Date of Gazette: 26 Sep. 1916
Place/Date of Birth: Wanstead, Essex — 29 Jul. 1894
Place/Date of Death: Bishopsteignton, Devon — 1 Feb. 1977
Memorials: — *Cremated at Torquay Crematorium*
Town/County Connections: Wanstead, Essex; Bishopsteignton, Devon
Remarks: — *VC in Worcestershire Regt Museum. Worcester.*
Account of Deed: On 9 Apr. 1916 at Sanna-i-Yat, Mesopotamia, Second Lieutenant Myles went
out alone several times in front of our advanced trenches and, under heavy rifle fire, at great personal risk, helped wounded men
lying in the open. On one occasion he carried in a wounded officer to a place of safety under circumstances of great danger.

No photograph available

MYLOTT, Patrick   909
Private (later Sergeant)   84th Regiment (later The York and Lancaster Regiment)
Other Decorations: —
Date of Gazette: 24 Dec. 1858
Place/Date of Birth: Hollymount, near Claremorris, Co. Mayo, Ireland — 1820
Place/Date of Death: Liverpool, Lancashire — 22 Dec. 1878
Memorials: —
Town/County Connections: Claremorris, Co. Mayo
Remarks: —
Account of Deed: From 12 Jul./25 Sep. 1857 in India, Private Mylott was conspicuous for gallant conduct — once for rushing across a road under a shower of musket balls to take an opposite enclosure, and at every engagement in which he was present with his unit. (Elected by the regiment.)

MYNARSKI, Andrew Charles   910
Warrant Officer II (promotion to Pilot Officer w.e.f. 11 Jun. 1944 notified posthumously)   419 Squadron, Royal Canadian Air Force
Other Decorations: —
Date of Gazette: 11 Oct. 1946
Place/Date of Birth: Winnipeg, Canada — 14 Oct. 1916
Place/Date of Death: Near Cambrai, France — 13 Jun. 1944
Memorials: Meharicourt Cemetery, Somme, France; Mynarski Lakes, Manitoba
Town/County Connections: —
Remarks: —
Account of Deed: On 12 Jun. 1944 over Cambrai, France, Pilot Officer Mynarski was mid-upper gunner of a Lancaster aircraft when fire broke out after an attack by enemy fighters and the captain ordered the crew to bale out. As Pilot Officer Mynarski went towards the escape hatch he saw that the rear gunner was trapped in his turret and immediately made his way through the flames to his assistance, but all his efforts were in vain. His own clothing was on fire and eventually being persuaded that nothing more could be done he returned to the escape hatch and jumped out. He was found by the French, but was so badly burned that he died of his injuries.

NAMDEO JADHAO,   911
Sepoy (later Havildar)   5th Mahratta Light Infantry, Indian Army
Other Decorations: —
Date of Gazette: 19 Jun. 1945
Place/Date of Birth: Nimaj Village, Admednagar District, Bombay, India — 18 Nov. 1921
Place/Date of Death: India — 2 Aug. 1984
Memorials: —
Town/County Connections: —
Remarks: PVSM (India)
Account of Deed: On 9 Apr. 1945 at the Senio River, when a small party were almost wiped out in an assault on the east floodbank of the river, Sepoy Namdeo Jadhao carried two wounded men under heavy fire through deep water, up a steep bank and through a mine belt to safety. Then, determined to avenge his dead comrades, he eliminated three enemy machine-gun posts. Finally, climbing on top of the bank he shouted the Mahratta war cry and waved the remaining companies across. He not only saved many lives but enabled the battalion to secure the bridgehead and ultimately to crush all enemy resistance in the area.

NAND SINGH   912
A/Naik (later Jemadar)   1/11th Sikh Regiment, Indian Army
Other Decorations: —
Date of Gazette: 6 Jun. 1944
Place/Date of Birth: Bahadur Village, Patiala State, Punjab, India — 24 Sep. 1914
Place/Date of Death: Uri, Kashmire — 12 Dec. 1947
Memorials: —
Town/County Connections: —
Remarks: —
Account of Deed: On 11/12 Mar. 1944 on the Maungdaw-Buthidaung Road, Burma, Naik Nand Singh, commanding a leading section of the attack, was ordered to recapture a position gained by the enemy. He led his section up a very steep knife-edged ridge under very heavy machine-gun and rifle fire and although wounded in the thigh, captured the first trench. He then crawled forward alone and, wounded again in the face and shoulder, nevertheless captured the second and third trenches.

NAPIER, William   **913**
Sergeant (later Sergeant-Major)   1st Bn., 13th Regiment (later The Somerset Light Infantry — Prince Albert's)
Other Decorations: —
Date of Gazette: 24 Dec. 1858
Place/Date of Birth: Bingley, Yorkshire — 1828
Place/Date of Death: Rochester, Victoria, Australia — 2 Jun. 1908
Memorials: Rochester Cemetery, Victoria, Australia
Town/County Connections: Bingley, Yorkshire
Remarks: —
Account of Deed: On 6 Apr. 1858 near Azimgurh, India, Sergeant Napier defended and finally rescued a private of his regiment who was severely wounded. The sergeant stayed with the wounded man at the risk of his own life. Surrounded by sepoys, he bandaged the wound and finally carried the man to safety.

NASH, William   **914**
Corporal (later Sergeant)   2nd Bn., The Rifle Brigade (Prince Consort's Own)
Other Decorations: —
Date of Gazette: 24 Dec. 1858
Place/Date of Birth: Newcastle, Co. Limerick, Ireland — 23 Apr. 1824
Place/Date of Death: Hackney, Middlesex — 29 Apr. 1875
Memorials: The Rifle Brigade Memorial, Winchester Cathedral
Town/County Connections: Newcastle, Co. Limerick
Remarks: —
Account of Deed: On 11 Mar. 1858 at Lucknow, India, Corporal Nash's company was engaged with a large number of the enemy near the Iron Bridge. At one stage a captain* found himself at the end of a street with only four of his men opposed to a considerable body of the enemy. One of the men was shot through both legs and Corporal Nash and a private* (who was himself severely wounded) lifted the man up and they then carried him for a considerable distance, the captain covering the retreat of the party. (*See also WILMOT, H. and HAWKES, D.)

NASMITH, Martin Eric (later Sir Martin Eric DUNBAR-)   **915**
Lieutenant Commander (later Admiral)   Royal Navy
Other Decorations: KCB, KCMG
Date of Gazette: 25 Jun. 1915
Place/Date of Birth: East Barnes, London — 1 Apr. 1883
Place/Date of Death: Elgin, Scotland — 29 Jun. 1965
Memorials: Buried in Elgin Cemetery
Town/County Connections: East Barnes, London; Weybridge, Surrey; Elgin, Scotland
Remarks: Knight Grand Cross of Orange Nassau and St. Olaf of Norway; Second Sea-Lord 1935-8; Commander-in-Chief Plymouth and Western Approaches 1938-41; Flag Officer in Charge, London 1942-46; after Second World War, Vice-Chairman, Imperial War Graves Commission
Account of Deed: During the period 20 May/8 Jun. 1915 in the Sea of Marmara, Dardanelles, Lieutenant-Commander Nasmith, in command of H.M. Submarine E.11, destroyed one large Turkish gunboat, two transports, one ammunition ship, three store ships and four other vessels. When he had safely passed the most difficult part of his homeward journey he returned to torpedo a Turkish transport.

NEAME, Philip (later Sir Philip)   **916**
Lieutenant (later Lieutenant General)   15th Field Coy., Corps of Royal Engineers
Other Decorations: KBE, CB, DSO
Date of Gazette: 18 Feb. 1915
Place/Date of Birth: Macknade, Faversham, Kent — 12 Dec. 1888
Place/Date of Death: Selling, near Faversham, Kent — 28 Apr. 1978
Memorials: Selling Church, Kent
Town/County Connections: Faversham, Kent
Remarks: Chevalier, Légion d'Honneur and Croix de Guerre (France); Croix de Guerre (Belgium); Knight of the Order of the White Lion (Czechoslovakia); Fellow of the Royal Geographical Society; Knight of the Order of St. John
Account of Deed: On 19 Jun. 1914 at Neuve Chapelle, France, Lieutenant Neame, in the face of very heavy fire, engaged the Germans in a single-handed bombing attack, killing and wounding a number of them. He was able to check the enemy advance for three-quarters of an hour and to rescue all the wounded whom it was possible to move.

NEEDHAM, Samuel — **917**

Private   1/5th Bn., The Bedfordshire Regiment
Other Decorations: —
Date of Gazette: 30 Oct. 1918
Place/Date of Birth: Great Limber, North Lincolnshire — 16 Aug. 1885
Place/Date of Death: Kantara, Egypt — 4 Nov. 1918
Memorials: Kantara War Memorial Cemetery, Egypt
Town/County Connections: Great Limber, North Lincolnshire
Remarks: —
Account of Deed: On 10/11 Sep. 1918 at Kefr Kasim, Palestine, one of our patrols was attacked by the enemy in considerable force, supported by very heavy fire. At a critical moment Private Needham ran back, turned to face a fresh body of the enemy which was approaching and fired rapidly at about 40 Turks at only 30 yards range. This action checked the enemy and just gave the patrol commander time to get his men together again. Half of the patrol were casualties but they managed to get back all their wounded. Private Needham's action in standing up to the enemy all alone did much to inspire the men and undoubtedly saved the situation.

NEELY, (usually mis-spelt NEELEY) Thomas — **918**

Corporal (Lance-Sergeant)   8th Bn., The King's Own (Royal Lancaster) Regiment
Other Decorations: MM
Date of Gazette: 14 Dec. 1918
Place/Date of Birth: Seacombe, Wallasey, Cheshire — 28 Mar. 1897
Place/Date of Death: Flesquieres, France — 1 Oct. 1918
Memorials: Masnieres British Cemetery, France; The Priory, Lancaster.
Town/County Connections: Seacombe, Wallasey, Cheshire; Liverpool, Lancashire
Remarks: —
Account of Deed: On 27 Sep. 1918 at Flesquieres, France, when his company was held up during the advance by heavy machine-gun fire, Corporal Neely realising the seriousness of the situation, at once under point-blank fire, dashed out with two men and rushed the gun positions, disposing of the garrisons and capturing three machine-guns. Subsequently, on two occasions, he rushed concrete strong points, killing or capturing the occupants. His actions enabled his company to advance 3,000 yards along the Hindenberg support line. He was killed three days later.

NELSON, David — **919**

Sergeant (later Major)   'L' Bty., Royal Horse Artillery
Other Decorations: —
Date of Gazette: 16 Nov. 1914
Place/Date of Birth: Deraghland, Stradnnoden, Co. Monaghan, Ireland — 3 Apr. 1886
Place/Date of Death: Lillers, France — 8 Apr. 1918
Memorials: Lillers Communal Cemetery, France
Town/County Connections: Deraghland, Stradnnoden, Co. Monaghan
Remarks: —
Account of Deed: On 1 Sep. 1914 at Nery, France, Sergeant Nelson helped to bring the guns into action (with an officer and a warrant officer*) under heavy fire and in spite of being severely wounded. He remained with the guns until all the ammunition was expended, although he had been ordered to retire to cover. (*See also BRADBURY, E.K. and DORRELL, G.T.)

NESBITT, Randolph Cosby — **920**

Captain (later Major)   Mashonaland Mounted Police, South African Forces
Other Decorations: —
Date of Gazette: 7 May 1897
Place/Date of Birth: Queenstown, Cape Colony, South Africa — 20 Sep. 1867
Place/Date of Death: Cape Town, South Africa — 23 Jul. 1956
Memorials: Ashes interred in Anglican Cathedral, Salisbury, Rhodesia
Town/County Connections: —
Remarks: —   (Mashonaland)
Account of Deed: On 19 Jun. 1896 near Salisbury, Rhodesia, Captain Nesbitt led a patrol consisting of only 13 men to go to the rescue of the miners at the Alice Mine in Mazoe Valley, who were surrounded by hordes of rebels. Captain Nesbitt and his patrol fought their way through the enemy and succeeded in getting the beleaguered party (including three women) back to Salisbury, in spite of heavy fighting in which three of the small rescue party were killed and five wounded.

NETRABAHADUR THAPA

921

A/Subadar 2nd Bn., 5th Royal Gurkha Rifles, Indian Army
Other Decorations: —
Date of Gazette: 12 Oct. 1944
Place/Date of Birth: Rahu Village, Bhirkot, Nepal — 8 Jan. 1916
Place/Date of Death: Near Bishenpur, Burma — 26 Jun. 1944
Memorials: The Rangoon Memorial, Burma
Town/County Connections: —
Remarks: —
Account of Deed: On 25/26 Jun. 1944 at Bishenpur, Burma, Subadar Netrabahadur Thapa was in command of a small isolated hill post, when the enemy attacked in force. The men, inspired by their leader's fine example, held their ground and the enemy were beaten off, but casualties were very heavy and reinforcements were requested. When these arrived some hours later they too became casualties, but the subadar, undeterred, retrieved the ammunition himself and took the offensive with grenades and kukris, until he was killed.

NETTLETON, John Dering

922

Squadron Leader (later Wing Commander)   44 Squadron, Royal Air Force
Other Decorations: —
Date of Gazette: 28 Apr. 1942
Place/Date of Birth: Nongoma, Natal, South Africa — 28 Jun. 1917
Place/Date of Death: Turin, Italy — 13 Jul. 1943
Memorials: The Runnymede Memorial, Surrey
Town/County Connections: —
Remarks: —
Account of Deed: On 17 Apr. 1942 over Augsberg, Germany, Squadron Leader Nettleton was the leader of one of two formations of six Lancaster bombers detailed to attack in daylight a diesel engine factory. Some time after crossing into enemy territory the formation was attacked by enemy fighters and four of the bombers were shot down, but the squadron leader held his two remaining aircraft on their course, and through intense anti-aircraft fire they flew low over rooftops and dropped their bombs. The second aircraft had to crash-land, but Squadron Leader Nettleton brought his Lancaster safely back to base, though riddled with holes.

No photograph available

NEWELL, Robert

923

Private   9th Lancers (The Queen's Royal)
Other Decorations: —
Date of Gazette: 24 Dec. 1858
Place/Date of Birth: Seaham, Co. Durham — 1835
Place/Date of Death: India — 11 Jul. 1858
Memorials: —
Town/County Connections: —
Remarks: —
Account of Deed: On 19 Mar. 1858 at Lucknow, India, Private Newell rescued a comrade whose horse had fallen, and took him to safety under heavy fire from a large number of the enemy.

NEWLAND, John Ernest

924

Captain (later Major)   12th Bn. (S.A., W.A. & Tasmania), Australian Imperial Force
Other Decorations: MSM
Date of Gazette: 8 Jun. 1917
Place/Date of Birth: Highton, Geelong, Victoria, Australia — 22 Aug. 1881
Place/Date of Death: Caulfield, Victoria, Australia — 19 Mar. 1948
Memorials: Brighton General Cemetery, Melbourne; Australian War Memorial, Canberra
Town/County Connections: —
Remarks: —
Account of Deed: On 7/9 Apr. 1917 at Bapaume, France, Captain Newland organized an attack by his company on an important objective and personally led a bombing attack under heavy fire, rallying his men who had suffered heavy casualties. The following night his company, holding the captured position, was heavily counter-attacked, but Captain Newland succeeded in regaining it. Later, on 15 Apr., north-east of Langnicourt, when one company was overpowered and his own was attacked from the rear, Captain Newland drove off several combined attacks and it was his tenacity and disregard for his own safety that encouraged his men to hold out.

NEWMAN, Augustus Charles   **925**
Lieutenant Colonel   The Essex Regiment, attd. No. 2 Commando
Other Decorations: OBE, TD
Date of Gazette: 19 Jun. 1945
Place/Date of Birth: Buckhurst Hill, Chigwell, Essex — 19 Aug. 1904
Place/Date of Death: Sandwich, Kent — 26 Apr. 1972
Memorials: Buried at Barham, Kent
Town/County Connections: Buckhurst Hill, Essex; Salford, Bedfordshire; Sandwich, Kent
Remarks: Légion d'Honneur and Croix de Guerre (France); MICE; Chairman of Federation of
Civil Engineering Contractors, 1957/58; DL, County of Essex
Account of Deed: On 27 Mar. 1942 in the attack on St. Nazaire, France, Lieutenant Colonel
Newman was in charge of the military forces and he was one of the first ashore, leading his men and directing operations quite
regardless of his own safety. Under his inspiring leadership the troops fought magnificently and held vastly superior numbers
of the enemy at bay until the demolition parties had done their work. The colonel then attempted to fight through into open
country and not until all the ammunition was spent were he and his men overwhelmed and taken prisoner.

NEWTON, William Ellis   **926**
Flight Lieutenant   22 Squadron, Royal Australian Air Force
Other Decorations: —
Date of Gazette: 19 Oct. 1943
Place/Date of Birth: St. Kilda, Victoria, Australia — 8 Jun. 1919
Place/Date of Death: Salamaua, New Guinea — 29 Mar. 1943
Memorials: Lae War Cemetery, New Guinea; Australian War Memorial, Canberra; St. Kilda
Presbyterian Church; Victoria Golf Club, Melbourne
Town/County Connections: —
Remarks: —
Account of Deed: On 16 Mar. 1943 in New Guinea, South-west Pacific, when leading an attack,
Flight Lieutenant Newton's aircraft was hit repeatedly, but in spite of this he flew through heavy fire and dropped his bombs
from low level on buildings and fuel dumps. He managed to get his crippled machine back to base and next day returned and
bombed a single building in the same area, but this time the aircraft burst into flames and with great difficulty he brought it
down in the sea. He and his flight sergeant were taken prisoner by the Japanese and later executed.

NGARIMU Moana-Nui-a-Kiwa   **927**
Second Lieutenant   28th Bn., 2nd N.Z.E.F.
Other Decorations: —
Date of Gazette: 4 Jun. 1943
Place/Date of Birth: Sir Apiraia Nata's Village, East Coast, New Zealand — 7 Apr. 1918
Place/Date of Death: Tunisia — 27 Mar. 1943
Memorials: Sfax War Cemetery, Tunisia; HQ, Dunedin RSA, New Zealand
Town/County Connections: —
Remarks: —
Account of Deed: On 26/27 Mar. during the action at Tobaga Gap, Tunisia, Second Lieutenant
Ngarimu, who was commanding a platoon in a vital hill feature strongly held by the enemy, led
his men straight up the face of the hill and was first on the crest. He personally destroyed two machine-gun posts and owing
to his inspired leadership several counter-attacks were beaten off during the night. He was twice wounded but refused to leave
his men. By morning when only two of his platoon remained unwounded, reinforcements arrived. When the next counter-
attack was launched, however, Second Lieutenant Ngarimu was killed.

NICHOLAS, Henry James   **928**
Private (later Sergeant)   1st Bn., Canterbury Infantry Regiment, N.Z.E.F.
Other Decorations: MM
Date of Gazette: 11 Jan. 1918
Place/Date of Birth: Lincoln, New Zealand — 11 Jun. 1891
Place/Date of Death: Vertigneul, France — 23 Oct. 1918
Memorials: Vertigneul Churchyard, France; HQ, Dunedin RSA, New Zealand
Town/County Connections: —
Remarks: —
Account of Deed: On 3 Dec. 1917 at Polderhoek, Belgium, Private Nicholas, who was one of a
Lewis gun section which was checked by heavy machine-gun and rifle fire from an enemy strong-
point, went forward followed by the remainder of his section at an interval of about 25 yards, shot the officer in command of
the strong-point and overcame the remainder of the garrison of 16 with bombs and bayonets, capturing four wounded
prisoners and a machine-gun. He captured the strong-point practically single-handed and thereby saved many casualties.
Subsequently he went out and collected ammunition under heavy machine-gun and rifle fire.

NICHOLLS, Harry   **929**
Lance-Corporal   3rd Bn., Grenadier Guards
Other Decorations: —
Date of Gazette: 30 Jul. 1940
Place/Date of Birth: Nottingham — 21 Apr. 1918
Place/Date of Death: Leeds, Yorkshire — 11 Sep. 1975
Memorials: —
Town/County Connections: Nottingham; Leeds
Remarks: —
Account of Deed: On 21 May 1940 near the River Escaut, Belgium, Lance Corporal Nicholls, although suffering from shrapnel wounds in his arm, continued to lead his section in a counter-attack against overwhelming opposition. He advanced over a ridge and when the position became critical, he rushed forward, putting three enemy machine-guns out of action. He then attacked massed enemy infantry beyond a second ridge until his ammunition ran out and he was taken prisoner.

NICKERSON, William Henry Snyder   **930**
Lieutenant (later Major General)   Royal Army Medical Corps, attd. Mounted Infantry
Other Decorations: CB, CMG
Date of Gazette: 12 Feb. 1901
Place/Date of Birth: Dorchester, New Brunswick, Canada — 27 Mar. 1875
Place/Date of Death: Cour, Kintyre, Scotland — 10 Apr. 1954
Memorials: —
Town/County Connections: Cour, Kintyre
Remarks: Served in the First World War 1914-18; Hon. Surgeon to The King 1925-33; Director, Medical Services in India 1929-33; Colonel Commandant, RAMC 1933-45; served in an Atlantic convoy 1940; Port of London River Emergency Service 1941; Home Guard 1941-45
Account of Deed: On 20 Apr. 1900 at Wakkerstroom, South Africa, during the advance of the infantry to support the mounted troops, Lieutenant Nickerson went under very heavy shell and rifle fire to attend a wounded man. He dressed his wounds and remained with him until he could be taken to a place of safety.

NICOLSON, Eric James Brindley   **931**
Flight Lieutenant (later Wing Commander)   249 Squadron, Royal Air Force
Other Decorations: DFC
Date of Gazette: 15 Nov. 1940
Place/Date of Birth: Hampstead, London — 29 Apr. 1917
Place/Date of Death: Bay of Bengal — 2 May 1945
Memorials: The Singapore Memorial
Town/County Connections: Hampstead, London; Tadcaster, Yorkshire
Remarks: The only Battle of Britain VC and the only fighter pilot to gain the award during the Second World War *Tonbridge School*
Account of Deed: On 16 Aug. 1940 near Southampton, Flight Lieutenant Nicolson's Hurricane was fired on by a Messerschmitt 110, injuring the pilot in one eye and one foot. His engine was also damaged and the petrol tank set alight. As he struggled to leave the blazing machine he saw another Messerschmitt, and managing to get back into the bucket seat, pressed the firing button continuing firing until the enemy plane dived away to destruction. Not until then did he bale out, and when he landed in a field, he was unable to release his parachute owing to his badly burned hands.

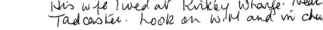

His wife lived at Kirkby Wharfe. Near Tadcaster. Look on wall and in chu

NOBLE, Cecil Reginald   **932**
A/Corporal   2nd Bn., The Rifle Brigade (Prince Consort's Own)
Other Decorations: —
Date of Gazette: 28 Apr. 1915
Place/Date of Birth: Bournemouth, Hampshire — 4 Jun. 1891
Place/Date of Death: Longuenesse, France — 13 Mar. 1915
Memorials: Longuenesse Souvenir Cemetery, France; The Rifle Brigade memorial, Winchester Cathedral
Town/County Connections: Bournemouth, Hampshire
Remarks: —
Account of Deed: On 12 Mar. 1915 at Neuve Chapelle, France, when the advance of the battalion was impeded by wire entanglements and by very severe machine-gun fire, Corporal Noble and another man* voluntarily rushed in front and succeeded in cutting the wires. They were both wounded, and Corporal Noble later died of his injuries. (*See also DANIELS, H.)

NORMAN, William   **933**
Private (later Corporal)   7th Regiment (later The Royal Fusiliers)
Other Decorations: —
Date of Gazette: 24 Feb. 1857
Place/Date of Birth: Warrington, Lancashire — 1832
Place/Date of Death: Salford, Lancashire — 13 Mar. 1896
Memorials: —
Town/County Connections: Warrington and Salford, Lancashire
Remarks: —
Account of Deed: On 19 Dec. 1854 in the Crimea, Private Norman was placed on single sentry duty some distance in front of the advanced sentries of an outlying picket in the White Horse Ravine, a post of much danger and requiring great vigilance. The Russian picquet was posted about 300 yards in front of him, and three Russians came reconnoitring under cover of the brushwood. Private Norman single-handed, took two of them prisoner without alarming the picquet.

NORTON, Gerard Ross   **934**
Lieutenant (later Captain)   Kaffrarian Rifles, South African Forces, attd. 1/4th Bn., The Hampshire Regiment (later The Royal Hampshire Regiment)
Other Decorations: MM
Date of Gazette: 26 Oct. 1944
Place/Date of Birth: Hershel, Cape Province, South Africa — 7 Sep. 1915
Place/Date of Death: — *Died 29.10.2004, probably in Harare, Zimbabwe.*
Memorials: —
Town/County Connections: —
Remarks: —
Account of Deed: On 31 Aug. 1944 during the attack on Monte Gridolfo, Italy, Lieutenant Norton's platoon was pinned down by heavy fire. On his own initiative and with complete disregard for his own safety, he advanced alone and attacked the first machine-gun emplacement, killing the crew of three. He then went on to the second position containing two machine-guns and 15 riflemen, and wiped out both machine-gun nests, killing or taking prisoner the remainder of the enemy. Throughout these attacks he was continuously under fire from a self-propelled gun, nevertheless he calmly went on to lead his platoon against the remaining enemy positions.

NORWOOD, John   **935**
Second Lieutenant (later Captain)   5th Dragoon Guards (Princess Charlotte of Wales's)
Other Decorations: —
Date of Gazette: 20 Jul. 1900
Place/Date of Birth: Beckenham, Kent — 8 Sep. 1876
Place/Date of Death: Sablonnieres, France — 8 Sep. 1914
Memorials: Sablonnieres New Communal Cemetery, France; St. Wilfred's Church, Haywards Heath, Sussex; 5th Dragoon Guards Memorial, Aldershot
Town/County Connections: Beckenham, Kent; Haywards Heath, Sussex
Remarks: —
Account of Deed: On 30 Oct. 1899 at Ladysmith, South Africa, Second Lieutenant Norwood went out in charge of a small patrol. They came under such heavy fire from the enemy, that when they had got to about 600 yards from them the patrol had to retire at full speed. One man dropped and Second Lieutenant Norwood galloped back through heavy fire, dismounted and, picking up the fallen trooper, carried him on his back, at the same time leading his horse with one hand. The enemy kept up an incessant fire during the whole of this time.

NUNNEY, Claude Joseph Patrick   **936**
Private   38th Bn., Eastern Ontario Regiment (Ottawa), C.E.F.
Other Decorations: DCM, MM
Date of Gazette: 14 Dec. 1918
Place/Date of Birth: Hastings, Sussex — 24 Dec. 1892
Place/Date of Death: Vis-en-Artois, France — 18 Sep. 1918
Memorials: Aubigny Communal Cemetery Extension, France
Town/County Connections: Hastings, Sussex
Remarks: —
Account of Deed: On 1 Sep. 1918 on the Drocourt-Queant Line, France, when his battalion which was preparing to advance, was heavily counter-attacked by the enemy, Private Nunney on his own initiative, went forward through the barrage to the company out-post lines, going from post to post and encouraging the men by his own fearless example. The enemy was repulsed and a critical situation saved. During the attack on 2 Sep. his leadership undoubtedly helped to carry his company forward to its objective and he again displayed the highest degree of valour until severely wounded.

NURSE, George Edward   **937**
Corporal (later Second Lieutenant)   66th Bty., Royal Field Artillery
Other Decorations: —
Date of Gazette: 2 Feb. 1900
Place/Date of Birth: Enniskillen, Ireland — 14 Apr. 1873
Place/Date of Death: Liverpool, Lancashire — 25 Nov. 1945
Memorials: —
Town/County Connections: Enniskillen, Ireland; Cobo, Guernsey; Liverpool, Lancashire
Remarks: —
Account of Deed: On 15 Dec. 1899, at the Battle of Colenso, South Africa, Corporal Nurse, with several others, tried to save the guns of the 14th and 66th Batteries, Royal Field Artillery, when the detachments serving the guns had all become casualties or been driven from their guns. Some of the horses and drivers were sheltering in a donga about 500 yards behind the guns and the intervening space was swept with shell and rifle fire. Corporal Nurse, with three officers* helped to hook a team into a limber and then to limber up a gun. Then, on his own, he managed to limber up a second gun. (*See also CONGREVE, W.N., ROBERTS, F.H.S. and SCHOFIELD, H.N.)

OCKENDEN, James   **938**
Sergeant   1st Bn., The Royal Dublin Fusiliers
Other Decorations: MM
Date of Gazette: 8 Nov. 1917
Place/Date of Birth: Portsmouth, Hampshire — 11 Dec. 1890
Place/Date of Death: Portsmouth, Hampshire — 29 Aug. 1966
Memorials: —
Town/County Connections: Portsmouth, Hampshire
Remarks: —
Account of Deed: On 4 Oct. 1917 east of Langemarck, Belgium, Sergeant Ockenden was acting as company sergeant-major, and seeing the platoon on the right held up by an enemy machine-gun, he immediately rushed the gun, regardless of his own safety and captured it, killing the crew. He then led a section to the attack on a farm, where under very heavy fire he rushed forward and called on the garrison to surrender. As the enemy continued to fire on him he opened fire, killing four, whereupon the remaining 16 surrendered.

O'CONNOR, Luke (later Sir Luke)   **939**
Sergeant (later Major General)   23rd Regiment (later The Royal Welch Fusiliers)
Other Decorations: KCB
Date of Gazette: 24 Feb. 1857
Place/Date of Birth: Elphin, Co. Roscommon, Ireland — 21 Jan. 1831
Place/Date of Death: London — 1 Feb. 1915 → *Phot 1100.*
Memorials: St. Mary's R.C. Cemetery, Kensal Rise, London; Portrait, R.W.F. Museum, *Caernarv* Caernarvon *Tablet in RC Church, Farm St. Mayfair.*
Town/County Connections: Elphin, Co. Roscommon; London
Remarks: First man of the Army to perform an action subsequently rewarded with the VC; served in the Indian Mutiny and Ashanti War; Hon. Colonel, The Royal Welch Fusiliers
Account of Deed: On 20 Sep. 1854, in the Crimea, at the Battle of the Alma, Sergeant O'Connor was advancing between two officers carrying the Colour, when one of them was mortally wounded. Sergeant O'Connor was also shot at the same time, but recovering himself, he snatched up the Colour from the ground and continued to carry it until the end of the action, although urged to retire to the rear on account of his wound. He also acted with great gallantry at the assault on the Redan (8 Sep. 1855) where he was shot through both thighs. *VC in RWF Museum. Caernarvon.*

No photograph available

ODGERS, William   **940**
Leading Seaman (later Quartermaster, Coast Guard Service)   Royal Navy
Other Decorations: —
Date of Gazette: 3 Aug. 1860
Place/Date of Birth: Falmouth, Cornwall — 14 Feb. 1834
Place/Date of Death: Saltash, Cornwall — 20 Dec. 1873
Memorials: —
Town/County Connections: Falmouth and Saltash, Cornwall
Remarks: —
Account of Deed: On 28 Mar. 1860 at Omata, New Zealand, Leading Seaman Odgers of HMS *Niger* displayed conspicuous gallantry when a party of officers, sailors and marines from the ship stormed a pass during operations against rebel natives. He was the first to enter the pass under heavy fire, and assisted in hauling down the enemy's colours.

O'HEA, Timothy   **941**
Private   1st Bn., The Rifle Brigade (Prince Consort's Own)
Other Decorations: —
Date of Gazette: 1 Jun. 1867
Place/Date of Birth: Skull, Bantry, Co. Cork, Ireland — 1846
Place/Date of Death: Sturt's Desert, Queensland, Australia — Nov. 1874
Memorials: Danville Town Hall, Quebec; The Rifle Brigade Memorial, Winchester Cathedral
Town/County Connections: —
Remarks: VC not awarded for bravery in time of war, but for extinguishing a fire in a railway car containing 2,000 lb. of ammunition.
Account of Deed: On 9 Jun. 1866 at Danville, Quebec, Canada, a fire broke out in a railway car containing ammunition, between Quebec and Montreal. The alarm was given and the car was disconnected at Danville Railway Station. While the sergeant in charge was considering what should be done, Private O'Hea took the keys from his hand, rushed to the car, opened it and called for water and a ladder. It was due to this man's example that the fire was suppressed.

O'KELLY, Christopher Patrick John   **942**
A/Captain (later Major)   52nd Bn., Manitoba Regiment, C.E.F.
Other Decorations: MC
Date of Gazette: 11 Jan. 1918
Place/Date of Birth: Winnipeg, Manitoba, Canada — 18 Nov. 1895
Place/Date of Death: Lac Seul, Ontario, Canada — 15 Nov. 1922
Memorials: Grave at Lac Seul, Ontario
Town/County Connections: —
Remarks: —
Account of Deed: On 26 Oct. 1917 at Passchendaele, Belgium, Captain O'Kelly led his company with extraordinary skill and determination. They captured six pill boxes, with 100 prisoners and 10 machine-guns. Later his company repelled a strong counter-attack, taking more prisoners, and subsequently during the night they captured a hostile raiding party consisting of one officer, 10 men and a machine-gun.

O'LEARY Michael   **943**
Lance-Corporal (later Major)   1st Bn., Irish Guards
Other Decorations: —
Date of Gazette: 18 Feb. 1915
Place/Date of Birth: Macroom, Inchigeela, Co. Cork, Ireland — 29 Sep. 1888
Place/Date of Death: London — 2 Aug. 1961
Memorials: Paddington Cemetery, Mill Hill, London
Town/County Connections: Inchigeela, Co. Cork; London
Remarks: Cross of the Order of St. George, 3rd Class (Russia); served in the Second World War — in The Middlesex Regiment 1940-44, Pioneer Corps 1944-45
Account of Deed: On 1 Feb. 1915 at Cuinchy, France, Lance-Corporal O'Leary was one of the storming party which advanced against the enemy's barricades. He rushed to the front and killed five Germans who were holding the first barricade, after which he attacked a second barricade 60 yards further on. This he captured after killing three of the enemy and taking two more of them prisoner. The lance-corporal thus practically took the position by himself and prevented the rest of the attacking party from being fired upon.

OLPHERTS William (later Sir William)   **944**
Captain (later General)   Bengal Artillery
Other Decorations: GCB
Date of Gazette: 18 Jun. 1858
Place/Date of Birth: Dartrey, Co. Armagh, Ireland — 8 Mar. 1822
Place/Date of Death: Upper Norwood, London — 30 Apr. 1902
Memorials: Richmond Cemetery, Surrey· *Grave·*
Town/County Connections: Dartrey, Co. Armagh; London (Norwood)
Remarks: Colonel Commandant of the Royal Artillery 1888
Account of Deed: On 25 Sep. 1857 at Lucknow, India, when the troops penetrated into the city, Captain Olpherts charged on horseback with the 90th Regiment when they captured two guns in the face of very heavy fire of grape. Afterwards he returned under severe fire of musketry to bring up limbers and horses to carry off the captured ordnance. (Elected by the Regiment.)

O'MEARA, Martin   **945**

Private   16th Bn. (S.A. & W.A.), Australian Imperial Force
Other Decorations: —
Date of Gazette: 5 Sep. 1916
Place/Date of Birth: Curcragha, Terryglass, Co. Tipperary, Ireland — 31 Dec. 1882
Place/Date of Death: Claremont, Perth, Western Australia — 20 Dec. 1935
Memorials: Karrakatta Cemetery, Perth; Australian War Memorial, Canberra
Town/County Connections: Lorra, Tipperary
Remarks: —
Account of Deed: Between 9/12 Aug. 1916 at Pozieres, France, during four days of very heavy fighting, Private O'Meara repeatedly went out and brought in wounded officers and men from "No Man's Land" under intense artillery and machine-gun fire. He also volunteered and carried up ammunition and bombs through a heavy barrage to a portion of the trenches which was being heavily shelled at the time. Throughout this period he showed utter contempt of danger and undoubtedly saved many lives.

O'NEILL, (or O'NIELL) John   **946**

Sergeant (later Lieutenant)   2nd Bn., The Prince of Wales's Leinster Regiment
Other Decorations: MM
Date of Gazette: 26 Dec. 1918
Place/Date of Birth: Airdrie, Lanarkshire, Scotland — 11 Feb. 1897
Place/Date of Death: Hoylake, Cheshire — 16 Oct. 1942
Memorials: Hoylake (Holy Trinity) Churchyard, Cheshire
Town/County Connections: Airdrie, Lanarkshire
Remarks: Médaille Militaire (France); served with The Pioneer Corps in the Second World War
Account of Deed: On 14 Oct. 1918 near Moorseele, Belgium, when the advance of his company was checked by two machine-guns and an enemy field battery firing over open sights, Sergeant O'Neill, with 11 men only, charged the battery, capturing four field guns, two machine-guns and 16 prisoners. Again, on the morning of 20 Oct. with one man he rushed an enemy machine-gun position, routing about 100 and causing many casualties.

ONIONS, George   **947**

Lance-Corporal (later Major)   1st Bn., The Devonshire Regiment
Other Decorations: —
Date of Gazette: 14 Dec. 1918
Place/Date of Birth: Bilston, Staffordshire — 2 Mar. 1883
Place/Date of Death: Birmingham — 2 Apr. 1944
Memorials: —   *Buried Quinton Cemetery, Northampton*
Town/County Connections: Bilston, Staffordshire; Birmingham
Remarks: —
Account of Deed: On 22 Aug. 1918 south of Achiet-le-Petit, France, Lance-Corporal Onions, having been sent out with one man to get in touch with the battalion on the right flank, saw the enemy advancing in large numbers. Seizing his opportunity, he boldly placed himself and his comrade on the flank of the advancing enemy and opened fire. When the enemy were about 100 yards from him the line wavered and some hands were thrown up, whereupon the lance-corporal rushed forward and helped by his comrade, took about 200 of the enemy prisoners and marched them back to his company commander.

ORMSBY John William   **948**

Sergeant   2nd Bn., The King's Own Yorkshire Light Infantry
Other Decorations: MM
Date of Gazette: 8 Jun. 1917
Place/Date of Birth: Dewsbury, Yorkshire — 11 Jan. 1881
Place/Date of Death: Dewsbury, Yorkshire — 29 Jul. 1952
Memorials: —   *Buried Dewsbury Cemetery.*
Town/County Connections: Dewsbury, Yorkshire
Remarks: —
Account of Deed: On 14 Apr. 1917 at Favet, France, during operations which culminated in the capture of an important position, Sergeant Ormsby, acting as company sergeant-major showed complete indifference to the heavy machine-gun and rifle fire and set a fine example. After clearing a village he pushed on and drove out many snipers from localities further forward. When the only surviving officer was wounded he took command of the company and led them forward under heavy fire for 400 yards to a new position, holding it until relieved.

O'ROURKE, Michael James **949**
Private   7th Bn., British Columbia Regiment, C.E.F.
Other Decorations: —
Date of Gazette: 8 Nov. 1917
Place/Date of Birth: Limerick, Ireland — 19 Mar. 1878
Place/Date of Death: Vancouver, British Columbia, Canada — 6 Dec. 1957
Memorials: Forest Lawn Burial Park, North Burnaby, British Columbia
Town/County Connections: Limerick, Ireland
Remarks: —
Account of Deed: During the period 15/17 Aug. 1917 at Hill 60 near Lens, France, Private O'Rourke, who was a stretcher-bearer, worked unceasingly for three days and nights bringing in the wounded, dressing their wounds and getting them food and water. During the whole of this period the area in which he worked was swept by heavy machine-gun and rifle fire and on several occasions he was knocked down and partially buried by enemy shells. His courage and devotion in carrying out his rescue work in spite of exhaustion and incessant heavy fire inspired all ranks and undoubtedly saved many lives.

OSBORN, John Robert **950**
Warrant Officer Class II (Company Sergeant-Major)   1st Bn., The Winnipeg Grenadiers, Canadian Infantry Corps
Other Decorations: —
Date of Gazette: 2 Apr. 1946
Place/Date of Birth: Foulden, near Thetford, Norfolk — 2 Jan. 1899
Place/Date of Death: Hong Kong — 19 Dec. 1941
Memorials: The Sai Wan Bay Memorial, Hong Kong; Osborn Barracks, Hong Kong
Town/County Connections: Foulden, Thetford, Norfolk
Remarks: Served with the Royal Naval Volunteer Reserve in the First World War
Account of Deed: On 19 Dec. 1941 during the attack on Mount Butler, Hong Kong, a part of one company led by Company Sergeant-Major Osborn, captured and held the hill until the position became untenable, when he helped stragglers to the new company position, exposing himself to heavy fire to cover their retirement. Later the enemy were hurling grenades which he picked up and threw back, until one landed in a position where it was impossible to return it in time, whereupon he shouted a warning and then threw himself on the grenade which exploded, killing him instantly.

OSBORNE, James **951**
Private   2nd Bn., The Northamptonshire Regiment
Other Decorations: —
Date of Gazette: 14 Mar. 1882
Place/Date of Birth: Wiggington, Tring, Hertfordshire — 13 Apr. 1857
Place/Date of Death: Near Tring, Hertfordshire — 2 Feb. 1928
Memorials: —
Town/County Connections: Wiggington, Tring, Hertfordshire
Remarks: —
Account of Deed: On 22 Feb. 1881 at Wesselstroom, South Africa, Private Osborne rode out under heavy fire, picked up a private who was lying wounded and carried him safely into camp.

O'SULLIVAN, Gerald Robert **952**
Captain   1st Bn., The Royal Inniskilling Fusiliers
Other Decorations: —
Date of Gazette: 1 Sep. 1915
Place/Date of Birth: Frankfield, Douglas, Co. Cork, Ireland — 8 Nov. 1888
Place/Date of Death: Suvla, Gallipoli — 21 Aug. 1915
Memorials: Helles Memorial, Gallipoli
Town/County Connections: Douglas, Co. Cork
Remarks: —
Account of Deed: On 1/2 Jul. 1915 south-west of Krithia, Gallipoli, Captain O'Sullivan volunteered to lead a party of bomb throwers to recapture a vital trench. He advanced in the open under very heavy fire and in order to throw his bombs with greater effect, got up on the parapet, completely exposed to the enemy occupying the position. He was finally wounded, but his example led his men to make further efforts which resulted in the recapture of the trench. Previously, on 18/19 Jun. he had saved a critical situation by his gallantry and leadership.

O'TOOLE, Edmund   **953**
Sergeant (later Captain)   Cape Frontier Light Horse, South African Forces
Other Decorations: —
Date of Gazette: 9 Oct. 1879
Place/Date of Birth: Grahamstown, South Africa — ?
Place/Date of Death: Salisbury, Rhodesia — 1891
Memorials: —
Town/County Connections: —
Remarks: First South African-born man serving with a South African unit under British Command to win the VC.
Account of Deed: On 3 Jul. 1879 at Ulundi, Zululand, during the retirement of a reconnoitring party, a captain* of the 9th Lancers went to the assistance of an NCO of the 24th Regiment whose horse had fallen and rolled on him. The Zulus were coming up quickly in great numbers, but the officer, with help from Sergeant O'Toole, managed to mount the injured man behind him. He was, however, so dizzy that the sergeant, who had been keeping back the enemy, gave up his carbine and rode alongside to hold him on. They all finally reached safety. (*See also BERESFORD, W.L. de la P.)

OWENS, James   **954**
Corporal (later Sergeant)   49th Regiment (later The Royal Berkshire Regiment — Princess Charlotte of Wales's)
Other Decorations: —
Date of Gazette: 24 Feb. 1857
Place/Date of Birth: Killaine, Baileyboro, Co. Cavan, Ireland — 1829
Place/Date of Death: Romford, Essex — 20 Aug. 1901
Memorials: —
Town/County Connections: Romford Essex
Remarks: Yeoman Warder at the Tower of London after leaving the 49th Regiment
Account of Deed: On 30 Oct. 1854 in the Crimea, Corporal Owens greatly distinguished himself in a personal encounter with the Russians, and gave noble assistance to a lieutenant of his regiment.

OXENHAM, William   **955**
Corporal   32nd Regiment (later The Duke of Cornwall's Light Infantry)
Other Decorations: —
Date of Gazette: 21 Nov. 1859
Place/Date of Birth: Tiverton, Devon — Jul. 1824
Place/Date of Death: Exeter, Devon — 29 Dec. 1874
Memorials: —
Town/County Connections: Tiverton and Exeter, Devon
Remarks: —
Account of Deed: On 30 Jun. 1857 at Lucknow, India, Corporal Oxenham saved the life of a Bengal Civil Servant by extricating him from the ruins of a verandah which had fallen on him. The corporal was exposed to heavy fire while effecting this rescue.

PALMER, Anthony   **956**
Private   3rd Bn., Grenadier Guards
Other Decorations: —
Date of Gazette: 24 Feb. 1857
Place/Date of Birth: Brereton, Congleton, Cheshire — 1819
Place/Date of Death: Crumpsall, Manchester, Lancashire — 12 Dec. 1892
Memorials: Heywood Cemetery, Rochdale, Lancashire *Grave · Plaque on wall of Cemetery chapel.*
Town/County Connections: Brereton, Cheshire; Manchester
Remarks: —
Account of Deed: On 5 Nov. 1854 at the Battle of Inkerman, Crimea, Private Palmer, with two other men were the first to volunteer to go with a brevet major* to dislodge a party of Russians from the Sandbag Battery. The attack succeeded. During this action Private Palmer shot down an assailant who was in the act of bayoneting the brevet major, and so saved his life. He was also one of a small band which, by a desperate charge against overwhelming numbers, saved the Colours of the battalion from capture. (*See also RUSSELL, C.)

PALMER, Frederick William   **957**
Lance-Sergeant (later Second Lieutenant)   22nd Bn., The Royal Fusiliers
Other Decorations: MM
Date of Gazette: 3 Apr. 1917
Place/Date of Birth: Hammersmith, London — 11 Nov. 1891
Place/Date of Death: Hordle, Hampshire — 10 Sep. 1955
Memorials: —
Town/County Connections: Hammersmith, London; Hordle, Hampshire
Remarks: —
Account of Deed: On 16/17 Feb. 1917 north of Courcelette, France, Lance-Sergeant Palmer assumed command of his company when all his officers had become casualties. Having cut his way under point-blank fire, through wire entanglements, he dislodged an enemy machine-gun and established a "block". He then collected some other men and held the barricade for nearly three hours against seven determined counter-attacks. While he was fetching more bombs an eighth counter-attack was delivered, threatening the advance of the whole flank. At this critical moment, although suffering from extreme exhaustion, he rallied his men, drove back the enemy and maintained his position.

PALMER, Robert Anthony Maurice   **958**
Squadron Leader   109 Squadron, Royal Air Force Volunteer Reserve
Other Decorations: DFC & Bar
Date of Gazette: 23 Mar. 1945
Place/Date of Birth: Gillingham, Kent — 7 Jul. 1920
Place/Date of Death: Near Cologne, Germany — 23 Dec. 1944
Memorials: Rheinberg War Cemetery, Germany
Town/County Connections: Gravesend and Gillingham, Kent
Remarks: —
Account of Deed: On 23 Dec. 1944 over Cologne, Germany, Squadron Leader Palmer was leading a formation of Lancaster bombers to attack the marshalling yards in daylight and it was his task to mark the target. Some minutes before reaching it he came under heavy anti-aircraft fire and two engines were set on fire, but disdaining the possibility of taking evading action and being determined to provide an accurate and easily seen aiming point for the other bombers, he managed to keep the badly damaged aircraft on a straight course, made a perfect approach and released his bombs. The Lancaster was last seen spiralling to earth in flames.

No photograph available

PARK, James   **959**
Gunner   Bengal Artillery
Other Decorations: —
Date of Gazette: 24 Dec. 1858
Place/Date of Birth: Barony, Glasgow — Jan. 1835
Place/Date of Death: Lucknow, India — 14 Jun. 1858
Memorials: —
Town/County Connections: Barony, Glasgow
Remarks: —
Account of Deed: During the whole of the period 14 to 22 Nov. 1857 at the Relief of Lucknow, India, Gunner Park acted with conspicuous gallantry. (Elected by the regiment.)

No photograph available

PARK, John   **960**
Sergeant   77th Regiment (later The Middlesex Regiment — Duke of Cambridge's Own)
Other Decorations: —
Date of Gazette: 24 Feb. 1857
Place/Date of Birth: Londonderry, Ireland — Feb. 1835
Place/Date of Death: Allahabad, India — 18 May 1863
Memorials: —
Town/County Connections: Ballymena, Antrim, Ireland
Remarks: —
Account of Deed: On 20 Sep. and 5 Nov. 1854 at the Battles of the Alma and Inkerman, Crimea, Sergeant Park showed great bravery. On 19 Apr. 1855 he also distinguished himself at the taking of the Russian Rifle Pits, during which he was severely wounded. He showed great resolution at both attacks on the Redan.

PARKASH SINGH

961

Havildar (later Major)   8th Punjab Regiment, Indian Army
Other Decorations: —
Date of Gazette: 13 May 1943
Place/Date of Birth: Sharikar, Jaranevala Tehsil, Lyallpur District, India — 31 Mar. 1913
Place/Date of Death: — *Died about 25.3.1991.*
Memorials: —
Town/County Connections: —
Remarks: PVSM (India)
Account of Deed: On 6 Jan. 1943 at Donbaik, Mayu Peninsula, Burma, Havildar Parkash Singh drove his own carrier forward and rescued the crews of two disabled carriers under very heavy fire. Again on 19 Jan. in the same area he rescued two more carriers which had been put out of action by an enemy anti-tank gun. He then went out yet again and brought to safety another disabled carrier containing two wounded men.

PARKASH SINGH (Jemadar) — see PRAKASH SINGH

PARKER, Charles Edward Haydon

962

Sergeant   'Q' Battery, Royal Horse Artillery
Other Decorations: —
Date of Gazette: 26 Jun. 1900
Place/Date of Birth: Birmingham — 11 Mar. 1870
Place/Date of Death: Coventry, Warwickshire — 5 Dec. 1918
Memorials: Coventry (London Road) Cemetery, Warwickshire
Town/County Connections: Birmingham and Coventry, Warwickshire
Remarks: — *Died SA 1936. Durban Cemetery?*
Account of Deed: On 31 Mar. 1900 at Korn Spruit, South Africa, two batteries of the Royal Horse Artillery were ambushed with the loss of most of the baggage column and five guns of the leading battery. When the alarm was given, 'Q' Battery went into action 1150 yards from the spruit, until the order to retire was received, when the major* commanding the battery ordered the guns and their limbers to be run back by hand to a safe place. This most exhausting operation was carried out by, among others, Sergeant Parker, a gunner and a driver* and when at last all but one of the guns and one limber had been moved to safety, the battery was reformed. (Award by ballot — *See also HORNBY, E.J. Phipps-, LODGE, I. and GLASOCK, H.H.)

PARKER, Walter Richard

963

Lance-Corporal   Royal Marine Light Infantry, Royal Naval Division
Other Decorations: —
Date of Gazette: 22 Jun. 1917
Place/Date of Birth: Grantham, Lincolnshire — 20 Sep. 1881
Place/Date of Death: Stapleford, Nottinghamshire — 28 Nov. 1936
Memorials: Stapleford Cemetery
Town/County Connections: Grantham, Lincolnshire; Stapleford, Nottinghamshire
Remarks: —
Account of Deed: On the night of 30 Apr./1 May 1915 at Gaba Tepe, Gallipoli, Lance-Corporal Parker, a volunteer stretcher-bearer, went out with a party of NCOs and men to take vital supplies to an isolated trench. Several men had already been killed in an attempt to reach the trench, and after crossing an area of about 400 yards swept by machine-gun and rifle fire, Lance-Corporal Parker was alone, the rest of the party having been killed or wounded. On his arrival he gave assistance to the wounded and when the trench was finally evacuated, he helped to remove and attend the casualties, although he himself was seriously hurt.

No photograph available

PARKES, Samuel

964

Private   4th Light Dragoons (later 4th Hussars — The Queen's Own)
Other Decorations: —
Date of Gazette: 24 Feb. 1857
Place/Date of Birth: Stafford, Staffordshire — 1813
Place/Date of Death: London — 14 Nov. 1864
Memorials: (Brompton Cemetery, London — unmarked grave).
Town/County Connections: Stafford; London
Remarks: — *Grave has been located and marked by a headstone of Queen's Roy Hussa*
Account of Deed: On 25 Oct. 1854 at Balaclava, Crimea, (Charge of the Light Brigade) the trumpet major's horse fell and dismounted him and he lost his sword. He was being attacked by two Cossacks when Private Parkes, whose horse had been shot, saved his life by placing himself between them and the trumpet major and drove them away with his sword. While attempting to follow the Light Cavalry Brigade in retreat, they were attacked by six Russians whom Parkes kept at bay, fighting and defending the trumpet major until he was deprived of his sword by a shot.

PARSLOW, Frederick Daniel   **965**
Lieutenant   Royal Naval Reserve
Other Decorations: —
Date of Gazette: 24 May 1919
Place/Date of Birth: London — 14 Apr. 1856
Place/Date of Death: At sea, near Queenstown, Ireland — 4 Jul. 1915
Memorials: Buried at Queenstown; Tower Hill Memorial, London
Town/County Connections: Islington, London
Remarks: —
Account of Deed: On 4 Jul. 1915 in the Atlantic, south-west of Queenstown, Ireland, HM Horse Transport *Anglo-Californian*, commanded by Lieutenant Parslow, was attacked by a submarine which made occasional hits although the lieutenant kept altering course. At last, on the point of abandoning ship in order to save lives, a message was received to hold on as long as possible and *Anglo-Californian* got under way again, whereupon the U-boat opened a very heavy fire, doing great damage. Lieutenant Parslow remained on the bridge throughout the attack, entirely without protection and was killed when the bridge was wrecked.

PARSONS, Francis Newton   **966**
Lieutenant   1st Bn., The Essex Regiment
Other Decorations: —
Date of Gazette: 20 Nov. 1900
Place/Date of Birth: Dover, Kent — 23 Mar. 1875
Place/Date of Death: Driefontein, South Africa — 10 Mar. 1900
Memorials: —
Town/County Connections: Dover, Kent
Remarks: —
Account of Deed: On 18 Feb. 1900 at Paardeberg, South Africa, a private of The Essex Regiment was wounded and while trying to take cover was wounded again. Lieutenant Parsons went to his assistance, dressed his wounds under heavy fire, fetched water from the river nearby, still under heavy fire, and then carried him to a place of safety. The lieutenant was killed in action a short time later.

PARSONS, Hardy Falconer   **967**
T/Second Lieutenant   14th (S) Bn., The Gloucestershire Regiment
Other Decorations: —
Date of Gazette: 17 Oct. 1917
Place/Date of Birth: Rishton, Blackburn, Lancashire — 13 Jun. 1897
Place/Date of Death: Near Epehy, France — 21 Aug. 1917
Memorials: Villers-Faucon Communal Cemetery, France
Town/County Connections: Bristol
Remarks: —
Account of Deed: On 20/21 Aug. 1917 near Epehy, France, during a night attack by the enemy on a bombing post held by his command, the bombers holding the post were forced back, but Second Lieutenant Parsons remained at his post. Single-handed and although severely scorched and burnt by liquid fire, he continued to hold up the enemy with bombs until severely wounded. His gallant action held the enemy long enough for the defence of the position to be consolidated. Second Lieutenant Parsons died of his wounds.

PARTRIDGE, Frank John   **968**
Private   8th Bn. (Victoria), Australian Military Forces
Other Decorations: —
Date of Gazette: 22 Jan. 1946
Place/Date of Birth: Grafton, New South Wales, Australia — 29 Nov. 1924
Place/Date of Death: Bellinger, New South Wales, Australia — 23 Mar. 1964
Memorials: Marksville Cemetery, New South Wales; Australian War Memorial, Canberra
Town/County Connections: —
Remarks: —
Account of Deed: On 24 Jul. 1945 at Bougainville, Solomon Islands, Private Partridge's section came under heavy machine-gun fire and suffered severe casualties, including the Bren gunner who was killed. Private Partridge, in spite of having been badly wounded, retrieved the Bren gun from the dead gunner and handed it to another man to provide covering fire while he rushed a bunker and silenced the machine-gun with a grenade. He killed the only living occupant and attacked another bunker, but weakness from loss of blood then compelled him to halt. Later he re-joined the fight and remained in action while the platoon withdrew from an untenable situation.

PATON, George Henry Tatham   **969**
A/Captain   4th Bn., Grenadier Guards
Other Decorations: MC
Date of Gazette: 13 Feb. 1918
Place/Date of Birth: Innellan, Argyllshire, Scotland — 3 Oct. 1895
Place/Date of Death: Gonnelieu, France — 1 Dec. 1917
Memorials: Metz-en-Couture Communal Cemetery, British Extension, France
Town/County Connections: Innellan, Argyllshire; Hallingbury, Essex
Remarks: — *Name on family grave. Putney Vale Cemetery*
Account of Deed: On 1 Dec. 1917 at Gonnelieu, France, when a unit on Captain Paton's left was driven back, thus leaving his flank in the air and his company practically surrounded, he walked up and down adjusting the line, within 50 yards of the enemy, under a withering fire. He personally removed several wounded men and was the last to leave the village. Later he again adjusted the line and when the enemy counter-attacked four times, each time sprang on to the parapet, deliberately risking his life, in order to stimulate his men. He was eventually mortally wounded.
Name on W. Memorials at Little Hallingbury, Essex. Brass in St. Columba Church, Pont St. Chelsea. Portrait in St. Stephens Church, Nova Boro. Pictures of him in Bryant & May HQ in Bow.

PATON, John   **970**
Sergeant   93rd Regiment (later The Argyll and Sutherland Highlanders — Princess Louise's)
Other Decorations: —
Date of Gazette: 24 Dec. 1858
Place/Date of Birth: Stirling, Scotland — 23 Dec. 1833
Place/Date of Death: Sydney, New South Wales, Australia — 1 Apr. 1914
Memorials: Rookwood Cemetery, Sydney
Town/County Connections: Stirling, Scotland
Remarks: —
Account of Deed: On 16 Nov. 1857 at Lucknow, India, Sergeant Paton went alone round the Shah Nujjiff and under extemely heavy fire discovered a breach in the opposite side. He afterwards led the Regiment to this breach and the important position was taken. (Elected by the regiment.)

PATTISON, John George   **971**
Private   50th Bn., Alberta Regiment (Calgary Regiment), C.E.F.
Other Decorations: —
Date of Gazette: 2 Aug. 1917
Place/Date of Birth: Woolwich, London — 8 Sep. 1875
Place/Date of Death: Lens, France — 3 Jun. 1917
Memorials: La Chaudiere Military Cemetery, France
Town/County Connections: Deptford, London
Remarks: — *look on Deptford W.M. and in church*
Account of Deed: On 10 Apr. 1917 at Vimy Ridge, France, when the advance of our troops was held up by an enemy machine-gun which was inflicting severe casualties, Private Pattison, with utter disregard of his own safety sprang forward and jumping from shell-hole to shell-hole reached cover within 30 yards of the enemy gun. From this point, in the face of heavy fire he hurled bombs killing and wounding some of the crew, and then rushed forward overcoming and bayoneting the surviving five gunners. His initiative and valour undoubtedly saved the situation.

PAYNE, Keith   **972**
Warrant Officer Class II   Australian Army Training Team, Vietnam
Other Decorations: —
Date of Gazette: 19 Sep. 1969
Place/Date of Birth: Ingham, Queensland, Australia — 30 Aug. 1933
Place/Date of Death: —
Memorials: Australian War Memorial, Canberra
Town/County Connections: —
Remarks: Vietnamese Cross of Gallantry with Bronze Star; U.S. Meritorious Unit Citation; Vietnamese Unit Citation Cross of Gallantry with Palm
Account of Deed: On 24 May 1969 in Vietnam, Warrant Officer Class Two Payne showed outstanding courage and leadership in saving the lives of many of the soldiers under his command, leading his men to safety under most difficult circumstances after an attack by the enemy in superior strength.

PEACHMENT, George Stanley **973**
Private   2nd Bn., The King's Royal Rifle Corps
Other Decorations: —
Date of Gazette: 18 Nov. 1915
Place/Date of Birth: Parkhills, Bury, Lancashire — 5 May 1897
Place/Date of Death: Hulluch, France — 25 Sep. 1915
Memorials: Loos Memorial, France
Town/County Connections: Bury, Lancashire
Remarks: —
Account of Deed: On 25 Sep. 1915 near Hulloch, France, during very heavy fighting, when the front line was compelled to retire in order to reorganise, Private Peachment saw his company commander lying wounded and crawled to help him. The enemy fire was intense but although there was a shell-hole quite close in which a few men had taken cover, Private Peachment never thought of saving himself. He knelt in the open by his officer and tried to help him, but while doing so was first wounded by a bomb and a minute later mortally wounded by a rifle bullet.

PEARKES, George Randolph (later The Hon. George) **974**
A/Major (later Major General)   5th Canadian Mounted Rifles Bn., Quebec Regiment, C.E.F.
Other Decorations: CB, DSO, MC
Date of Gazette: 11 Jan. 1918
Place/Date of Birth: Watford, Hertfordshire — 26 Feb. 1888
Place/Date of Death: Victoria, British Columbia — 30 May 1984
Memorials: Holy Trinity Cemetery, Victoria
Town/County Connections: Watford, Hertfordshire
Remarks: GOC 1st Canadian Division 1940; GOC-in-C Pacific Command, Canada 1942-45; CC (Canada); Legion of Merit (USA); Minister of National Defence, Canadian Government 1957-60; Lieut-Governor, British Columbia 1960-68; Overseas Vice-Chairman VC & GC Association 1956-68
Account of Deed: On 30/31 Oct. 1917 near Passchendaele, Belgium, Major Pearkes, although wounded in the right thigh, continued to lead his men with the utmost gallantry, despite many obstacles. It was entirely due to his determination and fearless personality that he was able to maintain his objective with the small number of men at his command against repeated enemy counter attacks. His appreciation of the situation and the reports rendered by him were invaluable to his commanding officer. He showed throughout a supreme contempt of danger and wonderful powers of command and leadership.

PEARSE, Samuel George **975**
Sergeant   45th Bn., The Royal Fusiliers
Other Decorations: MM
Date of Gazette: 23 Oct. 1919
Place/Date of Birth: Penarth, Glamorganshire, Wales — 16 Jul. 1897
Place/Date of Death: Near Emtsa, North Russia — 29 Aug. 1919
Memorials: Archangel Allied Cemetery, Russia; Australian War Memorial, Canberra
Town/County Connections: Penarth, Glamorganshire
Remarks: Served with 1st Machine-Gun Bn., Australian Imperial Force 1914/18
Account of Deed: On 24 Aug. 1919, north of Emtsa, North Russia, Sergeant Pearse cut his way through enemy barbed wire under very heavy machine-gun and rifle fire and cleared a way for the troops to enter an enemy battery position. He then charged a blockhouse which was harrassing the advance and causing casualties, and killed the occupants with bombs. A minute later he was killed, but it was due to him that the position was carried with so few casualties. *Name on Memorial to those who died in Russia. Brookwood Military Cemetery, Surrey.*

PEARSON, James **976**
Private (later Sergeant)   86th Regiment (later The Royal Irish Rifles)
Other Decorations: —
Date of Gazette: 28 Apr. 1860
Place/Date of Birth: Rathdowney, Queen's Co. (later Leix), Ireland — 2 Oct. 1822
Place/Date of Death: India — 23 Jan. 1900
Memorials: —
Town/County Connections: Rathdowney, Queen's Co. (Leix)
Remarks: Rode in the Light Brigade Charge at Balaclava
Account of Deed: On 3 Apr. 1858 at Jhansi, India, Private Pearson attacked a number of rebels, one of whom he killed and bayoneted two others. He was himself wounded in the attack. He also brought into Calpee, under heavy fire, a private who afterwards died of his wounds.

PEARSON, John　　977

Private (later Sergeant)　8th Hussars (The King's Royal Irish)
Other Decorations: —
Date of Gazette: 26 Jan. 1859
Place/Date of Birth: Leacroft, Leeds, Yorkshire — 19 Jan. 1825
Place/Date of Death: Ontario, Canada — 18 Apr. 1892
Memorials: Plaque in Memorial Park, Lion's Head, Ontario, Canada
Town/County Connections: Leeds, Yorkshire
Remarks: —
Account of Deed: On 17 Jun. 1858 at Gwalior, India, Private Pearson (together with a captain, a sergeant and a farrier)* was in a gallant charge made by a squadron of the 8th Hussars when, supported by a division of the Bombay Horse Artillery and the 95th Regiment, they routed the enemy. Charging through a rebel camp into two batteries, they captured and brought into their own camp two of the enemy's guns, under a heavy and converging fire from the fort and town. (*See also HENEAGE, C.W., WARD, Joseph and HOLLIS, G.)

PECK, Cyrus Wesley　　978

Lieutenant Colonel　Comd. 16th Bn., Manitoba Regiment (Canadian Scottish), C.E.F.
Other Decorations: DSO & Bar
Date of Gazette: 15 Nov. 1918
Place/Date of Birth: Hopewell Hill, New Brunswick, Canada — 26 Apr. 1871
Place/Date of Death: Sidney, Vancouver, British Columbia, Canada — 27 Sep. 1956
Memorials: New Westminster Cemetery, British Columbia
Town/County Connections: —
Remarks: Member, House of Commons, Canada 1917-21; Member, Provincial Parliament, British Columbia 1924
Account of Deed: On 2 Sep. 1918 at Cagnicourt, France, when Lieutenant Colonel Peck's command, after capturing the first objective, was held up by enemy machine-gun fire, he went forward and made a personal reconnaissance under very heavy fire. Returning, he reorganised his battalion and pushed them forward. He then went out, under the most intense artillery and machine-gun fire and intercepted the tanks, giving them the necessary directions, pointing out where they were to make for, and thus paving the way for an infantry battalion to push forward. To this battalion he subsequently gave the necessary support.

PEEL William (later Sir William)　　979

Captain　Royal Navy (Naval Brigade)
Other Decorations: KCB
Date of Gazette: 24 Feb. 1857
Place/Date of Birth: London — 2 Nov. 1824
Place/Date of Death: Cawnpore, India — 27 Apr. 1858
Memorials: Statues in Painted Hall, Greenwich Hospital, Sandy Church, Bedfordshire, Eden Gardens, Calcutta, India and Dublin, Ireland
Town/County Connections: London (Mayfair)　*Harrow School.*
Remarks: Légion d'Honneur (France)
Account of Deed: On 18 Oct. 1854 at Sebastopol, Crimea, Captain Peel took up a live shell with the fuse still burning from amongst several powder cases and threw it over the parapet. The shell burst as it left his hands. On 5 Nov. at the Battle of Inkerman he joined some of the officers of the Grenadier Guards and helped to defend the Colours of the regiment when they were hard pressed. On 18 Jun. 1855 he led the first scaling party at the assault on the Redan, and was himself severely wounded. On each of these occasions Captain Peel was accompanied by a young midshipman* as ADC. (*See also DANIEL, E.St.J.)

PEELER, Walter　　980

Lance-Corporal (later Sergeant)　3rd Pioneer Bn., Australian Imperial Force
Other Decorations: BEM
Date of Gazette: 26 Nov. 1917
Place/Date of Birth: Castlemaine, Melbourne, Victoria, Australia — 9 Aug. 1887
Place/Date of Death: Caulfield, Victoria, Australia — 23 May 1968
Memorials: Brighton Cemetery, Melbourne; Australian War Memorial, Canberra
Town/County Connections: —
Remarks: Served in Second World War
Account of Deed: On 20 Sep. 1917, east of Ypres, Belgium, during the first wave of an attack, Lance-Corporal Peeler encountered an enemy party sniping the advancing troops. He immediately rushed their position and accounted for nine of them, clearing the way for the advance. He repeated this action on two subsequent occasions, and each time accounted for a number of the enemy. During the operations he was directed to an enemy machine-gun which was firing on our troops. He located and killed the gunner and then bombed out the remainder from a dug-out where they had taken shelter.

PENNELL, Henry Singleton   **981**
Lieutenant (later Captain)   2nd Bn., The Derbyshire Regiment (later The Sherwood Foresters,
The Nottinghamshire and Derbyshire Regiment)
Other Decorations: —
Date of Gazette: 20 May 1898
Place/Date of Birth: Dawlish, Devon — 18 Jun. 1874
Place/Date of Death: St. Moritz, Switzerland — 19 Jan. 1907
Memorials: —
Town/County Connections: Dawlish, Devon
Remarks: —
Account of Deed: On 20 Oct. 1897 during the attack on the Dargai Heights, Indian Frontier (Tirah
Campaign), when a captain of The Derbyshire Regiment was struck down, Lieutenant Pennell ran to his assistance and made
two attempts, under a hail of bullets, to carry and drag him back to cover. The lieutenant only gave up when he found that the
wounded officer was dead.

PERCY, The Hon. Henry Hugh Manvers (later Lord Henry)   **982**
Colonel (later General)   3rd Bn., Grenadier Guards
Other Decorations: KCB
Date of Gazette: 5 May 1857
Place/Date of Birth: Cobham, Surrey — 22 Aug. 1817
Place/Date of Death: London — 3 Dec. 1877
Memorials: St. Nicholas Chapel, Westminster Abbey; Cross on wall of The Falconer's Tower,
Alnwick Castle, Northumberland
Town/County Connections: Cobham, Surrey; Alnwick, Northumberland
Remarks: Légion d'Honneur; MP for North Northumberland 1865-68
Account of Deed: On 5 Nov. 1854 at the Battle of Inkerman, Crimea, Colonel Percy was with a
number of men from various regiments who had charged too far, were nearly surrounded by the enemy and without
ammunition. Although wounded, the colonel extricated some 50 of the men, passing under heavy fire from the enemy and
bringing them to a place of safety, where they obtained fresh ammunition and were able to continue fighting.

No photograph available

PERIE, John   **983**
Sapper   Corps of Royal Engineers
Other Decorations: —
Date of Gazette: 24 Feb. 1857
Place/Date of Birth: Huntly, Aberdeenshire, Scotland — Aug. 1829
Place/Date of Death: Aberdeen, Scotland — 17 Sep. 1874
Memorials: —
Town/County Connections: Huntly, Aberdeen
Remarks: Médaille Militaire (France)
Account of Deed: On 18 Jun. 1855 at Sebastopol, Crimea, Sapper Perie showed conspicuous
gallantry, with a lieutenant* in leading a ladder party at the assault on the Redan. He also
volunteered to go with the lieutenant to help bring in a wounded sailor lying in the open, even though he was himself suffering
from a musket wound in the side. (*See also GRAHAM, G.)

PETERS, Frederick Thornton   **984**
A/Captain   Royal Navy
Other Decorations: DSO, DSC & Bar
Date of Gazette: 18 May 1943
Place/Date of Birth: Charlottetown, Prince Edward Island, Canada — 17 Sep. 1889
Place/Date of Death: Near Gibraltar — 13 Nov. 1942
Memorials: Portsmouth Naval Memorial, Hampshire
Town/County Connections: —
Remarks: —
Account of Deed: On 8 Nov. 1942 at Oran Harbour, North Africa, Captain Peters, commanding
HMS *Walney*, led his force through the boom towards the jetty in the face of point-blank fire from
shore batteries, a destroyer and a cruiser. Blinded in one eye, he alone of 17 officers and men on the bridge survived. *Walney*
reached the jetty disabled and ablaze and went down with her colours flying. Captain Peters and a handful of men managed to
reach the shore, but he was killed in an air crash five days later.

PHILLIPPS Everard Aloysius Lisle **985**
Ensign   11th Bengal Native Infantry
Other Decorations: —
Date of Gazette: 21 Oct. 1859 & 15 Jan. 1907
Place/Date of Birth: Coleorton, Leicestershire — 28 May 1835   *Grace Dieu Manor.*
Place/Date of Death: Delhi, India — 18 Sep. 1857
Memorials: Oscott College, Birmingham
Town/County Connections: Dishley, Leicestershire
Remarks: —
Account of Deed: From 30 May to 18 Sep. 1857 at the time of the Siege of Delhi, India, Ensign
Phillipps performed many gallant deeds, and during this time he was wounded on three occasions.
At the assault on the city he captured the Water Bastion with a small party and was killed in the streets on 18 September.

PHILLIPS Robert Edwin **986**
T/Lieutenant (later Captain)   13th Bn., The Royal Warwickshire Regiment, attd. 9th (S) Bn.
Other Decorations: —
Date of Gazette: 8 Jun. 1917
Place/Date of Birth: Hill Top, West Bromwich, Staffordshire — 11 Apr. 1895
Place/Date of Death: St. Veep, Lostwithiel, Cornwall — 23 Sep. 1968
Memorials: —   *Buried St Veep Parish Church*
Town/County Connections: West Bromwich, Staffordshire
Remarks: —
Account of Deed: On 25 Jan. 1917 near Kut, Mesopotamia, Lieutenant Phillips went to the
assistance of his commanding officer* who was lying in the open mortally wounded while leading
a counter-attack. The lieutenant went out with a comrade and, under the most intense fire, they succeeded in bringing their
commanding officer back to our lines. (*See also HENDERSON, E.E.D.)

PHIPPS-HORNBY, Edmund John — see **HORNBY,** Edmund John PHIPPS-

PICKARD, Arthur Frederick **987**
Lieutenant (later Colonel)   Royal Regiment of Artillery
Other Decorations: CB
Date of Gazette: 22 Sep. 1864
Place/Date of Birth: Forest Hill, Northamptonshire — 12 Apr. 1841
Place/Date of Death: Cannes, France — 1 Mar. 1880
Memorials: —
Town/County Connections: Forest Hill, Northamptonshire
Remarks: —
Account of Deed: On 20 Nov. 1863, at Rangiriri, New Zealand, during an assault on the enemy's
position, Lieutenant Pickard, together with an assistant surgeon,* exposed themselves to
imminent danger in crossing the entrance to the Maori Keep, at a point upon which the enemy were concentrating their fire, in
order to render assistance to the wounded. Lieutenant Pickard crossed and re-crossed the parapet to procure water for the
wounded, when none of the men could be induced to perform this service, as the space to be traversed was exposed to enemy
cross-fire. (*See also TEMPLE, W.)

PITCHER, Ernest Herbert **988**
Petty Officer (later Chief Petty Officer)   Royal Navy
Other Decorations: DSM
Date of Gazette: 2 Nov. 1917
Place/Date of Birth: Mullion, Cornwall — 31 Dec. 1888
Place/Date of Death: Sherborne, Dorset — 10 Feb. 1946
Memorials: Swanage (Northbrook) Cemetery, Dorset; Parish Church, Swanage
Town/County Connections: Mullion, Cornwall; Swanage, Dorset
Remarks: Médaille Militaire and Croix de Guerre (France); served in the Second World War
Account of Deed: On 8 Aug. 1917 in the Bay of Biscay, Petty Officer Pitcher was the 4-inch gun-
layer on HMS *Dunraven* (one of the 'Q' or 'mystery' ships) when she was shelled by an enemy
submarine. He and the rest of the crew waited while the battle went on overhead and all round them. When the magazine below
them caught fire they took up cartridges and held them on their knees to prevent the heat of the deck igniting them and when
the magazine finally blew up they were all blown into the air. (Award by ballot. See also BONNER, C.G.)

PITCHER, Henry William   **989**
Lieutenant (later Captain)   4th Punjab Infantry, Indian Army
Other Decorations: —
Date of Gazette: 16 Jul. 1864
Place/Date of Birth: ?Bath, Somerset — 1841
Place/Date of Death: Dehra Ghazeekhan, Punjab, India — 5 Jul. 1875
Memorials: —
Town/County Connections: Kensington, London
Remarks: —
Account of Deed: On 30 Oct. 1863 during the Umbeyla Campaign, North-West India, Lieutenant Pitcher led a party to recapture the Crag Picquet after its garrison had been driven in by the enemy and 60 of them killed. He led the party up the narrow path to the last rock until he was knocked down and stunned by a large stone thrown from above. On 16 Nov. the lieutenant displayed great courage in leading a party to the Crag Picquet when it had again fallen into enemy hands. He led the first charge, but was wounded in the action. (See also FOSBERY, G.V.)

PITTS, James   **990**
Private (later Corporal)   1st Bn., The Manchester Regiment
Other Decorations: MSM
Date of Gazette: 26 Jul. 1901
Place/Date of Birth: Blackburn, Lancashire — 26 Feb. 1877
Place/Date of Death: Blackburn, Lancashire — 18 Feb. 1955
Memorials: —
Town/County Connections: Blackburn, Lancashire
Remarks: Served with The Manchester Regiment in Second World War
Account of Deed: On 6 Jan. 1900 during an attack on Caesar's Camp, Natal, South Africa, 16 men of "D" Company were defending one of the slopes of the hill. The defenders were under heavy fire all day, the majority being killed and their positions occupied by the enemy. At last only Private Pitts and one other man* remained. They held their post for 15 hours without food or water, all the time exchanging deadly fire with the enemy, until relief troops had retaken the lost ground and pushed the enemy off the hill. (*See also SCOTT, R.)

PLACE, Basil Charles Godfrey   **991**
Lieutenant (later Rear-Admiral)   Royal Navy
Other Decorations: CB, DSC
Date of Gazette: 22 Feb. 1944
Place/Date of Birth: Little Malvern, Worcestershire — 19 Jul. 1921
Place/Date of Death: — *About 30.12.1994*
Memorials: — *Lived in Sherborne.*
Town/County Connections: Little Malvern, Worcestershire; Sherborne, Dorset
Remarks: Polish Cross of Valour; Chief Staff Officer to Flag Officer Aircraft Carriers 1958-60; Deputy Director of Air Warfare 1960-62; command of frigate *Rothesay*, and Captain (F) 6th Frigate Squadron 1962-64; Captain of *Ganges* 1964-66; command of carrier *Albion* 1966-68; Admiral commanding Reserves 1968-70. Chairman, VC and GC Association 1971
Account of Deed: On 22 Sep. 1943 at Kaafjord, North Norway, Lieutenant Place, commanding Midget Submarine X.7, and another lieutenant* commanding Midget Submarine X.6, carried out a most daring and successful attack on the German Battleship *Tirpitz*. The two submarines had to travel at least 1,000 miles from base, negotiate a mine field, dodge nets, gun defences and enemy listening posts. Having eluded all these hazards they finally placed the charges underneath the ship where they went off an hour later, doing so much damage that *Tirpitz* was out of action for months. (*See also CAMERON, D.)

POLLARD, Alfred Oliver   **992**
Second Lieutenant   1st Bn., Honourable Artillery Company
Other Decorations: MC & Bar, DCM
Date of Gazette: 8 Jun. 1917
Place/Date of Birth: Wallington, Surrey — 4 May 1893
Place/Date of Death: Bournemouth, Hampshire — 5 Dec. 1960
Memorials: —
Town/County Connections: Wallington, Surrey; Bournemouth, Hampshire
Remarks: — *Merchant Taylors School. Northwood, Middx*
Account of Deed: On 29 Apr. 1917 at Gavrelle, France, the troops of various units had become disorganised owing to the heavy casualties from shell fire and a subsequent determined attack with very strong forces caused further confusion and retirement. Second Lieutenant Pollard realised the seriousness of the situation and with only four men he started a counter-attack with bombs pressing it home until he had broken the enemy attack and regained all that had been lost and much ground in addition. This officer's splendid example inspired courage into every man who saw him.

POLLOCK, James Dalgleish   **993**
Corporal (later Captain)   5th Bn., The Queen's Own Cameron Highlanders
Other Decorations: —
Date of Gazette: 18 Dec. 1915
Place/Date of Birth: Tillicoultry, Clackmannanshire, Scotland — 3 Jun. 1890
Place/Date of Death: Ballochyle, Ayreshire, Scotland — 10 May 1958
Memorials: —
Town/County Connections: Tillycoultry, Clackmannanshire; Ballochyle, Ayrshire
Remarks: Cousin of Corporal J.L. Dawson, VC.
Account of Deed: On 27 Sep. 1915 near the Hohenzollern Redoubt, France, at about noon the enemy's bombers in superior numbers were successfully working up "Little Willie" Trench towards the Redoubt. Corporal Pollock, after obtaining permission, got out of the trench alone and walked along the top edge with complete disregard for danger, and compelled the enemy bombers to retire by bombing them from above. He was under heavy machine-gun fire the whole time, but contrived to hold up the progress of the Germans for an hour before he was at length wounded.

POOLL, Arthur Hugh Henry BATTEN-   **994**
Lieutenant (later Captain)   3rd Bn., The Royal Munster Fusiliers
Other Decorations: MC
Date of Gazette: 5 Aug. 1916
Place/Date of Birth: Knightsbridge, London — 25 Oct. 1891
Place/Date of Death: Ivybridge, Devon — 21 Jan. 1971
Memorials: Buried at Woolverton, near Bath, Somerset
Town/County Connections: London; Ivybridge, Devon; Woolverton, Bath
Remarks: — *Eton College.*
Account of Deed: On 25 Jun. 1916 near Colonne, France, Lieutenant Batten-Pooll was in command of a raiding party when, on entering the enemy's lines he was severely wounded by a bomb which broke and mutilated all the fingers of his right hand. In spite of this he continued to direct operations with unflinching courage. Half an hour later during the withdrawal, while personally assisting in the rescue of other wounded men, he received two further wounds, but refusing assistance, he walked to within 100 yards of our lines when he fainted and was carried in by the covering party.

POPE, Charles   **995**
Lieutenant   11th Bn. (W.A.), Australian Imperial Force
Other Decorations: —
Date of Gazette: 8 Jun. 1917
Place/Date of Birth: Mile End, London — 5 Mar. 1883
Place/Date of Death: Louveral, France — 15 April 1917
Memorials: Moeuvres Communal Cemetery Extension, France; Australian War Memorial, Canberra
Town/County Connections: Mile End, London
Remarks: —
Account of Deed: On 15 Apr. 1917 at Louveral, France, Lieutenant Pope was in command of a very important picquet post, with orders to hold it at all costs. The enemy in greatly superior numbers attacked and surrounded the post and ammunition was running short. Lieutenant Pope, in a desperate bid to save the position, was seen to charge with his men into the very superior enemy force, by which they were overpowered, although heavy losses were inflicted. This gallant officer had obeyed the order to hold out to the last and his body, with those of most of his men, was found in close proximity to 80 enemy dead.

PORTEOUS, Patrick Anthony   **996**
T/Captain (later Colonel)   Royal Regiment of Artillery
Other Decorations: —
Date of Gazette: 2 Oct. 1942
Place/Date of Birth: Abbottabad, North-west Frontier, India — 1 Jan. 1918
Place/Date of Death: — *About 10.10.2000*
Memorials: —
Town/County Connections: Fleet, Hampshire; Chichester, Sussex
Remarks: Colonel, Junior Leaders Regiment, Royal Artillery 1960-63; Commander, Rheindahlen Garrison 1966-69
Account of Deed: On 19 Aug. 1942 at Dieppe, France, Captain Porteous was liaison officer between two detachments whose task was to attack the heavy coast defence guns. During the initial assault Captain Porteous, with the smaller detachment was shot through the hand, but he nevertheless disarmed and killed his assailant, thereby also saving the life of a British sergeant. In the meantime the two officers of the other detachment had been killed and the Troop Sergeant Major seriously wounded, so Captain Porteous, in the face of withering fire, dashed across open ground to take command and led the men in a successful charge against the enemy, when he was severely wounded for the second time. He continued to the final objective, however, but eventually collapsed after the last gun had been destroyed.

POTTS, Frederick William Owen   997

Private (later Lance-Corporal) 1/1st The Berkshire Yeomanry
Other Decorations: —
Date of Gazette: 1 Oct. 1915
Place/Date of Birth: Reading, Berkshire — 18 Dec. 1892
Place/Date of Death: Reading, Berkshire — 3 Nov. 1943
Memorials: —
Town/County Connections: Reading, Berkshire
Remarks: —
Account of Deed: On 21 Aug. 1915 in the attack on Hill 70, Gallipoli, Private Potts, although wounded in the thigh, remained for over 48 hours under the Turkish trenches with another private from his regiment who was severely wounded, and unable to move. He finally fixed a shovel to the equipment of his wounded comrade and using this as a sledge, dragged the man back over 600 yards to safety, being under fire all the way.

POULTER, Arthur   998

Private 1/4th Bn., The Duke of Wellington's (West Riding) Regiment
Other Decorations: —
Date of Gazette: 28 Jun. 1918
Place/Date of Birth: Kilgrambridge, East Witton, North Yorkshire — 16 Dec. 1893
Place/Date of Death: Leeds, Yorkshire — 29 Aug. 1956
Memorials: — *Buried Wortley Cemetery, Leeds*
Town/County Connections: Leeds, Yorkshire
Remarks: —
Account of Deed: On 10 Apr. 1918 at Erquinghem, Lys, France, Private Poulter, who was acting as a stretcher-bearer, on 10 occasions carried badly wounded men on his back through particularly heavy artillery and machine-gun fire. Two of the wounded were hit a second time whilst on his back. Again, after a withdrawal over the river had been ordered, Private Poulter returned in full view of the enemy and carried back another man who had been left behind wounded. He bandaged 40 men under fire and was seriously wounded when attempting another rescue in the face of the enemy.

PRAKASH SINGH   999

Jemadar 4/13th Frontier Force Rifles, Indian Army
Other Decorations: —
Date of Gazette: 1 May 1945
Place/Date of Birth: Kahna Chak Village, Kathua District, Kashmir — 1 Jul. 1919
Place/Date of Death: Kanlan Ywathit, Burma — 17 Feb. 1945
Memorials: The Rangoon Memorial, Burma
Town/County Connections: —
Remarks: —
Account of Deed: On 16/17 Feb. 1945 at Kanlan Ywathit, Burma, Jemadar Prakash Singh was commanding a platoon which took the main weight of fierce enemy attacks. He was wounded in both ankles and relieved of his command, but when his second-in-command was also wounded, he crawled back and took command again, directing operations and encouraging his men. Being again wounded in both legs, he continued to direct the defence, dragging himself from place to place by his hands. When wounded a third time and dying, he lay shouting the Dogra war-cry, so inspiring his company that the enemy were finally driven off.

PREMINDRA SINGH BHAGAT   1000

Second Lieutenant (later Lieutenant General) Corps of Indian Engineers, attd. Royal Bombay Sappers and Miners
Other Decorations: —
Date of Gazette: 10 Jun. 1941
Place/Date of Birth: Bhagat Kot, Mussourie, India — 14 Oct. 1918
Place/Date of Death: ? — 23 May 1975
Memorials: —
Town/County Connections: —
Remarks: PVSM (India)
Account of Deed: On 31 Jan./1 Feb. 1941 after the capture of Gallabat in Abyssinia, Second Lieutenant Premindra Singh Bhagat cleared Italian mine-fields while chasing the enemy. In four days he covered 55 mine-ridden miles, was twice blown up in his carrier, was ambushed and had one of his ear drums shattered. There were casualties too, amongst his men, but he would not rest until the mine clearing had been completed.

PRENDERGAST, Harry North Dalrymple (later Sir Harry)   **1001**
Lieutenant (later General)   Madras Engineers
Other Decorations: GCB
Date of Gazette: 21 Oct. 1859
Place/Date of Birth: Madras, India — 15 Oct. 1834
Place/Date of Death: Richmond, Surrey — 24 Jul. 1913
Memorials: Richmond Cemetery, Surrey, *Grave*
Town/County Connections: Richmond, Surrey
Remarks: Commandant Western District (India) 1880; Officiating Resident in Mysore and Chief Commissioner of Coorg 1887-89 and 1891-92
Account of Deed: On 21 Nov. 1857 at Mundisore, India, Lieutenant Prendergast saved the life of another lieutenant at the risk of his own, by attempting to cut down a Velaitee who was covering the officer with his piece from only a few yards to the rear. Lieutenant Prendergast was wounded in this affair by the discharge of the piece and would have probably been killed had not the rebel been killed by a major who came to the rescue. Lieutenant Prendergast also distinguished himself by his gallantry in the actions at Ratgurh and Betwa, when he was severely wounded.

PRETTYJOHN John   **1002**
Corporal (later Colour-Sergeant)   Royal Marine Light Infantry
Other Decorations: —
Date of Gazette: 24 Feb. 1857
Place/Date of Birth: Dean Prior, Ashburton, Devon — 11 Jun. 1823
Place/Date of Death: Manchester, Lancashire — 20 Jan. 1887
Memorials: (Buried in Manchester)
Town/County Connections: Dean Prior and Plymouth, Devon
Remarks: —
Account of Deed: On 5 Nov. 1854 at the Battle of Inkerman, Corporal Prettyjohn's platoon went to clear out some caves which were occupied by snipers. In doing so they used up almost all their ammunition, and then noticed fresh parties of Russians creeping up the hillside in single file. Corporal Prettyjohn gave instructions to his men to collect as many stones as possible which they could use instead of ammunition. When the first Russian appeared he was seized by the corporal and thrown down the slope. The others were greeted by a hail of stones and retreated.

PRICE-DAVIS, Llewellyn Alberic Emilius — see **DAVIES,** Llewellyn Alberic Emilius PRICE-

PRIDE, Thomas   **1003**
Captain of the After Guard   Royal Navy
Other Decorations: —
Date of Gazette: 21 Apr. 1865
Place/Date of Birth: Oldbridge, Wareham, Dorset — 29 Mar. 1835
Place/Date of Death: Parkstone, Dorset — 16 Jul. 1893
Memorials: All Saints' Churchyard, Branksome, Dorset
Town/County Connections: Oldbridge and Longfleet, Poole, Dorset
Remarks: —
Account of Deed: On 6 Sep. 1864 at Shimonoseki, Japan, Captain of the After Guard Pride was one of the two colour sergeants who accompanied the midshipman* from HMS *Euryalus* when they carried the Queen's Colour into action in the capture of the enemy's stockade. They kept the flag flying in spite of the fierce fire which killed the other colour sergeant and severely wounded Pride. He and the midshipman, however, did not falter and were only finally prevented from going further forward by direct orders from their superior officer. (*See also entry for BOYES, D.G.)

PROBYN, Dighton MacNaghton (later Sir Dighton)   **1004**
Captain (later General)   2nd Punjab Cavalry
Other Decorations: GCB, GCSI, GCVO, ISO
Date of Gazette: 18 Jun. 1858
Place/Date of Birth: Marylebone, London — 21 Jan. 1833
Place/Date of Death: Sandringham, Norfolk — 20 Jun. 1924   *→ Grave.*
Memorials: Kensal Green Cemetery, London; Sandringham Church, Norfolk
Town/County Connections: London; Sandringham, Norfolk
Remarks: Comptroller and Treasurer to King Edward VII when Prince of Wales 1877-91; Keeper of Privy Purse and Extra Equerry to King Edward 1901-10; Comptroller to Queen Alexandra 1910-24.
Account of Deed: On many occasions during the period 1857-58 in India, Captain Probyn performed gallant and daring acts. On one occasion, at the Battle of Agra, when his squadron charged the rebel infantry, he was sometimes separated from his men and surrounded by five or six Sepoys. He defended himself and, before his own men had joined him, had cut down two of his assailants.

PROCTER, Arthur Herbert   **1005**
Private (later The Reverend)   1/5th Bn., The King's (Liverpool) Regiment
Other Decorations: —
Date of Gazette: 5 Aug. 1916
Place/Date of Birth: Bootle, Lancashire — 11 Aug. 1890
Place/Date of Death: Sheffield, Yorkshire — 27 Jan. 1973
Memorials: Sheffield Cathedral
Town/County Connections: Bootle, Lancashire; Sheffield, Yorkshire
Remarks: Served as a Chaplain with the Royal Air Force during the Second World War, having been ordained in 1927
Account of Deed: On 4 Jun. 1916 near Ficheux, France, Private Procter noticed some movement on the part of two wounded men who were lying in full view of the enemy about 75 yards in front of the trenches. He at once went out on his own initiative and, although heavily fired at, ran and crawled to the two men, got them under cover of a small bank, dressed their wounds and promised that they would be rescued after dark. He left them with warm clothing and then returned to the trenches, again being heavily fired at. The men were rescued at dusk.

PROCTOR, Andrew Frederick Weatherby BEAUCHAMP-   **1006**
A/Captain   84 Squadron, Royal Air Force
Other Decorations: DSO, MC & Bar, DFC
Date of Gazette: 30 Nov. 1918
Place/Date of Birth: Mossel Bay, Cape Province, South Africa — 4 Sep. 1894
Place/Date of Death: Upavon, Wiltshire — 21 Jun. 1921
Memorials: Mafeking Cemetery, South Africa, European Section
Town/County Connections: —
Remarks: —
Account of Deed: During the period 8 Aug./8 Oct. 1918 over France, Captain Proctor was victorious in 26 air combats, but from his first victory in November 1917 in all he destroyed 22 enemy aircraft, 16 kite balloons and drove down a further 16 enemy machines completely out of control. In addition, his work in attacking enemy troops on the ground and in reconnaissance during the advance of the Allied armies, commencing on 8 Aug. was almost unsurpassed in its brilliancy.

PROSSER, Joseph   **1007**
Private   2nd Bn., 1st Regiment (later The Royal Scots — The Lothian Regiment)
Other Decorations: —
Date of Gazette: 24 Feb. 1857
Place/Date of Birth: Monegal, King's Co. (later Offaly), Ireland — 1828
Place/Date of Death: Tipperary, Ireland — 1869
Memorials: —
Town/County Connections: Monegal, King's Co. (Offaly); Tipperary
Remarks: —
Account of Deed: On 16 Jun. 1855 at Sebastopol, Crimea, when on duty in the trenches, Private Prosser pursued and apprehended (while exposed to enemy cross-fire) a soldier in the act of deserting to the enemy. On 11 Aug. he left the most advanced trench and helped to carry to safety a severely wounded soldier of the 95th Regiment who was unable to move. This act was performed under very heavy fire from the enemy.

PROWSE, George   **1008**
Chief Petty Officer   Royal Naval Volunteer Reserve (Drake Bn., Royal Naval Division)
Other Decorations: DCM
Date of Gazette: 30 Oct. 1918
Place/Date of Birth: Bath or Paulton, Somerset — 1886
Place/Date of Death: Near Arleux, France — 27 Sep. 1918
Memorials: Vis-en-Artois Memorial, France   *Panels 1. and 2.*
Town/County Connections: Gorseinon, Carmarthenshire and Swansea, Wales   *May be on W.M.*
Remarks: — *He lived at 60, Treharne Road, Landore, Swansea.*
Account of Deed: On 2 Sep. 1918 at Pronville, France, Chief Petty Officer Prowse led a small party of men against an enemy strong point, capturing it, together with 23 prisoners and 5 machine-guns. On three other occasions he displayed great heroism in dealing with difficult and dangerous situations, and at one time he dashed forward and attacked and captured two machine-gun posts, killing six of the enemy and taking 13 prisoners and two machine-guns. He was the only survivor of this gallant party, but his action enabled the battalion to push forward in comparative safety.

PRYCE, Thomas Tannatt **1009**
A/Captain   4th Bn., Grenadier Guards (S.R.)
Other Decorations: MC & Bar
Date of Gazette: 22 May 1918
Place/Date of Birth: The Hague, Holland — 17 Jan. 1886
Place/Date of Death: Vieux Berquin, France — 13 Apr. 1918 → *Panel 1.*
Memorials: Ploegsteert Memorial, Belgium; Llandysilio Church and War Memorial, Montgomeryshire; Stock Exchange War Memorial. *Name on W.M. Maidenhead. Ber*
Town/County Connections: Llandysilio, Montgomeryshire, Wales; Maidenhead, Berkshire
Remarks: — *Shrewsbury School. Lived at Craufurd Lodge, Maidenhead.*
Account of Deed: On 11 Apr. 1918 at Vieux Berquin, France, Captain Pryce led two platoons in a successful attack on a village. Early next day he was occupying a position with some 40 men, the rest having become casualties. He beat off four attacks during the day, but by evening the enemy were within 60 yards of his trench. A bayonet charge led by Captain Pryce drove them back some 100 yards, but he had only 17 men left and no ammunition when yet another attack came. He again led a bayonet charge and was last seen engaged in a fierce hand-to-hand struggle against overwhelming odds. *Name on Stock Exchange W.M. Name on W.M at Four Crosses, Llandysilio. Mer. and in the church. VC in Guards Museum*

No photograph available

PURCELL, John **1010**
Private   9th Lancers (The Queen's Royal)
Other Decorations: —
Date of Gazette: 15 Jan. 1858
Place/Date of Birth: Kilcommon, Oughterard, Co. Galway, Ireland — 1814
Place/Date of Death: Delhi, India — 19 Sep. 1857
Memorials: —
Town/County Connections: Oughterard, Co. Galway
Remarks: —
Account of Deed: On 19 Jun. 1857 at Delhi, India during the Mutiny, when a wagon of one of the batteries was blown up and the horse of a brigadier was shot, Private Purcell with another private* and a sowar of the 4th Irregular Cavalry stayed with the officer until he could be dragged to safety by the sowar's horse. Private Purcell's horse was killed under him and the other private was severely wounded. (*See also HANCOCK, T.)

PYE, Charles Colquhoun **1011**
Sergeant-Major (later Captain)   53rd Regiment (later The King's Shropshire Light Infantry)
Other Decorations: —
Date of Gazette: 24 Dec. 1858
Place/Date of Birth: Rickerscote, Staffordshire — 22 Nov. 1822
Place/Date of Death: Edmonton, London — 17 Aug. 1890
Memorials: —
Town/County Connections: Rickerscote and Clifton Campville, Staffs.; Edmonton, London
Remarks: —
Account of Deed: On 17 Nov. 1857 at Lucknow, India, Sergeant-Major Pye acted with great fearlessness under fire when bringing up ammunition to the Mess House and on every occasion when the Regiment was engaged. (Elected by the regiment.)

QUERIPEL, Lionel Ernest **1012**
Captain   The Royal Sussex Regiment, attd. 10th Parachute Bn.
Other Decorations: —
Date of Gazette: 1 Feb. 1945
Place/Date of Birth: Winterbourne Monkton, Dorset — 13 Jul. 1920
Place/Date of Death: Arnhem, Holland — 19 Sep. 1944
Memorials: Arnhem Oosterbeek War Cemetery, Holland; The Royal Sussex Regimental Chapel, Chichester Cathedral.
Town/County Connections: Winterbourne Monkton, Dorset; Tunbridge Wells, Kent
Remarks: —
Account of Deed: On 19 Sep. 1944 at Arnhem, Holland, Captain Queripel displayed the highest standard of gallantry during the whole of a period of nine hours of bitter and confused fighting. Under heavy fire he carried a wounded sergeant to the regimental aid post and was himself wounded in the face. Later, when it became necessary to withdraw he insisted, despite the protests of his men, in remaining behind to cover their withdrawal, armed only with his pistol and a few hand grenades. This was the last occasion on which he was seen.

QUIGG, Robert   1013
Rifleman (later Sergeant)   12th Bn., The Royal Irish Rifles
Other Decorations: —
Date of Gazette: 9 Sep. 1916
Place/Date of Birth: Ardihennon, Giant's Causeway, Co. Antrim, Ireland — 28 Feb. 1885
Place/Date of Death: Ballycastle, Co. Antrim, Ireland — 14 May 1955
Memorials: Billy Parish Churchyard, Co. Antrim
Town/County Connections: Giant's Causeway, Bushmills and Ballycastle, Co. Antrim
Remarks: Medal of the Order of St. George, 4th Class (Russia)
Account of Deed: On 1 Jul. 1916, at Hamel, France, Rifleman Quigg advanced to the assault with his platoon three times. Early next morning, hearing a rumour that his platoon officer was lying wounded, he went out seven times to look for him under heavy shell and machine-gun fire, each time bringing back a wounded man. The last man he dragged in on a waterproof sheet from within a few yards of the enemy's wire. He was engaged for seven hours in this most gallant work and finally was so exhausted that he had to give it up.

RABY, Henry James   1014
Lieutenant (later Rear-Admiral)   Royal Navy (Naval Brigade)
Other Decorations: CB
Date of Gazette: 24 Feb. 1857
Place/Date of Birth: Boulogne, France — 26 Sep. 1827
Place/Date of Death: Southsea, Hampshire — 13 Feb. 1907
Memorials: Highland Road Cemetery, Portsmouth, Hampshire
Town/County Connections: Llanelly Carmarthenshire, Wales; Southsea, Hampshire
Remarks: First man to actually receive the VC from The Queen at the first investiture (26 Jun. 1857); Légion d'Honneur (France) *Sherborne School*
Account of Deed: On 18 Jun. 1855, in the Crimea, immediately after the assault on Sebastopol; a soldier of the 57th Regiment, who had been wounded in both legs, was observed sitting up and calling for help. At once Lieutenant Raby and two seamen* left the shelter of their battery works and ran forward a distance of 70 yards, across open ground, through heavy gunfire and succeeded in carrying the wounded man to safety. (*See also CURTIS, Henry and TAYLOR, J.)
Road in Llanelly named after his family. VC in RN Museum, Portsmouth.

No photograph available

RAMAGE, Henry   1015
Sergeant   2nd Dragoons (Royal Scots Greys)
Other Decorations: —
Date of Gazette: 2 Jun. 1858
Place/Date of Birth: Morningside, Edinburgh — 1827
Place/Date of Death: Newbridge, Co. Kildare, Ireland — 29 Dec. 1859
Memorials: —
Town/County Connections: Edinburgh; Newbridge, Kildare
Remarks: —
Account of Deed: On 25 Oct. 1854 at Balaclava, Crimea, Sergeant Ramage galloped out to the assistance of a private who was surrounded by seven Russians. The sergeant dispersed them and saved his comrade's life. On the same day, he brought in a prisoner from the Russian line and also, when the Heavy Brigade was covering the retreat of the Light Cavalry, lifted from his horse a private who was badly wounded and carried him safely to the rear under heavy cross-fire.

RAMBAHADUR LIMBU   1016
Lance-Corporal (later Captain)   2nd Bn., 10th Princess Mary's Gurkha Rifles
Other Decorations: MVO
Date of Gazette: 21 Apr. 1966
Place/Date of Birth: Chyangthapu Village, Yangrop Thum, East Nepal — Jul./Aug. 1939
Place/Date of Death: —
Memorials: —
Town/County Connections: —
Remarks: —
Account of Deed: On 21 Nov. 1965 in Sarawak, Lance-Corporal Rambahadur Limbu was in an advance party of 16 Gurkhas when they encountered about 30 Indonesians holding a position on the top of a jungle-covered hill. The lance-corporal went forward with two men, but when they were only 10 yards from the machine-gun, the sentry opened fire, whereupon the NCO rushed forward and killed him with a grenade. The enemy then opened fire on the small party wounding the two men with the lance-corporal who, under heavy fire, made two journeys into the open to drag his comrades to safety.

RAM SARUP SINGH   1017

A/Subadar   1st Punjab Regiment, Indian Army
Other Decorations: —
Date of Gazette: 8 Feb. 1945
Place/Date of Birth: Khere, Patiale State, India — 13 Apr. 1919
Place/Date of Death: Kennedy Peak, Burma — 25 Oct. 1944
Memorials: The Rangoon Memorial, Burma
Town/County Connections: —
Remarks: —
Account of Deed: On 25 Oct. 1945 at Kennedy Peak in the Tiddim area, Burma, two platoons were ordered to attack a particularly strong enemy position. The platoon commanded by Subadar Ram Sarup Singh attained its objective, completely routing the enemy, and although the subadar was wouned in both legs he insisted on carrying on. Later, the enemy's fierce counter-attack was only halted by Subadar Ram Sarup Singh's dashing counter-charge in which he killed four of the enemy himself. He was again wounded, in the thigh, but continued to lead his men, killing two more of the enemy, until he was mortally wounded.

RAMSDEN, Horace Edward   1018

Trooper   Protectorate Regiment (N.W. Cape Colony) South African Forces
Other Decorations: —
Date of Gazette: 6 Jul. 1900
Place/Date of Birth: Chester — 15 Dec. 1878
Place/Date of Death: Wynberg, Cape, South Africa — 3 Aug. 1948
Memorials: —
Town/County Connections: Chester
Remarks: VC awarded for saving his brother's life.
Account of Deed: On 26 Dec. 1899 near Mafeking, South Africa, during the action at Game Tree, after the order to retire had been given, Trooper Ramsden picked up his brother who had been shot through both legs and was lying some 10 yards from the Boer trenches. He carried him about 600 to 800 yards under heavy fire (putting him down from time to time to rest) until help arrived and the injured man was carried to a place of safety.

RANDLE, John Neil   1019

T/Captain   2nd Bn., The Royal Norfolk Regiment
Other Decorations: —
Date of Gazette: 12 Dec. 1944
Place/Date of Birth: Benares, India — 22 Dec. 1917
Place/Date of Death: Kohima, Assam, India — 6 May 1944
Memorials: Kohima War Cemetery, India; St. Peter's Church, Petersham, Surrey.
Town/County Connections: Richmond and Petersham, Surrey; Radlett, Hertfordshire
Remarks: Brother-in-law of Flying Officer L.T. Manser, VC.
Account of Deed: During the period 4/6 May 1944 at Kohima, Assam, India, Captain Randle took command of the company when his company commander had been wounded and in spite of being wounded himself inspired his men with his initiative and courage. On 6 May he led an attack which was almost immediately held up by heavy machine-gun fire from an enemy bunker and, realising the importance of destroying it, charged the post single-handed. Although mortally wounded, he silenced the gun with a grenade thrown through the bunker slit, and then flung his body across the slit so that the aperture should be completely sealed.

RANKEN, Harry Sherwood   1020

Captain   Royal Army Medical Corps, attd. 1st Bn., The King's Royal Rifle Corps
Other Decorations: —
Date of Gazette: 16 Nov. 1914
Place/Date of Birth: Glasgow — 3 Sep. 1883
Place/Date of Death: Braine, France — 25 Sep. 1914
Memorials: Braine Communal Cemetery, France   *S.E. of Soissons*
Town/County Connections: Glasgow; Irvine, Ayrshire, Scotland
Remarks: —
Account of Deed: On 19 and 20 Sep. 1914 at Haute-Avesnes, France, Captain Ranken was severely wounded in the leg whilst attending to his duties on the battlefield under shrapnel and rifle fire. He arrested the bleeding from this and bound it up, then continued to dress the wounds of his men, sacrificing his own chance of survival to their needs. When he finally permitted himself to be carried to the rear his case had become almost desperate and he died within a short period.

RATCLIFFE, William   **1021**
Private   2nd Bn., The South Lancashire Regiment (The Prince of Wales's Volunteers)
Other Decorations: —
Date of Gazette: 2 Aug. 1917
Place/Date of Birth: West Derby, Lancashire — 21 Mar. 1882
Place/Date of Death: Liverpool, Lancashire — 26 Mar. 1963
Memorials: —
Town/County Connections: West Derby and Liverpool, Lancashire
Remarks: —
Account of Deed: On 14 Jun. 1917 at Messines, Belgium, after an enemy trench had been captured, Private Ratcliffe located an enemy machine-gun which was firing on his comrades from the rear, and single-handed, on his own initiative, he immediately rushed the machine-gun position and bayoneted the crew. He then brought the gun back into action in the front line. Private Ratcliffe had displayed similar gallantry and resource on previous occasions.

RATTEY, Reginald Roy   **1022**
Corporal (later Sergeant)   25th Bn., Australian Military Forces
Other Decorations: —
Date of Gazette: 26 Aug. 1945
Place/Date of Birth: Barmedman, New South Wales, Australia — 28 Mar. 1918
Place/Date of Death: West Wyalong, N.S.W., Australia — 8 Jan. 1986
Memorials: Australian War Memorial, Canberra
Town/County Connections: —
Remarks: —
Account of Deed: On 22 Mar. 1945 at Bougainville, Solomon Islands, an attack by a company of Australian Infantry on a strongly held enemy position was met by extremely heavy fire. Corporal Rattey, realizing that any advance would be halted by this fire and heavy casualties inflicted, dashed forward firing his Bren gun from the hip and completely neutralized the enemy fire from three forward bunkers. Then, having silenced a bunker with one grenade, he fetched two more with which he silenced the other two bunkers. The company was then able to continue its advance. Later Corporal Rattey captured another machine-gun and 2000 rounds of ammunition.

RAVENHILL, George   **1023**
Private   2nd Bn., The Royal Scots Fusiliers
Other Decorations: —
Date of Gazette: 4 Jun. 1901
Place/Date of Birth: Birmingham — 21 Feb. 1872
Place/Date of Death: Birmingham — 14 Apr. 1921
Memorials: —
Town/County Connections: Birmingham
Remarks: —
Account of Deed: On 15 Dec. 1899 at Colenso, South Africa, Private Ravenhill went several times under heavy fire from his sheltered position as one of the escort to the guns, to assist the officers and drivers who were trying to withdraw a number of guns when the detachments serving them had all been killed, wounded or driven from them by infantry fire at close range. Private Ravenhill also helped to limber up one of the guns which was saved.

RAYFIELD, Walter Leigh   **1024**
Private   7th Bn., British Columbia Regiment, C.E.F.
Other Decorations: —
Date of Gazette: 14 Dec. 1918
Place/Date of Birth: Richmond, Surrey — 7 Oct. 1881
Place/Date of Death: Toronto, Canada — 19 Feb. 1949
Memorials: Soldiers' Plot, Prospect Cemetery, Toronto
Town/County Connections: Richmond, Surrey
Remarks: —
Account of Deed: From 2/4 Sep. 1918 during the operations east of Arras, France, Private Rayfield, ahead of his company, rushed a trench occupied by a large party of the enemy, bayoneting two and taking 10 prisoners. Later, after engaging with great skill an enemy sniper, he rushed the section of the trench from which the sniper had been operating and so demoralised the enemy that 30 others surrendered to him. Subsequently, regardless of personal safety, he left cover under heavy machine-gun fire and carried in a badly wounded comrade.

RAYMOND, Claud   **1025**

Lieutenant   Corps of Royal Engineers
Other Decorations: —
Date of Gazette: 28 Jun. 1945
Place/Date of Birth: Mottistone, Isle of Wight — 2 Oct. 1923
Place/Date of Death: Talaku, Burma — 22 Mar. 1945
Memorials: Taukkyan War Cemetery, Burma
Town/County Connections: Mottistone, Isle of Wight
Remarks: —
Account of Deed: On 21 Mar. 1945 at Talaku, Burma, Lieutenant Raymond was second-in-command of a reconnaissance patrol when they were fired on by a strongly entrenched enemy detachment and the lieutenant at once led his men towards the position. He was first wounded in the shoulder and then in the head, but continued leading his men forward, when he was hit a third time, his wrist being shattered. He still carried on into the enemy defences where he was largely responsible for capturing the position. In spite of the gravity of his wounds, he refused medical aid until all the other wounded had received attention. He died next day.

RAYNES, John Crawshaw   **1026**

A/Sergeant (later Battery Sergeant-Major)   'A' Bty., 71 Brigade, Royal Field Artillery
Other Decorations: —
Date of Gazette: 18 Nov. 1915
Place/Date of Birth: Ecclesall, Sheffield, Yorkshire — 28 Apr. 1887
Place/Date of Death: Leeds, Yorkshire — 13 Nov. 1929
Memorials: —
Town/County Connections: Sheffield and Leeds, Yorkshire
Remarks: —
Account of Deed: On 11 Oct. 1915 at Fosse 7 de Bethune, France, Sergeant Raynes went to the assistance of another sergeant who was lying wounded. He bandaged the injured man and returned to his gun, then, when the battery ceased firing, carried the wounded man to a dug-out and when gas shelling started, put his own gas helmet on his injured comrade and, badly gassed himself, went back to his gun. The next day he was buried, with others, under a house which had been shelled. As soon as he had been extricated he insisted on helping to rescue the others, then, having had his wounds dressed, reported for duty.

No photograph available

RAYNOR, William   **1027**

Lieutenant (later Captain)   Bengal Veteran Establishment
Other Decorations: —
Date of Gazette: 18 Jun. 1858
Place/Date of Birth: Plumtree, Nottinghamshire — Jul. 1795
Place/Date of Death: Ferozepore, India — 13 Dec. 1860
Memorials: Tablet over Gateway, Delhi Magazine
Town/County Connections: Plumtree, Nottinghamshire
Remarks: Thought to be the oldest winner of the VC — 61 years 10 months
Account of Deed: On 11 May 1857 at Delhi, India, Lieutenant Raynor was one of nine men who defended the Magazine for more than five hours against large numbers of rebels and mutineers, until, on the wall being scaled and there being no hope of help, they fired the Magazine. Five of the gallant band died in the explosion and one shortly afterwards, but many of the enemy were killed. (See also BUCKLEY, J. and FORREST, G.)

READ, Anketell Moutray   **1028**

Captain   1st Bn., The Northamptonshire Regiment
Other Decorations: —
Date of Gazette: 18 Nov. 1915
Place/Date of Birth: Bampton, Devon — 27 Oct. 1884
Place/Date of Death: Hulloch, France — 25 Sep. 1915
Memorials: Dud Corner Cemetery, France; War Memorial, Cheltenham, Gloucestershire; Bampton Church, Devon.
Town/County Connections: Bampton, Devon; Cheltenham, Gloucestershire
Remarks: — *Memorial in Bampton church*
Account of Deed: On 25 Sep. 1915 near Hulloch, France, Captain Read, although partially gassed, went out several times in order to rally parties of different units which were disorganised and retiring. He led them back into the firing line and regardless of danger to himself, moved about under withering fire, encouraging them, but he was mortally wounded while carrying out this gallant work. He had shown conspicuous bravery on other occasions, particularly on the night of 29/30 Jul. when he carried out of action an officer who was mortally wounded, under a hot fire of rifle and grenades.

READE, Herbert Taylor　　　　　　　　　　　　　　　　　　　　**1029**
Surgeon (later Surgeon General)　61st Regiment (later The Gloucestershire Regiment)
Other Decorations:　CB
Date of Gazette:　5 Feb. 1861
Place/Date of Birth:　Perth, Upper Canada — 20 Sep. 1828
Place/Date of Death:　Bath, Somerset — 23 Jun. 1897
Memorials: — *Buried Bath Cemetery*
Town/County Connections:　Bath, Somerset
Remarks:　Hon. Surgeon to Queen Victoria 1895
Account of Deed:　On 14 Sep. 1857, during the Siege of Delhi, India, while Surgeon Reade was attending the wounded at the end of one of the streets, a party of rebels advanced and having established themselves started firing from the roofs of the houses. The wounded were thus in very great danger, but Surgeon Reade drew his sword and, calling on the few soldiers who were near to follow, succeeded in dislodging the rebels. At the assault on Delhi, on 16 Sep. Surgeon Reade was one of the first up at the breach in the magazine and he, with a sergeant, spiked one of the enemy's guns.

READITT, John　　　　　　　　　　　　　　　　　　　　　　　**1030**
Private (later Sergeant)　6th Bn., The South Lancashire Regiment (The Prince of Wales's Volunteers)
Other Decorations: —
Date of Gazette:　5 Jul. 1917
Place/Date of Birth:　Manchester, Lancashire — 19 Jan. 1897
Place/Date of Death:　Clayton Bridge, Manchester — 9 Jun. 1964
Memorials:　Gorton Cemetery, Manchester. *Grave.*
Town/County Connections:　Manchester
Remarks: —
Account of Deed:　On 25 Feb. 1917 at Alqayat-al-Gaharbigah Bend, Mesopotamia, Private Readitt advanced five times along a water-course in the face of heavy machine-gun fire at very close range, being the sole survivor on each occasion. These advances drove the enemy back and about 300 yards of the water-course was made good in an hour. After his officer had been killed, Private Readitt, on his own initiative, made several more advances. On reaching the enemy barricade he was forced to retire, but gave ground slowly continuing to throw bombs. When support reached him he held a forward bend by bombing until the position was consolidated.

REED, Hamilton Lyster　　　　　　　　　　　　　　　　　　　**1031**
Captain (later Major General)　7th Bty. Royal Field Artillery
Other Decorations:　CB, CMG
Date of Gazette:　2 Feb. 1900
Place/Date of Birth:　Dublin — 23 May 1869
Place/Date of Death:　London, SW5 — 7 Mar. 1931
Memorials: —
Town/County Connections:　Dublin; London
Remarks:　Nephew of Lieutenant H.H. Lyster, VC; Legion of Honor, 3rd Class (USA); Croix de Guerre (France); served in the First World War — commanded 15th (Scottish) Division 1917-19; GOC 52nd (Lowland) Division, TA 1923-27
Account of Deed:　On 15 Dec. 1899 at the Battle of Colenso, South Africa, when so many horses had become casualties, Captain Reed brought three teams from his battery in an attempt to save the remaining guns. The shell and rifle fire was intense and he was wounded almost at once, as were five of the 13 men who rode with him. One was killed and 13 horses (including his own) out of 21, were killed before he got half way to the guns, and he was forced to retire.

REES, Ivor　　　　　　　　　　　　　　　　　　　　　　　　　**1032**
Sergeant (later Company Sergeant-Major)　11th Bn., The South Wales Borderers
Other Decorations: —
Date of Gazette:　14 Sep. 1917
Place/Date of Birth:　Felinfoel, near Llanelly, Carmarthenshire, Wales — 18 Oct. 1893
Place/Date of Death:　Llanelly, Carmarthenshire — 12 Mar. 1967
Memorials: — *Cremated*
Town/County Connections:　Llanelly, Carmarthenshire
Remarks:　Served with the Home Guard, as Sergeant-Major in Second World War
Account of Deed:　On 31 Jul. 1917 at Pilkem, Belgium, a hostile machine-gun opened fire at close range, inflicting many casualties. Sergeant Rees led his platoon forward by short rushes and gradually worked his way round to the rear of the main position. When he was about 20 yards away he rushed forward and killed two of the team. He then bombed the large concrete emplacement, killing five and capturing 30 prisoners, including two officers, in addition to an undamaged gun. *VC in SWB Museum, Brecon.*

REES, Lionel Wilmot Brabazon   1033
T/Major (later Group Captain)   Royal Regiment of Artillery and 32 Squadron, Royal Flying Corps
Other Decorations: OBE, MC, AFC
Date of Gazette: 5 Aug. 1916
Place/Date of Birth: Caernarvon, Wales — 31 Jul. 1884
Place/Date of Death: Andros, Bahamas — 28 Sep. 1955
Memorials: Nassau War Cemetery, Bahamas; St. George's Royal Garrison Church, Woolwich
Town/County Connections: Caernarvon, Wales
Remarks: Served in the Royal Air Force 1919-31; Assistant Commandant, RAF College, Cranwell
1923-24; ADC to King George V 1925-31; Group Captain in command of Headquarters RAF,
Transjordan and Palestine 1926-29; in command of RAF Depot at Uxbridge 1929-30; commanded
No. 21 Group 1930-31; sailed the Atlantic alone in a 34-foot ketch, autumn 1933 to Jan. 1934 (awarded Cruising Club of
America's 'Blue Water Medal'); served in RAF 1941-42; author of *Fighting in the Air.*
Account of Deed: On 1 Jul. 1916 at Double Crassieurs, France, Major Rees, whilst on flying duties, sighted what he thought
was a bombing party of our machines returning home, but were in fact enemy aircraft. Major Rees was attacked by one of them,
but after a short encounter it disappeared, damaged. The others then attacked him at long range, but he dispersed them,
seriously damaging two of the machines. He chased two others but was wounded in the thigh, temporarily losing control of his
aircraft. He righted it and closed with the enemy, using up all his ammunition, firing at very close range. He then returned home,
landing his aircraft safely. *VC in Eastbourne College*

No photograph available

REEVES, Thomas   1034
Seaman (later Captain of the Foretop)   Royal Navy (Naval Brigade)
Other Decorations: —
Date of Gazette: 24 Feb. 1857
Place/Date of Birth: Portsmouth, Hampshire — 1828
Place/Date of Death: Portsea, Hampshire — 4 Aug. 1862
Memorials: (Buried Portsea Island General Cemetery — now Mile End Gardens)
Town/County Connections: Portsmouth, Hampshire
Remarks: —
Account of Deed: On 5 Nov. 1854 at the Battle of Inkerman, Crimea, when the Right Lancaster
Battery was attacked and many of the soldiers were wounded, Seaman Reeves, with two other
seamen* and two others who were killed during the action, mounted the defence work banquette and, under withering attack
from the enemy, kept up a rapid, repulsing fire. Their muskets were re-loaded for them by the wounded soldiers under the
parapet and eventually the enemy fell back and gave no more trouble. (*See also GORMAN, J and SCHOLEFIELD, M.)

REID, Oswald Austin   1035
Captain (later Major)   1st Bn., The King's (Liverpool) Regiment, attd. 6th Bn., The Loyal North
Lancashire Regiment
Other Decorations: —
Date of Gazette: 8 Jun. 1917
Place/Date of Birth: Johannesburg, South Africa — 2 Nov. 1893
Place/Date of Death: Johannesburg — 27 Oct. 1920
Memorials: Braamfontein Cemetery, Johannesburg
Town/County Connections: — *Radley College, Berks.*
Remarks: —
Account of Deed: On 8/10 Mar. 1917 at Dailah River, Mesopotamia, Captain Reid consolidated a
small post with the advanced troops on the opposite side of the river to the main body, after his lines of communication had
been cut by the sinking of the pontoons. He maintained this position for 30 hours against constant attacks by bombs, machine-
gun and rifle fire, with the full knowledge that repeated attempts at relief had failed and that his ammunition was all but
exhausted. It was greatly due to his tenacity that the crossing of the river was effected the next night. During the operations he
was wounded.

REID, William   1036
A/Flight Lieutenant   61 Squadron, Royal Air Force Volunteer Reserve
Other Decorations: —
Date of Gazette: 14 Dec. 1943
Place/Date of Birth: Glasgow — 21 Dec. 1921
Place/Date of Death: — *Probably in Scotland around* 28.11.2001
Memorials: —
Town/County Connections: Glasgow
Remarks: —
Account of Deed: On 3 Nov. 1943 on the way to Dusseldorf, Germany, Flight Lieutenant Reid's
windscreen was shatterd by fire from a Messerschmitt and the gun turrets and cockpit badly
damaged. Saying nothing of his multiple injuries, he continued on his mission and soon afterwards was attacked again, his
navigator being killed and the wireless operator fatally wounded. He was wounded again, and also the flight engineer, while
the Lancaster received more serious damage. Pressing on to his target, Flight Lieutenant Reid released his bombs, then set
course for home and in spite of growing weakness from loss of blood, managed to land his crippled aircraft safely.

RENDLE, Thomas Edward　　　　　　　　　　　　　　　　　　　　　**1037**
Bandsman (later Sergeant)　1st Bn., The Duke of Cornwall's Light Infantry
Other Decorations:　—
Date of Gazette:　11 Jan. 1915
Place/Date of Birth:　Bedminster, Bristol — 14 Dec. 1884
Place/Date of Death:　Cape Town, South Africa — 1 Jun. 1946
Memorials:　—
Town/County Connections:　Bedminster, Bristol
Remarks:　Order of St. George, 4th Class (Russia)
Account of Deed:　On 20 Nov. 1914 near Wulverghem, Belgium, Bandsman Rendle attended to the wounded under very heavy rifle and shell fire and rescued men from the trenches in which they had been buried from the blowing in of the parapets by the fire of the enemy's heavy howitzers.

RENNIE, William　　　　　　　　　　　　　　　　　　　　　　　　**1038**
Lieutenant　90th Regiment (later The Cameronians — Scottish Rifles)
Other Decorations:　—
Date of Gazette:　24 Dec. 1858
Place/Date of Birth:　Elgin, Morayshire, Scotland — 31 Oct. 1822
Place/Date of Death:　Elgin, Morayshire — 22 Aug. 1896
Memorials:　—
Town/County Connections:　Elgin, Morayshire
Remarks:　—
Account of Deed:　On 21 Sep. 1857 at Lucknow, India, Lieutenant Rennie charged the enemy's guns in advance of the skirmishers of his regiment, under heavy musketry fire and prevented them from dragging off one gun, which was subsequently captured. On 25 Sep. he again charged in advance of the 90th column in the face of heavy grape fire, and forced the enemy to abandon their guns.

RENNY, George Alexander　　　　　　　　　　　　　　　　　　　　**1039**
Lieutenant (later Major General)　Bengal Horse Artillery
Other Decorations:　—
Date of Gazette:　12 Apr. 1859
Place/Date of Birth:　Riga, Russia — 12 May 1825
Place/Date of Death:　Bath, Somerset — 5 Jan. 1887
Memorials:　— *Buried Locksbrook Cemetery, Bath.*
Town/County Connections:　Bath, Somerset
Remarks:　—
Account of Deed:　On 16 Sep. 1857 at Delhi, India, after the capture of the magazine, vigorous attacks were made on the post by the enemy, who under cover of heavy cross-fire, set fire to a thatched roof. This fire was extinguished, but the roof was again set alight and Lieutenant Renny, with great gallantry, mounted to the top of the wall of the magazine and flung several sticks of shells with lighted fuses into the midst of the enemy, with immediate effect. The attacks became feeble and soon ceased altogether.

REYNOLDS, Douglas　　　　　　　　　　　　　　　　　　　　　　**1040**
Captain (later Major)　37th Bty., Royal Field Artillery
Other Decorations:　—
Date of Gazette:　16 Nov. 1914
Place/Date of Birth:　Clifton, Bristol — 20 Sep. 1882
Place/Date of Death:　Le Touquet, France — 23 Feb. 1916
Memorials:　Etaples Military Cemetery, France; War Memorial, Cheltenham, Gloucestershire; headstone Leckhampton Churchyard, Cheltenham.
Town/County Connections:　Clifton, Bristol; Cheltenham, Gloucestershire
Remarks:　—
Account of Deed:　On 26 Aug. 1914 at Le Cateau, France, Captain Reynolds took up two teams with volunteer drivers, to recapture two British guns and limbered up two guns under heavy artillery and infantry fire. Although the enemy was within 100 yards he managed, with the help of two drivers*, to get one gun away safely. On 9 Sep. at Pysloup, he reconnoitred at close range, discovered a battery which was holding up the advance and silenced it. (*See also DRAIN, J.H.C. and LUKE F.)

REYNOLDS, Henry

1041

T/Captain   12th Bn, The Royal Scots (The Lothian Regiment)
Other Decorations: MC
Date of Gazette: 8 Nov. 1917
Place/Date of Birth: Whilton, Northamptonshire — 16 Aug. 1879
Place/Date of Death: Carshalton, Surrey — 26 Mar. 1948
Memorials: St. Giles' Churchyard, Ashtead, Surrey
Town/County Connections: Whilton, Northamptonshire; Beckenham, Kent
Remarks: Superintendent and Steward, Sir Frederick Milner Homes, Beckenham, Kent 1930-48.
Account of Deed: On 20 Sep. 1917 near Frezenberg, Belgium, Captain Reynold's company were suffering heavy casualties from enemy machine-guns and a pill box. Captain Reynolds reorganised his men and then proceeded alone, rushing from shell-hole to shell-hole under heavy fire. When near the pill box he threw a grenade which should have fallen inside, but the entrance was blocked, so crawling to the entrance he forced a phospherous grenade in. This set the place on fire, killing three, and the remainder surrendered with two machine-guns. Afterwards, although wounded, Captain Reynolds captured another objective, with 70 prisoners and two more machine-guns.

REYNOLDS, James Henry

1042

Surgeon Major (later Lieutenant Colonel)   Army Medical Department (later Royal Army Medical Corps)
Other Decorations: —
Date of Gazette: 17 Jun. 1879
Place/Date of Birth: Kingstown, Co. Dublin — 3 Feb. 1844
Place/Date of Death: London — 4 Mar. 1932
Memorials: St. Mary's RC Cemetery, Kensal Rise, London
Town/County Connections: Kingstown, Dublin; London
Remarks: —
Account of Deed: On 22 and 23 Jan. 1879, at Rorke's Drift, Natal, South Africa, Surgeon Major Reynolds attended the wounded under fire and voluntarily carried ammunition from the store to the defenders of the hospital, exposing himself to cross-fire from the enemy in doing so.

REYNOLDS, William

1043

Private (later Corporal)   Scots (Fusilier) Guards
Other Decorations: —
Date of Gazette: 24 Feb. 1857
Place/Date of Birth: Edinburgh — 1827
Place/Date of Death: London — 20 Oct. 1869
Memorials: —
Town/County Connections: Edinburgh; London
Remarks: Légion d'Honneur (France)
Account of Deed: On 20 Sep. 1854 at the Battle of the Alma, Crimea, when the formation of the line was disordered, Private Reynolds behaved with conspicuous gallantry, in rallying the men round the Colours.

RHODES, John Harold

1044

Lance-Sergeant   3rd Bn., Grenadier Guards
Other Decorations: DCM & Bar
Date of Gazette: 26 Nov. 1917
Place/Date of Birth: Packmoor, Stoke-on-Trent, Staffordshire — 17 May 1891
Place/Date of Death: Fontaine Notre Dame, France — 27 Nov. 1917
Memorials: Rocquigny-Equancourt Road British Cemetery, France
Town/County Connections: Packmoor, Stoke-on-Trent, Staffordshire
Remarks: —
Account of Deed: On 9 Oct. 1917 near Houthulst Forest, east of Ypres, Belgium, Lance-Sergeant Rhodes was in charge of a Lewis gun section covering the consolidation of the right front company. He accounted for several of the enemy with his rifle as well as by Lewis-gun fire and upon seeing three of the enemy leave a pill-box he went alone through our barrage and hostile machine-gun fire and got into the pill-box. There he captured nine of the enemy including a forward observation officer connected by telephone to his battery. Lance-Sergeant Rhodes brought back these prisoners, together with valuable information.

RHODES-MOORHOUSE, William Bernard — see MOORHOUSE, William Bernard
RHODES-

RICHARDS, Alfred Joseph   **1045**
Sergeant   1st Bn., The Lancashire Fusiliers
Other Decorations: —
Date of Gazette: 24 Aug. 1915
Place/Date of Birth: Plymouth, Devon — 21 Jun. 1879
Place/Date of Death: Southfields, London — 21 May 1953
Memorials: Putney Vale Cemetery, London
Town/County Connections: Plymouth, Devon; Putney, London
Remarks: —
Account of Deed: On 25 Apr. 1915 west of Cape Helles, Gallipoli, three companies and the
Headquarters of the 1st Battalion, Lancashire Fusiliers, when landing on W Beach, were met by a
very deadly fire from hidden machine-guns which caused a large number of casualties. The survivors, however, rushed up and
cut the wire entanglements notwithstanding the terrific fire from the enemy and after overcoming supreme difficulties, the cliffs
were gained and the position maintained. (Sergeant Richards was one of six members of the regiment elected for the award.
See also BROMLEY, C., GRIMSHAW, J.E., KENEALLY, W., STUBBS, F.E., and WILLIS, R.R.)

RICHARDSON, Arthur Herbert Lindsay   **1046**
Sergeant   Lord Strathcona's Horse, Canadian Forces
Other Decorations: —
Date of Gazette: 14 Sep. 1900
Place/Date of Birth: Southport, Lancashire — 23 Sep. 1872
Place/Date of Death: Liverpool, Lancashire — 15 Dec. 1932
Memorials: St. James's Cemetery, Liverpool
Town/County Connections: Liverpool, Lancashire
Remarks: First man to win the VC while serving with a Canadian unit under British Command
Account of Deed: On 5 Jul. 1900 at Wolwespruit, Standerton, South Africa, a party of Lord
Strathcona's Horse (38 in number) came into contact and was engaged at close quarters with a
force of 80 of the enemy. When the order was given to retire Sergeant Richardson rode back under very heavy cross-fire, picked
up a trooper whose horse had been shot and who was badly wounded and rode with him out of fire. This act of gallantry was
performed within 300 yards of the enemy and Sergeant Richardson was himself riding a wounded horse.

RICHARDSON, George   **1047**
Private (later Sergeant)   34th Regiment (later The Border Regiment)
Other Decorations: —
Date of Gazette: 11 Nov. 1859
Place/Date of Birth: Derrylane, Killashandra, Co. Cavan, Ireland — 1 Aug. 1831
Place/Date of Death: London, Ontario, Canada — 28 Jan. 1923
Memorials: Veterans' Section, Prospect Cemetery, Toronto, Canada
Town/County Connections: Derrylane, Killashandra, Co. Cavan, Ireland
Remarks: —
Account of Deed: On 27 Apr. 1859 at Kewane Trans-Gogra, India, Private Richardson, although
severely wounded in one arm, closed with and secured an armed rebel sepoy.

RICHARDSON, James Cleland   **1048**
Piper   16th Bn., Mantioba Regiment (Canadian Scottish), C.E.F.
Other Decorations: —
Date of Gazette: 22 Oct. 1918
Place/Date of Birth: Bellshill, Lanarkshire, Scotland — 25 Nov. 1895
Place/Date of Death: Regina Trench, Somme, France — 9 Oct. 1916
Memorials: Adanac Military Cemetery, France
Town/County Connections: Bellshill, Lanarkshire
Remarks: —
Account of Deed: On 8 Oct. 1916 at Regina Trench, Somme, France, the company was held up
by very strong wire and came under intense fire. Piper Richardson, who had obtained permission
to play the company 'over the top' strode up and down outside the wire playing his pipes, which so inspired the company that
the wire was rushed and the position captured. Later the piper was detailed to take back a wounded comrade and some
prisoners, but after proceeding some distance he insisted on turning back to recover his pipes which he had left behind. He was
never seen again.

RICHHPAL RAM, 1049

Subadar 6th Rajputana Rifles, Indian Army
Other Decorations: —
Date of Gazette: 4 Jul. 1941
Place/Date of Birth: Tehsil, Patiala State, Rajputana, India — 27 Aug. 1899
Place/Date of Death: Keren, Eritrea — 12 Feb. 1941
Memorials: Keren Cremation Memorial, Eritrea
Town/County Connections: —
Remarks: —
Account of Deed: On 7 Feb. 1941 at Keren, Eritrea, Subadar Richhpal Ram led a successful attack on the enemy and subsequently repelled six counter-attacks and then, without a shot left, brought the few survivors of his company back. Five days later, when leading another attack, his right foot was blown off, but he continued to encourage his men until he died.

RICKARD, William Thomas 1050

Quartermaster (later Chief Officer of Coast Guards) Royal Navy
Other Decorations: CGM
Date of Gazette: 24 Feb. 1857
Place/Date of Birth: Stoke Damerel, near Devonport, Devon — 10 Feb. 1828
Place/Date of Death: Ryde, Isle of Wight — 21 Feb. 1905
Memorials: — *Buried Ryde Cemetery, I.O.W.*
Town/County Connections: Devonport, Devon; Ryde, Isle of Wight
Remarks: Légion d'Honneur (France)
Account of Deed: On 11 Oct. 1855 in the Sea of Azov, Crimea, Quartermaster Rickard went with the commander* of HMS *Weser* and a seaman to destroy large quantities of forage on the shore of the Sivash. After a difficult and dangerous journey they reached their objective — the magazine of corn — and managed to ignite the stacks, but the guards were alerted and immediately opened fire and gave chase. The pursuit was so hot that the seaman, through fatigue, fell into the mud and could not extricate himself. Rickard, however, although he was himself exhausted, went back and assisted him. The three men finally reached their ship and later the look-outs reported that the fodder store had burned to the ground. (*See also COMMERELL, J.E.)

RICKETTS, Thomas 1051

Private 1st Bn., Royal Newfoundland Regiment, C.E.F.
Other Decorations: DCM
Date of Gazette: 6 Jan. 1919
Place/Date of Birth: Middle Arm, White Bay, Newfoundland — 15 Apr. 1901
Place/Date of Death: St. John's, Newfoundland — 10 Feb. 1967
Memorials: Anglican Cemetery, Forest Road, St. John's Newfoundland
Town/County Connections: —
Remarks: Croix de Guerre with Golden Star (France)
Account of Deed: On 14 Oct. 1918 at Ledeghem, Belgium, Private Ricketts volunteered to go with his section commander and a Lewis gun in an attempt to out-flank an enemy battery causing casualties at point-blank range. Their ammunition was exhausted when still 300 yards from the battery and the enemy began to bring up their gun teams. Private Ricketts doubled back 100 yards under the heaviest machine-gun fire, procured ammunition and dashed back again to the Lewis gun. They then drove the enemy and gun teams into a farm and the platoon was able to advance. They captured four field guns, four machine-guns and eight prisoners.

RIDGEWAY, Richard Kirby 1052

Captain (later Colonel) Bengal Staff Corps and 44th Gurkha Rifles (later 1/8th Gurkha Rifles), Indian Army
Other Decorations: CB
Date of Gazette: 11 May 1880
Place/Date of Birth: Oldcastle, Co. Meath, Ireland — 18 Aug. 1848
Place/Date of Death: Harrogate, Yorkshire — 11 Oct. 1924
Memorials: —
Town/County Connections: Oldcastle, Co. Meath; Harrogate, Yorkshire
Remarks: —
Account of Deed: On 22 Nov. 1879 during the final assault on Konoma, Eastern Frontier of India, under heavy fire from the enemy, Captain Ridgeway rushed up to a barricade and attempted to tear down the planking surrounding it to enable him to effect an entrance. While doing this he was wounded severely in the right shoulder.

RIGGS, Frederick Charles   **1053**
Sergeant   6th Bn., The York and Lancaster Regiment
Other Decorations: MM
Date of Gazette: 6 Jan. 1919
Place/Date of Birth: Bournemouth, Hampshire — 28 Jul. 1888
Place/Date of Death: Epinoy, France — 1 Oct. 1918
Memorials: Vis-en-Artois Memorial, France
Town/County Connections: Bournemouth, Hampshire
Remarks: —
Account of Deed: On 1 Oct. 1918 near Epinoy, France, Sergeant Riggs, having led his platoon through strong uncut wire under severe fire, continued straight on and although losing heavily from flanking fire, succeeded in reaching his objective, where he captured a machine-gun. Later he handled two captured guns with great effect and caused 50 of the enemy to surrender. Subsequently, when the enemy again advanced in force, Sergeant Riggs cheerfully encouraged his men exhorting them to resist to the last, and while doing so was killed.

RIPLEY, John   **1054**
Corporal (later Sergeant)   1st Bn., The Black Watch (Royal Highlanders)
Other Decorations: —
Date of Gazette: 29 Jun. 1915
Place/Date of Birth: Keith, Banffshire, Scotland — 30 Aug. 1867
Place/Date of Death: St. Andrews, Fife, Scotland — 14 Aug. 1933
Memorials: —
Town/County Connections: St. Andrews, Fife; Keith, Banff
Remarks: —
Account of Deed: On 9 May 1915 at Rue du Bois, France, Corporal Ripley led his section on the right of the platoon in the assault and was the first man of the battalion to climb the enemy's parapet. From there he directed those following him to the gaps in the German wire entanglements. He then led his section through a breach in the parapet to a second line of trench. With seven or eight men he established himself, blocking other flanks, and continued to hold the position until all his men had fallen and he himself was badly wounded in the head.

RITCHIE, Henry Peel   **1055**
Commander (later Captain)   Royal Navy
Other Decorations: —
Date of Gazette: 10 Apr. 1915
Place/Date of Birth: Edinburgh — 29 Jan. 1876
Place/Date of Death: Edinburgh — 9 Dec. 1958
Memorials: —
Town/County Connections: Edinburgh
Remarks: —
Account of Deed: On 28 Nov. 1914 Commander Ritchie of HMS *Goliath* was in command of the searching and demolition operations at Dar-es-Salaam, East Africa. He had fitted out a steam pinnace for the execution of this task and, accompanied by two other small craft, entered the harbour. At first there was no reaction from the enemy, but suddenly they were met by a storm of shells and bullets from all directions. The commander was hit eight times in 20 minutes, but in spite of his wounds he carried on until at last he fainted from loss of blood.

RITCHIE, Walter Potter   **1056**
Drummer (later Drum-Major)   2nd Bn., The Seaforth Highlanders (Ross-shire Buffs, Duke of Albany's)
Other Decorations: —
Date of Gazette: 9 Sep. 1916
Place/Date of Birth: Glasgow — 27 Mar. 1892
Place/Date of Death: Edinburgh — 17 Mar. 1965
Memorials: —
Town/County Connections: Glasgow; Edinburgh
Remarks: —
Account of Deed: On 1 Jul. 1916 north of Beaumont Hamel, France, Drummer Ritchie, on his own initiative, stood on the parapet of an enemy trench and, under heavy machine-gun fire and bomb attacks, repeatedly sounded the "Charge" thereby rallying many men of various units who, having lost their leaders were wavering and beginning to retire. He also, during the day, carried messages over fire-swept ground.

RIVERS, Jacob   1057

Private   1st Bn., The Sherwood Foresters (The Nottinghamshire and Derbyshire Regiment)
Other Decorations: —
Date of Gazette: 28 Apr. 1915
Place/Date of Birth: Derby — 1881
Place/Date of Death: Neuve Chapelle, France — 12 Mar. 1915
Memorials: Le Touret Memorial, France
Town/County Connections: Derby
Remarks: —
Account of Deed: On 12 Mar. 1915, at Neuve Chapelle, France, Private Rivers, on his own initiative, crept to within a few yards of a very large number of the enemy who were massed on the flank of an advanced company of his battalion, and hurled bombs on them. His action caused the enemy to retire, and so relieved the situation. Private Rivers performed a second similar act of great bravery on the same day, again causing the enemy to withdraw. He was killed on this occasion.

ROBARTS, John   1058

Gunner, Royal Navy
Other Decorations: —
Date of Gazette: 24 Feb. 1857
Place/Date of Birth: Chacewater, Cornwall — 1818
Place/Date of Death: Southsea, Hampshire — 17 Oct. 1888
Memorials: — *Buried Highland Road Cemetery, Portsmouth*
Town/County Connections: Chacewater, Cornwall; Southsea, Hampshire
Remarks: —
Account of Deed: On 29 May 1855 in the Sea of Azov, Crimea, Gunner Robarts of HMS *Ardent* with two lieutenants*, one from HMS *Miranda* and the other from HMS *Swallow*, volunteered to land on a beach where the Russian army were in strength. They were out of covering gunshot range of the ships offshore and met considerable enemy opposition, but managed to set fire to corn stores and ammunition dumps and destroy enemy equipment before embarking again. (*See also BUCKLEY, C.W. and BURGOYNE, H.T.)

ROBERTS, Frank Crowther   1059

A/Lieutenant Colonel (later Major General)   Comd. 1st Bn., The Worcestershire Regiment
Other Decorations: DSO, OBE, MC
Date of Gazette: 8 May 1918
Place/Date of Birth: Highbury, Middlesex — 2 Jun. 1891
Place/Date of Death: Stanhope Bretby, Burton-on-Trent, Staffordshire — 12 Jan. 1982
Memorials: —
Town/County Connections: Southall, Middlesex
Remarks: —
Account of Deed: During the period 22 Mar./2 Apr. 1918 west of Somme and at Pargny, France, Lieutenant Colonel Roberts showed exceptional military skill in dealing with the many very difficult situations of the retirement and amazing endurance and energy in inspiring all ranks under his command. On one occasion the enemy attacked a village and had practically cleared it of our troops when Colonel Roberts got together an improvised party and led a counter-attack which temporarily drove the enemy out of the village, thus covering the retirement of troops on their flanks. The success of this action was entirely due to his personal valour and skill.

ROBERTS, The Hon. Frederick Hugh Sherston   1060

Lieutenant   The King's Royal Rifle Corps
Other Decorations: —
Date of Gazette: 2 Feb. 1900
Place/Date of Birth: Umballa, India — 8 Jan. 1872
Place/Date of Death: Chieveley, Natal, South Africa — 17 Dec. 1899
Memorials: The KRRC Memorial, Winchester Cathedral, Hampshire
Town/County Connections: —
Remarks: Son of Field-Marshal Earl Roberts, VC
Account of Deed: On 15 Dec. 1899 at the Battle of Colenso, South Africa, Lieutenant Roberts, with several others, tried to save the guns of the 14th and 66th Batteries, Royal Field Artillery, when the detachments serving the guns had all become casualties or been driven from their guns. Some of the horses and drivers were sheltering in a donga about 500 yards behind the guns and the intervening space was swept with shell and rifle fire. Lieutenant Roberts with two other officers* helped to hook a team into a limber and then to limber up a gun. While doing so, he fell badly wounded and later died of his wounds. (*See also CONGREVE, W.N. and SCHOFIELD, H.N.)

ROBERTS, (later Earl ROBERTS) Frederick Sleigh **1061**
Lieutenant (later Field Marshal)   Bengal Artillery
Other Decorations: KG, KP, GCB, OM, GCSI, GCIE, VD
Date of Gazette: 24 Dec. 1858
Place/Date of Birth: Cawnpore, India — 30 Sep. 1832
Place/Date of Death: France — 14 Nov. 1914 _→ Buried St. Paul's._
Memorials: St. Paul's Cathedral; equestrian statue Horse Guards Parade, London; Sanctum Crypt, St. Luke's Church, Chelsea, London
Town/County Connections: Waterford, Ireland
Remarks: Father of Lieutenant The Hon. F.H.S. Roberts, VC; Quartermaster General in India 1875-78; Commander-in-Chief Madras 1881-85; Commander-in-Chief India 1885-93; Commander, Forces in Ireland 1895; Commander-in-Chief South Africa 1899-1900; Commander-in-Chief 1901-04; Colonel-in-Chief Overseas and Indian Forces in Europe 1914; Colonel-Commandant, Royal Regiment of Artillery 1896; Colonel of the Irish Guards 1900; Knight of the Order of St. John
Account of Deed: On 2 Jan. 1858 at Khodagunge, India, on following up the retreating enemy, Lieutenant Roberts saw in the distance two sepoys going away with a standard. He immediately gave chase, overtaking them just as they were about to enter a village. Although one of them fired at him the lieutenant was not hit and he took possession of the standard, cutting down the man who was carrying it. He had also on the same day saved the life of a sowar who was being attacked by a sepoy.

No photograph available

ROBERTS, James Reynolds **1062**
Private   9th Lancers (The Queen's Royal)
Other Decorations: —
Date of Gazette: 24 Dec. 1858
Place/Date of Birth: Bow, London — 1826
Place/Date of Death: Marylebone, London — 1 Aug. 1859
Memorials: —
Town/County Connections: Bow, London
Remarks: —
Account of Deed: On 28 Sep. 1857 at Bolandshahr, India, Private Roberts brought in a comrade who was mortally wounded, under heavy musketry fire, although he himself was wounded.

ROBERTS, Peter Scawen Watkinson **1063**
Lieutenant   Royal Navy
Other Decorations: DSC
Date of Gazette: 9 Jun. 1942
Place/Date of Birth: Chesham Bois, Buckinghamshire — 28 Jul. 1917
Place/Date of Death: Newton Ferrers, Devon — 8 Dec. 1979
Memorials: —
Town/County Connections: Chesham Bois, Buckinghamshire; Newton Ferrers, Devon
Remarks: Served in Korea 1952-53
Account of Deed: On 16 Feb. 1942 north of Crete, HM Submarine *Thrasher*, after attacking and sinking a supply ship, was itself attacked, and later after surfacing, two unexploded bombs were discovered in the gun-casing. Lieutenant Roberts and a petty officer* removed the first one without too much difficulty, but the second was lying in a very confined space and they had to approach it lying full length. The petty officer then lay on his back with the bomb in his arms while the lieutenant dragged him along by the shoulders. It was 40 minutes before they got the bomb clear and dropped it over the side. (*See also GOULD, T.W.)

ROBERTSON, Charles Graham **1064**
Lance-Corporal   10th Bn., The Royal Fusiliers
Other Decorations: MM
Date of Gazette: 9 Apr. 1918
Place/Date of Birth: Penrith, Cumberland — 4 Jul. 1879
Place/Date of Death: Dorking, Surrey — 10 May 1954
Memorials: Dorking Cemetery, Surrey
Town/County Connections: Penrith, Cumberland; Dorking, Surrey
Remarks: —
Account of Deed: On 8/9 Mar. 1918 west of Polderhoek Chateau, Belgium, Lance-Corporal Robertson having repelled a strong attack by the enemy, realised that he was being cut off and sent for reinforcements, while remaining at his post with only one man, firing his Lewis gun and killing large numbers of the enemy. No reinforcements arrived, so he withdrew, and then was forced to withdraw again to a defended post where he got on top of the parapet with a comrade, mounted his gun and continued firing. His comrade was almost immediately killed and he was severely wounded, but managed to crawl back with his gun, having exhausted his ammunition.

ROBERTSON, Clement
1065

A/Captain   The Queen's Royal West Surrey Regiment, Special Reserve, Tank Corps
Other Decorations: —
Date of Gazette: 18 Dec. 1917
Place/Date of Birth: Pietermaritzburg, South Africa — 15 Dec. 1890
Place/Date of Death: Zonnebeke, Belgium — 4 Oct. 1917
Memorials: Oxford Road Cemetery, Ypres, Belgium
Town/County Connections: —
Remarks: — *Heileybury School.*
Account of Deed: On 4 Oct. 1917 at Zonnebeke, Belgium, Captain Robertson led his tanks in attack under heavy shell, machine-gun and rifle fire over ground which had been ploughed by shell-fire. He and his batman had spent the previous three days and nights going back and forth over the ground, reconnoitring and taping routes, and, knowing the risk of the tanks missing the way, he now led them on foot, guiding them carefully towards their objective, although he must have known that this action would almost certainly cost him his life. He was killed after the objective had been reached, but his skilful leading had already ensured success.

ROBERTSON, James FORBES-
1066

A/Lieutenant Colonel (later Brigadier General)   Comd. 1st Bn., The Border Regiment
Other Decorations: DSO & Bar, MC
Date of Gazette: 22 May 1918
Place/Date of Birth: Cheltenham, Gloucestershire — 7 Jul. 1884
Place/Date of Death: Bourton-on-the-Water, Gloucestershire — 5 Aug. 1955
Memorials: Cheltenham Cemetery
Town/County Connections: Strathpeffer, Ross and Cromarty; Bourton-on-the-Water, Glos.
Remarks: Commanded 152 Infantry Brigade 1932-34; DL, County of Sutherland
Account of Deed: On 11/12 Apr. 1918 near Vieux Berquin, France, four times Lieutenant Colonel Forbes-Robertson saved the line from breaking and averted a most serious situation. On one occasion, having made a reconnaissance on horseback in full view of the enemy under heavy fire, he led a counter-attack which was completely successful in establishing our line. When his horse was shot under him he continued on foot, steadying the men and inspiring confidence by his disregard for personal danger. On the second day he lost another horse and again continued on foot until he had established a line to which his own troops could withdraw.

ROBERTSON, James Peter
1067

Private   27th Bn., Manitoba Regiment (Winnipeg), C.E.F.
Other Decorations: —
Date of Gazette: 11 Jan. 1918
Place/Date of Birth: Albion Mines, Picton, Nova Scotia, Canada — 26 Oct. 1883
Place/Date of Death: Passchendaele, Belgium — 6 Nov. 1917
Memorials: Tyne Cot Cemetery, Passchendaele, Belgium
Town/County Connections: —
Remarks: —
Account of Deed: On 6 Nov. 1917 at Passchendaele, Belgium, when his platoon was held up by a machine-gun, Private Robertson rushed the gun, killed four of the crew and then turned the gun on the remainder. After inflicting more casualties and carrying the captured gun, he led his platoon to the final position and got the gun into action, firing on the retreating enemy. During the consolidation his use of the machine-gun kept down the enemy sniper fire. Later when two of our own snipers were wounded, he went out and carried one of them in under heavy fire but he was killed just as he returned with the second man.

ROBERTSON, William
1068

Sergeant-Major (later Lieutenant Colonel)   2nd Bn., The Gordon Highlanders
Other Decorations: CBE
Date of Gazette: 20 Jul. 1900
Place/Date of Birth: Dumfries, Scotland — 27 Feb. 1865
Place/Date of Death: Edinburgh — 6 Dec. 1949
Memorials: — *Buried Portobello Cemetery, Edinburgh*
Town/County Connections: Dumfries and Edinburgh
Remarks: Served in the First World War 1914-18; Légion d'Honneur (France); Recruiting Staff Officer, Scottish Command, after the war
Account of Deed: On 21 Oct. 1899 at the Battle of Elandslaagte, South Africa, during the final advance on the enemy's position, Sergeant-Major Robertson led each successive rush, exposing himself fearlessly to the enemy's artillery and rifle fire to encourage the men. After the main position had been captured, he led a small party to seize the Boer camp. Though exposed to a deadly cross-fire from the enemy's rifles, he gallantly held on to the position captured, and continued to encourage the men until he was dangerously wounded.

ROBINSON, Edward   **1069**
Able Seaman   Royal Navy (Naval Brigade)
Other Decorations: —
Date of Gazette: 24 Dec. 1858
Place/Date of Birth: Portsea, Hampshire — 17 Jun. 1838
Place/Date of Death: Windsor, Berkshire — 2 Oct. 1896
Memorials: Old Windsor Cemetery, Windsor, Berkshire · *St. Peter & St. Andrew Churchyard*
Town/County Connections: Portsea, Hampshire; Windsor, Berkshire
Remarks: —
Account of Deed: On 13 Mar. 1858 at Lucknow, India, some sandbags on top of the earthworks
were on fire. The enemy were only 50 yards away at this time, but Able Seaman Robinson, under
heavy fire, jumped up and extinguished the fires in some of the bags and threw others clear. He was severely wounded.

ROBINSON, Eric Gascoigne   **1070**
Lieutenant-Commander (later Rear-Admiral)   Royal Navy
Other Decorations: OBE
Date of Gazette: 16 Aug. 1915
Place/Date of Birth: Greenwich, London — 16 May 1882
Place/Date of Death: Haslar, Hampshire — 20 Aug. 1965
Memorials: —
Town/County Connections: Greenwich, London; Langrish, Hampshire
Remarks: Order of the Nile (Egypt); Order of St. Anne (Russia); recalled to the Royal Navy in the
Second World War for duty as a Commodore of Convoy, 1939-41
Account of Deed: On 26 Feb. 1915 in the Dardanelles, Lieutenant-Commander Robinson of HMS
Vengeance was in charge of a demolition party which was landed at Kum Kale. They were held up by heavy fire and Lieutenant-
Commander Robinson told his sailors to stay where they were as their white uniforms made them conspicuous, and went on
alone with a charge of gun-cotton. He found the A.A. Battery deserted and having blown up one gun, he went back for another
charge and blew up the second. He later took part in four attacks on the mine fields, always under heavy fire.

ROBINSON William Leefe   **1071**
Lieutenant   The Worcestershire Regiment and 39 Squadron, Royal Flying Corps
Other Decorations: —
Date of Gazette: 5 Sep. 1916
Place/Date of Birth: Tollideta, South Coorg, India — 14 Jul. 1895
Place/Date of Death: Stanmore, Middlesex — 31 Dec. 1918
Memorials: Harrow Weald (All Saints') Churchyard Extension, Middlesex
Town/County Connections: Harrow Weald, Middlesex
Remarks: —
Account of Deed: On the night of 2/3 Sep. 1916 over Cuffley, Hertfordshire, Lieutenant Robinson
sighted a German airship — one of 16 which had left bases in Germany on a mass raid over
England. The lieutenant made an attack at a height of 11,500ft. approaching from below and, closing to within 500ft., raked the
aircraft (a wooden-framed Schutte Lanz) with gunfire. As he was preparing for another attack, the airship burst into flames and
crashed in a field.

ROBSON, Henry Howey   **1072**
Private   2nd Bn., The Royal Scots (The Lothian Regiment)
Other Decorations: —
Date of Gazette: 18 Feb. 1915
Place/Date of Birth: South Shields, Co. Durham — 27 May 1894
Place/Date of Death: Toronto, Canada — 4 Mar. 1964
Memorials: York Cemetery, Military Section, Toronto
Town/County Connections: South Shields and Shotton Bridge, Co. Durham
Remarks: —
Account of Deed: On 14 Dec. 1914 near Kemmel, France, during an attack on a German position,
Private Robson left his trench under very heavy fire and rescued a wounded NCO. Subsequently,
during another attack, he tried to bring a second wounded man into cover, while exposed to heavy fire. In this attack he was
wounded almost at once, but persevered in his efforts until wounded a second time.

ROCHFORT, George Arthur BOYD-   1073
Second Lieutenant (later Captain)   Scots Guards (Special Reserve, attd. 1st Bn.)
Other Decorations:
Date of Gazette: 1 Sep. 1915
Place/Date of Birth: Middleton, Co. Westmeath, Ireland — 1 Jan. 1880
Place/Date of Death: Dublin — 11 Aug. 1940
Memorials: —
Town/County Connections: Castletown, Westmeath
Remarks: — Eton College.
Account of Deed: On 3 Aug. 1915 between Cambrin and La Bassee, France, a German trench-
mortar bomb landed on the side of the parapet of the communication trench in which Second
Lieutenant Boyd-Rochfort was standing close to a small working party of his battalion. Instead of stepping back into safety he
shouted to his men to look out, rushed at the bomb, seized it and hurled it over the parapet where it at once exploded. This
combination of presence of mind and courage saved the lives of many of the working party.

RODDY, Patrick   1074
Ensign (later Colonel)   Bengal Army
Other Decorations: —
Date of Gazette: 12 Apr. 1859
Place/Date of Birth: Elphin, Roscommon, Ireland — 17 Mar. 1827
Place/Date of Death: Jersey, Channel Islands — 21 Nov. 1895
Memorials: —
Town/County Connections: Elphin, Roscommon; Dublin; Jersey
Remarks: —
Account of Deed: On 27 Sep. 1858 on the return from Kuthirga, India of the Kupperthula
Contingent, Ensign Roddy, who was serving with that force, charged an armed rebel whom the
cavalry was afraid to approach, as each time they moved the rebel knelt, covering the horseman nearest him. This, however,
did not deter Ensign Roddy, who went boldly in, and although his horse was shot under him and the rebel tried to cut him down
the ensign seized and killed him with his sword.

No photograph available

RODGERS, George   1075
Private   71st Regiment (later The Highland Light Infantry)
Other Decorations: —
Date of Gazette: 11 Nov. 1859
Place/Date of Birth: Govan, Glasgow — Jan. 1829
Place/Date of Death: Glasgow — 9 Mar. 1870
Memorials: —
Town/County Connections: Glasgow, Scotland
Remarks: —
Account of Deed: On 16 Jun. 1858 at Marar, Gwalior, India, Private Rodgers attacked, by himself,
a party of seven rebels, one of whom he killed. This was a particularly valuable action, as the party
of rebels were well armed and strongly posted in the line of advance of a detachment of the 71st Regiment.

ROGERS, James   1076
Sergeant (later Captain)   South African Constabulary
Other Decorations: —
Date of Gazette: 18 Apr. 1902
Place/Date of Birth: Riverina, New South Wales, Australia — 2 Jun. 1875
Place/Date of Death: Sydney, New South Wales, Australia — 28 Oct. 1961
Memorials: Heywood, Victoria, Australia; Australian War Memorial, Canberra
Town/County Connections:
Remarks: Served in First World War 1914-16.
Account of Deed: On 15 Jun. 1901 at Thaba 'Nchu, South Africa, during a skirmish, a party of the
rearguard, consisting of a lieutenant, Sergeant Rogers and six men, was attacked by about 60
Boers. When the lieutenant's horse was shot, Sergeant Rogers rode back, took the lieutenant up behind and carried him for half
a mile on his own horse. The sergeant then returned to within 400 yards of the enemy and rescued two other men who had lost
their horses. Afterwards, he caught two horses and helped their owners to remount. This was done under heavy fire.

ROGERS, Maurice Albert Windham   **1077**
Sergeant   2nd Bn., The Wiltshire Regiment (Duke of Edinburgh's)
Other Decorations: MM
Date of Gazette: 10 Aug. 1944
Place/Date of Birth: Bristol — 17 Jul. 1919
Place/Date of Death: Anzio, Italy — 3 Jun. 1944
Memorials: Beach Head War Cemetery, Anzio, Italy
Town/County Connections: Bristol; Plaistow, Essex
Remarks: —
Account of Deed: On 3 Jun. 1944 at Anzio, Italy, a carrier platoon was held up by barbed wire and intense machine-gun fire only 70 yards from the objective. Sergeant Rogers, with his Thompson machine-gun, crashed through the wire, ran across a mine-field beyond, and accounted for two of the enemy posts. This action so inspired his platoon, now 100 yards behind, that they advanced to the assault, but before they could reach the sergeant he had been wounded in the leg. Undaunted, he continued to advance until he was shot and killed at point blank range.

ROGERS, Robert Montresor   **1078**
Lieutenant (later Major General)   44th Regiment (later The Essex Regiment)
Other Decorations: CB
Date of Gazette: 13 Aug. 1861
Place/Date of Birth: Dublin — 4 Sep. 1834
Place/Date of Death: Maidenhead, Berkshire — 5 Feb. 1895   *Buried All Saints churchyard. Maidenhead*
Memorials: —
Town/County Connections: Dublin; Maidenhead, Berkshire
Remarks: —
Account of Deed: On 21 Aug. 1860 at the Taku Forts, China, Lieutenant Rogers, together with a private of his regiment and a lieutenant of the 67th Regiment* displayed great gallantry in swimming the ditches and entering the North Taku Fort by an embrasure during the assault. They were the first of the English troops established on the walls of the Fort. (*See also McDOUGALL, J. and LENON, E.H.)

ROLLAND, George Murray   **1079**
Captain (later Major)   1st Bombay Grenadiers, Indian Army, employed Berbera-Bohotle Flying Column
Other Decorations: —
Date of Gazette: 7 Aug. 1903
Place/Date of Birth: Wellington, India — 12 May 1869
Place/Date of Death: Nagpur, India — 9 Jul. 1910
Memorials: St. Stephen's Church, South Kensington, London
Town/County Connections: —   *Harrow School.*
Remarks: —
Account of Deed: On 22 Apr. 1903 after the action at Daratoleh, Somaliland, the rearguard got considerably behind the rest of the column. Captain Rolland and another captain*, with four other men were with a fellow officer when he fell badly wounded and Captain Rolland ran back some 500 yards to get help while the others stayed with the casualty, endeavouring to keep off the enemy who were all round. This they succeeded in doing, and when the officer in charge of the column* arrived they managed to get the wounded man on to a camel. He was, however, hit again and died immediately. (*See also WALKER, W.G. and GOUGH, J.E.)

ROOM, Frederick George   **1080**
A/Lance-Corporal   2nd Bn., The Royal Irish Regiment
Other Decorations: —
Date of Gazette: 17 Oct. 1917
Place/Date of Birth: Ashley, Bristol — 31 May 1895
Place/Date of Death: Bristol — 19 Jan. 1932
Memorials: —   *Buried Greenbank Cemetery Bristol*
Town/County Connections: Bristol
Remarks: —
Account of Deed: On 16 Aug. 1917 at Frezenberg, Belgium, when the company which was holding a line of shell-holes and short trenches had many casualties, Lance-Corporal Room was in charge of the stretcher-bearers. He worked continuously under intense fire, dressing the wounded and helping to evacuate them. Throughout this period, with complete disregard for his own life, he showed unremitting devotion to his duties.

ROOPE, Gerard Broadmead   **1081**
Lieutenant-Commander   Royal Navy
Other Decorations: —
Date of Gazette: 10 Jul. 1945
Place/Date of Birth: Hillbrook Trull, near Taunton, Somerset — 13 Mar. 1905
Place/Date of Death: West Fjord, Norway — 8 Apr. 1940
Memorials: Portsmouth Naval Memorial, Hampshire
Town/County Connections: Taunton, Somerset; Weymouth, Dorset
Remarks: First VC winner of the Second World War.
Account of Deed: On 8 Apr. 1940 in the Norwegian Sea, Lieutenant-Commander Roope commanding HMS *Glowworm* (1,345 tons) fought an unequal duel with the German cruiser *Admiral Hipper* (10,000 tons). In the encounter *Glowworm* was soon battered and burning and eventually, as a last gesture of defiance, her commander decided to ram the cruiser, which resulted in a good deal of damage to the latter. *Glowworm* then fired one more salvo, scoring a hit, before she capsized and sank. One officer and 30 men were picked up by *Admiral Hipper's* captain, but Lieutenant-Commander Roope was drowned.

ROSAMUND, Matthew   **1082**
Sergeant-Major (later Lieutenant)   37th Bengal Native Infantry
Other Decorations: —
Date of Gazette: 23 Aug. 1858
Place/Date of Birth: Eaton Socon, Huntingdonshire — 13 Jul. 1823
Place/Date of Death: The Red Sea — 14 Jul. 1866
Memorials: —
Town/County Connections: Eaton Socon, Huntingdonshire
Remarks: —
Account of Deed: On 4 Jun. 1857 at Benares, India, Sergeant-Major Rosamund volunteered to accompany his commanding officer to the right of the lines in order to set fire to them and so drive out the sepoys. He also volunteered to go with another sergeant-major and a private* to rescue a paymaster, and his family from their bungalow and to take them to the safety of the barracks. (*See also GILL, P. and KIRK, John.)

ROSS, John   **1083**
Corporal (later Sergeant)   Corps of Royal Engineers
Other Decorations: —
Date of Gazette: 24 Feb. 1857
Place/Date of Birth: Inch, Stranraer, Wigtownshire, Scotland — 1822
Place/Date of Death: London — 23 Oct. 1879
Memorials: Finchley Cemetery, London   *Grave.*
Town/County Connections: London
Remarks: —
Account of Deed: On 21 Jul. 1855 at Sebastopol, Crimea, Corporal Ross went out at night in charge of a working party of 200 men each carrying an entrenching tool and a gabion, and before morning they had connected the 4th parallel right attack with an old Russian rifle-pit in front. On 23 Aug. the corporal was in charge of the advance from the 5th parallel right attack on the Redan in placing and filling 25 gabions under a very heavy fire. Again, on 8 Sep. he crept up to the Redan at night and returned to report its evacuation, bringing with him a wounded man.

ROUPELL, George Rowland Patrick   **1084**
Lieutenant (later Brigadier)   1st Bn., The East Surrey Regiment
Other Decorations: CB
Date of Gazette: 23 Jun. 1915
Place/Date of Birth: Tipperary, Ireland — 7 Apr. 1892
Place/Date of Death: Shalford, Surrey — 4 Mar. 1974
Memorials: Regimental Chapel, Parish Church, Kingston-upon-Thames, Surrey
Town/County Connections: Shalford, Surrey · *Rossall School, Fleetwood, Lancs*
Remarks: Croix de Guerre (France); Order of St. George, 4th Class (Russia); served in the Second World War — commanded 36 Infantry Brigade and 105 Infantry Brigade; DL, County of Surrey.
Account of Deed: On 20 Apr. 1915 at Hill 60, Belgium, Lieutenant Roupell was commanding a company which was being subjected to a most severe bombardment. Although wounded several times, he remained at his post and led his company in repelling a strong German assault. During a lull he had his wounds dressed but immediately returned to his trench which was again being fiercely bombarded. Towards evening he went back to battalion headquarters and fetched reinforcements, passing backwards and forwards over ground swept by heavy fire. With these reinforcements, he was able to hold his position throughout the night and until relieved next morning.

ROWLANDS, Hugh (later Sir Hugh)   **1085**
Captain (later General)   41st Regiment (later The Welch Regiment)
Other Decorations: KCB
Date of Gazette: 24 Feb. 1857
Place/Date of Birth: Llanrug, Caernarvonshire, Wales — 6 May 1828
Place/Date of Death: Llanrug, Caernarvonshire — 1 Aug. 1909
Memorials: St. Michael's Churchyard, Llanrug, Caernarvon
Town/County Connections: Llanrug, Caernarvon
Remarks: Légion d'Honneur (France); Quartermaster General 1880; comd. 1st Class District,
India 1884-89; Lieutenant, Tower of London 1893; comd. Scottish District 1893-96
Account of Deed: On 5 Nov. 1854 in the Crimea at Inkerman, Captain Rowlands rescued the
colonel of the 47th Regiment who had been wounded and surrounded by Russian soldiers. He also acted with great gallantry
in holding the ground occupied by his advanced picquet against the enemy at the commencement of the Battle of Inkerman.

VC. in Welch Regiment Museum, Cardiff Castle

RUSHE, David   **1086**
Troop Sergeant-Major (later Regimental Sergeant-Major)   9th Lancers (The Queen's Royal)
Other Decorations: —
Date of Gazette: 24 Dec. 1858
Place/Date of Birth: Woburn, Bedfordshire — 28 Apr. 1827
Place/Date of Death: Great Marlow, Buckinghamshire — 6 Nov. 1886
Memorials: Marlow Churchyard, Buckinghamshire
Town/County Connections: Marlow, Buckinghamshire; Woburn, Bedfordshire
Remarks: —
Account of Deed: On 19 Mar. 1858 at Lucknow, India, Troop Sergeant-Major Rushe displayed
conspicuous bravery when, with another soldier, he attacked eight of the mutineers posted in a
nullah and killed three of them.

RUSSELL, Sir Charles   **1087**
Bt/Major (later Lieutenant Colonel)   3rd Bn., Grenadier Guards
Other Decorations: —
Date of Gazette: 24 Feb. 1857
Place/Date of Birth: Sothern Hill, near Reading, Berkshire — 22 Jun. 1826
Place/Date of Death: Reading, Berkshire — 13 Apr. 1883
Memorials: —
Town/County Connections: Reading, Berkshire
Remarks: DL, County of Berkshire; Hon. Colonel, Middlesex Volunteers 1877
Account of Deed: On 5 Nov. 1854 at the Battle of Inkerman, Crimea, Brevet Major Russell offered
to dislodge a party of Russians from the Sandbag Battery if anyone would follow him. A sergeant and
two privates* (one of whom was subsequently killed) were the first to volunteer. The party met much resistance and several times
seemed to be on the point of annihilation but their skill, especially with the bayonet, finally brought success. Major Russell himself
fought with great valour and in single combat wrenched the rifle out of the grasp of a powerful Russian. (*See also PALMER, A.)

RUSSELL, John Fox   **1088**
Captain   Royal Army Medical Corps attd. 1/6th Bn., The Royal Welch Fusiliers
Other Decorations: MC
Date of Gazette: 11 Jan. 1918
Place/Date of Birth: Holyhead, Anglesey — 27 Jan. 1893   → *Plot F. Grave 31.*
Place/Date of Death: Tel-el-Khuweilfeh, Palestine — 6 Nov. 1917
Memorials: Beersheba War Cemetery, Palestine; War Memorial, Holyhead; Middlesex
Hospital, London; RAMC HQ, London
Town/County Connections: Holyhead, Anglesey
Remarks: — *Name on W.M. Aldeburgh. Suffolk.*
Account of Deed: On 6 Nov. 1917 at Tel-el-Khuweilfeh, Palestine, Captain Russell repeatedly
went out to attend to the wounded under murderous fire from snipers and machine-guns. In many cases where no other means
were at hand he carried casualties in himself, although almost exhausted. He was, at last, fatally wounded.

Memorials: St. Bees School. Holyhead W.M.   *Magdalen College, Oxford.*
VC in RAMC Museum. Aldershot   *Middlesex Hospital*

RUTHERFORD, Charles Smith   **1089**
Lieutenant (later Captain)   5th Canadian Mounted Rifles Bn., Quebec Regiment, C.E.F.
Other Decorations: MC, MM
Date of Gazette: 15 Nov. 1918
Place/Date of Birth: Haldimand Township, Ontario, Canada — 9 Jan. 1892
Place/Date of Death: — *Ottawa. About 12.6.1989.*
Memorials: —
Town/County Connections: —
Remarks: —   *Last of the Great War VC's to die.*
Account of Deed: On 26 Aug. 1918 at Monchy, France, Lieutenant Rutherford, commanding an assaulting party, found himself a considerable distance ahead of his men and at the same moment saw a fully armed strong enemy party outside a pill box in front of him. By masterly bluff he managed to persuade the enemy that they were surrounded and the whole party of 45, including two officers and three machine-guns, surrendered. The lieutenant then observed that gun fire from another pill box was holding up the assault, so with a Lewis gun section he attacked it capturing another 35 prisoners and their guns.

RUTHVEN, (later The Earl of GOWRIE) The Hon. Alexander Gore Arkwright HORE-   **1090**
Captain (later Brigadier General)   3rd Bn., The Highland Light Infantry
Other Decorations: CB, GCMG, DSO & Bar
Date of Gazette: 26 Feb. 1899
Place/Date of Birth: Windsor, Berkshire — 6 Jul. 1872
Place/Date of Death: Shipton Moyne, Gloucestershire — 2 May 1955
Memorials: — *Buried in the Churchyard*
Town/County Connections: Windsor, Berkshire; Shipton Moyne, Gloucestershire
Remarks: Croix de Guerre (France and Belgium); Governor General of Australia 1936-44; Deputy Constable and Lieutenant Governor of Windsor Castle 1945-53
Account of Deed: On 22 Sep. 1898 during the action at Gedarif, Sudan, Captain Hore-Ruthven saw an Egyptian officer lying wounded within 50 yards of the advancing Dervishes who were firing and charging. He picked up the wounded officer and carried him towards the 16th Egyptian Battalion. He had to drop his burden several times in order to fire upon the Dervishes and check their advance, but his action undoubtedly saved the officer's life.

RUTHVEN, William   **1091**
Sergeant (later Major)   22nd Bn. (Victoria), Australian Imperial Force
Other Decorations: —
Date of Gazette: 11 Jul. 1918
Place/Date of Birth: Collingwood, Melbourne, Victoria, Australia — 21 May 1893
Place/Date of Death: Victoria, Australia — 12 Jan. 1970
Memorials: Fawkner Crematorium, Victoria; Australian War Memorial, Canberra
Town/County Connections: —
Remarks: —
Account of Deed: On 19 May 1918 during the attack on Ville-sur-Ancre, France, when his company commander was severely wounded, Sergeant Ruthven took charge of company headquarters and rallied the men. He captured one machine-gun, then wounded two of the enemy and captured six others coming out of a shelter. Subsequently he went out and rushed a stubborn enemy position, shooting two who refused to leave the dug-outs. He then, single-handed, mopped up this post, taking 32 prisoners. During the remainder of the day, he continued to inspire and encourage his men.

No photograph available

RYAN, John   **1092**
Private (later Sergeant)   1st Madras Fusiliers (later The Royal Dublin Fusiliers)
Other Decorations: —
Date of Gazette: 18 Jun. 1858
Place/Date of Birth: Kilkenny, Ireland — 1823
Place/Date of Death: Cawnpore, India — 4 Mar. 1858
Memorials: —
Town/County Connections: Kilkenny, Ireland
Remarks: —
Account of Deed: On 26 Sep. 1857 at Lucknow, India, a party of men was shut up and besieged in a house in the city. Private Ryan, in conjunction with another private*, dashed into the street and took a wounded captain out of a dhooly and carried him into the house in spite of heavy fire in which the captain was again wounded. In addition to this Private Ryan devoted himself during the day to rescuing the wounded in the neighbourhood from being massacred. (*See also McMANUS, P.).

RYAN, John   **1093**
Private 55th Bn. (N.S.W.), Australian Imperial Force
Other Decorations: —
Date of Gazette: 26 Dec. 1918
Place/Date of Birth: Tumut, New South Wales, Australia — Feb. 1890
Place/Date of Death: Melbourne, Australia — 3 Jun. 1941
Memorials: Springvale Cemetery, Melbourne; Australian War Memorial, Canberra
Town/County Connections: —
Remarks: —
Account of Deed: On 30 Sep. 1918 at the Hindenberg Defences, France, when the enemy
succeeded in establishing a bombing party in the rear of the battalion's recently-won position,
Private Ryan, on his own initiative, organized and led a party of men with bombs and bayonets against the enemy. He reached
the position with only three men and they succeeded in driving the enemy back. Private Ryan cleared the last of them alone,
finally falling wounded himself.

No photograph available

RYAN John   **1094**
Lance-Corporal 65th Regiment (later The York and Lancaster Regiment)
Other Decorations: —
Date of Gazette: 16 Jan. 1864
Place/Date of Birth: Barnsleigh, Tipperary, Ireland — 1839
Place/Date of Death: Tuakan, New Zealand — 29 Dec. 1863
Memorials: —
Town/County Connections: Barnsleigh, Tipperary
Remarks: —
Account of Deed: On 7 Sep. 1863 near Cameron Town, New Zealand, Lance-Corporal Ryan, with
two privates, removed the body of a captain from the field of action after he had been mortally
wounded and remained with it all night in the bush, surrounded by the enemy. Lance-Corporal Ryan was drowned in December
of the same year, while trying to rescue a comrade.

No photograph available

RYAN, Miles   **1095**
Drummer 1st Bn., European Bengal Fusiliers (later The Royal Munster Fusiliers)
Other Decorations: —
Date of Gazette: 24 Dec. 1858
Place/Date of Birth: Londonderry, Ireland — 1826
Place/Date of Death: ?Bengal, India — Jan. 1887
Memorials: —
Town/County Connections: Londonderry; Templemore, Tipperary
Remarks: —
Account of Deed: On 14 Sep. 1857 at Delhi, India, when the troops were waiting at the Kabul
Gate, reserve ammunition was being carried up on to the ramparts to be put into a small
magazine, but before it could be safely stowed away, three boxes exploded and two were set on fire by enemy shot. Drummer
Ryan and a sergeant* who were part of the ammunition guard, seeing the danger of the fire spreading, seized the two boxes
which were alight and threw them over the ramparts into the canal, thus saving many lives. (*See also McGUIRE, J.)

RYDER, Robert Edward   **1096**
Private (later Sergeant) 12th Bn., The Middlesex Regiment (Duke of Cambridge's Own)
Other Decorations: —
Date of Gazette: 26 Nov. 1916
Place/Date of Birth: Harefield, Middlesex — 17 Dec. 1895
Place/Date of Death: Hucknall, Nottinghamshire — 1 Dec. 1978
Memorials: Buried at Harefield, Middlesex; plaque inside Middlesex Guildhall, Westminster
Town/County Connections: Harefield, Middlesex; Hucknall, Nottinghamshire
Remarks: IBM (Italy); served with The Royal Sussex Regiment in the Second World War until
1940 and then with a Derbyshire unit
Account of Deed: On 26 Sep. 1916 at Thiepval, France, Private Ryder's company was held up by
heavy rifle fire and all his officers had become casualties. For want of leadership the attack was flagging when Private Ryder,
realising the situation and without a moment's thought for his own safety dashed, absolutely alone, at the enemy trench and
by skilful handling of his Lewis gun succeeded in clearing the trench. This very gallant act inspired his comrades, made the
subsequent advance possible and turned what could have been failure into success.

RYDER, Robert Edward Dudley   **1097**
Commander (later Captain)   Royal Navy
Other Decorations: —
Date of Gazette: 21 May 1942
Place/Date of Birth: India — 16 Feb. 1908
Place/Date of Death: At sea — 29 Jun. 1986
Memorials: — *lived at Inkpen, Berks*
Town/County Connections: Uxbridge, Middlesex; Camberley, Surrey; Wolferton, Norfolk
Remarks: Naval Attaché, Oslo 1948-50; Member of Parliament for Merton & Morden 1950-55;
author of *The Attack on St. Nazaire*, and *Coverplan*
Account of Deed: On 28 Mar. 1942 in the attack on St. Nazaire, France, Commander Ryder,
commanding the Naval force, led HMS *Campbeltown* in under intense fire. When the main objective of the expedition had been accomplished and *Campbeltown* had been beached, Commander Ryder remained on the spot evacuating men from *Campbeltown* and conducting operations while exposed to heavy fire, and did not withdraw until it was certain that his ship could be of no more use. His motor gun boat (MGB. 314), full of dead and wounded, survived by a miracle and managed to withdraw through an intense barrage of fire.

SADLIER, Clifford William King   **1098**
Lieutenant   51st Bn. (Victoria), Australian Imperial Force
Other Decorations: —
Date of Gazette: 11 Jul. 1918
Place/Date of Birth: Camberwell, Victoria, Australia — 1892
Place/Date of Death: Busselton, Western Australia — 28 Apr. 1964
Memorials: Karrakatta Cemetery, Perth, Western Australia; Australian War Memorial, Canberra
Town/County Connections: —
Remarks: —
Account of Deed: On 24/25 Apr. 1918 at Villers-Bretonneux, France, Lieutenant Sadlier's platoon
had to advance through a wood where a strong enemy machine-gun post was causing casualties and preventing the advance. Although he was himself wounded, Lieutenant Sadlier at once collected his bombing section and led them against the machine-guns, killing the crews and capturing two of the guns. By this time his party were all casualties and alone he attacked a third enemy machine-gun with his revolver, killing the crew and taking the gun. In doing so, he was again wounded.

SAGE, Thomas Henry   **1099**
Private   8th Bn., The Somerset Light Infantry (Prince Albert's)
Other Decorations: —
Date of Gazette: 18 Dec. 1917
Place/Date of Birth: Tiverton, Devon — 8 Dec. 1882
Place/Date of Death: Tiverton, Devon — 20 Jul. 1945
Memorials: — *Buried Tiverton Cemetery* *Sage Grove, Wilcombe Estate,*
Town/County Connections: Tiverton, Devon · *named after him*
Remarks: —
Account of Deed: On 4 Oct. 1917 at Tower Hamlets Spur, east of Ypres, Private Sage was in a
shell-hole with eight other men, one of whom was shot while throwing a bomb which fell back into the shell-hole. Private Sage, with great presence of mind, immediately threw himself on it, and so saved the lives of several of his comrades, although he himself was severely wounded.

SALKELD, Philip   **1100**
Lieutenant   Bengal Engineers
Other Decorations: —
Date of Gazette: 18 Jun. 1858
Place/Date of Birth: Fontmell Magna, Dorset — 13 Oct. 1830
Place/Date of Death: Delhi, India — 10 Oct. 1857
Memorials: Kashmir Gate, Delhi; parish churchyard, Fontmell Magna; St. Paul's Cathedral,
Calcutta
Town/County Connections: Fontmell Magna, Dorset; Cumberland
Remarks: —
Account of Deed: On 14 Sep. 1857 at Delhi, India, Lieutenant Salkeld, with another lieutenant, a
sergeant and a bugler* showed conspicuous gallantry in the desperate task of blowing in the Kashmir Gate in broad daylight under heavy and destructive musket fire, preparatory to the assault. (*See also HOME, D.C., SMITH, John (No. 1164) and HAWTHORNE, R.)

SALMON, Nowell (later Sir Nowell)   **1101**
Lieutenant (later Admiral)   Royal Navy (Naval Brigade)
Other Decorations: GCB
Date of Gazette: 24 Dec. 1858
Place/Date of Birth: Swarraton, Hampshire — 20 Feb. 1835
Place/Date of Death: Southsea, Hampshire — 14 Feb. 1912
Memorials: Curdridge, Hampshire
Town/County Connections: Swarraton and Curdridge, Hampshire
Remarks: C-in-C Portsmouth 1894-97 (commanded the Diamond Jubilee Review); Admiral of
the Fleet 1899-1905
Account of Deed: On 16 Nov. 1857 at Lucknow, India, volunteers were called for to climb a tree
near the wall of the Shah Nujeff mosque in order to spot the enemy's position and then to dislodge the mutineers who were
throwing grenades and firing on the gun crews below. Lieutenant Salmon, a leading seaman* and an able seaman responded
to the call and succeeded in performing this dangerous service, but Lieutenant Salmon was wounded in the thigh and the able
seaman was killed. (*See also HARRISON, J. — No. 537)

SAMSON, George McKenzie   **1102**
Seaman (later Petty Officer)   Royal Naval Reserve
Other Decorations: —
Date of Gazette: 16 Aug. 1915
Place/Date of Birth: Carnoustie, Angus, Scotland — 7 Jan. 1889
Place/Date of Death: Bermuda — 28 Feb. 1923
Memorials: Military Cemetery, Bermuda
Town/County Connections: Carnoustie, Angus
Remarks: —
Account of Deed: On 25 Apr. 1915 during the landing at V Beach, Cape Helles, Gallipoli, Seaman
Samson, with three other men* was assisting the commander* of their ship HMS *River Clyde*, at
the work of securing the lighters. He worked all day under very heavy fire, attending wounded and getting out lines. He was
eventually dangerously wounded by Maxim fire. (*See also UNWIN, E., DREWRY, G.L., MALLESON, W.St.A., and WILLIAMS, W.C.)

SANDERS, George   **1103**
Corporal (later Captain)   1/7th Bn., The West Yorkshire Regiment (The Prince of Wales's Own)
Other Decorations: MC
Date of Gazette: 9 Sep. 1916
Place/Date of Birth: New Wortley, Leeds, Yorkshire — 8 Jul. 1894
Place/Date of Death: Leeds, Yorkshire — 4 Apr. 1950
Memorials: —   *Cremated Cottingley Crematorium, Leeds*
Town/County Connections: Leeds, Yorkshire
Remarks: —
Account of Deed: On 1 Jul. 1916 near Thiepval, France, after an advance into the enemy's
trenches, Corporal Sanders found himself isolated with a party of 30 men. He organised his
defences, detailed a bombing party, and impressed upon the men that his and their duty was to hold the position at all costs.
Next morning he drove off an attack by the enemy, rescuing some prisoners who had fallen into their hands. Later two bombing
attacks were driven off, and he was finally relieved after 36 hours. All this time his party had been without food and water,
having given their water to the wounded during the first night.

SANDERS, William Edward   **1104**
A/Lieutenant (later Lieutenant-Commander)   Royal Naval Reserve
Other Decorations: DSO
Date of Gazette: 22 Jun. 1917
Place/Date of Birth: Auckland, New Zealand — 7 Feb. 1883
Place/Date of Death: At sea, near S. Ireland — 14 Aug. 1917
Memorials: Plymouth Naval Memorial; Sanders Cup, New Zealand's premier sailing trophy;
HQ, Dunedin RSA, New Zealand.
Town/County Connections: —
Remarks: —
Account of Deed: On 30 Apr. 1917 about 180 miles south of Ireland, Lieutenant Sanders was in
command of HMS *Prize*, a three-masted topsail schooner (one of the 'Q' or 'mystery' ships) when she was attacked by a German
U-boat and badly damaged. After the 'Panic party' had taken to the boats and the ship appeared to be sinking, the U-boat
approached to within 80 yards of her port quarter, whereupon the White Ensign was hoisted and *Prize* opened fire. Within a few
minutes the submarine was on fire and her bows rose in the air. *Prize* in spite of her damage, was later towed into harbour.

SANDES, Arthur James Terence FLEMING-　　　　　　　　　　　　　　　**1105**
T/Second Lieutenant (later Major)　2nd Bn., The East Surrey Regiment
Other Decorations: —
Date of Gazette:　18 Nov. 1915
Place/Date of Birth:　Tulse Hill, London — 24 Jun. 1894
Place/Date of Death:　Romsey, Hampshire — 24 May 1961
Memorials: —
Town/County Connections:　Tulse Hill, London; Romsey, Hampshire
Remarks:　Judge of High Court, Sudan 1935-44, acting Chief Justice on occasions; Judge Advocate-General, Sudan Defence Force 1942-44; Chairman, Pensions Appeal Tribunal 1945-58.
Account of Deed:　On 29 Sep. 1915 at the Hohenzollern Redoubt, France, Second Lieutenant Fleming-Sandes was sent to command a company which was in a very critical postion. His men, very much shaken by continual bombing and machine-gun fire, were beginning to retire, but the second lieutenant collected a few bombs and jumping on the parapet in full view of the Germans, only 20 yards away, threw them. Although severely wounded almost at once, he continued to advance and throw bombs until he was again wounded. This act put new heart into his men and saved the situation.

SANDFORD, Richard Douglas　　　　　　　　　　　　　　　　　　　　**1106**
Lieutenant　Royal Navy
Other Decorations: —
Date of Gazette:　23 Jul. 1918
Place/Date of Birth:　Exmouth, Devon — 11 May 1891
Place/Date of Death:　Grangetown, Yorkshire — 23 Nov. 1918
Memorials:　Eston Cemetery, Yorkshire; Exeter Cathedral
Town/County Connections:　Exmouth, Devon
Remarks:　Légion d'Honneur (Belgium)
Account of Deed:　On 22/23 Apr. 1918 at Zeebrugge, Belgium, Lieutenant Sandford commanding HM Submarine C.3, skilfully placed the vessel between the piles of the viaduct which connected the Mole with the shore, before laying his fuse and abandoning her. He disdained to use the gyro steering which would have enabled him and his crew to abandon the submarine at a safe distance, but preferred to make sure that his mission would be successful.

SARTORIUS, Euston Henry　　　　　　　　　　　　　　　　　　　　　**1107**
Captain (later Major General)　59th Regiment (later The East Lancashire Regiment)
Other Decorations:　CB
Date of Gazette:　16 May 1881
Place/Date of Birth:　Cintra, near Lisbon, Portugal — 6 Jun. 1844
Place/Date of Death:　Chelsea, London — 19 Feb. 1925
Memorials: —
Town/County Connections:　Chelsea, London
Remarks:　Brother of Major R.W. Sartorius, VC
Account of Deed:　On 24 Oct. 1879 at Shahjui, (Afghan War), Captain Sartorius led a party of four or five men against a number of the enemy who were occupying an almost inaccessible position on the top of a precipitous hill. The nature of the ground made any regular formation impossible, and Captain Sartorius and his men were fired on by the enemy as they reached the top of the steep pathway. The action was, however, a complete success owing to the gallant and cool bearing of the captain, although one of his men was killed and he himself was wounded by sword cuts in both hands.

SARTORIUS, Reginald William　　　　　　　　　　　　　　　　　　　**1108**
Major (later Major General)　6th Bengal Cavalry, Indian Army
Other Decorations:　CMG
Date of Gazette:　26 Oct. 1874
Place/Date of Birth:　?Portugal — 8 May 1841
Place/Date of Death:　Cowes, Isle of Wight — 7 Aug. 1907
Memorials:　Buried Baddesley, Hampshire
Town/County Connections:　Cowes, Isle of Wight
Remarks:　Brother of Captain E.H. Sartorius, VC
Account of Deed:　On 17 Jan. 1874 during the attack on Abogu, Ashanti, West Africa, Major Sartorius removed, under heavy fire, a Houssa non-commissioned officer who was mortally wounded, and placed him under cover.

SAUNDERS, Arthur Frederick   **1109**
Sergeant   9th (S) Bn. The Suffolk Regiment
Other Decorations: —
Date of Gazette: 30 Mar. 1916
Place/Date of Birth: Ipswich, Suffolk — 23 Apr. 1879
Place/Date of Death: Ipswich, Suffolk — 30 Jul. 1947
Memorials: —   *Buried Ipswich Borough Cemetery.*
Town/County Connections: Ipswich, Suffolk
Remarks: —
Account of Deed: On 26 Sep. 1915 near Loos, France, when his officer had been wounded during the attack, Sergeant Saunders took charge of two machine-guns and a few men and, although severely wounded in the thigh, closely followed the last four charges of another battalion, giving them all possible support. Later, when the remains of the battalion which he had been supporting was forced to retire, he stuck to one of his guns and in spite of his wound, continued to give clear orders. By keeping his gun in action he helped to cover the retirement.

SAVAGE, Dickson Cornelius — see **TRAVIS,** Richard Charles

SAVAGE, William Alfred   **1110**
Able Seaman   Royal Navy
Other Decorations: —
Date of Gazette: 21 May 1942
Place/Date of Birth: Smethwick, Staffordshire — 30 Oct. 1912
Place/Date of Death: St. Nazaire, France — 28 Mar. 1942
Memorials: Falmouth Cemetery, Cornwall
Town/County Connections: Smethwick, Staffordshire; Birmingham
Remarks: —   *Road in Dargate Wood, Chatham named after him.*
Account of Deed: On 28 Mar. 1942 in the attack on St. Nazaire, France, Able Seaman Savage who was a gun-layer of a pom-pom in MGB. 314, engaged enemy positions ashore, shooting with great accuracy. Although he had no gun-shield and was in a most exposed position, he continued firing with great coolness until at last he was killed at his gun. The Victoria Cross was awarded not only for his own gallantry, but for the valour shown by many others unnamed, in motor launches, motor gun boats and torpedo boats who carried out their duties in entirely exposed positions against enemy fire at very close range.

SAYER, John William   **1111**
Lance-Corporal   8th Bn., The Queen's Royal West Surrey Regiment
Other Decorations: —
Date of Gazette: 9 Jun. 1919
Place/Date of Birth: Ilford, Essex — 12 Apr. 1879
Place/Date of Death: Le Cateau, France — 18 Apr. 1918
Memorials: Le Cateau Military Cemetery, France
Town/County Connections: Ilford, Essex
Remarks: —
Account of Deed: On 21 Mar. 1918 at Le Verguier, France, Lance-Corporal Sayer held the flank of a small isolated post for two hours. Owing to mist the enemy approached from both sides to within 30 yards before being discovered, but the lance-corporal, on his own initiative without assistance, beat off a succession of attacks, inflicting heavy losses. During the whole time he was exposed to heavy fire but his contempt of danger and skill in the use of his fire-arms enabled the post to hold out until nearly all the garrison had been killed and he himself wounded and captured. He died as a result of wounds four weeks later.

SCARF, Arthur Stewart King   **1112**
Squadron Leader   62 Squadron, Royal Air Force
Other Decorations: —
Date of Gazette: 21 Jun. 1946
Place/Date of Birth: Wimbledon, Surrey — 14 Jun. 1913
Place/Date of Death: Alor Star, Malaya — 9 Dec. 1941
Memorials: Taiping War Cemetery, Malaya
Town/County Connections: Wimbledon, Surrey
Remarks: —
Account of Deed: On 9 Dec. 1941 in Malaya, near the Siam border, all available aircraft had been ordered to make a daylight raid on Singora, in Siam. Squadron Leader Scarf, as leader of the raid, had just taken off from the base at Butterworth when enemy aircraft swept in destroying or disabling all the rest of the machines. The Squadron Leader decided nevertheless to fly alone to Singora. Despite attacks from roving fighters he completed his bombing run and was on his way back when his aircraft became riddled with bullets and he was severely wounded. He managed to crash-land the Blenheim at Alor Star, without causing any injury to his crew, and was rushed to hospital where he died two hours later.

SCHIESS, Ferndnand Christian — **1113**
Corporal   Natal Native Contingent, South African Forces
Other Decorations: —
Date of Gazette: 29 Nov. 1879
Place/Date of Birth: Bergedorf, Berne, Switzerland — 7 Apr. 1856
Place/Date of Death: At sea, near Angola — 14 Dec. 1884
Memorials: —
Town/County Connections: —
Remarks: First man serving with South African Forces under British Command to win the VC
Account of Deed: On 22 Jan. 1879 at Rorke's Drift, Natal, South Africa, Corporal Schiess, in spite of having been wounded in the foot a few days previously, displayed great gallantry when the garrison had retired to the inner line of defence and the Zulus had occupied the wall of mealie bags which had been abandoned. He crept along the wall in order to dislodge one of the enemy and succeeded in killing him and two others before returning to the inner defences.

SCHOFIELD, Harry Norton — **1114**
Captain (later Lieutenant Colonel)   Royal Field Artillery
Other Decorations: —
Date of Gazette: 30 Aug. 1901
Place/Date of Birth: Audenshaw, Ashton-under-Lyne, Lancashire — 29 Jan. 1865
Place/Date of Death: London — 10 Oct. 1931
Memorials: —
Town/County Connections: Ashton-under-Lyne, Lancashire; London
Remarks: Served in the First World War 1914-18 (Commandant of Lines of Communication, BEF 1915-17); Member of Hon. Corps of Gentlemen-at-Arms
Account of Deed: On 15 Dec. 1899, at the Battle of Colenso, South Africa, Captain Schofield with several others tried to save the guns of the 14th and 66th Batteries, Royal Field Artillery, when the detachments serving the guns had all become casualties or been driven from their guns by infantry fire at close range. Captain Schofield went out with two other officers and a corporal* when the first attempt was made to extricate the guns and helped in withdrawing the two that were saved. (*See also CONGREVE, W.N., ROBERTS, F.H.S. and NURSE, G.E.)

SCHOFIELD, John — **1115**
T/Second Lieutenant   2/5th Bn., The Lancashire Fusiliers
Other Decorations: —
Date of Gazette: 28 Jun. 1918
Place/Date of Birth: Blackburn, Lancashire — 4 Mar. 1892
Place/Date of Death: Givenchy, France — 9 Apr. 1918
Memorials: Vielle-Chapelle Military Cemetery, France
Town/County Connections: Blackburn, Lancashire
Remarks: —
Account of Deed: On 9 Apr. 1918 at Givenchy, France, Second Lieutenant Schofield led a party of nine men against a strong-point and was attacked by about 100 of the enemy, but his skilful use of men and weapons resulted in the taking of 20 prisoners. This officer, having made his party up to ten, then proceeded towards the front line, where he met large numbers of the enemy, on whom his party opened fire. He climbed on the parapet under point-blank machine-gun fire and by his fearless demeanour forced the enemy to surrender. As a result 123 of them, including several officers, were captured. He himself was killed a few minutes later.

No photograph available

SCHOLEFIELD, Mark — **1116**
Seaman (later Quartermaster and Petty Officer)   Royal Navy (Naval Brigade)
Other Decorations: —
Date of Gazette: 24 Feb. 1857
Place/Date of Birth: London — 16 Apr. 1828
Place/Date of Death: At Sea — 15 Feb. 1858
Memorials: —
Town/County Connections: —
Remarks: —
Account of Deed: On 5 Nov. 1854 at the Battle of Inkerman, Crimea, when the Right Lancaster Battery was attacked and many of the soldiers were wounded, Seaman Scholefield, with two other seamen* and two others who were killed during the action, mounted the defence work banquette and, under withering attack from the enemy, kept up a rapid, repulsing fire. Their muskets were re-loaded for them by the wounded soldiers under the parapet and eventually the enemy fell back and gave no more trouble. (*See also GORMAN, J. and REEVES, T.)

No photograph available

SCOTT, Andrew   **1117**

Captain (later Major)   Bengal Staff Corps, Indian Army
Other Decorations: —
Date of Gazette: 16 Jan. 1878
Place/Date of Birth: ?Devon — 22 Aug. 1840
Place/Date of Death: Srinagar, Kashmir — 5 Sep. 1882
Memorials: —
Town/County Connections: —
Remarks: —
Account of Deed: On 26 Jul. 1877 at Quetta, India, Captain Scott was on duty at the regimental parade ground in the evening when he heard that British officers were being killed and immediately rushed to the rescue. He found one lieutenant cut down and another hard pressed and wounded but being protected by a sepoy. Captain Scott bayoneted two of the assailants and closed with a third, who fell with him to the ground and was killed by the sepoys of the regiment. This action saved the life of the wounded lieutenant.

SCOTT, Robert   **1118**

Private   1st Bn., The Manchester Regiment
Other Decorations: —
Date of Gazette: 26 Jul. 1901
Place/Date of Birth: Haslingden, Lancashire — 4 Jun. 1874
Place/Date of Death: Downpatrick, Co. Down, Ireland — 22 Feb. 1961
Memorials: —
Town/County Connections: Haslingden, Lancashire; Downpatrick, Co. Down
Remarks: —
Account of Deed: On 6 Jan. 1900 during an attack on Caesar's Camp, Natal, South Africa, 16 men of "D" Company were defending one of the slopes of the hill. The defenders were under heavy fire all day, the majority being killed and their positions occupied by the enemy. At last only Private Scott and one other man* remained. They held their post for 15 hours without food or water, all the time exchanging deadly fire with the enemy, until relief troops had retaken the lost ground and pushed the enemy off the hill. (*See also PITTS, J)

SCOTT, Robert George   **1119**

Sergeant (later Lieutenant-Colonel)   Cape Mounted Riflemen, South African Forces
Other Decorations: DSO
Date of Gazette: 1 Oct. 1880
Place/Date of Birth: Whittlesey, near Peterborough, Cambridgeshire — 22 Apr. 1857
Place/Date of Death: Wynberg, Cape, South Africa — 3 Oct. 1918
Memorials: —
Town/County Connections: Whittlesey, Peterborough
Remarks: Served in South African War 1899-1902 and First World War 1914-15
Account of Deed: On 8 Apr. 1879 during an attack on Morosi's Mountain, South Africa (Basuto War), Sergeant Scott volunteered to throw time-fuse shells as hand grenades over a wall of stone barricades from behind which the enemy were bringing heavy fire to bear on the Colonial troops. Sergeant Scott made his men take cover in case the shells burst prematurely, before making two attempts to throw shells over it. At the second attempt the shell exploded almost in his hands, blowing his right hand to pieces and wounding him severely in the leg.

SCRIMGER, Francis Alexander Caron   **1120**

Captain   Canadian Army Medical Corps, attd. 14th Bn., (Royal Montreal Regiment), C.E.F.
Other Decorations: —
Date of Gazette: 23 Jun. 1915
Place/Date of Birth: Montreal, Canada — 10 Feb. 1880
Place/Date of Death: Montreal, Canada — 13 Feb. 1937
Memorials: Mount Royal Cemetery, Montreal
Town/County Connections: —
Remarks: —
Account of Deed: On 25 Apr. 1915 at St. Julien, Belgium, Captain Scrimger was in charge of an advanced dressing station. He directed the removal of the wounded under heavy fire and carried a wounded officer out of a stable in search of a place of greater safety. When he was unable to carry him any further, he remained with the wounded man until help could be obtained.

SEAGRIM, Derek Anthony

1121

T/Lieutenant Colonel   Comd. 7th Bn., The Green Howards (Alexandra, Princess of Wales's Own Yorkshire Regiment)
Other Decorations: —
Date of Gazette: 13 May 1943
Place/Date of Birth: Bournemouth, Hampshire — 24 Sep. 1903
Place/Date of Death: Tunisia — 6 Apr. 1943
Memorials: Sfax War Cemetery, Tunisia; War Memorial and Whissonsett Church, Norfolk
Town/County Connections: Bournemouth, Hampshire; Whissonsett, Norfolk
Remarks: The only instance to date of the VC and GC being awarded to the same family. His brother, Major H.P. Seagrim was posthumously awarded the GC for gallantry in Burma, during the period Feb. 1943/Feb. 1944.
Account of Deed: On 20/21 Mar. 1943 at the Mareth Line, Tunisia, Lieutenant Colonel Seagrim's courage and leadership led directly to the capture of an important objective. When it appeared that the attack on the position would fail owing to the intensity of enemy fire, he placed himself at the head of his battalion and led them forward. He personally helped to place a scaling ladder over an anti-tank ditch and was the first across. Leading an attack on two machine-gun posts, he accounted for 20 of the enemy and when a counter-attack was launched next day he moved from post to post quite unperturbed, until it was defeated.

SEAMAN, Ernest

1122

Lance-Corporal   2nd Bn., The Royal Inniskilling Fusiliers
Other Decorations: MM
Date of Gazette: 15 Nov. 1918
Place/Date of Birth: Heigham, Norwich — 16 Aug. 1893
Place/Date of Death: Terhand, Belgium — 29 Sep. 1918
Memorials: Tyne Cot Memorial, Belgium; Scole, Norfolk
Town/County Connections: Scole, Norfolk; Trimley and Felixstowe, Suffolk
Remarks: —
Account of Deed: On 29 Sep. 1918 at Terhand, Belgium, when the right flank of his company was held up by enemy machine-guns, Lance-Corporal Seaman went forward under heavy fire with his Lewis gun and engaged the position single-handed, capturing two machine-guns and 12 prisoners, and killing one officer and two men. Later in the day he again rushed another enemy machine-gun post, capturing the gun under very heavy fire. He was killed immediately afterwards, but it was due to his gallant conduct that his company was able to push forward to its objective.

SEELEY, William Henry Harrison

1123

Ordinary Seaman   Royal Navy
Other Decorations: —
Date of Gazette: 21 Apr. 1865
Place/Date of Birth: Topsham, Maine, USA — 1 May 1840
Place/Date of Death: Dedham, Massachusetts, U.S.A. — 1 Oct. 1914
Memorials: Evergreen Cemetery, Stoughton, Massachusetts
Town/County Connections: —
Remarks: First American citizen to win the VC.
Account of Deed: On 6 Sep. 1864 at Shimonoseki, Japan, during the capture of the enemy's stockade, Ordinary Seaman Seeley of HMS *Euryalus* distinguished himself by carrying out a daring reconnaissance to ascertain the enemy's position, and then, although wounded, continuing to take part in the final assault on the battery.

SELLAR, George

1124

Lance-Corporal (later Sergeant)   The Seaforth Highlanders (Ross-shire Buffs, Duke of Albany's)
Other Decorations: —
Date of Gazette: 18 Oct. 1881
Place/Date of Birth: Keith, Banffshire, Scotland — Dec. 1850
Place/Date of Death: Lairg, Sutherland, Scotland — 1 Nov. 1889
Memorials: Lairg Cemetery, Sutherland
Town/County Connections: Keith, Banffshire
Remarks: —
Account of Deed: On 14 Dec. 1879 at the Asmai Heights, near Kabul, (Afghan War), Lance-Corporal Sellar led the attack under heavy fire and dashing on in front of the party up a slope, engaged in desperate conflict with one of the enemy who sprang out to meet him. In this encounter Lance-Corporal Sellar was severely wounded.

SEPHTON, Alfred Edward — 1125
Petty Officer   Royal Navy
Other Decorations: —
Date of Gazette: 2 Dec. 1941
Place/Date of Birth: Warrington, Lancashire — 19 Apr. 1911
Place/Date of Death: At sea, South of Crete — 19 May 1941
Memorials: Portsmouth Naval Memorial
Town/County Connections: Warrington, Lancashire; Wolverhampton, Staffordshire
Remarks: —
Account of Deed: On 18 May 1941 in the Mediterranean, south of Crete, Petty Officer Sephton was a director layer on HMS *Coventry* when she went to the assistance of a hospital ship which was being attacked by German dive-bombers. When the enemy engaged *Coventry*, raking her with machine-gun fire, Petty Officer Sephton was mortally wounded, a bullet actually passing through his body and injuring an able seaman beside him. Although in great pain and partially blinded, nevertheless he stuck to his instruments and carried out his duties until the attack was over. He died of his injuries next day.

SEWELL, Cecil Harold — 1126
Lieutenant   The Royal West Kent Regiment, attd. 3rd (Light) Bn., Tank Corps
Other Decorations: —
Date of Gazette: 30 Oct. 1918
Place/Date of Birth: Greewich, London — 27 Jan. 1895
Place/Date of Death: Fremicourt, France — 29 Aug. 1918
Memorials: Vaulx Hill Cemetery, France; Charlton Cemetery, Woolwich, London (family memorial); Toc H lamp at Bovington Garrison Church
Town/County Connections: Greenwich, London   *Dulwich College*
Remarks: — *Name on Blackheath W.M.*
Account of Deed: On 29 Aug. 1918 at Fremicourt, France, Lieutenant Sewell, who was in command of a section of whippet light tanks, got out of his own tank and crossed open ground under heavy machine-gun fire to rescue the crew of another whippet of his section which had side-slipped into a shell-hole, overturned and caught fire. The door of the tank had become jammed against the side of the shell-hole, but Lieutenant Sewell, unaided, dug away the entrance to the door and released the crew.

SEXTON, Gerald — see **BUCKLEY,** Maurice Vincent

SHAHAMAD KHAN, — 1127
Naik (later Jemadar)   89th Punjab Regiment, Indian Army
Other Decorations: —
Date of Gazette: 26 Sep. 1916
Place/Date of Birth: Takhti, near Rawalpindi — 1 Jul. 1879
Place/Date of Death: Takhti, Pakistan — 28 Jul. 1947
Memorials: —
Town/County Connections: —
Remarks: —
Account of Deed: On 12/13 Apr. 1916 near Beit Ayeesa, Mesopotamia, Naik Shahamad Khan was in charge of a machine-gun covering a gap in our new line within 150 yards of the entrenched enemy. He beat off three counter-attacks and worked his gun single-handed after all his men, except two belt-fillers, had become casualties. For three hours he held the gap under very heavy fire and when his gun was knocked out, he and his two belt-fillers held their ground with rifles until ordered to withdraw. With help he then brought back his gun, ammunition and one severely wounded man, and finally all remaining arms and equipment.

SHAND, Stewart Walker LOUDOUN- — 1128
T/Major   10th Bn., The Yorkshire Regiment (Alexandra, Princess of Wales's Own)
Other Decorations: —
Date of Gazette: 9 Sep. 1916
Place/Date of Birth: Ceylon — 8 Oct. 1879
Place/Date of Death: Fricourt, France — 1 Jul. 1916
Memorials: Norfolk Cemetery, France
Town/County Connections: Dulwich, London   *Dulwich College; Name on Dulwich W.M*
Remarks: Served in the Boer War with the Pembrokeshire Yeomanry
Account of Deed: On 1 Jul. 1916 near Fricourt, France, when Major Loudoun-Shand's company attempted to climb over the parapet to attack the enemy's trenches, they were met by very fierce machine-gun fire which temporarily stopped their progress. The major immediately leapt on the parapet, helped the men over it and encouraged them in every way until he was mortally wounded. Even then, he insisted on being propped up in the trench and went on encouraging his men until he died.

SHANKLAND, Robert 1129
Lieutenant (later Lieutenant Colonel)   43rd Bn., Manitoba Regiment, C.E.F.
Other Decorations: DCM
Date of Gazette: 18 Dec. 1917
Place/Date of Birth: St. Quivox, Ayr, Scotland — 10 Oct. 1887
Place/Date of Death: Vancouver, British Columbia, Canada — 20 Jan. 1968
Memorials: Garden of Remembrance, Mountain View Cemetery, Vancouver, British Columbia;
lamp-post in Valour Road, Winnipeg
Town/County Connections: Ayr, Scotland
Remarks: —
Account of Deed: On 26 Oct. 1917 at Passchendaele, Belgium, having gained a position,
Lieutenant Shankland rallied the remnants of his own platoon and men of other companies, disposed them to command the
ground in front and inflicted heavy casualties on the retreating enemy. Later he dispersed a counter-attack and then personally
communicated to headquarters an accurate and valuable report as to the position on the brigade frontage. He then rejoined his
command and carried on until relieved. His courage and splendid example inspired all ranks.

SHARPE, Charles Richard 1130
A/Corporal (later Company Sergeant-Major)   2nd Bn., The Lincolnshire Regiment
Other Decorations: —
Date of Gazette: 29 Jun. 1915
Place/Date of Birth: Pickworth, near Sleaford, Lincolnshire — 2 Apr. 1889
Place/Date of Death: Workington, Cumberland — 18 Feb. 1963
Memorials: Newport Cemetery, Lincoln
Town/County Connections: Pickworth and Bourne, Lincolnshire
Remarks: Served with The Leicestershire Regiment for a time in the Second World War and
afterwards as a member of the ARP in Bourne
Account of Deed: On 9 May 1915 at Rouges Bancs, France, Corporal Sharpe was in charge of a
blocking party sent forward to take a portion of the German trench. He was the first to reach the enemy's position and using
bombs with great effect he himself cleared them out of a trench 50 yards long. By this time all his party had fallen and he was
then joined by four other men with whom he attacked the enemy with bombs and captured a further trench 250 yards long.

SHAUL, John David Francis 1131
Corporal (later Bugle Major)   1st Bn., The Highland Light Infantry
Other Decorations: —
Date of Gazette: 28 Sep. 1900
Place/Date of Birth: King's Lynn, Norfolk — 11 Sep. 1873
Place/Date of Death: Boksburg, South Africa — 14 Sep. 1953
Memorials: Commemorative plaque in Windsor Terrace, King's Lynn.
Town/County Connections: King's Lynn, Norfolk
Remarks: —
Account of Deed: On 11 Dec. 1899 during the battle of Magersfontein, South Africa, Corporal
Shaul was in charge of stretcher-bearers, but at one period of the battle he was seen encouraging
men to advance across the open. He was most conspicuous during the day in dressing men's wounds and in one case he came,
under fire, to a man who was lying wounded in the back, and with the utmost coolness sat down beside him and proceeded to
dress his wound. This act of gallantry was performed under continuous fire as calmly as if there had been no enemy near.

SHAW, Hugh 1132
Captain (later Major General)   18th Regiment (later The Royal Irish Regiment)
Other Decorations: CB
Date of Gazette: 28 Nov. 1865
Place/Date of Birth: Madras, India — 4 Feb. 1839
Place/Date of Death: Southsea, Hampshire — 25 Aug. 1904
Memorials: —   *Buried Highland Road cemetery, Portsmouth*
Town/County Connections: Southsea, Hampshire
Remarks: —
Account of Deed: On 24 Jan. 1865 at Nukumaru, New Zealand, Captain Shaw went, under heavy
fire, with four privates who had volunteered to accompany him, to within 30 yards of that part of
the bush occupied by the rebels, in order to rescue a comrade who was severely wounded.

SHAW, Same (John)   **1133**
Private (later Corporal)   3rd Bn., The Rifle Brigade (Prince Consort's Own)
Other Decorations: DCM
Date of Gazette: 26 Oct. 1858
Place/Date of Birth: Prestonpans, East Lothian, Scotland — ?
Place/Date of Death: At sea — 27 Dec. 1859
Memorials: Rifle Brigade Memorial, Winchester Cathedral, Hants.
Town/County Connections: Prestonpans, East Lothian
Remarks: —
Account of Deed: On 13 Jun. 1858 at Lucknow, India, an armed man (a Ghazee) was seen to enter a tope of trees and a party of officers and men went after him. Private Shaw, coming upon him, drew his short sword and after a struggle, during which the private received a severe tulwar-wound, the Ghazee was killed.

No photograph available

SHEBBEARE, Robert Haydon   **1134**
Lieutenant (later Captain) 60th Bengal Native Infantry
Other Decorations: —
Date of Gazette: 21 Oct. 1859
Place/Date of Birth: Clapham, London — 13 Jan. 1827
Place/Date of Death: At sea, South of Shanghai, China — 16 Sep. 1860
Memorials: — *Window in St. Mark's Church, Surbiton, Surrey*
Town/County Connections: Clapham, London
Remarks: —
Account of Deed: On 14 Sep. 1857 at Delhi, India, Lieutenant Shebbeare, leading the Guides with the 4th Column of the assault, twice charged the wall of the loopholed serai, under murderous fire, but failed to attain a breach. Despite a bullet through his cheek and a bad scalp wound he conducted a most successful retreat.

SHEPHERD, Albert Edward   **1135**
Rifleman (later Corporal) 12th (S) Bn., The King's Royal Rifle Corps
Other Decorations: —
Date of Gazette: 13 Feb. 1918
Place/Date of Birth: Royston, near Barnsley, Yorkshire — 11 Jan. 1897
Place/Date of Death: Royston, near Barnsley, Yorkshire — 24 Oct. 1966
Memorials: — *Memorial Gate in churchyard at Royston, Yorks*
Town/County Connections: Royston, Yorkshire
Remarks: —
Account of Deed: On 20 Nov. 1917 at Villers Plouich, France, when his company was held up by a machine-gun at point-blank range, Private Shepherd volunteered to rush the gun and although ordered not to, rushed forward and threw a Mills bomb killing two gunners and capturing the gun. The company, continuing its advance, came under heavy enfilade machine-gun fire and when the last officer and NCO had become casualties, Private Shepherd took command of the company, ordered the men to lie down and went back some 70 yards to get the help of a tank. He then returned to his company and led them to their last objective.

SHEPPARD (or SHEPHERD) John   **1136**
Boatswain's Mate (later Boatswain First Class) Royal Navy (Naval Brigade)
Other Decorations: CGM
Date of Gazette: 24 Feb. 1857
Place/Date of Birth: Hull, Yorkshire — 22 Sep. 1817
Place/Date of Death: Padstow, Cornwall — 17 Dec. 1884
Memorials: Padstow Churchyard, Cornwall
Town/County Connections: Hull, Yorkshire
Remarks: Légion d'Honneur (France); Al Valore Militari (Sardinia)
Account of Deed: On 15 Jul. 1855 at Sebastopol, Crimea, Boatswain's Mate Sheppard went into the harbour at night, in a punt which he had especially constructed for the purpose, with an explosive device with which he intended to blow up one of the Russian warships. He managed to get past the enemy's steamboats at the entrance of Careening Bay, but was prevented from getting further by a long string of boats carrying enemy troops. He made a second attempt on 16 Aug. but although both these actions were unsuccessful, they were boldly conceived and carried out in the face of great danger.

No photograph available

SHERBAHADUR THAPA 1137

Rifleman 1st Bn., 9th Gurkha Rifles, Indian Army
Other Decorations: —
Date of Gazette: 28 Dec. 1944
Place/Date of Birth: Ghalechap Village, Tannu District, Nepal — 20 Nov. 1921
Place/Date of Death: San Marino, Italy — 19 Sep. 1944
Memorials: Rimini Gurkha War Cemetery, Italy
Town/County Connections: —
Remarks: —
Account of Deed: On 18/19 Sep. 1944 at San Marino, Italy, when a company of the 9th Gurkha Rifles encountered bitter opposition from a German prepared position, Rifleman Sherbahadur Thapa and his section commander, who was afterwards badly wounded, charged and silenced an enemy machine-gun. The rifleman then went on alone to the exposed part of a ridge where, ignoring a hail of bullets, he silenced more machine-guns, covered a withdrawal and rescued two wounded men before he was killed.

SHERBROOKE, Robert St. Vincent 1138

Captain (later Rear-Admiral) Royal Navy
Other Decorations: CB,DSO
Date of Gazette: 12 Jan. 1943
Place/Date of Birth: Oxton, Newark, Nottinghamshire — 8 Jan. 1901
Place/Date of Death: Oxton, Nottinghamshire — 13 Jun. 1972
Memorials: —
Town/County Connections: Oxton, Nottinghamshire
Remarks: Gentleman Usher of the Scarlet Rod 1953; High Sheriff of Nottingham 1958.
Account of Deed: On 31 Dec. 1942 off North Cape, Barents Sea, Captain Sherbrooke in HMS *Onslow* was senior officer in command of destroyers escorting an important convoy for North Russia, when he made contact with a vastly superior enemy force. Four times the enemy tried to attack the convoy but was forced back each time. Early in the action Captain Sherbrooke was seriously wounded in the face and temporarily blinded. Nevertheless he continued to direct the ships under his command and even when the next senior officer had assumed control, he insisted on receiving all reports of the action until the convoy was out of danger.

No photograph available

SHER SHAH 1139

Lance-Naik 16th Punjab Regiment, Indian Army
Other Decorations: —
Date of Gazette: 8 May 1945
Place/Date of Birth: Gkikeraraia Village, Mianwali District, Punjab, India — 14 Feb. 1917
Place/Date of Death: Kaladan, Burma — 20 Jan. 1945
Memorials: The Rangoon Memorial, Burma
Town/County Connections: —
Remarks: —
Account of Deed: On 19/20 Jan. 1945 at Kyeyebyin, Kaladan, Burma, Lance-Naik Sher Shah was commanding a left forward section of his platoon when it was attacked by overwhelming numbers of Japanese. He broke up two attacks by crawling right in among the enemy and shooting at point blank range. On the second occasion he was hit and his leg shattered, but he maintained that his injury was only slight and when the third attack came, he again crawled forward engaging the enemy until he was shot through the head and killed.

SHERWOOD-KELLY, John — see KELLY, John SHERWOOD-

No photograph available

SHIELDS, Robert 1140

Corporal 23rd Regiment (later The Royal Welch Fusiliers)
Other Decorations: —
Date of Gazette: 24 Feb. 1857
Place/Date of Birth: Cardiff — 1827
Place/Date of Death: Bombay — 23 Dec. 1864
Memorials: —
Town/County Connections: Cardiff
Remarks: —
Account of Deed: On 8 Sep. 1855 at Sebastopol, Crimea, near the Redan, Corporal Shields volunteered to go out with an assistant surgeon to an exposed and dangerous part of the front, to bring in an officer who was wounded, and was afterwards found to be mortally so. (See also SYLVESTER, W.H.T.)

SHORT, William Henry   1141
Private 8th Bn., The Yorkshire Regiment (Alexandra, Princess of Wales's Own)
Other Decorations: —
Date of Gazette: 9 Sep. 1916
Place/Date of Birth: Eston, near Middlesbrough, Yorkshire — 4 Feb. 1887
Place/Date of Death: Contalmaison, France — 6 Aug. 1916
Memorials: Contalmaison Chateau Cemetery, France; Eston Cemetery, Middlesbrough
Town/County Connections: Eston, Middlesbrough, Yorkshire
Remarks: —
Account of Deed: On 6 Aug. 1916 at Munster Alley, France, Private Short was foremost in the attack, bombing the enemy with great gallantry, when he was wounded in the foot. He was urged to go back, but refused, and continued to throw bombs. Later his leg was shattered by a shell and he was unable to stand, so he lay in the trench, adjusting detonators and straightening the pins of bombs for the other men to throw. He died before he could be carried out of the trench.

SHOUT, Alfred John   1142
Captain 1st Bn. (N.S.W.), Australian Imperial Force
Other Decorations: MC
Date of Gazette: 15 Oct. 1915
Place/Date of Birth: New Zealand — 8 Aug. 1882
Place/Date of Death: Lone Pine, Gallipoli — 11 Aug. 1915
Memorials: Lone Pine Memorial, Gallipoli; Australian War Memorial, Canberra
Town/County Connections: —
Remarks: —
Account of Deed: On 9 Aug. 1915, at Lone Pine, Gallipoli, Captain Shout, with a very small party, charged down trenches strongly occupied by the enemy, and personally threw four bombs among them, killing eight and routing the remainder. In the afternoon of the same day, from the position gained in the morning, he captured a further length of trench under similar conditions and continued to bomb the enemy at close range under very heavy fire, until he was severely wounded. He died of his wounds shortly afterwards.

SIDNEY, (later Viscount DE L'ISLE) William Philip   1143
T/Major 5th Bn., Grenadier Guards
Other Decorations: KG, GCMG, GCVO
Date of Gazette: 30 Mar. 1944
Place/Date of Birth: Chelsea, London — 23 May 1909
Place/Date of Death: — *Died about 6.4.91. Tunbridge Wells.*
Memorials: —
Town/County Connections: Penshurst, Kent
Remarks: Son-in-law of Field Marshal Viscount Gort, VC: Parliamentary Secretary, Ministry of Pensions 1945; Secretary of State for Air 1951-55; Governor General of Australia 1961-65; Chancellor, Order of St. Michael and St. George 1968-84; President, Freedom Association 1975; DL, County of Kent; Deputy President, VC and GC Association 1983
Account of Deed: During the period 7/8 Feb. 1944 at the Anzio beachhead, Italy, Major Sidney led a successful attack which drove the enemy out of a gully. Later he led another counter-attack and dashed forward, engaging the enemy with his tommy gun at point-blank range, forcing a withdrawal. When the attack was renewed, Major Sidney and one guardsman were wounded and another killed, but he would not consent to have his wounds dressed until the enemy had been beaten off and the battalion's position was consolidated. During this time, although extremely weak from loss of blood, he continued to encourage and inspire his men.

SIFTON, Ellis Welwood   1144
Lance-Sergeant 18th Bn., Western Ontario Regiment, C.E.F.
Other Decorations: —
Date of Gazette: 8 Jun. 1917
Place/Date of Birth: Wallacetown, Ontario, Canada — 12 Oct. 1891
Place/Date of Death: Vimy, France — 9 Apr. 1917
Memorials: Lichfield Crater, Thelus, France
Town/County Connections: —
Remarks: —
Account of Deed: On 9 Apr. 1917 at Neuville-St.-Vaast, France, during an attack on enemy trenches, Lance-Sergeant Sifton's company was held up by machine-gun fire which inflicted many casualties. The sergeant located the gun and charged it alone, killing all the crew. A small enemy party then advanced down the trench but he managed to hold them off with bayonet and clubbed rifle until his comrades arrived and ended the unequal fight, but in carrying out this gallant act he was killed. His conspicuous valour undoubtedly saved many lives and contributed largely to the success of the operation.

SIMPSON, John   **1145**
Quartermaster-Sergeant   42nd Regiment (later The Black Watch (Royal Highlanders))
Other Decorations: —
Date of Gazette: 27 May 1859
Place/Date of Birth: Edinburgh — 29 Jan. 1826
Place/Date of Death: St. Martin's, Perth, Scotland — 27 Oct. 1883
Memorials: —
Town/County Connections: Perth, Scotland
Remarks: —
Account of Deed: On 15 Apr. 1858 during the attack on Fort Ruhya, India, Quartermaster-Sergeant Simpson volunteered to go to an exposed point within 40 yards of the parapet of the fort under a heavy fire and brought in first a lieutenant and then a private, both of whom were dangerously wounded.

SIMPSON, Rayene Stewart   **1146**
Warrant Officer Class II   Australian Army Training Team, Vietnam
Other Decorations: DCM
Date of Gazette: 29 Aug. 1969
Place/Date of Birth: Redfern, New South Wales, Australia — 16 Feb. 1926
Place/Date of Death: Tokyo, Japan — 17 Oct. 1978
Memorials: — Yokohama War Cemetery, Japan; Australian War Memorial, Canberra
Town/County Connections: —
Remarks: Silver Star and Bronze Star (USA)
Account of Deed: On 6 May 1969 in Vietnam, Warrant Officer Class Two Simpson rescued a wounded fellow Warrant Officer and carried out an unsuccessful attack on a strong enemy position. On 11 May he fought alone against heavy odds to cover the evacuation of a number of casualties.

SIMPSON, Walter — see **EVANS,** Arthur

SIMS, John Joseph   **1147**
Private   34th Regiment (later The Border Regiment)
Other Decorations: —
Date of Gazette: 24 Feb. 1857
Place/Date of Birth: Bloomsbury, London — Feb. 1836
Place/Date of Death: Birmingham — 14 Sep. 1881
Memorials: —
Town/County Connections: Bloomsbury, London; Birmingham
Remarks: —
Account of Deed: On 18 Jun. 1855 at Sebastopol, Crimea, after the regiment had retired into the trenches from the assault on the Redan, Private Sims went out under very heavy fire in broad daylight and brought in wounded soldiers outside the trenches.

SINNOTT, John   **1148**
Lance-Corporal (later Sergeant)   84th Regiment (later The York and Lancaster Regiment)
Other Decorations: —
Date of Gazette: 24 Dec. 1858
Place/Date of Birth: Wexford, Ireland — 1829
Place/Date of Death: Clapham, London — 20 Jul. 1896
Memorials: —
Town/County Connections: London
Remarks: —
Account of Deed: On 6 Oct. 1857 at Lucknow, India, Lance-Corporal Sinnott went out with two sergeants and a private to bring in a captain who had been mortally wounded while trying to extinguish a fire in the breastwork. They brought in the body under heavy fire and the lance-corporal was twice wounded. He had previously repeatedly accompanied the captain when he was attempting to extinguish the fire. (Elected by the regiment.)

SINTON, John Alexander
Captain (later Brigadier), Indian Medical Service
Other Decorations: OBE
Date of Gazette: 21 Jun. 1916
Place/Date of Birth: British Columbia, Canada — 2 Dec. 1884
Place/Date of Death: Cookstown, Co. Tyrone, Ireland — 25 Mar. 1956
Memorials: —
Town/County Connections: Cookstown, Co. Tyrone
Remarks: Fellow of the Royal Society; Consultant malariologist to War Office 1942; Order of St. George (Russia); Served in the Second World War 1939-45; High Sheriff for Tyrone, Ireland 1953
Account of Deed: On 21 Jan. 1916 at Orah Ruins, Mesopotamia, Captain Sinton attended to the wounded under very heavy fire and although he was shot through both arms and through the side he refused to go to hospital, remaining on duty as long as daylight lasted. In three previous actions he had also displayed the utmost bravery.

SKINNER, John
A/Company Sergeant-Major   1st Bn., The King's Own Scottish Borderers
Other Decorations: DCM
Date of Gazette: 14 Sep. 1917
Place/Date of Birth: Pollockshields, Glasgow — 26 Oct. 1881
Place/Date of Death: Vlamertinghe, Belgium — 17 Mar. 1918
Memorials: Vlamertinghe New British Cemetery, Belgium
Town/County Connections: Pollockshields, Glasgow
Remarks: —
Account of Deed: On 18 Aug. 1917 at Wijdendrift, Belgium, when his company was held up by machine-gun fire, Company Sergeant-Major Skinner, although wounded in the head, collected six men and with great courage and determination worked round the left flank of three block-houses from which the machine-gun fire was coming, and succeeded in bombing and taking the first block-house single-handed. Then leading his six men towards the other two block-houses he cleared them, taking 60 prisoners, three machine-guns and two trench mortars.

SLEAVON, Michael
Corporal   Corps of Royal Engineers
Other Decorations: —
Date of Gazette: 11 Nov. 1859
Place/Date of Birth: Magheraculmoney, Fermanagh, Ireland — 1827
Place/Date of Death: Ederney, Fermanagh — 14 Aug. 1902
Memorials: —
Town/County Connections: Co. Fermanagh, Ireland
Remarks: —
Account of Deed: On 3 Apr. 1858 at Jhansi, India, Corporal Sleavon maintained his position at the head of a sap during the attack on the Fort and continued to work under a very heavy fire with cool and steady determination.

SMITH, Alfred
Gunner   Royal Regiment of Artillery
Other Decorations: —
Date of Gazette: 12 May 1885
Place/Date of Birth: London — 1861
Place/Date of Death: Plumstead, Kent — 6 Jan. 1932
Memorials: Plumstead Cemetery, Kent
Town/County Connections: Plumstead, Kent
Remarks: —
Account of Deed: On 17 Jan. 1885 at Abu Klea, Sudan, Gunner Smith saved a lieutenant who was being attacked by a native. The officer was superintending his gun at the time and had no weapon in his hand, but Gunner Smith warded off the thrust of the spear, giving the lieutenant time to draw his sword and bring the assailant to his knees. The latter, however, made a wild thrust at the officer with a long knife, which Gunner Smith again warded off, but not before the lieutenant was wounded. The gunner then managed to kill the native before he could attack again.

SMITH, Alfred Victor   1153
Second Lieutenant   1/5th Bn., The East Lancashire Regiment
Other Decorations: —
Date of Gazette: 3 Mar. 1916
Place/Date of Birth: Guildford, Surrey — 22 Jul. 1891
Place/Date of Death: Helles, Gallipoli — 23 Dec. 1915
Memorials: Twelve Tree Copse Cemetery, Gallipoli; St. Catherine's Church, Burnley,
Lancashire; St. John's Church, Blackpool, Lancashire
Town/County Connections: Guildford, Surrey *, Name on Guildford W. M. in Castle grounds*
Remarks: *— Portrait in Towneley Hall Museum, Burnley*
Account of Deed: On 23 Dec. 1915 at Helles, Gallipoli, Second Lieutenant Smith was in the act of
throwing a grenade when it slipped from his hand and fell to the bottom of the trench close to several officers and men. He
immediately shouted a warning and jumped clear to safety. He then saw that the officers and men were unable to find cover
and knowing that the grenade was due to explode at any moment, he returned and flung himself upon it. He was instantly killed
by the explosion.

SMITH, Archibald Bissett   1154
T/Lieutenant   Royal Naval Reserve
Other Decorations: —
Date of Gazette: 24 May 1919
Place/Date of Birth: Cults, Aberdeenshire, Scotland — 19 Dec. 1878
Place/Date of Death: Atlantic — 10 Mar. 1917
Memorials: Tower Hill Memorial, London
Town/County Connections: Cults, Aberdeenshire
Remarks: —
Account of Deed: On 10 Mar. 1917 in the Atlantic, the *SS Otaki*, whose armament consisted of
one 4.7-inch gun, commanded by Lieutenant Smith, sighted a German raider who was armed with
four 5.9-inch, one 4.1-inch and two 22-pounder guns. The raider called on *Otaki* to stop, but on Lieutenant Smith refusing to do
so, a duel ensued, during which *Otaki* secured a number of hits and caused considerable damage, but she herself sustained
much damage and was on fire. Lieutenant Smith therefore ordered his crew to abandon ship, but he himself stayed on board
and went down with his ship.

SMITH, Clement Leslie   1155
Lieutenant (later Brigadier General)   2nd Bn., The Duke of Cornwall's Light Infantry, attd. 5th
Somaliland Light Infantry
Other Decorations: MC
Date of Gazette: 7 Jun. 1904
Place/Date of Birth: Whippingham, Isle of Wight — 17 Jan. 1878
Place/Date of Death: Alassio, Italy — 14 Dec. 1927
Memorials: English Cemetery, Alassio, Italy
Town/County Connections: Whippingham, Isle of Wight
Remarks: Served in the First World War 1914-18
Account of Deed: On 10 Jan. 1904 at the commencement of the fight at Jidballi, Somaliland,
Lieutenant Smith and a medical officer tried to rescue a hospital assistant who was wounded. The rapidity of the enemy's fire,
however, made this impossible and the hospital assistant was killed. Lieutenant Smith then did all that was possible to bring
out the medical officer, helping him to mount a horse and, when this was shot, a mule. This also was shot and the medical officer
was killed, but the lieutenant stayed with him to the end, trying to keep off the enemy with his revolver.

SMITH, Edward   1156
Lance-Sergeant (later Lieutenant)   1/5th Bn., The Lancashire Fusiliers
Other Decorations: DCM
Date of Gazette: 22 Oct. 1918
Place/Date of Birth: Maryport, Cumberland — 10 Nov. 1898
Place/Date of Death: France — 12 Jan. 1940
Memorials: Beuvry Communal Cemetery Extension, Pas-de-Calais, France; Maryport War
Memorial
Town/County Connections: Maryport, Cumberland
Remarks: Served with 2nd Bn., The Lancashire Fusiliers in the Second World War
Account of Deed: During the period 21/23 Aug. 1918 east of Serre, France, Lance-Sergeant Smith
while in command of a platoon, personally took a machine-gun post, rushing the garrison with his rifle and bayonet. The enemy
on seeing him coming, scattered to throw hand grenades at him, but heedless of all danger and almost without halting in his
rush, this NCO shot at least six of them. Later, seeing another platoon needing assistance, he led his men to them, took
command and captured the objective. During an enemy counter-attack the following day he led a section forward and restored
a portion of the line.

SMITH, Ernest Alvia **1157**
Private (later Sergeant)   The Seaforth Highlanders of Canada, Canadian Infantry Corps
Other Decorations: —
Date of Gazette: 20 Dec. 1944
Place/Date of Birth: New Westminster, British Columbia, Canada — 3 May 1914
Place/Date of Death: — *3. 8. 2005*
Memorials: —
Town/County Connections: —
Remarks: —
Account of Deed: On the night of 21/22 Oct. 1944 at the River Savio, North Italy, Private Smith was in the spearhead of the attack which established a bridgehead over the river. With a P.I.A.T. gun he put an enemy tank out of action at a range of 30 feet, and while protecting a wounded comrade, he destroyed another tank and two self-propelled guns, as well as routing a number of the enemy infantry.

SMITH, Frederick Augustus **1158**
Captain (later Lieutenant Colonel)   43rd Regiment (later The Oxfordshire and Buckinghamshire Light Infantry)
Other Decorations: —
Date of Gazette: 4 Nov. 1864
Place/Date of Birth: Dublin — 18 Nov. 1826
Place/Date of Death: Duleek, Co. Meath, Ireland — 22 Jul. 1887
Memorials: —
Town/County Connections: Navan, Meath, Ireland
Remarks: —
Account of Deed: On 21 Jun. 1864 at Tauranga, New Zealand, Captain Smith led an attack on the enemy's position and although wounded before reaching the rifle pits, he jumped down and began a hand-to-hand encounter with the enemy, setting a fine example to his men.

No photograph available

SMITH, Henry **1159**
Lance-Corporal (later Sergeant)   52nd Regiment (later The Oxfordshire and Buckinghamshire Light Infantry)
Other Decorations: —
Date of Gazette: 24 Apr. 1858
Place/Date of Birth: Thames Ditton, Surrey — 1825
Place/Date of Death: Gwalior, India — 18 Aug. 1862
Memorials: —
Town/County Connections: Thames Ditton, Surrey
Remarks: —
Account of Deed: On 14 Sep. 1857 at Delhi, India, on the morning of the assault, Lance-Corporal Smith carried a wounded comrade under heavy fire of grape and musketry to a place of safety.

SMITH, Issy **1160**
A/Corporal (later Sergeant)   1st Bn., The Manchester Regiment
Other Decorations: —
Date of Gazette: 23 Aug. 1915
Place/Date of Birth: East London — 16 Sep. 1886   *Maybe Hackney*
Place/Date of Death: Melbourne, Australia — 11 Sep. 1940
Memorials: Fawkner Cemetery, Victoria, Australia
Town/County Connections: Manchester   *Name on board in Hackney Town Hall*
Remarks: —
Account of Deed: On 26 Apr. 1915 at St. Julien, Belgium, Corporal Smith left his company on his own initiative and went forward towards the enemy's position to help a severely wounded man, whom he carried a distance of 250 yards into safety. When casualties were very heavy later in the day Corporal Smith again displayed great gallantry in helping to bring in more wounded men and attending them, regardless of personal risk.

No photograph available

SMITH, J.   1161

Private   1st Madras Fusiliers (later The Royal Dublin Fusiliers)
Other Decorations: —
Date of Gazette: 24 Dec. 1858
Place/Date of Birth: London (St. Luke's Parish) — Jul. 1822
Place/Date of Death: Taujore, Trichinopoly, India — 6 May 1866
Memorials: —
Town/County Connections: London
Remarks: —
Account of Deed: On 16 Nov. 1857 at Lucknow, India, Private Smith was one of the first to enter Secundra Bagh when the gateway on the north side had been burst open. He was immediately surrounded by the enemy but notwithstanding the fact that he received a sword cut on the head, a bayonet wound on the left side and bruising from the butt-end of a musket, he fought his way out and continued to perform his duties for the rest of the day. (Elected by the regiment.)

SMITH, James   1162

Corporal (later Colour-Sergeant)   The East Kent Regiment (The Buffs)
Other Decorations: —
Date of Gazette: 21 Apr. 1899
Place/Date of Birth: Maidstone, Kent — 1871
Place/Date of Death: Dartford, Kent — 18 Mar. 1946
Memorials: —
Town/County Connections: Maidstone and Dartford, Kent
Remarks: —
Account of Deed: On the night of 16/17 Sep. 1897, in the Mamund Valley, N.W. India, Corporal Smith, with other men, responded to a call for volunteers and followed two officers of the Royal Engineers* into the burning village of Bilot, in an attempt to dislodge the enemy. Afterwards, although wounded, Corporal Smith continued fighting steadily and coolly, and also helped to carry the wounded to the place prepared for them. When one of the officers left in order to get help, the corporal held the position until his return, exposing himself to great danger and directing the fire of his men. (*See also COLVIN, J.M.C. and WATSON, T.C.)

SMITH, James (real name James Alexander GLENN)   1163

Private   3rd Bn., The Border Regiment, attd. 2nd Bn.
Other Decorations: —
Date of Gazette: 18 Feb. 1915
Place/Date of Birth: Workington, Cumberland — 5 Jan. 1881
Place/Date of Death: Middlesbrough, Yorkshire — 21 May 1968
Memorials: —
Town/County Connections: Workington, Cumberland; Middlesbrough, Yorkshire
Remarks: —
Account of Deed: On 21 Dec. 1914 at Rouges Bancs, France, Private Smith and another private* voluntarily went out from their trench and rescued a wounded man who had been lying exposed against the enemy's trenches for 75 hours. On the same day they again left their trench under heavy fire to bring in another wounded man. They were under fire for 60 minutes whilst conveying the wounded men to safety. (*See also ACTON, A.)

No photograph available

SMITH, John   1164

Sergeant   Bengal Sappers and Miners
Other Decorations: —
Date of Gazette: 27 Apr. 1858
Place/Date of Birth: Ticknall, Derbyshire — Feb. 1814
Place/Date of Death: Jullundur, India — 26 Jun. 1864
Memorials: Artillery Cemetery, Jullundur
Town/County Connections: Ticknall, Derbyshire
Remarks: —
Account of Deed: On 14 Sep. 1857 at Delhi, India, Sergeant Smith with two lieutenants and a bugler* showed conspicuous gallantry in the desperate task of blowing in the Kashmir Gate in broad daylight under heavy and destructive musket fire, preparatory to the assault. (*See also HOME, D.C., SALKELD, P. and HAWTHORNE, R.)

SMITH, John Manners   **1165**
Lieutenant (later Lieutenant Colonel)   Indian Staff Corps and 5th Gurkha Rifles, Indian Army
Other Decorations: CIE, CVO
Date of Gazette: 12 Jul. 1892
Place/Date of Birth: Lahore, India — 30 Aug. 1864
Place/Date of Death: London — 6 Jan. 1920
Memorials: Plaque in sanctum crypt, St. Luke's church, Chelsea, London
Town/County Connections: London
Remarks: —
Account of Deed: On 20 Dec. 1891 near Nilt Fort, India (Hunza Campaign), Lieutenant Smith led the storming party at the attack and capture of a strong position occupied by the enemy. For nearly four hours on the face of the cliff which was almost precipitous, he moved his handful of men from point to point, and during this time he was unable to defend himself from any attack which the enemy chose to make. He was the first man to reach the summit within a few yards of one of the enemy's sangars, which was immediately rushed, the lieutenant pistolling the first man.

No photograph available

SMITH, Philip   **1166**
Corporal (later Sergeant)   17th Regiment (later The Leicestershire Regiment)
Other Decorations: —
Date of Gazette: 24 Feb. 1857
Place/Date of Birth: Lurgan, Co. Armagh, Ireland — 1825
Place/Date of Death: Harold's Cross, Dublin — 16 Jan. 1906
Memorials: —
Town/County Connections: Lurgan, Co. Armagh
Remarks: Médaille Militaire (France)
Account of Deed: On 18 Jun. 1855 in the Crimea, Corporal Smith went out repeatedly in front of the advanced trenches against the Great Redan, under heavy fire, after the column had retired from the assault, and brought in wounded comrades.

SMYTH, John George (later The Rt. Hon. Sir John, Bt.)   **1167**
Lieutenant (later Brigadier)   15th Ludhiana Sikhs, Indian Army
Other Decorations: MC
Date of Gazette: 29 Jun. 1915
Place/Date of Birth: Teignmouth, Devon — 24 Oct. 1893
Place/Date of Death: London — 26 Apr. 1983
Memorials: (Cremated Golders Green, London)
Town/County Connections: Teignmouth, Devon
Remarks: Order of St. George (Russia); raised 19th London Division in India 1941 and commanded 17th Division in Burma 1942 (A/Major General); Member of Parliament for Norwood 1950-66; Founder-Chairman, VC and GC Association 1956-71; Life-President, VC and GC Association 1971-83. Author of *The Story of the Victoria Cross, The Story of the George Cross,* etc., etc.
Account of Deed: On 18 May 1915 near Richebourg L'Aouve, France, with a volunteer bombing party of 10 men, Lieutenant Smyth conveyed a supply of 96 bombs to within 20 yards of the enemy's position over exceptionally dangerous ground, after the attempts of two other parties had failed. Lieutenant Smyth succeeded in taking the bombs to the desired position with the help of two of his men (the other eight having been killed or wounded). To achieve this purpose he had to swim a stream, being exposed the whole time to howitzer, shrapnel, machine-gun and rifle fire.

SMYTH, Nevill Maskelyne (later Sir Nevill)   **1168**
Captain (later Major General), 2nd Dragoon Guards (Queen's Bays)
Other Decorations: KCB
Date of Gazette: 15 Nov. 1898   *13, Victoria St.*
Place/Date of Birth: Westminster, London — 14 Aug. 1868
Place/Date of Death: Balmoral, Victoria, Australia — 21 Jul. 1941
Memorials: Balmoral Cemetery, Victoria, Australia
Town/County Connections: Marazion, Cornwall   · *Family lived at Marazion*
Remarks: Served in the First World War 1914-18; Cross of Commander of Order of Leopold and Croix de Guerre (Belgium); Légion d'Honneur (France); commanded 1st Australian Infantry Brigade at the Dardanelles operation and 2nd Australian Division on the Western Front
Account of Deed: On 2 Sep. 1898 at the Battle of Khartoum, Sudan, Captain Smyth galloped forward and attacked an Arab who had run amok among some War Correspondents. Captain Smyth received the Arab's charge, and killed him, being wounded in the arm while doing so, but he saved the life of at least one of the War Correspondents.

SMYTHE, Quentin George Murray   **1169**
Sergeant (later Captain)   Royal Natal Carabineers, South African Forces
Other Decorations: —
Date of Gazette: 11 Sep. 1942
Place/Date of Birth: Nottingham Road, Natal, South Africa — 6 Aug. 1916
Place/Date of Death: — *About 22.10.1997 in South Africa, probably Natal*
Memorials: —
Town/County Connections: —
Remarks: —
Account of Deed: On 5 Jun. 1942 in the Alem Hamza area, Western Desert, during an attack on an enemy strong point in which his officer was severely wounded, Sergeant Smythe took command of the platoon although he was himself wounded in the head. When our troops came under enfilade fire from an enemy machine-gun nest he attacked it with hand grenades, capturing the crew. Although weak from loss of blood, he continued to lead the advance and stalking an anti-tank position, he again attacked and captured it single-handed killing several of the enemy.

SOMERS, James   **1170**
Sergeant, 1st Bn., The Royal Inniskilling Fusiliers
Other Decorations: —
Date of Gazette: 1 Sep. 1915
Place/Date of Birth: Belturbet, Co. Cavan, Ireland — 12 Jun. 1884
Place/Date of Death: Cloughgordon, Tipperary, Ireland — 7 May 1918
Memorials: Modreeny Church of Ireland churchyard, Tipperary, Ireland
Town/County Connections: Belturbet, Co. Cavan
Remarks: —
Account of Deed: On 1/2 Jul. 1915, in Gallipoli, when, owing to hostile bombing, some of our troops had retired from a sap, Sergeant Somers remained alone there until a party brought up bombs. He then climbed over into the Turkish trench and bombed the Turks with great effect. Later on, he advanced into the open under heavy fire and held back the enemy by throwing bombs into their flank until a barricade had been established. During this period, he frequently ran to and from our trenches to obtain fresh supplies of bombs.

SPACKMAN, Charles Edward   **1171**
Sergeant   1st Bn., The Border Regiment
Other Decorations: MM
Date of Gazette: 11 Jan. 1918
Place/Date of Birth: Fulham, London — 11 Jan. 1891
Place/Date of Death: Southampton, Hampshire — 7 May 1969
Memorials: —
Town/County Connections: Fulham, London; Southampton, Hampshire
Remarks: —
Account of Deed: On 20 Nov. 1917 at Marcoing, France, the leading company was checked by heavy fire from a gun mounted on a position which covered the approaches. Sergeant Spackman, realising that it would be impossible for the troops to advance, went through heavy fire to the gun, where he succeeded in killing all but one of the gun crew and then captured the gun.

SPALL, Robert   **1172**
Sergeant   Princess Patricia's Canadian Light Infantry, Eastern Ontario Regiment, C.E.F.
Other Decorations: —
Date of Gazette: 26 Oct. 1918
Place/Date of Birth: Brentford, Middlesex — 5 Mar. 1890
Place/Date of Death: Parvillers, France — 13 Aug. 1918
Memorials: Vimy Memorial, France
Town/County Connections: Brentford, Middlesex
Remarks: —
Account of Deed: On 12/13 Aug. 1918 near Parvillers, France, during an enemy counter-attack, Sergeant Spall's platoon became isolated, whereupon he took a Lewis gun and standing on the parapet, fired upon the advancing enemy, inflicting many casualties. He then came down from the trench and directed his men into a sap 75 yards away, after which he picked up another Lewis gun, again climbed the parapet and held up the enemy with his fire, but while doing so was killed. Owing to Sergeant Spall, who deliberately gave his life, the platoon was saved.

SPEAKMAN, William   **1173**
Private (later Sergeant)   The Black Watch (Royal Highlanders), attd. 1st Bn., The King's Own
Scottish Borderers
Other Decorations: —
Date of Gazette: 28 Dec. 1951
Place/Date of Birth: Altrincham, Cheshire — 21 Sep. 1927
Place/Date of Death: —
Memorials: —
Town/County Connections: Altrincham, Cheshire
Remarks: —
Account of Deed: On 4 Nov. 1951 in Korea, when the section holding the left shoulder of the
company's position had been seriously depleted by casualties and was being over-run by the enemy Private Speakman, on his
own initiative, collected six men and a pile of grenades and led a series of charges. He broke up several enemy attacks, causing
heavy casualties and in spite of being wounded in the leg continued to lead charge after charge. He kept the enemy at bay long
enough to enable his company to withdraw safely.

SPENCE, David   **1174**
Troop Sergeant-Major (later Regimental Sergeant-Major)   9th Lancers (The Queen's Royal)
Other Decorations: —
Date of Gazette: 24 Dec. 1858
Place/Date of Birth: Inverkeithing, Fife, Scotland — 1818
Place/Date of Death: Lambeth, London — 17 Apr. 1877
Memorials: Streatham Cemetery, London
Town/County Connections: Inverkeithing, Fife; Lambeth, London
Remarks: Yeoman of the Guard after he left the 9th Lancers
Account of Deed: On 17 Jan. 1858 at Shunsabad, India, Troop Sergeant-Major Spence went to
the assistance of a private who had been wounded and his horse disabled, and rescued him from
a large number of rebels.

No photograph available

SPENCE, Edward   **1175**
Private   42nd Regiment (later The Black Watch (Royal Highlanders))
Other Decorations: —
Date of Gazette: 27 May 1859 & 15 Jan. 1907
Place/Date of Birth: Dumfries, Scotland — 28 Dec. 1830
Place/Date of Death: Ruhya, Oude, India — 17 Apr. 1858
Memorials: —
Town/County Connections: Dumfries, Scotland
Remarks: —
Account of Deed: On 15 Apr. 1858 during the attack on Fort Ruhya, India, Private Spence
volunteered, with others, to assist a captain* in bringing in the body of a lieutenant from the top
of the glacis. Private Spence deliberately placed himself in an exposed position, so as to cover the party bearing away the body.
He died on 17 Apr. of a wound which he received on this occasion. (*See also CAFE, W.M. and THOMPSON, A.)

STAGPOOLE, Dudley   **1176**
Drummer   57th Regiment (later The Middlesex Regiment — Duke of Cambridge's Own)
Other Decorations: DCM
Date of Gazette: 22 Sep. 1864
Place/Date of Birth: Killunan, Co. Galway, Ireland — 1838
Place/Date of Death: Ware, Hertfordshire — 1 Aug. 1911
Memorials: Hendon Park Cemetery, London   *Grave*
Town/County Connections: Limerick, Ireland; Ware, Hertfordshire
Remarks: —
Account of Deed: On 2 Oct. 1863 at Pontoko, New Zealand, Drummer Stagpoole volunteered to
go with an ensign* to rescue a wounded comrade from the rebel natives. They succeeded in
bringing in this wounded man who was lying about 50 yards from the bush, although the enemy kept up a very heavy fire at
short range and from fallen logs close at hand. (*See also DOWN, J.T.)

STANLAKE, (or STANLACK, or STANLOCK) William   **1177**
Private   Coldstream Guards
Other Decorations: DCM
Date of Gazette: 24 Feb. 1857
Place/Date of Birth: Halwill, near Okehampton, Devon — 31 Oct. 1830
Place/Date of Death: Camberwell, London — 24 Apr. 1904
Memorials: Camberwell Old Cemetery, London
Town/County Connections: Halwill, Okehampton, Devon; Camberwell, London
Remarks: —
Account of Deed: On 26 Oct. 1854 near Inkerman, Crimea, Private Stanlake, when employed as a sharpshooter, volunteered to reconnoitre, and although warned of the dangers he would encounter, crawled to within six yards of a Russian sentry and brought back such information that the officer in charge of the party was able to make a surprise attack.

STANNARD, Richard Been   **1178**
Lieutenant (later Captain)   Royal Naval Reserve
Other Decorations: DSO
Date of Gazette: 16 Aug. 1940
Place/Date of Birth: Blyth, Northumberland — 21 Aug. 1902
Place/Date of Death: Sydney, New South Wales, Australia — 22 Jul. 1977
Memorials: Rookwood Cemetery, Sydney
Town/County Connections: Blyth, Northumberland; Bexleyheath, Kent
Remarks: Norwegian War Cross; Member of Hon. Company of Master Mariners 1943; Marine Superintendent, P & O. Orient Lines of Australia 1960
Account of Deed: From 28 Apr. to 2 May 1940 at Namsos, Norway, HMS *Arab* survived 31 bombing attacks in five days. On one occasion during this period Lieutenant Stannard and two of his crew tackled for two hours a fire on the jetty caused by a bomb igniting ammunition. Part of the jetty was saved, which proved invaluable at the subsequent evacuation. Later feats included the destruction of a Nazi bomber whose pilot, thinking that he had HMS *Arab* at his mercy, ordered that she be steered into captivity.

STARCEVICH, Leslie Thomas   **1179**
Private, 2/43rd Bn. (S.A.), Australian Military Forces
Other Decorations: —
Date of Gazette: 8 Nov. 1945
Place/Date of Birth: Subiaco, Western Australia — 5 Sep. 1918
Place/Date of Death: — Died about 18.11.1989, Carnamah, Western Australia
Memorials: Tablet at Beaufort, North Borneo (scene of the action); Australian War Memorial, Canberra
Town/County Connections: —
Remarks: —
Account of Deed: On 25 May 1945 during the capture of Beaufort, North Borneo, the leading section came under fire from two enemy machine-gun posts and suffered casualties. Private Starcevich, a Bren gunner, moved forward and assaulted each post in turn, killing five of the enemy and putting the rest to flight. Later, when the section was again held up, he adopted similar tactics and single-handed captured two more posts, disposing of seven of the enemy.

STATTON, Percy Clyde   **1180**
Sergeant, 40th Bn. (Tasmania), Australian Imperial Force
Other Decorations: MM
Date of Gazette: 27 Sep. 1918
Place/Date of Birth: Beaconsfield, Tasmania — 21 Oct. 1890
Place/Date of Death: Hobart, Tasmania — 5 Dec. 1959
Memorials: Cornelian Bay Crematorium, Hobart; Australian War Memorial, Canberra
Town/County Connections: —
Remarks: —
Account of Deed: On 12 Aug. 1918, near Proyart, France, Sergeant Statton engaged two machine-gun posts with Lewis gun fire, enabling the rest of the battalion to advance. Then, the advance of the battalion on his left having been stopped by heavy machine-gun fire, he rushed four machine-gun posts in succession, armed only with a revolver, putting two out of action and killing five of the enemy.

STEELE, Gordon Charles   **1181**
Lieutenant (later Commander)   Royal Navy
Other Decorations: —
Date of Gazette: 11 Nov. 1919
Place/Date of Birth: Exeter, Devon — 1 Nov. 1892
Place/Date of Death: Winkleigh, Okehampton, Devon — 4 Jan. 1981
Memorials: — *Buried All Saints churchyard, Winkleigh.*
Town/County Connections: Exeter and Winkleigh, Devon
Remarks: Captain-Superintendent of HMS *Worcester* (training ship) 1929-57; served as Anti-Submarine Commander and Inspector Anti-Submarine Equipment in the Second World War. Author of *Electrical Knowledge for Ships' Officers* and *The Story of the Worcester*.
Account of Deed: On 18 Aug. 1919 at Kronstadt, Russia, Lieutenant Steele was second-in-command of Coastal Motor Boat 88. After this boat had entered the harbour her commanding officer was killed and the boat thrown off course. Lieutenant Steele took the wheel and steadied the boat, lifting the dead officer away from the steering and firing position, and torpedoed the battleship *Andrei Pervozanni* at 100 yards range. He then manoeuvred the CMB in a very confined space to get a clear shot at the other battleship *Petropavlosk* before making for the safety of the bay. (See also DOBSON, C.C.)

STEELE, Thomas   **1182**
Sergeant   1st Bn., The Seaforth Highlanders (Ross-shire Buffs, Duke of Albany's)
Other Decorations: —
Date of Gazette: 8 Jun. 1917
Place/Date of Birth: Oldham, Lancashire — 6 Feb. 1891
Place/Date of Death: Springhead, Oldham, Lancashire — 11 Jul. 1978
Memorials: —
Town/County Connections: Oldham, Lancashire; Saddleworth, Yorkshire
Remarks: —
Account of Deed: On 22 Feb. 1917 near Sanna-y-Yat, Mesopotamia, at a critical moment when a strong enemy counter-attack had temporarily regained some of the captured trenches, Sergeant Steele helped a comrade to carry a machine-gun into position. He kept this gun in action until relieved and was mainly instrumental in keeping the rest of the line intact. Some hours later another counter-attack enabled the enemy to reoccupy a portion of the captured trenches and Sergeant Steele rallied the troops, encouraging them to remain in their trenches and leading a number of them forward, helped to re-establish our line. On this occasion he was severely wounded.

No photograph available

STEWART, (or STEUART)   William George Drummond   **1183**
Captain   93rd Regiment (later The Argyll and Sutherland Highlanders — Princess Louise's)
Other Decorations: —
Date of Gazette: 24 Dec. 1858
Place/Date of Birth: Grandtully, Perth, Scotland — Feb. 1831
Place/Date of Death: Hythe, Kent — 19 Oct. 1868
Memorials: —
Town/County Connections: Grandtully, Perth
Remarks: —
Account of Deed: On 16 Nov. 1857 at Lucknow, India, Captain Stewart led an attack, with a small force, on two of the enemy's guns which were maintaining a heavy flanking fire and which covered the approach to the barracks. Captain Stewart captured the guns and was able to gain possession of the barracks. (Elected by the regiment.)

STOKES, James   **1184**
Private   2nd Bn., The King's Shropshire Light Infantry
Other Decorations: —
Date of Gazette: 17 Apr. 1945
Place/Date of Birth: Hutchesontown, Lanark, Scotland — 6 Feb. 1915
Place/Date of Death: Kervenheim, Rhineland — 1 Mar. 1945
Memorials: Reichswald Forest War Cemetery, Cleves, Germany
Town/County Connections: Glasgow, Scotland
Remarks: —
Account of Deed: On 1 Mar. 1945 during an attack on Kervenheim, Rhineland, a platoon was pinned down by intense rifle and machine-gun fire from a farm building. Private Stokes dashed into the building firing from the hip and reappeared with 12 prisoners. During the operation he was wounded but refused to go to the regimental aid post and continued the advance with his platoon and rushed another house, taking five more prisoners. Now severely injured he insisted on taking part in the advance on the final objective, but fell mortally wounded 20 yards from the enemy position.

STONE, Charles Edwin   **1185**
Gunner (later Bombardier) 'C' Bty., 83rd Brigade, Royal Field Artillery
Other Decorations: MM
Date of Gazette: 22 May 1918
Place/Date of Birth: Denby, near Belper, Derbyshire — 4 Feb. 1889
Place/Date of Death: Derby — 29 Aug. 1952
Memorials: —
Town/County Connections: Denby and Belper, Derbyshire
Remarks: —
Account of Deed: On 21 Mar. 1918 at Caponne Farm, France, after working at his gun for six hours under heavy gas and shell fire, Gunner Stone was sent back to the rear with an order. He delivered it and then, under a very heavy barrage, returned with a rifle to assist in holding up the enemy on a sunken road. First lying in the open under very heavy machine-gun fire and then on the right flank of the two rear guns he held the enemy at bay. Later he was one of the party which captured a machine-gun and four prisoners.

STONE, Walter Napleton   **1186**
A/Captain 3rd Bn., The Royal Fusiliers, attd. 17th (S) Bn.
Other Decorations: DSO, MC
Date of Gazette: 13 Feb. 1918
Place/Date of Birth: Blackheath, London — 7 Dec. 1891
Place/Date of Death: Moeuvres, near Cambrai, France — 30 Nov. 1917
Memorials: Cambrai Memorial, France
Town/County Connections: Blackheath, London
Remarks: — *Harrow School*
Account of Deed: On 30 Nov. 1917 in the Cambrai Sector, France, Captain Stone, commanding an isolated company 1000 yards in front of our main line, saw the enemy massing for an attack and sent invaluable information to battalion headquarters. He was ordered to withdraw, leaving a rearguard to cover the withdrawal. As the attack developed with unexpected speed, he sent three platoons back and remained with the rearguard. He stood on the parapet with the telephone, under terrific bombardment, sending back vital information until the line was cut on his orders. The rearguard was eventually cut to pieces, and Captain Stone was seen fighting to the last.

STORKEY, Percy Valentine   **1187**
Lieutenant (later Captain), 19th Bn. (N.S.W.), Australian Imperial Force
Other Decorations: —
Date of Gazette: 7 Jun. 1918
Place/Date of Birth: Napier, Hawkes Bay, New Zealand — 9 Sep. 1893
Place/Date of Death: Teddington, Middlesex — 3 Oct. 1969 · *Cremated at SW Middlesex Crematorium, Hanworth*
Memorials: Australian War Memorial, Canberra
Town/County Connections: Teddington, Middlesex
Remarks: Became a Judge, District Court Northern Circuit, New South Wales, Australia
Account of Deed: On 7 Apr. 1918 at Hangard Wood, France, Lieutenant Storkey, together with another officer and ten other ranks, charged an enemy position containing 80 to 100 men, driving them out, killing and wounding about 30 and capturing three officers and 50 men, also one machine-gun. Lieutenant Storkey's courage and initiative, together with his skilful method of attack against such heavy odds, removed a dangerous obstacle and inspired the remainder of the troops.

STRACHAN, Harcus   **1188**
Lieutenant (later Lieutenant Colonel) Fort Garry Horse, C.E.F.
Other Decorations: MC
Date of Gazette: 18 Dec. 1917
Place/Date of Birth: Borrowstounness, West Lothian, Scotland — 7 Nov. 1884
Place/Date of Death: Vancouver, Canada — 1 May 1982
Memorials: —
Town/County Connections: Borrowstounness (Bo'ness), West Lothian
Remarks: Commanded 1st Bn., Edmonton Fusiliers in the Second World War.
Account of Deed: On 20 Nov. 1917 at Masnieres, France, Lieutenant Strachan took command of a squadron of his regiment when the squadron leader, approaching the German front line at a gallop, was killed. Lieutenant Strachan led the squadron through the enemy line of machine-gun posts and then, with the surviving men, led the charge on the German battery, killing seven of the gunners with his sword. When all the gunners were killed and the battery silenced, he rallied his men and fought his way back at night through the enemy's lines, bringing all unwounded men safely in, together with 15 prisoners.

STRINGER, George   **1189**

Private   1st Bn., The Manchester Regiment
Other Decorations: —
Date of Gazette: 5 Aug. 1916
Place/Date of Birth: Manchester, Lancashire — 24 Jul. 1889
Place/Date of Death: Manchester — 22 Nov. 1957
Memorials: Philips Park Cemetery, Manchester
Town/County Connections: Manchester, Lancashire
Remarks: —
Account of Deed: On 8 Mar. 1916 at Es Sinn, Mesopotamia, after the capture of an enemy position, Private Stringer was posted on the extreme right of his battalion to guard against any hostile attack. His battalion was subsequently forced back by an enemy counter-attack, but Private Stringer held his ground single-handed and kept back the enemy until all his grenades were used up. His gallant stand saved the flank of his battalion and made a steady withdrawal possible.

STRONG, George   **1190**

Private   Coldstream Guards
Other Decorations: —
Date of Gazette: 24 Feb. 1857
Place/Date of Birth: Odcombe, Yeovil, Somerset — 30 Nov. 1835
Place/Date of Death: Sherston Magna, Wiltshire — 25 Aug. 1888
Memorials: Church of the Holy Cross churchyard, Sherston, Wiltshire
Town/County Connections: Odcombe, Yeovil, Somerset
Remarks: —
Account of Deed: In Sep. 1855, in the Crimea, when on duty, Private Strong picked up a live shell which had fallen into the trench, and threw it over the parapet. He was well aware of the extreme danger involved, and his action saved many lives.

STUART, Ronald Niel (or Neil)   **1191**

Lieutenant (later Captain)   Royal Naval Reserve
Other Decorations: DSO, RD
Date of Gazette: 20 Jul. 1917
Place/Date of Birth: Liverpool, Lancashire — 26 Aug. 1886
Place/Date of Death: Charing, Kent — 8 Feb. 1954
Memorials: Charing Cemetery, Kent
Town/County Connections: Liverpool; Charing, Kent
Remarks: Croix de Guerre avec Palmes (France); United States Navy Cross; Captain of the CPR *Empress of Britain* and Commodore of the CPR Fleet 1934
Account of Deed: On 7 Jun. 1917 in the Atlantic, Lieutenant Stuart was serving in HMS *Pargust* (one of the 'Q' or 'mystery' ships) which was inviting an attack by U-boats. At about 8am a U-boat fired a torpedo at close range and damaged *Pargust's* engine room. The 'Panic party' went away and the U-boat surfaced, its captain thinking that a merchant vessel had been hit, but when the U-boat was only about 50 yards away, the commander of *Pargust* gave the order to fire. The submarine tried to get away, but had received a great number of direct hits and blew up and sank almost at once. (Award by ballot. See also WILLIAMS, W.)

STUBBS, Frank Edward   **1192**

Sergeant   1st Bn., The Lancashire Fusiliers
Other Decorations: —
Date of Gazette: 15 Mar. 1917
Place/Date of Birth: Walworth, London — 12 Mar. 1888
Place/Date of Death: Krithia, Gallipoli — 25 Apr. 1915
Memorials: Helles Memorial, Gallipoli
Town/County Connections: Walworth and Peckham, London
Remarks: —
Account of Deed: On 25 Apr. 1915 west of Cape Helles, Gallipoli, three companies and the Headquarters of the 1st Battalion, Lancashire Fusiliers, when landing on W Beach, were met by a very deadly fire from hidden machine-guns which caused a large number of casualties. The survivors, however, rushed up and cut the wire entanglements notwithstanding the terrific fire from the enemy and after overcoming supreme difficulties, the cliffs were gained and the position maintained. (Sergeant Stubbs was one of the six members of the regiment elected for the award. See also BROMLEY, C., GRIMSHAW, J.E., KENEALLY, W., RICHARDS, A.J. and WILLIS, R.R.)

SUKANAIVALU, Sefanaia   **1193**
Corporal   3rd Bn., Fijian Infantry Regiment
Other Decorations: —
Date of Gazette: 2 Nov. 1944
Place/Date of Birth: Yathata Island, Fiji — ?
Place/Date of Death: South Mawakana, Bougainville — 23 Jun. 1944
Memorials: Rabaul (Bita Paka) War Cemetery, New Britain; memorial in Civic Buildings, Suva
Town/County Connections: —
Remarks: —
Account of Deed: On 23 Jun. 1944 at Bougainville, Solomon Islands, Corporal Sukanaivalu crawled forward to rescue some wounded men. He brought in two successfully and went out to fetch a third, but on the way back was seriously wounded in the groin and thigh and unable to move the lower part of his body. Several attempts were made to rescue him, but these resulted in further casualties. Knowing that his men would not withdraw as long as he was alive, Corporal Sukanaivalu deliberately raised himself in full view of the enemy and died riddled with bullets.

SULLIVAN, Arthur Percy   **1194**
Corporal, 45th Bn., The Royal Fusiliers
Other Decorations: —
Date of Gazette: 29 Sep. 1919
Place/Date of Birth: Crystal Brook, South Australia — 27 Nov. 1896
Place/Date of Death: Westminster, London — 9 Apr. 1937
Memorials: Ashes interred at Sydney, New South Wales; Australian War Memorial, Canberra
Town/County Connections: —
Remarks: —
Account of Deed: On 10 Aug. 1919, at Sheika River, North Russia, the platoon to which Corporal Sullivan belonged, after fighting a rearguard covering action, had to cross the river by means of a narrow plank, and during the passage an officer and three men fell into a deep swamp. Without hesitation, Corporal Sullivan, under intense fire, jumped into the river and rescued all four, bringing them out singly. But for this gallant action, the men would undoubtedly have drowned, as all ranks were exhausted and the enemy was less than 100 yards away.

SULLIVAN, John   **1195**
Boatswain's Mate (later Chief Boatswain's Mate)   Royal Navy (Naval Brigade)
Other Decorations: CGM; Royal Humane Society's Silver Medal
Date of Gazette: 24 Feb. 1857
Place/Date of Birth: Bantry, Cork, Ireland — 10 Apr. 1830
Place/Date of Death: Kinsale, Co. Cork, Ireland — 28 Jun. 1884
Memorials: —
Town/County Connections: Bantry and Kinsale, Co. Cork
Remarks: Légion d'Honneur (France); Al Valore Militari (Sardinia)
Account of Deed: On 10 Apr. 1855 in the Crimea, Boatswain's Mate Sullivan, as captain of one of the guns at Greenhill Battery, volunteered to place a flagstaff on a mound to act as an aiming point. He carried out this dangerous task undeterred by continuous fire from enemy sharpshooters, and his action enabled the battery to open fire on hitherto concealed enemy guns which were doing great damage to some of the advanced works.

SUTTON, William   **1196**
Bugler   1st Bn., 60th Rifles (later The King's Royal Rifle Corps)
Other Decorations: —
Date of Gazette: 20 Jan. 1860
Place/Date of Birth: Ightham, Kent — 1830
Place/Date of Death: Ightham, Kent — 16 Feb. 1888
Memorials: Ightham Church, Kent _Grave_
Town/County Connections: Ightham, Kent
Remarks: —
Account of Deed: On 13 Sep. 1857 at Delhi, India, on the night previous to the assault, Bugler Sutton volunteered to reconnoitre the breach. His conduct was conspicuous throughout the operations, especially on 2 Aug. 1857 on which occasion during an attack he rushed over the trenches and killed one of the enemy's buglers, who was in the act of sounding. (Elected by the regiment.)

SWALES, Edwin
Captain   South African Air Force, serving with 582 Squadron, Royal Air Force
Other Decorations: DFC
Date of Gazette: 24 Apr. 1945
Place/Date of Birth: Inanda, Natal, South Africa — 3 Jul. 1915
Place/Date of Death: Limburg, Belgium — 23 Feb. 1945
Memorials: Leopoldsburg War Cemetery, Limburg, Belgium
Town/County Connections: —
Remarks: —
Account of Deed: On 23 Feb. 1945 over Pforzheim, Germany, Captain Swales was leading the raid when he was attacked by an enemy fighter, one engine, fuel tanks and the rear gun turret being badly damaged. Unperturbed, he carried on, but was again attacked and his port engine was put out of action. Nevertheless he still remained over the target until satisfied that the attack had achieved its purpose. He finally managed to get his crippled Lancaster back to Allied-occupied territory before ordering his crew to bail out but as the last crew-member jumped, the aircraft plunged to earth. Captain Swales was found dead at the controls.

SYKES, Ernest
Private   27 (S) Bn., The Northumberland Fusiliers
Other Decorations: —
Date of Gazette: 8 Jun. 1917
Place/Date of Birth: Mossley, Saddleworth, Yorkshire — 4 Apr. 1885
Place/Date of Death: Lockwood, Yorkshire — 3 Aug. 1949
Memorials: Regimental Museum of The Northumberland Fusiliers, Alnwick Castle (name plate from LMS engine)
Town/County Connections: —
Remarks: —
Account of Deed: On 19 Apr. 1917, near Arras, France, the battalion in attack was held up by intense fire from front and flank, and suffered heavy casualties. Private Sykes, despite this heavy fire, went forward and brought back four wounded. He then made a fifth journey and remained out under conditions which appeared to be certain death, until he had bandaged all those too badly injured to be moved.

SYLVESTER, William Henry Thomas
Assistant Surgeon (later Surgeon Major)   23rd Regiment (later The Royal Welch Fusiliers)
Other Decorations: —
Date of Gazette: 20 Nov. 1857
Place/Date of Birth: Devizes, Wiltshire — 16 Apr. 1831
Place/Date of Death: Paignton, Devon — 13 Mar. 1920
Memorials: Paignton Cemetery, Devon. *Grave 2614*
Town/County Connections: Devizes, Wiltshire; Paignton, Devon
Remarks: Légion d'Honneur (France). He knew and worked with Florence Nightingale at Sebastopol and Scutari Hospitals. Served in the Indian Mutiny 1857-58
Account of Deed: On 8 Sep. 1855, at Sebastopol, Crimea, near the Redan, Assistant Surgeon Sylvester went with a corporal* to the aid of an officer who was mortally wounded and remained with him, dressing his wounds, in a most dangerous and exposed situation. Again, on 18 Sep. this officer was at the front, under heavy fire, attending the wounded. (*See also SHIELDS, R.) *VC in RAMC Museum, Aldershot.*

SYMONS, George
Sergeant (later Captain)   Royal Regiment of Artillery
Other Decorations: —
Date of Gazette: 20 Nov. 1857, amendment 1 Dec. 1857
Place/Date of Birth: South Hill, Cornwall — 18 Mar. 1826
Place/Date of Death: Bridlington, Yorkshire — 18 Nov. 1871
Memorials: — *Buried St. Marys Churchyard. Bridlington.*
Town/County Connections: South Hill, Cornwall; Bridlington, Yorshire
Remarks: —
Account of Deed: On 6 Jun. 1855 at Inkerman, Crimea, Sergeant Symons volunteered to unmask the embrasures of a five-gun battery in the advanced Right Attack. He did this under terrific fire from the enemy, which increased with the opening of each embrasure, until he came to the last one when he boldly mounted the parapet and threw down the sand-bags. As he was doing this an enemy shell burst and wounded him severely.

SYMONS, William John 1201

Second Lieutenant (later Lieutenant Colonel)   7th Bn. (Victoria), Australian Imperial Force
Other Decorations: —
Date of Gazette: 15 Oct. 1915
Place/Date of Birth: Eaglehawk, Bendigo, Victoria, Australia — 10 Jul. 1889
Place/Date of Death: London — 24 Jun. 1948
Memorials: Golders Green Cemetery, London; Australian War Memorial, Canberra
Town/County Connections: London
Remarks: Served with the Home Guard in the Second World War
Account of Deed: On 8/9 Aug. 1915 at Lone Pine, Gallipoli, Second Lieutenant Symons was in command of a section of newly captured trenches and repelled several counter-attacks with great coolness. An enemy attack on an isolated sap early in the morning resulted in six officers becoming casualties and part of the sap being lost, but Second Lieutenant Symons retook it, shooting two Turks. The sap was then attacked from three sides and this officer managed, in the face of heavy fire, to build a barricade. On the enemy setting fire to the head cover, he extinguished it and rebuilt the barricade. His coolness and determination finally compelled the enemy to withdraw.

TAIT, James Edward 1202

Lieutenant   78th Bn., Manitoba Regiment (Winnipeg Grenadiers), C.E.F.
Other Decorations: MC
Date of Gazette: 27 Sep. 1918
Place/Date of Birth: Greenbrae, Dumfries, Scotland — 27 May 1886
Place/Date of Death: Near Amiens, France — 11 Aug. 1918
Memorials: Fouquescourt British Cemetery, France
Town/County Connections: Dumfries, Scotland
Remarks: —
Account of Deed: During the period 8/11 Aug. 1918 at Amiens, France, when the advance had been checked by intense machine-gun fire, Lieutenant Tait rallied his company and led them forward with consummate skill under a hail of bullets. He then went forward alone to a machine-gun which was causing many casualties and killed the gunner. This so inspired his men that they rushed the position, capturing 12 machine-guns and 20 prisoners. Later, when the enemy counter-attacked our position under intense artillery bombardment, this officer displayed outstanding courage and although mortally wounded, continued to direct his men until his death.

TANDEY, Henry 1203

Private (later Sergeant)   5th Bn., The Duke of Wellington's (West Riding) Regiment
Other Decorations: DCM, MM
Date of Gazette: 14 Dec. 1918
Place/Date of Birth: Leamington, Warwickshire — 30 Aug. 1891
Place/Date of Death: Coventry, Warwickshire — 20 Dec. 1977
Memorials: —
Town/County Connections: Leamington and Coventry, Warwickshire
Remarks: Served with the Green Howards 1910-Aug. 1918; served as a Recruiting Sergeant during the Second World War.
Account of Deed: On 28 Sep. 1918 at Marcoing, France, during the counter-attack after the capture of the village and crossings, when Private Tandey's platoon was held up by machine-gun fire, he crawled forward, located the gun and with a Lewis gun team, knocked it out. Arriving at the crossings, he restored the plank bridge under a hail of bullets. Later in the evening, during an attack he, with eight comrades, was surrounded by an overwhelming number of the enemy. Although the position seemed hopeless, he led a bayonet charge, fighting so fiercely that 37 of the enemy were driven into the hands of the remainder of the company.

No photograph available

TAYLOR, John 1204

Captain of the Forecastle   Royal Navy (Naval Brigade)
Other Decorations: —
Date of Gazette: 24 Feb. 1857
Place/Date of Birth: Bristol — Jan. or Feb. 1822
Place/Date of Death: Woolwich, London — 25 Feb. 1857
Memorials: Woolwich Cemetery · *Headstone Ceremony 20.2.1996*
Town/County Connections: Bristol; Woolwich, London
Remarks: Légion d'Honneur (France)
Account of Deed: On 18 Jun. 1855 in the Crimea, immediately after the assault on Sebastopol, a soldier of the 57th Regiment, who had been wounded in both legs, was observed sitting up and calling for help. At once the second-in-command of the scaling party, another seaman* and Captain of the Forecastle Taylor left the shelter of their battery works and ran forward a distance of 70 yards, across open ground, through heavy gunfire and succeeded in carrying the wounded man to safety. (*See also CURTIS, Henry and RABY, H.J.)

TEESDALE, Christopher Charles (later Sir Christopher) **1205**
Lieutenant (later Major General)   Royal Regiment of Artillery
Other Decorations: KCMG, CB
Date of Gazette: 25 Sep. 1857
Place/Date of Birth: Grahamstown, Cape of Good Hope, South Africa — 1 Jun 1833
Place/Date of Death: Bognor, Sussex — 1 Dec. 1893
Memorials: —
Town/County Connections: Bognor, Sussex
Remarks: Légion d'Honneur (France)
Account of Deed: On 29 Sep. 1855 at Kars, Crimea, Lieutenant Teesdale volunteered to take command of the force engaged in the defence of the most advanced part of the works. He threw himself into the midst of the enemy and encouraged the garrison to make an attack so vigorous that the Russians were driven out. During the hottest part of the action he induced the Turkish artillerymen to return to their post from which they had been driven by enemy fire and after the final victorious charge he saved from the fury of the Turks a considerable number of the enemy wounded — an action gratefully acknowledged by the Russian Staff.

TEMPLE, William **1206**
Assistant Surgeon   Royal Regiment of Artillery
Other Decorations: —
Date of Gazette: 22 Sep. 1864
Place/Date of Birth: Monaghan, Co. Monaghan, Ireland — 7 Nov. 1833
Place/Date of Death: Tunbridge Wells, Kent — 13 Feb. 1919
Memorials: —
Town/County Connections: Monaghan, Ireland; Tunbridge Wells, Kent
Remarks: —
Account of Deed: On 20 Nov. 1863 at Rangiriri, New Zealand, during an assault on the enemy's position, Assistant Surgeon Temple, together with another officer* exposed themselves to imminent danger in crossing the entrance to the Maori keep at a point upon which the enemy were concentrating their fire, in order to render assistance to the wounded. Both officers showed great calmness under most trying circumstances. (*See also PICKARD, A.F.)

THACKERAY, Edward Talbot (later Sir Edward) **1207**
Second Lieutenant (later Colonel)   Bengal Engineers
Other Decorations: KCB
Date of Gazette: 29 Apr. 1862
Place/Date of Birth: Broxbourne, Hertfordshire — 19 Oct. 1836
Place/Date of Death: Garassio, Italy — 3 Sep. 1927
Memorials: —
Town/County Connections: Broxbourne, Hertfordshire
Remarks: Commanded Bengal Sappers and Miners 1879-85; Chief Commissioner, Order of St. John of Jerulalem 1893-98; Knight of Grace of the Order
Account of Deed: On 16 Sep. 1857 at Delhi, India, Second Lieutenant Thackeray, extinguished a fire in the Magazine enclosure under close and heavy musketry-fire from the enemy at the imminent risk to his own life from the explosion of combustible stores in the shed in which the fire occurred.

THAMAN GURUNG **1208**
Rifleman   1st Bn., 5th Royal Gurkha Rifles, Indian Army
Other Decorations: —
Date of Gazette: 22 Feb. 1945
Place/Date of Birth: Singla Village, No. 2 Thehsil, West Nepal — 2nd Oct. 1924
Place/Date of Death: Monte San Bartolo, Italy — 11 Nov. 1944
Memorials: Rimini Gurkha War Cemetery, Italy
Town/County Connections: —
Remarks: —
Account of Deed: On 10 Nov. 1944 at Monte San Bartolo, Italy, Rifleman Thaman Gurung was acting as a scout to a fighting patrol. It was undoubtedly due to his superb gallantry that his platoon was able to withdraw from an extremely difficult position without many more casualties than were in fact incurred and that some very valuable information was obtained which resulted in the capture of the feature three days later. The rifleman's bravery cost him his life.

No photograph available

THOMAS, Jacob   1209
Bombardier (later Quartermaster-Sergeant)   Bengal Artillery
Other Decorations: —
Date of Gazette: 24 Dec. 1858
Place/Date of Birth: Llanwinio, Carmarthen, Wales — 1833   *Darjeeling 5.3.1911.?*
Place/Date of Death: ?Hooghly, India — ?24 Apr. 1896   *Darjeeling 5.3.1911.?*
Memorials: —
Town/County Connections: *VC with 55th (The Residency) Field Battery . R.A*
Remarks: —
Account of Deed: On 27 Sep. 1857 at Lucknow, India, a soldier of the Madras Fusiliers, who was with a party returning to the Residency from a sortie, was wounded and in danger of falling into the hands of the enemy. Bombardier Thomas rescued him under heavy fire and under circumstances of considerable difficulty.

THOMAS, John   1210
Lance-Corporal   2/5th Bn., The North Staffordshire Regiment (The Prince of Wales's)
Other Decorations: —
Date of Gazette: 13 Feb. 1918
Place/Date of Birth: Openshaw, Manchester — 10 May 1886
Place/Date of Death: Stockport, Cheshire — 28 Feb. 1954
Memorials: Stockport Borough Cemetery; Garrison Church, Whittington Barracks, Lichfield, Staffordshire
Town/County Connections: Stockport, Cheshire; Openshaw, Manchester
Remarks: —
Account of Deed: On 30 Nov. 1917 at Fontaine, France, Lance-Corporal Thomas saw the enemy making preparations for a counter-attack so with a comrade and on his own initiative decided to make a close reconnaissance. They went off in full view of the enemy and under heavy fire. His comrade was hit almost immediately, but Lance-Corporal Thomas went on alone and finally reached a building used by the enemy as a night post. He was able to see where their troops were congregating and after staying for an hour, sniping the enemy, returned with information of the utmost value, which enabled plans to be made to meet the counter-attack.

THOMPSON, Alexander   1211
Lance-Corporal (later Sergeant)   42nd Regiment (later The Black Watch (Royal Highlanders))
Other Decorations: —
Date of Gazette: 27 May 1859
Place/Date of Birth: Edinburgh — 1824
Place/Date of Death: Perth, Scotland — 29 Mar. 1880
Memorials: —
Town/County Connections: Perth, Scotland
Remarks: —
Account of Deed: On 15 Apr. 1858 during the attack on Fort Ruhya, India, Lance-Corporal Thompson volunteered, with others to assist a captain* in carrying in the body of a lieutenant from the top of the glacis, in a most exposed position under a very heavy fire. (*See also CAFE, W.M. and SPENCE, E.)

THOMPSON, George   1212
Flight Sergeant   9 Squadron, Royal Air Force Volunteer Reserve
Other Decorations: —
Date of Gazette: 20 Feb. 1945
Place/Date of Birth: Trinity Gask, Perthshire, Scotland — 23 Oct. 1920
Place/Date of Death: Belgium — 23 Jan. 1945
Memorials: Brussels Town Cemetery, Evere-Les-Bruxelles, Belgium
Town/County Connections: Perth, Scotland
Remarks: —
Account of Deed: On 1 Jan. 1945 in an attack on the Dortmund-Ems Canal, Germany, a Lancaster bomber, after releasing its bombs, was hit by two shells and raging fire broke out. Flight Sergeant Thompson, wireless operator, seeing that both gun turrets were ablaze, went at once to help the two gunners to a place of relative safety, extinguishing their burning clothing with his bare hands. Then, despite his shocking state of burns and charred clothing, he went through the burning fuselage to report to the pilot. The crippled aircraft finally crash-landed; one of the gunners survived, the other died. Flight Sergeant Thompson died of his injuries three weeks later.

THOMPSON, James   **1213**
Private   1st Bn., 60th Rifles (later The King's Royal Rifle Corps)
Other Decorations: —
Date of Gazette: 20 Jan. 1860
Place/Date of Birth: Yoxall, Burton, Staffordshire — 1830
Place/Date of Death: Walsall, Staffordshire — 5 Dec. 1891
Memorials: Old Cemetery, Walsall
Town/County Connections: Walsall, Staffordshire
Remarks: —
Account of Deed: On 9 Jul. 1857 at Lucknow, India, Private Thompson saved the life of his captain by dashing forward to his relief when that officer was surrounded by a number of the enemy. The private killed two of the assailants before further assistance arrived. He was also commended for conspicuous gallantry throughout the siege. (Elected by the regiment.)

THROSSELL, Hugo Vivian Hope   **1214**
Second Lieutenant (later Captain)   10th Light Horse Regiment, Australian Imperial Force
Other Decorations: —
Date of Gazette: 15 Oct. 1915
Place/Date of Birth: Northam, Western Australia — 27 Oct. 1884
Place/Date of Death: Perth, Western Australia — 19 Nov. 1933
Memorials: Memorial plaque, Greenmount, Western Australia; Australian War Memorial, Canberra
Town/County Connections: —
Remarks: —
Account of Deed: On 29/30 Aug. 1915 at Kaiakij Aghala (Hill 60), Gallipoli, Second Lieutenant Throssell, although severely wounded in several places, refused to leave his post during a counter-attack or to obtain medical assistance until all danger was passed, when he had his wounds dressed and returned to the firing line until ordered out of action by the Medical Officer. By his personal courage and example he kept up the spirits of his party and was largely instrumental in saving the situation at a critical period.

TILSTON, Frederick Albert   **1215**
A/Major   The Essex-Scottish Regiment, Canadian Infantry Corps
Other Decorations: —
Date of Gazette: 22 May 1945
Place/Date of Birth: Toronto, Canada — 11 Jun. 1906
Place/Date of Death: — *Died about 24.9.1992*
Memorials: —
Town/County Connections: —
Remarks: Commander of the Order of St. John of Jerusalem
Account of Deed: On 1 Mar. 1945 in the Hochwald Forest, Germany, Major Tilston, although wounded in the head, led his company in the attack, through a belt of wire 10 feet deep, to the enemy trenches, personally silenced a machine-gun and was the first to reach the enemy position. Pressing on to the second line he was severely wounded in the hip but carried on, his unshakeable confidence and enthusiasm so inspiring his men that they held firm against great odds. Even when wounded for a third time and hardly conscious, he refused medical attention until he had given complete instructions for holding the position.

TISDALL, Arthur Walderne St. Clair   **1216**
Sub-Lieutenant   Royal Naval Volunteer Reserve (Anson Bn., Royal Naval Division)
Other Decorations: —
Date of Gazette: 31 Mar. 1916
Place/Date of Birth: Bombay, India — 21 Jul. 1890
Place/Date of Death: Achi Baba, Gallipoli — 6 May 1915
Memorials: Helles Memorial, Gallipoli; St. George's Churchyard, Deal, Kent
Town/County Connections: Deal, Kent
Remarks: —
Account of Deed: On 25 Apr. 1915 at V Beach, Gallipoli, during the landing from HMS *River Clyde*, Sub-Lieutenant Tisdall, hearing wounded men on the beach calling for help, jumped into the water, and pushing a boat in front of him, went to their rescue. He found, however, that he could not manage alone, but with help from other naval personnel he made four or five trips from the ship to the shore and was responsible for rescuing several wounded men under heavy and accurate fire.

TOLLERTON, Ross   **1217**
Private   1st Bn., The Queen's Own Cameron Highlanders
Other Decorations: —
Date of Gazette: 19 Apr. 1915
Place/Date of Birth: Hurlford, Ayr, Scotland — 6 May 1890
Place/Date of Death: Irvine, Ayrshire — 7 May 1931
Memorials: —
Town/County Connections: Irvine, Ayrshire
Remarks: —
Account of Deed: On 14 Sep. 1914 at the Battle of the Aisne, France, Private Tollerton carried a wounded officer, under heavy fire, as far as he was able, into a place of greater safety. Then, although he himself was wounded in the head and hand, he struggled back to the firing line where he remained until his battalion retired. He then returned to the wounded officer and stayed with him for three days until they were both rescued.

TOMBS, Henry (later Sir Henry)   **1218**
Major (later Major General)   Bengal Horse Artillery
Other Decorations: KCB
Date of Gazette: 24 Apr. 1858
Place/Date of Birth: Calcutta, India — 10 Nov. 1825
Place/Date of Death: Newport, Isle of Wight — 2 Aug. 1874 → *Grave*
Memorials: Carisbrook Cemetery, Isle of Wight; Garrison Church, Woolwich, London
Town/County Connections: Newport, Isle of Wight
Remarks: Commanded Allahabad Division of Army 1871; Regimental Colonel of Artillery 1872
Account of Deed: On 9 Jul. 1857 at the Siege of Delhi, India, Major Tombs twice went to the rescue of one of his junior officers*. On the first occasion one of the enemy was about to kill the young officer with his own sword when Major Tombs rushed in and shot the man. A second attack on the subaltern resulted in his being cut down with a sword wound to the head, and he would undoubtedly have been killed if Major Tombs had not put his sword through the assailant. (*See also HILLS, S)

TOMBS, Joseph Harcourt   **1219**
Lance-Corporal (later Corporal)   1st Bn., The King's (Liverpool) Regiment
Other Decorations: —
Date of Gazette: 24 Jul. 1915
Place/Date of Birth: Melbourne, Victoria, Australia — 1884
Place/Date of Death: Toronto, Canada — 28 Jun. 1966
Memorials: Pine Hill Cemetery, East Toronto
Town/County Connections: Grantham, Lincolnshire
Remarks: —
Account of Deed: On 16 Jun. 1915 near Rue du Bois, France, Lance-Corporal Tombs, on his own initiative, crawled out repeatedly under very heavy shell and machine-gun fire to bring in wounded men who were lying about 100 yards in front of our trenches. He rescued four men, one of whom he dragged back by means of a rifle sling placed round his own neck and the man's body.

TOPHAM, Frederick George   **1220**
Corporal   1st Canadian Parachute Battalion
Other Decorations: —
Date of Gazette: 3 Aug. 1945
Place/Date of Birth: Toronto, Canada — 10 Aug. 1917
Place/Date of Death: Canada — 31 May 1974
Memorials: —
Town/County Connections: —
Remarks: —
Account of Deed: On 24 Mar. 1945 east of the Rhine, North-West Europe, when two medical orderlies had been killed while attending to a wounded man lying in the open, Corporal Topham, on his own initiative, went out and while he was attending to the casualty, was shot through the nose. In spite of his wound he carried on, bringing the wounded man in under continuous fire, and refusing to have medical treatment until all the casualties had been cleared. Later in the day he rescued three men from a carrier which had been hit, regardless of the fact that the carrier's own ammunition was exploding.

TOWERS, James   **1221**
Private   2nd Bn., The Cameronians (Scottish Rifles)
Other Decorations: —
Date of Gazette: 6 Jan. 1919
Place/Date of Birth: Broughton, Preston, Lancashire — 9 Sep. 1897
Place/Date of Death: Preston, Lancashire — 24 Jan. 1977
Memorials: —
Town/County Connections: Broughton, Lancashire
Remarks: —
Account of Deed: On 6 Oct. 1918 at Mericourt, France, when five runners had failed to deliver an important message, Private Towers, while aware of the fate of those who had already attempted the task, volunteered for the duty. In spite of heavy fire opened on him as soon as he moved, he went straight through from cover to cover and eventually delivered the message. His determination and disregard of danger was an inspiring example.

TOWNER, Edgar Thomas   **1222**
Lieutenant (later Major)   2nd Bn., Australian Machine-Gun Corps
Other Decorations: MC
Date of Gazette: 14 Dec. 1918
Place/Date of Birth: Glencoe Station, Queensland, Australia — 19 Apr. 1890
Place/Date of Death: Australia — 18 Aug. 1972
Memorials: Longreach Town Cemetery, Queensland; Australian War Memorial, Canberra
Town/County Connections: —
Remarks: Croix de Guerre (France); Fellow of the Royal Geographical Society (Australia); Fellow of the Royal Historical Society (New South Wales)
Account of Deed: On 1 Sep. 1918 at Mont St. Quentin, near Peronne, France, Lieutenant Towner located and captured single-handed an enemy machine-gun, turning it on the enemy and inflicting heavy losses. Subsequently he captured 25 prisoners. Later, by fearless reconnaissance under heavy fire he gave valuable support to the infantry advance. Again when short of ammunition he secured an enemy machine-gun which he fired in full view of the enemy, making them retreat, and although wounded and under intense fire, he kept on firing. Throughout the night he kept close watch on enemy movements and was finally evacuated 30 hours after being wounded.

TOWSE, Ernest Beachcroft Beckwith (later Sir Ernest)   **1223**
Captain   1st Bn., The Gordon Highlanders
Other Decorations: CBE
Date of Gazette: 6 Jul. 1900
Place/Date of Birth: Regents Park, London — 23 Apr. 1864
Place/Date of Death: Goring-on-Thames, Berkshire — 21 Jun. 1948
Memorials: — Wellington College, Berks
Town/County Connections: London; Goring-on-Thames, Berkshire
Remarks: Served in the First World War 1914-18 (as Hon. Staff Captain for Base Hospitals); Sergeant-at-Arms in Ordinary to The King 1901; Hon. Corps of Gentlemen-at-Arms 1903-39; Knight of the Order of St. John.
Account of Deed: On 11 Dec. 1899 at Magersfontein, South Africa, during a retirement, Captain Towse helped a mortally wounded colonel and although close to the front of the firing line, supported him until help arrived. On 30 Apr. 1900 Captain Towse and 12 men confronted a party of about 150 Boers on the top of Mount Thaba, far from any support. The greatly outnumbered group were called on to surrender, but the captain ordered his men to open fire and remained firing himself until he was severely wounded (both eyes shattered) and they succeeded in driving off the enemy.

TOYE, Alfred Maurice   **1224**
A/Captain (later Brigadier)   2nd Bn., The Middlesex Regiment (Duke of Cambridge's Own)
Other Decorations: MC
Date of Gazette: 8 May 1918
Place/Date of Birth: Aldershot, Hampshire — 15 Apr. 1897
Place/Date of Death: Tiverton, Devon — 6 Sep. 1955
Memorials: —
Town/County Connections: Aldershot, Hampshire; Tiverton, Devon
Remarks: Assistant Commandant and Chief Instructor, Royal Egyptian Military College, Cairo 1925-35; Commandant War Office Schools of Chemical Warfare 1940-42; commanded 6th Airborne Division 1943-44; served at GHQ Middle East 1945-48; Commandant Home Office Civil Defence School 1949 until retirement.
Account of Deed: On 25 Mar. 1918 at Eterpigny Ridge, France, Captain Toye displayed conspicuous bravery and fine leadership. He three times re-established a post which had been captured by the enemy and when his three other posts were cut off he fought his way through the enemy with one officer and six men. He counter-attacked with 70 men and took up a line which he maintained until reinforcements arrived. In two subsequent operations he covered the retirement of his battalion and later re-established a line that had been abandoned before his arrival. He was twice wounded but remained on duty.

TRAIN, Charles William   **1225**
Corporal (later Sergeant)   2/14th (County of London) Bn., The London Regt. (London Scottish)
Other Decorations: —
Date of Gazette: 27 Feb. 1918
Place/Date of Birth: Finsbury Park, London — 21 Sep. 1890
Place/Date of Death: Vancouver, British Columbia, Canada — 28 Mar. 1965
Memorials: Field of Honour, Forest Lawn Memorial Park, Burnaby, British Columbia, Canada
Town/County Connections: Finsbury Park, London
Remarks: —
Account of Deed: On 8 Dec. 1917 at Air Karim, near Jerusalem, when his company was unexpectedly engaged at close range by a party of the enemy with two machine-guns and brought to a standstill, Corporal Train on his own initiative rushed forward and engaged the enemy with rifle grenades and succeeded in putting some of the team out of action by a direct hit. He shot and wounded an officer and killed or wounded the remainder of the team. After this he went to the assistance of a comrade who was bombing the enemy from the front and killed one of them who was carrying the second machine-gun out of action.

TRAVERS, James   **1226**
Colonel (later General)   2nd Bengal Native Infantry
Other Decorations: CB
Date of Gazette: 1 Mar. 1861
Place/Date of Birth: Cork, Ireland — 6 Oct. 1820
Place/Date of Death: India — 1 Apr. 1884
Memorials: —
Town/County Connections: —
Remarks: Commanded Central India Horse 1861; Brigadier-General commanding Sangor District 1865; commanded Mirat Division 1869.
Account of Deed: In July 1857 when the Presidency at Indore, India, was suddenly attacked by the enemy, Colonel Travers charged the guns with only five men to support him, and drove the gunners from the guns. This created a diverson so that many of the Europeans who were fugitives to the Residency were able to escape from slaughter. Time was also gained for the faithful Bhopal Infantry to man their guns.

TRAVIS (real name SAVAGE), Richard Charles (real names Dickson Cornelius)   **1227**
Sergeant   2nd Bn., Otago Infantry Regiment, N.Z.E.F.
Other Decorations: DCM, MM
Date of Gazette: 27 Sep. 1918
Place/Date of Birth: Otara, Opotiki, Southland, New Zealand — 6 Apr. 1884
Place/Date of Death: Rossignol Wood, France — 25 Jul. 1918
Memorials: Couin New British Cemetery, France; HQ Dunedin RSA, New Zealand
Town/County Connections: —
Remarks: —
Account of Deed: On 24 Jul. 1918 at Rossignol Wood, north of Hebuterne, France, it was necessary to destroy an impassible wire block and Sergeant Travis volunteered for this duty. In broad daylight and in close proximity to enemy posts he crawled out, successfully bombing the block and the attacking parties were able to pass through. A little later when a bombing party was held up by machine-guns Sergeant Travis rushed the position, capturing the guns and killing the crew, also an officer and three men who attacked him, thus enabling the bombing party to advance. He was killed next day while going from post to post encouraging his men.

TRAYNOR, William Bernard   **1228**
Sergeant   2nd Bn., The West Yorkshire Regiment (The Prince of Wales's Own)
Other Decorations: —
Date of Gazette: 17 Sep. 1901
Place/Date of Birth: Hull, Yorkshire — 31 Dec. 1870
Place/Date of Death: Dover, Kent — 20 Oct. 1956
Memorials: Charlton Cemetery, Kent
Town/County Connections: Hull, Yorkshire; Dover, Kent
Remarks: Served as Barrack Warden at Dover during First World War.
Account of Deed: On 6 Feb. 1901 at Bothwell Camp, South Africa, during a night attack, Sergeant Traynor ran out of a trench, under extremely heavy fire, to help a wounded man. While running he was wounded, and being unable to carry the man himself, called for assistance. A lance-corporal came to him and between them they carried the wounded soldier into shelter. Afterwards, in spite of his wounds, Sergeant Traynor remained in command of his section, encouraging his men until the attack failed.

TRENT, Leonard Henry   **1229**
Squadron Leader (later Group Captain)   Royal New Zealand Air Force, serving with 487
Squadron, Royal Air Force
Other Decorations: DFC
Date of Gazette: 1 Mar. 1946
Place/Date of Birth: Nelson, New Zealand — 14 Apr. 1915
Place/Date of Death: Auckland, New Zealand — 18 May 1986
Memorials: HQ, Dunedin RSA, New Zealand
Town/County Connections: —
Remarks: Transferred to Royal Air Force after the war; ADC to The Queen 1962-65
Account of Deed: On 3 May 1943 during a daylight raid on Amsterdam power station, Squadron
Leader Trent's force of 11 Venturas was attacked by very large numbers of enemy fighters and by the time they reached the
target he was left with only two accompanying aircraft, one of which was shot down as they approached and when his own
bombs had been released the second one had also disappeared. Immediately afterwards his own aircraft was hit, went into a
spin and broke up. Squadron Leader Trent and his navigator were thrown clear and became prisoners. He had displayed cool,
unflinching courage in the face of overwhelming odds.

TREVOR, William Spottiswoode   **1230**
Major (later Major General)   Bengal Engineers, Indian Army
Other Decorations: —
Date of Gazette: 31 Dec. 1867
Place/Date of Birth: India — 9 Oct. 1831
Place/Date of Death: London — 2 Nov. 1907
Memorials: Kensal Green Cemetery, London
Town/County Connections: London
Remarks: Held appointments in India: Provincial Chief Engineer, Director-General of Railways,
Secretary to Government of India.
Account of Deed: On 30 Apr. 1865 at Dewan-Giri, Bhootan, India, a number of the enemy, about
200 strong, had barricaded themselves in the blockhouse, which they continued to defend after the main body was in retreat.
The blockhouse, which was loopholed, was the key of the enemy's position and on the orders of the general in command, Major
Trevor and another officer* had to climb a 14ft. wall and then go head first through an opening only 2 feet wide. The two officers
scaled the wall, followed, after they had set the example, by the Sikh soldiers, but they were both wounded. (*See also
DUNDAS, J.)

TREWAVAS, Joseph   **1231**
Seaman (later Able Seaman)   Royal Navy
Other Decorations: CGM
Date of Gazette: 24 Feb. 1857
Place/Date of Birth: Mousehole, Cornwall — 14 Dec. 1835
Place/Date of Death: Mousehole, Cornwall — 20 Jul. 1905
Memorials: —
Town/County Connections: Mousehole, Cornwall
Remarks: —
Account of Deed: On 3 Jul. 1855 in the Straits of Genitchi, Sea of Azov in the Crimea, Seaman
Trewavas of HMS *Beagle* was sent in a 4-oared gig to destroy a bridge, and so cut the Russian's
main supply route. This was the third attempt, the first two having failed. As the gig ground against the bridge, Seaman
Trewavas leapt out with an axe and began to hew away at the hawsers holding the pontoons together, and although the enemy
kept up a heavy fire, particularly on Trewavas himself, he continued until his task was completed, and the two severed ends of
the pontoon began to drift apart. He was wounded as he got back into the gig.

TRIGG, Lloyd Allan   **1232**
Flying Officer   Royal New Zealand Air Force, serving with 200 Squadron, Royal Air Force
Other Decorations: DFC
Date of Gazette: 2 Nov. 1943
Place/Date of Birth: Houhora, New Zealand — 5 Jun. 1914
Place/Date of Death: Atlantic, West of West Africa — 11 Aug. 1943
Memorials: The Malta Memorial, Malta, GC; HQ, Dunedin RSA, New Zealand
Town/County Connections: —
Remarks: —
Account of Deed: On 11 Aug. 1943 while on sea patrol in the Atlantic, Flying Officer Trigg sighted
a surfaced U-boat which he immediately prepared to attack. During the approach, his aircraft
received many hits from the submarine's anti-aircraft guns and was set on fire. The flying officer nevertheless continued his
attack, diving to less than 50 feet and dropping his bombs with great accuracy. The crippled aircraft, with its crew, then crashed
into the sea and the U-boat sank within 10 minutes.

TRIQUET, Paul   1233
Captain (later Major)   Royal 22e Regiment, Canadian Army
Other Decorations: —
Date of Gazette: 6 Mar. 1944
Place/Date of Birth: Cabano, Quebec, Canada — 2 Apr. 1910
Place/Date of Death: Quebec City — 4 Aug. 1980
Memorials: —
Town/County Connections: —
Remarks: Commanded 8th Militia Group 1954-59; Hon. ADC to Governor-General of Quebec;
Provincial Commissioner, St. John Ambulance Corps; President L'Association du 22e Inc.
Account of Deed: On 14 Dec. 1943 during the attack on Casa Berardi, Italy, when all the other
officers and half the men of his company had been killed or wounded, Captain Triquet dashed forward and, with the remaining
men, broke through the enemy resistance. He then forced his way on with his small force — now reduced to two sergeants and
15 men — into a position on the outskirts of Casa Berardi. They held out against attacks from overwhelming numbers until the
remainder of the battalion relieved them next day. Throughout the action Captain Triquet's utter disregard for danger and his
cheerful encouragement were an inspiration to his men.

TUBB, Frederick Harold   1234
Lieutenant (later Major)   7th Bn. (Victoria), Australian Imperial Force
Other Decorations: —
Date of Gazette: 15 Oct. 1915
Place/Date of Birth: St. Helena, Longwood, Victoria, Australia — 28 Nov. 1881
Place/Date of Death: Polygon Wood, Ypres, 20 Sep. 1917
Memorials: Lijssenthoek Military Cemetery, Belgium; Australian War Memorial, Canberra
Town/County Connections: —
Remarks: —
Account of Deed: On 9 Aug. 1915 at Lone Pine, Gallipoli, Lieutenant Tubb held a newly captured
trench which was being counter-attacked by the enemy. They blew in a sand-bag barricade,
leaving only a foot of it standing, but Lieutenant Tubb led his men back, repulsed the enemy and rebuilt the barricade. Twice
more the enemy blew in the barricade, but on each occasion this officer, although wounded in the head and arm, held his
ground and assisted by two corporals*, rebuilt it. They succeeded in maintaining the position under very heavy fire. (*See also
BURTON, A.S. and DUNSTAN, W.)

TULBAHADUR PUN   1235
Rifleman (later Warrant Officer Class 1)   3rd Bn., 6th Gurkha Rifles, Indian Army
Other Decorations: —
Date of Gazette: 9 Nov. 1944
Place/Date of Birth: Banduk Village, Parbat District, Nepal — 23 Mar. 1923
Place/Date of Death: —
Memorials: —
Town/County Connections: —
Remarks: —
Account of Deed: On 23 Jun. 1944 at Mogaung, Burma, during an attack on the railway bridge,
a section of one of the platoons was wiped out with the exception of Rifleman Tulbahadur Pun, his
section commander and one other. The section commander immediately led a charge on the enemy position but was at once
badly wounded, as was the third man. Rifleman Tulbahadur Pun, with a Bren gun continued the charge alone in the face of
shattering fire and reaching the position, killed three of the occupants and put five more to flight, capturing two light machine-
guns and much ammunition. He then gave accurate supporting fire, enabling the rest of his platoon to reach their objective.

TURNBULL, James Youll   1236
Sergeant   17th Bn., The Highland Light Infantry
Other Decorations: —
Date of Gazette: 25 Nov. 1916
Place/Date of Birth: Glasgow — 24 Dec. 1883
Place/Date of Death: Authuille, France — 1 Jul. 1916
Memorials: Lonsdale Cemetery, France
Town/County Connections: Glasgow; Oban, Argyllshire, Scotland
Remarks: —
Account of Deed: On 1 Jul. 1916 at Leipzig Salient, Authuille, France, Sergeant Turnbull's party
captured a post of apparent importance to the enemy who immediately began heavy counter-
attacks which were continued throughout the day. Although his party was wiped out and replaced several times, Sergeant
Turnbull never wavered in his determination to hold the post, the loss of which would have been very serious. Almost single-
handed he maintained his position, displaying the highest degree of valour and skill in the performance of his duty. Later in the
day he was killed while engaged in a bombing counter-attack.

TURNER, Alexander Buller   **1237**

Second Lieutenant   3rd Bn., The Royal Berkshire Regt. (Princess Charlotte of Wales's), attd. 1st Bn.
Other Decorations: —
Date of Gazette: 18 Nov. 1915
Place/Date of Birth: Reading, Berkshire — 22 May 1893
Place/Date of Death: Near Chocques, France — 1 Oct. 1915
Memorials: Chocques Military Cemetery, France
Town/County Connections: —
Remarks: Brother of Lieutenant Colonel V.B. Turner, VC; Family connection with General Sir Redvers Buller, VC
Account of Deed: On 28 Sep. 1915 at Fosse 8, near Vermelles, France, when the regimental bombers could make no headway, Second Lieutenant Turner volunteered to lead a new bombing attack. He made his way down the communication trench practically alone, throwing bombs incessantly with such dash and determination that he drove off the Germans about 150 yards without a check. His action enabled the reserves to advance with very little loss and subsequently covered the flank of his regiment in its retirement, thus probably averting the loss of some hundreds of men. Second Lieutenant Turner died of the wounds received in this action.

TURNER, Hanson Victor   **1238**

A/Sergeant   1st Bn., The West Yorkshire Regiment (The Prince of Wales's Own)
Other Decorations: —
Date of Gazette: 17 Aug. 1944
Place/Date of Birth: Andover, Hampshire — 17 Jul. 1910
Place/Date of Death: Ningthoukong, Burma — 7 Jun. 1944
Memorials: Imphal War Cemetery, India
Town/County Connections: Ormesby and Halifax, Yorkshire
Remarks: —
Account of Deed: On 6/7 Jun. 1944 at Ninthoukhong, Burma, when Sergeant Turner's platoon was obliged to give ground before strong enemy forces, he reorganised his party and withdrew 40 yards. Although the enemy tried repeatedly to dislodge them, they held the position throughout the night, repelling all attacks. Next day Sergeant Turner decided to take the initiative in driving the enemy off and went forward alone, armed with grenades which he used with devastating effect. When his supply was exhausted he went back for more — five times he did this and it was on the sixth occasion that he was killed while throwing a grenade.

TURNER, Richard Ernest William (later Sir Richard)   **1239**

Lieutenant (later Lieutenant General)   Royal Canadian Dragoons
Other Decorations: KCB, KCMG, DSO
Date of Gazette: 23 Apr. 1901
Place/Date of Birth: Quebec, Canada — 25 Jul. 1871
Place/Date of Death: Quebec, Canada — 29 Jun. 1961
Memorials: Mount Hermon Cemetery, Sillery, Quebec City
Town/County Connections: —
Remarks: Légion d'Honneur and Croix de Guerre avec Palme (France); Order of White Eagle with Swords (Russia); served in First World War; commanded Canadian Brigade of Infantry and 2nd Canadian Division; GOC Canadian Forces in England 1916-18
Account of Deed: On 7 Nov. 1900 during the action at Komati River, South Africa, when the guns were in danger of being captured, Lieutenant Turner, although he had already been twice wounded, dismounted and deployed his men at close quarters and drove off the enemy, thus saving the guns.

No photograph available

TURNER, Samuel   **1240**

Private   1st Bn., 60th Rifles (later The King's Royal Rifle Corps)
Other Decorations: —
Date of Gazette: 20 Jan. 1860
Place/Date of Birth: Witnesham, Ipswich, Suffolk — Feb. 1826
Place/Date of Death: Meerut, India — 13 Jun. 1868
Memorials: —
Town/County Connections: Witnesham, Ipswich, Suffolk
Remarks: —
Account of Deed: On 19 Jun. 1857 at Delhi, India, during a severe conflict with the enemy at night, Private Turner carried off on his shoulder, under heavy fire, a mortally wounded officer of the Indian Service. Private Turner himself was wounded by a sabre-cut in the right arm. His gallant conduct saved the officer from the fate of others, whose mangled remains were not recovered until the following day.

TURNER, Victor Buller   **1241**
T/Lieutenant Colonel   The Rifle Brigade (Prince Consort's Own)
Other Decorations: CVO
Date of Gazette: 20 Nov. 1942
Place/Date of Birth: Thatcham, near Newbury, Berkshire — 17 Jan. 1900
Place/Date of Death: Ditchingham, near Bungay, Suffolk — 7 Aug. 1972
Memorials: (Cremated at Horsham St. Faith, Norfolk); The Rifle Brigade Memorial, Winchester
Cathedral
Town/County Connections: Thatcham, Newbury, Berkshire; Bungay, Suffolk
Remarks: Brother of Second Lieut. A.B. Turner, VC; family connection with General Sir Redvers
Buller, VC; Served with Yeomen of the Guard 1950-67; Lieut. of H.M. Body Guard 1967-70.
Account of Deed: On 27 Oct. 1942, at El Aqqaqir (Kidney Ridge), Western Desert, Lieutenant Colonel Turner was commanding
a battalion of the Rifle Brigade. After overcoming a German position, the battalion fought off desperate counter-attacks by 90
tanks, destroying or immobilising more than 50 of them. During the action, one of the 6-pounder guns was left with only one
officer and a sergeant, so Colonel Turner joined them as loader, and between them they destroyed another five tanks. Not until
the last tank had been repulsed did he consent to having a wound in his head attended to.

TURRALL, Thomas George   **1242**
Private   10th Bn., The Worcestershire Regiment
Other Decorations: —
Date of Gazette: 9 Sep. 1916
Place/Date of Birth: Hay Mills, Birmingham — 5 Jul. 1885
Place/Date of Death: Birmingham — 21 Feb. 1964
Memorials: —
Town/County Connections: Birmingham
Remarks: —
Account of Deed: On 3 Jul. 1916 at La Boiselle, France, during a bombing attack by a small party
against the enemy, the officer in charge was badly wounded and the party was compelled
eventually to retire. Private Turrall remained with the wounded officer for three hours under continuous and heavy fire from
machine-guns and bombs. Notwithstanding that both he and the officer were at one time completely cut off from our troops,
he held his ground with determination and finally carried the officer to our lines after a counter-attack had made this possible.

TYTLER, John Adam   **1243**
Lieutenant (later Brigadier General)   66th Bengal Native Infantry (later 1st Gurkha Rifles)
Other Decorations: CB
Date of Gazette: 23 Aug. 1858
Place/Date of Birth: Monghyr, Bengal, India — 29 Oct. 1835
Place/Date of Death: Thal, Kurram Valley, North-west Frontier — 14 Feb. 1880
Memorials: —
Town/County Connections: —
Remarks: —
Account of Deed: On 10 Feb. 1858 at Choorpoorah, India, when the attacking parties were
experiencing heavy fire of round shot, grape and musketry, Lieutenant Tytler dashed on
horseback, alone, up to the enemy's guns where he engaged in hand-to-hand combat until the guns were taken. He was
wounded three times during the encounter.

UMRAO SINGH   **1244**
Havildar (later Subadar-Major)   Royal Indian Artillery
Other Decorations: —
Date of Gazette: 31 May 1945
Place/Date of Birth: Palra Village, Jrajur, Rhotak, Punjab — 11 Jul. 1920
Place/Date of Death: —   *Died 22.11.2005 probaldy in his home vil*
Memorials: —   *of Palra in the Punjab.*
Town/County Connections: —
Remarks: —
Account of Deed: On 15/16 Dec. 1944 in the Kaladan Valley, Burma, Havildar Umrao Singh, who
was in charge of a gun in an advanced section of his battery, repeatedly beat off enemy attacks.
In the final assault on the objective he struck down three of the enemy in hand-to-hand fighting and later, when found exhausted
and wounded beside his gun there were 10 of the enemy lying dead around him. The gun was still in working order and was in
action again that day.

UNWIN Edward
1245

Commander (later Captain)   Royal Navy
Other Decorations: CB, CMG
Date of Gazette: 16 Aug. 1915
Place/Date of Birth: Fawley, Hythe, Hampshire — 17 Mar. 1864
Place/Date of Death: Hindhead, Surrey — 10 Apr. 1950
Memorials: Buried at Grayshott, Surrey
Town/County Connections: Hythe, Hampshire; Hindhead, Surrey; Ashbourne, Derbyshire
Remarks: Order of the Nile (Egypt)
Account of Deed: On 25 Apr. 1915 during the landing at V Beach, Cape Helles, Gallipoli, Commander Unwin of HMS *River Clyde* left the ship and under murderous fire attempted, with the help of four other men* to get the lighters into position. He worked until, suffering from the effects of cold and immersion he was obliged to return to the ship for treatment. He then returned to his work against the doctor's orders and completed it. He was later attended by the doctor for three wounds, but once more left the ship, this time in a life-boat, and rescued three men, wounded, in the shallow water. (*See also DREWRY, G.L., MALLESON, W. St. A., SAMSON, G.M. and WILLIAMS, W.C.)

UPHAM, Charles Hazlitt
1246

Second Lieutenant (later Captain)   20th Bn., 2nd N.Z.E.F. (The Canterbury Regiment)
Other Decorations: —
Date of Gazette: 14 Oct. 1941 and BAR 26 Sep. 1945
Place/Date of Birth: Christchurch, New Zealand — 21 Sep. 1908
Place/Date of Death: — *Died about 23.11.1994 probably in N.Z.*
Memorials: HQ, Dunedin RSA, New Zealand
Town/County Connections: —
Remarks: Family connection with Captain N.G. Chavasse, VC & Bar, MC.
Account of Deed: Between 22 and 30 May 1941 in Crete, Second Lieutenant Upham displayed outstanding leadership and courage in the very close-quarter fighting. He was blown up by one mortar shell and badly wounded by another. He was also wounded in the foot, but in spite of his wounds and a severe attack of dysentery, he refused to go to hospital. He carried a wounded man back to safety when his company was forced to retire on 22 May and on 30 May he beat off an attack at Sphakia, 22 Germans falling to his short-range fire.

BAR: On 14/15 Jul. 1942 at El Ruweisat Ridge, Western Desert, Captain Upham, in spite of being twice wounded, insisted on remaining with his men. Just before dawn he led his company in a determined attack, capturing the objective after fierce fighting; he himself destroyed a German tank and several guns and vehicles with hand grenades. Although his arm had been broken by a machine-gun bullet, he continued to dominate the situation and when at last, weak from loss of blood, he had his wounds dressed, he immediately returned to his men, remaining with them until he was again severely wounded and unable to move.

UPTON, James
1247

Corporal   1st Bn., The Sherwood Foresters (The Nottinghamshire and Derbyshire Regiment)
Other Decorations: —
Date of Gazette: 29 Jun. 1915
Place/Date of Birth: Lincoln — 3 May 1888
Place/Date of Death: Uxbridge, Middlesex — 10 Aug. 1949
Memorials: —
Town/County Connections: Lincoln; Nottingham; Uxbridge, Middlesex
Remarks: —
Account of Deed: On 9 May 1915 at Rouges Bancs, France, Corporal Upton displayed great courage all day in rescuing the wounded while exposed to very heavy rifle and artillery fire, going close to the enemy's parapet regardless of his own safety. One wounded man was killed by a shell while the corporal was carrying him. When not actually carrying the wounded he was engaged in dressing and bandaging the serious cases in front of our parapet.

VALLENTIN, John Franks
1248

Captain   1st Bn., The South Staffordshire Regiment
Other Decorations: —
Date of Gazette: 18 Feb. 1915
Place/Date of Birth: Lambeth, London — 14 May 1882
Place/Date of Death: Zillebeke, Belgium — 7 Nov. 1914
Memorials: Menin Gate Memorial, Belgium; St. Leonard's Parish Church, Hythe, Kent; Garrison Church, Whittington Barracks, Lichfield, Staffordshire
Town/County Connections: Lambeth, London; Hythe, Kent
Remarks: — *Wellington College, Berks.*
Account of Deed: On 7 Nov. 1914 at Zillebeke, Belgium, when leading an attack against the Germans under very heavy fire, Captain Vallentin was struck down and on rising to continue the attack, was immediately killed. The capture of the enemy's trenches which immediately followed was in a great measure due to the confidence which the men had in their captain, arising from his many previous acts of great bravery and ability.

VANN, Bernard William   **1249**

A/Lieutenant Colonel   1/8th Bn., The Sherwood Foresters (The Nottinghamshire and Derbyshire Regiment), comd. 1/6th Bn.
Other Decorations: MC & Bar
Date of Gazette: 14 Dec. 1918
Place/Date of Birth: Rushden Northamptonshire — 9 Jul. 1887
Place/Date of Death: Rammicourt, France — 3 Oct. 1918
Memorials: Bellicourt British Cemetery, France
Town/County Connections: —
Remarks: Croix de Guerre avec Palme (France)
Account of Deed: On 29 Sep. 1918 at Bellenglise and Lehaucourt, France, Lieutenant Colonel Vann led his battalion with great skill across the Canal du Nord through a very thick fog and under heavy fire. When the attack was held up by fire of all descriptions from the front and right flank, the colonel, realising the importance of the advance going forward with the barrage, rushed up to the firing line and led the line forward himself. Later he rushed a field gun single-handed and knocked out three of the detachment. He was killed four days later leading his battalion in attack.

VEALE, Theodore William Henry   **1250**

Private (later Corporal)   8th Bn., The Devonshire Regiment
Other Decorations: —
Date of Gazette: 9 Sep. 1916
Place/Date of Birth: Dartmouth, Devon — 11 Nov. 1892
Place/Date of Death: Hoddesdon, Hertfordshire — 6 Nov. 1980
Memorials: —
Town/County Connections: Dartmouth, Devon; Hoddesdon, Hertfordshire
Remarks: —
Account of Deed: On 20 Jul. 1916 east of High Wood, France, Private Veale, hearing that a wounded officer was lying in the open within 50 yards of the enemy, went out and dragged him into a shell hole and then took him water. As he could not carry the officer by himself, he fetched volunteers, one of whom was killed almost at once, and heavy fire necessitated leaving the wounded man in a shell hole until dusk when Private Veale went out again with volunteers. When an enemy patrol approached, he went back for a Lewis gun with which he covered the party while the officer was carried to safety.

VICKERS, Arthur   **1251**

Private (later Sergeant)   2nd Bn., The Royal Warwickshire Regiment
Other Decorations: —
Date of Gazette: 18 Nov. 1915
Place/Date of Birth: Aston, Birmingham — 2 Feb. 1882
Place/Date of Death: Birmingham — 27 Jul. 1944
Memorials: —
Town/County Connections: Birmingham
Remarks: —
Account of Deed: On 25 Sep. 1915 at Hulloch, France, during an attack by his battalion on the first line German trenches, Private Vickers on his own initiative, went forward in front of his company under very heavy shell, rifle and machine-gun fire and cut the wires which were holding up a great part of his battalion. Although it was broad daylight at the time, he carried out this work standing up and his gallant action contributed largely to the success of the assault.

VICKERS, Charles Geoffrey (later Sir Geoffrey)   **1252**

T/Captain (later Colonel)   1/7th Bn., The Sherwood Foresters (The Nottinghamshire and Derbyshire Regiment)
Other Decorations: —
Date of Gazette: 18 Nov. 1915
Place/Date of Birth: Nottingham — 13 Oct. 1894
Place/Date of Death: Goring-on-Thames, Oxfordshire — 16 Mar. 1982
Memorials: —
Town/County Connections: Nottingham; Leicester; Rugby, Warwickshire; Aston, Birmingham
Remarks: Croix de Guerre (Belgium); U.S. Medal of Freedom; served in the Second World War; Deputy Director-General, Ministry of Economic Warfare (and member Joint Intelligence Committee of Chiefs of Staff 1941-45); legal adviser to National Coal Board 1946-48; Board member in charge of manpower, training, education, health and welfare 1948-55; Council, Law Society 1944-48; Medical Research Council 1952-60; Chairman, Research Committee of Mental Health Research Fund 1951-67.
Account of Deed: On 14 Oct. 1915 at the Hohenzollern Redoubt, France, when nearly all his men had been either killed or wounded and there were only two men available to hand him bombs, Captain Vickers held a barrier for some hours against heavy German bomb attacks. Regardless of the fact that his own retreat would be cut off, he ordered a second barrier to be built behind him in order to secure the safety of the trench. Finally he was severely wounded, but not before his courage and determination had enabled the second barrier to be completed.

VICKERY, Samuel   **1253**
Private (later Corporal)   1st. Bn., The Dorsetshire Regiment
Other Decorations: —
Date of Gazette: 20 May 1898
Place/Date of Birth: Wambrook, Chard, Somerset — 6 Feb. 1873
Place/Date of Death: Cardiff —20 Jun. 1952
Memorials: —
Town/County Connections: Wambrook, Chard, Somerset; Cardiff
Remarks: —
Account of Deed: On 20 Oct. 1897 during the attack on the Dargai Heights, Tirah, India, Private Vickery ran down the slope and rescued a wounded comrade under heavy fire, bringing him back to cover. He subsequently distinguished himself in the Waran Valley, killing three of the enemy who attacked him when he was separated from his company.

VOUSDEN, William John   **1254**
Captain (later Major General)   5th Punjab Cavalry and Bengal Staff Corps, Indian Army
Other Decorations: CB
Date of Gazette: 18 Oct. 1881
Place/Date of Birth: Perth, Scotland — 20 Sep. 1845
Place/Date of Death: Lahore, India — 12 Nov. 1902
Memorials: —
Town/County Connections: Perth, Scotland
Remarks: Commanded Punjab Frontier Force 1901-2
Account of Deed: On 14 Dec. 1879 on the Asmai Heights, near Kabul, (Afghan War), Captain Vousden charged with a small party into the centre of the line of the retreating Kohistani Force, by whom they were greatly outnumbered. After rapidly charging through and through the enemy backwards and forwards several times, Captain Vousden and his party swept off round the opposite side of the village and joined the rest of the troops.

WADESON, Richard   **1255**
Lieutenant (later Colonel)   75th Regiment (later The Gordon Highlanders)
Other Decorations: —
Date of Gazette: 24 Dec. 1858
Place/Date of Birth: Lancaster — 31 Jul. 1826
Place/Date of Death: Chelsea, London — 24 Jan. 1885
Memorials: Brompton Cemetery, London; Royal Hospital, Chelsea
Town/County Connections: Chelsea, London
Remarks: Lieutenant-Governor of the Royal Hospital, Chelsea 1881-5
Account of Deed: On 18 Jul. 1857 at Delhi, India, when the regiment was engaged in the Subjee Mundee, Lieutenant Wadeson saved the life of a private when he was being attacked by a sowar of the enemy's cavalry. Also, on the same day he rescued another private of the regiment when he was wounded and helpless, and being attacked by a cavalry sowar. In both cases Lieutenant Wadeson killed the sowars who were attacking the privates.

WAIN, Richard William Leslie   **1256**
A/Captain   'A' Bn., Tank Corps
Other Decorations: —
Date of Gazette: 13 Feb. 1918
Place/Date of Birth: Penarth, Glamorganshire, Wales — 5 Dec. 1896
Place/Date of Death: Marcoing, France — 20 Nov. 1917
Memorials: Cambrai Memorial, France; Llandaff Cathedral, South Wales
Town/County Connections: Penarth, Glamorganshire
Remarks: —
Account of Deed: On 20 Nov. 1917 at Marcoing, near Cambrai, France, Captain Wain and one man were the only survivors when his tank was disabled by a direct hit near an enemy strong point which was holding up the attack. Although bleeding profusely, Captain Wain refused the attention of the stretcher bearers, rushed from behind the tank with a Lewis gun and captured the strong point, taking about half the garrison prisoners. Despite his severe wounds he then picked up a rifle and continued to fire at the enemy until he received a fatal wound in the head.

WAKEFORD, Richard   1257

T/Captain   (later Major)   2/4th Bn., The Hampshire Regiment (now The Royal Hampshire Regt.)
Other Decorations: —
Date of Gazette: 13 Jul. 1944
Place/Date of Birth: London — 23 Jul. 1921
Place/Date of Death: Leatherhead, Surrey — 27 Aug. 1972
Memorials: —
Town/County Connections: London (Fulham and Kensington)
Remarks: Appointed a Master of the Chancery Division of the Supreme Court 1964.
Account of Deed: On 13 May 1944 near Cassino, Italy, Captain Wakeford, accompanied only by his orderly and armed with a revolver, went forward and killed several of the enemy and took 20 prisoners. When attacking a hill feature the following day his company came under heavy fire, but although wounded in the face and both arms, Captain Wakeford pressed home the attack. He was wounded again, but reached the objective and consolidated the position.

WAKENSHAW, Adam Herbert   1258

Private   9th Bn., The Durham Light Infantry
Other Decorations: —
Date of Gazette: 11 Sep. 1942
Place/Date of Birth: Newcastle upon Tyne, Northumberland — 9 Jun. 1914
Place/Date of Death: Mersa Matruh, Egypt — 27 Jun. 1942
Memorials: El Alamein War Cemetery, Egypt
Town/County Connections: Newcastle upon Tyne, Northumberland
Remarks: —
Account of Deed: On 27 Jun. 1942 south of Mersa Matruh, Western Desert, Private Wakenshaw was a member of a crew of a 2-pounder anti-tank gun, when the enemy attacked, silencing the gun and killing or seriously wounding all the crew. Private Wakenshaw's left arm was blown off but he crawled back to his gun, loaded it with one arm and fired five more rounds with considerable effect. He was then blown away from the gun by an enemy shell and was again severely wounded, but he still managed to crawl back and was preparing to fire again when a direct hit on the ammunition killed him and destroyed the gun.

WALFORD, Garth Neville   1259

Captain   Royal Regiment of Artillery
Other Decorations: —
Date of Gazette: 23 Jun. 1915
Place/Date of Birth: Frimley, Surrey — 27 May 1882
Place/Date of Death: Sedd-el-Bahr, Gallipoli — 26 Apr. 1915
Memorials: V. Beach Cemetery, Gallipoli; Chagford Church, Devon; Exeter Cathedral
Town/County Connections: Chagford, Devon; Frimley, Surrey; Kensington, London
Remarks: — *Harrow School*
Account of Deed: On 26 Apr. 1915 after a landing had been made on the beach on a point of the Gallipoli Peninsula, during which the brigadier general and the brigade major had been killed, Captain Walford and another officer* organised and made an attack through and on both sides of the village of Sedd-el-Bahr on the Old Fort at the top of the hill. The enemy's position was very strongly entrenched and defended, but mainly due to the initiative, skill and great gallantry of the two officers the attack was a complete success. Both were killed in the moment of victory. (*See also entry for WYLIE, C.H.M. Doughty-)

WALKER, Mark (later Sir Mark)   1260

Lieutenant (later General)   30th Regiment (later The East Lancashire Regiment)
Other Decorations: KCB
Date of Gazette: 2 Jun. 1858
Place/Date of Birth: Gore Port, Finca, Co. Westmeath, Ireland — 24 Nov. 1827
Place/Date of Death: Arlington, Devon — 18 Jul. 1902
Memorials: Cheriton Road Cemetery, Folkestone, Kent; Canterbury Cathedral, Kent
Town/County Connections: Finca, Co. Westmeath; Folkestone, Kent
Remarks: —
Account of Deed: On 5 Nov. 1854 at Inkerman, Crimea, Lieutenant Walker jumped over a wall in the face of two battalions of Russian Infantry which were marching towards it. This act was to encourage the men, by his example, to advance against such odds — which they did and succeeded in driving back both battalions.

WALKER, William George   **1261**
Captain (later Major General)   4th Gurkha Rifles, Indian Army, employed Bikanir Camel Corps
Other Decorations: CB
Date of Gazette: 7 Aug. 1903
Place/Date of Birth: Naini Tal, India — 28 May 1863
Place/Date of Death: Seaford, Sussex — 16 Feb. 1936
Memorials: (Cremated at Woodvale Cemetery, Brighton)
Town/County Connections: Seaford, Sussex
Remarks: Served in the First World War 1914-17.
Account of Deed: On 22 Apr. 1903 after the action at Daratoleh, Somaliland, the rearguard got considerably behind the rest of the column. Captain Walker and another captain* with four other men were with a fellow officer when he fell badly wounded, and while one went for assistance, Captain Walker and the rest stayed with him, endeavouring to keep off the enemy. This they succeeded in doing, and when the officer in command of the column* arrived, they managed to get the wounded man on to a camel. He was, however, hit a second time and died immediately. (*See also ROLLAND, G.M. and GOUGH, J.E.)

WALKER-HENEAGE, Clement — see **HENEAGE,** Clement Walker

WALLACE, Samuel Thomas Dickson   **1262**
T/Lieutenant (later Captain)   'C' Bty., 63rd Brigade, Royal Field Artillery
Other Decorations: —
Date of Gazette: 13 Feb. 1918
Place/Date of Birth: Thornhill, Dumfries-shire, Scotland — 7 Mar. 1892
Place/Date of Death: Moffat, Scotland — 2 Feb. 1968
Memorials: —
Town/County Connections: Thornhill, Dumfries-shire
Remarks: Deputy Director of Agriculture for Central Province, India 1919-32. Flight Lieutenant, Royal Air Force Volunteer Reserve 1940-43.
Account of Deed: On 30 Nov. 1917 at Gonnelieu, France, when the personnel of Lieutenant Wallace's battery were reduced to five, having lost their commander and five sergeants, and were surrounded by enemy infantry, he maintained the firing of the guns by swinging the trails close together, the men running and loading from gun to gun. He was in action for eight hours firing the whole time and inflicting severe casualties on the enemy. Then, owing to the exhausted state of his men, he withdrew when infantry supports arrived, taking with him all essential gun parts and all wounded.

No photograph available

WALLER, George   **1263**
Colour-Sergeant   1st Bn., 60th Rifles (later The King's Royal Rifle Corps)
Other Decorations: —
Date of Gazette: 20 Jan. 1860
Place/Date of Birth: West Horsley, Guildford, Surrey — Jun. 1827
Place/Date of Death: Cuckfield, Sussex — 10 Jan. 1877
Memorials: —
Town/County Connections: West Horsley, Surrey; Cuckfield, Sussex
Remarks: —
Account of Deed: On 14 Sep. 1857 at Delhi, India, Colour-Sergeant Waller charged and captured the enemy's guns near the Kabul Gate. On 18 Sep. he showed conspicuous bravery in the repulse of a sudden attack made by the enemy on the gun near the Chaudney Chouk. (Elected by the regiment.)

WALLER, Horace   **1264**
Private   10 (S) Bn., The King's Own Yorkshire Light Infantry
Other Decorations: —
Date of Gazette: 8 Jun. 1917
Place/Date of Birth: Batley Carr, Dewsbury, Yorkshire — 23 Sep. 1897
Place/Date of Death: Heninel, France — 10 Apr. 1917
Memorials: Cojeul British Cemetery, France
Town/County Connections: Dewsbury, Yorkshire
Remarks: —
Account of Deed: On 10 Apr. 1917 south of Heninel, France, Private Waller was with a bombing section forming a block in the enemy line. A very violent counter-attack was made by the enemy on this post and although five of the garrison were killed, Private Waller continued for more than an hour to throw bombs and finally repulsed the attack. In the evening the enemy again counter-attacked and all the garrison became casualties except Private Waller who, although wounded later, continued to throw bombs for another half an hour until he was killed.

WALLER, William Francis Frederick   **1265**
Lieutenant (later Colonel)   25th Bombay Light Infantry
Other Decorations: —
Date of Gazette: 25 Feb. 1858
Place/Date of Birth: Dagoolie, India — 20 Aug. 1840
Place/Date of Death: Bath, Somerset — 29 Jan. 1885
Memorials: —
Town/County Connections: Bath, Somerset
Remarks: —
Account of Deed: On 20 Jun. 1858 at Gwalior, India, Lieutenant Waller, with another lieutenant who was killed during the action, were the only Europeans present at the storming of the fortress. With a handful of men they climbed on to the roof of a house, shot the gunners who opposed them and took the fort, killing everyone in it.

No photograph available

WALTERS, George   **1266**
Sergeant   49th Regiment (later The Royal Berkshire Regiment — Princess Charlotte of Wales's)
Other Decorations: —
Date of Gazette: 24 Feb. 1857
Place/Date of Birth: Newport Pagnell, Buckinghamshire — 29 Jan. 1831
Place/Date of Death: Marylebone, London — 3 Jun. 1872
Memorials: Marylebone Cemetery, London, *City of Westminster Cemetery, Finch*
Town/County Connections: Guildford, Surrey   *Headstone erected in November 1997*
Remarks: Joined the London Police Force after leaving the Army   *the Royal Glos. Berks & H Reg*
Account of Deed: On 5 Nov. 1854 at the Battle of Inkerman, Crimea, Sergeant Walters rescued a brigadier general who was surrounded by the enemy, one of whom the sergeant bayoneted.

WANKLYN, Malcolm David   **1267**
Lieutenant-Commander   Royal Navy
Other Decorations: DSO & 2 Bars
Date of Gazette: 16 Dec. 1941
Place/Date of Birth: Calcutta, India — 28 Jun. 1911
Place/Date of Death: Gulf of Tripoli, North Africa — 14 Apr. 1942
Memorials: Portsmouth Naval Memorial
Town/County Connections: Southsea, Hampshire
Remarks: —
Account of Deed: On 24 May 1941 in the Mediterranean, south of Sicily, Lieutenant-Commander Wanklyn, commanding HM Submarine *Upholder*, torpedoed a troopship which was with a strongly protected convoy. The troopship sank and *Upholder* then endured a strong counter-attack in which 37 depth charges were dropped in 20 minutes, before she got clear. By the end of 1941 Lieutenant-Commander Wanklyn had sunk nearly 140,000 tons of enemy shipping, including a destroyer and troopships, tankers, supply and store ships.

WANTAGE, Lord — see **LINDSAY,** Robert James

WARBURTON-LEE, Bernard Armitage Warburton — see **LEE,** Bernard Armitage
Warburton WARBURTON-

WARD, Charles   **1268**
Private (later Company Sergeant-Major)   2nd Bn., The King's Own Yorkshire Light Infantry
Other Decorations: —
Date of Gazette: 28 Sep. 1900
Place/Date of Birth: Hunslet, Leeds, Yorkshire — 10 Jul. 1877
Place/Date of Death: Bridgend, Glamorgan, Wales — 30 Dec. 1921
Memorials: St. Mary's Churchyard, Whitchurch, Cardiff *Grave*
Town/County Connections: Leeds, Yorkshire; Bridgend, Glamorgan; Cardiff
Remarks: Last winner of the VC to be decorated by Queen Victoria
Account of Deed: On 26 Jun. 1900 at Lindley, South Africa, a picquet of the regiment was surrounded on three sides by about 500 Boers and the majority of them were either killed or wounded. Private Ward volunteered to take a message asking for reinforcements to the signalling post about 150 yards away. He was eventually allowed to go, although it seemed certain that he would be shot, and he managed to get across through a storm of bullets. Having delivered his message, he returned to his commanding officer across the fire-swept ground, and was severely wounded, but his gallant action saved the post from capture.

WARD, Henry   **1269**
Private (later Quartermaster-Sergeant)   78th Regiment (later The Seaforth Highlanders —
Ross-shire Buffs, Duke of Albany's)
Other Decorations: —
Date of Gazette: 18 Jun. 1858
Place/Date of Birth: Harleston, Norfolk — 1826
Place/Date of Death: Great Malvern, Worcestershire — 21 Sep. 1867
Memorials: War Memorial, Harleston, Norfolk
Town/County Connections: Harleston, Norfolk; Great Malvern, Worcestershire
Remarks: —
Account of Deed: On 25 and 26 Sep. 1857 at Lucknow, India, Private Ward stayed with a dhooly
in which an officer of the 10th Foot and a private of the 78th had taken refuge. Although under heavy cross-fire of ordnance and musketry, Private Ward remained at the side of the dhooli, inspiring the bearers to carry their double load, and encouraging them with the same steadiness as if on parade. Both wounded men were taken to the safety of the Baillie Guard.

WARD, James Allen   **1270**
Sergeant   Royal New Zealand Air Force, serving with 75 Squadron, Royal Air Force
Other Decorations: —
Date of Gazette: 5 Aug. 1941
Place/Date of Birth: Wanganui, New Zealand — 14 Jun. 1919
Place/Date of Death: Hamburg, Germany — 15 Sep. 1941
Memorials: Ohlsdorf Cemetery, Hamburg, Germany; HQ Dunedin RSA, New Zealand
Town/County Connections: —
Remarks: —
Account of Deed: On 7 Jul. 1941 after an attack on Munster, Germany, fire broke out in the
Wellington bomber in which Sergeant Ward was second pilot. The skipper of the aircraft having told him to try to put out the fire, the sergeant crawled out through a narrow astro-hatch, scrambled to the back of the starboard engine which was alight, and smothered the flames with an engine cover. His crawl back over the wing in which he had previously torn hand and foot-holes, was more dangerous than the outward journey, but he managed it with the help of the aircraft's navigator. The bomber was eventually landed safely.

No photograph available

WARD, Joseph   **1271**
Sergeant   8th Hussars (The King's Royal Irish)
Other Decorations: —
Date of Gazette: 26 Jan. 1859
Place/Date of Birth: Kinsale, Co. Cork, Ireland — 1832
Place/Date of Death: Longford, Ireland — 23 Nov. 1872
Memorials: —
Town/County Connections: Kinsale, Co. Cork
Remarks: —
Account of Deed: On 17 Jun. 1858 at Gwalior, India, Sergeant Ward (together with a captain, a
farrier and a private)* was in a gallant charge made by a squadron of the 8th Hussars when, supported by a division of the Bombay Horse Artillery and the 95th Regiment, they routed the enemy. Charging through a rebel camp into two batteries, they captured and brought into their own camp two of the enemy's guns, under a heavy and converging fire from the fort and town. (*See also HENEAGE, C.W., HOLLIS, G. and PEARSON, John)

WARE, Sidney William   **1272**
Corporal   1st Bn., The Seaforth Highlanders (Ross-shire Buffs, Duke of Albany's)
Other Decorations: —
Date of Gazette: 26 Sep. 1916
Place/Date of Birth: Whitchurch, Dorset — 11 Nov. 1892
Place/Date of Death: Persian Gulf — 16 Apr. 1916
Memorials: Amara War Cemetery, Iraq
Town/County Connections: Whitchurch and Milton Abbas, Dorset
Remarks: — *Name on WM Milton Lilbourne, Wilts*
Account of Deed: On 6 Apr. 1916 at Sanna-i-Yat, Mesopotamia, when an order was given to
withdraw to a communication trench, Corporal Ware, whose cool gallantry had been very marked during an advance, was one of the few men remaining unwounded. He picked up a wounded man and carried him some 200 yards to cover and then returned for others, moving to and fro under very heavy fire for more than two hours until he had brought in all the wounded, and was completely exhausted.

WARING, William Herbert   **1273**
Lance-Sergeant   25th Bn., The Royal Welch Fusiliers
Other Decorations: MM
Date of Gazette: 31 Jan. 1919
Place/Date of Birth: Welshpool, Montgomeryshire, Wales — 13 Oct. 1885
Place/Date of Death: Le Havre, France — 8 Oct. 1918   *Division 62. Plot 5. Row 1.*
Memorials: Ste. Marie Cemetery, Le Havre, France   *Grave 3*
Town/County Connections: Welshpool, Montgomeryshire   *Name on his parents grave at Christ v*
Remarks: — *Name on Welshpool W.M. Name on his parents grave at Christ v   Welshpool.*
Account of Deed: On 18 Sep. 1918 at Ronssoy, France, Lance-Sergeant Waring led an attack against enemy machine-guns and in the face of devastating fire, single-handed rushed a strong point, bayoneting four of the garrison and capturing two, with their guns. The lance-sergeant then reorganised his men leading and inspiring them for another 400 yards when he fell mortally wounded. *VC in Welshpool Borough Castle*

WARK, Blair Anderson   **1274**
Major (later Lieutenant Colonel)   32nd Bn. (S.A. & W.A.), Australian Imperial Force
Other Decorations: DSO
Date of Gazette: 26 Dec. 1918
Place/Date of Birth: Bathurst, New South Wales, Australia — 27 Jul. 1894
Place/Date of Death: Puckapungel, Victoria, Australia — 13 Jun. 1941
Memorials: Eastern Suburbs Crematorium, Sydney, New South Wales; Australian War Memorial, Canberra
Town/County Connections: —
Remarks: —
Account of Deed: During the period 29 Sep. to 1 Oct. 1918, at Bellicourt and the advance through to Joncourt, France, Major Wark moved fearlessly at the head of and at times far in advance of his troops, cheering them on and showing great gallantry in attack. At one time, leading his assaulting companies, he rushed a battery of 77mm guns, capturing four of them and 10 of the crew. Then, with only two NCOs, he surprised and captured 50 of the enemy near Magny La Fosse. Subsequently, he again, at great personal risk, silenced machine-guns which were causing heavy casualties.

WARNEFORD, Reginald Alexander John   **1275**
Flight Sub-Lieutenant   Royal Navy (1 Squadron, Royal Naval Air Service)
Other Decorations: —
Date of Gazette: 11 Jun. 1915
Place/Date of Birth: Darjeeling, India — 15 Oct. 1891
Place/Date of Death: Versailles, France — 17 Jun. 1915
Memorials: Brompton Cemetery, London; St. Michael's Church, Highworth, Wiltshire
Town/County Connections: Highworth, Wiltshire
Remarks: Légion d'Honneur (France) *VC & Medals in FAA Museum. Yeovilton*
Account of Deed: On 7 Jun. 1915 at Ghent, Belgium, Flight Sub-Lieutenant Warneford attacked and completely destroyed a German airship in mid air. He had chased the airship from the coast near Ostend, and succeeded in dropping his bombs on it, the last of which set the airship on fire, but the explosion overturned the attacking plane and stopped its engine. Having no alternative, Flight Sub-Lieutenant Warneford had to land in hostile country, but after 35 minutes spent on repairs, he managed to restart the engine and returned to base.

WARNER, Edward   **1276**
Private   1st Bn., The Bedfordshire Regiment
Other Decorations: —
Date of Gazette: 29 Jun. 1915
Place/Date of Birth: St. Albans, Hertfordshire — 18 Nov. 1883
Place/Date of Death: Near Ypres, Belgium — 2 May 1915
Memorials: Menin Gate Memorial, Belgium
Town/County Connections: St. Albans, Hertfordshire   *. Christ church, St. Albans*
Remarks: —
Account of Deed: On 1 May 1915 near Hill 60, Ypres, Belgium, when a trench had been vacated by our troops after a gas attack, Private Warner entered it alone in order to prevent the enemy taking possession. Reinforcements were sent to him but could not reach him owing to the gas. However he then went back and brought up more men, by which time he was completely exhausted, but the trench was held until the enemy attack ceased. Private Warner died shortly afterwards from the effects of gas poisoning.

WASSALL, Samuel   **1277**
Private   80th Regiment (later The South Staffordshire Regiment)
Other Decorations: —
Date of Gazette: 17 Jun. 1879
Place/Date of Birth: Aston, Warwickshire — 28 Jul. 1856
Place/Date of Death: Barrow-in-Furness, Lancashire — 31 Jan. 1927
Memorials: Barrow-in-Furness Cemetery; Garrison Church, Whittington Barracks, Lichfield,
Staffordshire   *grave*
Town/County Connections: Barrow-in-Furness, Lancashire
Remarks: —
Account of Deed: On 22 Jan. 1879 at Isandhlwana, Zululand, when the camp was taken by the
enemy, Private Wassall retreated towards the Buffalo River, in which he saw a comrade struggling and apparently drowning.
He rode to the bank and dismounted, leaving his horse on the Zulu side. He then rescued the man mounted his horse and
dragged his comrade across the river under a heavy shower of bullets.

WATERS, Arnold Horace Santo (later Sir Arnold)   **1278**
A/Major   218th Field Coy., Corps of Royal Engineers
Other Decorations: CBE, DSO, MC
Date of Gazette: 13 Feb. 1919
Place/Date of Birth: Plymouth, Devon — 23 Sep. 1886
Place/Date of Death: Four Oaks, Sutton Coldfield, Warwickshire — 22 Jan. 1981
Memorials: —
Town/County Connections: Plymouth, Devon; Four Oaks, Sutton Coldfield, Warwickshire
Remarks: President of the Institute of Structural Engineers 1933; Divisonal Food Officer for West
Midlands 1939-45; Chairman of the South Staffordshire Waterworks Co. 1959; DL, County of
Warwick.
Account of Deed: On 4 Nov. 1918 near Ors, France, Major Waters, with his Field Company, was bridging the Oise-Sambre
Canal under artillery and machine-gun fire at close range, the bridge being damaged and the building party suffering severe
casualties. All Major Waters' officers had been killed or wounded and he at once went forward and personally supervised the
completion of the bridge, working on cork floats while under such intense fire that it seemed impossible that he could survive.
The success of the operation was entirely due to his valour and example.

WATKINS, Tasker (later Sir Tasker)   **1279**
Lieutenant (later Major)   1/5th Bn., The Welch Regiment
Other Decorations: —
Date of Gazette: 2 Nov. 1944
Place/Date of Birth: Nelson, Glamorgan, Wales — 18 Nov. 1918
Place/Date of Death: —
Memorials: —
Town/County Connections: Nelson, Glamorgan
Remarks: Various legal appointments, including Recorder, Merthyr Tydfil (1968-70), Swansea
(1970-71); Leader, Welsh and Chester Circuit 1970-71; Judge, High Court of Justice (Queen's
Bench Division) 1974; a Lord Justice of Appeal 1980; Senior Presiding Judge for England and
Wales 1983; Hon. LLD, Wales 1979; DL County of Glamorgan 1956-
Account of Deed: On 16 Aug. 1944 at Barfour, Normandy, Lieutenant Watkins' company came under murderous machine-gun
fire while advancing through corn fields set with booby traps. The only officer left, Lieutenant Watkins led a bayonet charge with
his 30 remaining men against 50 enemy infantry, practically wiping them out. Finally, at dusk, separated from the rest of the
battalion, he ordered his men to scatter and after he had personally charged and silenced an enemy machine-gun post, he
brought them back to safety. His superb leadership not only saved his men, but decisively influenced the course of the battle.

WATSON, John (later Sir John)   **1280**
Lieutenant (later General)   1st Punjab Cavalry
Other Decorations: GCB
Date of Gazette: 16 Jun. 1859
Place/Date of Birth: Chigwell Row, Essex — 6 Sep. 1829
Place/Date of Death: Finchampstead, Berkshire — 23 Jan. 1919
Memorials: —
Town/County Connections: Chigwell Row, Essex; Finchampstead, Berks.
Remarks: —
Account of Deed: On 14 Nov. 1857 at Lucknow, India, Lieutenant Watson, with his own squadron
and that under another lieutenant, came upon a body of rebel cavalry. The ressaidar in command
of them, with about half-a-dozen, rode out and confronted Lieutenant Watson and in the fierce fighting which ensued the
lieutenant received several disabling blows and cuts from tulwars. He continued to defend himself, however, until his own men
joined in the melée and utterly routed the enemy.

WATSON, Oliver Cyril Spencer   **1281**
A/Lieutenant Colonel   Reserve of Officers, 1st County of London Yeomanry, comd. 5th Bn., The King's Own Yorkshire Light Infantry
Other Decorations: DSO
Date of Gazette: 18 May 1918
Place/Date of Birth: Cavendish Square, London — 7 Sep. 1876
Place/Date of Death: Rossignol Wood, France — 28 Mar. 1918
Memorials: Arras Memorial, France; St. Mary's Church, Wargrave, Berkshire
Town/County Connections: Kensington, London; Wargrave, Berkshire
Remarks: Served with The Green Howards in the Tirah Expedition 1897-8 and the China Expedition 1900; retired 1904

Account of Deed: On 28 Mar. 1918 at Rossignol Wood, north of Hebuterne, France, a counter-attack had been made against the enemy position which at first achieved its object, but as they were holding out in two improvised strong points, Lieutenant Colonel Watson saw that immediate action was necessary and he led his remaining small reserve to the attack, organising bombing parties and leading attacks under intense fire. Outnumbered, he finally ordered his men to retire, remaining himself in a communication trench to cover the retirement. The assault he led was at a critical moment and without doubt saved the line, but he was killed covering the withdrawal.

WATSON, Thomas Colclough   **1282**
Lieutenant (later Lieutenant-Colonel)   Corps of Royal Engineers
Other Decorations: —
Date of Gazette: 20 May 1898
Place/Date of Birth: Velsen, Holland — 11 Apr. 1867
Place/Date of Death: London — 15 Jun. 1917
Memorials: (Cremated Golders Green, London)
Town/County Connections: Dovercourt, Essex
Remarks: Served in First World War 1914-15
Account of Deed: On the night of 16/17 Sep. 1897 in the Mamund Valley, N.W. India, Lieutenant Watson with another lieutenant* collected a party of volunteers* and led them into the dark and burning village of Bilot, to try to dislodge the enemy who were inflicting losses on our troops. After being wounded and driven back by very heavy fire at close quarters, Lieutenant Watson made a second attempt to clear the village and only gave up after a second repulse and being again severely wounded. (*See also COLVIN, J.M.C. and SMITH, James — No. 1162).

WATT, Joseph   **1283**
Skipper (later Chief Skipper)   Royal Naval Reserve
Other Decorations: —
Date of Gazette: 29 Aug. 1917
Place/Date of Birth: Gardenstown, Gamrie, Banff, Scotland — 25 Jun. 1887
Place/Date of Death: Fraserburgh, Scotland — 13 Feb. 1955
Memorials: Kirktown Cemetery, Fraserburgh
Town/County Connections: Fraserburgh, Aberdeenshire
Remarks: Croix de Guerre (France); Military Medal for Valour (Italy).
Account of Deed: On 15 May 1917 in the Straits of Otranto, when HM Drifter *Gowan Lea* was attacked by an Austrian light cruiser and called on to surrender, Skipper Watt ordered full speed ahead and called upon his crew to fight to the finish. The cruiser was then engaged, but after only one round had been fired a shot from the enemy disabled *Gowan Lea's* gun. The gun's crew struggled to repair the gun, under heavy fire, and after the cruiser had passed on, thinking that the drifter was sinking, Skipper Watt took her alongside the badly damaged drifter *Floandi* and helped to remove the dead and wounded.

WEALE, Henry   **1284**
Lance-Corporal (later Sergeant)   14th Bn., The Royal Welch Fusiliers
Other Decorations: —
Date of Gazette: 15 Nov. 1918
Place/Date of Birth: Flint, Wales — 2 Oct. 1897
Place/Date of Death: Rhyl, Wales — 13 Jan. 1959
Memorials: Rhyl Cemetery. *Grave*
Town/County Connections: Shotton and Rhyl, Flintshire, Wales
Remarks: — *VC with RWF Museum. Caernarvon Castle*
Account of Deed: On 26 Aug. 1918 at Bazentin-le-Grand, France, when the advance of the adjacent battalion was held up by enemy machine-guns, Lance-Corporal Weale was ordered to deal with hostile posts. When his Lewis gun failed him, on his own initiative, he rushed the nearest post and killed the crew, then went for the others, the crews of which fled on his approach. His dashing action cleared the way for the advance, inspired his comrades and resulted in the capture of all the machine-guns.

WEARNE, Frank Bernard **1285**
Second Lieutenant   3rd Bn., The Essex Regiment, attd. 11th Bn.
Other Decorations: —
Date of Gazette: 2 Aug. 1917
Place/Date of Birth: Kensington, London — 1 Mar. 1894
Place/Date of Death: Loos, France — 28 Jun. 1917
Memorials: Loos Memorial, France
Town/County Connections: Worcester Park, Surrey; London
Remarks: —
Account of Deed: On 28 Jun. 1917 east of Loos, France, Second Lieutenant Wearne, commanding
a small party in a raid on the enemy's trenches, had gained his objective in the face of fierce
opposition and managed to maintain his position against repeated counter-attacks. Then, realising that if the left flank was lost
his men would have to give way, he leaped on to the parapet and followed by his left section, ran along the top of the trench
firing and throwing bombs. While doing this he was severely wounded, but continued directing operations until he received
two more wounds, the second mortal.

WEATHERS, Lawrence Carthage **1286**
T/Corporal   43rd Bn., (S.A), Australian Imperial Force
Other Decorations: —
Date of Gazette: 26 Dec. 1918
Place/Date of Birth: Te Koparu, New Zealand — 14 May 1890
Place/Date of Death: North-east of Peronne, France — 29 Sep. 1918
Memorials: Unicorn Cemetery, France; Australian War Memorial, Canberra
Town/County Connections: —
Remarks: —
Account of Deed: On 2 Sep. 1918, north of Peronne, France, when the attack was held up by a
strongly held enemy trench, Corporal Weathers went forward alone and attacked the enemy with
bombs. Returning for more bombs, he again went forward with three comrades and attacked under heavy fire. Regardless of
personal danger, he mounted the enemy parapet and bombed the trench; 180 prisoners and three machine-guns were taken.

WELCH, James **1287**
Lance-Corporal (later Sergeant)   1st Bn., The Royal Berkshire Regiment (Princess Charlotte of
Wales's)
Other Decorations: —
Date of Gazette: 27 Jun. 1917
Place/Date of Birth: Stratfield Saye, near Silchester, Hampshire — 7 Jul. 1889
Place/Date of Death: Bournemouth, Hampshire — 28 Jun. 1978
Memorials: —
Town/County Connections: Stratfield Saye, Silchester, Hampshire
Remarks: —
Account of Deed: On 29 Apr. 1917 near Oppy, France, Lance-Corporal Welch entered an enemy
trench and killed one man after a severe hand-to-hand struggle. Then, armed only with an empty revolver, he chased four of
the enemy across the open and captured them single-handed. He handled his machine-gun with the utmost fearlessness, and
more than once went into the open, exposed to heavy fire, to search for and collect ammunition and spare parts in order to keep
his guns in action, which he succeeded in doing for over five hours, until wounded by a shell.

WELLS, Harry **1288**
Sergeant   2nd Bn., The Royal Sussex Regiment
Other Decorations: —
Date of Gazette: 18 Nov. 1915
Place/Date of Birth: Herne, Kent — 19 Sep. 1888
Place/Date of Death: Loos, France — 25 Sep. 1915
Memorials: Dud Corner Cemetery, France; War Memorial, Herne, Kent; Regimental Memorial,
Chichester Cathedral
Town/County Connections: Herne, Kent
Remarks: —
Account of Deed: On 25 Sep. 1915 near Le Rutoire, Loos, France, when the platoon officer had
been killed, Sergeant Wells took command and led his men forward to within 15 yards of the German wire. Nearly half the
platoon were killed or wounded and the remainder were much shaken but Sergeant Wells rallied them and led them on. Finally,
when very few were left, he stood up and urged them forward once again and while doing this he was killed.

WELLS, John Stanhope COLLINGS-   **1289**
A/Lieutenant Colonel   Comd. 4th Bn. The Bedfordshire Regiment
Other Decorations: DSO
Date of Gazette: 24 Apr. 1918
Place/Date of Birth: Caddington, Bedfordshire — 19 Jul. 1880
Place/Date of Death: Near Albert, France — 27 Mar. 1918
Memorials: Bouzincourt Ridge Cemetery, France; St. Ethelreda's Church, Hatfield, Herts.
Town/County Connections: Markyate, Hertfordshire; Caddington, Bedfordshire
Remarks: —
Account of Deed: In the period 22/27 Mar. 1918 during the fighting from Marcoing to Albert, France, when the rearguard was in great danger of being captured, Lieutenant Colonel Collings-Wells called for volunteers who remained behind and held up the enemy for 1½ hours whilst the remainder of the rearguard withdrew. During this time the colonel moved amongst his men guiding and encouraging them. On a subsequent occasion when ordered to counter-attack, and knowing that his men were extremely tired, he personally led them, and even when twice wounded, continued to lead and encourage them, until he was killed at the moment of gaining the objective.

WEST, Ferdinand Maurice Felix   **1290**
Captain (later Air Commodore)   8 Squadron, Royal Air Force
Other Decorations: CBE, MC
Date of Gazette: 8 Nov. 1918
Place/Date of Birth: London — 29 Jan. 1896
Place/Date of Death: — *Died about 9.7.1988.*
Memorials: — *Buried Holy Trinity churchyard, Church Road, Sunningda*
Town/County Connections: London
Remarks: Air Attaché to Finland, Estonia and Latvia 1936-39; Air Attaché, British Embassy in Rome 1940, then to the British Legation at Berne until the end of the Second World War. Commander, Order of the Orange Nassau (Netherlands); Légion d'Honneur (France)
Account of Deed: On 10 Aug. 1918 north east of Roye, France, Captain West, who had spent the two previous days on reconnaissance patrols and attacking the enemy from tree level, found a huge concentration of troops and transport. He had noted the strength of the enemy formation when he was attacked by several German scouts, receiving five bullets in his left leg which was partially severed. In a rapidly weakening state and in great pain he managed to bring his aircraft back to safety, and on landing, despite waves of unconsciousness, insisted on giving in his report before being taken to hospital.

WEST, Richard Annesley   **1291**
A/Lieutenant Colonel   The North Irish Horse (S.R), seconded to 6th Bn., Tank Corps
Other Decorations: DSO & Bar, MC
Date of Gazette: 30 Oct. 1918
Place/Date of Birth: Cheltenham, Gloucestershire — 26 Sep. 1878
Place/Date of Death: Vaulx Vraucourt, France — 2 Sep. 1918
Memorials: Mory Abbey Military Cemetery, France
Town/County Connections: Cheltenham, Gloucestershire; White Park, Fermanagh, Ireland
Remarks: —
Account of Deed: On 21 Aug. 1918 at Courcelles, France, during an attack, the infantry lost their bearings in dense fog and Lieutenant Colonel West at once collected any men he could find and led them to their objective, in face of heavy machine-gun fire. On 2 Sep. at Vaulx Vraucourt, he arrived at the front line when the enemy were delivering a local counter-attack. The infantry battalion had suffered heavy officer casualties and realizing the danger if they gave way, and despite the enemy being almost upon them, Colonel West rode up and down in face of certain death, encouraging the men. He fell riddled with bullets. His magnificent bravery at a critical moment so inspired the infantry that the hostile attack was defeated.

WESTON, William Basil   **1292**
Lieutenant   The Green Howards attd. 1st Bn. The West Yorkshire Regiment
Other Decorations: —
Date of Gazette: 15 May 1945
Place/Date of Birth: Ulverston, Lancashire — 3 Jan. 1924
Place/Date of Death: Meiktila, Burma — 3 Mar. 1945
Memorials: Taukkyan War Cemetery, Burma; St. Mary's RC Church, Ulverston
Town/County Connections: Ulverston, Lancashire
Remarks: —
Account of Deed: On 3 Mar. 1945 during the attack on Meiktila, Burma, Lieutenant Weston was commanding a platoon which, together with the rest of the company, had to clear an area of the town of the enemy. In the face of fanatical opposition he led his men superbly, encouraging them from one bunker position to the next. When he came to the last, particularly well-defended bunker, he fell wounded in the entrance. Knowing that his men would not be able to capture the position without heavy casualties he pulled the pin out of one of his grenades as he lay on the ground and deliberately blew himself up with the occupants of the bunker.

WHEATLEY, Francis **1293**
Private   1st Bn., The Rifle Brigade (Prince Consort's Own)
Other Decorations: DCM
Date of Gazette: 24 Feb. 1857
Place/Date of Birth: Ruddington, Nottinghamshire — 1822
Place/Date of Death: Eversley, Hampshire — 21 May 1865
Memorials: The Rifle Brigade Memorial, Winchester Cathedral
Town/County Connections: Ruddington, Nottinghamshire; Elvetham, Eversley, Hampshire
Remarks: Légion d'Honneur (France)
Account of Deed: On 10 Nov. 1854 in the Crimea, in the trenches, Private Wheatley tackled a live shell which fell in the midst of the riflemen. He first tried to knock out the burning fuse with the butt of his rifle, but as he was unsuccessful in this, he deliberately picked up the shell and threw it over the parapet where it immediately exploded.

WHEATLEY, Kevin Arthur **1294**
Warrant Officer Class II   Australian Army Training Team, Vietnam
Other Decorations: —
Date of Gazette: 13 Dec. 1966
Place/Date of Birth: Sydney, New South Wales, Australia — 13 Mar. 1937
Place/Date of Death: Tra Bong, Vietnam — 13 Nov. 1965
Memorials: Pine Grove Memorial Park, Blacktown, NSW; Australian War Memorial, Canberra
Town/County Connections: —
Remarks: —
Account of Deed: On 13 Nov. 1965 in Vietnam, Warrant Officer Class Two Wheatley insisted on staying with a wounded comrade against overwhelming odds and in spite of ample opportunity to make good his escape. He was killed while defending his comrade.

WHEELER, George Campbell **1295**
Major (later Lieutenant Colonel)   2nd Bn., 9th Gurkha Rifles, Indian Army
Other Decorations: —
Date of Gazette: 8 Jun. 1917
Place/Date of Birth: Tokyo, Japan — 7 Apr. 1880
Place/Date of Death: Barton-on-Sea, Hampshire — 26 Aug. 1938
Memorials: —
Town/County Connections: Barton-on-Sea, Hampshire
Remarks: —
Account of Deed: On 23 Feb. 1917 at Shumran on the River Tigris, Mesopotamia, Major Wheeler, together with one Gurkha officer and eight men crossed the river and rushed the enemy's trench in the face of very heavy fire. Having obtained a footing on the far bank, he was almost immediately counter-attacked by the enemy with a party of bombers. Major Wheeler at once led a charge, receiving in the process a severe bayonet wound in the head. In spite of this, however, he managed to disperse the enemy and consolidate his position.

WHEELER, George Godfrey Massy **1296**
Major   7th Hariana Lancers, Indian Army
Other Decorations: —
Date of Gazette: 1 Sep. 1915
Place/Date of Birth: Chakrata, United Provinces, India — 31 Jan. 1873
Place/Date of Death: Near Shaiba, Mesopotamia — 13 Apr. 1915
Memorials: Basra War Cemetery, Iraq; St. Alban's Church, Hindhead, Surrey
Town/County Connections: Hove, Sussex
Remarks: —
Account of Deed: On 12 Apr. 1915 at Shaiba, Mesopotamia, Major Wheeler took out his squadron in an attempt to capture a flag which was the centre-point of a group of the enemy who were firing on one of our picquets. He advanced, attacked the enemy's infantry with the lance, and then retired while the enemy swarmed out of hidden ground, and formed an excellent target for the Royal Artillery guns. On 13 Apr. Major Wheeler led his squadron to the attack of the North Mound. He was seen far ahead of his men, riding straight for the enemy's standards but was killed in the attack.

No photograph available

WHIRLPOOL, (born CONKER, alias JAMES, Frederick Humphrey) Frederick **1297**
Private   3rd Bombay European Regiment (later The Prince of Wales's Leinster Regiment)
Other Decorations: —
Date of Gazette: 21 Oct. 1859
Place/Date of Birth: Liverpool — 1829
Place/Date of Death: Near Windsor, New South Wales, Australia — 24 Jun. 1899
Memorials: Presbyterian Cemetery, McGrath Hill, New South Wales
Town/County Connections: Liverpool, Lancashire; Dundalk, Louth, Ireland
Remarks: —
Account of Deed: On 3 Apr. 1858 in the attack on Jhansi, India, Private Whirlpool volunteered to
return and carry to safety several killed and wounded. He did this twice under very heavy fire. On
2 May he rushed to the rescue of a lieutenant of his regiment who was dangerously wounded. Private Whirlpool himself
received 17 severe wounds, one of which nearly severed his head from his body. The gallant example shown by this man was
considered to have greatly contributed to the success of the day.

WHITCHURCH, Harry Frederick **1298**
Surgeon Captain (later Surgeon Major)   Indian Medical Service
Other Decorations: —
Date of Gazette: 16 Jul. 1895
Place/Date of Birth: Sandown, Isle of Wight — 22 Sep. 1866
Place/Date of Death: Dharmsala, Punjab, India — 16 Aug. 1907
Memorials: —
Town/County Connections: Sandown, Isle of Wight
Remarks: —
Account of Deed: On 3 Mar. 1895 at Chitral Fort, North-west Frontier, India, Surgeon-Captain
Whitchurch went to the assistance of a captain who had been mortally wounded 1½ miles from
the fort. The captain was placed in a dhooly, but on the return journey three of the bearers were killed and a fourth severely
wounded, so the Surgeon-Captain took the injured man on his back and carried him for some distance. The rescue party was
fired on incessantly the whole way, but Surgeon-Captain Whitchurch eventually succeeded in getting them back to the fort,
although nearly all were wounded.

WHITE, Albert **1299**
Sergeant   2nd Bn., The South Wales Borderers
Other Decorations: —
Date of Gazette: 27 Jun. 1917
Place/Date of Birth: Kirkdale, Liverpool, Lancashire — 1896 *or 1889*
Place/Date of Death: Monchy-le-Preux, France — 19 May 1917
Memorials: Arras Memorial, France *Bay 6.*
Town/County Connections: Kirkdale, Liverpool, Lancashire
Remarks: —
Account of Deed: On 19 May 1917 at Monchy-le-Preux, France, Sergeant White, realizing during
an attack, that one of the enemy's machine guns, which had previously been located, would hold
up the whole advance of his company, dashed ahead to capture the gun. When within a few yards of it, he fell riddled with
bullets, having willingly sacrificed his life in an attempt to secure the success of the operation.

WHITE, Archie Cecil Thomas **1300**
T/Captain (later Colonel)   6th Bn., The Yorkshire Regiment (Alexandra, Princess of Wales's Own)
Other Decorations: MC
Date of Gazette: 26 Oct. 1916
Place/Date of Birth: Boroughbridge, Yorkshire — 5 Oct. 1890
Place/Date of Death: Camberley, Surrey — 20 May 1971
Memorials: — *Cremated Woking Crematorium, Surrey.*
Town/County Connections: Boroughbridge, Yorkshire
Remarks: Army Educational Corps 1920-47; Principal, City Literary Institute 1948-56; Member of
Senate, University of London 1953-56; Deputy Colonel-Commandant, Royal Army Educational
Corps 1960-69; Officier d'Academie FKC
Account of Deed: During the period 27 Sep.—1 Oct. 1916 at Stuff Redoubt, France, Captain White was in command of the
troops which held the southern and western faces of a redoubt. For four days and nights by skilful disposition he held the
position under heavy fire of all kinds and against several counter-attacks. Although short of supplies and ammunition, his
determination never wavered and when the enemy attacked in greatly superior numbers and had almost ejected our troops
from the redoubt, he personally led a counter-attack which finally cleared the enemy out of the southern and western faces.

WHITE, Geoffrey Saxton   **1301**
Lieutenant-Commander   Royal Navy
Other Decorations: —
Date of Gazette: 24 May 1919
Place/Date of Birth: Bromley, Kent — 2 Jul. 1886
Place/Date of Death: Dardanelles — 28 Jan. 1918
Memorials: Portsmouth Naval Memorial
Town/County Connections: Bromley, Kent
Remarks: —
Account of Deed: On 28 Jan. 1918 in the Dardanelles, Lieutenant-Commander White, commanding
H.M. Submarine E.14 was under instructions to find the German battle cruiser *Goeber*, reported
aground. She was not found, however, and E.14 turned back, but after firing a torpedo at an enemy ship a heavy explosion
occurred, badly damaging the submarine. Lieutenant Commander White, after submerging for a time, was forced to bring E.14
to the surface where she was hit again and again until eventually the lieutenant-commander decided to try to ground her to give
the crew a chance of being saved. He himself remained on deck until killed by a shell.

WHITE, George Stuart (later sir George)   **1302**
Major (later Field Marshal)   92nd Regiment (later The Gordon Highlanders)
Other Decorations: GCB, OM, GCSI, GCMG, GCIE, GCVO
Date of Gazette: 2 Jun. 1881
Place/Date of Birth: Ballymena, Co. Antrim, Ireland — 4 Jul. 1835
Place/Date of Death: Chelsea, London — 24 Jun. 1912   *Bradfied School, Berkshire*
Memorials: Statue, Portland Place, London; Royal Military College, Camberley, Surrey
Town/County Connections: Portstewart, Co. Londonderry, Ireland; Chelsea, London
Remarks: Governor of Gibraltar 1900-04; Governor of Chelsea Hospital from 1904
Account of Deed: On 6 Oct. 1879 at Charasiah, (Afghan War), Major White led an attack on a
strongly fortified hill where the enemy force outnumbered the major's by about eight to one.
When his men became exhausted and immediate action seemed necessary, he took a rifle and, running foward alone, shot the
enemy leader. This decided the issue and the enemy fled. Again, at the battle of Kandahar Major White led the final charge and
personally captured one of the two guns held by the enemy, immediately after which the latter retired.

WHITE, Jack   **1303**
Private (later Lance-Corporal)   6th Bn., The King's Own (Royal Lancaster) Regiment
Other Decorations: —
Date of Gazette: 27 Jun. 1917
Place/Date of Birth: Leeds, Yorkshire — 23 Dec. 1896
Place/Date of Death: Manchester, Lancashire — 27 Nov. 1949
Memorials: The Priory, Lancaster   *Buried Jewish Cemetery, Blackly.*
Town/County Connections: Leeds; Manchester
Remarks: —
Account of Deed: On 7/8 Mar. 1917 on the Dialah River, Mesopotamia, Private White, a signaller,
during an attempt to cross the river, saw the two pontoons ahead of him come under very heavy
fire with disastrous results. When his own pontoon had reached mid-stream, with every man except himself either dead or
wounded, and not being able, by himself, to control the boat the private tied a telephone wire to the pontoon, jumped overboard
and towed it to the shore, thereby saving an officer's life and bringing to land the wounded and also the rifles and equipment
of all the men in the boat.

WHITE, William Allison   **1304**
T/Second Lieutenant (later Captain)   38th Bn., Machine Gun Corps
Other Decorations: TD
Date of Gazette: 15 Nov. 1918
Place/Date of Birth: Mitcham, Surrey — 19 Oct. 1894
Place/Date of Death: Wellington, Shropshire — 13 Sep. 1974
Memorials: (Cremated at Shrewsbury)
Town/County Connections: Mitcham, Surrey
Remarks: —
Account of Deed: On 18 Sep. 1918 at Gouzeaucourt, France, when the advance was held up by
enemy machine-guns, Second Lieutenant White rushed a gun position single-handed, shot the
three gunners and captured the gun. Later he attacked a gun position accompanied by two men, both of whom were
immediately shot down. He went on alone to the gun, killing the team and capturing the gun. On a third occasion when the
advance was again held up this officer collected a small party and rushed the position, inflicting heavy losses on the garrison.
Subsequently he consolidated the position by the skilful use of captured enemy and his own machine guns.

WHITFIELD, Harold   **1305**
Private (later Sergeant)   10th Bn., The King's Shropshire Light Infantry
Other Decorations: —
Date of Gazette: 8 May 1918
Place/Date of Birth: Oswestry, Shropshire — 11 Jun. 1886
Place/Date of Death: Oswestry, Shropshire — 19 Dec. 1956
Memorials: —
Town/County Connections: Oswestry, Shropshire
Remarks: —
Account of Deed: On 10 Mar. 1918 at Burj El Lisaneh, Egypt, during the first of three counter-attacks made by the enemy on the position which had just been captured by his battalion, Private Whitfield, single-handed, charged and captured a Lewis gun, killed the whole gun team and turned the gun on the enemy, driving them back with heavy casualties. Later he organised and led a bombing attack on the enemy, again inflicting many casualties and by establishing his party in their position saved many lives and materially assisted in the defeat of the counter-attack.

WHITHAM, Thomas   **1306**
Private   1st Bn., Coldstream Guards
Other Decorations: —
Date of Gazette: 6 Sep. 1917
Place/Date of Birth: Fulledge, Burnley, Lancashire — 11 May 1888
Place/Date of Death: Oldham, Lancashire — 24 Oct. 1924
Memorials: Inghamite Burial Ground, Nelson, Lancashire . *Buried Wheatley Lane Cemetery, Burnley*
Town/County Connections: Worsthorne, Burnley, Lancashire
Remarks: — *Portrait in Townley Hall Museum, Burnley*
Account of Deed: On 31 Jul. 1917 at Pilkem, Belgium, during an attack an enemy machine-gun was seen to be enfilading the battalion on the right. Private Whitham on his own initiative immediately worked his way from shell-hole to shell-hole through our own barrage, reached the machine-gun and, although under very heavy fire captured it, together with an officer and two other ranks. This bold action was of great assistance to the battalion and undoubtedly saved many lives.

WHITTLE, John Woods   **1307**
Sergeant   12th Bn., (S.A., W.A & Tasmania), Australian Imperial Force
Other Decorations: DCM
Date of Gazette: 8 Jun. 1917
Place/Date of Birth: Huon Island, Tasmania — 3 Aug. 1883
Place/Date of Death: Glebe, Sydney, New South Wales, Australia — 2 Mar. 1946
Memorials: Rookwood Cemetery, Sydney; Australian War Memorial, Canberra
Town/County Connections: —
Remarks: —
Account of Deed: On 9 Apr. 1917, near Boursies, France, Sergeant Whittle was in command of a platoon when the enemy, under cover of an intense artillery barrage, attacked the small trench he was holding and, owing to their numbers, succeeded in entering it. Sergeant Whittle collected his men, charged the enemy and regained the position. On a second occasion, when the enemy broke through our line and tried to bring up a machine gun to enfilade the position, Sergeant Whittle rushed across the fire-swept ground and attacked the enemy with bombs, killing all of them and capturing the gun.

WILCOX, Alfred   **1308**
Lance-Corporal   2/4th Bn., The Oxfordshire and Buckinghamshire Light Infantry
Other Decorations: —
Date of Gazette: 15 Nov. 1918
Place/Date of Birth: Aston, Birmingham — 16 Dec. 1884
Place/Date of Death: Birmingham — 30 Mar. 1951
Memorials: —
Town/County Connections: Birmingham
Remarks: —
Account of Deed: On 12 Sep. 1918 near Laventie, France, when his company was held up by enemy machine-gun fire at short range, Lance-Corporal Wilcox rushed to the nearest enemy gun, bombing it and killing the gunner. Being then attacked by an enemy bombing party, the corporal picked up enemy stick bombs and led his company against the next gun, finally capturing and destroying it. Then, left with only one man he continued bombing and captured a third gun. Going up the trench, bombing as he went, he captured a fourth gun and then returned to his platoon.

WILKINSON, Alfred Robert   **1309**
Private (later Lieutenant) 1/5th Bn., The Manchester Regiment
Other Decorations: —
Date of Gazette: 6 Jan. 1919
Place/Date of Birth: Leigh, Lancashire — 5 Dec. 1896
Place/Date of Death: Leigh, Lancashire — 23 Oct. 1940
Memorials: —
Town/County Connections: Leigh, Lancashire
Remarks: —
Account of Deed: On 20 Oct. 1918 at Marou, France, during the attack, four runners had been killed in attempting to deliver a message to the supporting company and Private Wilkinson volunteered for the duty. He succeeded in delivering the message although the journey involved exposure to extremely heavy machine-gun and shell fire for 600 yards. He showed magnificent courage and complete indifference to danger and throughout the remainder of the day continued to do splendid work.

WILKINSON, Thomas   **1310**
Bombardier (later Sergeant Instructor in Auxiliary Forces) Royal Marine Artillery
Other Decorations: —
Date of Gazette: 24 Feb. 1857
Place/Date of Birth: York — 1832
Place/Date of Death: York — 22 Sep. 1887
Memorials: York Cemetery
Town/County Connections: York
Remarks: Légion d'Honneur (France)
Account of Deed: On 7 Jun. 1855 at Sebastopol, Crimea, Bombardier Wilkinson was especially recommended for gallant conduct with the advanced batteries. He worked at the task of placing sandbags to repair damage done to the defences under a most galling fire.

WILKINSON, Thomas   **1311**
T/Lieutenant Royal Naval Reserve
Other Decorations: —
Date of Gazette: 17 Dec. 1946
Place/Date of Birth: Widnes, Lancashire — 1 Aug. 1898
Place/Date of Death: Java Sea — 14 Feb. 1942
Memorials: Widnes War Memorial, Liverpool Naval Memorial
Town/County Connections: Widnes, Lancashire
Remarks: —
Account of Deed: On 14 Feb. 1942 in the Java Sea, HMS *Li Wo*, a patrol vessel, formerly a passenger steamer, commanded by Lieutenant Wilkinson, sighted two enemy convoys, one escorted by Japanese warships. The lieutenant told his crew he had decided to engage the convoy and fight to the last in the hope of inflicting some damage — this decision drew resolute support from the whole ship's crew. In the action which followed a Japanese transport was set on fire and abandoned, and *Li Wo* stayed in action against a heavy cruiser for over an hour before being hit at point-blank range and sunk. Lieutenant Wilkinson ordered his crew to abandon ship, but he went down with *Li Wo*.

WILKINSON, Thomas Orde Lauder   **1312**
T/Lieutenant 7th Bn., The Loyal North Lancashire Regiment
Other Decorations: —
Date of Gazette: 26 Sep. 1916
Place/Date of Birth: Bridgnorth, Shropshire — 29 Jun. 1894
Place/Date of Death: La Boiselle, France — 5 Jul. 1916
Memorials: Thiepval Memorial, France
Town/County Connections: Bridgnorth, Shropshire; Milford, Surrey
Remarks: —Wellington College, Berks.
Account of Deed: On 5 Jul. 1916 at La Boiselle, France, during an attack, when a party of men from another unit were retiring without their machine-gun, Lieutenant Wilkinson with two of his men, got the gun into action and held up the enemy until relieved. Later he forced his way forward during a bombing attack and found four or five men from different units stopped by a wall of earth over which the enemy was throwing bombs. He at once mounted the machine-gun on top of the parapet and dispersed the bombers. Subsequently, in trying to bring in a wounded man, he was killed.

WILLIAMS (born FIELDING)   John   **1313**
Private   2nd Bn., 24th Regiment (later The South Wales Borderers)
Other Decorations: —
Date of Gazette: 2 May 1879
Place/Date of Birth: Abergavenny, Monmouthshire — 24 May 1857
Place/Date of Death: Cwmbran, Monmouthshire — 25 Nov. 1932
Memorials: Llanfihangel Churchyard, Llantarnam, Monmouthshire . *Grave.*
Town/County Connections: Abergavenny and Cwmbran, Monmouthshire
Remarks: —   *VC with SWB Museum, Brecon*
Account of Deed: On 22/23 Jan. 1879 at Rorke's Drift, Natal, South Africa, Private Williams and two other men held a distant room of the hospital for more than an hour until they had no ammunition left, when the Zulus burst in and killed one of the men and two patients. Meanwhile Private Williams had succeeded in knocking a hole in the partition and took the two remaining patients through into the next ward. He was there joined by another man*, and working together (one holding the enemy at bayonet point while the other broke through three more partitions) they were able to bring eight patients into the inner line of defence. (*See also HOOK, A.H.)

WILLIAMS, John Henry   **1314**
Company Sergeant-Major   10th Bn., The South Wales Borders
Other Decorations: DCM, MM & Bar
Date of Gazette: 14 Dec. 1918
Place/Date of Birth: Nantyglo, Monmouthshire — 29 Sep. 1886
Place/Date of Death: Newport, Monmouthshire — 6 Mar. 1953   *Buried Ebbw Vale Cemetery*
Memorials: Ebbw Vale Council Chamber and General Offices, Richard, Thomas & Baldwin
Town/County Connections: Nantyglo and Ebbw Vale, Glamorgan
Remarks: Médaille Militaire (France); Served in Home Guard in Second World War, with rank of captain.
Account of Deed: On 7/8 Oct. 1918 at Villers Outreaux, France, Company Sergeant-Major Williams, seeing that his company was suffering heavy casualties from an enemy machine-gun, ordered a Lewis gun to engage it, and went forward under heavy fire to the flank of the enemy post, which he rushed single-handed, capturing 15 of the enemy. The prisoners, realizing that he was alone, then turned on him and one of them gripped his rifle. He managed to break away and killed five of the enemy, whereupon the remainder again surrendered. This action enabled not only his own company but those on the flank to advance.   *VC with SWB Museum, Brecon.*

WILLIAMS, William   **1315**
Seaman   Royal Naval Reserve
Other Decorations: DSM & Bar
Date of Gazette: 20 Jul. 1917
Place/Date of Birth: Amlwch Port, Anglesey — 30 Oct. 1890
Place/Date of Death: Holyhead — Anglesey — 23 Oct. 1965
Memorials: Amlwch, Anglesey . *Various memorials in Amlwch*
Town/County Connections: Amlwch, Anglesey
Remarks: Médaille Militaire (France).
Account of Deed: On 7 Jun. 1917 HMS *Pargust* (one of the 'Q' or 'mystery' ships) was out in the Atlantic when her engine room was damaged by a torpedo fired from a U-boat. The 'Panic party' went away and the U-boat surfaced, thinking that *Pargust* was a merchant vessel. When the U-boat was about 50 yards away, the Commander of *Pargust* gave the order to fire and the submarine blew up and sank. The explosion when *Pargust* was torpedoed loosened the gun covers and Seaman Williams with great presence of mind took the whole weight on himself and physically prevented the covers from falling and betraying the ship to the enemy. (Award by ballot. *See also STUART, R.N.)

WILLIAMS, William Charles   **1316**
Able Seaman   Royal Navy
Other Decorations: —
Date of Gazette: 16 Aug. 1915
Place/Date of Birth: Stanton Lacy, Shropshire — 15 Sep. 1880
Place/Date of Death: V. Beach, Gallipoli — 25 Apr. 1915
Memorials: Portsmouth Naval Memorial; Chepstow Parish Church
Town/County Connections: Stanton Lacy, Shropshire; Chepstow, Monmouthshire
Remarks: —   *Gun in Beaufort Square, Chepstow.*
Account of Deed: On 25 Apr. 1915 during the landing on V Beach, Cape Helles, Gallipoli, Able Seaman Williams, with three other men* was assisting the commander* of their ship, HMS *River Clyde* at the work of securing the lighters. He held on to a rope for over an hour, standing chest deep in the sea, under continuous fire. He was eventually dangerously wounded and later killed by a shell whilst his rescue was being affected by the commander who described him as the bravest sailor he had ever met. (See also UNWIN, E., DREWRY, G.L., MALLESON, W. St.A. and SAMSON, G.M.)

WILLIS, Richard Raymond   **1317**
Captain (later Major)   1st Bn., The Lancashire Fusiliers
Other Decorations: —
Date of Gazette: 24 Aug. 1915
Place/Date of Birth: Woking, Surrey — 30 Oct. 1876
Place/Date of Death: Cheltenham, Gloucestershire — 9 Feb. 1966
Memorials: (Cremated Cheltenham) *Harrow School.*
Town/County Connections: Woking, Surrey; Cheltenham, Gloucestershire
Remarks: RAF Education Officer 1923-29; Fellow of the Royal Geographical Society
Account of Deed: On 25 Apr. 1915 west of Cape Helles, Gallipoli, three companies and the Headquarters of the 1st Battalion, Lancashire Fusiliers, when landing on W Beach, were met by a very deadly fire from hidden machine-guns which caused a large number of casualties. The survivors, however, rushed up and cut the wire entanglements notwithstanding the terrific fire from the enemy and after overcoming supreme difficulties, the cliffs were gained and the position maintained. (Captain Willis was one of the six members of the regiment elected for the award. See also BROMLEY, C., GRIMSHAW, J.E., KENEALLY, W., RICHARDS, A.J. and STUBBS, F.E.)

WILMOT, Henry (later Sir Henry)   **1318**
Captain (later Colonel)   2nd Bn., The Rifle Brigade (The Prince Consort's Own)
Other Decorations: —
Date of Gazette: 24 Dec. 1858
Place/Date of Birth: Chaddesden, Derbyshire — 3 Feb. 1831
Place/Date of Death: Bournemouth, Hampshire — 7 Apr. 1901
Memorials: Chaddesden Church; The Rifle Brigade Memorial, Winchester Cathedral
Town/County Connections: Chaddesden, Derbyshire
Remarks: Judge Advocate-General to Forces during Chinese War 1860-61; Member of Parliament for South Derbyshire 1869-85; Colonel in command of North Midland Volunteer Brigade 1888-95
Account of Deed: On 11 Mar. 1858 at Lucknow, India, Captain Wilmot's company was engaged with a large number of the enemy near the Iron Bridge. That officer found himself at one stage, at the end of a street with only four of his men opposed to a considerable body of the enemy. One of his men was shot through both legs and two* of the others lifted him and although one of them was severely wounded they carried their comrade for a considerable distance, Captain Wilmot firing with the men's rifles and covering the retreat of the party. (*See also HAWKES, D. and NASH, W.)

WILSON, Arthur Knyvet (later Sir Arthur)   **1319**
Captain (later Admiral)   Royal Navy (Naval Brigade)
Other Decorations: GCB, OM, GCVO
Date of Gazette: 21 May 1884
Place/Date of Birth: Swaffham, Norfolk — 4 Mar. 1842
Place/Date of Death: Swaffham, Norfolk — 25 May 1921
Memorials: Swaffham Parish Church
Town/County Connections: Swaffham, Norfolk
Remarks: Lord Commissioner of the Admiralty and Comptroller of the Navy 1897-1901; Commandant, Channel Squadron 1901-03; Commander-in-Chief Home and Channel Fleets 1903-07; Admiral of the Fleet 1907; First Sea Lord 1909-12.
Account of Deed: On 29 Feb. 1884 at the Battle of El Teb, Sudan, Captain Wilson of HMS *Hecla* attached himself, during the advance, to the right half-battery, Naval Brigade, in place of a lieutenant who was mortally wounded. As the troops closed on the enemy battery, the Arabs charged out on the detachment which was dragging one of the guns, whereupon Captain Wilson sprang to the front and engaged in single combat with some of the enemy, and so protected the detachment until men of the York and Lancaster Regiment came to his assistance.

WILSON, Eric Charles Twelves   **1320**
A/Captain (later Lieutenant Colonel)   The East Surrey Regiment, attd. Somali Mounted Infantry
Other Decorations: —
Date of Gazette: 14 Oct. 1940
Place/Date of Birth: Sandown, Isle of Wight — 2 Oct. 1912
Place/Date of Death: —
Memorials: —
Town/County Connections: Sandown, Isle of Wight
Remarks: Administrative Officer, HM Overseas Civil Service, Tanganyika 1949-61.
Account of Deed: From 11 to 15 Aug. 1940 at Observation Hill in Somaliland, Captain Wilson kept a machine-gun post in action in spite of being wounded and suffering from malaria. Some of his guns were blown to pieces by the enemy's field artillery fire, and he himself was taken prisoner, but was freed later when Eritrea was conquered.

WILSON, George   1321
Private   2nd Bn., The Highland Light Infantry
Other Decorations: —
Date of Gazette: 5 Dec. 1914
Place/Date of Birth: Edinburgh — 29 Apr. 1886
Place/Date of Death: Edinburgh — 22 Apr. 1926
Memorials: —
Town/County Connections: Edinburgh
Remarks: —
Account of Deed: On 14 Sep. 1914 near Verneuill, France, Private Wilson went with a rifleman to try to locate a machine-gun which was holding up the advance of the 2nd Battalion, Highland Light Infantry. When the rifleman was killed, Private Wilson went on alone and, when he reached his target shot six of the enemy, bayoneted the officer and then captured the gun.

WOOD, Harry Blanshard   1322
Corporal (Lance-Sergeant)   2nd Bn. Scots Guards
Other Decorations: MM
Date of Gazette: 14 Dec. 1918
Place/Date of Birth: Newton-on-Derwent, Yorkshire — 21 Jun. 1881
Place/Date of Death: Bristol — 15 Aug. 1924
Memorials: —
Town/County Connections: Newton-on-Derwent, Yorkshire; Bristol
Remarks: —
Account of Deed: On 13 Oct. 1918 at St. Python, France, when the advance was desperately opposed and the streets of the village were raked by fire, Corporal Wood's platoon sergeant was killed and he took command of the leading platoon. The River Selle had to be crossed and the ruined bridge gained, although the space in front of it was full of snipers, so the corporal carried a very large brick into the open space, lay down behind it and, firing continuously on the snipers, covered his men while they worked their way across. Later in the day he repeatedly drove off enemy counter-attacks.

WOOD, Henry Evelyn (later Sir Evelyn)   1323
Lieutenant (later Field Marshal)   17th Lancers (Duke of Cambridge's Own)
Other Decorations: GCB, GCMG
Date of Gazette: 4 Sep. 1860
Place/Date of Birth: Cressing, Essex — 9 Feb. 1838
Place/Date of Death: Harlow, Essex — 2 Dec. 1920
Memorials: St. Paul's Cathedral
Town/County Connections: Cressing and Harlow, Essex; London
Remarks: Légion d'Honneur (France). Joined the Royal Navy 1852 and served in the Crimea with the Naval Brigade; Quartermaster to the Forces 1893-97; Adjutant General 1897-1901; commanded 2 Army Corps 1901-04; Constable of the Tower of London 1911-19.
Account of Deed: On 19 Oct. 1858 during an action at Sinwaho, India, Lieutenant Wood was in command of a troop of light cavalry and attacked almost single-handed a body of rebels, whom he routed. He also subsequently at Sindhora, rescued, with the help of a duffadar and a sowar, a Potail from a band of robbers who had captured the man and carried him into the jungle where they intended to hang him.

WOOD, John Angustus   1324
Captain (later Colonel)   20th Bombay Native Infantry
Other Decorations: —
Date of Gazette: 3 Aug. 1860
Place/Date of Birth: Fort William, Scotland — 10 Jun. 1818
Place/Date of Death: Poona, India — 23 Jan. 1878
Memorials: —
Town/County Connections: Fort William, Scotland
Remarks: —
Account of Deed: On 9 Dec. 1856 at Bushire, Persia, Captain Wood led a Grenadier Company which formed the head of the assaulting column and was the first man on the parapet of the fort, where he was immediately attacked by a large number of the garrison. A volley was fired at Captain Wood and the head of the storming party at very close range but although the captain was hit by seven musket balls he at once threw himself upon the enemy, killing their leader. He was closely followed by the men of his company and speedily overcame all opposition.

WOOD, Wilfred **1325**
Private   10th Bn., The Northumberland Fusiliers
Other Decorations: —
Date of Gazette: 27 Nov. 1918
Place/Date of Birth: Stockport, Cheshire — 2 Feb. 1897
Place/Date of Death: Hazel Grove, near Stockport — 3 Jan. 1982
Memorials: Name-plate (from a LMS engine) in Regimental Museum of The Northumberland Fusiliers, Alnwick Castle, Northumberland.
Town/County Connections: Stockport, Cheshire
Remarks: —
Account of Deed: On 28 Oct. 1918 near Casa Vana, Italy, when the advance was being held up by hostile machine-guns and snipers, Private Wood on his own initiative worked forward with his Lewis gun, enfiladed the enemy machine-gun nest and caused 140 men to surrender. Later, when a hidden machine-gun opened fire at point-blank range, Private Wood charged the gun, firing his Lewis gun from the hip at the same time. He killed the machine-gun crew and, without further orders, pushed on and enfiladed a ditch from which three officers and 160 men subsequently surrendered.

WOODALL, Joseph Edward **1326**
Lance-Sergeant (later Captain)   1st Bn., The Rifle Brigade (Prince Consort's Own)
Other Decorations: —
Date of Gazette: 28 Jun. 1918
Place/Date of Birth: Winton, Eccles, Manchester — 1 Jun. 1896
Place/Date of Death: Dun Laoghaire, Ireland — 2 Jan. 1962
Memorials: The Rifle Brigade Memorial, Winchester Cathedral
Town/County Connections: Eccles, Manchester; Southall, Middlesex
Remarks: —
Account of Deed: On 22 Apr. 1918 at La Pannerie, France, Lance-Sergeant Woodall was in charge of a platoon which was held up during an advance by a machine-gun. On his own initiative he rushed forward and single-handed captured the gun and eight men. He then collected 10 men and rushed a farmhouse from which heavy fire was coming, taking 30 prisoners. Shortly afterwards when the officer in charge was killed, he took entire command, reorganising and disposing the two platoons most skilfully. Throughout the day this NCO was constantly encouraging the men and finding out and sending back invaluable information.

WOODCOCK, Thomas **1327**
Private (later Corporal)   2nd Bn., Irish Guards
Other Decorations: —
Date of Gazette: 17 Oct. 1917
Place/Date of Birth: Wigan, Lancashire — 19 Mar. 1888
Place/Date of Death: Bullecourt, France — 27 Mar. 1918
Memorials: Douchy-les-Ayette British Cemetery, France
Town/County Connections: Wigan, Lancashire
Remarks: —
Account of Deed: On 12/13 Sep. 1917 north of Broenbeek, Belgium, when an advanced post had held out for 96 hours and was finally forced to retire, the lance-sergeant* in charge of the party and Private Woodcock covered the retirement. After crossing the stream themselves, Private Woodcock heard cries for help behind him — he returned and waded into the stream amid a shower of bombs and rescued another member of the party whom he carried across open ground in daylight towards our front line, regardless of machine-gun fire. (*See also MOYNEY, J.)

WOODEN, Charles **1328**
Sergeant-Major (later Lieutenant and Quartermaster)   17th Lancers (Duke of Cambridge's Own)
Other Decorations: —
Date of Gazette: 26 Oct. 1858
Place/Date of Birth: Germany — 24 Mar. 1827
Place/Date of Death: Dover, Kent — 24 Apr. 1876
Memorials: St. James's Cemetery, Dover
Town/County Connections: Dover, Kent
Remarks: Rode in the Charge of the Light Brigade.
Account of Deed: On 26 Oct. 1854, in the Crimea, at Balaclava, Sergeant-Major Wooden went out with a surgeon* to the assistance of an officer who was lying seriously wounded in an exposed position, after the retreat of the Light Cavalry. He helped to dress the officer's wounds under heavy fire from the enemy. (*See also MOUAT, J.)

WOODROFFE, Sidney Clayton
1329

Second Lieutenant   8th Bn., The Rifle Brigade (Prince Consort's Own)
Other Decorations: —
Date of Gazette: 6 Sep. 1915
Place/Date of Birth: Lewes, Sussex — 17 Dec. 1895
Place/Date of Death: Hooge, Belgium — 30 Jul. 1915
Memorials: Menin Gate, Belgium; The Rifle Brigade Memorial, Winchester Cathedral
Town/County Connections: Lewes, Sussex; Bournemouth, Hampshire
Remarks: — *Marlborough College, Wilts*
Account of Deed: On 30 Jul. 1915 at Hooge, Belgium, when the enemy had broken through the centre of our front trenches, Second Lieutenant Woodroffe's position was heavily attacked with bombs from the flank and subsequently from the rear, but he managed to defend his post until all his bombs were exhausted. He then skilfully withdrew his remaining men and immediately led them forward in a counter-attack under intense rifle and machine-gun fire, and was killed whilst in the act of cutting the wire obstacles in the open.

WOODS, James Park
1330

Private   48th Bn. (S.A.), Australian Imperial Force
Other Decorations: —
Date of Gazette: 26 Dec. 1918
Place/Date of Birth: Gawler, South Australia — 2 Jan. 1891
Place/Date of Death: Claremont, Western Australia — 18 Jan 1963
Memorials: Karrakatta Cemetery, Perth; Australian War Memorial, Canberra
Town/County Connections: —
Remarks: —
Account of Deed: On 18 Sep. 1918, near Le Verguier, north-west of St. Quentin, France, Private Woods, with a weak patrol, attacked and captured a formidable enemy post, which, with two comrades, he held against heavy counter-attacks. Jumping on to the parapet he fired, and kept on firing, inflicting severe casualties and holding up the enemy until help arrived.

WOOLLEY, Geoffrey Harold
1331

Second Lieutenant (later Captain)   9th (County of London) Bn., The London Regt. (Queen Victoria's Rifles)
Other Decorations: OBE, MC
Date of Gazette: 22 May 1915
Place/Date of Birth: Bethnal Green, London — 14 May 1892
Place/Date of Death: West Chiltington, Sussex — 10 Dec. 1968
Memorials: —
Town/County Connections: Bethnal Green, London; West Chiltington, Sussex
Remarks: Ordained after the First World War; served as a Chaplain of the Forces during the Second World War in North Africa; Vice-Chairman (UK) of the VC and GC Association 1956-68.
Account of Deed: During the night of 20/21 Apr. 1915 on Hill 60, Belgium, Second Lieutenant Woolley was the only officer on the hill at the time, but with very few men he successfully resisted all attacks on his trench, and continued throwing bombs and encouraging his men until relieved. His trench during all this time was being heavily shelled and bombed.

No photograph available

WRIGHT, Alexander
1332

Private   77th Regiment (later The Middlesex Regiment — Duke of Cambridge's Own)
Other Decorations: —
Date of Gazette: 24 Feb. 1857
Place/Date of Birth: Ballymena, Co. Antrim, Ireland — 1826
Place/Date of Death: Calcutta, India — 28 Jul. 1858
Memorials: —
Town/County Connections: Ballymena, Co. Antrim
Remarks: —
Account of Deed: On 22 Mar. 1855 in the Crimea, Private Wright distinguished himself in repelling a sortie. On 19 Apr. he showed great bravery at the taking of the Russian Rifle Pits and was particularly noticed for the encouragement he gave the other men while holding the Pits under very heavy fire; he was wounded in this action. He again showed great courage on 30 Aug. 1855, and throughout the war.

WRIGHT, Peter Harold   **1333**
Company Sergeant-Major   3rd Bn., Coldstream Guards
Other Decorations: —
Date of Gazette: 7 Sep. 1944
Place/Date of Birth: Mettingham, Bungay, Suffolk — 10 Aug. 1916
Place/Date of Death: — *Died about 9.4.1990 in Suffolk, possibly in the*
Memorials: —   *Mettingham or Wenhaston area.*
Town/County Connections: Mettingham and Wenhaston, Suffolk
Remarks: —
Account of Deed: On 25 Sep. 1943 near Salerno, Italy, a steep, wooded hill was being assaulted by the 3rd Bn. Coldstream Guards, and Company Sergeant-Major Wright's company, most of its officers killed, was held up near the crest. Sergeant-Major Wright took charge and single-handed he silenced with grenades and bayonet three Spandau posts and then led his men to consolidate the position. He then beat off a counter-attack, and disregarding the heavy fire, brought up extra ammunition.

WRIGHT, Theodore   **1334**
Captain   57th Field Coy., Corps of Royal Engineers
Other Decorations: —
Date of Gazette: 16 Nov. 1914
Place/Date of Birth: Brighton, Sussex — 15 May 1883
Place/Date of Death: Vailly, France — 14 Sep. 1914
Memorials: Vailly British Cemetery, France
Town/County Connections: Brighton, Sussex
Remarks: — *Name on W.M. in Albury Church, Surrey.*
Account of Deed: On 23 Aug. 1914 at Mons, Belgium, Captain Wright tried to connect up the lead to demolish a bridge, under heavy fire and although wounded in the head, he made a second attempt. At Vailly, France, on 14 Sep. he assisted the passage of the 5th Cavalry Brigade over the pontoon bridge and was mortally wounded whilst helping a wounded man into shelter.

WRIGHT, Wallace Duffield   **1335**
Lieutenant (later Brigadier General)   1st Bn., The Queen's Royal West Surrey Regiment, employed Northern Nigeria Regiment
Other Decorations: CB, CMG, DSO
Date of Gazette: 11 Sep. 1903
Place/Date of Birth: Gibraltar — 20 Sep. 1875
Place/Date of Death: Chobham, Surrey — 25 Mar. 1953
Memorials: —
Town/County Connections: Chobham, Surrey
Remarks: Served with The Queen's Own Cameron Highlanders 1914-18; commanded 8th Infantry Brigade 1918-22; Légion d'Honneur (France); HM's Body Guard of Hon. Corps of Gentlemen-at-Arms 1932-50; served with the Home Guard 1940-45.
Account of Deed: On 26 Feb. 1903 in West Africa, Lieutenant Wright, with only one other officer and 44 men sustained the determined charges of 1,000 horse and 2,000 foot for two hours and when the enemy, after heavy losses, fell back in good order, Lieutenant Wright continued to follow them until they were in full retreat. The personal example of this officer, as well as his skilful leadership, contributed largely to the brilliant success of the affair.

WYATT, George Harry   **1336**
Lance-Corporal (later Lance-Sergeant)   3rd Bn., Coldstream Guards
Other Decorations: —
Date of Gazette: 18 Nov. 1915
Place/Date of Birth: Worcester — 5 Sep. 1886
Place/Date of Death: Doncaster, Yorkshire — 22 Jan. 1964
Memorials: Cadeby Churchyard, near Doncaster, S. Yorkshire
Town/County Connections: Worcester; Doncaster, Yorkshire
Remarks: Order of St. George (Russia). Joined the Police Force in Yorkshire after leaving the Army, serving in Barnsley and over 20 years in Doncaster.
Account of Deed: On 25/26 Aug. 1914 at Landrecies, France, part of Lance-Corporal Wyatt's battalion was hotly engaged close to some farm buildings, when the enemy set alight some straw sacks in the farmyard. The lance-corporal twice dashed out under very heavy fire from the enemy, only 25 yards away, and extinguished the burning straw, making it possible to hold the position. Later, although wounded in the head, he continued firing until he could no longer see owing to the blood pouring down his face. The medical officer bound up his wound and ordered him to the rear, but he returned to the firing line and went on fighting.

WYLIE, Charles Hotham Montagu DOUGHTY-   **1337**
Lieutenant Colonel   The Royal Welch Fusiliers, attd. HQ Mediterranean Expeditionary Force
Other Decorations: CB, CMG
Date of Gazette: 23 Jun. 1915
Place/Date of Birth: Theberton, Leiston, Suffolk — 23 Jul. 1868
Place/Date of Death: Sedd-el-Bahr, Gallipoli — 26 Apr. 1915
Memorials: V Beach Cemetery, Gallipoli; St. Peter's Church, Theberton; War Memorial,
Theberton Churchyard
Town/County Connections: Theberton and Southwold, Suffolk
Remarks: VC in RWF Museum, Caernarvon.
Account of Deed: On 26 Apr. 1915 after a landing had been made on the beach on a point of the
Gallipoli Peninsula, during which the brigadier general and the brigade major had been killed, Lieutenant Colonel Doughty-Wylie and another officer* organised and made an attack through and on both sides of the village of Sedd-el-Bahr on the Old Fort at the top of the hill. The enemy's position was very strongly entrenched and defended, but mainly due to the initiative, skill and great gallantry of the two officers the attack was a complete success. Both were killed in the moment of victory. (*See also WALFORD, G.N.)

WYLLY, Guy George Egerton   **1338**
Lieutenant (later Colonel)   Tasmanian Imperial Bushmen
Other Decorations: CB, DSO
Date of Gazette: 23 Nov. 1900
Place/Date of Birth: Hobart, Tasmania — 17 Feb. 1880
Place/Date of Death: Camberley, Surrey — 9 Jan. 1962
Memorials: (St. John's Crematorium, Woking, Surrey); Australian War Memorial, Canberra
Town/County Connections: —
Remarks: He and private J.H. Bisdee were the first Australian-born men to win the VC while serving with an Australian Unit under British Command. Served with the Australian Imperial Force in the First World War 1914-18; on North-west Frontier, India 1919, 1930 (Commandant 6th DCO Lancers 1926-29); Assistant Adjutant and Quartermaster General, Peshawur District 1929-33; ADC to The King 1926-33.
Account of Deed: On 1 Sep. 1900 near Warm Baths, Transvaal, South Africa, Lieutenant Wylly was one of the advance scouting party passing through a narrow gorge, when the enemy suddenly opened fire at close range and six out of the party of eight were wounded, including Lieutenant Wylly, who, seeing that one of his men was badly wounded in the leg and that his horse was shot, went back to him. He made the wounded man take his horse while he, the lieutenant, opened fire from behind a rock to cover the retreat of the others, at the imminent risk of being cut off himself.

YATE, Charles Allix Lavington   **1339**
Major   2nd Bn., The King's Own Yorkshire Light Infantry
Other Decorations: —
Date of Gazette: 25 Nov. 1914
Place/Date of Birth: Madeley, Shropshire — 14 Mar. 1872
Place/Date of Death: Germany — 20 Sep. 1914
Memorials: Berlin South Western Cemetery, Germany
Town/County Connections: Madeley, Shropshire
Remarks: —
Account of Deed: On 26 Aug. 1914 at Le Cateau, France, Major Yate commanded one of the two companies that remained to the end in the trenches, and when all other officers had been killed or wounded and ammunition exhausted, he led his 19 survivors against the enemy in a charge in which he himself was severely wounded. He was picked up by the enemy and subsequently died as a prisoner of war.

YESHWANT GHADGE   **1340**
Naik   5th Mahratta Light Infantry, Indian Army
Other Decorations: —
Date of Gazette: 2 Nov. 1944
Place/Date of Birth: Phalasgaon Village, Kolaba District, Bombay — 16 Nov. 1921
Place/Date of Death: Morlupo, Italy — 10 Jul. 1944
Memorials: The Cassino Memorial, Italy
Town/County Connections: —
Remarks: —
Account of Deed: On 10 Jul. 1944 in the Upper Tiber Valley, Italy, a rifle section commanded by Naik Yeshwant Ghadge came under heavy machine-gun fire at close range which killed or wounded all members of the section except the commander. Without hesitation Naik Yeshwant Ghadge rushed the machine-gun position, first throwing a grenade which knocked out the machine-gun and firer and then he shot one of the gun crew. Finally, having no time to change his magazine, he clubbed to death the two remaining members of the crew. He fell mortally wounded, shot by an enemy sniper.

YOUENS, Frederick   **1341**
T/Second Lieutenant   13th Bn., The Durham Light Infantry
Other Decorations: —
Date of Gazette: 2 Aug. 1917
Place/Date of Birth: High Wycombe, Buckinghamshire — 14 Aug. 1895
Place/Date of Death: Near Hill 60, Belgium — 9 Jul. 1917
Memorials: Railway Dugouts Burial Ground, Belgium; High Wycombe Parish Church
Town/County Connections: High Wycombe, Buckinghamshire
Remarks: —
Account of Deed: On 7 Jul. 1917 near Hill 60, Belgium, it was reported that the enemy were preparing to raid our trenches and Second Lieutenant Youens, who had already been wounded, immediately set out to rally a Lewis gun team which had become disorganised. While doing this an enemy bomb fell on the Lewis gun position without exploding. The second lieutenant picked it up and hurled it over the parapet, but soon after another bomb fell near the same place and again he picked it up, but it exploded in his hand, severely wounding him and some of his men. This gallant officer later succumbed to his wounds.

YOULL, John Scott   **1342**
T/Second Lieutenant   1st Bn., The Northumberland Fusiliers, attd. 11th (S) Bn.
Other Decorations: —
Date of Gazette: 25 Jul. 1918
Place/Date of Birth: Thorncroft, Thornley, Co. Durham — 6 Jun. 1897
Place/Date off Death: River Piave, Italy — 27 Oct. 1918
Memorials: Giavera British Cemetery, Italy
Town/County Connections: Thornley, Co. Durham
Remarks: —
Account of Deed: On 15 Jun. 1918 south west of Asiago, Italy, Second Lieutenant Youll was commanding a patrol which came under heavy enemy fire. Sending his men back to safety he remained to watch the situation and then, unable to rejoin his company, he reported to a neighbouring unit where he took command of a party of men from different units, holding his position against enemy attack until a machine-gun opened fire behind him. He rushed and captured the gun, killing most of the team and opened fire, inflicting heavy casualties. He then carried out three separate counter-attacks, driving the enemy back each time.

YOUNG, Alexander   **1343**
Sergeant-Major (later Lieutenant)   Cape Police, South African Forces
Other Decorations: —
Date of Gazette: 8 Nov. 1901
Place/Date of Birth: Ballinona, Clarinbridge, Co. Galway, Ireland — 27 Jan. 1873
Place/Date of Death: Somme, France — 19 Oct. 1916
Memorials: Thiepval Memorial, France
Town/County Connections: Clarinbridge, Co. Galway
Remarks: Served with the South African Scottish Regiment in the First World War
Account of Deed: On 13 Aug. 1901 at Ruiterskraal, South Africa, towards the close of the action, Sergeant-Major Young, with a handful of men, rushed some kopjes which were being held by about 20 Boers. On reaching their objective, the enemy were seen galloping back to another kopje held by the Boers. Sergeant-Major Young then galloped on some 50 yards ahead of his party and closing with the enemy, shot one of them and captured the commandant, the latter firing three times at point-blank range before being taken prisoner.

YOUNG, Frank Edward   **1344**
Second Lieutenant   1st Bn., The Hertfordshire Regiment
Other Decorations: —
Date of Gazette: 14 Dec. 1918
Place/Date of Birth: Cherat, North West Province, India — 2 Oct. 1895
Place/Date of Death: Near Havrincourt, France — 18 Sep. 1918
Memorials: Hermies Hill British Cemetery, France; War Memorial in St. Mary's Churchyard, Hitchin, Hertfordshire
Town/County Connections: —
Remarks: —
Account of Deed: On 18 Sep. 1918 south-east of Havrincourt, France, during an enemy counter-attack and throughout intense enemy fire, Second Lieutenant Young visited all posts, warned the garrisons and encouraged the men. In the early stages of the attack he rescued two of his men who had been captured and bombed and silenced an enemy machine-gun. Then he fought his way back to the main barricade and drove out a party of the enemy assembling there. Throughout four hours of heavy fighting this officer set a fine example and was last seen fighting hand-to-hand against a considerable number of the enemy.

YOUNG, John Francis   **1345**
Private   87th Bn., Quebec Regiment (Canadian Grenadier Guards), C.E.F.
Other Decorations: —
Date of Gazette: 14 Dec. 1918
Place/Date of Birth: Kidderminster, Worcestershire — 14 Jan. 1893
Place/Date of Death: Quebec, Canada — 7 Nov. 1929
Memorials: Mount Royal Cemetery, Montreal, Canada
Town/County Connections: Kidderminster, Worcestershire
Remarks: —
Account of Deed: On 2 Sep. 1918 in the Dury-Arras Sector, France, when his company had
suffered heavy casualties, Private Young, a stretcher-bearer, went forward to dress the wounded
in open ground swept by machine-gun and rifle fire. He did this for over an hour displaying absolute fearlessness, and on more
than one occasion, having used up all his stock of dressings, he returned to company headquarters for a further supply. Later
in the day he organised and led stretcher-bearers to bring in the wounded whom he had dressed.

YOUNG (real name MORRELL), Thomas   **1346**
Private   9th Bn., The Durham Light Infantry
Other Decorations: —
Date of Gazette: 4 Jun. 1918
Place/Date of Birth: Boldon, Co. Durham — 28 Jan. 1895
Place/Date of Death: Whickham, Co. Durham — 15 Oct. 1966
Memorials: Buried at St. Patrick, High Spen, Co. Durham
Town/County Connections: Boldon and High Spen, Co. Durham
Remarks: —
Account of Deed: During the period 25/31 Mar. 1918 at Bucquoy, France, Private Young, a
stretcher-bearer, worked unceasingly, evacuating the wounded from seemingly impossible
places. On nine different occasions he went out in front of our lines in broad daylight, under heavy rifle, machine-gun and shell
fire and brought back wounded to safety. Those too badly wounded to be moved before dressing, he dressed under fire and
then carried them back unaided to our lines. He saved nine lines in this manner.

YOUNG, Thomas James   **1347**
Lieutenant (later Captain)   Royal Navy (Naval Brigade)
Other Decorations: —
Date of Gazette: 1 Feb. 1859
Place/Date of Birth: ? — 1827
Place/Date of Death: Caen, France — 20 Mar. 1869
Memorials: Protestant Cemetery in the Rue du Magazin à Poudre, Caen, France
Town/County Connections: —
Remarks: Brother-in-law of Midshipman D.G. Boyes, VC; Order of Medjidie, 5th Class
Account of Deed: On 16 Nov. 1857 at Lucknow, India, naval guns were brought up close to the
Shah Nujeff mosque, and the gun crews kept up a steady fire in an attempt to breach the walls,
while a hail of musket balls and grenades from the mutineers inside the mosque caused heavy casualties. Lieutenant Young
moved from gun to gun giving encouragement, and when he and an able seaman* were the only survivors, all the rest being killed
or wounded, Lieutenant Young took the last gunner's place and between them they loaded and fired the gun. (*See also HALL, W.)

YOUNG, William   **1348**
Private   8th (S) Bn., The East Lancashire Regiment
Other Decorations: —
Date of Gazette: 30 Mar. 1916
Place/Date of Birth: Maryhill, Glasgow — 1 Jan. 1876
Place/Date of Death: Aldershot, Hampshire — 27 Aug. 1916
Memorials: Preston (New Hall Lane) Cemetery, Lancashire
Town/County Connections: Glasgow; Preston, Lancashire
Remarks: —
Account of Deed: On 22 Dec. 1915, East of Fonquevillers, France, Private Young saw from his
trench that one of his company's NCOs was lying wounded in front of the wire. Acting without
orders and heedless of his exposure to enemy fire, he climbed over the parapet and went to the rescue of his sergeant. He was
hit by two bullets, one shattered his jaw and the other entered his chest. Undeterred, he went on and, with another soldier who
came to assist, brought the wounded sergeant back to safety. Later Private Young walked back to the village dressing station
to have his injuries attended to.

YOUNGER, David Reginald   1349

Captain   1st Bn., The Gordon Highlanders
Other Decorations: —
Date of Gazette: 8 Aug. 1902
Place/Date of Birth: Edinburgh — 17 Mar. 1871
Place/Date of Death: Lechochoek, Transvaal, South Africa — 11 Jul. 1900
Memorials: —
Town/County Connections: Edinburgh and Leith, Scotland
Remarks: —
Account of Deed: On 11 Jul. 1900 near Krugersdorp, South Africa, Captain Younger took out a party which successfully dragged an artillery waggon under cover of a small kopje, though exposed to very heavy and accurate enemy fire. He also accompanied a second party who went out to try to bring in the guns, but during the afternoon he was mortally wounded, dying shortly afterwards. (See also GORDON, W.E.)

ZENGEL, Raphael Louis   1350

Sergeant   5th Bn., Saskatchewan Regiment, C.E.F.
Other Decorations: MM
Date of Gazette: 27 Sep. 1918
Place/Date of Birth: Faribault, Minnesota, U.S.A. — 11 Nov. 1894
Place/Date of Death: British Columbia, Canada — 22 Feb. 1977
Memorials: —
Town/County Connections: —
Remarks: —
Account of Deed: On 9 Aug. 1918 east of Warvillers, France, Sergeant Zengel was leading his platoon forward to the attack when he realised that an enemy machine-gun was firing into the advancing line. He rushed forward ahead of the platoon to the gun emplacement, killed the officer and operator of the gun and dispersed the crew. Later in the day he was rendered temporarily unconscious by an enemy shell but on recovering continued to direct harassing fire on the enemy. His utter disregard for personal safety and the confidence he inspired in all ranks greatly assisted in the successful outcome of the attack.

THE AMERICAN UNKNOWN WARRIOR   1351

He is buried at Arlington National Cemetery, Washington, D.C. The Cross is inscribed *The Unknown Warrior of the United States of America* and dated 28th October 1921

Town & County Connections

Aberdeen, Scotland 239, 280, 788
Aberdour, Fife, Scotland 690
Abergavenny, Mon. 881, 1313
Aberystwyth, Cardigan, Wales 390
Abingdon, Berkshire 209
Abram, Wigan, Lancashire 498
Acton, London 327, 474
Airdrie, Lanark, Scotland 185, 946
Aldershot, Hampshire 1224
Alloa, Clackmannan, Scotland 141
Alnwick, Northumberland 982
Alton, Hampshire 12, 594
Altrincham, Cheshire 114, 1173
Alverstoke, Hampshire 175
Amlwch Port, Anglesey 1315
Anderson, Blandford, Dorset 703
Anderston, Glasgow 787
Anerley, Bromley, Kent 655
Ardersier, Inverness, Scotland 814
Ardwick, Lancashire 659
Argyllshire, Scotland 182, 753
Armadale, West Lothian 33
Arrabeg, Offaly, Ireland 505
Ascot, Berkshire 113
Ash, Hampshire 540
Ashbourne, Derbyshire 1245
Ashington, Northumberland 171
Ashton-under-Lyne, Lancs. 1114
Ashwell, Rutland 6
Aston, Birmingham 1252
Athboy, Co. Meath, Ireland 542
Atherstone, Warwickshire 635
Athlone, Westmeath 354, 414
Athy, Co. Kildare, Ireland 581
Awbridge, Hampshire 292
Ayr, Scotland 1129
Ayrshire, Scotland 107

Bagnalstown, Carlow, Ireland 754
Bagshot, Surrey 27
Balcarres, Fife, Scotland 745
Ballinacor, Wicklow, Ireland 443
Ballinrobe, Co. Mayo, Ireland 638
Balloch, Dunbarton, Scotland 404
Ballochyle, Ayrshire, Scotland 993
Ballybeggan, Tralee, Kerry 670
Ballycastle, Antrim, Ireland 1013
Ballymena, Antrim 960, 1332
Ballyragget, Kilkenny, Ireland 56
Bampton, Devon 1028
Bangor, Down, Ireland 90, 237, 819
Bantry, Co. Cork, Ireland 1195
Banwell, Axbridge, Somerset 825
Bardwell, Suffolk 8
Barking, Essex 348
Barnet, Hertfordshire 291, 856
Barnsleigh, Tipperary, Ireland 1094
Barony, Glasgow, Scotland 959
Barrow-in-Furness, Lancs. 419, 852, 1277
Barton-on-Sea, Hampshire 1295
Barton Regis, Bristol 333

Bath, Somerset 165, 421, 640, 1029, 1039, 1265
Battersea, London 234
Bayswater, London 841
Beaminster, Dorset 888
Beckenham, Kent 532, 935, 1041
Beddington, Surrey 650
Bedford 422
Bedlington, Northumberland 644
Bedminster, Bristol 1037
Beeston, Nottinghamshire 442
Belfast, Ireland 77, 184, 821
Bellshill, Lanark, Scotland 1048
Belper, Derbyshire 1185
Belturbet, Co. Cavan, Ireland 1170
Berkeley, Gloucestershire 158
Bermondsey, London 585 798
Bethnal Green, London 1331
Bewdley, Worcestershire 721
Bexleyheath, Kent 1178
Bideford, Devon 37
Billingford, Norfolk 415
Bilston, Staffordshire 53, 947
Bingley, Yorkshire 913
Birmingham 23, 252, 402, 416, 450, 677 947, 962, 1023, 1110, 1147, 1242, 1251, 1308
Birr, Offaly, Ireland 168, 907
Birstall, Leicestershire 525
Bishop Auckland, Co. Durham 504
Bishopscourt, Kildare, Ireland 409
Bishopsteignton, Devon 908
Blaby, Leicestershire 281
Black Rock, Dublin, Ireland 763
Blackburn, Lancs. 319, 497, 990, 1115
Blackheath, London 228, 383, 1186
Blandford, Dorset 263
Bloomsbury, London 1147
Blyth, Northumberland 1178
Bodmin, Cornwall 31, 435
Bognor, Sussex 1205
Bolden, Co. Durham 1346
Bolton, Lancashire 388
Bootle, Lancashire 78, 1005
Boroughbridge, Yorkshire 1300
Borrisokane, Tipperary 386, 387
Borrowstounness (Bo'ness), West Lothian, Scotland 1188
Boscombe, Hampshire 851
Bosham, Sussex 449
Bourne, Lincolnshire 1130
Bournemouth, Hants. 813, 825, 884, 887, 932, 992, 1053, 1121, 1329
Bourtie, Aberdeen, Scotland 477
Bourton-on-the-Water, Glos. 642
Bow, London 1062
Bowes Park, London 104
Bracklesham, Sussex 21
Bradford, Yorks. 26, 198, 604, 853
Bramhall, Cheshire 214
Bray, Dublin, Ireland 322
Brecon, Wales 756

Brentford, Middlesex 1172
Brentwood, Essex 860
Brereton, Cheshire 956
Bridge of Allan, Stirling 462
Bridgend, Glamorgan, Wales 1268
Bridgnorth, Shropshire 1312
Bridlington, Yorkshire 1200
Brierley Hill, Staffordshire 103
Brigg, Lincolnshire 575
Brighton, Sussex 67, 104, 110, 278, 305, 516, 563, 833, 1334
Brill, Aylesbury, Bucks. 373
Bristol 79, 150, 305, 738, 739, 967, 1077, 1080, 1204, 1322
Brockenhurst, Hampshire 650
Bromley, Kent 471, 1301
Broomelton, Lanark, Scotland 13
Broughton, Lancashire 1221
Broughty Ferry, Dundee 826
Broxbourne, Hertfordshire 1207
Buckhurst Hill, Essex 925
Buckie, Banffshire, Scotland 788
Buckley, Flintshire, Wales 91
Bungay, Suffolk 1241
Burnham, Buckinghamshire 426
Burnley, Lancashire 237, 355
Burslem, Staffordshire 59, 235
Burton, Cheshire 241, 242
Burton-on-Trent, Staffs. 235
Bury, Lancashire 973
Bushmills, Antrim, Ireland 1013

Caddington, Bedfordshire 1289
Caerleon, Monmouthshire 163
Caernarvon, Wales 1033
Cahir, Tipperary, Ireland 903
Cahirbane, Co. Clare, Ireland 271
Calcott, Somerset 145
Camberley, Surrey 283, 521, 857, 898, 1097
Camberwell, London 61, 192, 255, 1177
Cambridge 234, 346, 618
Cambusnethan, Lanarkshire 873
Canterbury, Kent 164, 833
Cardiff 57, 1140, 1253, 1268
Carlingford, Louth, Ireland 885
Carlisle, Cumberland 113, 232
Carlow, Ireland 761
Carluke, Lanarkshire 33, 172, 176
Carnoustie, Angus 634, 1102
Carrickfergus, Co. Antrim 174, 273
Carrington, Nottinghamshire 103
Cashel, Co. Tipperary, Ireland 444
Castleblaney, Co. Monaghan 605
Castleborough, Co. Wexford 537
Castlecomer, Kilkenny, Ireland 163
Castleford, Yorkshire 140
Castletown, Donegal, Ireland 245
Castletown, Isle of Man 169
Castletown, Co. Westmeath 1073
Catford, Kent 704

Cavendish, Suffolk 209
Cawdor, Nairn, Scotland 180, 782
Chacewater, Cornwall 1058
Chaddesden, Derbyshire 1318
Chagford, Devon 1259
Chalfont St. Giles, Bucks. 485
Chalfont St. Peter, Bucks. 352
Charing, Kent 1191
Chatham, Kent 669, 893
Chatteris, Cambridgeshire 216
Cheadle Hulme, Cheshire 699
Cheddah, Galway, Ireland 473
Chelmsford, Essex 634, 897
Chelsea, London 1107, 1255, 1302
Chelford, Cheshire 380
Cheltenham, Gloucestershire 112, 288, 519, 566, 695, 706, 773, 832, 1028, 1040, 1291, 1317
Chepstow, Monmouth 743, 1316
Chertsey, Surrey 680
Chesham, Buckinghamshire 154
Chesham Bois, Bucks. 1063
Cheshunt, Hertfordshire 346
Chester 209, 898, 1018
Chesterfield, Derbyshire 227, 486
Chesterton, Oxfordshire 444
Chevening, Kent 106
Chewton Mendip, Somerset 738
Chichester, Sussex 342, 617, 736, 996
Chigwell Row, Essex 1280
Chilworth, Surrey 429
Chipping Sodbury, Glos. 582
Chirbury, Shropshire 139, 310
Chiswick, London 400, 574
Chobham, Surrey 1335
Chorley, Lancashire 836, 871
Chudleigh, Devon 221
Church Crookham, Hants. 642, 653
Churcham, Gloucestershire 592
Clackmannan, Scotland 771
Clandon, Surrey 492
Clapham, London 835, 1134
Claremorris, Mayo, Ireland 909
Clarinbridge, Galway, Ireland 1343
Claygate, Surrey 74
Clearwell, Coleford, Glos. 867
Clifton, Bristol 300, 312, 1040
Clifton Campville, Staffs. 1011
Cloghan, Offaly, Ireland 886
Clonmel, Tipperary, Ireland 468
Coalville, Leicestershire 71
Cobham, Surrey 982
Cobo, Guernsey, C.I. 937
Cockenzie, East Lothian 166
Coleford, Gloucestershire 142
Collon, Drogheda, Co. Louth 382
Colonsay, Argyll, Scotland 812
Comber, Co. Down, Ireland 325
Compton Bassett, Wiltshire 560
Comrie, Perthshire, Scotland 269
Congleton, Cheshire 368
Congreve, Staffordshire 241

continued overleaf

349

Family VCs

Gough
Major C.J.S. Gough and Lieut. H.H. Gough (Indian Mutiny 1857-8) — *brothers.*
Major J.E. Gough (Somaliland 1903) — *son of Major C.J.S. Gough, nephew of Lieut. H.H. Gough.*

Sartorius
Major R.W. Sartorius (Ashanti 1874) and Captain E.H. Sartorius (Afghanistan 1879) — *brothers.*

Bradford
Lieut-Col. R.B. Bradford (France 1916) and Lieut-Cdr. G.N. Bradford (Zeebrugge 1918) — *brothers.*

Turner
Second-Lieut. A.B. Turner (France 1915) and Lieut-Col. V.B. Turner (W. Desert 1942) — *brothers.*

Roberts
Lieut. F.S. Roberts (Indian Mutiny 1858) and Lieut. the Hon. F.H.S. Roberts (S. Africa 1899) — *father and son.*

Congreve
Captain W.N. Congreve (S. Africa 1899) and Major W. La T. Congreve (France 1916) — *father and son.* Both in The Rifle Brigade.

Esmonde
Captain T. Esmonde (Crimea 1855) and Lieut-Cdr. E.K. Esmonde (Straits of Dover 1942) — *great-uncle and great-nephew.*

Grieve
Sergeant-Major J. Grieve (Crimea 1854) and Captain R.C. Grieve (Belgium 1917) — *uncle and nephew.*

Chavasse and Upham Capt. Noel Chavasse VC and Bar (Flanders 1916-1917) had family connections with S/Lieut. Charles Upham VC and Bar (Crete 1941 – Western Desert 1942)

Lyster and Reed
Lieut. H.H. Lyster (Indian Mutiny 1858) and Captain H.L. Reed (S. Africa 1899) — *uncle and nephew.*

Gifford and Butler
Lieut. Lord Gifford (Ashanti 1873-4) and Captain J.F.P. Butler (Cameroons 1914) — *uncle and nephew.*

Blair
Captain J. Blair and Lieut. R. Blair (Indian Mutiny 1857) — *cousins.*

Dawson and Pollock
Cpl. J.L. Dawson and Cpl. J.D. Pollock (France 1915) — *cousins.*

Cadell and Lawrence
Lieut. T. Cadell and Lieut. S.H. Lawrence (Indian Mutiny 1857) — *cousins.*

Maude
Bt. Lieut-Col. F.F. Maude (Crimea 1855) and Captain F.C. Maude (Indian Mutiny 1857) — *cousins.*

Young and Boyes
Lieut. T.J. Young (Indian Mutiny 1857) and Midshipman D.G. Boyes (Japan 1864) — *brothers-in-law.*

Gort and Sidney
Lieut-Col. Viscount Gort (France 1918) and Major W.P. Sidney (Italy 1944) — *father-in-law and son-in-law.* Both in Grenadier Guards.

Cubitt, Hills and Evans, L.P.
Lieut. W.G. Cubitt and Second-Lieut. J. Hills (Indian Mutiny 1857) — *brothers-in-law.*
Lieut-Col. L.P. Evans (Belgium 1917) *nephew of Lieut. W.G. Cubitt.*

Manser and Randle
Flying Officer L.T. Manser (Germany 1942) and Captain J.N. Randle (Assam 1944) — *brothers-in-law.*

Town & County Connections continued

Unusual VCs

Two VCs were won by men who saved the lives of their brothers: **Major C.J.S. Gough** saved the life of his brother **Lieut. H.H. Gough** (who already had a VC) during the Indian Mutiny, and **Trooper H.E. Ramsden** saved his brother's life in the South African War in 1899.

VCs awarded for actions other than in time of war against the enemy were awarded to:

> **Pte. D. Bell, Pte. J. Cooper, Assistant Surgeon C.M. Douglas, Pte. W. Griffiths, Pte. T. Murphy** (all from the 24th Regt., later The South Wales Borderers) — for bravery at sea in saving life in a storm off the Andaman Islands, 1867.

> **Pte. T. O'Hea** (The Rifle Bde.) — for extinguishing a fire in a railway car containing 2,000 lb. of ammunition at Danville Railway Station, Quebec, Canada, in 1866.

The oldest VC winner, according to the records, is thought to be **Lieut. W. Raynor,** of The Bengal Veteran Establishment, at Delhi during the Indian Mutiny (May, 1857) at the age of 61 years, 10 months.

The youngest VC winners are acknowledged to be: **Hospital Apprentice A. FitzGibbon,** Indian Medical Establishment at Taku Forts, China (Aug. 1860), and **Drummer T. Flinn,** 64th Regt. (later The North Staffordshire Regt.) at Cawnpore during the Indian Mutiny (Nov. 1857) — both aged 15 years, 3 months.

Three men have won Bars to their VCs:

> **Surgeon-Captain A. Martin-Leake,** South African Constabulary, in South Africa (1902) and Bar as a Lieutenant in the Royal Army Medical Corps in Belgium (1914). He died on 22nd June, 1953, at Ware, Herts.

> **Captain N.G. Chavasse,** Royal Army Medical Corps, attd. 10th Bn. The King's (Liverpool) Regt., in France (1916) and Bar in Belgium (1917). He was killed in action two days later.

> **Second-Lieutenant C.H. Upham,** 20th Bn., 2nd N.Z.E.F. in Crete (May 1941) and Bar as a Captain in the Western Desert (July 1942). He lives in New Zealand.

Non-British VCs

Captain **B.S. Hutcheson** *(American)*; Lance-Corporal **W.H. Metcalf** *(American)*; Sergeant **G.H. Mullin** *(American)*; Ordinary Seaman **W.H.H. Seeley** *(American)*; Sergeant **R.L. Zengel** *(American)*; Lieut-Colonel **A. Carton de Wiart** *(Belgian)*; Stoker **W. Johnstone** *(German)*; Sergeant-Major **C. Wooden** *(German)*; Corporal **F.C. Schiess** *(Swiss)*; Trooper **P. Brown** *(Swedish)*; Private **T. Dinesen** *(Danish)*; Private **J.C. Jensen** *(Danish)*; Major **A.F.E.V.S. Lassen** *(Danish)*; Corporal **F. Konowal** *(Russian)*. And the American Unknown Warrior, who is buried at Arlington National Cemetery. It was presented on behalf of King George V by Admiral of the Fleet Lord Beatty at the same time that he laid the King's wreath on the tomb, on 11th November, 1921.

The United States Government bestowed a Congressional Medal of Honor on the British Unknown Warrior buried in Westminster Abbey.

Civilian VCs

Five civilians have won the VC: **Mr. R.L. Mangles, Mr. W.F. McDonell** and **Mr. T.H. Kavanagh** of the Bengal Civil Service, **Mr. G.B. Chicken,** a volunteer of the Indian Naval Brigade and the **Rev. J.W. Adams** of the Bengal Ecclesiastical Department. The first four were in the Indian Mutiny in 1857 and the fifth in Afghanistan in 1879.

BIBLIOGRAPHY

The Air VCs, W.E. Johns (Hamilton, 1935); *Britain's Role of Glory*, D.H. Parry (Cassells, 1906); *British Gallantry Awards*, P.E. Abbot and J.M.A. Tamplin (Guinness Superlatives & B.A. Seaby, 1971 and Nimrod Dix & Co. 1981); *The Bronze Cross*, F.C. Roe (Cawthorn, 1945); *The Evolution of the Victoria Cross*, M.J. Crook (Midas Books, 1975, in association with The Ogilby Trusts); *For Valour: The Air VCs*, C. Bowyer (Kimber, 1978); *For Valour: The History of South Africa's Victoria Cross Heroes*, I.S. Uys (Uys, Johannesburg, 1973); *'Gainst All Disaster*, A. Stannistreet (Picton Publishing (Chippenham) Ltd., 1986); *Heroes of the Victoria Cross*, Colour-Sergeant T.E. Toomey (Newnes, 1895); *History of the Victoria Cross*, P.A. Wilkins (Constable, 1904); *Illustrated Handbook of the Victoria Cross and George Cross*, Imperial War Museum (IWM, 1970); *The Kashmir Gate — Lieutenant Home and the Delhi VCs*, Roger Perkins (Picton Publications, 1983); List of Recipients of the Victoria Cross, War Office (mimeographed, 1953); Stories of the Victoria Cross awards during Second World War up to June 1943, Ministry of Information (Robinson, 1943); *The Story of the Victoria Cross*, Brigadier The Rt. Hon. Sir John Smyth, Bt., VC, MC (Muller, 1963); *Submariners VC*, Sir W.S. James (Peter Davis, 1962); *They Dared Mightily*, L. Wigmore and B. Harding (Australian War Memorial, Canberra, 1963); *Valiant Men: Canada's VC and GC Winners*, H. Swettenham (Hakkert, Toronto, 1973); *The Victoria Cross*, R. Stewart (Hutchinson, 1928); *Victoria Cross Battles of the Second World War*, C.E. Lucas-Phillips (Heinemann, 1973); *The Victoria Cross* — booklet issued for Centenary Exhibition at Marlborough House, 1956; *The Victoria Cross and the Crimea*, W.W. Knollys (Dean, 1877); *The VC and DSO, Vol.1*, General Sir O'Moore Creagh and H.M. Humphris (Standard Art Book Co., 1924, reprint by J.B. Hayward & Son, 1985); *The Victoria Crosses and George Crosses of the Honourable East India Company and Indian Army 1856-1945*, National Army Museum (N.A.M. 1962); *The Victoria Cross — India's VCs in Two World Wars*, India G.H.Q. (Civil & Military Gazette, Lahore, 1945); *The Victoria Cross in India, How and by Whom Won*, W.W. Knollys (Dean, 1878); *Victoria Cross and How Won*, Colour-Sergeant T.E. Toomey (Boot, 1890); *The Victoria Cross at Sea*, J. Winton (Michael Joseph, 1978); *The VCs of Wales and the Welsh Regiments*, W. Alister Williams (Bridge Books, Wrexham, 1984).